Physical Education Activity Handbook

Related Benjamin Cummings Kinesiology Titles

Austin/Crawford, *Therapeutic Recreation: An Introduction*, Third Edition (2001)

Bishop, *Fitness through Aerobics*, Fifth Edition (2002)

Darst/Pangrazi, *Dynamic Physical Education for Secondary School Students*, Fourth Edition (2002)

Darst/Pangrazi, *Lesson Plans for Dynamic Physical Education for Secondary School Students* (2002)

Freeman, *Physical Education and Sport in a Changing Society*, Sixth Edition (2001)

Fronske, *Teaching Cues for Basic Sports Skills for Elementary and Middle School Children* (2002)

Fronske, *Teaching Cues for Basic Sports Skills*, Second Edition (2001)

Powers/Dodd, *Total Fitness: Exercise, Nutrition, and Wellness*, Second Edition (1999)

McGown/Fronske/Moser, *Coaching Volleyball* (2001)

Metzler, *Badminton* (2001)

Metzler, *Golf* (2001)

Metzler, *Raquetball* (2001)

Carr/Metzler, *Soccer* (2001)

Metzler, *Tennis* (2001)

Poole/Metzler, *Volleyball* (2001)

Mosston/Ashworth, *Teaching Physical Education*, Fifth Edition (2002)

Pangrazi, *Dynamic Physical Education for Elementary School Children*, Thirteenth Edition (2001)

Pangrazi, *Lesson Plans for Dynamic Physical Education for Elementary School Children*, Thirteenth Edition (2001)

Plowman/Smith, *Exercise Physiology for Health, Fitness, and Performance*, Second Edition (2003)

Silva/Stevens, *Psychological Foundations of Sport* (2002)

Check out these and other Benjamin Cummings Kinesiology titles at: www.aw.com/bc.

Physical Education Activity Handbook

Tenth Edition

Neil Schmottlach
Ball State University

Jerre McManama
Ball State University

Benjamin
Cummings

San Francisco   Boston   New York
Cape Town   Hong Kong   London   Madris   Mexico City
Montreal   Munich   Paris   Singapore   Sydney   Tokyo   Toronto

Publisher: Daryl Fox
Acquisitions Editor: Deirdre McGill
Publishing Assistant: Michelle Cadden
Managing Editor, Production: Wendy Earl
Production Editor: Leslie Austin
Illustrations: Karl Miyajima
Cover Design: Brad Greene
Text Design: Brad Greene
Copy Editor: Sally Peyrefitte
Proofreader: Martha Ghent
Marketing Manager: Sandra Lindelof
Manufacturing Buyer: Megan Cochran, Stacey Weinberger
Compositor: Cecelia G. Morales
Cover Photographs (clockwise from large photo):
          © Corbis Corporation/Petse Saloutos, 2001
          © Corbis Corporation/David Stoecklein, 2001
          © Rommel/Masterfile, 2001
          © Ed Gifford/Masterfile, 2001
          © David Schmidt/Masterfile, 2001

Library of Congress Cataloging-in-Publication Data

Library of Congress Cataloging-in-Publication Data

Schmottlach, Neil.
    The physical education activity handbook/Neil Schmottlach, Jerre
McManama.—10th ed.
        p. cm.
    Rev. ed. Of Physical eduation handbook. 9th ed. C 1997.
    Includes bibliographical references.
    ISBN 0-205-34401-1 (pbk. : alk. paper)
    Physical education and trainingóStudy and teaching. I.
McManama, Jerre L. II. Schmottlach, Neil. Physical education handbook.
III. Title.
    GV361 .P49 2001
    796--dc21

                    2001047345

ISBN 0-205-34401-1
2 3 4 5 6 7 8 9 10—CRK—05 04 03 02
www.aw.com/bc

This edition is dedicated to our wives, children, and the many people who would enjoy a lifetime of active participation.

Contents

Teachers, recreational leaders, volunteer scout trainers, and similar personnel are often called upon to "start the ball rolling" or to teach an activity with which they are not completely familiar. Many instructors have only a few specializations and it would take them too long to master all the present offerings in physical education. Some activities, too, are more familiar to men than to women, and vice versa. Yet with the changes brought about by Title IX and laws regarding participation by special populations, today's teaching personnel must be able to give instruction in a great variety of activities. This is particularly true of individual and team sports such as golf, orienteering, cycling, speedball, flag football, field hockey, and soccer.

To meet these needs, the *Physical Education Activity Handbook*, 10th edition, has been written to serve as a teaching and reference tool for several types of people: physical educators, student teachers, recreational leaders, sports enthusiasts, physical education majors, and all high school and college students who are interested in sports activities and physical fitness.

In deciding what changes to make for this edition, we relied on a survey of previous users who expressed their needs and activity interests. We also conducted a focus group session of college physical education teachers who are in teacher training programs. Previous users of the *Handbook* will find new changes and updates throughout. One primary change has been to the title, *Physical Education Activity Handbook*, a name that best reflects its content. In addition, Fencing, Modern Dance, Appendix A (Sources of Rules), Appendix C (Selected National Health Goals for the Year 2000), and material previously contained in the preface have been dropped. The first section of the *Handbook* (Chapter One) has been revised and a section added that describes how best to use the *Activity Chapter* formats for more effective instruction. A new feature of the *Handbook* includes a section at the end of each chapter that identifies Web Sites of interest. These sites are included to help the user obtain additional information and keep abreast of the current issues and changes concerning a particular activity. The sites also contain helpful instructional information and hints that will aid in your understanding of an activity. A new chapter on Yoga has been added to address one of the fastest growing and most popular activities found in many college physical education and recreation programs. A new Appendix A, "An Overview of and Resources for Contemporary Activities," has been added. The activities included are based on the results of our previously mentioned focus group session. The eight new activities have been outlined, including essential equipment needs, a list of beginning skills a learner would expect to encounter, and an extensive list of references, organizations, and web sites of interest.

All activity chapters have been updated including new pictures added where appropriate, sections added (Flying Disc in Recreational Activities), and references updated. Hints for special populations have been expanded and refined.

To derive maximum utility from the *Handbook*, it is essential to begin with a careful study of the introductory chapters. Chapter 1, "Considerations for Effective Skill Learning," covers four basic areas which contribute to a person's skill development. First, the mechanical (movement) aspects underlie the principles that affect good skill development for each activity in the Handbook. Second, the psychological aspect (motor learning) of learning enhances the developmental process when applied by an instructor. Third, the organizational structure (format) systematically provides direction and details for becoming a skilled participant for each activity presented. Fourth, the technology advances introduces a challenge for instructors with many new aids for instruction and skill learning. Additionally, the dual goals of skill and fitness development between programs call for creative approaches in methods if both are to be attained. Chapter 2, "Principles of Physical Fitness," provides the foundation that the remaining chapters must draw upon, for integrating fitness within activities. Physical training and skill training are paramount for effective participation.

These two introductory chapters constitute the backbone and sinews of this *Handbook*; they also provide both the meaningful principles and the practical suggestions needed for applying these principles for effective teaching and learning.

ACKNOWLEDGMENTS

We are indebted to the following professors and instructors who so graciously contributed their knowledge and expertise to the *Physical Education Activity Handbook.*

DR. ARNO WITTIG, Ball State University
Psychological Aspects of Physical Education

DR. GALE GEHLSEN, Ball State University
Mechanical Aspects of Physical Education

DR. LEONARD KAMINSKY, Ball State University
Physical Fitness Programs

JUDY DONAHUE, LEE EDGREN-STOHLER, and MARGE HOBLEY, Ball State University
Aerobic Dance

DR. SUNG-JAE PARK, Ball State University
Archery; Team Handball

WILLIAM NICHOLS
Badminton

DEBBIE POWERS, Ball State University
Basketball

SHARON BURGESS, Ball State University
Cycling

TERRY WHITT BAILEY, Ball State University
Dance (Folk, Square, Social)

YAAKOV EDEN, Ball State University
Western Line Dance

PENNY JUSTIN, Ball State University
Gymnastics and Tumbling

DALE SCRIVNOR, Ball State University
Golf

DR. RON DAVIS, Ball State University
Modifications for Special Populations

DR. REBECCA WOODARD, Ball State University
Modifications for Special Populations

DR. WARREN VANDER HILL, Ball State University
Angling

KAREN FITZPATRICK, Ball State university
Field Hockey

TERRY HITCHCOCK
Handball and Racquetball

JERRY RUSHTON, Ball State University
Orienteering; Track and Field

DR. MARILYN BUCK, Ball State University
Softball; Technology and Future of Physical Education Programs of the Future

JOHN WINGFIELD
Swimming

PAUL FAWCETT, Ball State University
Swimming; Canoeing and Kayaking

SCOTT B. PERELMAN
Tennis

DR. DAVID PEARSON, Ball State University
Weight Training

LEE EDGREN-STOHLER, Ball State University
Yoga

CAROL REED, Ball State University
Skin Diving; SCUBA Diving

We would also like to thank the following people for their valuable assistance:

KATHY BULL, Head, Women's Tennis Coach, Ball State University, for her assistance on the Tennis chapter.

JANE SCHMOTTLACH, for her typing assistance.

ANNEMARIE KENNEDY, Allyn and Bacon, for her assistance in keeping us informed and on track.

Physical Education Activity Handbook

CHAPTER 1

Considerations for Effective Skill Learning

- Mechanical Aspects
- Psychological Aspects
- Activity Chapter Format
- Technology and Physical Education Programs of the Future

Nature and Purpose

Many considerations come to play in learning the skills involved in physical activities. Foremost among these considerations are the mechanical and psychological aspects that affect skill development. Each specific activity has unique attributes, rules, equipment, skills/techniques, safety considerations, strategies/tactics, etiquette or playing courtesies, terminology and modifications for special populations. All of these considerations affect planning or organization for progressive learning (Figure 1-1).

Physical activity, when planned and taught properly, is "education through the physical." That is, the activity serves as a medium through which a total learning experience takes place. Do you recall the first time you ever got up on water skis, or jogged a mile or two, or first rode a bicycle? If you have been successful at some relatively difficult and strenuous physical feat, what happened to your self-esteem as a result? In all likelihood, your achievement created a more positive outlook of yourself. In addition, you may have been encouraged to try other types of activities. Researchers have determined that such experiences improve our total being. In other words, physical activity not only improves our physical health, but also enhances our emotional outlook and even stimulates our intellectual activity and ability. In short, it improves our "wellness" in that it improves us totally.

Effective skill learning focuses on teaching skills, acquiring knowledge, and developing attitudes through movement. Public schools, Boys and Girls Clubs, Scouting programs, and other educational venues recognize the importance of physical activity by making it a part of their curricular plans. School physical education and wellness programs provide each person with various opportunities—from the assessment of fitness levels and the appropriate activi-

ties that will help overcome personal weaknesses to the acquisition of lifetime fitness-type activities. Physical activity programs remain a vital part of the total process of "education through the physical" by using games, sports, aquatics, dance and other vigorous activities to help the individual achieve physical well-being.

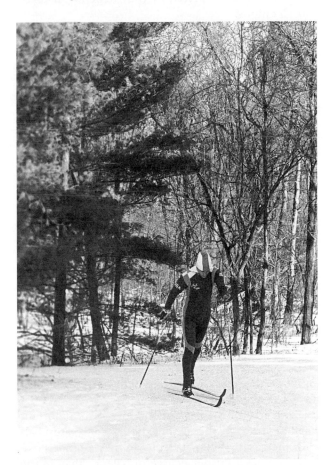

Figure 1-1 Some skills provide a lifetime of pleasurable activity.

We begin Chapter 1 by examining two important components of effective skill learning that affect participation and practice in physical activities: the mechanical and the psychological aspects of learning a skill. The third section of Chapter 1 outlines the organizational structure of each succeeding chapter and the relationship of planning and organization to effective skill learning. The fourth and final section examines the future of physical education programs as they relate to technology and the development of a physically educated person.

MECHANICAL ASPECTS

This section examines selected positions and movements found in everyday and sport activities such as standing, sitting, walking, lifting, carrying, pulling, pushing, running, jumping, throwing, catching, and striking. Discussion will focus on the mechanical aspects related to basic movement skills. The presentation is divided into two sections: the first part deals with static and semistatic activities for which balance considerations are the main concern; the second part describes dynamic activities that depend on force considerations.

Balance Considerations

Basic to all activity, both ordinary and sports-related, is understanding how the body maintains a balanced position. A body's degree of stability or balance depends upon several factors, including (a) the area of the base of support, (b) the height of the center of gravity, and (c) the proximity of the center of gravity within the supporting base.

A balanced position is defined as a position wherein the center of gravity is placed over the support base. The center of gravity is the point around which the body balances in all directions. The base of support includes not only the feet in contact with the ground but also the area between the feet. If the center of gravity is placed outside the supporting base, the body loses balance and downward motion results. The body can regain balance by reestablishing the support under the center of gravity. Locomotion, therefore, is accomplished by a continuous process of placing the center of gravity outside the base, thus losing balance and then regaining balance by placing the foot under the center of gravity.

The area of the base of support is an important stability factor. As the area of the base increases, balance increases. When standing in a side-stride position, one has a greater degree of balance than in the feet-together position. A side-stride position increases balance in a lateral direction; a forward-stride position increases balance in an anterior-posterior direction.

The degree of balance is also influenced by the height of the center of gravity: a low center of gravity increases balance, and a high center of gravity decreases balance. In athletic activity, the body often can increase in balance by bending the knees to lower center of gravity.

If the center of gravity falls over the middle of the supporting base, equal balance on all sides of the body is established. However, if the center of gravity is placed over the back edge of the base, the degree of balance increases toward the front of the body and decreases toward the back edge of the supporting base. In other words, as the horizontal distance from the center of gravity to the front edge of the support increases, balance increases. For the body to stop quickly and maintain balance, the center of gravity should be moved to the back edge of the supporting base. For the body to move quickly in the forward direction, the center of gravity should be placed toward the front edge of the base. This allows the balance to be destroyed very quickly because the center of gravity only has to be moved a short distance to be outside the supporting base.

Standing

Standing posture varies among individuals and is affected by such factors as health (including mental attitude), body build, and occupation. Although there is no single description of good standing posture, proper body alignment is an essential element. The body is not one solid mass, but is composed of a series of segments. Each segment is connected to the next segment by joints that are held together by muscle tendons and ligaments. If the segments of the trunk are stacked so that the line of gravity passes directly through the center of each segment, less stress will be placed upon the muscles and ligaments. There is little stress on the muscles and ligaments because the segments are perfectly balanced one over the other. Therefore, a good standing position is one in which each body segment is centered over the segment immediately below it (Figure 1-2).

In the standing position with perfect alignment, a straight line should pass through the ear lobe, center of shoulder joint, slightly behind the hip joint, slightly in front of the center of the knee joint, and in front of the ankle joint. The total picture of the best standing posture shows shallow curves of the upper and lower back, a slight tilt forward-upward of the pelvis to help decrease the curve of the lower back, the head back and the chin comfortably down, the abdominal wall flattened, the chest lifted, and the shoulders relaxed and back. This posture is not only mechanically sound but also attractive in appearance.

In good standing position, the feet are usually placed parallel, 4 to 6 inches apart. Although some

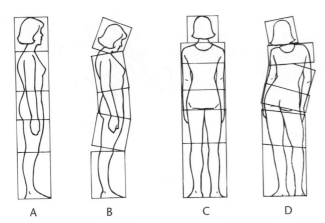

Figure 1-2 In (A) and (C) each segment is balanced above the segment below. In (B) and (D) the alignment is unbalanced.

authorities consider a toeing-out position to be normal, those who advocate the parallel position appear to have sounder reasons. In this latter position, the base is firm in both forward-backward and lateral directions as compared with the weaker triangular foot position (smaller base) resulting from the toeing-out position. The parallel foot position also places less strain on the leg muscles, and the body weight can be transferred along the entire longitudinal arch of the foot.

Sitting

On average, individuals spend over 60 percent of their waking hours in a sitting position. As in the standing position, body alignment and balance are the two essential considerations in sitting and in the act of getting into and out of a chair.

In preparing to sit down, stand near and in front of the chair. This is necessary so that in the act of sitting, the trunk and upper body will move in an almost erect position with the leg muscles controlling the action. As the body is lowered, the trunk should bend slightly forward from the hip joint. This will keep the center of gravity over the supporting base. The body weight should first be placed on the front edge of the chair, thus establishing a new base of support, and then pushed back in the seat (chair).

When sitting on a straight chair, make full use of the chair seat and the chair lower back for support. Sit with the buttocks well back into the seat with the body against the back of the chair. The upper torso should rest slightly against the upper back of the chair. As in standing, the major criterion for good sitting position is good alignment of the body segments.

To get up from the chair, reverse the order for sitting down. Place one leg in front of the other, slide forward, and bend the trunk forward from the hips. When the center of gravity is over the feet, lift the body upward.

Lifting and Carrying

Considerations of balance and body alignment also apply in lifting and carrying. Keeping an aligned position will avoid strain and stress on muscles and joints.

When lifting an object from below, stand close to it, place one foot slightly in front of the other, keeping the back straight and the ankles, knees, and hips flexed. In this position the entire body remains over the center of the supporting base. To straighten up, use the strong leg muscles (not the weak back muscles) to lift the body and object to the erect position.

During lifting, the weight of the object alters the location of the body's center of gravity. The object is momentarily a part of the body and tends to move the body's center of gravity in the direction of the object. Therefore, a wider supporting base is required.

A weight carried on one side of the body should be carried close to the body with only a slight shift of the center of gravity. If the weight must be carried away from the body, raising the arm on the opposite side will move the center of gravity back toward the middle of the base. A weight carried in front of the body necessitates a backward shift of the center of gravity. The shift should be only enough to keep the center of gravity over the base. The most economical way to carry a load is on top of the head, directly in line with the body.

Pushing and Pulling

Many pushing and pulling tasks are not strenuous, but several involve the application of considerable force. Therefore, economy of effort and avoidance of strain are prime considerations. The more nearly the body segments are aligned to apply the force of either pushing or pulling and the better the base over which the body moves, the easier the task. The height and weight of the object to be pushed or pulled determine how much the body's center of gravity must be lowered. To push a heavy object, place the hands in line with the object's center of gravity. The body should be in line with the arms. If the object tends to tip, lower the position of the hands.

In pulling, the body should be inclined in the direction of motion. In this position the body exerts its force most economically by using the strong leg muscles. The force should be applied as nearly as possible in the direction of the desired movement. Whenever the force is applied at an angle to the line of movement, only the component of the force in the direction of movement is effective in accomplishing the desired result.

Force Considerations

All locomotor tasks (running, jumping, skipping, etc.) propel the body by applying a force against the ground. The force that actually moves the body is a reaction force (ground reaction force) that is reacting to the muscular force applied to the ground in accordance with Newton's Third Law: For every action there is an equal and opposite reaction. The greater the force pushing against the ground, the greater will be the reaction force pushing the body forward. Therefore, the key to increasing the vertical ground reaction force and thus increasing the speed of movement is the development of explosive leg movements. Explosive leg movements provide the body with a positive acceleration. This positive acceleration is directly proportional to increased ground reaction forces (Newton's Second Law).

The direction in which the force is applied is another factor that contributes to speed and efficiency of locomotion. In almost all locomotor tasks (except some forms of hopping and jumping), the muscular force is applied to the ground in a backward-downward direction; the reaction force results then in a forward and upward direction. The upward (vertical) component is effective in lifting and supporting the body against the pull of gravity; the forward (horizontal) force component results in the forward movement of the body. If the body can apply only a limited amount of force and if the force is exerted in two directions, then it is better to divide the force unequally, putting more force in the desired direction. In running and walking, in which the vertical force is greater than the horizontal, the body appears to bounce upward with each step. A greater horizontal force provides more speed in the horizontal direction, giving the motion an appearance of smoothness. An increase in the forward lean allows the body to pull more backward than upward, thus increasing the horizontal force component.

In some locomotor activities (walking, skipping, galloping, and sliding), the forward foot strikes the ground well ahead of the body's center of gravity. This action exerts a backward and upward reaction force against the body. The backward component of this force provides a resisting action to the body's forward momentum and makes it possible to stop the forward progress. This retarding force component remains in action to a lessening degree until the foot is directly under the center of gravity. From this point until the foot leaves the ground, the propelling forward-upward reaction force is invoked (Figure 1-3).

Friction, a force that opposes motion, tends to influence the ground reaction force. In order to move the body forward, there must be sufficient friction between the foot and the ground to invoke the ground reaction force. Everyone knows that it is easier to walk or run on a hard, solid surface than on a slippery surface or on a surface that gives. In the latter situation, the foot slides backward against the sur-

Figure 1-3 (A) Backward component of pushing force, (B) downward component of pushing force, (C) forward component of reaction force, (D) upward component of reaction force.

face or the surface moves, thereby reducing the ground reaction force. That is why rubber-soled shoes or cleats are used in athletics: to provide adequate friction, thereby ensuring the best possible ground reaction force.

Walking

Walking is the process of locomotion in which the body weight is transferred from one forward swinging leg and foot to the other. It differs from other locomotor tasks in that at no time is there lack of contact with the floor. The outstanding characteristic of the walk is the period of double support. For clarity, the walk will be described in terms of leg action and arm swing.

Leg Action. From the double support position with one leg in front of the other, the back leg moves backward until it breaks contact with the ground. Then the knee and the hip begin to bend, starting the forward swing of the leg. The leg moves in the shape of an arc, more or less. When the approximate midpoint of the arc is reached, there is more flexion of the knee and hip to permit clearance from the ground. The leg is then extended and the heel contacts the floor. As the heel of the swinging leg touches the floor, the leg extends; the body then shifts forward, and the cycle is repeated.

In ideal foot placement the toes are pointed straight ahead. This provides the best possible position to apply force in a direction opposite the desired movement. A toeing-in or a toeing-out position not only places undue stress on the ankle and knee joints but also is less efficient because the force is applied at an angle to the foot.

Arm Swing. In walking, the arms hang relaxed at the sides and swing forward and backward in opposition to the leg movements. This oppositional action occurs in all movements and is controlled at the reflex level of the nervous system. It is possible to interfere with this reflex through conscious control of movement. However, it is not desirable to do so because this oppositional action of the arms and shoulder girdle counterbalance the rotation of the hips, and the resultant forces are applied straight ahead.

In efficient walking, the heel should first contact the ground (toes pointed straight ahead), and the body weight should be transferred to the outer border of the foot and then the ball, followed by a push off from the toes. Foot placement is considered best when the inner border of each foot falls closely (within one to two inches) along an imaginary line. Care should be taken not to cross this line in a weaving motion.

In summary, a natural walk is one in which the arms and legs swing easily, although the length of the stride and the frequency of steps taken will vary with the individual. The essential factors causing this variation are the individual's height, particularly the leg length, and speed of walking. An increase in walking speed is accomplished by either increasing the stride length (distance covered per stride) or increasing the frequency of steps, or both. In most people the stride length is increased until a given acceleration, at which time stride length is decreased and the stride frequency increases.

There should be little up and down bouncing movement of the body caused by the vertical force component. Increased walking speed is also accompanied by increasing body inclination. Horizontal movement is facilitated by this position because (1) the body is more in line with the driving leg, (2) the center of gravity is shifted forward to the front edge of the supporting base and gravity is used to assist in overcoming the body's inertia, and (3) the stride length is increased from the center of gravity to the release.

Running

Running, like walking, is a locomotor task in which the body weight is transferred from one forward-swinging foot to the other. Running differs from walking, however, in that there is a short period of nonsupport (no contact with the ground), whereas in walking there is always contact with the ground. Running is generally divided into three phases: (1) recovery phase, (2) support phase, and (3) driving phase.

The recovery phase starts the instant the rear, or driving, leg leaves the ground and ends when the same leg has moved forward and again contacts the ground beneath the individual's center of gravity. As the foot leaves the ground (the beginning of the recovery phase), the hip begins its forward movement and the lower leg folds up toward the upper leg. As the speed of running increases, there is a greater tendency for the heel to kick up toward the buttock. This kick-up action is not a fault as was once thought. The kick-up shortens the lever of the leg and permits the swinging leg a smaller moment of inertia. The advantage of the small moment of inertia is that it can be moved very quickly without a great deal of muscular force.

As the leg continues forward in the recovery phase, the height to which the knee is lifted depends upon the running speed. The lift is highest in sprinting and lowest in jogging. The forward swinging leg reaches its highest point as the rear leg completes its full extension. After reaching the limit of its forward swing, the recovery leg (front leg) reverses its direction and moves the foot first forward and then downward. The recovery phase is completed as the foot strikes the ground. Several factors must be considered in the foot striking. First the foot should be placed under the center of gravity and moving backward at moment of contact. This positioning of the foot enables upward and forward ground reaction forces to be invoked. Overstriding is characterized by the foot contacting the ground in front of the center of gravity and by the forward movement of the foot at contact. The foot should be moving backward at the time of contact in order to invoke the forward ground reaction force. The contact of the foot in front of the center of gravity tends to create a backward driving force or blocking action that will determine the running momentum.

The support phase of running begins with the landing of the forward foot and ends when the center of gravity passes in front of the supporting foot. As the foot contacts the ground, the knee bends to absorb the shock of landing, which is the first function of the support phase. The second function of the support phase is to arrest the body against the force of gravity. The final function of this phase is to move the body to a position for an effective driving phase.

The driving phase begins as the supporting phase ends—as the foot leaves the ground. In this phase, the body is propelled forward by exerting muscular leg force against the ground and behind the center of gravity. As the body progresses forward, the heel is lifted, the knee extends, and finally the ankle and toe extend well behind the body. Failure to obtain complete extension of the driving leg is a common characteristic of the poor runner.

Arms. In running, the upper body (shoulders and arms) moves in opposition to the leg action in order to balance the rotation effect of the leg swing on the trunk. The upper arms move relatively straight backward and forward. However, the lower arms move in a slight cross-body direction in front but do not cross an imaginary vertical plane bisecting the body into right and left halves.

In sprinting, the elbows tend to be bent at an angle of approximately 90 degrees. This angle increases as the hand swings in front of the body and decreases as the hand passes the hip to the rear. The smaller moment of inertia (small lever arm) allows the arms to be moved very rapidly. The amount of bend in the arms decreases as the running speed decreases. The distance that the arms are carried away from the side of the body (lateral distance) seems to be dependent on the width of the hips. The heavier the hips in relation to the arms, the farther from the body the arms must be carried. The hands are usually carried in a relaxed, cupped position.

Body Lean. When the rate of acceleration of a runner is the greatest, the forward lean of the trunk is the greatest. Thus a sprinter has a tremendous lean at the start of a race. From the instant the sprinter starts to reach top speed, the rate of acceleration is gradually diminished and the forward lean becomes less and less. The body lean at a uniform rate of speed is nearly erect. This slight lean is necessary in order to maintain balance; i.e., to keep the body from rotating or falling forward.

Stride Length–Stride Frequency. The speed at which a runner moves depends upon two factors: (1) the stride length and (2) the stride frequency. The stride length is the horizontal distance translated from the toe of one foot to the toe of the other foot. The frequency is the number of strides taken per unit of time. If a runner has a stride length of 2 meters per stride and a frequency of 3 strides per second, the running speed (distance per time) equals 6 meters per second. Any increase or decrease of these two elements will cause a corresponding change in the running speed. Biomechanics research over the past decade indicates that stride length is the major running speed factor at speeds from 3 to 6 m/s. At running speeds from 6 m/s to 11 m/s, stride length levels off and stride frequency becomes the important speed factor. The skilled runner has the ability to produce larger forces against the ground in a short period of time. Explosive leg strength is needed to produce large forces in a short period of time.

Jumping, Hopping, Leaping

The jump, hop, and leap are all forms of locomotion that involve projecting the body into the air. The hop is defined as any movement involving a takeoff and landing on the same foot. In the leap, there is a takeoff from one foot and a landing on the other. For the jump, the takeoff is from one foot or both feet, and the landing is on both feet simultaneously. Many sports skills involve a form of jumping, hopping, and/or leaping.

The essential factors to be considered in jumping, hopping, and leaping are (1) initial force, (2) angle of takeoff, and (3) gravity.

In preparing to jump, hop, or leap, the legs bend in preparation for the strong, explosive leg action. The depth of the bend of the legs (or crouch) depends upon the strength of the leg muscles and the nature of the sport skill. A deep crouch requires a great deal of leg strength and a long period of time to lift the body. Therefore, in most situations the crouch should never form a 90-degree angle at the knee. The angles between 65 and 90 degrees tend to produce the best jumps.

The initial force is produced by the explosive leg action pushing down against the ground. In accordance with Newton's Third Law, an equal and opposite ground reaction force is produced that pushes the body into the air. The height reached by the body's center of gravity is proportional to the magnitude of the vertical ground reaction forces at takeoff. An arm swing in an upward direction produces an increase in the ground reaction forces and a transfer of momentum.

If the purpose of the jump, hop, or leap is to move the body upward as far as possible (i.e., a vertical jump), all force should be applied straight down against the ground, with the center of gravity directly over the feet. This will produce a ground reaction force with only a vertical component, and all energies are used to lift the body vertically. If, however, the purpose of the task is to propel the body forward and upward, the force should be applied against the ground at an angle. The forward lean of the body and the arm swing forward contribute to this angle of projection. When the takeoff force is applied at a 45-degree angle, half of the ground reaction force is used to move the body upward and half is used to move the body forward. A higher angle of pushoff, for example 70 degrees, provides a greater vertical force than horizontal; a lower angle, for example 30 degrees, provides greater horizontal motion and less vertical motion. Thus the angle of takeoff depends upon the goal of the skill.

Once the body is projected into the air, gravity will slow its vertical velocity and bring the body back to earth. The height that a body will achieve depends only on the magnitude of the ground reaction force and the angle of application. An angle of projection of 90 degrees will provide the greatest amount of time in the air because all available force is in a direction to resist gravity. Any other angle divides the ground reaction force vertically and horizontally, producing less time in the air.

Any movement in the airborne phase of a jump, hop, or leap will create an equal and opposite reaction. However, it is possible to create a momentary pause at the high point of a jump by lowering the position of the center of gravity within the body. This may be achieved by lowering the arms or bending the legs at the top of the jump.

In landing from a jump, hop, or leap, the force must be absorbed in order to avoid injury. A force can be absorbed by its gradual slowing over the greatest possible time and distance (i.e., giving with the force). Therefore, all joints of the legs must "give" in sequence as contact with the ground is made.

Catching

Catching is a skill that requires the body to stop the momentum of a moving object. The mechanical considerations are (1) absorbing the force over the greatest possible distance, i.e., "give," and (2) absorbing the force over the greatest possible surface area.

The absorption of the force over the greatest possible distance involves exerting a force on the object in the opposite direction of the moving object. This can be accomplished by (1) moving in line with the oncoming object, (2) reaching out as far as possible to meet the object, and (3) contacting and slowly allowing the object to move toward the body. A step taken in the direction of the oncoming object not only increases balance but also, for an increase in the distance and time, permits the object's velocity to be reduced.

For balls that are to be caught above the waist, the thumbs of both hands should be placed together and the fingers pointed upward. For objects to be caught below waist level, the little fingers should be placed together and pointed downward. These positions are important in order to avoid injury and to present the largest possible surface area. In baseball, the padded glove increases the area over which the force is received.

Throwing

Throwing an object involves the transfer of momentum from the body to the object. An object held in the hand acquires the speed and direction of the hand and, when released, continues to move at this velocity and in the same direction until acted upon by other forces, such as gravity and air resistance. Of primary concern are the methods for developing speed and controlling the direction of the hand.

The faster the hand is moving when a ball is released, the greater the speed of the throw. The speed of hand movement can be increased by increasing the period of time the ball is moving in the direction of the throw—in other words, increasing the length of the backswing. To increase the backswing (1) turn the side opposite the throwing arm toward the direction of the throw, (2) rotate the body away from the direction of the throw, and (3) place the feet in a stride position with the foot opposite the throwing arm forward.

An essential factor to throwing velocity is the length of the external lever arm or the perpendicular distance from the axis of rotation to the throwing hand. Holding the ball in the finger tips and holding the arm farther away from the body are two ways to increase the lever arm.

The total effective force is the sum of the force produced by all the muscle groups contributing to the action. The contributing body parts brought into action in timed sequence provide more speed. The sequence is step, rotate, throw. The step should be taken in the direction of the throw. The rotation refers to the rotation of the trunk, and the throw refers to the forward arm swing. Any movement of the body in the direction of the throw adds to the velocity of the throw. A run up or hop preceding the throw gives the body added momentum that is transferred to the thrown object. Follow-through, a gradual reduction of the body's momentum, is essential to avoid injury and to ensure maximum transfer of momentum to the object.

In addition to the speed of release, such factors as angle of release, air resistance, gravity, height of release, and spin will affect the distance an object can be thrown. For example, top spin on a ball will cause a ball to have a shorter period of flight. When throwing for distance, the ball must be released at an angle no greater than 45 degrees. The greater the distance the ball is released, above the ground, the lower the projectile angle should be. The angle of release should also be decreased when throwing against high air resistance.

Striking

As in throwing, the effectiveness of striking is judged in terms of the speed, distance, and direction of the struck object. All the factors that apply to a thrown ball apply similarly to striking. Momentum must be developed in the body, transferred to the hand and then to the implement held in the hand (or foot, as in kicking), and then transferred to the ball or object.

The speed that can be developed by the striking implement depends upon (1) the length of the striking implement, (2) the mass of the striking implement and the mass of the ball, (3) the velocity of the striking implement and the ball, and (4) the firmness of the striking implement and the point of contact between the striking implement and the struck object at the time of contact.

A longer striking implement will provide a longer lever arm, which will increase the struck object's velocity. The longer the implement, the faster the distal end of the object will travel, and the more velocity will be imparted to the ball. However, the longer lever is more difficult to control. In many cases, choking up on the striking implement will increase control but decrease the optimal velocity of the struck object.

The heavier the striking implement, up to the point of loss of movement speed, the greater the momentum transfer possible. If a bat, for example, is so heavy that the speed of the swing is reduced, the resulting momentum will be decreased rather than increased by weight. The opposite is true of the struck object—the lighter the object being struck, the greater the resultant velocity.

The firmer the striking surface, the greater the force imparted to the struck object. The striking implement must not be allowed to "give" at the moment of contact. Any loosening of the grip or lack of a firm wrist at contact will absorb and reduce the magnitude of the imparted force. If a flat open hand is used to strike a ball, as in volleyball, some of the force being transferred to the ball will be absorbed by the hand. The hand, constructed of many small bones and muscles, cannot be kept completely firm and absorbs some of the forces at contact. The use of a closed hand, or heel of the hand, provides a firmer striking surface.

The more nearly the ball is contacted in line with its center of gravity, the greater the force transferred to the ball in the desired direction. Any force applied at a distance from the object's center of gravity will create an angular force (spin) in addition to a reduced linear force. The angle at which the ball leaves the striking surface also depends upon the angle at which it hits the surface of the striking implement. The ball will generally rebound at an angle equal and opposite to the one with which it strikes the implement surface (the angle of incidence is equal to the angle of reflection).

In addition to the above factors, successful striking movements like throwing movements depend on the length of the backswing, number of contributing muscles, correct sequence of muscular contraction, weight shift, and follow-through. Each factor contributes significantly to optimal striking ability.

The above discussion of the mechanical aspects of physical activity is intended to provide an overview of movement biomechanics. For additional information, see the following further reading selections in the interrelated fields of anatomy, kinesiology, and biomechanics.

Further References

Adrian, M. J. and Cooper, J. M. *The Biomechanics of Human Movement*. Indianapolis, IN: Benchmark Press, Inc., 1989.

Enoka, R. M. *Neuromechanical Basis of Kinesiology*. Champaign, IL: Human Kinetics Books, 1988.

Gowitzke, B. A. and Milner, M. *Scientific Bases of Human Movement*. 3rd ed. Baltimore, MD: Williams and Wilkins, 1984.

Hay, J. G. *The Biomechanics of Sports Techniques*. 3rd ed. Englewood Cliffs, NJ: Prentice Hall, 1985.

Hay, J. and Reid, J. G. *Anatomy, Mechanics and Human Motion*. 2nd ed. Englewood Cliffs, NJ: Prentice Hall, 1988.

Kreighbaum, E. and Barthels, K. M. *Biomechanics*. 3rd ed. New York, NY: Macmillan Publishing Co., 1990.

Rasch, P. J. *Kinesiology and Applied Anatomy*. 7th ed. Philadelphia, PA: Lea and Febiger, 1989.

PSYCHOLOGICAL ASPECTS

Psychology is the study of behavior and cognitive processes. As such, it is concerned with all aspects of physical and mental behavior. There are many areas of study in psychology, but in this handbook we concentrate on principles that are most relevant for teachers and coaches, particularly those concerning motivation, learning, personality, and social interaction.

Motivation

Whatever behavior is being studied, one important consideration is the motivation prompting it. *Motivation* is any condition that energizes, guides, and sustains responding. Motives may be unlearned, such as hunger and thirst, or learned, such as the desire for friendship or for accomplishment.

Needs and Drives. Psychologists view *needs* as the physiological or psychological deficits a person experiences; *drives* are the states resulting from needs. Motives are often viewed as the product of needs and drives.

Physiological needs include hunger or thirst, need for air, or need for relief from pain. Physical education instructors may not be concerned with the first two, but the latter two provide good illustrations of problems that may prove important. For example, teaching swimming may be very difficult if the learner has a strong fear of suffocation and refuses to put his or her head in the water. And many runners experience painful "stitches" and simply stop participating.

Psychological deficits may be more difficult to identify. If not expressed by the learner, it may be extremely hard for the instructor to realize the type of achievement "need" being felt and the resultant drive produced. For example, research has shown that the key reasons for children's participation in sports or physical activities include wanting to achieve improvement in skills and ability, have fun, and enjoy the social and sportsmanship aspects of the events. If the instructor believes the children's primary desire is to win, the wrong kinds of achievement may be stressed and rewarded. Indeed, for people of all ages, taking part in sports or physical activities often is prompted by a desire to be "part of the group." If the instructor fails to support this, an important psychological motive may not be satisfied. Children or adults who do not experience satisfaction may be likely to leave the learning (physical activity) situation and not return.

Level of Motivation.   Regardless of the type of motive being investigated, psychologists have tried to find ways to express the strength of the motive. This is sometimes accomplished by measuring *deprivation,* that is, how much time has passed since last satisfying the motive. An avid recreational jogger who has been prevented from running for several weeks because of a nagging illness would be thought to have experienced considerable deprivation and be likely to have high motivation to start jogging again.

Another quite common way of investigating the level of motivation is to use standardized tests. Many versions exist, some attempting to identify current motive states and others concentrating on what are thought to be enduring traits. For example, *state anxiety* is thought to be the prevailing level of anxiety being experienced as a result of conditions existing in the environment at the moment. By contrast, *trait anxiety* is thought to be a more permanent characteristic of an individual, a general way of responding in many different situations. As an illustration, a child who is extremely deft when playing in the backyard may not show these skills when asked to perform in front of the whole class. The difference in circumstance creates a difference in the level of state anxiety. (Note: The child who is upset about having to play in *any* circumstance would be described as having a high level of state anxiety.)

Psychologists have studied the relationship between the level of motivation and the resultant performance. For many years, the results, illustrated in Figure 1-4, were thought to represent the most common findings, often called the "inverted-U curve." Performance was thought to be best at moderate levels of motivation, with poorer performance expected when motive levels were low (laziness, for example) or too high ("choking").

More recently, psychologists have modified their beliefs about level of motivation, finding that each

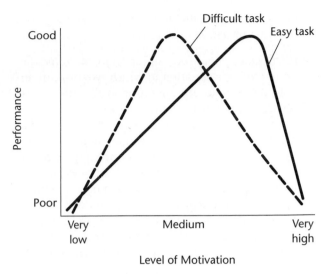

Figure 1-4 Inverted-U curve.

individual may have a level of motivation that is best for him or her. Based on the work of Russian psychologist Yuri Hanin, psychologists interested in physical activities and sport behaviors now often talk about the zone of optimal functioning (ZOF). The ZOF theory proposes that each person will perform best at a motivation level that matches individual characteristics; that is, while many people *will* show best performance when experiencing moderate levels of motivation, others will do equally well when highly aroused or when in a very relaxed or passive state. According to this theory, coaches who previously accepted the concept that all players should be "psyched up" before a competition should modify that concept to recognize that each player may need individualized consideration.

Functional Autonomy.   *Functional autonomy* refers to a situation in which a response is first made to satisfy some external motivating condition, but after being repeated a number of times, comes to be motivating in and of itself. One example of functional autonomy found in physical education or recreation may be a life-long sport such as tennis. Many school-age students begin playing tennis because it is required in a class, while many adults take up the activity to get in shape, lose weight, stop smoking, or obey doctor's orders. Yet many players come to appreciate the playing just for its own sake. Indeed, just as joggers who are kept from playing by bad weather, job pressures, or other reasons, feel deprived, so do avid tennis players when they are unable to play.

A number of studies have found that a vigorous bout of exercise is followed by an improved mood state, the "feeling good" reaction to a workout. Although there are some questions as to whether everyone can experience such reactions and what causes the mood state change, this phenomenon is one that argues for including physical activity as a regular part of school or work.

Conflict. One other aspect of the study of motivation is that of *conflict,* a situation in which two or more incompatible motives are operating at the same time. Resolving any conflict usually involves choosing a response that satisfies the strongest of the motives. For example, a person who starts to play tennis may experience both positive motivators, such as passing the class or getting in shape, and negative ones, such as experiencing some discomfort or pain or of having to change one's daily schedule. Instructors will want to try to strengthen the positive motives and reinforce those aspects that lead the person to resolve a conflict of such positive and negative values by choosing the exercise alternative.

Learning

Assuming a person is motivated to attempt some behavior, instructors then must facilitate learning the behavior properly. *Learning* is defined as a relatively permanent change in behavior that occurs as a result of experience. This definition does not negate the importance of physical development. Physical growth often is a necessary condition for learning to take place, but physical growth alone is not sufficient. Experience must also occur.

Learning-Performance Distinction. *Performance* is the actual behavior shown by the person. It must be recognized that what is observed does not necessarily reveal what has been learned. For example, research has shown that junior high school girls will often "defer" to the boys in physical activities even when the girls are more skilled, letting the boys perform at a better level rather than violate what are seen to be important social standards. The girls' observable performance would not show the learning they actually have acquired.

A variation of the concern with performance has been the choice of *process,* or how a response is made, versus *product,* or what result turns out. This debate is often expressed as "That's not the right way to do that!" versus "But it works!" Instructors are constantly faced with this concern. It is very hard to tell the bowler with a high average that her approach steps are not smooth—the product is successful, even though the process is not what might be considered ideal. (Note: Instructors working in adapted physical activity with participants who are disabled or handicapped in some manner often confront this type of conflict and must adjust instruction to maximize the results obtained.)

Effects of Practice. Some people are able to realize the effects of poor form. A swimmer, for example, may come to understand that a flutter kick that creates big splashes may look like it is very active and productive, but that "rebuilding" the kick to be smoother and more efficient will lead to even more success. Changing the practice patterns to include drills that enable making this change should eventually lead to a better performance.

Many students and athletes grow up believing that "practice makes perfect." This is an inaccurate statement unless the response being performed *is* perfect, or is being modified constantly to approach perfection. Instructors should recognize that a more appropriate viewpoint is that "practice makes *permanent.*" As with the swimmer, an instructor's task is to try to help any student or athlete make permanent the very best response possible.

Reinforcement

The condition that satisfies a motive is called a reinforcer. Although often thought of as a reward, psychologists use the term *reinforcement* in a broader sense, defining it as any condition that increases or maintains the strength of a response.

Positive Reinforcement. The conditions usually described as rewards are called *positive reinforcements,* events that, when present, increase or maintain the strength of the response. These may include anything from a few words of praise to stars pasted on a chart on the classroom wall.

Negative Reinforcement. Another form of reinforcement is *negative reinforcement,* in which the removal or absence of some stimulus increases or maintains the strength of the response. The unpleasant condition being removed is called an *aversive stimulus.* Negative reinforcement is *not* punishment. *Punishment* occurs when a response *leads* to an aversive stimulus, whereas negative reinforcement occurs when the aversive stimulus does not occur or is stopped.

Instructors often use negative reinforcers as well as punishers. Particularly good responses are reinforced by the removal of some unpleasant condition, for example, cancelling the laps to be run at the end of class. On the other hand, if the responses have been especially poor, the instructor may punish the class by not allowing the usual period of free play typically enjoyed at the end of class.

Extinction, Counterconditioning, and Spontaneous Recovery. When a response is no longer followed by a reinforcer, the response tends to become weaker. *Extinction* is both the procedure of no longer presenting the reinforcement and the result of this process, that is, the weakening of the response strength. When a replacement response is desired in the same stimulus situation, *counterconditioning*— reinforcing a substitute response—is often employed. Interestingly, sometimes an extinguished response will reappear after a period of rest has followed the extinction procedure. This is called *spontaneous recovery* of the response, and it occurs when stimulus conditions provoke the response although there is no reinforcement present.

All three of these principles should be familiar to instructors. For example, many young children learn to throw ineffectively, placing the forward foot on the same side of the body as the throwing hand. An instructor hoping to change this pattern may have to devote quite a bit of time to praising an appropriate response (counterconditioning) and extinguishing (not reinforcing) the less efficient pattern. Despite this instruction, sometimes after children have been away from instruction for some period of time, the inefficient form may reappear. Just why this spontaneous recovery occurs is not understood. Regardless, instructors must realize that if it does, additional practice such as that described above will be necessary.

Partial Reinforcement Effect. One condition that works against extinction is *partial reinforcement*, that is, following a response with reinforcement only part of the time. The result of partial reinforcement is called the partial reinforcement effect (PRE). Responses learned under partial reinforcement conditions are more resistant to extinction than responses learned under continuous reinforcement.

This works to the advantage of the instructor if the response is a productive or efficient one. However, an inefficient response, such as the throwing response mentioned above, *will* work some of the time. In such cases, eliminating the response may be quite difficult. This points to the need for effective instruction for motor responses very early in a child's life. When appropriate response patterns can be taught, they can become very resistant to extinction and probably will be maintained throughout life. By contrast, lack of instruction or poor instruction may allow inefficient or inappropriate responses to be learned that will work against the pleasures and successes that could be experienced. For example, if the young child does learn to throw with the "wrong" foot forward, this pattern may generalize to other activities, such as serving a tennis ball or bowling, in which case those activities will be less well done and less pleasurable than they might otherwise be.

Shaping

One of the most common ways of using reinforcement to improve responding is to shape the preferred response. *Shaping* is defined as reinforcing closer and closer approximations of a desired behavior, for example, when teaching a young child to make a forward roll. To begin with, the child is encouraged whenever the head is tucked and the body completes a rotation. Step by step, the child is taught more control, so that eventually the child learns the complete forward roll, including smoothly returning to one's feet. The same reinforcing of closer and closer approximations of the desired response can be extended to teach the child how to do a forward roll on the much smaller surface of a balance beam.

Modeling

Modeling occurs when a person observes the behavior of another, then performs some or all of that observed response (Figure 1-5). The instructor teaching the forward roll first demonstrates how it is done. The child then tries to imitate what he or she saw. If modeling is combined with shaping, the instructor reinforces each imitation that gets closer to the ultimately desired performance.

Another concern in modeling is *vicarious learning*, which occurs when the learner observes both the response and the consequences of the response. For example, vicarious learning occurs when the learner imitates the form of an expert archer who consistently hits the bull's-eye. In some cases, observing an unsuccessful response may instruct a student how to *avoid* making an ineffectual response. For example, if a companion attempts to cast a fishing line while standing too close to a tree, thus snagging the line, the observer learns to avoid that response without actually having to perform it.

Superstitious Responding. Occasionally, a response is followed by a reinforcement that is *not* contingent upon the response being made. Nevertheless, the performer may come to believe there is a contingency. The result, called *superstitious responding*

Figure 1-5 Modeling is an important instructional principle.

because of this inaccurate belief, is repetition of this response pattern. Unfortunately, infrequent response-reinforcement sequences, although not contingent relationships, are enough to sustain the superstition, illustrating the partial reinforcement effect.

While many superstitions may appear harmless, even seemingly silly ones, such as *having* to have three pennies in a pocket while playing a recreational round of golf, may influence the pleasure of the day. The player who believes that he will not be able to play well without those pennies probably will adopt a defeatist attitude and, indeed, will not play well. The "Now I *can't* play well because I didn't follow the superstition" attitude can be extremely destructive, despite its complete falseness.

Attention

Almost any sport or activity environment has many aspects of stimulation. Response acquisition may depend on the person's attention to the stimuli that are important for correct learning.

A popular way of conceptualizing attention in physical activities has been proposed by Robert Nideffer,[1] who suggests that attention can be viewed as having both width and direction. *Width* refers to whether the performer must focus in a broad or narrow range, while *direction* refers to either an internal or external focus. Combining these two dimensions, physical activities can then be viewed as broad-external, such as a field hockey player who must pay attention to the positioning and movement of both teammates and opponents when deciding where to try to pass the ball; broad-internal, such as when an experienced shuffleboard player considers the several strategies available before deciding what kind of play will be attempted; narrow-external, such as the concentration a cross-country skier must give to the terrain and snow conditions; and narrow-internal, such as is required by the kind of focus used by weight-lifters.

Analysis of each physical activity or sport may help instructors instill appropriate attentional focus into participants. For example, if the person learning how to putt a golf ball is distracted by shadows or sounds, the instructor may teach how to focus only on the line of the putt and other relevant cues. Eventually, the goal would be to reach a level of habitual responding where attending to the necessary and appropriate cues is done in a manner that makes correct responding relatively automatic.

Generalization and Discrimination. Attention may be influenced by *stimulus generalization*— responding not only to the original stimulus, but also to other similar stimuli—and *discrimination* (or *differentiation*), when the response is made to one stimulus but not made to other stimuli that are judged to be dissimilar.

Skiing provides examples of both principles. The novice skier may judge all snow conditions to be the same, that is, generalize that all slopes or trails have "snow." The more experienced skier may discriminate among the several types of snow that can be encountered and adjust responses accordingly.

Other General Acquisition Principles

While many factors such as those mentioned above influence acquisition, there are a number of other variables that affect learning. This section presents some that seem most appropriate for physical education.

Overlearning. *Overlearning* is associated with the "practice makes permanent" concept. If some criterion is used to decide when learning has occurred, overlearning refers to the amount of time or number of trials spent practicing beyond that criterion level. Even if the young child seemingly has mastered the forward roll, repeated practice will ensure the learning.

Transfer of Training. When task acquisition is affected by some previous learning, *transfer of training* has taken place. Instructors should strive for *positive transfer,* that is, when learning one task facilitates the acquisition of another. As mentioned before, learning the correct motion involved in throwing a ball (opposite hand-foot pattern) may provide positive transfer for the subsequent acquisition of activities such as serving a volleyball, serving in tennis, or rolling a bowling ball. Some situations generate *negative transfer,* when already knowing one task interferes with the acquisition of a second. Something as simple as learning the rules regarding out-of-bounds illustrates how negative transfer can occur. In baseball, tennis, and a number of other sports, on the line is in-bounds. The ball must be completely beyond the line to be out-of-bounds. But in football and basketball, on the line is out-of-bounds. In soccer, if the ball crosses the line completely, it is judged to be out-of-bounds, even if it does this while in the air and later returns to field of play before landing. In golf, the ball may cross the out-of-bounds area, as long as its final resting place is within bounds at the end of the shot. Obviously, learning in any one of these cases may be detrimental to learning the same type of rule for some other activity.

There will be some instances in which no transfer takes place, either positive or negative; that is, one task has no bearing upon another.

Knowledge of Results. Also called feedback, *knowledge of results* is the information about success or failure a person receives after performing some response. In general, knowledge of results facilitates acquisition of a response, especially if it is provided immediately after the response is made rather than delayed.

Many physical activities provide knowledge of results automatically. If a person tries a new type of turn while skiing and falls, there is immediate feedback about the response. Other circumstances require the feedback provided by an outside observer, such as comments about position on the playing area or time elapsed for a particular distance.

A popular way to provide feedback about physical activities is the use of film or videotape. One advantage of this type of feedback is that it can be used repeatedly, allowing the learner the certainty of understanding the point being made.

Distribution of Practice. A summary of research supports the finding that holding relatively short practice periods and distributing them over some period of time will produce the best acquisition of a response. This is often called *distributed practice,* as opposed to *massed practice,* where practice periods are bunched together. (Note: The concern here is with acquiring a response; longer practice periods for already-learned responses may be necessary to obtain desired conditioning levels.)

Many instructors take advantage of distributed practice by scheduling a variety of tasks during any one session. The tasks may be repeated over several days, but are not practiced long enough in any one session to produce boredom or fatigue. Distributed practice also seems to allow for consolidation of learning to take place during the interim periods.

Active versus Passive Attitude. A principle that seems to apply to almost any acquisition situation in physical education (or in sport situations) is that an *active* approach to learning will produce better acquisition than will a *passive* attitude. However, it should be recognized that the activity may be physical or mental or both. Recent investigations in cognitive psychology have shown that some forms of both approaches may combine to produce improved acquisition and excellent performance. For example, instructors who combine active physical practice with *mental imagery,* the relatively passive mental rehearsal of a task, often appear to produce learning benefits for their students. Those who teach their students to create images of the responses to be made and how those responses will be executed frequently generate improved acquisition and performance from their students when compared with those students taught only with active practice that does not employ imagery as well.

Instructors should explore the many possibilities that may lead to improved acquisition and performance. An illustration would be to use a videotape of an excellent performer as an introduction to a task (a potential modeling situation). After viewing the tape, the learners then might try to create mental images matching their intended performance with those seen on the tape. The positive transfer resulting from the modeling and imagery should produce better learning and performance of the response.

Context of Learning. Evidence indicates that people often develop what is called *state-dependent learning,* in which the response is attached to the physical environment or emotional condition in which it is learned. This factor is one that is important for both the acquisition and retention of the response. "Dress rehearsal" practices are conducted to try to satisfy this factor. For instance, summer recreational swim clubs will often do this by holding intrasquad competition before any actual meets are held against other clubs, trying to match the conditions that will exist when retention is actually demanded.

Retention and Forgetting

Of major concern to instructors in all areas is whether responses that have been learned will be retained or forgotten. *Retention* is the storage of learning over some period of time, often called the *retention interval. Forgetting* refers to the loss of retention, or the inability to retrieve a response from storage. It should be noted that we must always measure retention in some manner, not forgetting. Forgetting is only inferred from what appears to not be retained.

Storage. *Storage,* or the maintenance of a memory over the retention interval, has several forms. All are well illustrated by the life-long activity of bicycling. Stimuli encountered while riding may be kept briefly in *sensory storage,* in which information is held in an unprocessed form for several seconds or less. These might include such things as the visual scene, the sound of a car's horn, or the kinesthetic sensations produced by the seating position on the bicycle. Some stimuli may be incorporated into *short-term storage,* in which information is given some initial processing, then may be processed further or simply discarded. For example, the rider may be given directions and hold these in memory only long enough to execute them, or may further process them into *long-term storage,* in which information is encoded, rehearsed, or treated in some manner so that retention extends over some longer period of time. Long-term storage may last a lifetime, and the rider may always remember the appropriate way to follow the route. Of course, the act of riding the bicycle itself is good evidence for life-long, long-term storage of a series of responses. It has often been said that once one learns to ride a bicycle, the responses are never forgotten. Much evidence exists to indicate this is correct.

Failure to Retrieve. The two most common explanations for failure to retrieve information from storage are that (1) a person is given the wrong cue to initiate the retrieval and (2) the cue is correct, but some other interfering response is produced instead. As an example of inappropriate retrieval cues, consider the dance instructor who asks her young students to "start with the tango you learned last Friday." If the students practiced different dances at that last session, they may be unable to make the correct response. They may know the tango and may indeed remember the dance, but are confused by the retrieval cues given.

Interference suggests that retention of one response conflicts or interferes with the retention of some other response. This may be previous learning interfering with the retention of something learned later (often called proactive interference) or later learning interfering with something learned before (called retroactive interference). In either case, more than one stored response can be elicited by the retrieval cue and, if the inappropriate response is given, forgetting will seem to have occurred. For example, someone who has just learned flycasting often has difficulty because so many other recreational sports involve considerable movement in the wrist, something that is inappropriate to this particular activity. The old learning interferes with the newly acquired learning and makes it appear that the person has forgotten the instruction.

Problem Solving in Physical Education

The Problem-Solving Sequence. *Problem solving,* that is, establishing a goal and then seeking ways to achieve that goal, is typified by a fairly common sequence of events. The five steps are (1) recognizing there is a problem, (2) defining the problem accurately, (3) producing hypotheses about the problem's solution, (4) testing the hypotheses, and (5) selecting the best solution.

Recognizing that a problem exists may be a major step in initiating problem solving because, logically, lack of understanding stops the sequence before it gets started. For example, not realizing that the rules of a game are misunderstood means the problem is not recognized and the game continues to be played incorrectly. If recognition occurs, defining the problem accurately requires identifying the most relevant concepts. When rules are misunderstood, discovering which are not grasped is essential if they are to be learned properly.

Once the areas to be worked on have been identified, hypotheses about how to resolve the problem can be generated. Generating as many solutions as possible before testing any or making judgments about any of the approaches (often called *brainstorming*) may help to guarantee that the best possible solution will be found. For example, the instructor may suggest holding rules classes, giving a rule book to each student, showing videotapes depicting the rules, or taking the students to a game in which the rules are being enforced properly. Each of these possible solutions might be suggested before any evaluation or decision is made.

Testing means confirming or disconfirming each hypothesis. If the hypothesis is disconfirmed (that is, the students would not learn the rules if they tried that solution), it is discarded as unworkable. If the hypothesis is confirmed, the solution should be compared with any other confirmed ones to determine which is most acceptable. Taking the students to a game might be an acceptable hypothesis but prohibitively expensive when compared with renting a videotape. The latter solution would be more likely to be adopted.

Variables Affecting Problem Solving. The reader is invited to review earlier sections of this chapter and try to develop applications of the principles presented to a problem-solving situation. To illustrate the complexity of problem solving and how many variables may be important, consider the instructor trying to help novice swimmers learn to make a flip-turn. The heightened motivational level generated by submersion and disorientation may reduce performance effectiveness considerably. Repeated practice almost certainly will be needed. The instructor may use modeling as one solution and use the principles of shaping as well. Knowledge of results will show how a well-executed flip-turn reduces the turn-around time required at the end of the pool. Finally, interference may exist in the form of other rolling-motion activities or other turns the swimmers have learned previously. What may seem to be a fairly simple goal to achieve may actually be rather complicated and require thorough study before the instructor initiates a practice plan.

Personality and Social Concerns in Physical Education

Although it is beyond the scope of this handbook to consider personality variables or social interactions in great detail, it should be recognized that the characteristics of each individual and the ways in which individuals interact will have pronounced effects on the behaviors seen in learning or performing physical activities. The study of personality considers the characteristics of each person individually, whereas social psychology studies the behavior of the individual within the group setting.

Personality. *Personality,* the enduring characteristics that represent a person's behavior, develops from the combined effects of environmental and hereditary influences. Aspects of personality that have been studied in relation to performing physical activities include anxiety, aggression, gender role orientation, racial differences, mood states, and sociability. Personality can influence the performance of participants at every level, from the beginning child to the elite adult athlete.

Many of the topics overlap with those already discussed; for example, several researchers have devoted considerable study to the attributes of people who participate in high-risk sports such as hanggliding and parachuting. These people plainly operate at motivational levels unlike those of the typical person, and studies have identified them as being high in need for achievement, dominance, and courage, while low in need for order. They are often described as sensation-seeking or stress-seeking individuals, ones who appreciate a high level of arousal. Having such a student in class would certainly present a challenge to the instructor, if for no other reason than having to try to blend this person with those with more usual motivational levels.

Stereotypes provide another example of personality and social concerns that may be of importance to the participant or instructor. Researchers have found, for instance, that certain physical activities are considered socially "wrong" either for females or males. Depending on whether such stereotypes are accepted or rejected by the student or outside observers, participation in such physical activities may be limited, or met with disapproval, such as from parents of the student. An instructor must be ready to deal with such reactions.

These examples illustrate the kinds of personality research being done with regard to physical activity. There is also a large body of research dealing with the relationship between personality characteristics and performance in competitive sports. Whether for class, recreational, or competitive activities, characteristics have been identified that appear to distinguish the type of person who may succeed in particular activities. Instructors should realize that personality variables may have pronounced influence on the activities preferred and the performance and success of potential participants. Instructors are encouraged to explore these possibilities more thoroughly through additional study.

Social Interaction. Many recreational pursuits, games, and organized sports involve the participation of more than one person at the same time. *Social interaction*—how people interact and what effects these interactions have upon their behaviors— is of major importance in many physical activities. The phenomena of *social facilitation* and *social interference* refer to the effects the presence of other participants or of observers such as a class, an audience, or a crowd may have upon performance. Both provide good illustrations of social interaction.

Social facilitation means that the presence of others tends to make performance better than when others are not present; social interference refers to situations in which the presence of others tends to make performance poorer than when others are not present. Obvious examples of these phenomena occur when performance is required in front of a class or when a crowd is present for an athletic contest.

In general, studies have shown that social facilitation is most likely to occur when the response to be performed is one that has been well learned. Social interference occurs more frequently with relatively new responses. Again, instructors who understand these results can try to establish conditions that create facilitation and avoid interference. The implied reinforcement of social facilitation or punishment of social interference can be expected to affect later performances.

Social Expectations. *Social expectations* may influence a person's behavior, especially when the behavior appears to occur in order to satisfy some previously expressed expectation. Instructors should be particularly careful to avoid repetitive, demeaning remarks when dealing with behaviors that are easily changed. Comments such as "You'll never get it right!" become the expectation and yield inadequate performances. Guarding against peer group ridicule is equally important, for it can produce the same kind of effect. Correspondingly, establishing positive expectations often will generate improved performance. The "You're getting better; I know you'll get it soon" attitude can be expected to produce improved responding.

Competition and Cooperation. *Competition* is the attempt to do something better than someone else. Competition often requires a positive attitude, whether the someone else involved is another person or the previous accomplishments of the person competing. Research indicates that a successful competitor strives for and expects accomplishments that an unsuccessful competitor does not expect. Additionally, studies have shown that anxiety about competition varies as a function of many variables, including perceived threat, level of motivation, or gender role endorsement. It may be wise to evaluate competitive anxiety before establishing contest strategies.

Cooperation refers to working with or helping someone else in hopes of achieving some mutual goal. Both competition and cooperation often are fostered by game or sport situations. Cooperation often refers to collaboration with classmates or teammates, but cooperation with instructors, officials, opponents, or even spectators also may be a part of a situation.

One problem often faced by instructors or coaches is the competition versus cooperation dilemma. The person who has a high level of competitive motivation may find it difficult to cooperate with others, even though cooperation would facilitate pursuit of the goal desired. Psychologists call such a situation, in which one protects a self-interest and by doing so actually loses, a *social trap*. In effect, what the person experiences can be described as a social conflict, when two incompatible social motives are operating at the same time. For example, in class, some students appear to have a need to be the "star." These students compete against classmates for recognition even when the very nature of the activity requires cooperation and a star system will lead to a poorer result. Convincing students that both competition and cooperation are possible simultaneously is often difficult. Because social motives such as achievement and friendship can be extremely powerful and create social conflict situations, instructors are cautioned to evaluate such possibilities when working with their students.

Summary

This brief look at psychological principles is sufficient to indicate the need for instructors to be aware of the many variables that may affect learning and performance. The references listed below will help the reader explore in more detail those areas that are of particular interest.

Further References

Anshel, M. H. *Sport Psychology: From Theory to Practice.* Scottsdale, AZ: Gorsuch Scarisbrick, 1990.

Cox, R. H. *Sport Psychology: Concepts and Applications.* 3rd ed. Madison, WI: Brown & Benchmark, 1994.

Kremer, J. M. D. and Scully, D. M. *Psychology in Sport.* London/Bristol, PA: Taylor & Francis, 1994.

LeUnes, A. D. and Nation, J. R. *Sport Psychology: An Introduction.* Chicago, IL: Nelson-Hall, 1989.

Murphy, S. M. (ed.). *Sport Psychology Interventions.* Champaign, IL: Human Kinetics, 1995.

Russell, G. W. *The Social Psychology of Sport.* New York: Springer-Verlag, 1993.

Suinn, R. M. *Seven Steps to Peak Performance.* Toronto: Hans Huber Publishers, 1986.

Williams, J. M. (ed.). *Applied Sport Psychology: Personal Growth to Peak Performance.* Mountain View, CA: Mayfield, 1993.

In addition, the reader may want to consult any one of the many good introductory psychology textbooks available for understanding of the basic psychological principles presented.

Periodicals

Journals that particularly emphasize the relationship between psychology and physical activity include the following: *Journal of Sport and Exercise Psychology, Journal of Teaching in Physical Education, Journal of Applied Psychology, The Sport Psychologist, Research Quarterly*, and *Journal of Motor Behavior*. In addition, instructors especially interested in working with students with disabilities or handicaps will want to look at *Adapted Physical Activity Quarterly and Palaestra*.

ACTIVITY CHAPTER FORMAT

To assist the instructor in planning and continuity, the chapters follow a definite structural format. Because of the variety of activities and the length allocated to each, a chapter may not include all the elements listed in the format. For example, there is no "Playing Strategy/Tactics" topic in gymnastics nor "Scoring/Rules" for dance. However, the order and elements, as they relate to each activity, are consistent in structure.

Chapter Format Elements and Order

- Chapter Objectives
- Nature and Purpose
- Scoring/Rules
- Equipment
- Suggested Learning Sequence
- Skills and Techniques
  - Learning/Helpful Hints
  - Practice/Organizational Suggestions
- Safety Considerations
- Playing Strategies/Tactics
- Etiquette/Playing Courtesy
- Modifications for Special Populations
- Terminology
- References
- Web Sites

Each element is presented in the text to assist in effective skill learning as follows:

Chapter Objectives: These highlight the chapter's main concepts and features. They provide direction for the learner and provide objectives for assessing understanding.

Nature and Purpose: Provides a brief overview of the activity, nuances that make the activity different from or similar to others, and historical implications. This information provides a basic understanding and foundation as the learner starts the activity.

Scoring/Rules: Identifies the parameters for participating in the activity; what is expected, allowed, and not allowed; and defines the area where the activity takes place. Rules often vary slightly according to ability levels, sexes, or governing bodies. The rules presented define the basics of activity, and modifications are possible. They are used as a guide for the learners as they practice skills, progress to limited application in modified play, and culminate in actual game-like conditions.

Equipment: Provides official specifications, identifies items for safety and protection, and suggests the minimum equipment needed for participation. This information helps the learner identify what is necessary to start the activity.

Suggested Learning Sequence: Identifies the beginning to intermediate skills/techniques which assist in participating in the acitivity effectively.

Skills and Techniques: Identifies the mechanical breakdown of each skill for developing correct execution. The learner should consult "Mechanical Aspects" in Chapter 1 of the text, which describes basic movements underlying quality skill development.

Learning/Helpful Hints: Provides knowledge, strategies, and suggestions regarding the mechanics of developing each skill listed for the activity.

Practice/Organizational Suggestions: Identifies specific methods, drills, and/or suggestions for the learner to use when practicing each of the skills.

Safety Considerations: Suggests ways the learners can protect themselves and other participants from injury or harm while participating in the activity.

Playing Strategies/Tactics: Provides factors (formations, alignments, principles, etc.) that lead to skillful, organized, controlled play when the learner applies the skills in competition or participation.

Etiquette/Playing Courtesy: Identifies specific suggestions for factors that make the activity more enjoyable for oneself and others, defines any code of ethics, and cities characteristics for good sportsmanship.

Modifications for Special Populations: Suggests ways that the orthopedically impaired, cognitively impaired, or sensory-impaired individual might be included in the activity with other participants.

Terminology: Defines basic terms that help the learner understand the activity and develop a professional vocabulary for communication.

References: Lists books, periodicals, and audiovisual materials for the learner who desires more extensive knowledge about the activity.

Web Sites: Identifies computer sites where the participant can locate additional information about the activity.

The foregoing elements provide systematic and complete information for each activity so the learner can develop beginning to intermediate skills and knowledge. There are sources provided if additional information is needed.

TECHNOLOGY AND PHYSICAL EDUCATION PROGRAMS OF THE FUTURE

Only recently has the traditional classroom begun to change. The classroom of 150 years ago had desks facing the chalkboard in the front of the room. Today's classroom looks much the same, except that computers have been added in some, but not all, classrooms. In the early 1980s Goodlad observed that schools had responded slowly to the technological revolution.[2] Physical education has been even slower to respond. A typical gymnasium and the activities that occur there have changed very little over the past several decades, but society and the recognized needs of students have changed considerably. Changes in schools also are becoming more evident, especially in the area of technology. Schools are becoming equipped with computer labs, and many classrooms have at least one computer. Videotapes and films have been used for many years to enhance instruction. In 1993 a survey of computer use in one state revealed that only 42.6 percent of physical education teachers used a computer in their classes or as a tool to enhance learning.[3]

Physical education is at what some are calling a critical crossroads.[4] The next few years will determine the face of physical education and even the mere existence of physical education classes in the schools of the future. The inclusion of technology in the gymnasium is only one of the contributing factors. Three other areas of current concern in education that also are affecting physical education are financial constraints, educational reform, and teacher accountability for student learning. Physical education teachers can allow each of the above-mentioned items to eliminate physical education programs, or they can use this situation as an opportunity to enhance physical education. For example, the educational reform movement provides an opportunity to review the physical education curriculum and to design a curriculum that is appropriate for each student at each level. The movement also opens lines of communication between teachers in a particular school across grade levels and disciplines. Each of the above will enhance the physical education program. All teachers will need to address positively the issues that are affecting their schools and communities.

Professional organizations are providing guidance and leadership in directing the changes that need to occur in physical education. The National Association for Sport and Physical Education (NASPE), an association of the American Alliance for Health, Physical Education, Recreation and Dance (AAHPERD), has taken a leadership role in helping shape the future of physical education. In 1990 the definition of the physically educated person was published. Benchmarks to measure progress toward the definition followed. In the early 1990s, on the national educational level, academic areas were charged with the task of developing their individual content standards. In 1995 NASPE completed the content standards for physical education, which are as follows.

A physically educated person

1. Demonstrates competency in many movement forms and proficiency in a few movement forms.
2. Applies movement concepts and principles to the learning and development of motor skills.
3. Exhibits a physically active lifestyle.
4. Achieves and maintains a health-enhancing level of physical fitness.
5. Demonstrates responsible personal and social behavior in physical activity settings.
6. Demonstrates understanding and respect for differences among people in physical activity settings.
7. Understands that physical activity provides opportunities for enjoyment, challenge, self-expression, and social interaction.[5]

This document also includes guidelines and ideas for assessing the content standards. The guidelines are provided for selected grade levels throughout the K–12 experience.

NASPE has also published a series of position statements, including guidelines for elementary, middle school, and high school physical education. Other position statements discuss developmentally appropriate activities for various age groups. Program appraisal checklists are available to evaluate the quality of physical education programs.[6]

The issues facing education today require physical educators to promote their programs. Teacher education programs need to provide training in marketing and public relations. NASPE has developed an advocacy kit to provide materials and ideas for physical educators to use to increase support for their programs.[7]

No one knows exactly what physical education will be like in the future, but the present provides some clues. Teachers will be held accountable for student learning in all disciplines and for providing programs to meet the needs of all students. The physical fitness levels of students have been questioned recently. Interest in raising fitness levels is high. Much discussion in the profession has focused on whether to emphasize improving fitness or skills in physical education classes.

A look at the past indicates that for various reasons physical educators have found it difficult to address physical fitness adequately within their programs. One challenge is to determine how to organize physical fitness within the multiactivity program structure (sports, dance, aquatics, gymnastics, fitness, etc.) and how to address teaching it.

One approach educators have tried is to vary activities into a set length of instruction. This approach, however, does not work because physical fitness takes time to develop and needs to be maintained. A traditional 3-week unit (15 meetings) in aerobic dance followed by a 3-week unit in volleyball does not allow sufficient time to develop nor to maintain fitness. Conversely, devoting an entire semester to weight training can make students bored and, moreover, does not address other factors of physical fitness, such as aerobic capacity.

Because of the length of a typical class period (50 minutes), it is impossible to allocate sufficient time for fitness, sport instruction/practice, and dressing (20 to 30 minutes suggested for each). Block scheduling provides enough time daily but in most cases, only a certain period, such as a semester or six weeks, is allotted to physical education; thereafter, students go on to a different subject in some other discipline. Even when physical education has been allotted enough time to develop students' aerobic fitness, until recently, it has been difficult for educators to determine the optimal intensity of the fitness work.

Heart rate monitor technology is an instrument for measuring the effectiveness of instruction when the goal is improvement of cardiovascular fitness. In addition, the monitors allow for individualization of instruction because each student can be told to work at an appropriate heart rate level. This begins the process of meeting the needs of all students. No longer must all students work at the same pace. Some may actually be walking and working at the same effort level as others who are running. Heart rate monitors now provide the assurance that students are working at an appropriate level.

One recently suggested method for teaching fitness is to incorporate it into all motor skill classes, with the goal of developing skill and fitness simultaneously. It had been thought that both fitness and skills could not be improved concurrently. A 1995 study[8] focused on the question. Two beginning volleyball classes were used in the study. One was taught in a traditional manner. In the other class, fitness was infused into the class activities by adding movements to all drills and games that are part of successful volleyball playing. Students wore heart rate monitors to evaluate the effectiveness of the instruction in maintaining heart rate levels at appropriate intensities and for sufficient durations for cardiovascular gains to occur. Pretests and posttests were administered to measure skill levels, playing ability, and fitness components. Class instruction occurred 3 days a week for 8½ weeks. Posttests revealed that the classes had no significant difference in skill levels and that each class had improved at the same rate. No difference existed in any other measure except for cardiovascular fitness. In 8½ weeks a significant difference in cardiovascular fitness gains had occurred. The study indicated that there is no need to continue the discussion of which area—fitness or skill—to emphasize in physical education classes but that physical educators should simply be taught how to infuse fitness into skill instruction in all fitness component areas.

For physical education to be part of the future, new creative ideas, such as fitness infusion, will need to be included. If physical education is no more than a recreation program, physical education will not be part of the educational future. Communities can develop and administer quality recreation programs for less expense than the costs of a physical education program. Students will be expected to learn and will be provided with new knowledge and experiences each year. Technological advances will make this easier.

Currently technology is used in a variety of ways in the gymnasium, ranging from video cameras to body composition analyzers. Computers can be used to teach rules, to simulate games, to access information all over the world, and to assess fitness levels (Figures 1-6, 1-7) as well as for word processing, grading, and other administrative functions. Compact Disc-Interactive (CD-I) and CD-ROM technology allow the student to interact with the computer in such a way that the student's responses indicate what path the computer will go in presenting new information or in reviewing previously presented material. In addition to that already mentioned, technology available now includes heart rate monitors, computerized blood pressure systems, laser discs, stress assessment systems, and more. Computers can be connected to the Internet (the information super highway), providing access to electronic bulletin boards, listserves, and computers and files of information from all over the world. Software, video material, and sound also can be transferred by way of the Internet to an individual personal computer. Students can communicate with other students anywhere in the world via this system.

Complementing the technology is computer software that can analyze fitness results, teach rules and strategies of games and concepts such as exercise physiology and motor learning, demonstrate biomechanical principles, and carry out many administrative functions required of teachers. Video material is available for much of the above in the form of videotapes, laser discs, and CD-ROMs.

The following is a scenario describing a possible physical education class of the future.

As the class enters the gymnasium, two or three students go to the blood pressure computer station to check each other's blood pressure. Students do this on a rotating basis so that the students and the teacher can see if any trends are developing.

Another student moves to the biofeedback equipment (Figure 1-8) to work on stress reduction strategies. The student will be able to visually see the effects of various music or videos on his stress levels. The student can then determine the types of activities that can be used to regularly reduce stress.

The fitness self-assessment area will be the destination of another group of students. The students will assess all fitness components and enter the results into a computer program, Body and Mind.[9] They will then prepare an individual exercise program from the information learned. Some of the students will do their own programs at home, some with their families, while others will use the fitness room during the hours it is open before and after school and in the evenings.

Heart rate monitors will be placed on another group of students to monitor the intensity level of their work during the class (Figure 1-9). Students in the school and parent volunteers have been trained to download the heart rate monitor information into a computer (Figure 1-10) and print the curves (Figure 1-11) and other information generated by the software.

The heart rate monitor group and all other students will log onto an assigned computer station. (All stations are networked so the teacher has access to all of the class data from any one station.) At the beginning of each unit of instruction, when the students log onto the computer, they are given a series of pre-assessment tasks. When the tasks are completed, the student enters the data into the computer. The pre-assessment results are analyzed by the computer and

Figure 1-6 MicroFit fitness assessment system.

Ball State Teacher Education
MicroFit Fitness Profile

Age:	19 years	Standard data:	20-29 yr	Sex: Female
Height:	74.0 in	Current weight:	162.5 lbs	21-Nov-1995
		Prior weight:	lbs	

Score Poor Unfit Average Fit Excellent

Measure	Score									
Percent body fat (%)	23.9 *	37.0	32.0	30.0	28.0	26.0	24.0	22.0	20.0	18.0
Biceps strength (lbs)	66 *	20	25	30	38	48	58	68	75	80
Back flexibility (units)	17 *	12	14	16	18	19	20	21	22	23
Resting heart rate (bpm)	66 *	90	83	80	77	74	71	68	66	62
Systolic blood pressure (mmHg)	128 *	168	159	148	139	115	112	109	105	99
Diastolic blood pressure (mmHg)	78 *	104	99	94	89	72	69	67	64	59
Aerobic fitness (ml/kg/min)	47.1 *	22.0	24.0	28.0	31.0	34.0	37.0	42.0	48.0	51.0
Push-ups (maximum)	* *	5	9	11	14	16	20	22	26	32
R&L hand grip strength (kg)	* *	50	53	56	59	62	64	67	70	74
Total fitness score	61 *	10	20	30	40	50	60	70	80	90

Bike test data	21-Nov-1995		Skinfold data	21-Nov-1995
Workload (kp)	2.0		Triceps	21.9
Heartrate	138		Suprailium	14.8
			Thigh	24.7

Figure 1-7 Example of a fitness assessment using the MicroFit system.

used to determine the drills and learning experiences appropriate for each student. The student is assigned a partner or group, depending upon the activity. The group views a demonstration and cues presented on the computer. This material has been prepared using the best pedagogical knowledge available. The group will go to their assigned area, perform the assigned tasks, and complete a self-check assignment. When finished, they return to the computer and input the results of the self-check. The results will determine if the next assignments made by the computer are extensions (tasks of increasing or decreasing difficulty),

Figure 1-8 Biofeedback equipment in use by a student.

Figure 1-9 Heart rate monitor transmitter and receiver.

Figure 1-10 Student downloading heart rate monitor data.

Time: 00:00:00   a:\16vb2-4.raw
Heart Rate: 94 bpm
STUDENT 16 VBSTUDY 11:00 CLASS DAY 5--3 ON
3 PLAY 2-4-94

Figure 1-11 Heart rate monitor printout.

refinements (additional tasks at the same level of difficulty), or applications (lead-up games, for example). Each student works at a pace designed especially for him.

All students will be given an assignment to communicate with their electronic "pen pal" over the Internet. The next unit will be international games, and each student is required to teach a game he has learned from the international pen pal. Part of the student's presentation will include a video message from the pen pal and a video of children in the other country playing the game. All of this will be downloaded from the information super highway.

The teacher's role is that of a facilitator. The teacher is free to help any student who needs extra help without slowing down the learning process for any of the other students. The teacher has the opportunity to interact with each student individually. Students are working independently at an individually designed pace.

The technology necessary for this scenario to occur is already available. All that is lacking is the design and production of the individualized learning units. Other possible scenarios may include simulators or virtual reality equipment. The physical education class of the future will be determined by the creativity of the physical educators of the present.

What is known about the future is that technology in some form will need to be used for physical education to survive and adjust to the demands of the 21st century. Teachers who have already incorporated technology into their physical education programs have reported increased student learning and motivation. Parents have also increased support for physical education classes as they see the curriculum changing.

The time has arrived for all physical education programs to move out of the past and into the exciting world of the future. Technology is definitely part of that future.

References

1. Nideffer, R. M. A Test of Attentional and Interpersonal Style. *Journal of Personality and Social Psychology,* 34: 395–404, 1976.
2. Goodlad, J. *A Place Called School.* New York: McGraw-Hill, 1983.
3. Buck, M. M. and Assmann, N. Computer Usage by Indiana Public School Physical Education Teachers: Part II. *Indiana Journal for Health, Physical Education, Recreation and Dance,* 23(3):9–12, 1994.
4. Rink, J. E. (ed.). *Critical Crossroads: Middle and Secondary School Physical Education.* Reston, VA: National Association for Sport and Physical Education, 1993.
5. NASPE. *Moving into the future. National Standards for Physical Education: A Guide to Content and Assessment.* St. Louis: Mosby, 1995, p. 1.
6. Contact NASPE at 1900 Association Drive, Reston, VA 22091, for information on ordering copies of the above-mentioned items.
7. NASPE. *Sport and Physical Education Advocacy Kit* (SPEAK). Reston, VA: NASPE, 1994.
8. Buck, M. M. and McManama, J. Improving fitness and skill concurrently: Can it be done? Presentation at the 1995 ICHPERSD World Congress, Gainesville, FL, 1995.
9. Body & Mind: Interactive Technology for Fitness Education. Designed by Fitness Lifestyle Design, Inc., 1995.

APPENDIX: TECHNOLOGY RESOURCES

Computer Programs

1. Baudville, 1001 Medical Park Dr., SE, Grand Rapids, MI 49506; 800-728-0888
   Award Maker Software
2. Bonnie's Fitware, 18832 Stefani Ave., Cerritos, CA 90701; 310-924-0835
   Software designed for use with the Sharp Wizard handheld computer
   Portfolio software, variety of other software
3. CompTech Systems, P.O. Box 516, Hastings, MN 55033; 800-343-2406
   Variety of software for physical education
4. Cramer Software Group, 153 W. Warren, Gardner, KS 66030; 800-255-6611
   Fit-N-Dex fitness software
5. Fitness Lifestyle Design, 2317 Eastgate Way, Tallahassee, FL 32308; 904-391-7212
   Body and Mind CD-ROM software for Macintosh computers
6. Institute for Aerobics Research, 12330 Preston Rd., Dallas, TX 75230; 214-701-6885
   Fitness Gram Software
7. Intellimedia Sports Inc., Two Piedmont Center, Suite 300, Atlanta, GA 30305; 404-261-8330
   CD-ROM "Let's Play" series, including golf, football, baseball, soccer, tennis, basketball, skiing, and more
8. MAZE Products, 2610 Commonwealth Dr., Charlottesville, VA 22901
   Observation, Analysis and Recording System (OARS) Software
9. MECC, 3490 Lexington Ave., North, St. Paul, MN 55126; 800-228-3504
   Puzzle and Poster software
10. Micro Computer Software, Virginia Tech, Department of Physical Education, Blacksburg, VA 24061
    ALT-PE software
11. Mindscape, Inc., 1345 Diversey Pkwy., Chicago, IL 60614; 800-829-1900
    Crossword puzzle software
12. Persimmon Software, 1901 Gemway Dr., Charlotte, NC 28216; 704-398-1309
    Variety of physical education–related titles
13. Springboard Software, 7808 Creekridge Circle, Minneapolis, MN 55435; 612-944-3912
    Certificate Maker software
14. Softshare, AAPHERD, 1900 Association Dr., Reston, VA 22091; 800-213-7193
    Variety of titles for use with IBM-compatible, Apple, and Macintosh computers
15. SISU Software, Inc., P. O. Box 2305, Renton, WA 98056-2305; 800-228-5385
    Interactive CD-ROM series, including volleyball, soccer, softball, track and field, and tennis

Other Resources

1. Heart Rate Monitors
   Polar Vantage XL ($259–$289)
   Favor ($85)
   Interface, software, cable ($389)
   POLAR; Laura Delgado, 800-227-1314
   Creative Health Products, 800-742-4478
   Bike Wave, 317-471-1117
2. EMG Stress Assessment
   Biofeedback Microlab
   Apple ($325)
   IBM ($320); Required interface card for IBM ($100); 25 percent discount on six or more
   Creative Health Products, 800-742-4478
   Queue, Inc., Distributors, 800-232-2224

3. Dynapulse 200M
   Educational Version—curriculum and five labs
   ($295) (unlimited database)
   Pulse Metric; Willis Lee, 800-927-8573; FAX
   619-546-9470
4. Digiscore
   Automated scoring system, including hand held
   keypads, docking station, and software
   Fleetwood, P.O. Box 1259, Holland, MI 49422;
   800-257-6390

5. Voice-It
   Digital voice recorder: 45-second version ($30);
   90-second version ($40); 3-minute version ($55)
   Available at Target Stores and Service
   Merchandise
6. MicroFit, Inc., Mountain View, CA 94043; 415-
   969-7296
   Computerized fitness assessment system

CHAPTER 2

Principles of Physical Fitness

This chapter discusses

- Skill-related versus health-related physical fitness
- The need for and benefits of physical fitness
- Components of the pre-exercise program screening
- The principles of exercise training
- Exercise for weight (fat) loss
- Supplemental training programs (interval and circuit training)

If ten people were asked to define physical fitness, it would not be surprising to get ten different answers that are all partially correct. This variation occurs because physical fitness can be categorized into two types—skill-related and health-related—with each type having various components. Skill-related physical fitness includes power, speed, agility, balance, coordination, and reaction time. Prior to 1980, the majority of physical education programs evaluated primarily the skill-related components of physical fitness by using a battery of tests that included sit-ups, pull-ups, shuttle run, 50-yard dash, softball throw, and 600-yard run/walk. However, beginning in 1980, the American Alliance for Health, Physical Education, Recreation, and Dance (AAHPERD) began using a health-related physical fitness test that included a one-mile run/walk, skinfold measurements, sit and reach measurement, and a sit-up test.[1] In 1988, AAHPERD added a pull-up test to the assessment as part of their *Physical Best* program.[2] Health-related fitness includes the following five components:

1. *Cardiorespiratory Endurance*—the ability of the heart, respiratory, and circulatory systems to supply oxygen and nutrients to, and to remove waste products from, the working muscles
2. *Muscular Strength*—the ability of the muscles to exert a force to move an object or to develop tension to resist the movement of an object
3. *Muscular Endurance*—the ability of a muscle to sustain repeated contractions or to maintain a submaximal contraction
4. *Body Composition*—the relative proportion of body fat or fat-free body tissues (muscle, bone, organs) to total body weight

5. *Flexibility*—the ability to move a body part fluidly through a complete range of motion about a joint

This chapter will focus on health-related physical fitness programs, specifically related to the cardiorespiratory endurance and body composition components (muscular strength, muscular endurance, and flexibility training will be discussed in later chapters). Information concerning the need for and benefits of health-related physical fitness will be presented. This will be followed by concerns for pre-exercise screening and then specific types of training programs.

Current Physical Fitness Characteristics

The mechanization of many American industries in the early through mid-20th century decreased the occupational activity level of many individuals. As the technology explosion continued, the automation of products for home and recreation further decreased the activity levels of Americans. This has led to a substantial number of unfit Americans.

Youth. Data from the National Children and Youth Fitness Study II (NCYFS)[3] conducted in the mid-1980s revealed that a majority of the youth in the United States had low levels of physical fitness. Some specific findings were that 50 percent of the children could not run one mile in less than 10 minutes; 55 percent of girls and 40 percent of boys could not perform more than one pull-up; 40 percent of boys could not reach beyond their toes on a sit and reach test; obesity and superobesity (triceps skinfold > 85th and 95th percentile, respectively) increased 54 percent and 98 percent in youth aged 6 to 11 years old.[4] These data are not surprising given reports that only 50 percent of the youth exercised at appropriate frequency, intensity, and duration to stimulate cardiorespiratory endurance; a minority of children had daily physical education; and a majority of physical education class time was spent doing little or no exercise.

The American College of Sports Medicine issued a Position Stand in 1988 on the Physical Fitness in Children and Youth.[5] This is must reading for all professionals working with this population. Among the major points made in this position stand were that youth should have 20 to 30 minutes a day of *vigorous* exercise, that programs should promote life-long exercise behaviors, and that recreational and fun aspects of exercise should be emphasized. Recently, some physical educators have developed programs requiring children to wear pulse rate monitors during workouts to assure that they are of a vigorous nature. Although these types of programs provide important research data, caution is needed to make sure that children understand that all physical fitness programs do not need to be highly structured. The challenge to physical educators is to develop creative programs that provide all children with the necessary amount of vigorous exercise in an environment that is fun and conducive to becoming a life-long activity. Indeed both the 1992 "Statement on Exercise" from the American Heart Association[6] and the "Physical Activity and Health" report from the Surgeon General[7] recommend that schools offer these types of programs. Three specific objectives set in the Healthy People 2010 report from the U.S. Department of Health and Human Services are (1) to increase the proportion of the nation's public and private schools that require daily physical education for all students; (2) to increase to at least 50 percent the proportion of children and adolescents in ninth through twelfth grade who participate in daily physical education; (3) to increase to at least 50 percent the proportion of school physical education class time that students spend being physically active, preferably engaged in lifetime physical activities;[8] (4) to increase to at least 35 percent the proportion of adolescents who engage in moderate physical activity for at least 30 minutes on 5 or more of the previous 7 days; and (5) to increase to at least 35 percent the proportion of adolescents who engage in vigorous physical activity that promotes cardiorespiratory fitness 3 or more days per week for 20 or more minutes per occasion.

Adults. Data from the third National Health and Nutrition Examination Survey (NHANES III) conducted from 1988 to 1991 reported that only 29 percent of U.S. adults participate in daily physical activities.[9]

Twenty-two percent of the population surveyed reported not doing any leisure-time physical activity. Based on findings from these national surveys the Healthy People 2010 report made the following specific physical activity recommendations: to reduce to no more than 20 percent the proportion of adults who engage in no leisure-time physical activity; to increase to at least 30 percent the proportion of adults who engage regularly, preferably daily, in moderate physical activity for at least 30 minutes per day; to increase to at least 30 percent the proportion of adults who engage in vigorous physical activity that promotes the development and maintenance of cardiorespiratory fitness 3 or more days per week for 20 or more minutes per occasion: to increase to at least 30 percent the proportion of adults who perform physical activities that enhance and maintain muscular strength and endurance; and to increase to at least 43 percent the proportion of adults who perform physical activities that enhance and maintain flexibility.

Preliminary data from NHANES III also suggests that the prevalence of obesity among adults is on the rise (age-adjusted rates for men of 32 percent and for women of 35 percent, compared with rates of 24 and 27 percent for men and women, respectively, from 1976–1980).[10] It has been shown that the prevalence rate is higher (40%) in those who perform no leisure-time physical activity and lower (28%) in those who report being active at least 3 days per week.[11]

Approximately 50 percent of the U.S. adult population had total cholesterol concentrations above the desirable level of 200 mg/dL.[12] However, there are indications that the National Cholesterol Education Program (NCEP), which was launched in 1987, has had the intended effect of increasing individuals' knowledge of their cholesterol levels and that population levels are beginning to decrease. Additionally, data from NHANES III suggests that approximately 50 million U.S. adults have hypertension (systolic blood pressure $\geq$ 140 mmHg and/or diastolic blood pressure $\geq$ 90 mmHg, or taking antihypertensive medication).[13]

Consequences. The lack of physical fitness has been associated with a number of health problems. The term *hypokinetic disease,* meaning "a condition related to, or caused by, a lack of regular physical activity,"[14] has been used to describe this problem. Specific diseases and health problems associated with inactivity are coronary heart disease, cancer, hypertension, hyperlipidemia, obesity, and low back pain/injury. Coronary heart disease (CHD) is the leading cause of death in the United States, accounting for 36 percent of all deaths. Cancer is the second leading cause, accounting for 22 percent of all deaths. In 1992 the

American Heart Association made a major pronouncement when they added physical inactivity as the fourth primary risk factor for coronary artery disease.[6] Prior to this time, the value of exercise as a preventive tool in the battle against heart disease was considered to be of far less importance than getting people to stop smoking, lower their blood cholesterol, or lower their blood pressure. Research evidence has accumulated that now suggests that becoming regularly active is of equal importance as an independent factor to changes in any of the other three primary risk factors. Regular exercise may actually be the most important to the population at large, as it is associated with beneficial improvements in each of the other three risk factors.

Benefits of Physical Fitness

A regular exercise program will result in numerous physiological adaptations. A summary of some of the physiological changes that occur with aerobic exercise training is provided in Table 2-1. Although most tests of physical fitness emphasize improvements in maximal capabilities (e.g., maximal oxygen uptake is used as the principle measure of cardiorespiratory fitness), the most important benefits to the individual are the ability to perform daily tasks with increased ease and the ability to perform more total work throughout the day. The most generic of definitions of physical fitness suggests it to be the ability to perform daily activities without undue fatigue.[15]

Physiological Adaptations

The beneficial effects of exercise on the cardiovascular system are evident. The heart, which in essence is a muscular pump, becomes stronger and more efficient. Cardiac output, the amount of blood pumped from the heart each minute, is a product of stroke volume and heart rate. The heart adapts to regular aerobic exercise training by increasing the amount of blood it pumps with each beat (stroke volume), thus becoming a stronger, more effective pump. Consequently, at submaximal workloads the heart does not have to beat as often, thus reducing the demand on the heart. One can easily recognize this training effect by simply monitoring the decrease in resting heart rate or the heart rate during a fixed submaximal work task. The body also responds by increasing the total blood volume and the hemoglobin content in the blood. These two adaptations allow the individual to deliver more blood and more oxygen to the working muscles during exercise.

Changes also take place within the muscles themselves. Basically, the "metabolic machinery" of the muscle cell is built up so that it can produce more energy. The muscle can extract more oxygen from

Table 2-1 Physiological effects of training

At Rest	Increase	Decrease	No Change
During Rest and/or Submaximal Exercise			
Lactic acid accumulation		X	
Heart rate		X	
Stoke volume	X		
Cardiac output			X
VO$_2$			X
Fat utilitization	X		
Ventilatory efficiency	X		
Carbohydrate utilization		X	
During Maximal Exercise			
Lactic acid accumulation	X		
Heart rate		X or	X
Stoke volume	X		
Cardiac output	X		
VO$_2$	X		
Ventilatory efficiency	X		
Other Changes			
Body fat		X	
Serum cholesterol		X	
Serum triglycerides		X	
Serum high-density lipoproteins	X		
Serum low-density lipoproteins		X	
Resting metabolic rate	X or		X

the blood, and the enhanced circulation through the muscle helps to remove the additional waste products produced.

The physiological measure of these adaptations is that of maximal oxygen consumption (VO$_2$ max). This is also termed the individual's maximal aerobic power or the functional capacity (i.e., the maximal ability of the body to produce energy and thus perform work). Factors such as muscle fiber-type make-up (determined by genetics) and pre-training VO$_2$ max level will determine the potential to improve one's maximal aerobic power; however, improvements in the range of 20 to 30 percent are possible following three months of appropriate aerobic training. Training will also increase the individual's "anaerobic threshold," the point in metabolism at which lactic acid begins to accumulate in the blood. Lactic acid accumulation, with the resultant decrease in muscle and blood pH, is a key factor associated with fatigue. Increasing the anaerobic threshold allows the individual to work at a higher absolute submaximal workload without fatiguing.

Regular aerobic exercise training can also improve an overfat individual's body composition. Through training, the muscles and bones are stimulated, which helps the body maintain muscle tissue and increase the integrity of bone. At the same time, the increased energy expenditure of training promotes the loss of body fat stores. Exercise for weight loss will be discussed in more detail later in this chapter.

Blood lipids and hypertension are also favorably changed after regular aerobic exercise training. Total cholesterol, low-density lipoprotein (LDL), and especially triglycerides may all decrease, and high-density lipoprotein (HDL) can increase following training. The most consistent effects of training are changes in triglyceride and HDL levels. The lipoproteins serve as carriers of lipids (fats) in blood and have been found to play a major role in the process of developing fatty deposits in walls of blood vessels. Basically, LDL is used to transport cholesterol from the liver to various tissues in the body to serve important purposes, such as structure of cell membranes. In excess, LDL can promote the development of atherosclerotic plaques within the coronary blood vessels. HDLs, on the other hand, function to transport unneeded cholesterol from the tissues to the liver. Thus, HDLs can prevent the build-up of fatty deposits in the blood vessels. It should be noted that recent evidence suggests that only individuals with unfavorably high total cholesterol and/or low HDL see marked improvement in these lipid concentrations following aerobic training. Training can also help reduce blood pressure in those with borderline hypertension. Thus, the risk of coronary heart disease can be reduced by improving physical fitness.

Reduced Mortality. Evidence is mounting that physically fit individuals or those who are regularly active have a reduced death rate from coronary heart disease compared with the unfit and inactive population. The recent findings from the Aerobics Research Institute[16] reported that the largest reduction in coronary heart disease deaths, as well as deaths from all causes, was between the lowest fitness category and those in the moderate fitness category. A follow-up study demonstrated that these same benefits are obtained when previously unfit men improved their physical fitness.[17]

Many of the earlier studies on CAD mortality demonstrated favorable effects from moderate increases in physical activity/fitness. Based on these studies, the Surgeon General's report offered the following recommendations.

Significant health benefits can be obtained by in-cluding a moderate amount of physical activity on most, if not all days of the week. . . . Additional health benefits can be gained through greater amounts of physical activity. People who can maintain a regular regimen of activity that is of longer duration or of more vigorous intensity are likely to derive greater benefit.

Thus, it is now clear that health benefits accrue from moderate amounts of physical activity and that regular exercise provides even more benefits (in both health and fitness).

In fact, studies from the Ball State Adult Fitness Cohort,[18] the British Civil Servants Study,[19] and the Harvard Alumni[20] suggest that vigorous physical activity/fitness may be most beneficial. Additional research is needed to clarify the threshold levels of physical activity/fitness necessary for optimal health benefits. At the present, it is prudent to advise individuals to engage in at least a moderate amount of activity on a daily basis and, if possible, to include a program of regular exercise.

Psychological and Sociological Values

Regular exercise affects not only the body but also the mental and emotional states. Exercise can serve as an outlet for pent-up emotions through socially accepted channels. Stress, anxiety, and depression may be relieved by exercise, without the ills and side effects of mood-altering drugs. Physically fit individuals speak of their enhanced mental acuity, mental energy, concentration, and feelings of well-being. These feelings have been documented in several studies. In addition, physically fit individuals have an enhanced self-image, a definite sign of excellent mental health.

The late President Kennedy, an exponent of the strenuous life, summed it up in this way:

Physical fitness is not only one of the most important keys to a healthy body, it is the basis of dynamic and creative intellectual activity. The relationship of the body and the activities of the mind is subtle and complex. Much is not yet understood, but we do know what the Greeks knew: that intelligence and skill can only function at the peak of their capacity when the body is healthy and strong; that hardy spirits and tough minds usually inhabit sound bodies.

In this sense, physical fitness is the basis of all the activities of our society. And if the body grows soft and inactive, if we fail to encourage physical development and prowess, we will undermine our capacity for thought, for work, and for the use of those skills vital to an expanding and complex America. Thus, the physical fitness of our citizens is a vital prerequisite to America's realization of its full potential as a nation, and to the opportunity of each individual citizen to make full and fruitful use of her capabilities.

Pre-exercise Screening

Although exercise is a safe activity for most individuals, for some it should be avoided (at least temporarily), and for others some special considerations may need to be followed. In order to identify those who may have an unfavorable response to exercise, some simple procedures should be followed prior to beginning the physical activity. An essential procedure to use is a health history questionnaire that asks for items that could present problems during exercise (e.g., heart problems, diabetes, asthma, etc.). Many of these questionnaires have been published, and most can use a closed-answer, check-off type response format. However, instructors can construct their own questionnaire to fit their specific program needs.

A second step that is advisable, especially if concerns arise during the health history review, is a medical examination. A medical exam is particularly important for individuals who have been diagnosed with a disease such as diabetes or asthma. Although it is safe and appropriate for these individuals to participate in exercise programs, physicians may have instructions about specific needs or precautions for their patients. A medical exam is also a recommended procedure for sedentary adults before they begin an exercise program.

Finally, the individual's current level of fitness should be assessed prior to beginning the training program. This allows the instructor to design the program to meet the individual's weaknesses and to provide an evaluation of the effectiveness of the training program. As mentioned previously, AAHPERD recommends a battery of tests to assess cardiorespiratory endurance, muscular strength and endurance, body composition, and flexibility of school-age children in the *Physical Best* program. Alternative tests of cardiorespiratory endurance for college-age students are a 1.5-mile run, a step test, and a submaximal cycle test. Likewise, muscular strength can be assessed by weight-lifting tests. These tests are relatively crude markers of cardiorespiratory fitness and have relatively high measurement errors associated with them. At best, they can provide an indication of the student's fitness classification (i.e., poor, fair, average, etc.). For adults, when time and expense are less of an issue, cardiorespiratory fitness can be measured directly during maximal exercise tests. A more complete fitness assessment of these components would include tests of various muscle groups and joints throughout the body.

When programs are being designed for adults, the guidelines established by the American College of Sports Medicine should be followed for screening individuals.[21] Depending on age and health status, the guidelines provide recommendations for a physical exam and exercise testing before the individual begins an exercise program. Evaluation of individuals' muscular strength can be obtained from weight-lifting tests.

Exercise Programming

Regardless of the type of training to be used, all exercise training sessions should have the same basic structure. The session begins with a *warm-up* period, proceeds with the specific type of training, and finishes with a *cool-down* period. The purpose of the warm-up is to prepare the body for the training session by gradually increasing the heart rate and blood circulation to the active musculature. Walking, calisthenic-type exercises, and stretching are appropriate warm-up activities. Although documentation is lacking, many believe that warm-up activities help prevent injury.

The cool-down helps restore the body to its pre-exercise condition. Initially the cool-down consists of walking, which is then followed by stretching exercises. It is believed that the cool-down is the optimal time for making flexibility improvements because the muscles are warm and the joints are most supple. Although many flexibility exercises are available, a basic routine would include neck rotations, arm pullovers, side stretches, one-legged sit and reach, hip and knee flexion, and ankle rotation (Figures 2-1 to 2-6).

When designing the training session of the program, the instructor should employ the basic principles of specificity and overload, as well as individualization. The principle of *specificity* states that adaptations to training will be specific to the muscle groups trained, the specific movement patterns and speed of contractions used, and the metabolic energy systems stressed. This principle is most applicable to training for sport; however, it is also important to consider when evaluating improvements in physical fitness. For example, cycling, jogging, and swimming are all appropriate activities to condition the cardiorespiratory systems. However, the one-mile run/walk test will only accurately reflect cardiorespiratory improvements for those in a jogging program. Those in a cycling or swimming program would have their cardiorespiratory endurance underestimated with such a test. The *overload* principle means that in order for a muscle or system to adapt, it must be stressed beyond a level to which it is normally accustomed. Overload is derived by manipulating the following factors: intensity, duration, and frequency. The American College of Sports Medicine has specific recommendations for training guidelines for healthy adults.[22]

Intensity. Intensity refers to the percentage of the maximal capabilities that are being required for the

Figure 2-1 Neck rotations.

Figure 2-2 Arm pull-overs.

Figure 2-3 Side stretches.

Figure 2-4 One-legged sit and reach.

Figure 2-5 Hip and knee flexion.

Figure 2-6 Ankle rotations.

activity. Research has established that for cardiorespiratory improvements, an intensity level of at least approximately 40 to 50 percent of VO_2 reserve must be achieved (note: severely deconditioned individuals will make improvements at lower intensities). Additional improvements are achieved through intensities up to 85 percent of VO_2 reserve. This intensity can be monitored by palpating a pulse rate during the exercise session. Pulse rates of approximately 75 to 85 percent of maximum are the equivalent of 70 to 80 percent of VO_2 reserve. Maximal heart rate can be measured during a maximal exercise test; however, an estimate can be made from the formula of 220 – age. For example, the training intensity for a 15-year-old would be calculated as follows:

$$(220 - 15) \times .75 = 154 \text{ bpm} - (220 - 15) \times .85 = 174 \text{ bpm}$$

It should be noted that although this equation is widely used, it has a large measurement error associated with it (95 percent confidence levels ± 30 bpm).[23] This means that some individuals' "true" target heart rates (exercise intensity) will actually be much higher or lower than that estimated using the age-predicted maximal heart rate formula.

To monitor the intensity of the exercise session, the individual should momentarily stop the exercise (after at least 5 minutes of activity) and immediately count the pulse rate. It is advisable to keep walking or walk in place during this time. The pulse can be palpated using the index and middle fingers at either the radial artery on the wrist or one of the carotid arteries on either side of the neck (Figure 2-7). Some precautions need to be followed if the carotid artery

is used. First, it is important to palpate only on one side of the neck (i.e., do not put the thumb on one side of the neck and the fingers on the other side). Also, the individual should not press too hard to palpate the carotid artery as a reflex lowering of the heart rate could occur. The pulse count is taken for a 10-second count (start the count with zero), and the training range can be determined by dividing the training heart rate by 6 (examples: $154 \div 6 = 26$; $174 \div 6 = 29$). The pulse should also be monitored at the end of the training session. Exercising within the training heart rate range will produce optimal physiological adaptations. Highly motivated individuals sometimes have a tendency to train above the training heart rate range (i.e., the feeling that if some is good, then more must be better); however, this should be discouraged because the additional benefits

Figure 2-7 Radial and carotid pulse palpation.

are relatively small and the risk for injury increases at these high intensities.

Duration.   The duration of the program is the amount of time spent in the training part of the exercise session (not including warm-up and cool-down time). The minimum duration necessary to stimulate physiological adaptations is 20 minutes, with further increases seen through 60 minutes of activity. The recommended duration range for most individuals is 30 to 40 minutes.

Frequency.   The frequency of the training program refers to how often the training should take place, usually described in terms of days per week. Training needs to be performed at least 3 days per week to derive physiological benefits. Further increases are seen with more frequent training; however, for health-related physical fitness training, more than 5 days per week is of little value. In fact, the body needs rest time between training sessions to make the adaptations. Training 6 to 7 days per week increases the individual's risk for injury. It should be noted that these "off" days do not have to be totally sedentary; indeed, alternative types of physical activities and recreation should be encouraged.

Figure 2-8 shows various combinations of frequency, intensity, and duration that would theoretically derive the same training benefit. The data are hypothesized for a person with a VO_2 max of 3 L/min. The minimal threshold level as recommended

Figure 2-8 Frequency, intensity, and duration of exercise combinations for minimal (1,000 kcal/week) and optimal (2,000 kcal/week) cardiorespiratory fitness.

by the American College of Sports Medicine is 1,000 kcal/week.[21] An example of two different combinations to meet the minimal thresholds would be exercising at 55 percent intensity, 5 days per week for 24 minutes per session, or exercising at 85 percent intensity, 3 days per week, for 26 minutes per session. It should also be recognized that greater amounts of energy expenditure (i.e., > 1,000 kcal/week) will result in additional training benefits.

Table 2-2   Two-week walking/jogging program

WALKING PROGRAM

	Mon.	Tues.	Thur.	Fri.
First Week	Walk 20 min.	Walk 20 min.	Walk 24 min.	Walk 24 min.
Second Week	Walk 28 min.	Walk 28 min.	Walk 32 min.	Walk 32 min.

JOG/WALK PROGRAM

	Mon. and Tues.	Thur. and Fri.
First Week	Walk 20 min.	Walk 17 min.
	Jog/Walk ½, ½, ½, ½	Jog/walk ½, ½, ½, ½, ½, ½
	Walk 10 min.	Walk 10 min.
Second Week	Walk 15 min.	Walk 12 min.
	Jog/walk ½, ½, ½, ½, ½, ½, ½, ½, ½	Jog/walk ½, ½, ½, ½, ½, ½
	Walk 10 min.	Walk 10 min.

JOGGING PROGRAM

	Mon.	Tues.	Thur.	Fri.
First Week	Jog 2 miles	Jog 4 miles	Jog 3 miles	Jog 5 miles
Second Week	Jog 3 miles	Jog 4 miles	Jog 2 miles	Jog 5 miles

*Note: ½ = 110 yds. or 30 to 45 sec. Individual should alternate on the Jog/Walk routine—i.e., Jog ½, Walk ½, Jog ½, etc.

Individualization. Intensity, duration, and frequency of training are interrelated. This allows for designing an exercise program to meet the individual's physical capabilities and psychological perceptions of the comfort of the exercise program. Also, factors such as availability of facilities, work or school schedules, weather, and medical restrictions can influence the exercise training program. To be effective, regular exercise must become an integral part of one's lifestyle.

If an intensity level of 75 to 85 percent HR max is found to be undesirably strenuous, the training program can be modified by reducing the intensity level to 65 to 75 percent and either increasing the duration by 5 to 10 minutes per session or the frequency by one day per week.

Individualization can also take place by considering the type of exercise being utilized for the training. Aerobic exercise types are those that use the large muscle groups (i.e., legs or arms and legs) in a rhythmical, dynamic fashion. Activities such as walking, jogging, swimming, cycling, rowing, and cross-country skiing are examples of aerobic exercise types.

A final consideration is the need to begin an exercise program at the reduced intensity and duration and to progress slowly. As one becomes acquainted with the exercise program structure and techniques used, he can gradually increase the intensity and duration of the training session. This helps to reduce injuries at the beginning of the program and also increases the individual's self-confidence. Table 2-2 represents an example of a start-up walk/jog program. Dr. Bud Getchell, the founder of the Adult Fitness Program at Ball State University, has developed protocols for beginning and progressing in programs of walking, running, cycling, and swimming.[24]

Recreational Activities. A question that often is asked is whether one can use recreational activities for training. In general, one should "get in shape to play the game, not play the game to get in shape." However, once an acceptable level of physical fitness is obtained, recreational activities can be useful as a supplement to the training program to maintain the desired level. Table 2-3 shows the caloric equivalents of different recreational activities as well as the standard aerobic training modes for comparison purposes. Recreational activities can provide the necessary variety to the training program to make the long-term commitment to regular exercise solid.

Exercise for Weight Loss. As mentioned previously, from one-third to one-half of adult Americans are overweight or obese. Body weight is determined by the balance between energy intake and energy expenditure (Figure 2-9). If intake exceeds expenditure, weight will increase, and if expenditure exceeds

Table 2-3   Energy requirements of various activities

Activity		kcal/min.	
		123 lb.	150 lb.
Aquatic Games		7.2	8.7
Archery		3.6	4.4
Badminton		5.4	6.6
Basketball		7.7	9.4
Bicycling		5.6	6.8
Bowling		3.7	4.0
Canoeing		2.5	3.0
Cycling	10 mile/hour	6.5	7.0
Football: Touch/Flag		5.4	6.0
Golf (walking)		4.8	5.8
Handball		7.8	9.5
Hiking		5.5	6.3
Racquetball		7.8	9.5
Running	12 min/mile	8.1	9.9
	11 min/mile	8.7	10.7
	10 min/mile	9.5	11.6
	9 min/mile	10.3	12.7
	8 min/mile	11.6	14.2
	7 min/mile	13.1	16.0
	6 min/mile	15.1	18.5
Skiing: Cross-Country		13.7	15.1
Skiing: Downhill		8.7	10.0
Soccer		7.8	9.5
Softball		3.6	4.7
Swimming		7.2	8.7
Table Tennis		3.8	4.6
Tennis		6.1	7.4
Volleyball		2.8	3.4

Note: A heavier person (150 vs. 123 lb.) must do more work to transport his/her body weight, thus requiring more energy.

intake, weight will decrease. Although energy intake is easy to quantify and regulate (increase or decrease food intake), energy expenditure is more difficult to understand, because the body can become more or less energy conservative, depending on how it responds to different stresses.

The goal for weight-loss programs is the loss of excess body fat. Weight can be lost if energy intake is decreased (dieting), if energy expenditure is increased

Energy Intake	Energy Expenditure
	Resting metabolic rate
Food	Physical activity
Beverages	Thermic effect of food

Figure 2-9 Body weight balance.

(principally by increased physical activity), or by both dieting and exercising. Intervention programs for obesity have not been very successful, as most have concentrated only on the energy intake side of the body weight balance equation. The majority of diet programs require substantial caloric restrictions, which are actually counterproductive to long-term weight loss because they result in a decrease in resting metabolic rate (the largest component of daily energy expenditure). The more successful weight-loss programs use the "exchange" principle for reducing calorie intake. They recommend that individuals exchange their intake of much of the dietary fat, which has 9 kcal/gm, for complex carbohydrates (fruits and vegetables), which have only 4 kcal/gm. This essentially reduces the energy intake but still allows the individual to consume *normal quantities* of food. Successful programs also realize that energy expenditure must be increased for long-term maintenance with weight loss. The types of activities used does not really matter; what is important is that the total amount of physical activity be increased. The increased physical activity level actually serves two purposes: (1) It results in an increase in caloric expenditure due directly to the activity, and (2) it maintains or may slightly increase the resting metabolic rate.

Estimates of how much weight should be lost can be made from the following equation:

$$\text{Desired Body Weight} = \frac{\text{Fat-free body weight}}{1 - (\text{desired body fat \%} \div 100)}$$

Note that this equation requires knowledge of the individual's body fat percentage and also what percent is a normal or desired body fat. For example, consider a 200-lb. man with 25 percent body fat and a goal of 15 percent body fat. The desired body weight would be calculated as follows:

$$\frac{200(1 - 25 \div 100)}{1 - (15 \div 100)} = \frac{150 \text{ lb.}}{0.85} = 175.5 \text{ lb.}$$

Thus, this individual would need to lose 24.5 lbs. of fat to achieve his desired body composition. Since one pound of fat holds 3,500 kcal, 82,250 kcals must be expended to achieve the desired goal. At first glance this may seem like an insurmountable task. However, success in weight (fat)-loss programs is achieved by using the *long-haul* approach. For example, say this man exchanged one-third of his 133 gm of daily fat intake for carbohydrates; this would result in a daily decrease of 220 kcal/day [44 gm/day × (9 − 4 kcal/gm)]. Additionally, he began a 4-day/week exercise program and expended 300 kcal/session (approxi-

mately 2.5 miles of walking or jogging) and increased his daily activity level to expend an additional 100 kcal/day. Over a week he would have burned an additional 3,440 kcal, or approximately the equivalent of 1 lb. of fat. Thus, it would take him about half a year to attain his goal; however, during this time he likely developed lifestyle dietary and exercise habits that will help him maintain his desired body weight over the long term. Additionally, the exercise training program would also improve total physical fitness. Note that the maximal safe rate of weight loss is 1 to 2 lb. per week. Losing weight more rapidly will involve losing fat-free weight and decreasing resting metabolic rate.

Clothing and Equipment

Essentially the only piece of specialized clothing required for aerobic training is proper footwear. Good exercise shoes provide adequate support and cushioning to protect the feet and reduce the shock of the foot strike to the rest of the body. (Good shoes can take on a force of approximately three times the body weight.) The running/walking shoe industry has gone high-tech with literally hundreds of different shoes, available with variable features (outsole, midsole, heel counter, upper, foxing, toe box). One should shop for the shoes at a reputable dealer who has personnel that can explain the various features of the different types of shoes and thus assist in selecting the most appropriate shoe for the individual's needs.

In general, exercise clothing should be lightweight and should fit loosely. Fashionable exercise clothing has become very popular; however, care has to be taken to assure that the clothing is breathable and allows moisture to evaporate from the skin. Seasons will dictate how much to wear. In warm, humid weather, it is important to expose as much body surface area as possible to allow sweat the opportunity to evaporate and thus help keep body temperature down (Figure 2-10). In cold weather, layering lightweight clothing is most advantageous because this allows removal of a layer (or two) as the body heat production increases (Figure 2-11). In extremely cold conditions, protecting the extremities is a must. A hat that covers the ears and either gloves or mittens are needed. Additionally, some individuals find using a breathing filter-type mask helps to moisturize the cold, dry air.

One myth related to exercise clothing is that rubberized sweat suits are helpful for exercise and weight-loss programs. It is true that one can lose a substantial amount of weight in an exercise session by wearing a rubberized suit. However, the weight lost is from body water, *not* body fat, and thus is quickly regained. These suits are not only ineffective

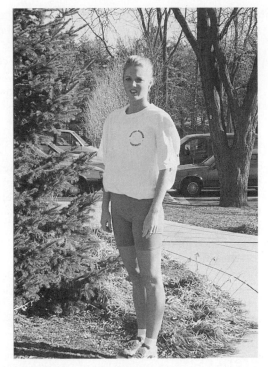

Figure 2-10 Clothing for warm weather.

Figure 2-11 Clothing for cold weather. Dress in layers of clothing.

for reducing excess body fat, but are also potentially dangerous because dehydration can raise body temperature to dangerous levels.

Exercise equipment sales have been tremendous in recent years. Claims that particular machines provide the "best" workout in the shortest period of time have helped fuel sales. As a result of technological advances, computer-aided features such as monitors for heart rate, estimations of caloric expenditure, and interval-type training sessions can be found on some of these exercise devices. Indeed, many of these exercise machines can make the exercise session more enjoyable by adding some variety to the workout. However, the individual must still perform the work (i.e., same specificity and overload principles apply) to achieve the physiological benefits. The other factor to consider is the expense of much of this equipment. Individuals should be counseled to test thoroughly a piece of equipment before purchasing it. Too often an individual purchases a piece of exercise equipment for home use and uses it only for a short period of time before moving into a closet or out to the garage for storage.

Supplementary Training

Once the major cardiorespiratory adaptations have been made, some individuals like to modify their training program for maintenance of the adaptations. One modification is to supplement their regular aerobic training with one or two interval training sessions a week. *Interval training* involves doing repeated cycles of high-intensity exercise followed by a brief recovery period. This type of training is used widely in athletics and can produce excellent fitness benefits. The principal advantage of this type of training is that it allows high-quality training stimulus in a relatively short duration. For aerobic training, work intervals of .25, .5, and/or .75 miles are recommended, with a work-recovery ratio of 1:1 (i.e., if the work interval is 2 minutes, the recovery time is 2 minutes). These distances are run at a pace faster than the average time for that distance based on the individuals' best mile time. For example, if the best mile time is 8 minutes, the average .25 mile time is 2 minutes, thus the interval training pace for the .25-mile interval run would be less than 2 minutes. A complete description of interval training is beyond the scope of this chapter.[25]

Circuit training involves a series of exercises designed to improve muscular endurance and muscular strength that are completed within a set time frame. The individual moves quickly between each exercise station and then begins the next type of exercise. Some stations may involve aerobic exercise, such as stationary cycling, running, and rope skipping. These types of programs are useful ways to add some variety to the exercise program if it is becoming "stale" and also assure that the muscular strength and endurance components of fitness are stimulated. A typical circuit could involve two sets of the following exercise stations (one minute per station):

Station	Activity
1	jumping jacks
2	bicep curls
3	modified sit-ups
4	bench press
5	running in place
6	leg press
7	stationary cycling
8	tricep curls
9	rope skipping or bench stepping
10	leg curls

It is important to remember that the appropriate program structure of beginning with a warm-up and finishing with a cool-down period also applies to these supplemental types of training.

Conclusion

A quote attributable to Hippocrates sums up the value of physical fitness:

All parts of the body which have a function, if used in moderation and exercised in labors in which each is accustomed, become thereby healthy, well-developed and age more slowly, but if unused and left idle they become liable to disease, defective in growth, and age quickly.[26]

Terminology

Aerobic training Exercise training performed at an intensity, duration, and frequency that stimulates adaptations of the aerobic energy system and the cardiorespiratory systems of the body.

Body composition The evaluation of the components of the body (e.g., water, muscle, bone, fat), with the determination of percentage of body fat the most common.

Calorie A unit of energy.

Cool-down A group of activities including walking, calisthenics, and flexibility exercises performed following the exercise training session to gradually return the body to its resting state.

Duration The amount of time spent in one exercise training session.

Exchange principle A diet modification that substitutes foods of lower caloric value, mainly high carbohydrate foods, for foods of higher caloric value (i.e., foods of high fat content).

Frequency The number of training sessions performed in a fixed period of time, usually one week.

Intensity The percentage of maximal capabilities that are being utilized (e.g., percentage of maximal heart rate).

Interval training Exercise training sessions that are characterized by alternating periods of vigorous exercise (work interval) with periods of relief (low-intensity exercise or rest interval).

Lipids Substances that are not soluble in water. The most important blood lipids include cholesterol and triglyceride.

Lipoproteins A compound formed by combining cholesterol and protein to allow the cholesterol to be soluble in fluid and thus transported in the blood.

Overload An exercise training principle that states that adaptations to training will only take place when the activity stresses the body's systems beyond what it is normally accustomed to.

Specificity An exercise training principle that states that adaptations to training are specific to the muscle groups utilized, the speed of contractions performed, the movement patterns employed, and the energy systems required to power the activity.

VO_2 The volume of oxygen consumed, used as an indirect measure of energy expenditure.

Warm-up A group of activities including walking, calisthenics, and flexibility exercises performed prior to the exercise training to prepare the body for vigorous physical activity.

References

1. American Alliance for Health, Physical Education, Recreation and Dance: *AAHPERD Health-Related Physical Fitness Test Manual.* Washington, D.C., AAHPERD, 1980.

2. American Alliance for Health, Physical Education, Recreation and Dance: *AAHPERD Physical Best Manual.* 1990 Association Drive, Reston, VA. AAHPERD, 1988.

3. Ross, J. G. and Pate, R. R. The National Children and Youth Fitness Study II: A Summary of Findings. *Journal of Physical Education, Recreation and Dance,* Nov./Dec.: 66–70, 1987.

4. Gortmaker, S. L. et al. Increasing Pediatric Obesity in the United States. *American Journal of Disabled Children,* 141:535–540, 1987.

5. American College of Sports Medicine. Opinion Statement on Physical Fitness in Children and Youth. *Medicine and Science in Sports and Exercise,* 20:422–423, 1988.

6. American Heart Association. Statement on Exercise. *Circulation,* 86:340–344, 1992.

7. U.S. Department of Health and Human Services. Physical Activity and Health: A Report of the Surgeon General. Atlanta, GA: U.S. Department of Health and Human Services, Centers for Disease Control and Prevention, National Center for Chronic Disease Prevention and Health Promotion, 1996.

8. U.S. Department of Health and Human Services. Healthy People 2010: Understanding and Improving Health. Washington, D.C.: U.S. Dept. of Health and Human Services. DHHS Publication No. 017-001-00550-9, 2000.

9. Crespo, C. J. and Wright, J. D. Prevalence of Sedentary Lifestyles and Frequency of Physical Activity from the Third National Health and Nutrition Examination Survey. *Medicine and Science in Sports and Exercise*, 26:S80, 1994.

10. U.S. Department of Health and Human Services. Strategic Development Workshop for Public Education on Weight and Obesity. Washington, D.C.: U.S. Dept. of Health and Human Services. NIH Publication No. 95-3314, 1995.

11. Crespo, C. J. and Wright, J. D. Prevalence of Overweight Among Active and Inactive Adults from the Third National Health and Nutrition Examination Survey. *Medicine and Science in Sports and Exercise*, 27:S73, 1995.

12. U.S. Department of Health and Human Services. Second Report of the Expert Panel on Detection, Evaluation, and Treatment of High Blood Cholesterol in Adults. Washington, D.C.: U.S. Dept. of Health and Human Services. NIH Publication No. 93-3095, 1993.

13. U.S. Department of Health and Human Services. The Sixth Report of the Joint National Committee on Detection, Evaluation, and Treatment of High Blood Pressure. Washington, D.C.: U.S. Dept. of Health and Human Services. NIH Publication No. 98-4080, 1997.

14. Miller, D. K. and Allen, T. E. *Fitness: A Lifetime Commitment*. 4th ed. New York: Macmillan Publishing Co., 1990, p. 3.

15. Miller, A. J., Grais, I. M., Winslow, E. and Kaminsky, L. A. The Definition of Physical Fitness. *Journal of Sports Medicine and Physical Fitness*, 31:639–640, 1991.

16. Blair, S. N. et al. Physical Fitness and All-Cause Mortality: A Prospective Study of Healthy Men and Women. *Journal of the American Medical Association*, 262:2395–2401, 1989.

17. Blair, S. N. et al. Changes in Physical Fitness and All-Cause Mortality. *Journal of the American Medical Association*, 273:1093–1098, 1995.

18. Kaminsky, L. A., Whaley, M. H., Miller, C. R. and Getchell, L. H. Vigorous Exercise Program Participation Associated with Reduced Cardiac Morbidity in Men. *Medicine and Science in Sports and Exercise*, 26:S218, 1994.

19. Morris, J. N. et al. Exercise in Leisure-time: Coronary Attack and Death Rates. *British Heart Journal*, 63:325–334, 1990.

20. Lee, I. M., Hsieh, C. C. and Paffenbarger, R. S. Exercise Intensity and Longevity in Men. *Journal of the American Medical Association*, 273: 1179–1184, 1995.

21. American College of Sports Medicine. *Guidelines for Exercise Testing and Prescription*. 6th ed. Baltimore: Lippincott, 2000.

22. American College of Sports Medicine. Position Stand: The Recommended Quantity and Quality of Exercise for Developing Cardiorespiratory and Muscular Fitness, and Flexibility in Healthy Adults. *Medicine and Science in Sports and Exercise*, 30:975–991, 1998.

23. Whaley, M. H., Kaminsky, L. A., Dwyer, G. B., Getchell, L. H. and Norton, J. A. Predictors of Over and Under-Achievement of Age-predicted Maximal Heart Rate. *Medicine and Science in Sports and Exercise*, 24:1173–1179, 1992.

24. Getchell, Bud. *The Fitness Book*. Indianapolis, IN: Benchmark Press, Inc., 1987.

25. For more information on designing interval training workouts, see E. L. Fox, *Sports Physiology*. New York: CBS College Publishing, 1984, pp. 378–380.

26. Wallace, A. G. Fitness, Health, and Longevity—A Question of Cause and Effect. *Inside Track*, 583, 1986.

Further References

American College of Sports Medicine. *Resource Manual for Guidelines for Exercise Testing and Prescription*. 4th ed. Philadelphia: Lea & Febiger, 2001.

Baechle, T. and Earl, R. (eds.) *Essentials of Strength Training and Conditioning: National Strength and Conditioning Assoc.* 2nd ed. Champaing, IL: Human Kinetics, 2000.

Bouchard, G., Shepard, R. J. and Stephens, T. (eds.). *Physical Activity, Fitness, and Health*. Champaign, IL: Human Kinetics, 1994.

Brubaker, P., Kaminsky, L., and Whaley, M. *Prevention and Rehabilitation of Coronary Artery Disease*. Champaign, IL: Human Kinetics, 2001.

Katch, F. L. and McArdle, W. D. *Nutrition, Weight Control, and Exercise*. 3rd ed. Philadelphia: Lea & Febiger, 1988.

Neiman, D. C. *Fitness and Sports Medicine*. 3rd ed. Palo Alto, CA: Bull Publishing Co., 1995.

Pollock, M. L. and Wilmore, J. H. *Exercise in Health and Disease*. 2nd ed. Philadelphia: W. B. Saunders Co., 1990.

CHAPTER 3

Aerobic Dance

This chapter will enable you to

- Communicate the benefits of regular participation in aerobic dance to your students
- Understand both the movement and safety elements that underlie the structure of an effective aerobic exercise class
- Distinguish between high-impact and low-impact movements and know which to use for any given class situation
- Understand the utility and importance of incorporating circuit and interval training in an aerobics class format
- Incorporate all the elements of an effective aerobics class—including safety, appropriate music, and step and movement combinations—in class design

Nature and Purpose

The fun of moving to music in a sociable group setting while obtaining a great cardiovascular workout has made aerobic dance one of the fastest growing leisure activities in the United States. Today's aerobics class, which may feature cardio funk, hip hop, yogaerobics, or slide aerobics, as well as more standard step and arm movements, has an interesting evolution that spans the years since the publication of Dr. Kenneth Cooper's *Aerobics* in 1968.

Cooper's research studies of Air Force personnel in the 1960s determined that the key to human fitness was the ability of an individual to take in and deliver oxygen to the entire body. His studies brought the importance of aerobic conditioning to national awareness. However, his emphasis was on more traditional forms of conditioning such as jogging, cycling, and swimming, which, for many people, seemed to be too much work and too little fun.

Around 1970, Jackie Sorensen, who studied Cooper's Air Force Aerobics Program and who attributed her excellent performance on the 12-minute run/walk test to her years of dance training, began combining her understanding of Cooper's aerobic principles and her knowledge of dance. Sorensen created a new form of aerobic movement set to music. This innovation, called aerobic dance, transformed aerobic exercise. Sorenson's aerobic dance was fun and social and it hid the hard work of aerobic conditioning under music and rhythm. Aerobic dance (also called "aerobics") had immediate appeal for many women and men turned off by the undisguised work or competition in other forms of aerobic exercise.

Judi Sheppard Missett is another early pioneer in the evolution of aerobics. Missett, the founder of Jazzercise, Inc., included fitness movements in her jazz dance classes, creating entertaining dance routines that could be followed with little or no explanation.

In the late 1980s, the addition of bench-stepping equipment by former gymnast Gin Miller further enhanced the applicability of aerobic dance to people with many different physical capabilities. Benches not only can allow for variation in the height of the step, creating different levels of intensity, but also provide creative instructors with greatly increased choreographic possibilities.

Today, professional aerobic dance associations are setting standards for instructor qualifications as well as access to more and more professional training. Organizations such as the International Association of Fitness Professionals (IDEA) and the Aerobic and Fitness Association of America (AFAA) provide training, exercise journals, conventions, and workshops, as well as instructor certification.

With each innovation, aerobic dance has become more fun, more diverse in form and style, and more responsive to the increase in knowledge about safe and effective forms of movement. Today, about 25 million people participate in some form of aerobics, enhancing their personal health and contributing to the growth of a multi-million-dollar industry that supports one of the fastest growing leisure activities in the United States.

Benefits

While regular participation in aerobic dance improves cardiovascular endurance, many other benefits appear simultaneously—and all are related to an improved ability to enjoy life. These benefits are both physical and mental, because a healthy body, good psychological health, and enjoyment of life are interrelated.

One major key to enjoying all the benefits that aerobic dance has to offer is an appropriate level of participation. A student can achieve maximum benefits by taking classes 3 to 7 times a week and does not take more than one class a day. Resting 1 day out of 7 will not slow your progress and may even help sustain freshness and enthusiasm. A second major key to enjoying the benefits of aerobic dance is staying with it long enough to see results. It takes 6 to 8 weeks to establish the habit of a program and to begin seeing both physical and psychological improvements.

The first benefit of aerobics has always been improved conditioning of the circulatory and respiratory systems, which results in a lowered risk of cardiovascular disease, better handling of stress, an improved ability to relax, and greater energy and vitality. Regular participants in well-taught classes should also experience stronger joints, firmer muscles, improved postural alignment, a decrease in body fat, and better digestion. As a student's physical health and physical appearance improve, self-esteem and self-confidence tend to improve as well. In addition, many studies have shown that regular aerobic exercise impacts the body's systems in ways that alleviate depression. Aerobic dance also develops coordination, balance, and memory.

The informality of most aerobic dance classes also promotes social interaction and may lead to the formation of lasting friendships. This is not as inconsequential as it might first appear; participants are more likely to continue exercising if they take classes with friends, and strong friendship networks foster longevity.

The Classroom

The setting in which a class is conducted will impact the success of the class. An ideal aerobics classroom will offer the following:

- A floor that provides traction, resilience, and stability. A hardwood sprung floor is ideal. Carpeted floors provide good traction and shock absorption, but foot-drag on this "slower" surface may increase the likelihood of injury.
- Adequate space for all participants. About 3 to 4 feet of empty space around each exerciser provides room to extend the arms and to move in any direction.

- Floor-to-ceiling mirrors on at least one of the classroom's long walls. Mirrors not only allow participants to see and correct themselves, but also allow instructors to monitor the entire class even while leading with the back turned toward the group.
- Adequate ventilation without drafty areas. A temperature above 60° F but below 70° F is generally comfortable.
- A good sound system and a good collection of tapes. A wireless microphone is a plus in all but the smallest studios and a necessity in larger rooms.
- Additional equipment such as mats, hand weights, rubber bands, and more, and a storage area where it, and the sound equipment, may be locked away.
- A raised platform for the instructor is helpful in large rooms accommodating many students.

Equipment

Shoes

Appropriate shoes are the most important piece of equipment in any aerobics setting. Shoes should be durable, flexible, and lightweight while providing enough cushion and support to help absorb movements that may generate forces of up to four times the participant's body weight. In general, bigger, heavier people need slightly heavier, sturdier shoes. The shoe should have adequate cushioning, especially under the ball of the foot. It should also provide good support and stability, as well as traction appropriate to the surface in the room. Greater traction is required on hardwood floors, less on carpeted floors. A mismatch in the shoe and the surface increases the likelihood of injury. It is very important not to try to substitute running or court shoes for aerobic shoes. The former are not designed to compensate for the stresses of aerobic dance's movement patterns and will not provide the needed safety, support, and traction.

Buying a high-quality, brand-name shoe that is well constructed will save money (and your body) in the end. If you have a limited budget, skimp on outfits, not on shoes. Make sure the shoes really fit. Try at least three different brands in the store, select the best-feeling one, then wear the shoe around a carpeted area in your home for at least an hour. If it doesn't feel good at the end of the hour, return that one and try again.

Many people have feet with high arches, flat arches, or other structural abnormalities and will need shoes designed for their special needs, another reason to have expert sales help when selecting shoes. If aches in the feet, knees, hips, or lower back occur while a student is participating in a class series, suggest that the student may want to consult a podiatrist.

Apparel

Fashion tends to dictate the look of the clothing worn by participants, but whatever the current fashion, aerobic apparel should provide mobility, comfort, and porosity. Among current fabric options, cotton fabrics, or cotton-Lycra fabrics with high cotton content are desirable because they absorb moisture, allow air to circulate to the skin (thus preventing overheating), and provide good durability. Cotton socks are cooler than wool socks, provide good absorption of perspiration, and also help prevent blisters. In general, T-shirts, leotards, knee-length tights, and fitness shorts worn either with a T-shirt or leotard provide both comfort and mobility. Teachers will want to encourage students to dress in layers, especially if the classroom is cool, and to remove outer layers as the body warms up. Reminding students that they have the freedom to discard the outer layers of clothing then becomes part of the structure of the class.

Teaching Aids

A good aerobic dance class can still be taught without any additional equipment, but most classes include some or all of the following (Figure 3-1).

> *Mats*—provide cushioning as well as a sense of personal space. A good mat keeps you from feeling the floor and is also easy to keep clean, transport, and store.
>
> *Exercise Bands*—add resistance to the strength exercises. Anyone who has a recent or pre-existing joint injury, or anyone who develops joint pain during a class series, should not use an exercise band. There are a wide variety of bands available.

> *Hand Weights*—are appropriately used by students working at the intermediate or advanced level. There should be no history of joint injury or disease, such as knee surgery, ligament damage, arthritis, or bursitis.
>
> *Steps (Benches)*—need to be stable, skid-proof, and of a height that requires a knee-bend of 90 degrees *or less*. Beginners will want to begin on a low (4-inch) bench and progress gradually to higher steps. Six-and 8-inch benches are most commonly used, with occasional use of the 10-inch bench for advanced workouts.
>
> *Pulse Readers*—give an electronic reading of the pulse at a glance. Those that clip on the earlobe or slip over the finger are generally unreliable.
>
> *Heart Rate Monitors*—are more accurate pulse readers, but require wearing a band that wraps around the chest. The monitor electrodes must touch the skin. They are somewhat inconvenient to wear with one-piece leotards.
>
> *Wireless Microphones with Headsets*—allow instructors to give audible cues without straining their vocal cords. When wireless mikes are used, instructors need to remember that they no longer need to shout to be heard. Amplification should be separate from that used for the music.

Program Fundamentals

A well-designed aerobic dance class is fun, appropriately challenging, and designed for each participant's safety. A good aerobics teacher will incorporate cardiovascular safety and conditioning principles in the structure of the class, monitor the individuals in the class as they work out, and keep the class motivated (as well as safe) by giving clear cues and choosing appropriate music. These are the considerations discussed in this section.

Class Structure

The structure of the class facilitates the body's preparation for and recovery from the cardiovascular conditioning that takes place during the most intense portion of the class.

The warm-up makes the body ready for the demands of the aerobic workout. Warming up seems to shorten the cardiovascular and muscular systems' adjustment to stress, allowing a shift from rest to activity without unnecessary strain on the heart. It is thought that warming up minimizes the risk of inadequate blood flow to the heart during the first bit of intense activity, also helping to prevent cardiac arrhythmias caused by the heart's attempts to provide increased blood circulation. Warming up also facilitates mental preparation.

Figure 3-1 Equipment options for aerobic classes. Left to right: Fit balls, adjustable slide, jump-stretch bands, and SPRI bands.

The *isolation* phase (1–1.5 min) of the warm-up focuses on exercising one body part at a time with simple movements. It helps to create body awareness and to focus attention on posture and alignment.

The *active warm-up* phase (3–4 min) involves full body movements such as simple calisthenics, brisk walking, or light jogging. It starts slowly and intensifies, elevating the heart rate and warming the muscles. When light perspiration begins, the participant is ready for more intense activity.

The third phase of the warm-up consists of *static stretching* (1–2.5 min). The five major muscle groups used during the full-intensity workout are subjected to slow, static stretches lasting anywhere from 10 to 30 seconds. It is important to avoid bouncing to stretch since this actually triggers a reflex that will tighten, rather than loosen, the muscle fibers.

The *aerobic warm-up* (5–10 min) begins with low- to moderate-intensity movements that are structured into simple routines that stress the use of the large muscle groups. A low-impact approach is usually desirable.

The *peak aerobics session* (20–30 min) may advance to high-impact movement or may increase the intensity of low-impact movements. In this phase students should be in their heart rate zones (defined as 50 to 85% of maximum capacity; see Chapter 2) and should monitor the pulse rate periodically to see that they do not drop below or exceed their personal limits.

Aerobic exercise results in the delivery of large quantities of blood to the working muscles. If exercise stops abruptly, the blood tends to pool in the lower extremities. Thus, *cooling down* (15 min) is a very important part of a well-balanced class. The cool-down should last until the heart rate is at or below 120 beats per minute (bpm), which usually takes about 5 minutes. Cool down is accomplished by keeping the arms below the level of the heart, gradually diminishing the intensity of all movements, slowing movement, and finally shifting to simple locomotion patterns.

Toning and conditioning exercises (5–20 min) are increasingly a part of most aerobics classes. Typically, exercises targeting the abdomen, chest, arms, buttocks, and thigh are included; frequently resistance equipment is used to add both difficulty and variety. As with every part of class, it remains important to pay attention to participants' body alignment and technique.

Final stretching for flexibility lasts from 5 to 10 minutes, improves or maintains flexibility and helps prevent muscle soreness. A flexible body is one that is less easily injured and also one that adapts more readily to stress. Deep stretching is facilitated at this time because the muscles are warm and pliable. As in the warm-up, the stretching is slow and static; stretches are held longer; and participants are encouraged to relax into the stretch, rather than straining to achieve an extreme stretch.

Relaxation, even if brief (5–8 min), is an important part of class. While it helps the body, it also teaches the mind that being able to let go, being able to rest, is as important a human activity as actively moving. It teaches the mind and the body to simply release effort and stress—at least for a short while.

Cueing

Cues are what keeps the class moving. If one wants to be an instructor that students rave about, learn to give good cues. With clear cues, participants have no doubt in their mind when, how, and where to move; without them, the class becomes fragmented, frustrated, and unmotivated.

Good cueing depends on good timing and on a combination of explicit and consistent visual and verbal messages. One must communicate the steps and the arm movements the students are to use *in advance* of their actually performing the movements. This can be done verbally, visually, or both. Since some students learn best from verbal instructions, and some from visual patterns, a combination of both will provide the strongest teaching style. Typically, cues are given on the last four beats of the measure preceding the one in which the new movement is to begin.

Verbal Cues. Griffith describes five different types of verbal cues. *Footwork cueing* indicates whether one should move the right or left foot; *rhythmic cueing* indicates the correct tempo of the routine; *numerical cueing* involves counting the rhythm, such as one, two, three, and four; *step cueing* refers to the name of the step, such as step touch; and *directional cueing* indicates whether the movement should be forward, back, or to the side. Instructors need to combine cues from all five categories for maximum impact.

Visual Cues. The instructor's body movements are a major visual cue, so one needs to model good technique in all movements. When facing the class, the instructor needs to mirror the movements that they want the class to make. For example, if the class is cued to move left, the instructor will move to the right. A second set of visual cues are the hand signals and other gestures that are used to communicate what the class is to do. Tamilee Webb designed a set of "Step 'Q' Signs," to help instructors communicate with their classes. There are about ten visual cues that are now widely used. For example, pointing to the eye means "watch me," holding the arm up with the palm facing forward signals "hold or stay." Learning these 'Q' signs will help you communicate with all learners, especially those who may be hearing impaired.

Music

Selecting music that both inspires students and keeps them moving at an appropriate rate is another creative opportunity for the aerobics instructor. Great music selections make the class exciting. Unfortunately, it doesn't matter how skilled an instructor is if the music does not motivate students to move.

Tempo. Tempo (or rate) at which music is performed is measured in beats per minute (bpm). The tempo of the music used needs to be appropriate to the level of work required during each phase of class. The following are useful guidelines:

Phase/Type of Class	bpm
Warm-up: Floor and step	110–140
Peak workout: Floor only	140–160
Peak workout: Step only	118–124
Peak workout: High impact	144–160
Toning and conditioning	110–130
Flexibility enhancement	100 or less
Relaxation	100 or less

It is wiser to increase intensity by using benches or arm movements rather than by increasing the speed of the music. Music that is too fast may lead students to lose control of their form and their movements.

Movement Groups. Music used in aerobics classes is almost always written in 4/4 meter—four beats to the measure, with the quarter note constituting one beat. In the aerobics world, a phrase of music is almost always 32 beats (or eight measures) long. Usually each phrase is divided into four different movements, each lasting eight counts (or two measures). This makes it easy to match the movements to the music. For example, have the class walk forward for eight counts, moving on the beat, backward for eight counts, slide right for eight counts, and slide left for eight counts, for a total of 32 beats.

Other Considerations. We favor the use of professionally produced audiotapes that usually have an aerobic side and a toning side, each lasting 45 minutes. There are a number of music services that provide complete audiotapes for all segments of an aerobics class. These tapes, available for approximately $20 to $30, give you an accurate bpm count, keep one in step with current music, and save the considerable time it takes to select and mix your own music. By subscribing to a service, one can choose among pop, rock, techno, Motown, funk, 50s, 60s, hip hop, Latin, and country music, all recorded in aerobic or step format. Having a selection of tapes also provides an easy way to set a theme for the class and to vary themes from class to class.

If one produces their own tapes (or uses student-produced tapes), they should preview them carefully. Popular tunes may have offensive lyrics that are not appropriate in a school setting.

Finally, if a wireless headset is used (as we recommend), be sure that the music and one's voice are amplified separately. This allows the instructor to keep the music volume up and the voice volume down.

Aerobic Dance Elements

Base Moves for Low- and High-Impact Dance, Step, Resistance, and Flexibility

The footwork patterns known as "base moves" form the choreographic foundation of any aerobic dance class. Successfully teaching each individual pattern, then creatively sequencing the base moves, and finally adding other movements to them are some of aerobics' most creative dimensions. Use the guidelines below for selecting and teaching base moves. This will provide a head start in creating a dynamic class that students will find fun and easy to follow.

➤ **Learning Hints—High Impact**

1. Give students ample time to grasp any base move.
2. Visually determine that most students can perform the move being taught before changing directions or going on to a new movement.
3. Teach the foot movements before adding any arm movements.
4. Be selective. Do not try to put everything you know in any one class. An effective class can be built with four combinations.
5. When beginners and advanced students are in the same class, have the beginners concentrate on the foot movements. Beginners need to master the foot moves before adding the arms.
6. Advanced students may increase the intensity of their work by using higher benches, by using a greater variety of arm movements, or by adding propulsion moves.
7. Vary the level of arm movements to prevent injury to the shoulder girdle. Keep students moving their arms from low to medium to high positions.

Base Moves—Low and High Impact
Dance
March/Walk/Step:

   Action: Transfer weight, one foot to the other, without losing contact with the floor.

Jog/Run:

   Action: Transfer weight, one foot to the other; momentary loss of contact with the floor.

Step Touch:

> **Action:** Step right foot to right side; tap ball of left foot next to right foot.
>
> **Tip:** Weight is not on tapping foot so the foot may be used again.

Hamstring Curl:

> **Action:** Step right foot to right side; lift and bend the left leg (heel toward buttocks).

Knee Lift:

> **Action:** Step right foot to right side; bend left knee while lifting knee up (perform to front, back, or side).
>
> **Tip:** Say, "step, knee up; step, knee up."

Taps (heel taps, toe taps, side taps):

> **Action:** Step right foot to right side; touch left heel in front (do not transfer weight). Step left foot to left side; touch right heel in front (do not transfer weight).
>
> **Tip:** To get back on the beat, tap both toes (or heels) of both feet.

Lunges:

> **Action:** Step right foot to right side; extend left leg backward (right leg bends at knee).
>
> **Tip:** As used in aerobic dance, feet are parallel.

Slides:

> **Action:** Right foot brushes floor (front, side, or back); momentary loss of contact with the floor as left replaces right.
>
> **Tip:** Uneven rhythm, "long, short."

Hops:

> **Action:** Lift weight off one foot and land on the same foot.

Jumps:

> **Action:** Take off on two feet and land on two feet. Momentary or sustained loss of contact with the floor.

Jumping Jack:

> **Action:** Start feet together, spring up, land feet opening to a straddle position; spring up, landing feet together.
>
> **Tip:** Since weight is even on both feet, this step may alternate or repeat on the same side.

Heel Jack:

> **Action:** Jump with feet together; jump, extending left heel to left side (left heel should touch floor); jump, landing both feet together. Repeat to other side.
>
> **Tip:** Since weight is even on both feet, this step may alternate or repeat on the same side.

Leaps:

> **Action:** An aerial movement from one foot to the other; sustained loss of contact with the floor.

Kicks:

> **Action:** Step right foot to right side; extend left leg forward (front kicks).
>
> **Tip:** For a flex kick, bend and then quickly extend the working leg (used in Charleston basic and kick ball-change). For a high kick, move the working leg from the hip. Do not bend the knee.

Dance Moves

Aerobics uses movements from the entire dance vocabulary—jazz, ballet, disco, funk, hip hop, Latin. Because most of aerobic dance is cued while the students are moving, short phrases are used to identify steps. In the list below are terms generally used in aerobic dance.

Grapevine:

> **Action:** Step right to right, cross left behind, step right to right, touch left next to right.
>
> **Tip:** May end with a jump, both feet together (weight even on both feet). Move can be repeated to same side.
>
> **Cue:** Step, behind, step, touch.

Mambo:

> **Action:** Step forward right, step in place left, step back on right, step in place left.
>
> **Tip:** This is a rocking step. To alternate leads take three quick steps in place.
>
> **Variation:** Latin-style step on bent knee, smoothly shifting hips.

Charleston:

> **Action:** Step forward with right leg, flex kick or swing left leg forward, step in place with left leg, touch right foot straight back (no weight).
>
> **Tip:** As used in aerobics, do not pivot on balls of feet for each count.

Kick Ball-Change:

> **Action:** Kick right leg forward, step (weight) on ball of right foot (behind left), step left foot in place.
>
> **Rhythm:** Slow, quick, quick.
>
> **Tip:** Use ball of foot with heel lifted; no time to put whole foot down.

Jazz Square, Box Step:

> **Action:** Cross right in front of left, step back on left, step right to right side, touch left next to right in front of right.

Tip: Bend knees especially on first step. Difficult step for beginners.

Cha Cha Cha:

Action: (Three small steps in place) Step right in place, step left in place, step right in place. As used in aerobics, not to be confused with the basic ballroom dance step.

Tip: Clap three times and say "cha, cha, cha" to help students with rhythm.

Pony:

Action: (Three small steps in place) Step right in place, step left slightly behind right, step right in place.

Tip: Variation: Close left beside right or cross left in front of right.

Pivot Turn:

Action: (As used in aerobics) Step forward right, then turn 180 degrees toward left to face the rear. Step forward right, then turn 180 degrees toward left to face front.

Tip: During the turn, make sure your weight is evenly distributed on both feet.

Step

Step aerobics incorporates benches ranging in height from 4 to 10 inches. Step work increases the intensity of any aerobics dance class, as well as expanding the choreographic possibilities. Using step benches is usually fun for both teachers and students. Step benches or platforms are easily incorporated in aerobic dance, circuit training, interval training, and muscular conditioning classes. By giving conditioned athletes higher steps and having beginners work either without a bench or on a very low one, students with all levels of skill can be appropriately challenged in the same class.

Warming up is usually done without actually stepping up onto the bench, although the bench can be used as a prop for stretching or calisthenics. Be sure students are thoroughly warmed up and stretched before beginning the step workout.

➤ Learning Hints—Step

1. Be sure students place the whole foot on the step.
2. Students should step softly to avoid unnecessary stress.
3. Students' knees should be slightly bent at all times when stepping up or down.
4. Give students ample time to grasp any base move.
5. Visually determine that most students can perform the move you are teaching before changing directions or going on to a new movement.
6. Teach the foot movements before you add any arm movements.
7. Be selective. Do not try to put everything you know in any one class. An effective class can be built with four combinations.
8. When beginners and advanced students are in the same class, have the beginners concentrate on the foot movements. Beginners need to master the foot moves before adding the arms.
9. Advanced students may increase the intensity of their work by using higher benches, by using a greater variety of arm movements, or by adding propulsion moves.
10. Vary the level of arm movements to prevent injury to the shoulder girdle. Keep students moving their arms from low to medium to high positions.

Base Moves—Step

Basic Step:

Position: Start at 6:00.

Action: Right foot up; left foot up; right foot down; left foot down. Cued: "up," "up," "down," "down."

V-Step:

Position: Start at 6:00 and step toward 3:00.

Action: Right foot up wide position; left foot up wide position; right foot down center; left foot down center.

A-Step:

Position: Face bench and approach from left end (7:00).

Action: Right foot up center; left foot up center; right foot down right end; left foot down right end.

L-Step:

Position: Face bench and approach from right end (5:00).

Action: Right foot up; left foot up; right foot down (moving sideways off right end 3:00); left foot down tap; left foot up (moving sideways to top); right foot up; left foot down; right foot down tap.

Turn Step:

Position: Start at 6:00.

Action: Stepping up onto the bench with a basic step, but as you step down make a quarter turn, ending at 7:00.

Up Tap Down Tap:

Position: Start at 6:00 and face 12:00.

Action: Right foot up; left foot up tap; left down; right tap.

Cued: "up," "tap," "down," "tap."

```
      11      12      1
  10  ┌──────────────┐  2
   9  │              │  3
   8  └──────────────┘  4
       7       6      5
```

Figure 3-2 Key directional approaches for step.

Knee Up:

Position: Start at 6:00 and face 12:00.

Action: Right foot up; left knee up; left foot down; right foot down. Reverse. For variety, instead of knee up use hamstring curl, side leg lifts, forward kick, or back kick.

Over the Top:

Position: Start 6:00 and face 9:00.

Action: The footwork is the same as your basic step, but you are moving over the top with your right shoulder toward the long side of the bench.

Repeater:

Position: Start at 6:00.

Action: A movement that is repeated. For example, right foot up; left knee up three times; left foot down; right foot down.

Straddle Down:

Position: Stand on top of the bench facing 9:00.

Action: Right foot down (straddling bench); left foot down; right foot up; left foot up.

See Figure 3-2 for the key directional approaches for step.

Resistance

Resistance training is usually part of the aerobic or step training class. Toning exercises can improve both muscular endurance and muscular strength and are essential to keeping the body looking taut and fit. While the aerobic portion of class burns fat, the resistance training portion gives the body shape and definition.

Pushing, pulling, or lifting a body part or weight are forms of resistance work. Resistance may be increased in a variety of ways. In the aerobics classroom, this is typically done by adding light weights, resistance tubing, performing the movements more slowly, or using a more difficult body position.

➤ Learning Hints—Resistance

1. It is important to communicate proper body alignment and technique to the student.

2. Always work the large muscle groups before working the smaller muscle groups.

3. Movements should be slow and controlled.

4. Be sure that opposing muscle groups are worked. For example, if one works the gastrocnemius, the tibialis anterior also needs to be worked. They do not need to be in exact sequence, but do need to be given equal time.

5. Students should never hold the breath. The exhalation should occur as the muscle is contracted, the inhalation during extension or relaxation.

6. Students should work through the full range of motion, being careful not to hyperextend or lock joints.

7. Always follow resistance training with stretching.

Base Moves—Resistance

Bicep Curls: Biceps—front of arms (Figure 3-3)

Major Muscles Used: Bicep Brachii

Position: Stand with legs shoulder-width apart and arms extended at your side.

Action: Bend the arms at the elbows until the hands come near your shoulders. Return to starting position.

Tips: 1. Keep upper arms stationary; move lower arms only.
2. Keep elbows close to body.
3. Do not rock, jerk, or swing body.
4. Exhale on upward movement, inhale on downward movement.

Tricep Extension: Tricep—back of arms (Figure 3-4)

Major Muscles Used: Tricep Brachii

Position: Stand with legs shoulder-width apart, knees bent, and one arm extending overhead.

Figure 3-3 Bicep curl: Tubing or free weights.

Figure 3-4 Tricep extension: Tubing or free weights.

Figure 3-6 Chest press: Free weights or tubing .

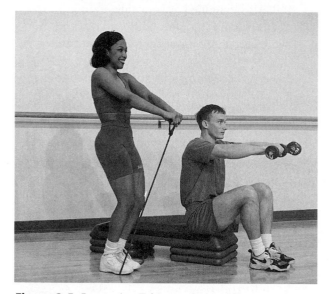

Figure 3-5 Front raise: Tubing or free weights.

Action: Bend the arm at the elbow and lower toward the upper back. Return to starting position. Support the arm with the opposite hand. Hold near the tricep in front of the chest.

Tip: Keep your working arm close to your ear.

Front Raise: Shoulders (Figure 3-5)

Major Muscle Used: Anterior Deltoid

Position: Arms extended downward in front of body.

Action: Raise extended arms up to shoulder level and lower to starting position.

Tip: Do not lock elbow joints or raise arms above shoulders.

Upright Rows: Shoulders and upper back

Major Muscles Used: Deltoid, Trapezius

Position: Stand with feet shoulder-width apart and knees slightly bent. Arms extended downward in front of body.

Action: Pull the hands upward until they reach the chin, elbows extending away from body.

Tips: 1. Keep your hands close together and near your body.

2. Elbows higher than wrist at the top of the exercise.

Chest Press: Chest (Figure 3-6)

Major Muscle Used: Pectoralis Major

Position: Stand with your feet shoulder-width apart. Elbows extended to sides with forearms pointed upward (elbows bent 90 degrees).

Action: Press the arms together in front of the body. Return to starting position.

Tip: Keep the upper arms lower than the shoulders.

Variation: Point the forearms forward and extend arms forward from chest position (very effective with tubing).

Pushups: Chest and Arms

Major Muscles Used: Tricep Brachii, Pectoralis Major

Position: Begin in the pushup position with hands on the floor, slightly wider than shoulder width, fingers facing forward. Legs are extended backward with weight resting on toes. To modify, rest weight on knees.

Action: Bend elbows to approximately 90 degrees. Then straighten elbows and return to starting position.

Tip: Keep the back straight; do not lock elbows at the top of the exercise.

Regular Crunch: Abdominals

Major Muscles Used: Rectus Abdominis, Internal and External Obliques

Position: Lie flat on the back with knees bent, feet flat on the floor and shoulder-width apart. Hands may be at sides, across the chest, or placed behind the head for support.

Action: Lift the upper body off the floor while pressing the lower back into the floor. Lower back down to starting position.

Tip: Focus eyes up toward ceiling; lift and curl naturally with the body and neck. Gently press head backward into hands to keep neck in neutral position.

Twisting Crunch: Abdominals and Obliques

Major Muscles Used: Rectus Abdominis, Internal and External Obliques

Position: Assume same position as regular crunch.

Action: Twist and lift the torso to one side as the back is lifted off the floor.

Tip: If hands are placed behind the head, leave one elbow on or near the floor when twisting and lifting with the opposite side of the body.

Squat: Buttocks and Thighs (Figure 3-7)

Major Muscles Used: Quadriceps, Hamstrings, Gluteus Maximus

Position: Stand with feet shoulder-width apart, knees slightly bent.

Figure 3-8 Four-count lunge: Free weights or arms only.

Action: Lower the buttocks to about 90 degrees. Sit backward as though trying to sit on a chair. Keep head and eyes forward.

Tip: Do not round your back.

4-Count Lunge: Thighs and Buttocks (Figure 3-8)

Major Muscles Used: Quadriceps, Hamstrings, Gluteus Maximus

Position: Head up, eyes forward. Stand with feet together.

Action: Step forward with right foot; left heel should be lifted. Lower left knee toward floor; (bending both knees); slowly extend legs. Push off using right foot to starting position. Reverse to left.

Tips: 1. Keep the knee and ankle of forward stepping foot in alignment.
2. Keep back and neck straight.
3. All movement should be slow and controlled.

Inner Thigh Lift: Inner Thigh and Hips

Major Muscles Used: Abductors

Position: Lie on side with head supported by bent arm or resting on straight arm. Bring top leg over extended bottom leg and relax top knee to floor.

Action: Lift and lower extended leg.

Tip: Do not lower working leg completely to floor.

Outer Thigh Lift: Outer Thigh and Hip

Major Muscles Used: Abductors

Position: Lie on side with head supported by bent arm or resting on straight arm. Bottom knee bent with top leg extended.

Action: Lift the top leg up and down, keeping the foot parallel to the floor.

Tip: Make sure your hips are in proper alignment.

Figure 3-7 Squats: Arms only or free weights.

Flexibility

Stretch Strategy. Stretching exercises are performed during both the warm-up and the cool-down. In both phases, static stretching is recommended. Warm-up stretches are generally done standing up and are held for only 10 to 30 seconds. Warm-up stretches help reduce resistance to vigorous movement, improve psychological readiness to workout, as well as improve the muscle's ability to extend.

Final stretches, performed to maintain or increase flexibility, are held for 30 to 60 seconds. The final stretching is generally easier because the body is warm and the joints are well lubricated. Many of the final stretches are done on the floor and emphasize an increased range of motion. Students should be encouraged to concentrate and relax during each stretch. All major muscle groups should be included—arms, shoulders, chest, back, hips, thighs, and calves. Instructors need to be particularly vigilant about form during final stretching.

➤ Learning Hints—Stretching

1. Avoid partner stretching; it can be dangerous unless performed by a skilled person.
2. Floor stretches are best done on warm, dry surfaces.
3. Breathing is very important. Full, deep breathing promotes mental and physical relaxation and helps to slow the heart rate and lower blood pressure.
4. Muscles should be stretched only to a point of tension, not to a point of pain.

Upper Body Stretch Moves

Upper Body Neck Isolations: Head Turn, Head Tilts, Chin to Chest, Head Tilts

Major Muscles Stretched: Trapezius, Sternocleidomastoid

Position: Standing erect, shoulders down, looking forward.

Head Turn:

Action: Turn head to right (focus eyes); return to center; turn head to left; return to center.

Chin to Chest:

Action: Slowly lower chin toward chest hold; return to erect position.

Head Tilt:

Action: Tilt head, right ear toward right shoulder; return to center; tilt head to left shoulder; return to center.

Tips: 1. Do not "look up" or "break" neck to the back.
2. Do not do neck circles. They may damage the cervical vertebrae.

Shoulders:

Major Muscles Stretched: Middle Deltoid, Posterior/Deltoid

Position: Standing erect, look forward

Action: 1. Shrug shoulders, lower shoulders
2. Shoulder circles backward
   a. Shoulder only
   b. Bend elbow, circling backward
   c. Whole arm circles backward as backstroke in swimming
3. Shoulder circles forward
   a. Shoulder only forward
   b. Bend elbow, circling forward
   c. Whole arm circles forward as free style in swimming

Across Body:

Major Muscles Stretched: Middle Deltoid, Posterior Deltoid, Latissimus Dorsi

Position: Standing erect, with feet in straddle position.

Action: Gently bring left arm across body. Hold and support with right arm. Slowly reverse and repeat.

Tips: 1. Keep the arm close to body, shoulders level. Do not lift arm above chest.
2. Do not hold at elbow or wrist joint. Support above or below.

Tricep Stretch Behind the Head:

Major Muscles Stretched: Triceps Brachii

Position: Standing erect, with feet in straddle position, extend left arm over head. Bend the arm at the elbow and lower toward upper back. Gently hold elbow with right hand.

Action: Hold left elbow with right hand; press head back slightly to intensify stretch.

Tips: 1. Keep spine long, abdominals pulled in.
2. Do not hold the elbow joint. This may cause undue stress to the joint.

Chest Stretch:

Major Muscles Stretched: Pectoralis Major, Anterior Deltoid

Position: Standing erect, feet parallel and directly under hips, knees slightly flexed, and hands clasped behind back.

Action: Clasping hands behind back, pull shoulder blades together to stretch chest.

Tips: 1. Keep abdominals lifted.
2. Keep lower back in rounded position.

Upper Back:

Major Muscles Stretched: Rhomboids, Erector Spinae, Trapezius

Position: Feet in straddle, hands clasped low in front of body, palms facing floor.

Action: Slowly raise clasped hands to front of body (parallel floor) and press palms forward.

Tip: Keep pelvis tipped forward, abdominals tight.

Lateral:

Major Muscles Stretched: Latissimus Dorsi, Triceps Brachii

Position: Stand with feet shoulder-width apart, feet rotated outward (10:00–2:00); arms reaching toward ceiling; shoulders pressing down.

Action: Looking up at lifted hands: bend right knee; right hand stretching up; hold position. Keeping right hand at that high level; stretch right hand up to meet this level, bending left knee; hold position.

Tip: Keep abdominals lifted, spine long. Keep straight leg rotated outward also.

Standing Cat Back:

Major Muscles Stretched: Erector Spinae

Position: Feet in a straddle position, with hands resting on thighs.

Action: Round the back and lift the abdominal muscles. Exhale as the back is rounded.

Tips: 1. Arms may give active support to increase "cat back."
2. May be done in hands and knee position on floor.

Lower Body Stretch Moves

Hamstrings:

Major Muscles Stretched: Hamstrings, Gastrocnemius, Soleus

Position: Standing, with feet shoulder-width apart.

Action: Extend right leg forward; left leg should be bent and right foot should be flexed with heel on floor. Place both hands on left thigh.

Tips: 1. Always place hands on the bent support leg.
2. Keep abdominals tight to avoid low back strain.

Standing Quadriceps:

Major Muscles Stretched: Quadriceps, Iliopsoas

Position: Face wall, left hand on wall for support. Standing on left foot, bend lower right leg behind body. Hold the right foot with the right hand.

Action: Slowly push right foot toward hand and hold.

Tips: 1. Maintain abdominal support and upright posture.
2. Do not compact the knee.
3. May be done lying down on left side, left arm fully extended on the floor.
4. Support leg should be bent. Avoid hyperextending the leg.

Calf Stretch:

Major Muscles Stretched: Gastrocnemius, Soleus, Achilles' Tendon

Position: Stand with feet together.

Action: Lift right foot and extend right leg backward, slowly pressing right heel toward floor. Left leg should be bent.

Tips: 1. Hands can be placed on the bent support leg.
2. Keep heels of both feet in contact with floor.
3. The knee and ankle of the forward leg should be vertically aligned.

Inner Thigh/Outer Thigh:

Major Muscles Stretched: Adductors, Abductors

Position: Stand in a wide straddle position with feet parallel. Place hands on floor beneath shoulders.

Action: Lean forward, shifting weight to hands. Straighten right leg as you bend left knee. Reverse.

Tip: Do not bend knees more than 90 degrees.

Toe Taps:

Major Muscles Stretched: Tibialis Anterior

Position: Feet parallel, one foot apart, knees bent.

Action: Tap toes slowly up and down.

Tips: 1. Both feet may be worked together or one at a time.
2. Deeper bend in the knees allows for greater stretch.

Floor Stretches

Knee to Chest:

Major Muscles Stretched: Hamstrings, Gluteus Maximus

Position: Lying on back, knees bent, and feet flat on the floor.

Action: Slowly bring your right knee toward your chest. Place hands behind knee.

Tips: 1. Placing hands directly on knee can cause undue stress to knee joint.
2. Contract abdominals and press lower back to floor.

Gluteal Stretch:

Major Muscles Stretched: Gluteus Maximus, Gluteus Medius, Gluteus Minumus, Hip Adductors

Position: Lying on back, with left leg bent and foot on floor, cross your right leg over and rest your ankle on your left knee.

Action: Slowly bring your left knee toward your chest and hold. Deepen stretch by using hands on back of left leg. Hold.

Tip: You can grasp your thigh when pulling your knee to chest.

Hamstring Stretch:

Major Muscles Stretched: Hamstrings, Gluteus Maximus

Position: Lying on back, with knees bent and feet flat on the floor.

Action: Bring the right knee toward the chest and extend the lower leg up. Gently bring the leg closer to the chest and hold.

Tip: The knee of the extended leg should not be hyperextended.

Inner Thigh Stretch:

Major Muscles Stretched: Adductors

Position: Lying on back, with both legs bent toward chest.

Action: Slowly extend legs overhead. Slowly open and slowly close legs.

Tip: End by returning knee to chest and placing feet on floor.

Quadriceps Stretch:

Major Muscles Stretched: Quadriceps

Position: Lying on side, with head supported by bent arm or resting on straight arm. Both legs extended.

Action: Bend top right leg and grasp foot with right hand. Gently press foot into hand.

Tip: Do not let hips roll forward or backward.

Low Cobra:

Major Muscles Stretched: Rectus Abdominis, Pectoralis Major

Position: Lying on floor in a prone position (face down). Hands placed beneath shoulders.

Action: Slowly press up, lifting your chest off the floor and arching your lower back.

Tips: 1. Keep hips and elbows on the floor and lower back relaxed.
2. Do not overarch lower back.
3. Do not extend elbows beyond 90 degrees.

Cat Stretch:

Major Muscles Stretched: Erector Spinae

Position: Hands and knees

Action: Drop the head, slowly tucking the chin toward the chest, as you curve the spine and contract the abdominal muscles. Hold this position. Return the back to a neutral position.

Standing Stretch Routine

Head Tilts
Shoulder Shrugs
Shoulder Stretch (R)
Tricep Stretch (R)
Shoulder Stretch (L)
Tricep Stretch (L)
Chest Stretch (hand clasped behind back)
Upper Back Stretch (hands clasped, in front)
Standing Cat Back
Calf Stretch (R and L)
Quadriceps (R and L)
Hamstring (R and L)
Tibialis Anterior (R and L)
Toe Taps

Floor Stretch Routine

Knee to Chest Stretch (R)
Ankle Flexion and Extension (R)
Ankle Circles (R)
Hamstring Stretch (R)
Gluteal Stretch (right leg resting on left knee)
Knee to Chest Stretch (L)
Ankle Flexion and Extension (L)
Ankle Circles (L)
Hamstring Stretch (L)
Gluteal Stretch (left leg resting on right knee)
Inner Thigh Stretch

Circuit and Interval Training with Aerobic Dance

Circuit and interval training have been around for a long time but have only recently been incorporated into the aerobic dance class. In circuit training, a series of stations is set up, and participants move from one station to the next with little or no rest between stations. Stations now range in number, but the classic circuit has nine to twelve stations. Whatever the number, exercises performed at each station are carefully selected and sequenced. Typically, each participant will perform a 15- to 45-second workout of 8 to 20 repetitions. Stations may incorporate exercise machines, hand-held weights, calisthenics, resistance bands, or any equipment combination. When a

30-second to 3-minute aerobics station is included, you have aerobic circuit training. Although the research has not yet substantiated the improvement of cardiorespiratory endurance through this type of training, it is enjoyable for both students and teachers. Aerobics stations may be inserted after any number of exercise stations.

Interval training alternates periods of intense work and rest. Typically a student may work at near maximal intensity for 3 minutes and then rest for 3 minutes. Theoretically, alternating work and relief may allow more cardiovascular work to be accomplished in any one training session. Interval training's effect on muscles may lead to more effective use of both fats and carbohydrates, as well as other positive changes in the muscle's blood-carrying capacity and enzyme activity.

It is a good idea to strive for a balance between both of these methods. When used in combination, interval and circuit training have many benefits, including

- Increased variety and therefore more enjoyment by participants
- The potential for more work in less time
- Improvement in both aerobic and anaerobic capacity
- Increased exercise adherence
- Enhanced sports performance

On a practical level, the following approach works well in the aerobics classroom. Alternate cardiovascular and strength stations. One or two exercises may be performed at each station. Students will exercise for 30 to 60 seconds, then rest for 10 to 15 seconds or use that time to move on to the next station. During peak intensity, use music with 120 bpm. Follow the guidelines for appropriate warm-up and cool-down tempos (see Music section, this chapter). Be sure to completely demonstrate the exercise (or exercises) to be performed at each station before starting any activity. Assign students to stations, then begin your group warm-up.

Provide a sign for each station, naming the exercise(s) to be performed there, and any cautions that are appropriate; if you have access to laminating equipment, it is worthwhile to photocopy a picture of the exercise(s), glue it on, and then laminate the entire sign. Signs that are computer generated on 8½-by-11-inch sheets of paper work well. Students may benefit from having color-coded signs that indicate whether they are doing primarily strength or cardiovascular work.

Circuits are easily designed for any class situation. Carefully select the work that you want your students to do, look at the number of students in your class and the size of your room, and decide whether you need to have one or two exercises performed at each station. There must be at least one station for every student. If you have more students than total stations, it is necessary to set up another *complete* circuit. Having empty stations will not disrupt the flow of the class, but having more students than stations is not workable. For example, alternating seven strength stations with seven cardiovascular stations and having students move around the circuit twice will provide approximately 30 minutes of peak-intensity work. With a brief group warm-up, a group cool-down, abdominal work, and brief final stretching, a class can be completed in 45 minutes.

Sample Circuit

This 16-station circuit has proved very popular with students. Either one or two complete circuits can be set up in a large classroom, accommodating anywhere from 16 to 32 students (Figure 3-9).

Equipment (Figure 3-10)

Resistance tubes or bands
Hand weights
Benches
Stopwatch
Music
118–126 bpm

Warm-up

Have students form a circle, moving around the room. Walk, walk on toes, walk on heels, walk backwards, easy jog, skip, gallop lead right, gallop lead left, slide, reverse slide direction.

Stations

1. Bench
2. Tricep extension with tube
3. Run
4. 4-count lunge
5. Bench
6. Bicep curl with weights
7. Run
8. Squats
9. Bench
10. Chest press with tube
11. Run
12. 4-count lunge
13. Bench
14. Upright rows with weights
15. Run
16. Squats

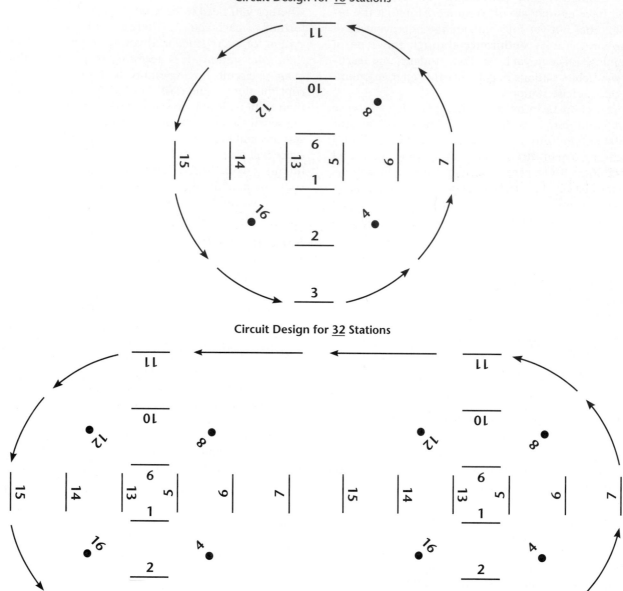

Figure 3-9 Circuit designs.

When at the run stations (3, 7, 11, and 15), students should travel counter-clockwise around the room.

Cardiovascular Cool-down

Walk around the room.

Abdominal Workout

Final Stretching and Relaxation

Safety Considerations

While being lively and engaging and providing a lot of fun, instructors also need to keep the safety of all participants uppermost in their minds. The vigilance does not need to show, but it does need to be present if class members are to avoid injury or harm. Here are some useful guidelines.

1. Screen every participant *before* they participate in class. They should obtain a medical history or pre-exercise health risk appraisal.

Figure 3-10 Cardio/resistance circuit.

2. Monitor participants' movements closely while you are teaching. Face the class and teach by mirror image, especially if you do not have a mirror to look in when you turn your back to the class. Students have an easier time following when your back is to them, but these periods should be brief unless you can continue to monitor the entire class by watching their movements in a mirror as you lead. Watch for flailing arm movements and incorrect directional movement that may lead to collision. Also watch for proper alignment: head up, shoulders back, chest up, buttocks tucked, and knees relaxed.

3. Keep potentially high-risk positions out of your class. These include sustained, unsupported forward flexion in a standing position (forward bends); trunk rotation against a fixed axis; or hyperextension of the neck, elbows, knees, or back. Other exercises to avoid include deep knee bends, the hurdler stretch, double leg raises, straight-leg sit-ups, and side leg lifts while on the knees and either hands or elbows.

Modifications for Special Populations

Orthopedically Impaired

1. Students using a wheelchair may do a variation of dance movements using upper body only.
2. Allow students who can push their wheelchairs to move forward, backward, or side to side to the beat of the music.
3. Students using crutches or walkers may be allowed to sit in a standard desk chair.
4. Students with a lower extremity amputation may be allowed to use the back of a standard desk chair for balance.

5. Students with ataxia should be allowed to move with more simple patterns, e.g., step forward, step back.

Cognitively Impaired

1. Use key words during directions and not entire phases, e.g., "Forward" instead of "Walk forward two beats, rock side to side, and now walk back." Keep your instructions short.
2. Use pictures whenever possible.
3. Allow students to follow at their own rate and pace.

Sensory Impaired

1. Students with visual impairments might need several physical prompts or "hand over hand" cues, i.e., assisting with arm patterns.
2. Students with hearing impairments should be positioned closer to the instructor. You might ask the student with a hearing impairment to teach you specific sign language for the various movements of the dance.

Contact Disabled Sports USA for more information regarding individuals with amputations or other orthopedic conditions: www.dsusa.org. Contact the United States Association of Blind Athletes for more information regarding individuals with visual impairments: www.usaba.org.

Resources
Professional Organizations

Aerobic dance is influenced by factors ranging from shifts in popular taste to new research findings in many specialized fields. Professional organizations monitor and evaluate changes and pass the information on to their members. To ensure teaching excellence, membership in one or more professional organizations is highly recommended. Professional organizations set standards of excellence for their members and offer certification programs for those willing to go through an often rigorous certification process. They also offer networking opportunities, workshops, and publications, and they frequently sponsor research.

Aerobic and Fitness Association of America (AFAA), 15250 Ventura Blvd., Suite 200, Sherman Oaks, CA 91403-3297

American College of Sports Medicine, P.O. Box 1440, Indianapolis, IN 46206-1440

American Council on Exercise, 5820 Oberlin Dr., Suite 102, San Diego, CA 92121-3787

American Aerobic Association International/ International Sports Medicine Association (AAAI/ISMA), P.O. Box 633, Richboro, PA 18954

Aquatic Exercise Association, P.O. Box 497, Port Washington, WI 53074

The Cooper Institute for Aerobic Research, 12330 Preston Rd., Dallas, TX 75230-2299

IDEA, The Health and Fitness Source, 6190 Cornerstone Ct. E., Ste. 204, San Diego, CA 92121-4701

Videos

There are hundreds of aerobic dance videos. What is right for you and the classes you teach? Reviews in journals and magazines help sort the good from the bad, as do previews that some publishers will arrange for teachers in educational institutions (colleges and universities, especially). Another good guide is the Collage Video Specialties' *Complete Guide to Exercise Videos,* published quarterly. Hundreds of tapes are reviewed in each issue.

The following questions help you evaluate any video. What are the qualifications of the presenter? How old is the tape? Does it provide adequate time to all phases of an aerobic class? Is it appropriate for your group? Does it have heart rate and other safety checks, clear cueing, high motivational value?

Finally, if one learns a routine from a videotape and then teaches it in a class, one must credit to the class the expert who developed the routine.

Creative Instructors Aerobics Educational Videos, 2314 Naudain St., Philadelphia, PA 19146

Collage Video Specialties, Inc., 5390 Main St., N.E., Dept. 1, Minneapolis, MN 55421

Music

It is highly recommended that one use professionally mixed audiotapes. The following are good sources, and most have 800 numbers. If you decide to mix your own music, remember music copyright laws. Contact the appropriate performing rights society for permission.

Music Services

Music Mixes, P.O. Box 533967, Orlando, FL 32853

Power Music, 560 W. 200 St., Suite 200, Salt Lake City, UT 84101

Dynamix Music Service, 9411 Philadelphia Road, Baltimore, MD 21237

Musicflex, P.O. Box 140435, Queens, NY 11414-0435

Serenity, 8016 Marion Dr., Maria Stein, OH 45860

Music Performing Rights Societies

ASCAP, 1 Lincoln Plaza, New York, NY 10023

BMI, 320 W. 57th St., New York, NY 10019

Instructor Purchase Programs

Many leading suppliers of fitness footwear and clothing offer instructor discount programs. Contact the following for information about their programs:

Reebok Professional Instructor Alliance, P.O. Box 1245001, 60 North Ronks Rd., Ronks, PA 17572-9987

Nike Instructor Network Program, P.O. Box 4455, Beaverton, OR 97076-4455

Avia Select Instructor, P.O. Box 1823, Beaverton, OR 97075-1823

Adidas Three Stripe Instructions, P.O. Box 25384, Portland, OR 97298

Rykä Instructor Trainer Alliance, 10200 Swallen, Suite 1, Beaverton, OR 97005

Terminology

Aerobic Oxygen-using.

Aerobic cool-down The period at the end of the aerobics segment of an exercise session in which intensity is reduced to begin lowering the heart rate.

Aerobic dance-exercise A method of exercising to music that conditions the cardiovascular system by using movements that create an increased demand for oxygen over an extended time.

Agonist A muscle that is directly responsible for the joint movement observed. Also referred to as a prime mover.

Alignment The relationship of the body segments to one another. Proper alignment features balanced agonist and antagonist muscle pairs.

Anaerobic Without oxygen.

Antagonist A muscle that acts in opposition to the action produced by an agonist muscle.

Atrophy Wasting of muscle size resulting from disuse.

Ballistic stretching A stretch using rapid, bouncing movements. Contraindicated.

Basic locomotor steps These are considered to be walking, running, hopping, and jumping.

Beats A pattern of strong and weak pulsations that have an even rhythm.

Cardiorespiratory fitness (CRF) Related to the capacity of the heart-lung system to deliver oxygen for sustained energy production, CRF is the ability to perform large muscle movement over a sustained period.

Carotid pulse An arterial pulse point located in the neck about one inch below the jaw line, next to the esophagus.

Concentric muscle action Contraction of muscle that causes the muscle to shorten.

Contraindication Any condition that makes any movement, activity, or treatment undesirable.

Cueing Hand and/or verbal signals that identify upcoming movement.

Directional cueing A visual or verbal technique that signals the direction in which to move.

Exercise intensity The specific level of physical activity at which a person exercises that can be quantified (e.g., heart rate, work, rate of perceived exertion) and is usually reflected as a percentage of one's maximal capacity to do work.

Flexibility The possible range of motion around any joint.

Footwork cueing A visual or verbal technique that signals which foot to move.

Freestyle method Spontaneous choreography by an instructor.

Muscular endurance The capacity of a muscle to exert repeated force.

Muscular strength The maximum force that can be exerted by a muscle or muscle group.

Numerical cueing A visual or verbal technique used by instructors to count the rhythm of the exercise.

Rating of perceived exertion (RPE) A scale that correlates the participant's perception of exercise effort with the actual intensity level.

Resting heart rate The number of heartbeats per minute after the body has been at complete rest for at least 10 minutes.

Rhythm A regular pattern of movement or sound.

Rhythmic cueing A visual or verbal technique that indicates the correct rhythm of an exercise or step.

Slide aerobics A type of training program in which a lateral movement trainer is used to perform aerobic conditioning movements and exercises.

Static stretching A long stretch that holds the desired muscle under tension without pain for at least 15 to 30 seconds.

Step cueing A verbal technique that refers to the name of the step in an aerobics routine, such as "grapevine" or "step touch."

Step workout A type of aerobic conditioning that incorporates a bench between 4 and 10 inches high.

Talk test A method for measuring exercise intensity using observation of respiration effort and the ability to talk while exercising.

Target heart rate The number of heartbeats per minute that indicates appropriate exercise intensity levels for each person. Also called training heart rate.

Target heart-rate range The exercise intensity that represents the minimum and maximum intensity for safe and effective exercise. Also referred to as training zone.

Tempo The rate of speed at which a musical composition is played.

Warm-up The early phase of a workout or exercise session designed to ready the body for vigorous motion.

Further References

American College of Sports Medicine. *ACSM Fitness Book*. Champaign, IL: Leisure Press, 1992.

American Council on Exercise. *Group Fitness Instructor Manual*. San Diego, CA, 2000.

Anderson, Bob. *Stretching*. Bolinas, CA: Shelter Publications, Inc., 1980.

Baechle, Thomas R. and Groves, Barney R. *Weight Training Steps to Success*. Champaign, IL: Leisure Press, 1992.

Bishop, Jan G. *Fitness Through Aerobics*. 3rd ed. Scottsdale, AZ: Gorsuch, Scarisbrick Publishers, 1995.

Cibrario, Mark. *A Complete Guide to Rubberized Resistance Exercises*. Buffalo Grove, IL: Spri Products, Inc.

Copeland, Candice. *Moves: The Fool Proof Formula for Creative Choreography*. Los Angeles, CA: CompuThink, 1987.

Gretchell, Bud. *Physical Fitness: A Way of Life*. 3rd ed. New York: Macmillan, 1983.

Hesson, James L. *Weight Training for Life*. 2nd ed. Englewood, CO: Morton Publishing, 1991.

Kam, Esther and Kraines, Minda G. *Keep Moving! It's Aerobic Dance*. 2nd ed. Mountain View, CA: 1992.

Kravitz, Len. *Anybody's Guide to Total Fitness*. Dubuque, IA: Kendall/Hunt Publishing, 1986.

Kravitz, Len. Circuits and Intervals. *IDEA Today for Fitness Professionals* (January): 33–43, 1996.

Mazzo, Karen. *Aerobic Dance A Way to Fitness*. Englewood, CO: Morton Publishing, 1993.

Mazzo, Karen. *Fitness Through Aerobics and Step Training*. Englewood, CO: Morton Publishing, 1993.

Mazzo, Karen and Mangili, Lauren. *Step Training Plus*. Englewood, CO: Morton Publishing, 1993.

Robbins, Gwen, Powers, Debbie and Burgess, Sharon. *A Wellness Way of Life*. 4th ed. Dubuque, IA: WCB McGraw-Hill, 1999.

VanGalen, Patricia. *Exercising With Dyna-Band Total Body Toner*. Hudson, OH: Gilliam Enterprises, Inc.

Web Sites

www.cooperinst.org The Cooper Institute for Aerobic Research—offers training and certification programs for fitness leaders and health professionals.

www.acefitness.org American Council on Exercise—leading provider of certification and education to the professional, commercial, and retail fitness markets.

www.afaa.com Aerobics and Fitness Association of America (AFAA)—offers training and certification and fitness facts.

www.afpafitness.com American Fitness Professionals & Association—offers health and fitness professionals a variety of certification programs, continuing education courses, home correspondence, and regional conventions.

www.acsm.org American College of Sports Medicine— offers certification and continuing education.

www.ideafit.com IDEA, The Health & Fitness Source— IDEA's home page, containing information on employment offerings, IDEA events, membership benefits, products, and more.

www.turnstep.com Turnstep/Choreography Web site— a choreography Web site with moves, choreography, and ideas, as well as listings of other Internet links and FAQ (frequently asked questions) page.

www.nsca-cc.org National Strength and Conditioning Association—certification body of the National Strength & Conditioning Association (NSCA).

CHAPTER 4

Archery

This chapter will enable you to
- Identify and demonstrate the ten basic steps of shooting in target archery
- Identify and demonstrate terms related to the bow and arrow
- Understand the basic terminology associated with target archery
- Identify and describe the rules associated with target archery
- Identify and observe the necessary safety precautions

Nature and Purpose

For the past several years, interest in archery has grown tremendously throughout the world, and many schools and colleges have added archery in their physical education programs. Consequently, archery has become a modern sport form. In the 1972 Olympic Games held at Munich, archery appeared as an Olympic event for the first time. Several archers from the United States have captured Olympic medals and medals from other international competitions.

Archery is an easy-to-learn activity, and it is possible for both sexes of all ages to develop proficiency in archery skills in a relatively short period of time. As an individual sport, it is relatively inexpensive and can be practiced year-round. The benefits of archery are both physical and emotional.

Rules of Target Archery

1. Any bow except a crossbow may be used for competition.
2. Arrows should have a distinctive crest in order to distinguish each archer's arrow.
3. After the signal to shoot, arrows should be nocked.
4. Arrows that fall from the bow and cannot be reached with the bow from the shooting line are considered to be shot.
5. Only six arrows may be shot at the designated target; if more than six are shot, only the lowest six scores are counted, and any arrow(s) shot at any other target shall not be scored.
6. An archer should shoot from the longest distance first, the second longest distance next, and so forth.

7. Scores are recorded from the highest score to the lowest score.
8. Arrows should be retrieved only after the signal to do so is given.

Scoring

The scoring values of target archery are 9 points for gold, 7 for red, 5 for blue, 3 for black, and 1 for white rings. An arrow that goes completely through the target or that bounces off the target counts 7 points regardless of the part of the target it passes or hits. An arrow that lands on the line between two rings counts as hitting the higher scoring ring.

All target archery rounds (competitions) are shot at a regulation 48-inch target face unless otherwise specified. The common target archery competitions are the American Round, Columbia Round, Hereford Round, York Round, Women's and Men's Metropolitan Rounds, and Scholastics Round. Each competition round differs in the number of arrows and the distance from which the arrows are shot.

For physical education classes, a modified institutional round should be implemented to enable a round to be completed within a given time period. For example, the Ball State Round consists of 12 ends: 4 ends each shooting from 20 yards, 25 yards, and 30 yards, and requiring approximately 60 minutes to complete. Each end consists of shooting five arrows. The scoring values of the Ball State Round are 5 points for gold, 4 points for red, 3 for blue, 2 for black, and 1 for white. This gives a maximum total of 300 points (5 arrows × 5 points × 12 ends = 300 points). If a class period is only 45 minutes, a round should consist of 8 ends: 4 ends from 25 yards and 4 ends from 30 yards.

Equipment

Archery equipment as a whole is known as "tackle." The minimum essential tackle for the beginning archer includes (1) a bow of correct length and weight, (2) one dozen matched arrows, (3) a finger tab or glove, (4) an arm guard, and (5) a target. The selection of a proper bow and matched arrows is the most important step for successful archery practice.

Bows

Bows are constructed of many materials, including wood, fiberglass, or laminated wood core and fiberglass. To overcome the disadvantages of the wooden or fiberglass bow, a laminated (composite) bow was designed. This bow is smooth-shooting and is not subject to changes due to weather.

Bow weight refers to the weight in pounds required to bring a bow to full draw. The most important factor in determining bow weight is the individual archer's muscular strength. For the beginner, it is best to start with a bow that is easier to draw and handle rather than using "overbow." The bow weight may be gradually increased as the archer improves shooting technique and develops muscular strength. Table 4-1 shows the recommended bow weights according to the standards established by the Archery Manufacturers Organization.

Arrows

Arrows are made of wood, fiberglass, or aluminum. The least expensive, wooden arrows, are used by most beginning archers; glass and aluminum arrows are used by more advanced archers. Each type of arrow has it own advantages and disadvantages, but it is very important that one select arrows closely matched in weight, length, and stiffness (spine).

A beginner should start to shoot with arrows that are 2 inches longer than the needed proper length in case of an overdraw. To determine the proper length, one should place the nock of the arrow on the center of one's chest and extend arms full length forward, palms facing, so that the point of the arrow extends past the fingertips. When purchasing a bow and arrows, one should seek advice from an expert to determine the proper bow and arrows that fit best.

Arm Guards

Arm guards have two main functions: (1) The most important is to protect the bow arm from the slap of the bow string; (2) the other is to keep a long sleeve close to the arm so it will not interfere with the bow string. The arm guard is worn on the inside of the forearm below the elbow, near the wrist of the bow arm. The arm guard is usually made of leather with elastic straps to hold the guard on the forearm.

Finger Tabs or Gloves

Friction between the fingers and the bow string can produce not only soreness to the fingers, but also an effect on proper shooting. Tabs or gloves will protect the fingers and aid in developing a smooth and consistent release. Many beginners have difficulty in using finger tabs or gloves but with a little patience and practice can overcome this difficulty.

Target

A target consists of a target face, a mat, and a stand. Ready-made targets can be purchased from a sporting goods dealer. Schools and colleges usually use a 48-inch target face. Target mats are easily made from tightly compressed hay and should measure at least 50 × 50 inches.

Suggested Learning Sequence

Open space with good lighting and a proper backdrop, well-organized lessons, and an emphasis on safety are all important aspects of creating a successful atmosphere for archery. Safety should be stressed from the very beginning. Instructions should include the care of the equipment (bow, bowstring, and arrows) and the ten essential steps for shooting described in this chapter. A good learning sequence is the following:

A. Introduction
B. Nature of the Activity
   1. Archery as a sport and family recreation
   2. Discussion of equipment
   3. Safety
C. Skills and Techniques—Ten Basic Steps of Shooting
   Static Stage: Practice without arrows
   1. Proper stance
   2. Nocking the arrow
   3. Setting the hook
   4. Holding the bow
   5. Raising the head
   6. Raising the unit

Table 4-1   Recommended bow weights

	Under 20 lbs	20 lbs	25 lbs	30 lbs	35 lbs	40 lbs	Over 40 lbs
Children 6–12	X	X					
Teen (girl)		X	X				
Teen (boy)		X	X	X			
Women		X	X	X			
Men					X	X	X	
Hunting							X

Dynamic Stage: Practice with arrows

   7. Drawing and anchoring

   8. Aiming and holding

   9. Releasing

 10. Follow-through

Participants should practice steps 7 and 8 several times before moving to steps 9 and 10.

    The first shooting practice should start from 15 yards, then 20 yards, 30 yards, and so on.

D. Rules and Scoring—Once they have achieved some proficiency in shooting technique, participants can be taught the rules governing target archery and the scoring method.

Skills and Techniques

String the Bow

Push-pull Method

1. Take the bow handle in your left hand with the back of the bow toward you.
2. Holding the left arm in front of the body and angling the bow's upper limb toward the right, place the lower nock against the instep of the left foot, but not touching the ground.
3. Place the right hand on the upper limb just below the upper loop of the bowstring; then keeping both arms straight, pull with the left hand and push with the heel of the right hand, and slide the string into the upper nock with fingers. While stringing, keep your face away from the bow.

Step-through Method

1. Hold the bow in your right hand and the string with the other hand.
2. Place the back of the lower limb of the bow across the ankle of your left foot.
3. Step through the bow with your right leg.
4. Place the bow handle high on your right thigh.
5. Press the upper limb of the bow forward with the open right hand and slide the string in the nock with the left hand. Always check both notches for proper string insertion and alignment after each stringing.

Shooting: The Ten Basic Steps

Archers should always follow the ten basic steps of the shooting sequence in their proper order. Consistency is very important for becoming a good archer. Repeating these ten steps will help you develop rhythm in shooting and become a satisfied archer. The steps described below are for the right-handed person; adjustments are required for left-handers.

Step 1—Establishing a Proper Stance

The stance establishes the foundation of good archery form; the square and open stances are the most commonly used. For both stances, the archer should spread both feet apart (approximately shoulder width) to achieve a comfortable feeling. The archer's weight should be equally distributed upon both feet, and the knees should be locked to maintain balance. Once you decide on a stance—either the square or open stance—you should take the same stance each time you shoot.

1. *Square Stance.* The square stance is recommended for beginning archers. In this stance, the archer's feet straddle the shooting line, with both feet parallel to each other, and toes line up with the center of the target. The body should be upright with head turned toward the target (Figure 4-1).
2. *Open (Oblique) Stance.* To assume the open stance, the archer draws the foot that is closer to the target back about 4 to 6 inches from the square stance. At the same time, hips and shoulders must also turn so that the body is at about a 45-degree angle to the target (Figure 4-2). The open stance is recommended for advanced archers.

Step 2—Nocking the Arrow

Nocking the arrow means placing the arrow on the bowstring in preparation for drawing.

Figure 4-1 Square stance.

Figure 4-2 Open stance.

► **Learning Hints**

1. Hold the bow with the left hand and the palm of the bow hand facing the ground.

2. With the right hand holding the shaft of the arrow, with index finger pointing upward, slip the nock onto the string at a 90-degree angle with the string. Make a small mark with ink on the string to ensure that the nocking is always done in the same place. If a bow with the nocking point is already fixed on the string, the arrow is usually nicked below the nocking point. After nocking, the archer makes sure there is no gap between the string and the throat of the nock.

Step 3—Setting the Hook

After nocking the arrow, the archer must establish a proper hook. The hook is set using three fingers (index, middle, and fourth fingers) of the archer's right hand. Hook the first three fingers around the string at the first knuckles of these fingers. Hold the arrow lightly between index and middle fingers but do not squeeze the arrows (Figure 4-3). The thumb and little finger of the right hand should be touching each other over the palm. After shooting for a while, relax the thumb and little finger. It is important to keep the back of the right hand straight.

Step 4—Establishing a Bow Hold

As in all other aspects of archery, consistency is also required in establishing a proper bow hold. First, extend your left arm at the shoulder height toward the target with the left hand in a "handshake" position; then place the pivot point of the bow handle (midsection of the bow) in the "V" formed by the thumb and index finger. Now the handle of the bow should rest against the base of the thumb, and the other fingers should be placed lightly around the handle. This keeps the bow from falling at release of the arrow. Make sure that you do not grip the bow. Before releasing the arrow, the elbow of the bow arm must be turned down to avoid slapping by the bowstring (Figure 4-4).

Step 5—Raising the Head

Before raising the unit (bow and arrow), the archer's head should be in a natural position, turned to look directly at the center of the target without any tilt (Figure 4-5).

Step 6—Raising the Unit

At this point, the archer has prepared mechanically for shooting by establishing a proper stance, nocking an arrow, setting the hook, establishing the grip, and raising the head. Now the archer is ready to do the dynamic parts of shooting. The archer raises the entire unit (bow with a nocked arrow) to shoulder height. The bow is now in an upright position facing the target, the bow arm is extended toward target, and the drawing arm is forming an extension of the arrow. The elbow of the drawing arm is better positioned slightly higher than lower in relation to the arrow (Figure 4-6).

Step 7—Drawing and Anchoring

Drawing is the act of pulling the bowstring into the shooting position, and anchoring is the point where the drawing hand is placed. The drawing and the

Figure 4-3 Setting the hook.

Figure 4-4 The bow hold.

Figure 4-5 Note head position.

Figure 4-6 Eyes on target, drawing arm slightly higher than arrow.

anchoring should be done with one smooth deliberate motion.

➤ **Learning Hints—Drawing**

1. Before drawing, keep in mind that the three fingers of the drawing hand are just hooked onto the string at the first knuckles.
2. Relax the drawing hand, giving special attention to relaxing the back of the hand.
3. The elbow of the drawing arm should be slightly elevated.
4. Now the archer draws the bow by letting the shoulder and back muscles do the pulling with one smooth and deliberate motion.
5. At the full draw, the string should make contact with the center of the nose, lips, and chin.

➤ **Learning Hints—Anchoring**

1. Anchoring must be done at the same point for each draw. This lets the arrow be drawn exactly the same distance and place each time.
2. The index finger of the drawing hand should be under the tip of the jawbone, with the thumb relaxed against the neck (low anchor point).
3. While drawing, take a deep breath, exhale about half of the air, and hold the rest until the arrow has been released (Figure 4-7).

Figure 4-7 Anchoring.

Step 8—Aiming and Holding

Three methods of aiming in archery are by using a bow sight attached to the bow, by "point of aim," and by "instinctive shooting."

1. Shooting with a bow sight is the most accurate aiming technique. The archer should line up the string and bow sight with the center of the target.

If the arrow hits high, move the sight up and if low, move the sight down. The sight can also be adjusted left or right.

2. Point-of-aim shooting is aiming at some spot with the point of the arrow. The spot may be in front of, on, or above the target. The selection of the aiming spot depends upon the height of the archer, length of the arrow, and bow weight. When shots are low, move the spot up; when shots are high, move the spot down. String alignment is also important and should be done directly in front of the right eye and lined up vertically with the bow.

3. Instinctive shooting is shooting without a sight or point-of-aim marker. The archer's eyes are focused on the center of target and the bow arm will adjust itself toward target. Accuracy of this technique depends upon the archer's shooting form, eyesight, depth perception, and kinesthetic awareness.

Concentration may be the single most important part of aiming. You should hold your breath and relax a few seconds until the arrow is released. You should also be aware that the sight will oscillate while you are aiming, but make sure it oscillates within the target center.

Step 9—Release
The arrow should be released with unconscious effort. Simply relax the entire drawing hand and let the string roll off the fingers by itself. No other parts of the body except the drawing hand should be moved. During the release, continue aiming and maintain the contraction of the upper back muscles. Furthermore, let neither the drawing hand move forward nor come off the anchor position to release the string.

Step 10—Follow-through
Follow-through is the act of maintaining the body position and mental condition assumed at release until the arrow hits the target. The bow arm is pushed slightly forward, and the drawing hand rubs the chin as it moves back behind your neck. During the act of release and follow-through, continue aiming at the target center rather than following the flight of the arrow and continue keeping the tension of the upper back muscles (Figure 4-8).

Retrieving Arrows
To retrieve an arrow from the target, place the palm of your left hand against the target face, with the arrow resting between the index and the middle finger, and push the target face lightly. With your right hand, grasp the arrow by the shaft close to the target and, twisting it slightly counterclockwise, pull the arrow directly backward. If the arrow goes through

Figure 4-8 Release and follow-through.

the target but the fletchings (feathers) remain inside the mat, go to the back of the target and pull the arrow carefully forward without any twisting motion.

Hints for Improving Technique
Upon release, movements of certain parts of the body will cause faulty arrow flights. Be aware of these movements so that you can avoid them.

1. *High arrow flights are usually caused by*
   a. Peeking (looking up to watch the arrow in flight)
   b. Heeling the bow (putting pressure on the low part of the bow handle with the low portion of the bow hand)
   c. Body leaning backward
   d. Overdraw (pulling arrows beyond normal anchor point)
2. *Low arrow flights are usually caused by*
   a. Creeping (letting the drawing hand move forward before arrow is released)
   b. Overhold (maintaining the hold position too long)
   c. String hitting the arm guard upon release
   d. Hunching the shoulder of the bow arm
3. *Arrow flights to the left are usually caused by*
   a. Cupping the drawing hand instead of having the back of the drawing hand relaxed and straight

b. Bringing the string away from the face (anchor point) to release the arrow

c. Improper alignment of the bow, body, or string

4. *Arrows falling off the arrow rest of the bow are caused by*

a. Pinching of the arrow nock with the fingers of the drawing hand. To remedy this, the archer should separate the index and middle fingers to ensure a light touch with the nock, hook the string with the first knuckles of drawing fingers, and utilize back muscles to draw

b. Tight finger tab

c. Cupping of the drawing hand

Safety

Bows and arrows are weapons capable of inflicting serious injury and should be handled with care. Here are some specific precautions to follow. Remember that the continued enjoyment of archery depends upon everyone observing these safety rules.

1. Always check the bow and string to see if it is properly placed at both ends of the string notch before starting to shoot.

2. Shoot only at the target.

3. Don't draw the bow when anyone is between you and the target area.

4. Never allow anyone to retrieve arrows until all arrows have been shot.

5. Never shoot into the air or in any direction where it might destroy property or endanger life.

6. Always be sure that the area in back of the target is clear or has an adequate back stop.

7. Do not overdraw the bow.

8. Be sure arrows are of the correct length and stiffness for the bow.

9. Do not release a fully drawn bow without an arrow.

10. Obey all commands given for shooting and retrieving arrows.

11. Always wear an arm guard and finger tab to prevent injury.

12. Do not wear bulky clothing or dangling jewelry when shooting.

13. No fooling around or horseplay on the shooting line.

14. Never run with arrows in your hand; when carrying arrows, keep the pile ends toward the ground.

15. When you have finished shooting, stand behind the other archers until the end has been completed.

Modifications for Special Populations

Orthopedically Impaired

1. Minimal modifications are needed for the student who uses a wheelchair and has good upper body strength and coordination.

2. Students with grasping difficulties should consider commercially purchased assistive devices, e.g., trigger, wrist, and mouthpiece releases.

Cognitively Impaired

1. Individual considerations must be taken into account to determine the appropriateness of archery for students who have very low cognitive abilities. Consult with Special Olympics.

Sensory Impaired

1. Students with visual impairments can be taught to feel the correct way to notch the arrow in the bow.

2. An audio signal could be used as a target.

3. A rope could be tethered to provide the student with a visual impairment with a guide for retrieving an arrow.

4. Students with hearing impairments or who are deaf require minimal adaptations.

Terminology

Addressing the target Standing ready to shoot with a proper shooting stance.

Anchor point Specific location on the archer's face to which the index finger comes while holding and aiming.

Archery golf An adaptation of the game of golf to the sport of archery. Players shoot for the holes and score according to the number of shots required to hit the target.

Arm guard A piece of leather or plastic that is worn on the inside of the forearm to protect the arm from the bowstring.

Arrow plate A protective piece of hard material set into the bow where the arrow crosses it.

Arrow rest A small projection at the top of the bow handle where the arrow rests.

Back The side of the bow away from the shooter.

Bow arm The arm that holds the bow; this would be the left arm for a right-handed person.

Bow sight A device attached to the bow through which the archer sights when aiming.

Bow weight Designates the amount of effort (in pounds) needed to pull a bowstring a specific distance (usually 28 inches).

Cant The act of holding the bow tilted or slightly turned while shooting.

Cast The distance a bow can shoot an arrow.

Clout shooting A type of shooting that uses a target 48 feet in diameter, laid on the ground at a distance of 180 yards for men and 140 or 120 yards for women. Usually 36 arrows (6 ends with 6 arrows) are shot per round.

Cock feather Now called the "index feather." The feather that is set at a right angle to the arrow nock; differently colored from the other two feathers.

Creeping Letting the drawing hand move forward at the release.

Crest The archer's identifying marks shown just below the fletchings on the arrow.

Draw The act of pulling the bow string back into the anchor position.

End A specified number of arrows shot at one time or from one position before retrieval of arrows.

Face The part of the bow facing the shooter.

Finger tab A leather flap worn on the drawing hand to protect the fingers and provide a smooth release of the bow string.

Fletchings The feathers of the arrow, which give guidance to its flight.

Flight shooting Shooting an arrow the farthest possible distance.

Handle The grip at the midsection of the bow.

Hen feathers The two feathers that are not set at right angles to the arrow nock. See *Cock feather.*

Hold Steadily holding the arrow at full draw before release.

Instinctive shooting Aiming and shooting instinctively, rather than using a bow sight or point-of-aim method.

Limbs Upper and lower parts of the bow; divided by the handle.

Nock The groove in the end of the arrow in which the string is placed.

Nocking point The point on the string at which the arrow is placed.

Notch The grooves of the upper and lower tips of the limbs into which the bow string is fitted.

Overbow Using too strong a bow that is too powerful to allow a bowstring to be pulled proper distance.

Overdraw Drawing the bow so that the pile of the arrow is inside the bow.

Petticoat That part of the target face outside the white ring.

Pile (point) The pointed metal tip of the arrow.

Pinch To squeeze the nock of the arrow.

Plucking Jerking the drawing hand laterally away from the face on the release, which will cause arrow flight to the left.

Point-blank range The only distance from the target at which the point of aim is right on the bull's eye.

Point-of-aim A method of aiming in which the pile of the arrow is aligned with the target.

Quiver A receptacle for carrying or holding arrows.

Recurve bow A bow that is curved on the ends.

Release The act of letting the bowstring slip off the fingertips.

Round The term used to indicate shooting a designated number of arrows at a designated distance or distances.

Roving Archery game played outdoors in which natural targets (stumps, trees, bushes, etc.) are selected for competition.

Serving The thread wrapped around the bowstring at the nocking point.

Shaft The long, body part of the arrow.

Spine The characteristic rigidity and flexibility of an arrow.

Tackle Archery equipment referred to as a whole.

Target face The painted front of a target, usually replaceable.

Trajectory The path of the arrow in flight.

Vane Plastic feather of an arrow.

Further References

Axford, R. *Archery Anatomy: An Introduction to Techniques for Improved Performance.* London, UK: Souvenir Press Limited, 1996.

The Basic Guide to Archery. Torrance, CA: Griffin Publishing, 1997.

Boga, S. *Archery.* Mechanicsburg, PA: Stackpole Books, 1997.

Falda, S. *Traditional Archery.* Mechanicsburg, PA: Stackpole Books, 1999.

Matthews, R. and Holden, J. *Archery in Ernest.* North Pomfert, VT: Trafalgar Square, 1998.

Reno, H. et al. *The Pocket Guide to Target and Field Archery.* Helena, MT: Greycliff Publishing, 1994.

Wise, L. and Wert, L. *The Comprehensive Guide to Equipment, Technique, and Competition.* Mechanicsburg, PA: Stackpole Books, 1992.

Audio-Visual Materials

Advanced Shooting Techniques. Writ. A. Henderson. Athletic Institute: North Palm Beach, FL, 1978 (motion picture).

An Invitation to Archery. Writ. A. Henderson. Athletic Institute: North Palm Beach, FL, 1978 (motion picture).

Archery. Champions on Film & Video, 745 State Circle, Box 1941, Ann Arbor, MI 48106. VHS.

Fundamentals of Archery: Basic Shooting Techniques. Writ. A. Henderson. Athletic Institute: North Palm Beach, FL, 1978 (motion picture).

Mastering the Bow and Arrow Sports. Writ. A. Henderson. Athletic Institute: North Palm Beach, FL, 1978 (motion picture).

On Target for Fun: Archery Skills and Techniques Demonstrated by Olympic Medal Winners. Athletic Institute, 200 Castlewood Dr., North Palm Beach, FL 33408.

Stream and Field: Bull's-Eye Archery. Champions on Film & Video, 745 State Circle, Box 1941, Ann Arbor, MI 48106. VHS.

Understanding Shooting Form. Champions on Film & Video, 745 State Circle, Box 1941, Ann Arbor, MI 48106. VHS.

Web Sites

www.usarchery.org A national association site with a comprehensive site index. For beginners, the site includes sections on rules, articles, history, publication links, equipment, a tutorial, and links to other Web sites.

www.homepage.ntlworld.com/joetapley An extensive site on bow mechanics with scientific explanations for instruction.

CHAPTER 5

Badminton

This chapter will enable you to

- Understand the fundamental techniques in various strokes used in the game of badminton
- Display an understanding of basic strategy in both singles and doubles
- Identify and understand the basic rules for singles and doubles
- Understand basic terminology used in the game of badminton

Nature and Purpose

The game of badminton has been around for a number of years. Historians believe that a very similar game (called *battledore*) was played in China over 2,000 years ago. However, badminton as it is currently known is believed to have originated from a game called *poona* that was played by English army officers stationed in India during the 17th century.

Badminton has steadily gained world-wide acceptance as being a very fast paced, highly skilled, competitive game. This is substantiated by the fact that badminton has now been included as a full-fledged medal sport in the Olympic Games. Badminton in America is also rapidly growing in popularity. At the beginning level, it is usually possible to keep the shuttle in play, which makes the game enjoyable and rewarding for most age groups. Singles, doubles, or mixed doubles may be played; thus badminton is an excellent coeducational activity.

Although courts can be set up outdoors, competitive badminton is generally played indoors where the wind and elements will not affect the shuttle.

Rules of Badminton

1. Toss for serve. Before a match begins, opponents can toss a coin, spin a racket, or toss a shuttle to determine who shall get the choice of "serve" or "side." If spinning a racket, identify a marking on the racket and have one person call the mark. If tossing a shuttle, the proper procedure is for one person to either hit or toss the shuttle in the air and let it land. The person toward whom the base of the shuttle is pointing gets the choice.

2. Men's singles and all doubles games are played to 15 points. Women's singles is played to 11 points. In a 15-point game, if the score becomes tied at 13–13, the player/team scoring 13 points first (the receivers) can elect to continue and finish the game to 15 points (which is termed "no set"), or they can elect to play 5 more points ("set") to finish the game. When tied at 14–14, the player/team scoring 14 points first can elect to continue and finish the game to 15 points, or they can elect to "set" the game at 3 points. In an 11-point game, if the game is tied at 9–9, the first player scoring 9 points has the choice of either finishing the game at 11 points ("no set") or "setting" the game at 3 points. If the game is tied at 10–10, the choice would be either to finish the game at 11 points or to "set" the game at 2 points. (Note: A player/team *does not* have to win by 2 points.)

3. The serve must be delivered into the diagonal service court and within its boundaries to be a legal serve. Any shuttle hitting the line is in. In singles, the shuttle must land in the long, narrow court; in doubles, it must land in the short, wide court. In doubles, once the serve has been returned, the full court (20 × 44 feet) is played.

4. The server is allowed only one trial to put the shuttle into play. The shuttle may hit the net and land in the proper court and be legal. In singles, the service is made from the right service court whenever the server's score is an even number (0, 2, 4, etc.). Whenever the server's score is an odd number (1, 3, 5, etc.), the service is made from the left service court. In doubles, the first serve is always started from the right court whenever a team acquires the service from their opponents.

The server will alternate service courts each time a point is made or until the serve is lost. Only one "hand" is allowed the side beginning the serve in doubles during the first "inning." Two hands are allowed each inning thereafter.

5. Matches consist of winning two out of three games. Players must change sides of the court after each game. The winner of the previous game starts the serve in the next game. If a third game is required, players will switch courts again at what is considered the half-way point: immediately after a player reaches 8 points in a 15-point game or immediately after a player reaches 6 points in an 11-point game.

6. It is a fault (loss of service or "hand out" for the serving side; or loss of point for the receiving side) when
   a. Service is illegal, i.e., the shuttle is struck when above the waist, or the head of the racket is higher than the lowest finger of the racket hand when contact is made.
   b. Service or played shot lands outside the specified court, passes through or under the net, or hits a player or obstruction outside the court.
   c. If server or receiver is standing outside of the proper court upon delivery of the serve or balks in any way before the service. Only the person served to may return the shuttle.
   d. The server or receiver steps forward, lifts, or drags a foot during the delivery of the serve.
   e. The server misses the shuttle in attempting to serve.
   f. A player reaches over the net to contact a shuttle. (The follow-through, however, may break the plane of the net.)
   g. A player touches the net with the racket or any part of the body while the shuttle is deemed to be in play.
   h. A player contacts the shuttle twice in one swing. (Referred to as a "double hit.")
   i. A player fails to return the shuttle to the opponent's proper court. (The opposing player cannot hit, catch, or be struck by a doubtful shuttle and then call it "out.")
   j. On a doubles serve, the server's partner unsights the server (does not allow receivers to view the service).
   k. In doubles, a shuttle is hit by a player and the player's partner successively.
   l. A player prevents or hinders an opponent from making a legal stroke where the shuttle is followed over the net (racket follow-through of the striker).

Equipment

The choice of equipment is important in badminton. High-quality rackets and shuttlecocks (birds) can have a favorable bearing on performance. When purchasing rackets and birds, buy the best you can afford.

Racket

Badminton rackets are quite light and can be made of wood, aluminum, metal, or synthetic materials such as graphite or carbon. Synthetic rackets are quite popular now because of their extreme lightness and strength.

The price of rackets also varies. There are "playable" rackets that can be purchased from $20 to $35 (excellent for the beginner or physical education classes) and other higher quality rackets for the "competitive" player, ranging from $45 to $150. The racket can be strung with either nylon or gut. Nylon string is sufficient for the beginning player because it usually costs less and lasts longer than gut.

In any case, choosing a racket is a matter of personal preference, and you should use what feels comfortable, not what looks good.

Shuttlecock

The "official" shuttlecock, usually called *shuttle* or *bird,* is made from goose feathers that are placed in a leather-covered cork head. Feather shuttles are quite expensive and can be damaged during play very quickly. They are used primarily in high-level tournament competition.

Shuttles are also made of either plastic or nylon. These shuttles last longer and are not as expensive as the feathered bird. There are several types of nylon or plastic birds that are very durable and excellent for class play.

Badminton Court

The official badminton court (shown in Figures 5-1 and 5-2) is 44 feet long. The doubles court is 20 feet wide, whereas the singles court is 17 feet wide. The net is 5 feet at the center and 5 feet 1 inch at the posts. A "½ court" practice/drill arrangement is shown in Figure 5-3.

Overhead clearance is an important factor in setting up a badminton court. Generally speaking, an overhead clearance of less than 20 feet would not be considered conducive for playing the game effectively. A clearance of at least 30 feet is required for all national and international competition.

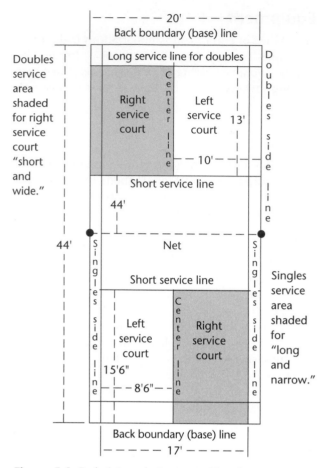

Figure 5-1 Badminton playing court: Top view.

Figure 5-3 "½ court" practice/drill areas. A1 practices/drills with partner A2; B1 practices/drills with B2.

Serving Court—Singles

The serving court for singles is bounded by the short service line, the centerline, the singles sideline, and the back boundary line of the court. The server must stand within this court, feet not touching any lines, and serve diagonally over the net into his opponent's singles service court in order to have a legal serve.

Serving Court—Doubles

The serving court for doubles is bounded by the short service line, the centerline, the doubles sideline, and the long service line for doubles. The server must stand within this court, feet not touching any lines, and serve diagonally over the net into her opponent's doubles service court in order to have a legal serve.

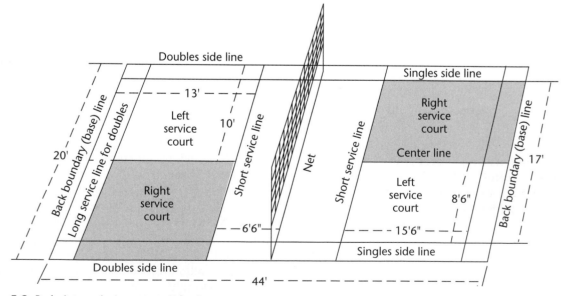

Figure 5-2 Badminton playing court: Side view.

Suggested Learning Sequence

After the students have acquired an understanding of the basic strategy, simplified rules, and court courtesies, playing should start immediately. Specific skills will be introduced as the learning sequence progresses. The following outline includes everything that needs to be covered, but the exact teaching sequence will vary according to circumstances.

A. Nature of the Game
   1. Demonstration or video of actual play (national or international competition)
   2. The playing court
B. The Singles Game
   1. Basic strategy
   2. Simplified rules and scoring
   3. Court courtesies
C. Grip
   1. Forehand
D. Play Games
E. Strokes
   1. Overhead clear
   2. Long serve
   3. Short serve
F. Introduce intra-class competition
   1. Ladder tournament
   2. Round robin, etc.
G. Strokes (continued)
   1. Smash
   2. Block (forehand and backhand)
H. Footwork and movement
   1. Backcourt
   2. Lateral (blocking)
   3. Forecourt
I. Strokes (continued)
   1. Around-the-head
     a. Clears
     b. Smashes
   2. Overhead drop
J. Grip
   1. Backhand
K. Strokes (continued)
   1. Net clears (forehand and backhand)
   2. Net drops (forehand and backhand)
L. The Doubles Game
   1. Basic strategy
   2. Simplified rules and scoring
   3. Alignments
     a. Side-by-side (defensive)
     b. Up-and-back (offensive)
     c. Circular rotation (combination of a and b above, depending upon the situation)

Skills and Techniques

A fundamentally sound badminton player must use many different skills and techniques. In this section we will describe each stroke or skill and give learning hints and practice/organizational suggestions for each.

The Grips

Forehand. To acquire the proper grip for a forehand stroke, hold the racket by the shaft in the left hand with the face of the racket perpendicular to the floor, and "shake hands" with the grip (Figure 5-4). Slide your hand down so that the fatty part rests comfortably against the "butt" of the handle. There will be a "V" formed by the juncture of your thumb and index finger. This 'V' should be slightly to the left of center for right-handed players. Grasp the handle lightly, with fingers spread slightly. The thumb wraps around the handle on the left side. Proper thumb placement is vital for stroking proficiently.

When not in the act of stroking the shuttle, your grip should be relaxed and fairly loose. As you start your stroke, you will tighten your grip somewhat—just enough to maintain control of the racket. The more forceful the shot, the tighter the grip.

Figure 5-4 Forehand grip.

Figure 5-5 Backhand grip.

This same grip may be used for most backhand shots. For our purposes, we will vary this grip only when stroking backhand net drops and net clears. (At the beginning level, asking players to change grips repeatedly during fast-paced volleys can be quite frustrating to most students).

Backhand. For backhand net drops and net clears you will move the racket a quarter turn clockwise from the forehand grip, so that your thumb moves farther behind the racket handle (Figure 5-5).

Home Base—Singles

"Home base" is referred to as the area in the court where a player would stand to best cover the entire court effectively. In singles, it is in the center of the court—an equal distance to all four corners.

After each shot is hit, the player should attempt to return to home base position as quickly as possible and prepare for her opponent's return. If you cannot return quickly enough prior to your opponent's return, you should stop, ready yourself, and then react to her return from wherever you are in the court. A player should not be moving at the moment an opponent contacts the shuttle.

The Ready Position

Moving efficiently around the court during play is of the utmost importance in badminton. Good move-

Figure 5-6 image appears at top of right column.

Figure 5-6 Ready position: Front.

ment begins with a proper "ready position." This is the position, or stance, a player should assume prior to maneuvering toward an opponent's return shot. The feet should be spread shoulder-width apart or slightly wider, the knees slightly bent, and your weight on the balls of your feet, ready for movement in any direction. A stagger stance with the racket-foot forward is used by most players (Figure 5-6).

Footwork

Efficient footwork is extremely important in badminton. You must be able to get to the shuttle as quickly as possible in order to set up for your next stroke. Generally speaking, long strides and lunging action should be emphasized in footwork. Using short steps to cover the court is time consuming and a waste of valuable energy.

For shots close to the net, always lunge with the racket-side foot reaching toward the shuttle at the moment of contact.

For lateral shots, push off with the foot that is farthest away from the shuttle and lunge with the other—pushing off with your right foot if you are moving to the left.

For shots hit deep into the backcourt, backward strides should be used. It is important to turn the body sideways to the net when hitting the shuttle, with the non-racket shoulder facing the net. This will allow full rotation of the upper body and hips in generating power. More advanced players will use a scissors kick (switching the legs) while in the act of striking the shuttle. This allows them to push off with the non–racket-side leg, gaining efficiency in returning to the home base position.

The Strokes

There are five basic groups of shots that should be learned at the beginning level of badminton: serves, clears, smashes, blocks, and drops. Each of these strokes is described below, followed by a sixth type: "around-the head" shots.

I. Serves

There are two basic badminton serves: the long serve, which is hit high and deep, and the short serve, which is hit low and short. The long serve is used primarily in singles play, and the short serve is used primarily in doubles play. The serving stances and areas are the same in both singles and doubles.

A. Long Serve (High and Deep). The object of the long serve is simply to move your opponent as far away from the net as possible. In singles play, this would be to the baseline, and in doubles play, it would be to the long service line for doubles.

When positioning yourself, stand approximately 3 to 4 feet behind the short service line and close to the centerline (Figure 5-7). Face your opponent's diagonal service court, stagger your stance (right foot behind the left if you are right-handed) with your weight on the back foot, stand tall, and relax (knees slightly bent).

Hold the shuttle with your fingers and thumb wrapped gently around the feathers and cork base

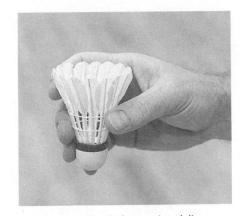

Figure 5-8 Holding shuttle for service delivery.

when starting the service (Figure 5-8). The shuttle arm is flexed at approximately 90 degrees and positioned across the body toward the racket-shoulder. When released, the shuttle is "set out" and dropped away from the body toward your racket side. It should not be allowed to "tumble" (flipped end-over-end) or "waver" after it is released because these actions will cause inconsistent flight patterns. The shuttle should be released from approximately shoulder height (refer to Figure 5-7).

The racket is in the backswing position with the racket head being held higher than the racket hand.

Figure 5-7 Service stance.

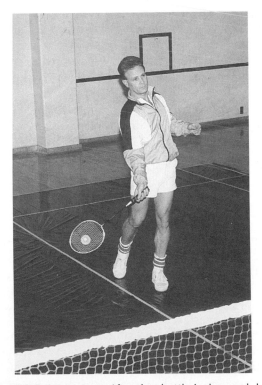

Figure 5-9 Long serve. After the shuttle is dropped, bring the racket downward and forward.

Figure 5-10 The follow-through position after a vigorous wrist snap and rotation of the forearm.

As you release the shuttle to start your serve, your weight shifts forward (to your front foot), and your racket is pulled down and through the shuttle (Figure 5-9). At the contact point, your wrist snaps, and the forearm rotates upward and forward in the direction of your serve. Contact point is about knee level. Hips and shoulders will rotate toward the net, and the racket arm will finish across the body (Figure 5-10).

The long serve can be described as a basic underhand motion with a vigorous wrist snap and forearm rotation.

➤ **Learning Hints**

1. Stand facing the receiver's court in a relaxed, upright, staggered serving stance.
2. Make sure the racket wrist is cocked as much as possible in the backswing position, elbow fairly close to the body.
3. Drop the shuttle before starting the swing.
4. Drop the shuttle in front of and to the side of your body far enough away to force the hitting arm to reach for it slightly.
5. Be as relaxed as possible and try to generate maximum racket head acceleration by snapping the wrist and rotating the forearm at point of contact.
6. Contact shuttle at about knee height.
7. Hit the shuttle up and out.

➤ **Practice/Organizational Suggestions**
(Figure 5-11)

Get as many shuttles as possible and hit the high, deep singles serve. You can practice serving diagonally if space permits, or you can practice serving straight across the net using the ½ court practice/play variation.

The two keys to look for are height and depth. Hit the shuttle high enough and hit it deeply enough to land in the back alley close to the base line. Remember, a long serve that is not high enough or deep enough will put you in a very defensive situation.

B. Short Serve (Short and Low). The object of the short serve is to force your opponent to "lift" the shuttle. (Lifting the shuttle—resulting most often from underhand strokes—is considered to be defensive as it will allow the opponent an opportunity to return the "lifted" shuttle downward.)

When positioning yourself, stand approximately three to four feet behind the short service line and close to the centerline. Face your opponent's diagonal service court, stagger your stance (right foot behind the left if you are right-handed) with your weight on the back leg, stand tall, and relax (knees slightly bent).

The racket is in the backswing position with the racket head being held higher than the racket hand. As you release the shuttle to start your serve, your weight shifts forward (to your front foot), and your racket is "pushed" (rather than pulled as in the long serve) through the shuttle. At the contact point, your wrist remains cocked with the racket-arm following through forward (in the direction of your serve)—as if pushing from behind to guide it over the net (Figure 5-12). Contact point is about thigh level. Minimum hip or shoulder rotation is utilized.

The idea is to hit the shuttle so that it will stay low and drop just behind the short service line. Because little power is needed to achieve this, the wrist remains in the cocked position throughout the stroke. The shuttle should reach its maximum height at the net and then immediately start to drop.

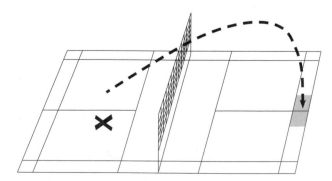

Figure 5-11 Long serve: Trajectory and target zones for singles play.

Figure 5-12 Notice the short follow-through in the direction of the flight.

Figure 5-13 Short serve: Trajectory and target zones for singles and doubles paly.

> **Learning Hints**
>
> 1. Stand facing the receiver's court in a relaxed, upright, staggered serving stance.
> 2. Make sure the racket wrist is cocked as much as possible in the backswing position, elbow close to the body.
> 3. Drop the shuttle before starting the swing.
> 4. Drop the shuttle in front of and to the side of your body.
> 5. Be as relaxed as possible and try to "push" the shuttle rather than "hitting" it.
> 6. Contact shuttle at about thigh height.
> 7. Keep the shuttle as low and short as possible.

> **Practice/Organizational Suggestions**
> (Figure 5-13)

Get as many shuttles as possible and hit the short, low serve. You can practice serving diagonally if space permits, or you can practice serving straight across the net using the ½ court practice/play variation.

The two keys to look for are low clearance of the net and shortness in depth. Hit the shuttle low enough, and hit it short enough to land just past the short service line. Remember, a short serve that is not low enough will put you in a very defensive situation.

Return of Service—Singles. The position for returning serves in singles is approximately 4 feet in back of the short service line (midcourt) and moved slightly to your backhand side in the service court.

Your stance will be a slightly exaggerated stagger with the non-racket leg forward (Figures 5-14 and 5-15). Stand tall with the majority of your weight on the forward leg. Hold your racket in front of your body about chin high.

For returning a long serve (high and deep), push off with your forward leg and backstride to position yourself under the oncoming shuttle. To return a short serve (low and short), lunge forward by moving your back leg quickly to the net. As you lunge, reach out with your racket to contact the shuttle at its highest point.

Return of Service—Doubles. The position for returning serves in doubles is approximately one foot in back of the short service line and moved slightly to your backhand side in the service court. This position puts you much closer to the net than in the singles return position. Your stance will be a slightly exaggerated stagger with the non-racket leg forward. Stand tall with the majority of your weight on the

Figure 5-14 Singles service return stance: Even court.

Figure 5-15 Singles service return stance: Odd court.

forward leg. Hold your racket in front of your body slightly higher than the position held for a normal singles return. This will allow you a quicker contact time for short serves—the serve that is used most often in doubles play.

The footwork used in returning doubles long serves is the same as that used for returning long serves in singles.

II. Clears

Clears are used as a defensive stroke to allow you time to return to the ready position and regroup, and to move your opponent as far away from the net as possible. There are two types of clears: overhead and underhand.

A. Overhead Clear. Overhead clears are usually taken from a backcourt position. From your home base position, move into a position under and slightly behind the oncoming shuttle. Prepare your racket for the stroke by bringing it back behind the shoulders into what is called the "back-scratching" position: arm bent, elbow parallel to the floor (Figure 5-16).

With your racket shoulder now in line with the shuttle, extend the arm to meet the shuttle at the highest point possible (Figure 5-17). At the moment

Figure 5-16 Overhead clear: Backswing (used for all overhead strokes).

Figure 5-17 Overhead clear: Contact.

Figure 5-18 Overhead clear: Follow-through.

Figure 5-19 Overhead clears: Trajectory and target zones for singles play.

of contact, your forearm rotates outward, and the wrist snaps quickly, causing the racket head to accelerate and drive the shuttle upward and outward deep into your opponent's court. The racket head will be facing slightly upward at contact. Follow-through with the racket arm crossing your body in the direction of your non-racket side (Figure 5-18).

➤ **Learning Hints**

1. Position yourself under and slightly behind the dropping shuttle.
2. Prepare the racket in the back-scratching position.
3. As you swing upward, rotate the forearm and extend the arm as high as possible, with the racket face pointing slightly upward.
4. At the moment of contact, snap the wrist quickly.
5. Hit the shuttle high (18 to 20 feet) and deep into your opponent's backcourt area.
6. Follow-through across your body.

➤ **Practice/Organizational Suggestions** (Figure 5-19)

1. *Straight clears using the ½ court area.* Partners hit continuous clears to each other, attempting to get the shuttle into the back alley.

2. *Crosscourt clears.* Partners hit continuous clears diagonally to each other, working on distance and accuracy. Each partner attempts to get the shuttle into the back alley and corner of the singles court.
3. *Side alley clears.* Partners hit continuous clears within the side alley boundaries, working on accuracy and distance.

B. Forehand Underhand (Net) Clear. Underhand clears are usually taken from a forecourt position. When your opponent hits a drop shot into your forecourt, or close to the net, it forces you to "lift" the shuttle and go on the defensive. Hitting an underhand clear in this situation will serve the same purpose as hitting an overhead clear in a backcourt situation. That is, it will allow you time to return to the ready position and regroup, and, it will move your opponent as far away from the net as possible.

As the shuttle is dropping toward your forehand side and in the forecourt area, from the ready position take a short first step with your non-racket leg and then a long lunge to the shuttle with the racket leg.

Reach for the shuttle with the wrist slightly cocked and your racket arm in as high a position as necessary to contact the bird at its highest point possible. At the moment of contact, rotate your forearm so that the racket is uncocked explosively up and through the shuttle (Figure 5-20). The follow-through is in the direction that you intend the shuttle to travel (Figure 5-21).

C. Backhand Underhand (Net) Clear. Change to a backhand grip. As the shuttle is dropping toward your backhand side and in the forecourt area, from the ready position take a short first step with your non-racket leg and then a long lunge to the shuttle with the racket leg.

Reach for the shuttle with the wrist slightly cocked and your racket arm in as high a position as necessary to contact the bird at its highest point possible. At the moment of contact, rotate your forearm

Figure 5-20 Forehand net clear: Contact.

Figure 5-22 Backhand net clear: Contact.

Figure 5-21 Forehand net clear: Follow-through.

Figure 5-23 Backhand net clear: Follow-through.

so that the racket is brought explosively up and through the shuttle (Figure 5-22). The follow-through is in the direction that you intend the shuttle to travel (Figure 5-23).

➤ **Learning Hints**
1. Lunge to the shuttle with your racket leg forward at contact.
2. Contact the shuttle at the highest point possible.
3. Lift the shuttle with a hard, explosive wrist action.
4. Hit the shuttle high (18 to 20 feet) and deep into your opponent's backcourt area.
5. Follow-through in the direction you intend the shuttle to travel.

➤ **Practice/Organizational Suggestions**
(Figure 5-24)

Straight underhand clears using the ½ court area. One player hits overhead drops from the back alley, while the partner hits underhand clears from the net area.

Note: See overhead drop "Practice/Organizational Suggestions" in Section V, Drop Shots.

D. Attacking Clear. Attacking clears are used primarily to drive your opponent to the backcourt (farthest point from the net) after she has come very close to the net, and you think you can "clear" the shuttle over her racket for a winner. They are stroked similar to the clears discussed above except that the trajectory is lower. This lower trajectory will cause the shuttle to reach the floor sooner, and in turn put your opponent in a very defensive situation (see Figure 5-19).

III. Smashes
The smash is the basic offensive shot in badminton. It is a very powerful stroke that is used primarily for getting the shuttle to land on your opponent's side of the court as quickly as possible. However, if the shuttle does not land on his court and end the volley as expected, it will force him to "lift" the shuttle—putting him in a very defensive situation. The smash is a shot that can be tremendously effective.

The body position is similar to the overhead clear stroke, with one exception: The shuttle should be lined up *ahead* of your racket-shoulder (Figure 5-25),

Figure 5-24 Net clear: Trajectory and target zones for singles play.

Figure 5-25 Smash. Notice that the contact point is forward of the racket shoulder.

farther ahead than the contact point of the overhead clear. By the same token, the racket face must be angling downward, as compared with upward for the overhead clear.

You should contact the shuttle at the highest point possible. The higher you contact the shuttle, the greater the angle down to your opponent's court. The greater the angle, the greater the chance you have for clearing the net. Your forearm and wrist will rotate and snap rapidly as the shuttle is contacted. Follow-through is similar to that for the overhead clear.

Unless you have an exceptionally strong smash, this stroke should be used only when you are in the front three-quarters of the court. Remember, smashing from the back alley area forces the shuttle to fly a greater distance to get to your opponent's side of the court. This will allow your opponent more time to react to your smash and increase his chances of returning the shuttle with some control.

➤ Learning Hints

As far as preparation and motion are concerned, the same learning cues apply to both the overhead clear and the smash. These additional key points apply to smashes:

1. Get into position so that contact can be made ahead of the racket shoulder, which is farther ahead than for an overhead clear.
2. The racket face should be angling downward at contact.
3. A sharp downward angle is just as important as shuttle speed.

➤ Practice/Organizational Suggestions (Figure 5-26)

Straight smashes using the ½ court area. One player hits short, underhand clears while the partner returns them with smashes.

Note: Also see "Practice/Organizational Suggestions" under Section IV, Blocks.

IV. Blocks (Figures 5-27, 5-28, 5-29)

Blocks are used as a defensive stroke in response to an opponent's smash. They are used primarily for returning a smash in an emergency situation. However, if effectively stroked, a block can also change your defensive situation into an offensive one. (An effective block will force your opponent to return the shuttle with an underhand stroke. Hopefully, this "lifting" action on the part of your opponent will enable you to regain the attack.)

The block shot is best accomplished by trying to get the racket head out in front of your body and to the shuttle as quickly as possible. Use the forehand

Figure 5-26 Smash: Trajectory and target zones for singles play.

Figure 5-27 Forehand block.

Figure 5-28 Backhand block.

Figure 5-29 High body block.

grip (see Figure 5-27). There is no backswing to this stroke, but merely a slight push of the shuttle to have it rebound from the racket and barely clear the net. The force of your push will depend upon the speed of your opponent's smash. The harder the smash, the less

the push. A mere rebound off of a stationary racket face—from a powerful smash—is often sufficient to accomplish this stroke. The object is to drop the shuttle over the net shallow in the opponent's forecourt.

> ➤ **Learning Hints**

1. Do not try to take the racket back, because this stroke does not require a backswing.
2. React as quickly as possible, trying to get the racket head out in front of your body and to the shuttle.
3. Try to keep the shuttle low, barely clearing the net.
4. Do not swing at the shuttle. Merely block with a slight push.

> ➤ **Practice/Organizational Suggestions**
> (Figure 5-30)

1. *Smash and block drill using the ½ court area.* One player hits a short, high underhand clear that the partner smashes. The returner attempts to block the smash and get it over the net shallow in the forecourt.
2. *2–1–1 Smash and block drill (½ court).* Player (A) hits a short, high underhand clear to start the drill.
   The partner (B) overhead clears.
   (A) smashes.
   (B) blocks.
   (A) underhand (net) clears, and the drill continues.
   Sequence: underhand clear, overhead clear, smash, block, repeat.
3. *3–1–1 Smash and Block drill (½ court).* Use the same sequence as the 2–1–1 except add in an extra overhead clear to this drill.
   Sequence: underhand clear, overhead clear, overhead clear, smash, block, (repeat).

V. Drop Shots

There are two types of drop shots: overhead and underhand. Underhand drop shots are taken from the

Figure 5-30 Block: Two flight patterns and target zones for blocking.

forecourt area, oftentimes close to the net, and are referred to as "net drops." Overhead drops are usually taken from the backcourt area and referred to as simply "drops." Drops are used to force your opponent to come to the net from her backcourt position, and to force her to "lift" the shuttle for her return. They can be described as soft shots that barely clear the net and then drop quickly into the opponent's forecourt area—preferably in front of the short service line.

A. Overhead Drop. Overhead drops are usually taken from a backcourt position. The object is to make your opponent think that you are going to clear or smash, and then execute a soft stroke that gently drops the shuttle over the net. As stated above, overhead drops are used to move your opponent to the forecourt, and to force a "lifting" return of the shuttle. If stroked deceptively enough, overhead drops can put your opponent into such an off-balance position that a decent return from him would be extremely difficult.

The body position used is similar to the overhead clear. The shuttle is contacted in front of the body, but the racket head will slow instead of accelerating at the moment of impact. As in the smash, the racket face must be angling downward. Follow-through is across your body and toward the non-racket side.

This shot depends to a great extent on finesse and deception. A backswing, stroke, and follow-through similar to the clear or smash are vital in the disguise of this stroke. Remember, *the shuttle is fully stroked and guided,* not pushed from the shoulder or tapped from a stiff, overhead, outstretched arm position.

> **Learning Hints**

1. Get into position so that contact can be made in front of the body.
2. Racket preparation has to be the same as if you were going to clear or smash.
3. Slow the speed of the racket head just before contacting the shuttle.
4. The racket face should be angling slightly downward on impact.
5. Gently guide the shuttle over the net with your wrist action and follow-through.

> **Practice/Organizational Suggestions** (Figure 5-31)

1. *Continuous straight drops using the ½ court area.* One player hits underhand clears while the partner returns them with overhead drops.
2. *2–1 overhead drop drill (½ court).* Player (A) hits a short, high underhand clear to start the drill. The partner (B) overhead clears. (A) overhead drops, and the drill continues.

Figure 5-31 Overhead drop: Trajectory and target zones for singles play.

Sequence: underhand clear, overhead clear, overhead drop, (repeat).

3. *3–1 overhead drop drill (½ court).* Use the same sequence as the 2–1 except add an extra overhead clear to this drill.
   Sequence: underhand clear, overhead clear, overhead clear, overhead drop, repeat.
   Note: Also see net drop "Practice/Organizational Suggestions," below.

B. Net Drop. Net (or underhand) drops are hit from the forecourt area and are used to draw your opponent close to the net after she has hit an overhead drop from her backcourt. They are also used to force an opponent to "lift" the shuttle.

Net drops taken on the forehand side are stroked using the forehand grip. Net drops taken on the backhand side are stroked using the backhand grip previously described. The object is to lift slightly or push the shuttle gently over the top of the net so that it falls below the white tape level as quickly as possible. If stroked properly, the shuttle will fall very close to the net. This will force your opponent to travel the greatest distance possible from her present position in the court.

Getting to the shuttle quickly is of the utmost importance. The idea is to contact the shuttle as close to the top of the net as possible. The lower the contact point, the more "lift" you will have to put on your shot. You would rather "push" your drop over the net than "lift" it over. Lifting the shuttle forces you into an uncertain defensive situation. Remember, a shuttle that is lifted too hard (too high) will put you in terrible trouble. A shuttle that is lifted too softly (not high enough) will result in a bird that didn't make it over the net. Pushing and guiding your net drop will eliminate the uncertainty of "lifting."

Lunge toward the shuttle with your racket-side leg. With your arm and racket out in front of your body and as high as necessary to contact the shuttle at its highest point, gently push and guide the shuttle over the net. Have the shuttle just barely clear the

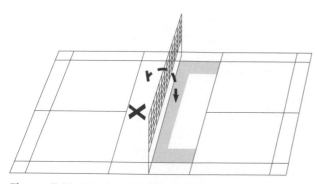

Figure 5-32 Net drop: Trajectory and target zones for singles play.

net so that your opponent will not have a chance to smash it back at you.

➤ Learning Hints (Figure 5-32)

1. Lunge with the racket-side leg toward the shuttle.
2. Contact the shuttle as near to the top of the net as possible.
3. Gently push and guide the shuttle over the net.
4. Have the shuttle just barely clear the net.

➤ Practice/Organizational Suggestions

1. *Toss and stroke drill using the ¹/₂ court area.* One player stands on the short service line and tosses a shuttle over the net, while the partner lunges toward the shuttle and net drops. Tosses should be directed to the forehand side for forehand practice, backhand side for backhand practice. The stroker should be in a ready position approximately 2 feet behind the short service line prior to each toss.
2. *Continuous net drops (¹/₂ court).* From behind the short service line, one player puts the shuttle into play with a short serve. Each player continues to hit net drops until a missed shot has occurred.
3. *2–1–1 overhead drop and net drop drill (¹/₂ court).* Player (A) hits an underhand clear to start the drill.
   The partner (B) overhead clears.
   (A) overhead drops.
   (B) net drops.
   (A) underhand clears, and the drill continues.
   Sequence: underhand clear, overhead clear, overhead drop, net drop, repeat.
4. *3–1–1 Overhead drop and net drop drill (¹/₂ court).* Use the same sequence as the 2–1–1 except add an extra overhead clear to this drill. Sequence: underhand clear, overhead clear, overhead clear, overhead drop, net drop, repeat.

VI. Around-the-Head Shots

Around-the-head strokes are used in place of the conventional overhead "backhand" stroke—a shot usually considered to be weak and very defensive.

Around-the-heads may be used for overhead clears, smashes, and overhead drops. If stroked properly they can be very powerful, attacking strokes. Although this stroke will be contacted on your backhand (non-racket) side, your grip will be a forehand grip.

Position yourself so that the shuttle is in alignment with your non-racket shoulder. The backswing is exactly the same as in the other overhead shots, but the contact point will be over your non-racket shoulder (Figure 5-33). There will be a bending of the waist in the direction of the backhand side. The racket arm is extended as fully as is necessary to contact the shuttle at its highest point possible.

Remember, the only difference between around-the-head shots and other overheads is that the shuttle is contacted over the non-racket shoulder in all around-the-heads.

At the beginning and intermediate levels, it is suggested that around-the-head strokes be strongly emphasized. This will not only encourage more aggressive stroking, but it will also deter players from stroking the weaker backhand shots (clears and drops) unnecessarily.

Figure 5-33 Around-the-head. Notice that the contact is on the backhand side of the body.

Playing Strategy

There is no set sequence of shots or strategic decisions that one can use to win a volley. However, with sound fundamentals, proficient strokes, and good strategy, you will win many matches.

Basically, shots made from below net level (the white tape), or what is termed "lifted," are considered to be *defensive,* and those made from above the net level, or stroked downward, are considered to be *offensive.*

Basic Strategy

1. Force your opponent to move as far as possible to return a shot.
2. Use attacking strokes whenever you get a chance.
3. Return to "home base" after every shot.
4. Play to your opponent's weakest side—generally the backhand.
5. When in doubt, hit a high, deep clear and hope for a weak return.

Singles Strategy

The game of singles demands a great deal of determination, hustle, quick reactions, and patience. Outsmarting your opponent by using good strategy and outhustling her through mere determination is very exciting and rewarding.

Serving

1. A long serve (high and deep) to the backcourt area near the centerline is used the majority of the time. This serve will put your opponent as far away from the net as possible and will force her to hit a very strong return to put you at any disadvantage whatsoever. Directing your serve to the centerline will cut down the angle of return.
2. A short serve can be used if your opponent is standing too deep in her receiving court to return your serve. Or, short serves can be used if your opponent has a very effective smash from the backcourt area, and you want to eliminate a smash return directly off your serve.

Return of Service

1. Return serves with shots that are straight ahead. Crosscourt shots take longer to travel and need to be hit harder due to the extra distance they have to fly.
2. Your service return should move your opponent out of her home base position.
3. Long serves are generally returned with an overhead clear or a drop shot in the near corner.
4. Short serves are generally returned with an underhand clear or a net drop (push) to the near corner.

The Volley

1. Move your opponent to the various corners of the court by varying your shot selection. Moving your opponent out of her home base position and to the different corners of the court will increase your chances of forcing a weak return and losing control of the volley.
2. Move your opponent to the various corners of the court, in diagonal patterns if possible. Moving your opponent diagonally forces her to travel greater distances in covering the court.
3. Force your opponent to "lift" the shuttle as often as possible. This will decrease your opponent's chances for returning the shuttle with a strong stroke and increase your chances for staying on the attack (hitting the shuttle downward).
4. Build your game on a pattern of drops and clears. If you are patient, this pattern will eventually force your opponent to hit a weak return. Then, use your smash to put the volley away.
5. Take advantage of any weakness your opponent may have. The backhand is usually the weaker side, so direct your shots to that side.
6. In defending a smash, block it to the opposite side of where the smash was originated.
7. If your opponent is moving to cover an open spot on the court when you are about to make your shot, play the bird to the position being vacated. The most difficult maneuver on the court is one that requires a quick change of direction in your movement. Retracing your steps demands the utmost agility and speed.
8. Do not play the sidelines too close with your shots. Give yourself about a 3-foot "safety" variance inside the sideline to reduce your chances of hitting the shuttle out-of-bounds.
9. If late in the game, and you are trailing your opponent, you might want to switch to a more conservative type of play. Direct your shots toward the center portion of the court. This will increase your chances of staying in-bounds and remaining "in the game." This does not, however, mean that you should become less aggressive in your stroking.

Doubles Strategy

It must be understood that doubles is a more complex game than singles. It is faster paced and demands considerable strategy and cohesive teamwork for partners to be effective. It is offense oriented, which means that attacking, energy-consuming strokes are used most of the time. With excellently placed strokes and long volleys, doubles can be a very strenuous game.

Serving

1. A short serve (low and short) to the "T" area (near corner) is used most of the time. This serve will force your opponents to "lift" the shuttle and will put them in a defensive situation directly off the serve.
2. Long serves (high, but not as deep as the singles long serve) can be used to move a strong forecourt player to the backcourt area, or they can be used to maneuver an opponent who has an ineffective smash to the backcourt. Remember, because long serves in doubles are not allowed to travel as far back into the playing court area as long serves in singles play, the long serve should be used very sparingly.
3. The server's partner should assume a position two feet forward of the long service line and straddling the centerline. This alignment is used in preparation for an attacking strategy (up-and-back).

Return of Service

1. The receiving position in doubles is slightly different for the receiver than in singles (see Return of Service—Singles). From this doubles receiving position, short serves can be played very quickly. This will, in turn, increase the possibility of using attacking strokes for short service returns.
2. Rush short serves. As soon as the shuttle is served, step forward with the racket foot and attempt to contact the shuttle while it is still above the net level. Stroke the shuttle downward if possible.
3. Drop returns should be directed to the near corner.
4. A push shot directed to the near side alley, midcourt depth, is an excellent return for a short serve.
5. Return long serves with a smash.
6. The receiver's partner should assume a position two feet forward of the long service line and straddling the centerline. This alignment is used in preparation for an attacking strategy (up-and-back).

The Volley

There are three basic alignments used for doubles play. These alignments are generally dependent upon the specific situation during the game or volley. There is a defensive alignment *side by side;* an offensive alignment, *up and back;* or, you can use a combination of these two alignments, called *circular rotation.* Circular rotation depends largely upon the situation your team is in (offensive or defensive) during the point being played.

Side-by-Side Alignment. This alignment is considered to be defensive. In this alignment, each partner is responsible for his half of the playing court (Figure

Figure 5-34 Doubles side-by-side alignment.

5-34). Whenever your opponents are in control of the volley (using attacking strokes or forcing you to "lift" the shuttle), the side-by-side alignment is the best strategy to use. With this alignment, it will be harder for your opponents to stroke a smash past you because you and your partner will have the court covered laterally very efficiently. This alignment is also easy to understand and learn.

A disadvantage of this alignment is that it allows a team to play to the weaker player. It would be to your advantage, if aligned in this formation, to get back to an attacking (offensive) situation as soon as possible. This can be accomplished by either blocking your opponent's smashes to the side alleys or front corners, forcing them to "lift" the shuttle to you, or net dropping their overhead drops to the front corners, forcing them to "lift" and assume a defensive alignment. Remember, although the side-by-side alignment is a very effective defensive alignment, doubles is an attacking game. Very few points can be won directly from defensive strokes or defensive alignments.

Up-and-Back Alignment. This alignment is considered to be offensive. In this alignment one partner is responsible for the forecourt area (sideline to sideline, from the net to the "T") while his partner is responsible for the midcourt and backcourt area (sideline to sideline). Both players are situated along the centerline of the court, with one player positioned at the "T" and the other positioned approximately 2 feet forward of the long service line (Figure 5-35).

Whenever your team is in control of the volley (using attacking strokes or forcing your opponents to "lift" the shuttle), the up-and-back alignment is the best strategy to use. With this alignment, it will be harder for your opponents to block a smash or net drop effectively, because one partner will have the forecourt covered very efficiently. It will also decrease the effectiveness of your opponent's clears in that your partner will have the backcourt covered.

Figure 5-35 Doubles up-and-back alignment.

A disadvantage of the up-and-back alignment is that it allows a team to pass or drive a shot down the side alleys of the court.

The net player's (partner at the "T") responsibility is to intercept any shot by the opponents before that shot reaches his partner's midcourt or backcourt area. The net player is also responsible for stroking the shuttle downward, net dropping, or pushing the shuttle back over the net as quickly as possible from the forecourt area in response to an opponent's stroke. The net player should use any stroke that will keep the opponents in a defensive situation, or "lifting" the shuttle.

The backcourt player's responsibility is to attack the opponents with strokes that force "lifting" responses. Smashes and overhead drops used strategically will serve this purpose. He should direct these shots down the centerline or toward the side alleys. The backcourt partner should also direct these attacking strokes to the opponent that is the weaker player.

Remember, the up-and-back alignment is an offensive alignment and doubles is an attacking game. Points can be won directly from attacking strokes with players in offensive alignments.

Combination (Circular Rotation). The combination system combines the best of the other two systems, using the side-by-side alignment for defense and the up-and-back alignment for attacking. This system is generally used by more advanced players. It takes a great deal of teamwork, practice, and playing time to use this system effectively.

The basic principles to be followed in the combination system are as follows:

1. If the server serves short, the serving team will remain in the up-and-back alignment.
   Reason: A short serve forces your opponents to "lift" the shuttle. This will, in turn, allow the serving team to return the shuttle with downward, attacking strokes, keeping them in an offensive situation.

2. If the server serves long, the serving team will go to a side-by-side alignment. The server should drop back to his serving side. The partner will, in turn, move to the opposite side.
   Reason: A long serve allows the opponents to return the shuttle with attacking strokes, thereby putting your team in a defensive situation.

3. If the receiver of the serve is served short, and he net drops or pushes the shuttle downward back over the net, the receiving team should stay in an up-and-back alignment.
   Reason: The receiving team, with those returns, has just forced their opponents to start "lifting" the shuttle.
   If the receiver of the serve is served short, and he clears the shuttle, the receiving team should go to a side-by-side alignment.
   Reason: The receiving team has been forced to "lift" the shuttle. They are now in a defensive situation.
   If the receiver of the serve is served long, his partner should immediately go to the "T" to play the net, and the receiver should smash or overhead drop the shuttle to force his opponents to "lift." With these actions, they have now assumed the up-and-back offensive alignment.

4. On any shot that gives the opponents the advantage and opportunity to smash or overhead drop, the team making the stroke should take up the defensive side-by-side alignment. The player making the shot should cover the half of the court from which the shot was made.

5. When reverting from a defensive alignment to an offensive alignment, the player taking a backcourt stroke (attacking) that initiates the change will stay in the backcourt "back" position. The partner will then move to the "up" position and guard the net from the "T." If the stroke that initiates the change is taken from a forecourt position, the player taking that stroke will move to the "up" position at the net. The partner will then move to the "back" position in the backcourt.

► **Learning Hints for Doubles Strategy**

1. Attack as often as possible. Hit the shuttle downward and force your opponents to "lift" the shuttle.
2. When attacking, use the up-and-back alignment.
3. When "lifting" the shuttle, use the side-by-side alignment.
4. Rush short serves. Attack them if possible.
5. Smash long serves.
6. When opponents are in a defensive alignment, smash or overhead drop toward the centerline.

7. When opponents are in a defensive alignment, play to the weaker opponent.
8. When opponents are in an offensive alignment, direct your shots to the side alleys.
9. When you are in a defensive alignment, revert to an attacking situation as soon as the chance arises.
10. Use clears only in emergency situations. If you must clear, clear to the back corners.

Playing Courtesies

Badminton emphasizes good sportsmanship and playing courtesies. Use good judgment at all times with regard to your own behavior as well as to your attitude toward your opponent. Be cordial and respectful. As in any sport, be a good loser as well as a gracious winner. Try to maintain a positive rather than negative attitude, creating a more enjoyable game for all participants. The following are some courtesies specific to badminton.

1. If your opponent is unknown to you, introduce yourself and shake hands prior to the match.
2. The warm-up period should be gracious and uncompetitive.
3. The server should call the score prior to each serve—server's score first.
4. If in doubt about the shuttle's landing, always call it in favor of your opponent.
5. Inform your opponent of the call as quickly as possible.
6. Never question your opponent's calls.
7. If there is any question of your faulting, be sure to call it on yourself.
8. If a shuttle lands on your side and you are the receiver, pick it up and hit it back to the server so that she does not have to go out of her way to retrieve it.
9. Do not smash at your opponent if the point could be easily won by placing the shuttle elsewhere in the court.
10. Do not stall. Keep the play continuous.
11. If you are the receiver, get ready to receive the serve without any hesitation.
12. Compliment your opponent's exceptional shots.
13. Do not offer playing advice to your opponents.
14. Do not, under any circumstances, throw your racket or the shuttle in anger.
15. Always shake hands with your opponent after the match.

Modifications for Special Populations

Orthopedically Impaired

1. See modifications discussed in the chapters on handball, racquetball, and tennis.

2. Students with grasping difficulties should consider bracing or wrist devices to assist with gripping. The student could have the racket secured to the brace with an ace bandage.

Cognitively Impaired

1. Consult with Special Olympics, and use modifications from the chapters on handball, racquetball, and tennis from this text.

Sensory Impaired

1. Individual considerations must be taken into account to determine the appropriateness of badminton for students who are visually impaired. Students with this condition might be able to play a modified game using a tethered shuttlecock.
2. Students with hearing impairments will need minimal modifications. Make sure to face the student, speak slowly, and do not cover your mouth with hand gestures. Also avoid standing in front of a bright light, because this may produce shadows on your face.

Terminology

Alley The 1½-foot-wide area on each side of the court that is used for doubles. Often referred to as the "side alley."

Around-the-head stroke An overhead stroke used when hitting a forehand-like overhead stroke that is on the backhand side of the body.

Back alley The area between the doubles long service line and the baseline.

Backcourt The back third of the court.

Backhand A stroke made on the non-racket side of the body.

Baseline The back boundary line of the court.

Bird Another name for the shuttlecock.

Block A soft shot, used primarily in defense against a smash. Intercepting an opponent's smash and returning it back over the net.

Carry Called when the shuttle stays on the racket during a stroke. It is legal if the racket follows the intended line of flight. Also referred to as a "throw."

Centerline The mid-line separating the service courts.

Clear A high shot that goes over your opponent's head and lands close to the baseline.

Combination alignment Partners play both up-and-back and side-by-side during doubles games and/or volleys.

Crosscourt A shot hit diagonally into the opposite court.

Defense The team or player hitting the shuttle upward (lifting), usually from an underhand stroke.

Double hit An illegal shot in which the racket contacts the shuttle twice in one swing.

Doubles service court The short, wide area to which the server must serve in doubles play.

Down-the-line shot A shot hit straight ahead—usually down the sideline.

Drive A hard driven shot that travels parallel with the floor. This shot clears the net but does not go high enough for your opponent to smash.

Drop A shot that just clears the net, then falls close to it.

Face The string area of the racket.

Fault Any infraction of the rules. It results in the loss of serve or in a point for the server.

First serve A term used in doubles play to indicate that the server is the "first server" during an inning.

Foot fault Illegal position or movement of the feet by either the server or receiver.

Forecourt The front area of the court, usually considered to be between the net and the short service line.

Forehand Any stroke made on the racket side of the body.

Game point The point which, if won, allows the server to win the game.

Hand in The term used to indicate that the server retains the serve.

Hand out The term used in doubles to show that one player has lost the service.

Home base The position in the center of the court from which the player can best play any shot hit by an opponent.

Inning The time during which a player or team holds service.

Let The stopping of play due to some type of outside interference. The point is replayed.

Lifting the shuttle To stroke the bird underhanded and hit it upward.

Long serve A high, deep serve landing near the long service line in doubles or back boundary line (baseline) in singles.

Love The term used to indicate zero in scoring.

Match A series of games. In badminton, winning two out of three games will win the match.

Match point The point that, if won by the server, makes that person the winner of the match.

Midcourt The middle third of the court, usually considered to be between the short service line and the long service line for doubles.

Net shot A shot taken near the net.

Non-racket side The opposite side of the hand holding the racket.

Offense The team or player that is stroking the shuttle downward (attacking).

Overhead A motion used to strike the shuttle when it is above the head.

Racket foot or leg The foot or leg on the same side as the hand holding the racket.

Ready position The position a player assumes to be ready to move in any direction.

Receiver The player to whom the shuttle is served.

Second serve In doubles, the term indicates that one partner has lost the serve, and the other partner is now serving.

Server The player who puts the shuttle into play.

Setting Choosing how many more points to play when certain tie scores are reached.

Short serve A serve that barely clears the net and lands just beyond the short service line.

Shuttlecock (shuttle) The feathered, plastic, or nylon object that is volleyed back and forth over the net.

Side alley See *Alley.*

Side-by-side A defensive alignment used in doubles play. Each partner is responsible for one side of the court, from the net to the back boundary line.

Side out When a player or team loses the serve.

Smash An overhead stroke hit downward with great velocity and angle. The principal attacking stroke in badminton.

"T" The intersection of the centerline and the short service line.

Underhand A stroke that is hit upward when the shuttle has fallen below shoulder level.

Unsight Illegal position taken by the server's partner so the receiver cannot see the shuttle as it is hit.

Up-and-back An offensive alignment used in doubles. The "up" player is responsible for the forecourt, and the "back" player is responsible for the midcourt and backcourt.

Further References

Ballou, R. *Badminton for Beginners.* Englewood, CO: Morton Publishing Company, 1997.

Bloss, M. V. and Hale, R. S. *Badminton.* 8th ed. Dubuque, IA: William C. Brown, 2000.

Boga, S. *Badminton.* Mechanicsburg, PA: Stackpole Books, 1996.

Davis, P. *Play the Game.* London, UK: Cassell, 1998.

Edwards, J. *Badminton: Technique-Tactics-Training.* North Pomfert, VT: Trafalgar Square, 1997.

Paup, D. and Fernhill, B. *Skills, Drills, and Strategies for Badminton.* Scottsdale, AZ: Holcomb Hathaway, Inc., 2000.

Roper, B. *The Skills of the Game of Badminton.* North Pomfert, VT: Trafalgar Square, 1995.

Shaw, M. and French, L. *How to Play Badminton.* Cincinnati, OH: Seven Hills Book Distribution, 1993.

Periodicals

Badminton U.S.A. United States Badminton Association, 501 W. Sixth Street, Papillion, NE 68046.

World Badminton. The International Badminton Federation, 24 Winchcombe House, Winchcombe Street, Cheltenham, Gloucestershire, England GL52 2NA.

Audio-Visual Materials

Badminton Movies. Louisville Badminton Supply, 9411 Westport Road, Louisville, KY 40222.

C.B.A. Video Library. Canadian Badminton Association, 333 River Road, Toronto, Ontario M4W 1J5, Canada.

Champions on Film & Video, 745 State Circle, Box 1941, Ann Arbor, MI 48106. Badminton (VHS only, 14 minutes).

U.S.B.A. Video Library. United States Badminton Association, 501 W. Sixth Street, Papillion, NE 68046.

Web Sites

www.badmintoncentral.com Provides tips on technique, rules, a forum for addressing techniques with others, and other links.

www.intbadFed.org Lists the history, scientific reviews of skills, development, and rules/laws.

www.usabadminton,com Provides history, rules, links, badminton facts, and a video library.

www.badminton-interactive.com A great site for drills and tips; the interactive instruction is voice and visual for techniques.

CHAPTER 6

Basketball

This chapter will enable you to

- Know the playing court, equipment, and basic rules of basketball
- Practice and develop skill in the fundamentals of passing, dribbling, shooting, rebounding, individual offense, and individual defense
- Identify the objectives and strategies of team offense and defense

Nature and Purpose

Basketball is an extremely popular game, played in all parts of the world and at every conceivable level. In America, the extremes are evident—from rickety backboards attached to outdoor garages to multi-million-dollar arenas that hold thousands of spectators. Basketball can be played at a highly organized level or spontaneously at a neighborhood playground. Children can play on school teams, beginning with elementary school, and continuing through college. Highly skilled men and women can earn basketball scholarships to play for colleges and universities. There are amateur tournaments and professional leagues. The United States has men's and women's Olympic Basketball Teams. Recreationally, basketball is played in the YMCA, YWCA, Boys Club, church leagues, and community centers. It is a vital part of school intramural programs, sometimes even played coeducationally. Basketball presents the opportunity to learn ball skills, coordination, agility, and body control; participation in the game can contribute toward maintenance of an individual's total fitness. For these reasons, basketball is an attractive physical education class activity.

This original American sport has very broad applications: Large groups can participate at relatively low cost; the game can serve for competitive as well as recreational purposes; and it has the necessary appeal to make it a popular spectator sport.

Officially, a basketball team is composed of five players. However, in recreational play, two, three, or four players can play a game. The purpose of the game is to score a larger total number of points than the opponent. The score is compiled by shooting the ball through the basket either from the field (called a field goal) or from the free-throw line (called a free throw or a foul shot). The ball is passed, thrown, bounced, batted, or rolled from one player to another. A player in possession of the ball must maintain contact with the floor with one foot (called the pivot foot), unless the player is shooting, passing, or dribbling. Dribbling consists of a series of one-hand taps, causing the ball to bounce on the floor. Physical contact with an opponent can result in a foul if the contact impedes the desired movement of the player.

Court or Field of Play

The playing area of basketball is called the court. The rectangular court measures a maximum of 94 feet long and 50 feet wide, or a minimum of 74 feet long and 42 feet wide. The baskets are suspended 10 feet above the floor at the endline of each court. The court has three restraining circles and two free-throw areas (Figure 6-1). The court can be modified (made smaller) and the baskets lowered to accommodate younger participants. Basketball can be played on half of a court if large numbers of participants want to play in an intramural, class, or recreational situation.

Basic Rules

Two or sometimes three on-the-court officials regulate a basketball game. The game is divided into 20-minute halves for college and university teams and 8-minute quarters for high school teams. Teams composed of players younger than high school age should have 6-minute quarters. The length of the game in a recreational, class, or intramural situation can be adjusted by shortening the quarters or halves, or by having "running time," wherein the clock does not stop on the dead balls.

Figure 6-1 The basketball court.

There are slight variations of rules between high school and collegiate play, as well as between the men's and women's collegiate games. Nevertheless, there are basic rules of basketball governing play at any level.

Players

1. Even though only five players play at a time, any number of substitutions can be made at any dead ball during the game or during a timeout. Substitutes must report to the scorer and wait to be beckoned onto the court by an official.

2. One of the five players is the designated floor captain and may address the official on matters of interpretation or information. Any player may request a timeout.

Scoring and Timing

1. A goal is made when a live ball enters the basket from above and remains in or passes through except on a throw-in. A field goal counts *3 points* if the shot is made by a player situated beyond the 3-point field goal line. For a successful 3-point field goal, the player must have one or both feet on the floor and be beyond the 3-point line when attempting the shot. After releasing the ball, the shooter may land on or over the line. Touching the line before the release places the shooter in the 2-point area.

2. A goal from the field other than from the 3-point area counts *2 points*.

3. When a free throw is awarded for fouls, each successful free throw counts *1 point*.

4. If a player mistakenly scores a field goal in the opponent's basket, the goal is counted for the opponent.

5. Each team gets the same number of timeouts per game. Various organizing bodies (NCAA, high school, YMCA, etc.) dictate the number and length of these timeouts. They can vary from 20 seconds to 1 minute. Regardless of the length and time, timeouts can be requested only during a dead ball or anytime by the team in possession of the ball.

6. If the score is tied at the end of regulation time, play continues an extra period. As many extra periods are played as necessary to break the tie.

7. The clock stops each time an official blows the whistle indicating a dead ball (violation, personal foul, out-of-bounds). The clock keeps running after successful field goals.

Play

1. The ball is put into play at the beginning of the game and any overtime period by a jump ball in the center circle between two opponents. Each subsequent quarter or half starts with the team entitled to possession given the ball at the center division line. In jump ball situations, other than at the start of the game and start of extra periods, teams will alternate taking the ball out-of-bounds. The team not obtaining control of the

initial jump ball will start the alternating process. After each goal, the ball is put into play by the team that did not score from the out-of-bounds area at the end of the court at which the basket has been scored.

2. A player is out-of-bounds when touching the floor on or outside the boundary line.

3. The ball is out-of-bounds when it touches a player who is out-of-bounds or any other person, the floor, or any object on or outside a boundary, or the supports or back of the backboard.

4. The ball is caused to go out-of-bounds by the last player touching it before it goes out. The ball would be awarded out-of-bounds for a throw-in by the opposing team. The ball is awarded out-of-bounds after a violation, successful free throw or field goal, or a common foul until the bonus rule goes into effect.

5. While the ball is alive, an offensive player cannot remain for more than three seconds in that part of the free-throw lane between the endline, the free-throw line, and the free-throw lane lines.

6. If two opponents are both firmly holding the ball, or an offensive ball handler is closely guarded by the defense for five seconds, a jump ball is called.

7. Violations include causing the ball to go out-of-bounds, double dribbling, running with the ball, kicking the ball (positive act), striking the ball with the fist, interfering with the basket, illegal throw-in (taking more than 5 seconds or stepping on the line), and the 3-second lane rule.

8. Fouls are classified as (1) *personal*—involving pushing, charging, tripping, holding, body contact; or (2) *technical*—involving delay of game, unsportsmanlike conduct, illegal entry, excessive timeouts. For personal fouls, the offender is charged with one foul; a fifth personal foul results in disqualification. The offended player is awarded:
    a. one free throw if the foul occurred during a field goal attempt and the basket was made.
    b. two free throws if the foul occurred during a 2-point field goal attempt and the basket was missed.
    c. three free throws if the foul occurred during a 3-point field goal atempt and the basket was missed.
    d. no free throw, but the ball is awarded to the offended player's team out-of-bounds, if the foul occurred before the seventh common team foul of the half.
    e. one free throw plus a bonus free throw if the first one is made, when the fifth common foul or seventh common team foul (see (d) above) has occurred. This is called the bonus rule.
    f. two free throws for the remainder of the half when the tenth common team foul of the half has occurred. This is called the double bonus rule.

For technical fouls, the offended team is awarded two free throws as well as the ball out-of-bounds.

Equipment

The Ball. The official ball is spherical with a circumference of 29½ to 30 inches for men and 28½ to 29 inches for women. Smaller balls are available for younger participants. In competition, a ball of high-grade leather is used. Less expensive balls are made of rubber or synthetic materials.

The Basket. The basket consists of a simple metal ring, 18 inches in inside diameter. A white-cord net suspends from beneath the ring. The basket is securely attached to a rigid backboard. Most backboards used in competition are transparent glass and rectangular in shape. However, it is not uncommon for backboards to be fan-shaped and made of solid wood.

Suggested Learning Sequence—Beginners

A. Conditioning and stretching
B. Purpose of the game and general game concepts
C. Basic rules
D. Fundamental skills:
  1. Pivoting
  2. Catching and holding the ball
  3. Passing—chest, bounce, overhead
  4. Dribbling—high speed, low control
  5. Shooting—one-handed set, layup
  6. Rebounding—position, jumping
E. Individual offense:
  1. Cutting—V-cut, front
  2. Driving
F. Individual defense:
  1. Basic stance and movement
  2. Guarding a player with the ball
  3. Guarding a player without a ball
G. Team play:
  1. *Offense*—basic concepts on how to attack a player-to-player defense
  2. *Defense*—player-to-player
  3. *Other*—jump ball alignment, free-throw alignment

Suggested Learning Sequence—Intermediates

A. Conditioning and stretching
B. Additional rules
C. Review beginners unit
D. Intermediate skills:
   1. Passing—one-hand bounce, baseball
   2. Dribbling—crossover, reverse (spin)
   3. Shooting—free throw, jump shot, layup from various angles
   4. Rebounding—blocking out, outlet pass
E. Individual offense:
   1. Cutting—backdoor (reverse)
   2. Fakes and feints
F. Individual defense:
   1. Defense against a player one pass away and two passes away
   2. Denial defense
   3. Defense against a ball handler
G. Team play:
   1. *Offense*—basic concepts on how to attack a zone defense
   2. *Defense*—combatting picks and screens, zones
   3. *Other*—fast break, in-bounds plays

Skills and Techniques

Pivoting

Pivoting is the only legal maneuvering a player standing and holding the ball is allowed. One foot (the pivot foot) must be kept at its point of contact with the floor, while the other foot can step in any direction. A good technique for the beginner is to imagine that a spike has been driven through the pivot foot into the floor; this would afford faking movements with the opposite foot, but the spike can be removed only through dribbling, passing, or shooting. Illegally moving the pivot foot or taking too many steps while stopping constitutes "traveling." The result is a loss of possession of the ball for that team.

Passing

Good passing is necessary in order to maintain possession of the ball and be able to move into scoring position. The key to an effective offense is accuracy in passing, and passing is the quickest way to move the ball, thus *allowing the offense to catch the defense off balance or out of position.*

Chest Pass. This pass is probably the most commonly used pass. The ball is held in both hands, the fingers spread on the sides of the ball with the thumbs behind the ball. Held about chest high with the elbows held comfortably at the sides of the body, the ball is released by extending the arms fully, snapping the wrists, and stepping in the direction of the pass. The palms should be facing downward or slightly outward, with the elbow chest high on the follow-through. The chest pass should be received chest high.

Bounce Pass. This pass is a short-distance pass used to avoid a deflection or interception when a player is being closely guarded. It is executed in the same manner as the chest pass except the ball is bounced into the hands of the receiver. The ball should bounce at approximately two-thirds of the distance between the passer and receiver, and should rebound waist high. This pass can also be released with one hand by stepping out with the free foot to either side of a close defender and bouncing the ball around him. It is also possible to make this pass directly off of the dribble.

Overhead Pass. This pass is used to pass over a defensive player, usually to a post player or a cutter. The ball is held overhead with both hands, thumbs under the ball and fingers spread on the sides of the ball (Figure 6-2A). The passer steps forward toward the intended receiver and transfers the body weight to the front foot. The arms, which are slightly bent, are brought forward sharply, with a snap of the wrists releasing the ball (Figure 6-2B). This pass is best utilized by a player who is taller than the defending opponent.

One-Hand Overhead Pass (Baseball Pass). This pass is used most frequently to cover long distances, especially in initiating the fast break. When this pass is thrown with the right hand, the ball is brought back to the right ear, close to the head, with the fingers well spread in back of the ball. The left hand can steady the ball when it is in this position, ready to be thrown. The weight of the body is shifted to the right rear foot as the ball is brought back. The weight shifts forward to the left foot as the right arm is brought forward to release the ball. The ball is released about one foot in front of the body with the wrist snapping forward and downward.

➤ Learning Hints for Passing

1. Passes should be crisp, but not too hard to catch.
2. Use a pass appropriate for the specific situation.
3. Take a step in the direction of the pass.
4. Weight should be balanced when passing.
5. Do not "telegraph" the pass; be deceptive with your eyes.
6. Aim to hit your receiver between the waist and shoulders.
7. A fake before you pass may cause your defender to move, creating a better passing lane.

A   B

Figure 6-2 The overhead pass.

8. Put as little spin as possible on the pass.
9. Pass to the side of your teammate away from the defender.
10. Always pass ahead of a running teammate.
11. Learn to catch and pass in one motion.

Catching and Holding the Ball

Possession of the ball is so important that receiving and holding the ball are as essential as passing. A player should attempt to catch every pass regardless of how it is thrown. To help eliminate deflections, a player should cut sharply toward each pass to meet it, with the hands held out in front of the body to provide a target and to maintain balance when moving in any direction to meet the ball. It is also possible to hold one hand up in the air (the hand furthest from your defender) to provide a high target for a pass (Figure 6-3). The ball should be caught with the pads of the fingers and brought toward the body to protect it before dribbling, passing, or shooting. If a player must stand for a few moments in possession of the ball, it is best to step back slightly with your free foot, away from your defender, pulling the ball back with you. This places your body between the ball and the defender for added protection.

➤ **Learning Hints for Catching and Holding the Ball**

1. Provide the passer with a target by holding a hand up or both hands forward.
2. Move to meet passes thrown to you.

Figure 6-3 Preparing to catch a pass against a defender.

3. Hands should be comfortably spread and relaxed when catching.

4. Keep elbows flexed, not stiff, enabling absorption of the impact of the thrown ball.

5. Watch the ball all of the way into your hands.

6. Pull the ball in close to your body for protection.

7. Whenever possible, catch with two hands to ensure control.

➤ Practice/Organizational Suggestions for Passing and Catching

1. Stand approximately 8 feet from a wall. Execute different passes against the wall, concentrating on form and accuracy.

2. With a partner, stand in positions as either two guards, or as a guard and a forward. Pass back and forth, faking before each pass and practicing deception. Add two defenders. Add a cut to the basket after each pass to receive a return pass.

3. To practice the baseball pass, stand 30 feet from a partner. Pass back and forth. To practice this pass on the move, both players position themselves near the backboard. One player rebounds the ball off the board, dribbles toward the sideline, and releases a baseball pass to the other player cutting downcourt. Add defenders.

4. Three-player weave (Figure 6-4): Three players start on the endline approximately 15 feet apart. The player in the middle has a ball. This player passes to a wing and subsequently cuts behind the wing player. This receiver, in turn, passes to the third player and cuts behind this third player. The three players continue passing and moving

downcourt. Vary the passes. Add one, two, or three defenders.

5. Four corner passing (Figure 6-5): With players in a box formation, one player makes a long pass to the first player in the next line. This player follows the pass and receives a short pass back. The initial player hands off to the same player and goes to the end of that line. Continue with a long pass to the next corner.
Variation: Add another ball. Start them in opposite corners.

6. Shotgun passing (Figure 6-6): One player stands apart from a half-circle of teammates who are arranged so that two players are just in the peripheral vision of the single player. Using two balls, the half-circle players and the single player pass very quickly back and forth.

7. Reaction pass drill: One partner has a ball, while the other player stands approximately 15 feet away facing away from the partner. The player with the ball calls out the other player's first name, followed by a pass to the player. Upon hearing his name, the player quickly turns and attempts to catch the ball and gain control of it. The pass should vary, making the receiver jump, reach, stoop, etc., to secure every pass.

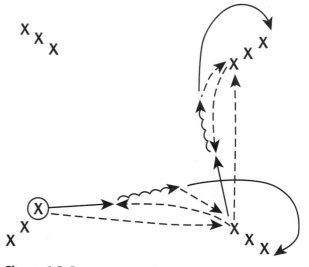

Figure 6-5 Four-corner passing.

Key to Maneuvers

Cut	——→
Pass	– – →
Pick or screen	——⊂
Dribble	∿∿∿

Figure 6-4 Three-player weave.

Figure 6-6 Shotgun passing.

8. Monkey in the middle: Players form a circle with one player ("monkey") in the middle. Using one ball and any type of pass, a player in the circle attempts to get the ball to any other player in the circle, other than the two players immediately on each side. The "monkey" attempts to touch, deflect, or intercept the pass. If successful, the "monkey" changes place with the passer.

9. Shuttle pass drill: Form two lines in a shuttle formation. The first player in one of the lines has a ball. The first person in the opposite line defends as the player attempts to pass across to the other line. Continue passing between the two lines with the passer each time becoming the next defender.

Dribbling

Dribbling is slower than passing as a means of moving the ball. Therefore it should not be overused. The dribble should be used only to (1) penetrate or drive toward the basket, (2) create a better passing lane, (3) get out of a crowd, and (4) bring the ball down the court. A good rule to remember is never to dribble the ball when a pass can be completed successfully.

With the hand cupped, the pads of the fingers control the direction of the ball, while the wrist and finger flexion provide the force. The ball should be pushed downward and slightly forward, with the body in a crouched position. The opposite arm and forward foot should provide protection between the ball and the opponent. There are basically two types of dribbles that are identifiable by observing the rebounding height of the ball and the proximity of the defender. These are the high-speed dribble and the low-control dribble.

High-Speed Dribble. The high-speed dribble is used when a player is unguarded and moving quickly—leading a fast break, driving to the basket, bringing the ball down the court without opposition. The body is erect, with only a slight forward crouch. The ball rebounds between the waist and chest. The dribbling arm pushes the ball forward and slightly to the side of the body. A full running stride is used, limited only by the dribbler's ability to control the ball.

Low-Control Dribble. This dribble is used when a player is closely guarded or in a congested area. Both the body and the ball should be kept low (Figure 6-7). The ball should rebound knee high and close to the dribbling side of the body. The more frequent contact with the ball allows for control and change of direction when under pressure.

Crossover Dribble. In order to change directions, the crossover dribble can be used. It is effective only

Figure 6-7 Low-control dribble.

if the defender is guarding loosely. The dribbler simply pushes the ball to the floor so that it rebounds across in front of the body to the opposite hand. This must be done very quickly and with only one low bounce in order to avoid an interception. The shoulder opposite the dribbling hand should always be lowered and brought forward to protect the ball. The dribbler can now continue dribbling in the opposite direction.

Reverse (Spin) Dribble. The reverse dribble allows a player to change directions against an opponent who is guarding closely. It provides good protection for the ball, but forces the dribbler to turn away from the basket and lose visual contact with teammates (Figure 6-8). To execute the reverse while dribbling with the right hand: plant the left foot, spin or pivot away from the defender, and rotate the head quickly to the right as the right foot swings out past the defender. Only one bounce of the ball is necessary to switch the dribble from the right hand to the left hand. The dribbler then continues dribbling toward the left with the left hand.

➤ Learning Hints for Dribbling

1. Keep your eyes and head up, facing the basket and your teammates as much as possible.
2. Be able to dribble with either hand.
3. Protect the ball with your body and opposite arm.
4. Control the dribble with your fingers and wrist, not the palm.
5. Push the ball; do not slap it.
6. Keep your knees bent for balance.
7. Dribble with the right hand when dribbling to the right, and dribble with the left hand when dribbling to the left, *especially* when being guarded.

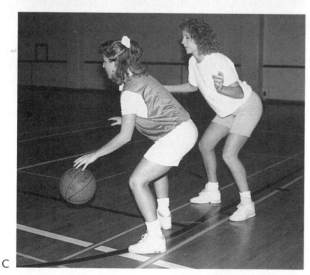

Figure 6-8 Reverse (spin) dribble (a 3-picture sequence).

➤ Practice/Organizational Suggestions for Dribbling and Ball Handling

(Work to keep your head up during all dribbling and ball-handling drills.)

1. Rotate the ball around the body, starting with the head. Go all the way down around the legs, and back up.
2. Rotate the ball around each ankle—right and left. Rotate the ball in a figure 8 around the ankles in a continuous motion.
3. Dribble the ball around the legs in a figure 8. Keep the ball low.
4. Straddle flip: With the legs shoulder-width apart, hold the ball low in front with both hands. Flip it up slightly between your legs, bringing your hands around behind the legs to catch the ball before it hits the ground. Flip it up again and bring the hands back to the front. Repeat as quickly as you can. *Variation:* Start with the hands alternately on the ball—one in front and one in back. Flip the ball up, alternating the hands quickly.
5. Dribble the ball around your body while on one knee, both knees, sitting, lying.
6. Standing two feet from a wall, tap the ball with the right or left hand high against the wall. *Variation:* Tap two balls simultaneously.
7. Circle keepaway: Within the boundaries of a restraining circle, try to dribble and maintain possession of a ball while another player attempts to steal it. *Variation:* Both players have a ball, trying to dribble *and* steal the other player's ball.
8. On a half court, try to dribble and maintain possession of a ball while two or three players try to pursue and steal the ball.
9. Dribble tag: On a half court, with all players dribbling a ball, play "tag." *Variations:* (1) More than one player is "it." (2) Restrict all players to use their nondominant hand. (3) Only half of the players have a ball, and others try to steal them (legally).
10. Column dribbling drills (players at the endline in three columns): Dribble the full length of the court:
    a. In a zigzag pattern, executing a crossover dribble or a reverse dribble at each corner.
    b. Doing a crossover, reverse, or stop on the coach's signal.
    c. Going around obstacles in a figure 8 pattern.
    d. Against a defender, trying to steal the ball.

Shooting

The primary objective of the game of basketball is to score goals. Therefore all players should be able to shoot. Being able to shoot a variety of shots from varying distances increases the effectiveness of any player.

Point of Aim. There are two targets that can be used in aiming at a basket—the rim or a spot on the backboard for a bank shot. The easiest point of aim for a beginner is the rim of the basket, due to its permanent position from anywhere on the floor. The player should concentrate on dropping the ball just beyond the front of the rim. The bank shot is typically used when a player is positioned at a 24- to 45-degree angle on either side of the basket. A spot on the backboard is sighted with the purpose of allowing the ball to hit this spot and rebound into the basket. Selecting the correct spot and judging the force to put on the ball makes this a skill for experienced players. A square box is painted on most backboards to aid in spot selection. In aiming, the brain sights the target, computes the distance, and determines the correct trajectory to put on the ball. It is important for the eyes to be focused on the target before each shot, during the release, and after the follow-through. It is obvious why shooting demands so much practice.

One-Handed Set Shot.   This shot is used for most long shots. The feet should be positioned in a forward-backward stride position, with the foot under the shooting hand slightly forward. The ankles, knees, and hips should be slightly flexed, with the weight easily balanced over the feet, and the shoulders square to the basket (Figure 6-9A). The ball is held below the chin (sighting the basket over the ball) or above the forehead (sighting the basket below the ball). It might be noted that the higher the ball is held, the less chance the defense has of blocking the shot. The ball should be held with the fingers, never in the palms of the hands. The shooting hand is behind and slightly under the ball with the fingers spread and wrist cocked (hyperextended). The elbow

of the shooting arm should be directly under the ball, making the forearm perpendicular to the floor.

The non-shooting or guide hand is placed on the side and slightly under the ball, with fingers spread. In executing the shot, the legs extend upward while the shooting arm extends toward the basket (Figure 6-9B). The wrist flexes forward, while the guide hand comes off of the ball. The wrist flexion releases the ball, with the fingertips coming off last, creating a slight backspin on the ball. A proper follow-through should have the guide hand held high, with the palm of the shooting hand facing the floor. The one-handed set shot is also used by most players when shooting free throws.

Jump Shot.   The jump shot is a very effective offensive weapon, due to its high point of release. The initial body position and the placement of the hands on the ball are the same as in the one-handed set shot. The shooter jumps into the air by pushing off with both legs. The ball is brought high above the forehead. At the apex of the jump, the body should be in a near-stationary, balanced position (Figure 6-10). Keeping the eyes focused on the basket, the shooting arm is uncocked and releases the ball with the same action as the one-handed position. Since the force for the jump shot is supplied primarily by the arms and wrist, the range of this shot is limited, as compared with the set shot, which incorporates leg power as well as arm strength.

Layup.   This shot is one of the highest percentage shots in the game, due to its closeness of range. It is used when a player has received a pass close to the

A   B

Figure 6-9 One-handed set shot.

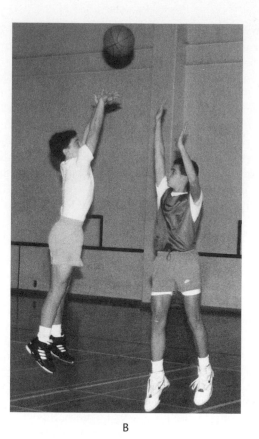

A   B

Figure 6-10 Jump shot (a 2-picture sequence).

basket, or has driven past the defense near the goal. It is best executed on a diagonal in relation to the basket, using the backboard to bank the ball in. At the last dribble, the ball is firmly grasped with the fingers of both hands and carried above the head. When shooting with the right hand, the player should take off with the left foot, while thrusting the right knee upward to achieve maximum height. At the same moment, the ball is set in the shooting hand and the left hand falls away. The shooting arm and fingers extend upward to "lay" the ball against the backboard. A proficient basketball player will develop the ability to shoot a layup with either hand being the dominant hand—the left hand when on the left side of the basket, the right hand when on the right side.

➤ Learning Hints for Shooting

1. Knees should bend to help generate power and provide balance. Shoulders should be square to the target.
2. Eyes should be focused on the target before, during, and after the shot.
3. The shooting arm's elbow should be directly under the ball.
4. Fingers should control every shot.
5. Use the backboard to bank a shot from an angle.
6. Maintain body balance; try not to lean or fall.
7. The shooting hand should follow through toward the basket after releasing the ball.

8. Backspin on the ball is desirable.
9. Generally, a higher arc on the ball results in greater accuracy and a better bounce off the rim if the shot is missed.

➤ Practice/Organizational Suggestions for Shooting

1. Add shooting to various passing and dribbling drills.
2. Column shooting drills (two lines of players facing the basket):
   a. One line shoots layups; the other line rebounds. Vary the angles for the layups. Add defensive pressure from the rebounding line.
   b. Same as (a), but use jump shots or set shots.
3. Around-the-world shooting: One player shoots, moving to a new spot after each shot, while another player rebounds and quickly passes to the shooter. *Variations:* (1) The passer-rebounder applies defensive pressure on each shot. (2) Have two rebounders and two balls, so the shooter must move and shoot more quickly.
4. Shuffle and shoot: Using two balls, a player shuffles between two spots, picking up the ball at each spot and shooting. Two rebounders work at rebounding the balls and replacing them at each spot (Figure 6-11).

Figure 6-11 Shuffle and shoot.

5. One-on-one: A player passes the ball to a player being guarded. The receiver practices various shots against the defender. *Variations:* (1) The receiver "posts up" to practice hook shots and moves with her back to the basket. (2) The receiver is allowed to use the passer again if she gets stuck.
6. Rebound-pass-shoot drill: Player X shoots from one of the spots, after receiving a pass from the passer. The rebounder rebounds and passes the ball to the passer. In the meantime, the shooter has moved to the next spot, ready to receive the pass there. Use two balls to make the action even more continuous. Vary the shooting spots and passing angle (Figure 6-12).
7. Follow the leader: Each player has a ball. One leader is designated. The leader shoots from various spots, while every player follows her.

8. Competitive shooting: Two teams compete against each other from various shooting spots. *Variations:* (1) Timed shooting. (2) Designated number of completed shots. (3) Least number of misses. (4) First team to finish.

Rebounding

Rebounding is gaining possession of the ball after an unsuccessful shooting attempt. Since approximately 60 percent of field goal attempts are missed, rebounding skill is essential to any team. Rebounding is categorized as being either defensive (at your opponent's basket) or offensive (at your own team's basket). The keys to effective rebounding are positioning, aggressiveness, and timing of the jump.

Positioning for the rebound is called "blocking out" or "boxing out" (Figure 6-13). The defensive player has a distinct advantage here, already being closer to the basket. With anticipation and a quick move, however, the offensive player can gain the inside position. Blocking out is done by pivoting to face the basket, putting the opponent behind you. It is important here to spread the feet far apart, bend the legs, lower the hips, and hold the elbows out away from the body. This helps to create a stable position, not allowing an opponent to get around. Since both the offensive player and the defensive player want the inside position, a player must be very aggressive in order to maintain this desired position. This means

Figure 6-12 Rebound-pass-shoot.

Figure 6-13 Blocking out.

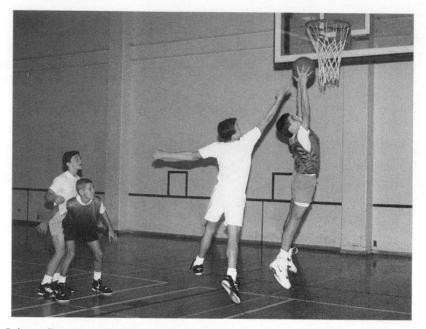

Figure 6-14 Rebounding. Note the blockout by the other player.

the player that is blocking out must slide and maintain physical contact with his opponent until the rebound is secured.

Once the inside position is attained, you must observe the ball and anticipate how and where it will rebound off of the rim or backboard. Jump high and grasp the ball firmly with both hands (Figure 6-14). On the downward move, after getting the ball, spread the legs and hold the ball high and away from the opponents. If it is a defensive rebound, pass (outlet) the ball away from the basket to a teammate near the sideline, or dribble the ball out away from the basket. An offensive rebound should be tipped back up to the basket, shot back up after landing on the ground, or passed to a teammate in better shooting position.

➤ **Learning Hints for Rebounding**

1. Work hard to attain or maintain the inside position closest to the basket.
2. Do not get pushed too far under the basket or backboard.
3. Be aggressive.
4. Jumping:
   a. Initiate the jump with the arms.
   b. Explode off of the floor by bending the legs.
   c. Reach high with both arms extended.
   d. Time the jump in order to grasp the ball as high as possible, attempting to keep the ball on line with the forehead.
5. Go for the ball; do not let it merely fall into your hands.
6. Keep a firm hold on the ball, jerking it down and away from any nearby opponents.
7. Land with feet comfortably spread and elbows out.

8. After landing, hold the ball high to keep opponents from getting it.
9. For a defensive rebound, get the ball away from the basket quickly (outlet). For an offensive rebound, try to get an immediate score out of it.

➤ **Practice/Organizational Suggestions for Rebounding**

1. Standing 20 to 25 feet from a partner, have her toss a ball high into the air toward you. Jump high and grasp the ball firmly with both hands, bringing it down aggressively.
2. Standing in front of the backboard, toss the ball high against the board. Jump and grasp the rebound, concentrating on good rebounding form. *Variations:* (1) Execute an outlet pass after rebounding (defensive rebound). (2) Shoot or tip the ball into the basket (offensive rebound).
3. Second-effort drill: Stand in front of the backboard with a partner holding a ball behind you. On your partner's command, jump high into the air as if rebounding. After you have jumped, the partner tosses the ball against the board, forcing you to spring back up immediately to rebound.
4. Circle blockout: Place a ball in the center of a restraining circle. Align three pairs of players around the outside of the circle—facing each other (one inside player with her back to the ball). On the whistle, the player on the inside turns and blocks out the other player, trying to keep him/her from touching the ball for approximately five seconds. *Variation:* Place a ball on the floor near each pair. Have each player block out her opponent from their ball for 30 seconds (Figure 6-15).

Figure 6-15 Circle blockout.

Figure 6-16 Three-on-three blockout.

5. Three-on-three blockout: With three offensive players and three defensive players positioned around the basket, the coach shoots the ball. Both teams attempt to secure the rebound. The offensive player should shoot the ball again or tip it in, while the defensive player should outlet the ball (Figure 6-16).

Individual Offense

To be a good basketball player, you must always be a threat to the opponents when your team has possession of the ball. This means being able to score when the ball is in your hands, as well as being able to move effectively on the floor without the ball in order to free yourself or a teammate.

Driving. Driving is a means of getting past opponents by faking them off balance, accelerating, and dribbling hard past them. It is important to dribble with the hand farthest from the defender when driving. Fakes can be executed with the head, ball, or free foot. By holding the ball close to your body, away from the defender, a series of "jab" steps (i.e., stepping forward and back) with the free foot may lure the opponent off balance so that you can drive. It is essential that a player not dribble immediately after receiving a pass. This would eliminate the fake and drive—a prime individual offensive weapon.

Cutting. Cutting is sharp, angular movement involving starting, stopping, and changes of direction, which enables a player without the ball to get free from defenders. All cuts should be preceded by a fake in the opposite direction. Cuts can be in front of the defender (front cut) or behind a defender (reverse or backdoor cut). A V-cut is a sharp, angular cut (in the shape of a V) used to clear an area for a pass.

All offensive movement should be purposeful—not aimless, wasted motion. An offensive player with the ball is constantly looking for open shots, passes, or drives. An offensive player without the ball is cutting and moving to get free or to set a screen for a teammate. Of course, offensive team patterns or plays are a means of regulating and structuring every player's movement on the floor.

Individual Defense

Defense involves preventing a team from scoring or, at least, limiting the maneuvering ability of the offensive team. Defense is as important as offense, but is considered less glamorous than scoring baskets. It requires hard work, concentration, and determination. Body balance is the key to good defense. The feet must be ready to move, preventing leaning and reaching with the upper body. It is a general rule (with only a few exceptions) that a defensive player should try to stay positioned between the offensive opponent and the basket. Foot movement is accomplished by sliding, keeping the feet as close to the floor as possible to enable quick shifts in direction.

There are two general situations to consider in individual defense: guarding a player with the ball (a ball handler) and guarding a player without the ball.

Defense Against a Player With the Ball. Note the fundamental defensive stance (Figure 6-17) of the player: weight low and evenly distributed on the balls

Figure 6-17 Defensive stance.

of the feet, head up, knees flexed, arms flexed, hands relatively close to the body, palms up. The eyes should be focused on the opponent's hips rather than on the eyes or the ball. This prevents being faked out of position. Rather than reaching with the hands, a player should constantly be sliding the feet to maintain good body position. The arms should extend upward or outward from the body only to deflect a pass or a shot. The distance between the defensive player and the ball handler depends on the quickness and shooting range of the offensive player. Once a player stops dribbling, a very close defensive position should be established, with arms extended to prevent passes or a shot.

Defense Against a Player Without the Ball. It makes sense that a player without the ball is not an immediate scoring threat. Thus, in playing defense, you must work hard to prevent your opponent from *receiving* the ball. This is accomplished by keeping the player you are guarding and the ball in view at all times. Also, one arm should constantly be extended between the ball and your defender to "deny" the pass (Figure 6-18). If your opponent is not close enough to the ball to receive a pass, you may have to open up your body position, using your peripheral vision to keep the ball and your opponent in view. This position allows you to "help out" a teammate who has been beaten by an offensive player. Again, like defending a ball handler, you try to dictate and thwart your opponent's moves.

➤ **Practice/Organizational Suggestions for Individual Offense and Defense**

(Either the *offensive* or *defensive* portion can be emphasized.)

1. Cutting: B attempts to free himself for a pass from A by executing V-cuts, front cuts, or reverse cuts (backdoors). X works to deny the pass (Figure 6-19).

Individual Offense: After receiving a pass from A, B must do three offensive maneuvers en route to the basket for a shot (Example: jab step, reverse dribble, head fake). May add a defender.

2. Zigzag: Divide the court into thirds. Staying in her third of the court, the offensive player dribbles in a zigzag pattern down the floor. The defensive player stays with her, practicing good defensive form and position. *Variation:* The dribbler stops her dribble en route, making the defensive player move closer, straighten, and extend her arms (Figure 6-20).
3. Denial Defense: Both defensive players (X) work hard to deny any pass to the player they are guarding. A and B pass the ball back and forth trying to get it to the offensive players (Figure 6-21).
4. Denial in a Box: Within a 10-to 15-foot square, X must work hard to deny B from receiving a pass from A (Figure 6-22).

Modified and Lead-Up Games
Half-Court Basketball

Using the general rules of basketball that govern fouls, penalties, and general playing situations, a half-court game can be played involving two-on-two, three-on-three, four-on-four, and even five-on-five. Both teams shoot at the same basket. A throw-in from the center circle is used to start the game and to restart play after each score. If the ball changes hands (after a missed shot, steal, or pass interception), the team gaining possession must take the ball behind the free-throw extended before working it in for a shot. Games can be shortened by either time or point limits, with teams rotating to various courts.

Figure 6-18 Defense against players without the ball. Note the "help"-position defensive player.

Figure 6-19 Cutting.

Figure 6-22 Denial in a box.

Ten Pass

Assign teams of three to six players to areas of the gym with designated boundaries. The offensive team attempts to score a point by completing ten consecutive passes between team members. The defensive team tries to intercept the ball (without fouling). Each time an interception or offensive team violation (traveling, double dribble, etc.) occurs, or a point is scored, the offensive and defensive teams reverse positions. A foul committed by the defense results in a point for the offensive team. Play continues until one team scores ten points.

Sideline Basketball

Divide the class into two teams. Five players from each team are on the court playing regulation basketball. The remaining team members stand on the sidelines (one team on each side of the court). The court players can pass the ball to their sideline teammates to help move the ball down the court. The sideline players may not shoot the ball or cross the sideline. They may pass only to court players, not to other sideline players. At the end of a designated time period or point total, *or* after each scored basket, the court players move to the end of the line at the sideline and five new players become court players.

Fifteen-Player Basketball

Fifteen or more players can participate in this continuous-action game. The game begins with three offensive players (Os) working together in an attempt to score against two defensive players (Ds). Once a shot is taken, whether made or missed, every player (Os and Ds) attempts to rebound the ball. The successful rebounder passes the ball out to one of the wing players (Ws) and joins with this player and the opposite wing player to take the ball down the court to attempt to score against the two wing players at the other end of the court who have stepped in to play defense (new Ds). Players who did not get the rebound fill in the wing lines at their end of the court. Play continues up and down the court, with the successful rebounder continually involved in the offense. An intercepted pass by a defender is treated just like a rebound, with that player passing the ball to a wing and getting to continue down the floor on offense. Because there are no distinct teams, no score is kept. If the ball goes out-of-bounds, the player who

Figure 6-20 Zigzag.

Figure 6-21 Denial defense.

Figure 6-23 Fifteen-player basketball.

hustles to recover it gets to pass to the wing and continue as an offensive player (Figure 6-23).

Playing Strategy

Team Offense

Offensive tactics in basketball vary according to the defensive tactics employed by the opposing team. Thus the offensive patterns will vary so that the most efficient attack may be developed against the particular defense. Generally speaking, there are two types of offense: (1) that which is employed against the player-to-player defense and (2) that which is employed against the zone defense.

Offense Against a Player-to-Player Defense. The offense used against the player-to-player defense is a combination of passing and player movement. Even though the offense consists of five players, it is most common for only two or three players to work together for a shot while the others employ decoying or

rebounding roles. Against a player-to-player defense, it only takes one defensive player to falter to enable an open shot for the opposing offensive player. Working together to accomplish this, it is possible to do a give-and-go, a backdoor cut, or a variety of screens/picks. These maneuvers employ only two or three players and confuse the defense, putting them out of good defensive position. Of course, individual offensive moves such as cutting and driving may be incorporated also (Figures 6-24, 6-25, 6-26, and 6-27).

These maneuvers can be incorporated into set plays or used spontaneously in a freelance situation. Thus, five-player plays are actually a combination of two-and three-player maneuvers.

Offense Against a Zone Defense. The offense used against the zone defense is primarily one of moving the ball with short, quick passes to force the defensive

Figure 6-24 Give-and-go.

Figure 6-25 Pick (on-the-ball).

Figure 6-26 Pick (off-the-ball).

Figure 6-27 Backdoor cut.

players out of their assigned positions in order that a good shot may be taken. The offensive players move to positions that will force the defense to alter their zone and thus weaken its strength. Even if an offensive player gets past a defender, in a zone defense there is another defender waiting to cover. Therefore, the following principles should guide the offense in defeating the zone defense:

1. Quick passing
2. Outside shooting
3. Penetrate the zone with a dribble or a pass, then quickly pass out to a free teammate
4. Cut through the zone, splitting two defenders
5. Overload one side of the zone with more offensive players than defensive players
6. Dribble very sparingly
7. Screen a shifting defensive player

Team Defense

The Zone Defense. This style of defense calls for the placement of the defensive players in designated areas in and around the defensive basket in order to give a maximum protection against good shots. The alignments are numbered. The alignment selected must take into consideration the size, speed, and abilities of the players, as well as the area of the court desired to be covered. The most common zone defenses are the 2–1–2, the 2–3, the 1–3–1, and the 1–2–2. Each player in zone defense is assigned a certain area on the court to cover and guards only that offensive player who comes into that area. The defense shifts in relation to the ball, rather than in relation to the position of the offensive players. The zone defense is valuable in securing rebounds, in cutting off inside shooting against taller opponents, and in protecting players who are tired, weak defensively, or in foul trouble (Figures 6-28 and 6-29).

The Player-to-Player Defense. The principle behind the player-to-player defense is the assignment of each player to guard one offensive player, and thus the area element that is prominent in the zone defense is eliminated. Instead of shifting as a unit in relation to the position of the ball, each player must follow one player all over the defensive court. This defense takes extraordinary skill, stamina, and teamwork, since any free offensive player is a scoring threat. Because the offensive team will be working screens, picks, and cuts to free a teammate, the defense must communicate and have tactics to avoid such maneuvers. One such tactic involves immediate on-the-floor switching of defensive assignments if an offensive player has gotten free. Another tactic involves defensive players allowing room for each

Figure 6-28 The 2–1–2 zone defense.

Figure 6-29 The shift of the 2–1–2 zone, with the ball passed to B.

other to slide through picks and screens, enabling them to stay with their assigned players.

The Pressing Defense. In recent years, pressing defenses have taken on great significance at all levels of basketball competition. The main objectives of pressing defenses are to harass opponents into ball-handling errors, to force opponents into changing their game strategy, and to force the offensive team to use up valuable time in bringing the ball down the court. The press can be administered full-court, ½ court, or ½ court, and can incorporate zone or player-to-player principles.

Modifications for Special Populations

Orthopedically Impaired

1. Contact the National Wheelchair Basketball Association for rules and specific information at their Web site, www.NWBA.org.
2. Students with difficulties grasing and releasing the ball can practice dropping smaller balls into hoops, wastebaskets, or buckets. Use beanbags or other small objects if student cannot grip a small ball.
3. For students with severe limitations, consider using commercial "Near Basketball" games.
4. Consider allowing students without disabilities to shoot from seated position on a bench or desk chair.
5. Make sure to discuss spacing issues if you allow the student using a wheelchair to participate on the floor during a game with those who are ambulatory. Wheelchair users need extra space so, for example, you might create a 3-foot rule; that

is, no one is allowed to guard the individual using a wheelchair by closer than 3 feet.

Cognitively Impaired

1. Special Olympics has a well-defined basketball program. Ask for their manual on basketball rules.
2. Concentrate on concepts of the game, such as offense, defense, and transition. Allow the students to "travel" if it promotes play. Specific rules of the game will evolve as the unit continues.

Sensory Impaired

1. Minimal modifications are needed for the student who is deaf or hearing impaired. Consider hand signals for your teaching prompts.
2. Individual considerations must be taken into account to determine the appropriateness of basketball for students who are visually impaired. Consider checking for resources on the game of Goalball for the blind or visually impaired. You can access that information at www.usaba.org.

Terminology

Backcourt players (Guards) Players who set up a team's offensive pattern; usually the smaller players on the team or the best ball handlers.

Backdoor An offensive maneuver whereby a player cuts toward the baseline to the basket, behind the defenders, and receives a pass for a field goal attempt.

Baseline The endline.

Blocking out (Boxing out) A term used to designate a player's position under the backboard that prevents an opposing player from achieving good rebounding position.

Charging Personal contact against a stationary defender by a player with the ball. This becomes a personal foul against the offensive player.

Corner players (Forwards) Tall players who are responsible for the rebounding and shooting phases of the team's operation. They usually position themselves closer to the basket than the guards.

Cut A quick offensive move by a player trying to get free for a pass.

Denial defense Aggressive individual defense where the defensive player works hard to keep the offensive player from receiving a pass.

Double foul When two opponents commit personal fouls against each other at the same time. The result is a throw-in for the team entitled, as a result of the alternating jump ball process.

Dribble Ball movement by a player in control who throws or taps the ball in the air or onto the floor and then touches it. The dribble ends when the dribbler touches the ball with both hands simultaneously, permits it to come to rest while in contact with it, or loses control.

Drive An aggressive move toward the basket by a player with the ball.

Fake (Feint) Using a deceptive move with the ball to pull the defensive player out of position.

Fast break Moving the ball quickly downcourt in order to score before the defense can set up.

Field goal A basket scored from the field.

Freelance No structure or set plays in the offense.

Free throw The privilege given a player to score one or two points by unhindered shots for a goal from within the free-throw circle and behind the free-throw line.

Give-and-go A maneuver in which the offensive player makes a pass to a teammate, and then immediately cuts in toward the basket for a return pass.

Held ball Occurs when two opponents have one or both hands firmly on the ball, and neither can gain possession without undue roughness. The result is a throw-in for the team entitled, as a result of the alternating jump ball process.

Inside player (Center, Post, Pivot) Most often the tallest player on the team. This player is situated near the basket, around the three-second lane area, and is responsible for rebounding and close-range shooting.

Jump ball A method of putting the ball into play to start the game or any overtime periods by tossing it up between two opponents in the center circle. In jump ball situations that occur (due to held ball, double foul, etc.) once the game has begun teams will alternate taking the ball out-of-bounds. The team not obtaining control of the initial jump ball will start the alternating process.

Outlet pass A term used to designate a direct pass from a rebounder to a teammate, with the main objective being the start of a fast break.

Overtime period An extra period of playing time (5 minutes in college; 3 minutes in high school) if the score is tied at the end of the regulation game.

Personal foul A player foul that involves contact with an opponent while the ball is alive or after the ball is in possession of a player for a throw-in.

Pick A special type of screen where an offensive player stands so the defensive player slides to make contact, freeing an offensive teammate for a shot or drive.

Pivot Takes place when a player who is holding the ball steps once or more than once in any direction with the same foot, the other foot, called the pivot foot, is kept at its point of contact with the floor. Also, another term for the inside player.

Posting up A player cutting to the three-second lane area, pausing, and anticipating a pass.

Rebound A term usually applied when the ball bounces off the backboard or basket after a missed shot.

Restraining circles Three circles of six-foot radius, one located in the center of the court and one located at each of the free-throw lines.

Running time Not letting the clock stop for fouls or violations, usually used in a recreational situation.

Screen An offensive maneuver where an offensive player is positioned between the defender and a teammate in order to free the teammate for an uncontested shot.

Switching A reversal of defensive guarding assignments.

Technical foul A noncontact foul by a player, team, or coach for unsportsmanlike behavior or failure to abide by rules regarding submission of lineups, uniform numbering, and substitution procedures.

Telegraphing a pass Indicating where you are going to pass by looking or signaling.

Throw-in A method of putting the ball in play from out-of-bounds.

Traveling When a player in possession of the ball within bounds progresses illegally in any direction (e.g., taking steps with the ball without dribbling).

Violation An infraction of the rules resulting in a throw-in from out-of-bounds for the opponents.

Further References

Basketball Rule Book, published yearly by the National Federation of State High School Associations, P.O. Box 690, Indianapolis, IN 46206.

Head-Summitt, P. and Jennings, D. *Basketball: Fundamentals and Team Play*. 2nd ed. New York: McGraw-Hill, 1996.

Krause, J. *Basketball*. New York: McGraw-Hill, 1999.

Krause, J., Meyer, D. and Meyer, J. *Basketball Skills and Drills*. 2nd ed. Champaign, IL: Human Kinetics, 1999.

NCAA Men's and Women's Basketball Rules and Interpretations, published yearly by the National Collegiate Athletic Association, P.O. Box 6222, Indianapolis, IN 46206.

Scott, J. *The Basketball Book*. Needham Heights, MA: Allyn & Bacon, 2001.

Stier, W. *Coaching Modern Basketball: Hints, Strategies and Tactics*. Needham Heights, MA: Allyn & Bacon, 1997.

Wissel, H. *Basketball: Steps to Success*. Champaign, IL: Human Kinetics, 1994.

Audio-Visual Materials

Duke Basketball Video Series. 1999. Titles include: *Team Defense, Transition Game* and *Championship Practices*. From Human Kinetics, P.O. Box 5076, Champaign, IL 61825-5076. 800-747-4457.

Interactive Basketball Skills and Drills. 2000. (CD-ROM: 2 discs) by Jerry Krause. From Human Kinetics, P.O. Box 5076, Champaign, IL 61825-5076. 800-747-4457.

National Basketball Association (NABC) video series. 2001. Titles include: *Shooting Fundamentals, Defending and Rebounding Fundamentals,* and *Ballhandling Fundamentals.* From Human Kinetics, P.O. Box 5076, Champaign, IL 61825-5076. 800-747-4457.

NCAA Basketball. 1992. Produced by the National Collegiate Athletic Association and featuring some of the league's top coaches, this video series teaches techniques and drills that have been used to train consistently top-ranked teams. The specific titles are *Individual Defense, Rebounding, Defense-Pivot Man, Ball Handling and Dribbling, Passing Techniques, Shooting,* and *Offensive Post Play.* From Insight Media, 2162 Broadway, P.O. Box 621, New York, NY 10024-0621. 800-233-9910.

Web Sites

www.findhoops.com Has over 5,000 basketball links to teams at all levels, statistics, products, books, players, software, officiating, and organizations.

www.ncaa.org The home page of the National Collegiate Athletic Association, the regulatory organization for all collegiate athletics, including basketball. Has photos, features, game results, schedules, interviews with players and coaches.

www.nfhs.org The home page of the National Federation of State High School Associations. Has current news, rules information, sports materials, publications, and resources for basketball.

CHAPTER 7

Bowling

This chapter will enable you to

- Select a proper fitting bowling ball and a pair of bowling shoes
- Bowl a game according to the official rules of the American Bowling Congress
- Practice and use the four-step approach and delivery, the straight ball, and the hook ball
- Score a complete game using the appropriate symbols to indicate the line score
- Improve your strategy by converting spares
- Understand the terminology, observe safety rules, and utilize proper etiquette associated with the sport

Nature and Purpose

Bowling appeals to people of all ages and is easily adapted for special populations. Because a relatively small expenditure of energy is required in bowling, it is not an activity that lends itself to the development of physical fitness. However, participants may bowl for years after more strenuous activities have been abandoned, and fortunately, any person who has a degree of motor fitness can enjoy bowling as a lifetime sport.

The typical bowling center has become an almost 24-hour enterprise. It caters to housewives' leagues in the morning, to junior leagues in the afternoon, to leagues (separate or mixed) for men and women in the evening, and to late-night–early-morning bowlers who work the second shift. Most establishments are clean and well kept, thus providing suitable entertainment places for the whole family.

The modern game of tenpins is played on indoor wooden lanes, 60 feet long from the foul line to the center of the number one pin, and 41 or not more than 42 inches wide (Figure 7-1). The tenpins are set up (or "spotted") in a diamond formation on pin spots 12 inches apart, center to center (Figure 7-2A). A regulation tenpin is 15 inches high, with a diameter of 2½ inches at the base. Pins are constructed of clear, hard maple and are usually coated with a plastic outer covering. They must conform to American Bowling Congress specifications. The object of the game is to roll the ball down the lane and knock down all the pins located in the diamond formation.

The lane is bordered on either side by gutters that prevent an errant ball from moving into an adjacent lane. It is constructed of two types of wood: maple, a hardwood to take the constant punishment of the ball, and pine, a soft wood that aids in gripping the ball. As shown in Figure 7-2B, a lane has several markings, some of which appear to be off the lane (the approach area). All of the marks serve as points of reference for the bowler. The initial sets of dots, found in the approach area, serve as a point of reference for the bowler. The set of points in arrow formation beyond the foul line serve as a point of reference for aiming the ball.

Equipment and Facilities

Bowling is one of the few sports that a participant can enjoy without having to buy expensive equipment. For the recreational or occasional bowler, bowling centers provide "house balls," and shoes may be rented for a small fee. However, if you are planning to become a regular bowler, it is best to own your own equipment. Studies indicate that men and women who own their own equipment have higher bowling averages. Basically, all the bowler needs is a ball, a carrying bag, and a good pair of bowling shoes.

For a school physical education class, it would be expensive and impractical to have bowling lanes in the gymnasium. Several companies manufacture bowling sets consisting of plastic bowling pins, a plastic sheet on which to place the pins for proper distance and placement, and a hollow rubber bowling ball containing several holes so the learner can properly fit the ball to the hand. Markings and distances can be measured and painted on the floor with a water-based paint for easy removal. Many techniques

Figure 7-1 Lane dimensions.

Figure 7-2 (A) Position and number of pins.
(B) Lane markings.

can be learned in the gymnasium before proceeding to the bowling center.

Bowling Ball

Choosing a Ball. Bowling balls are made of hard rubber or plastic and come in a variety of colors. The hard rubber ball is black and is the type of ball found in most bowling centers. Although all bowling balls are the same size, 27 inches in diameter, the weight varies from 8 to 16 pounds. When selecting a ball,

the beginner should choose the weight that feels most comfortable. Young junior bowlers use a light ball, women generally use a ball that weighs 10 to 13 pounds, and men usually use a ball weighing 14 to 16 pounds. The primary considerations in making your decision should be comfort and how well you can control the ball. If you consistently use a house ball, find a ball that best fits you. House balls are marked with an identification number and the weight; try to use the same ball each time you bowl.

Fitting the Ball. It is also important to select a ball equipped with holes that fit your fingers. Balls are drilled with three holes, one for the thumb and two for the third and fourth fingers. If you buy your own ball, the ball is fitted to your hand span. This ensures

Figure 7-3 Position of fingers in three-hole ball.

a proper fit that will allow you to handle the ball fairly easily. The holes should be large enough for the fingers to slip in and out with ease. The thumb hole should be comfortably loose. The bowler should be able to turn the ball around the thumb without binding, grabbing, or excessive rubbing of the skin.

To determine the proper fit, the bowler must decide the type of grip that will be used. There are three grips: the conventional, the semi-fingertip, and the full fingertip. Advanced bowlers use the latter two grips; beginners should use the conventional grip since it is the easiest to control. To determine proper hand span for the conventional grip, place the thumb completely in the thumb hole, keeping the fingers relaxed and spread over the finger holes. The crease of the second joint of the two middle fingers should extend ¼-inch beyond the inside edge of the finger holes (Figure 7-3). The finger holes are cut at a certain pitch or angle to aid the bowler in grasping the ball.

In practice bowling sets used in most schools, the hollow rubber ball generally comes with several finger holes in order to accommodate the various hand spans.

Bowling Shoes

Another important item on the bowler's list of equipment is proper footwear. At first glance, both shoes of a pair of bowling shoes look the same. Closer inspection of the soles of the shoe will reveal a difference. For the right-handed bowler, the left shoe should have a leather sole, to facilitate sliding at the release

point, and a rubber heel; the right shoe should have a rubber sole with a leather tip, and a rubber heel. For the left-handed bowler, the order is reversed. Most bowling centers have rental shoes for both right-handed and left-handed bowlers. Whether the bowler rents shoes or owns them, it is important to check the soles for any substance that will not allow the bowler to slide during the delivery. Fine sandpaper can be used to clean off sticky substances or rough places that may impede sliding.

For the physical education class, it is important that students wear smooth-soled shoes that enable sliding during the approach and release. Crepe soles or heavy-treaded rubber soles such as used in jogging shoes would be inappropriate.

Ball Bag

The serious bowler and the bowler who owns equipment should have a bag in which to store and carry the ball. Bags come in a variety of materials; those made of plastic, vinyl, or canvas are the least expensive. Many discount department stores have bags on sale regularly.

Basic Rules

In league or tournament play, two contiguous lanes are used, and the bowling of ten complete frames on these lanes constitutes an official game. Members of contesting teams successively and in regular order bowl one frame on one lane and the next frame on the other lane, so alternating frames until the game is completed. Each player bowls two balls in each frame. If a strike is made on the first ball, the second ball is not rolled (except that in the tenth frame if a strike or spare is made, the player immediately rolls on the same lane the additional balls or ball to which the strike or spare entitles him).

In case of a tie game, each team bowls an extra complete frame on the same lane in which the tenth frame was bowled. The extra frame is bowled and scored in exactly the same manner as the tenth frame. If a tie still exists at the completion of the first extra frame, the teams must change lanes for the additional frames that may be required to determine the winner.

It is a foul if a bowler permits any part of his foot, hand, or arm, while in contact with the lanes or runways, to rest upon or extend beyond the foul line at any time after the ball leaves his hands and passes beyond the foul line. No count is made on a foul ball, and any pins knocked down are immediately respotted. A foul ball counts as a ball bowled by the player. If a player commits a foul that is apparent to both captains, one or more members of each of the opposing teams competing in a league or tournament on the same pair of lanes where the foul is committed, and the foul is not seen by the foul judge or umpire, or recorded by an automatic foul-detecting device, a foul shall nevertheless be declared and so recorded.

Pinfall—Legal

Every ball delivered by the player shall count, unless declared a dead ball. Pins must then be respotted after the cause for declaring such dead ball has been removed.

1. Pins knocked down by another pin or pins rebounding in play from the side partition or rear cushion are counted as pins down.
2. If, when rolling at a full setup or in order to make a spare, it is discovered immediately after the ball has been delivered that one or more pins are improperly set, although not missing, the ball and resulting pinfall shall be counted. It is each player's responsibility to detect any misplacement of pins and have the setup corrected before he bowls.
3. Pins knocked down by a fair ball, and that remain lying on the lane or in the gutters, or that lean so as to touch kickbacks or side partitions, are termed dead wood and counted as pins down, and must be removed before the next ball is bowled.

Pinfall—Illegal

When any of the following incidents occur, the ball counts as a ball rolled, but pins knocked down shall not count.

1. When pins are knocked down or displaced by a ball that leaves the lanes before reaching the pins
2. When a ball rebounds from the rear cushion
3. When pins come in contact with the body, arms, or legs of a pinsetter and rebound
4. A standing pin that falls upon removing dead wood or that is knocked down by a pinsetter or mechanical pinsetting equipment shall not count and must be replaced on the pin spot where it originally stood before delivery of the ball.
5. Pins that are bowled off the lane, rebound, and remain standing on the lane must be counted as pins standing.
6. If in delivering the ball a foul is committed, any pins knocked down by such delivery shall not be counted.

Bowling on Wrong Lane

When only one player or the leadoff players of both teams bowl on the wrong lane and the error is discovered before another player has bowled, a dead ball shall be declared and the player, or players, required to bowl on the correct lane. When more than

one player on the same team has rolled on the wrong lane, the game shall be completed without adjustment, and the next game shall be started on the correctly scheduled lane.

Scoring

All players should learn how to score. It adds considerably to the enjoyment of the game if the player can keep an accurate record of the score as the game progresses. There are ten numbered boxes on the score sheet to correspond to the ten frames in a game. At the top of each frame box are two small squares in which to write the number of pins toppled with the first ball and the second ball. Some simple scoring rules must be remembered in order to score a game accurately.

1. The score that is entered from box to box is cumulative; i.e., it represents the total number of pins toppled up to that point.
2. If a bowler does not get a strike or spare in any frame, scoring is just a matter of adding on the number of pins knocked down in each frame.
3. If all pins are knocked down with the first ball, it is called a *strike* and a cross (X) is marked in the small square in the upper right-hand corner of the frame box. The strike will count 10 pins plus the number of pins knocked down on the next two successive balls. A score will not be entered in the frame box until those two balls have been rolled.
4. If all pins are knocked down with two balls, it is called a *spare* and is indicated by a diagonal mark (/). The spare will count 10 pins plus the number of pins knocked down on the next ball rolled. A score will not be entered in the frame box until the next ball has been rolled.
5. If you spare or strike in the tenth frame, then you roll one more ball if a spare, or two more balls if a strike, and add that to your total score.

In order to illustrate scoring, we will score a hypothetical game. But first let's review the symbols used and the scoring procedure.

(X) Indicates a *strike:* 10 plus the score of the next two balls.
(/) Indicates a *spare:* 10 plus the score of the next ball rolled.
(O) Indicates a *split:* score will depend on number of remaining pins knocked down by next ball rolled.
(Ø) Indicates a *converted split:* 10 plus the score of the next ball rolled.
(-) Indicates a *miss or error:* no score.
(F) Indicates a *foul:* no score.
(G) Indicates a *gutter ball.*

The score sheet of a completed game is shown and analyzed in Figure 7-4.

Frame	1st ball	2nd ball	Total score
1.	7 pins Enter score in first square	2 pins	9 pins
2.	5 pins	3 pins	17—cumulative score of first score of first two frames: 9 + 8 = 17
3.	Strike. Enter (X) in first square		46—2 strikes (20) + 9 pins (see frame five) + 17 = 46
4.	Strike (X)		65—Strike (10) + 9 + 46 = 65
5.	9 pins—add to the two consecutive strikes	Miss (–) no pins	74 (65 + 9)
6.	8 pins	Spare. Enter (/) in second square	89—Spare (10) + 5 pins + 74 = 98
7.	5 pins—add to spare from frame six	4 pins	89 + 9 pins = 98
8.	9 pins	(–) no pins	98 + 9 = 107
9.	7 pins—a split	(O) no pins, missed converting the split	107 + 7 = 114
10.	Strike (X)—Player rolls two more balls, which are also strikes		114 + 3 strikes (30) = 144

Figure 7-4 Scoring example and score sheet of a complete game.

Suggested Learning Sequence

A. Nature of the game
 1. Equipment
 2. Fitting a bowling ball
 3. Safety: Lane courtesy
B. Techniques. Rules should be introduced early in the learning progression to coincide with specific techniques.
 1. Stance
 2. Approach
 3. Straight ball
 4. Hook ball
C. Scoring. May be introduced as the situation warrants and is most appropriate.
D. Strategy
 1. Pin bowling and Spot bowling
 2. Making spares

Skills and Techniques

Bowling is a relatively easy game to learn, but like all sporting activities, it is important to learn the techniques involved in order to develop consistency. For the physical education teacher, much of the technique involving the grip, stance, approach, and release can be taught in the gymnasium. The basic skill to be learned is the swing coordinated with a specific number of steps.

The Stance

There is no definite or prescribed stance assumed by all bowlers preparatory for the start of the approach. However, there are some important points to remember.

1. Hold the ball with both hands in front of the body. For a man this may be waist high, for a woman a little higher in order to attain a longer swing for increased speed.
2. The feet are spread slightly apart, weight evenly distributed, perhaps one foot slightly ahead of the other.
3. Most of the weight of the ball should be supported by the nonthrowing hand at this point.
4. The ball is gripped with the thumb in a 12 o'clock position for a straight ball or the 10 o'clock position for a hook ball.

The Approach

Bowlers vary in the number of steps taken in the approach. The number of steps range from three to five, but most experts recommend the four-step approach. The beginning bowler should experiment with the delivery and determine which works best. The following discussion will center around the four-step approach for the right-handed bowler. The left-handed bowler will reverse the starting procedure.

In proper execution of the approach, the bowler will take a series of steps in a smooth, rhythmical manner, and will end with a slide and follow-through as the ball is released. Women bowlers begin on the 12-foot line with feet straddling the second dot from the right for right-handers or the second dot from the left for left-handers. The eyes should be fixed on the second arrow from the right (right-hander) or left (left-hander) located on the lane. Men will begin the approach approximately 18 inches farther back from the 12-foot line. As the steps are taken and the delivery is executed, it is important for the bowler to walk in a straight line. Let the dots near the foul line be your guide.

➤ Learning Hints

Step 1. The push away. Step with the right foot and at the same time push the ball out to an arm's length in front of the body. Do not overextend the push away, or loss of balance and direction may result.

Step 2. The ball moves to the bottom of the arc on the downswing as the left foot completes the second step.

Step 3. The ball reaches the top of the backswing (shoulder high) as the right foot completes the third step. The ball must swing in a straight line, shoulders square to the foul line.

Step 4. As the last step is taken, the ball swings forward, the wrist is firm, and the ball is released toward the target. The nonthrowing hand will help serve as a means of balance. The left toe will be pointing at the target.

If the timing is correct, the ball is released out in front of the body and laid rather than dropped on the lane. The bowling ball, when properly delivered, has a double motion. When first released, it slides and revolves, sliding in the direction toward the pins. After sliding a distance, once it reaches the nonoiled surface, friction increases, and the ball begins to revolve, causing it to hook, roll straight, or back up, depending on the type of ball that is thrown.

➤ Practice/Organizational Suggestions

1. Allow students to move to the ball rack and demonstrate proper technique for picking up the ball.
2. Pick up the ball and assume a good, well-balanced stance with ball held comfortably and in proper position.
3. From a designated line on the floor or on the approach, try a four-step approach without the ball. To determine the length of your approach, move to a position short of the foul line and take four steps toward the beginning position. Try to coordinate steps, arm swing, and follow-through without the ball. Check the line from step one to step four.
4. Bellisimo recommends a one-step delivery with a ball.[1] Place students in a position to take the last step. Allow them to first take a practice swing with a ball, then allow students to take the last step and delivery. Concentrate on a straight pendulum swing and a good follow-through with the hand finishing high.
5. Allow bowlers to try a four-step approach and delivery using the ball (Figure 7-5).

The Straight Ball

Beginning bowlers should concentrate first on perfecting a straight ball before attempting to roll a hook. It is also recommended that the woman bowler who lacks ball speed continue the use of a straight ball.

➤ Learning Hints

1. The thumb should be held in a 12 o'clock position with the fingers underneath the ball.
2. The hand position should be maintained throughout the swing, with no arm rotation during release of the ball.
3. The wrist remains firm, and the palm faces the pins as the ball is delivered; maintain a straight follow-through.
4. The ball should be started from the right side of the lane and directed toward the 1-3 pocket.

The Hook Ball

Most good bowlers use a hook ball; beginning bowlers will want to learn this delivery as soon as possible. To obtain maximum pin action, the ball should strike the pins at an angle, but the angle of the straight ball is limited by the width of the alley. The straight ball revolves forward, but the hook ball revolves at an angle, thus giving it greater pin splash or action by imparting a revolving action to the pins. This delivery is sometimes called the "handshake"

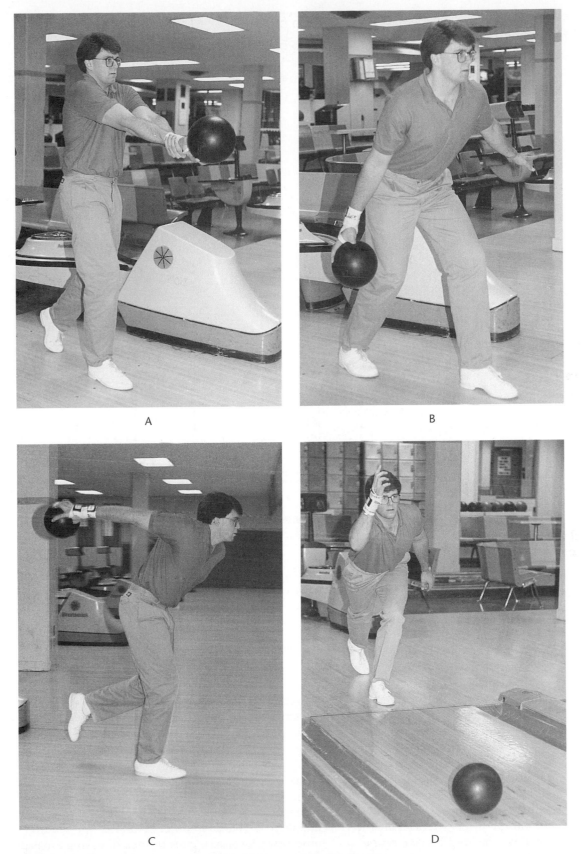

A

B

C

D

Figure 7-5 Four-step approach. Note shoulders squarely facing the pins.

delivery because the position of the hand is similar to that used in an ordinary handshake.

➤ Learning Hints

1. The wrist is firm, the thumb is in a 10:30 o'clock position. This position must be maintained throughout the swing.

2. As the ball is released, the thumb comes out first, and the fingers lift and impart a rotational effect to the ball.

3. Release the ball with the V formed by the thumb and forefinger pointing toward the target.

4. The hand should be carried upward and forward toward the pins in the follow-through. Do not side-wheel, twist the arm, or intentionally spin the ball.

There are two other types of deliveries: the curve ball and the backup ball. However, because of the difficulty of controlling them, they are not recommended for the beginning bowler.

➤ Practice/Organizational Suggestions

1. For the physical education class, use partners. Using a hollow plastic ball, roll a straight ball or a hook to each other. Concentrate on proper wrist and hand position as well as swing consistency.

2. At the lanes, practice the swing first, holding the ball in the correct position. Some experts recommend rolling the ball back and forth between partners to practice the proper release technique.

3. The bowler will continue to roll the ball over the second arrow from the right (right-hander). However, experiment with your starting position by moving over one or two boards toward the left to find the most consistent path for your hook (Figure 7-6).

Playing Strategy

Spot Bowling and Pin Bowling

An individual sport, bowling has no complicated playing strategies similar to those found in many team sports. You should plan your game so as to knock down the greatest number of pins possible. This is accomplished by individual control and accuracy, rather than cooperation with teammates in the execution of plays.

Playing strategy should include, first, a mastery of a definite approach and delivery style. The good bowler will settle upon a definite pattern as early as possible, making every effort to throw each ball with the same motion. Most bowlers are classified as "spot" or "pin" bowlers. The spot bowler selects a spot on the alley a few feet from the foul line and attempts to roll the first ball in each frame over that spot. The pin bowler looks at the pins while approaching and making the delivery. Whether you

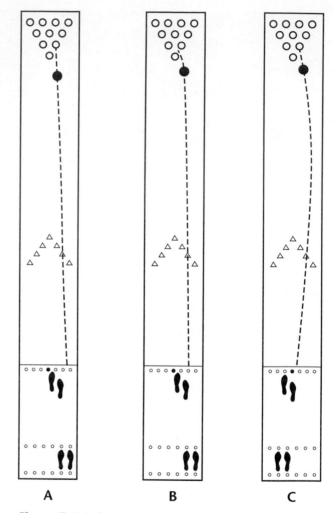

Figure 7-6 Paths of (A) straight ball, (B) hook ball, and (C) curve ball.

prefer throwing a hook or a straight ball, follow your selected style on all balls and concentrate on developing accuracy with a smooth and rhythmical delivery.

Spares

To bowl a good score, the bowler must pick up spares consistently. Accuracy is essential for good spare bowling. Unlike rolling a strike ball, the spare may force the bowler to vary the starting position and the spot over which the ball may be rolled. For the right-handed bowler, when pins are left on the right side of the lane—such as the 1, 3, 6, 10 or 3, 5, 6, 9, 10—the starting position should be on the left side of the lane. For pins on the left side, the ball will be delivered from the right side of the lane. Pins that are left one directly behind another should be hit head-on; otherwise, the bowler runs the risk of having the ball glance off the front pin, thereby missing the rear pin. Conversion of spares will make a marked difference in your scores; practice and experience are two important factors in increasing the score.

Modifications for Special Populations

Orthopedically Impaired

1. Use commercially adapted bowling ramps made from the following: wood, aluminum, or plastic. Consider making your own ramps using carpet roll cardboard cores. The diameter of the core will dictate the size of the ball used in the bowling session; for example, for a 5-inch core, you will use a tennis ball or softball.
2. Use push sticks, either commercial or home made.
3. Use special bowling balls made with retractable handles.

Cognitively Impaired

1. Minimal modifications are needed. You might use similar adaptations suggested in the previous section for those with orthopedic limitations.
2. Allow a lot of practice time.
3. Reinforce students with additional tactile and kinesthetic input during delivery.
4. Contact your local Special Olympics office for bowling leagues in your area.

Sensory Impaired

1. Use variations on the approach:
   a. Mark the pattern of approach with carpet squares or floor tape.
   b. Use the ramp previously mentioned; however, ask the student how to reposition the ramp after each delivery. The sighted aide should explain which pins still need to be knocked down, and the student with a visual impairment should be required to adjust the ramp using verbal cues.

Ot her Considerations

Lane Etiquette

As in other sporting activities, certain playing courtesies should be extended to your bowling competitors and teammates.

1. Do not talk to or otherwise disturb a bowler who is on the approach and ready to bowl.
2. Do not walk in front of a bowler to secure your ball from the rack when the bowler is ready to bowl. Wait for your ball to return.
3. When bowlers on adjacent lanes are both ready to bowl, the one on the right (as you face the pins) should always be permitted to bowl first.
4. Do not use a ball that is the personal property of an individual unless you have the owner's permission to do so.

5. Be at your post, ready to bowl, when your turn comes.
6. After delivering the ball and noting the result, turn and walk back immediately to the rear of the runway, being careful to stay in your approach lane.
7. Do not argue with the foul line judge over decisions even though you think an unjust call has been made against you.
8. Be punctual when scheduled to bowl. Nothing upsets a team more than having to wait for a late member.
9. Control your temper. Public exhibition of anger disturbs fellow bowlers and detracts from your efficiency.

Safety

Bowling is a relatively safe activity. Accidents are few, and good common sense will prevent them from occurring. The following are a few guidelines for safe bowling.

1. With a large class, plan formations well in advance so there is plenty of space between each participant during the approach, backswing, forward swing, and follow-through.
2. Be aware of people around you; swing the ball only on the designated alley.
3. Check to make sure the approaches are free of oily or rough substances that may interfere with the approach.
4. Use a towel to wipe the ball or dry your hands before each roll. A ball can become oily from the lanes, and the oil may get on your hands.
5. When picking up the ball from the rack, always keep your palms perpendicular to the sides of the bowling rack (Figure 7-7).

Figure 7-7 Proper method of picking up a ball from the rack.

6. Be aware of your fellow competitors; make sure the approach area is cleared before rolling the ball.

7. If students are used to set the pins, make sure the pinsetter is clear of the alley before rolling the ball.

Terminology

Anchor The person who shoots last on a team.

Baby split The 2-7 or 3-10 split.

Backup A reverse hook. The ball rotates toward the right for a right-handed bowler and toward the left for a left-handed bowler.

Bed posts The 7-10 split.

Blow An error; missing a spare that is not a split.

Box The same as a frame.

Brooklyn A cross-over ball, one that strikes the 1-2 pocket (i.e., crosses over to the other side of the head pin opposite the side it was thrown).

Bucket The 2-4-5-8 or 3-5-6-9 leaves after the first throw.

Cherry Chopping off the front pin on a spare.

Double Two strikes in succession.

Double pinochle The 4-6-7-10 split, also known as the *big four*.

Dutch 200 (Dutchman) A score of 200 made by alternating strikes and spares for entire game.

Foul To touch or go beyond the foul line in delivering the ball.

Frame The box in which scores are entered. There are ten frames to each game.

Gutter ball A ball that drops into either gutter. (Also a channel ball.)

Handicap A bonus score or score adjustment awarded to an individual or team based on averages.

Head pin The number one pin.

High hit Hitting the head pin full in the face or head-on.

Hook A ball that breaks to the left for a right-handed bowler. For a left-hander, a hook ball breaks to the right.

Jersey side Same as a Brooklyn.

Kegler Synonym for *bowler*, derived from the German *Kegel* (game of ninepins).

Lane A bowling alley.

Lane bed Surface on which the ball is rolled.

Leave Pin or pins left standing after a throw.

Light hit Hitting the head pin lightly to the right or left side.

Line A complete game as recorded on the score sheet.

LPBT Ladies Professional Bowlers Tour.

Mark making a strike or spare in a frame.

Open frame A frame in which no mark is made; at least one pin remains standing after rolling both balls in a frame.

PBA Professional Bowlers Association.

Pocket Space between the head pin and pins on either side (1-3 pins for the left-hander and the 1-2 pins for the right-hander).

Railroad Another term for a split. There are several kinds.

Sleeper A pin hidden from view.

Spare All pins knocked down on two balls.

Split A leave, after the first ball has been thrown, in which the number one pin plus a second pin are down, and eight pins remain standing. Indicated by 0 on score sheet.

Spot Series of dots or arrows on the alley at which a bowler aims.

Spot bowling Method using arrows or dots on the alley as targets as opposed to looking at the pins during the throw.

Strike All pins knocked down by the first ball.

Striking out Obtaining three strikes in the last frame.

Tap When a pin is left standing on an apparently perfect hit.

Turkey Three strikes in a row.

WIBC Women's International Bowling Congress.

Reference

1. Bellisimo, L. and Bennett, J. *The Bowler's Manual.* 4th ed. Englewood Cliffs, NJ: Prentice Hall, 1982, p. 10.

Further References

American Association for Health, Physical Education, Recreation, and Dance: Division of Girls' and Women's Sport. *Official Bowling, Fencing and Golf Guide.* Washington, D.C.: AAHPERD.

American Bowling Congress. *ABC Bowling Guide* (current ed.). Milwaukee: American Bowling Congress, 1572 East Capitol Drive.

Bellisimo, L. and Bennett, J. *The Bowlers Manual.* 4th ed. Englewood Cliffs, NJ: Prentice Hall, 1982.

Blassingame, C. and Ross, T. *Success in Bowling.* Dubuque, IA: Kendall/Hunt Publishing, 1991.

Bohn, Parker and Herbst, Dan. *Bowling: How to Master the Game.* Englewood, NJ: Universe Books, 2000.

Carlson, Gerald P. and Blackwith, E. Harold. *Bowling Basics: A Step by Step Approach.* 4th ed. Dubuque, IA: Kendall/Hunt Publishing, 1997.

Costello, P. and Glossbrenner, A. *Bowling.* New York: Mason/Charter, 1977.

Durbin, Mike and Herbst, Dan. *From Gutterballs to Strikes: Correcting 101 Common Bowling Errors.* Chicago: NTC/Contemporary Publishing, 1997.

Edgington, C. *Bowling.* Dubuque, IA: Eddie Bowers Publishing Co., Inc., 1992.

Grinfelds, V. and Hultstrand, B. *Right Down Your Alley: The Complete Book of Bowling.* 3rd ed. Englewood, CO: Morton Publishing Company, 1992.

Mackey, R. *Bowling.* 5th ed. Mountain View, CA: Mayfield Publishing, 1993.

Scott, T. M. and Carpenter, C. L. *Bowling Everyone.* Winston-Salem, NC: Hunter Books, 1985.

Showers, N. E. *Bowling.* Santa Monica, CA: Goodyear Publishing Co., 1980.

Strickland, R. H. *Bowling—Steps to Success.* 2nd ed. Champaign, IL: Leisure Press, 1996.

Werner, Doug. *Bowlers Start-up: A Beginners to Bowling.* San Diego, CA: Tracks Publishing, 1995.

Audio-Visual Materials

Champions on Film & Video, 745 State Circle, Box 1941, Ann Arbor, MI 48106. *Bowl to Win* (Earl Anthony) (VHS only).

Also from Champions on Film & Video: *Bowling* (Lyndon Lee) (VHS only, 13 minutes); *Let's Bowl* (Dick Weber) (VHS only, 40 minutes); *Teaching Kids Bowling* (Gordon Vadakin) (VHS only, 40 minutes).

RMI Media Productions, 2807 W. 47th St., Shawnee Mission, KS 66205. *Earl Anthony on Beginning Bowling* ($\frac{1}{2}$ inch VHS or Beta video, 61 minutes). Features equipment selection, proper delivery, and common errors to avoid.

Athletic Institute, 200 Castlewood Dr., North Palm Beach, FL 33408. *Four Steps to Better Bowling Series* ($\frac{3}{4}$ or $\frac{1}{2}$ inch video). Focuses on strikes and spares, fundamentals of footwork, fundamentals of arm-swing, shoe and ball selection and scoring, and approach and delivery.

Karol Videos, 350 North Pennsylvania Ave., Box 7600, Wilkes-Barre, PA 18766-7600. *Teaching Kids Bowling* (VHS, 40 minutes).

Also from Karol Videos: *Bowling with Nelson Burton Jr.* (60 minutes); *ESPN-Strike!: Consistent Bowling* (55 minutes).

Web Sites

www.vraket.com/bowling.htm Articles, tips, instruction, terminology, and more.

www.bowling.about.com/recreation/bowling/ History, humor, tips, organizations, online games, how to score.

www.tenpin.org/sites.htm Various bowling links: national and international.

www.bowl.com/template/BowlDotCom/index. html Bowling news, bowling events, tournaments, instruction, organizations.

www.bowlingindex.com Instruction by Bob Strickland, tips, links, coaches, camps, books, and videos.

CHAPTER 8

Cycling

This chapter will enable you to

- Use proper hand signals and follow bicycle safety rules
- Discuss the characteristics of various types of bicycles—touring, hybrid, recumbent, mountain, and utility bikes
- Select and fit a bicycle to individual needs
- Select equipment for everyday riding and repair
- Describe and apply the gearing theory to everyday cycling
- Demonstrate techniques for safe and efficient cycling in city and country, including ankling, balancing, body positioning, braking, cadence, emergency stops, group riding, mounting and dismounting, maneuvering, pacing, short radius turning, and straight roadside riding

Nature and Purpose

Bicycling is a wonderful lifetime activity. It can be enjoyed by young and old alike and is a great family recreational pastime. Many people today are finding many areas on which to ride. The national Rails-to-Trail Conservancy has been a proponent of establishing a vast network of parks and greenways appropriate for cyclists. Cycling offers relaxation, fitness, and occasional vacation touring or camping. A bicycle is not only a vehicle for pleasure and sport, but also a means of transportation to work or school—a role it has long played for millions of people throughout the world. While it is not likely to replace the automobile in this country, the bicycle is relatively inexpensive, durable, and cheap to operate and maintain. It does not use up natural resources nor pollute the atmosphere. This chapter will introduce the fundamentals of cycling. Mountain biking and racing enthusiasts will find additional information on these topics in the Further References section.

Bicycles and Equipment

Bicycles come in various models, styles, and colors, and with different components. They are priced from under $200 to over $3,000. Types of bicycles include touring and racing (road bikes) bikes, mountain bikes, hybrids, recumbent bikes, and utility bikes (Figure 8-1). When buying a bike, shop at a local bike store for the best selection, sizing, and service. A dealer will help you choose a bike that is best for you, based on the type of riding you wish to do.

Touring and Racing Bikes. If you want to cycle for fitness or for weekend or longer bike trips, choose a touring bike that has multiple gears (10-27). A touring model is durable, with a flexible frame that absorbs shock, and has a wide range of gears for climbing hills, caliper hand brakes, and a padded seat. Dropped handlebars take some weight off the seat and allow a wide range of riding positions. Avoid a racing bike unless you intend to race. Racing bikes are built for speed, with stiffer frames, less shock absorption, a narrow range of gears, and less padding.

Mountain Bikes. If you wish to do a significant amount of trail riding or off-road riding, then the heavier mountain bike is for you. A majority of bikes sold today fall in this category. The mountain bike is also fine for commuting around town or for shorter bike rides on the road. Mountain bikes have at least 18 gears; high ground clearance; fat, knobby tires; upright handle bars; and a sturdy frame. For further information on mountain biking, consult Further References at the back of this chapter.

Hybrid Bikes. If you wish to have a bike that can be used on the road as well as on some trails, then consider a hybrid bike. Hybrids have wider tires than a touring or racing bike, straight, upright handlebars, and larger wheels than a mountain bike. The upright position of the rider on the seat places greater pressure on the buttocks, arms, shoulders, wrists, and hands. Bicycling on a hybrid can be tiring on a long ride. Although you can ride trails, be advised that the trail should be compact or firm and relatively free of debris.

A   B

Figure 8-1 (A) A racing bike, touring bike, and hybrid bike. (B) A recumbent bike, mountain bike, and utility bike. (Courtesy of B&B Kirks Bicycle Shop, Muncie, IN)

Recumbent Bikes. If you want a bicycle that places you in a natural sitting position, then consider a recumbent bike ($650–$2,000). The recumbent is designed to maximize comfort and ride smoothly. The wheels are smaller than most bikes, the handlebars are above or below the seat, and the seat is much larger than a normal seat. Recumbent bikes have become more popular in recent years because of several features they offer: good, broad weight distribution on the back and buttocks; lack of pressure on the shoulders, neck, arms, wrist, and hands; and the comfortable ride. Although the turning radius is generally larger than most bikes, most riders enjoy them during long and extended tours.

Utility Bikes. Utility bikes with heavy frames, upright handlebars, wide tires, and wide padded seats are less expensive, take more abuse, and require less upkeep than the other bikes. The one-speed adult cruiser with its balloon tires is easy to handle and gives a very smooth ride. It is fine for off-road riding. The three-speed bike has lighter wheels, hand brakes, up right handlebars, and gears that can be shifted when stopped. It is good for commuting around town but is not good for long trips or climbing many hills.

Basic Parts of a Bicycle

The touring bicycle shown in Figure 8-2 illustrates the basic parts of the bicycle:

1. *Frame.* Heavy frames are welded steel. Better, costlier frames are double-butted, lugged, and brazed alloy. Frames come in different shapes and sizes and determine the quality of the bike.
2. *Brakes.* Either center- or side-pull hand caliper brakes are good on derailleur bikes. Coaster (pedal) brakes are used on one-speed models.

3. *Wheels* consist of hubs, spokes, rims, and tires, and come in standard, touring, and racing versions.
4. *Tires* come in two basic types. Clinchers are durable and inexpensive (recommended). A liner can be inserted between tire and tube to prevent punctures. Tubulars (sew-ups) are not advised for the general bicyclist. While thinner and lighter, they are expensive and prone to punctures.
5. *Handlebars* come in raised or dropped styles, and either version can be fitted on any bike. Upright bars allow good vision and are comfortable for many people. Dropped bars take shock off the spine and weight off the seat while allowing a wider range of riding positions. Handlebar padding may be added to reduce road shock, preventing arm and hand soreness.
6. *Crank set* in better bikes is alloy and cotterless (uses bolts or nuts to attach the crank arm to the axle).
7. *Derailleur* is a gear-changing device that lifts and pulls the chain from sprocket to sprocket. If you don't like shifting, click shifting is now widely available. It finds gears automatically, so you don't have to feel around for the next one.
8. *Pedals.* Rubber tread pedals are cheap. Metal platform or thin cage pedals allow use of toe clips.
9. *Saddle* (Seat). Leather or plastic, narrow or wide, padded or not, the seat should be comfortable right away.

➤ **Learning Hints**

1. See how many different types of bicycle components you can identify on different bicycles in class.
2. Visit a local bike shop and have the owner explain the advantages of different types of bicycle components.

Figure 8-2 Parts of a bicycle.

Fitting the Bicycle

A properly set up and well-maintained bike is a pleasure to ride, easier to control, and important in accident prevention. The most common problem for beginners is riding with the seat too low. Complete the Bicycle Inspection Checklist (Figure 8-3) to check the fit of your bike and to see if any preventive maintenance needs to be done before you hit the road.

➤ Practice/Organizational Suggestions

1. Check seat height. Locate the bolt (under the seat) that loosens the seat post. Mark on the stem current height, then, if needed, change seat height, and set at correct height and tighten bolt.
2. Locate bolts that adjust seat tilt. Loosen and remove saddle, then replace and retighten bolts.
3. Locate quick-release levers for front and rear brakes. Release front lever and squeeze front brakes. Close lever. Recheck front brakes.
4. Locate quick-release levers for front and rear wheels. Loosen front brake, release front wheel, remove. Replace front wheel, center between brake shoes, and close brake lever.

General Maintenance Tips

Regardless of the type of bicycle you have, it must be kept in good working order. Preventive maintenance, tightening loose bolts before they fall off, and lubricating cables before they rust and stick is better than finding yourself stuck miles from home with a broken bike. If you are not mechanically inclined, consult your local bike shop for a spring tuneup. Then, at least once a month, make the following checks: Investigate rattles and tighten loose bolts, if needed. Check tire pressure and inflate to the recommended pressure embossed on the sidewall. Lubricate cables and moving parts with a silicone lubricant, such as WD-40. In addition, spray the chain and clean it off by holding a rag against it as you turn the pedals. If anything is bent or broken, like spokes, rims, brakes, or gears, take it to a bicycle mechanic for repairs.

However, if you like learning how things work, you can save money and time by doing much of your own maintenance. The following tools are recommended: tire patch kit, tire irons, adjustable wrench or set of crescent wrenches (best), third hand (for brakes), screwdriver, tire gauge, silicone lubricant,

Bicycle Inspection Checklist

Name _____

Bicycle make & model _____

Serial No. _____

	OK	FIX
Frame Size		
Can you straddle frame with both feet flat on the ground? (Should be 1 to 2 inch space between crotch and top bar.)	___	___
Saddle		
Horizontal adjustment—Nose of the saddle should be 1 to 3 inches behind a vertical line drawn through the crank hangar. A cyclist 5'6" tall would position saddle 1 inch back; 5'10" tall: 2 inches back; and 6'3" tall: 3 inches back.	___	___
Vertical adjustment—Sit on bike with heel on pedal at lowest position. Knee should be straight, so when toe is on pedal, knee is slightly bent.	___	___
Tilt—Should be horizontal or slightly downtilted.	___	___
Is saddle tight and in good condition?	___	___
Handlebars		
Vertical adjustment—Top bar should be level with nose of saddle.	___	___
Horizontal adjustment—Place elbow on nose of saddle. Outstretched fingertips should just touch center of handlebars. (Length of stem may need to be changed.)	___	___
In line with wheel and symmetrical	___	___
Tight, no horizontal or vertical movement	___	___
Tubing ends plugged, grips tight	___	___
Tire pressure		
Check. Correct pressure for this bike is (Correct tire pressure is embossed on side of tire.) Check once a week.	___	___
Bolts		
Check bolts for looseness. Recheck monthly.	___	___

	OK	FIX
Hand brakes		
Adequate space between lever and handlebar when engaged? (if not, tighten cable.)	___	___
Cable: Should be taut, with no kinks, rust, or frayed ends.		
Brake shoes: Tight? Openings face rear?	___	___
Level with and no more than 1/4" from rim? At least 3/16" rubber remaining? (Replace if needed.)	___	___
Test operation of each brake separately. Must hold without catching: Front	___	___
Rear	___	___
Wheels		
Spin each wheel. It should run true (no wobbles)	___	
Should have no binding or looseness (bearings)	___	
Centered between forks (and chain stays in rear)	___	___
Rim: Not dented or kinked?	___	___
Spokes: All intact and tight?	___	___
Tire: Properly seated? Tread?	___	___
Derailleurs		
Turn bike upside down or have partner lift rear wheel while you crank pedal and shift through first the front then rear gears. (Shift only while pedal is turning!) Derailleur should shift chain smoothly from one sprocket to the next without skipping a gear, catching, or throwing chain off.	___	___
Chain condition (Clean with silicone spray if dirty.)	___	___
Sprocket teeth intact, not bent or broken.	___	___
Pedals		
Shake and spin to check bearings: no looseness or binding.	___	___
Pedals intact and tight?	___	___
Tread intact and tight?	___	___
Press down on both pedals at once. Tight?	___	___

Remarks:

G. Robbins, D. Powers, and S. Burgess, *A Wellness Way of Life* (Dubuque, IA: Wm. C. Brown Publishing Co., 1991), pp. 329–330.

Figure 8-3 Bicycle inspection checklist.

tire pump. Several of the bike books listed at the end of this chapter provide a complete section on bike repairs and should be consulted.

➤ **Practice/Organizational Suggestions**

1. Use wrench to check and tighten any loose bolts.
2. Lubricate cables and inside cable housing with spray silicone lubricant. Spray and wipe chain to clean. Spray pivot points of levers and calipers, but *do not spray bike rims.*
3. Use tire pressure gauge to check tire pressure. Find recommended pressure on tire sidewall and inflate carefully to correct pressure.

Accessories and Clothing

The most important accessory, a bicycle helmet, should be worn on every ride. Make sure that it is approved by the American National Standards Institute (ANSI) or the Snell Memorial Foundation. It should contain a dense liner made from stiff polystyrene which absorbs most of the impact in a crash. It should fit snugly and be fastened securely with the chin strap.

Toe clips are good because they enable a rider to pull up as well as push down each pedal stroke. However, they do take some getting used to, and must be worn loosely at first so you can get your foot out quickly. Some new safety pedals work like quick-release ski bindings, releasing the shoe with a twist of the foot.

Avoid the "suicide" or "safety" brake levers positioned on the top of handlebars. They decrease braking power and increase the distance needed to stop.

Other equipment that is recommended includes lock and chain, a water bottle, bike bag, tools, and gloves. Bicycles operated at night must have a headlamp that is visible from a distance of at least 500 feet to the front. New bicycles must have front, rear, pedal, and side reflectors. A patch kit, tire irons, and pump are useful for fixing flats on the road. If you encounter dogs frequently, you may wish to carry dog repellent spray.

Clothing worn depends on weather conditions. In warm weather, regular or bicycling shorts and a T-shirt are ideal. Also remember to wear a sunscreen with an SPF of at least 15. In cool weather, tights, T-shirts, sweatshirt or jersey, and windbreaker (or warmups) can be layered to keep you comfortable. Gloves are essential, and a stocking cap can be worn under the helmet and pulled down over the ears. If you wear long pants, you will need pants clips or a rubberband to keep them out of your chain. Rain calls for a rain cape, though a large plastic garbage bag may suffice in a pinch.

Rules of the Road and Safety Considerations

A bicycle is not a toy but a means of transportation. Bicycle drivers are subject to the same traffic laws as automobile drivers. In most bicycle-automobile accidents, it is the bicyclist who is at fault. Riding on the road requires maturity, knowledge, and ability to follow rules of the road. The police issue traffic tickets to careless cyclists. Rules for safe cycling include the following:

1. Wear an ANSI- or Snell-approved bicycle helmet and brightly colored clothing for maximum visibility in traffic.
2. Obey all traffic regulations, stop signs, stop signals, one-way streets, and traffic control signs.
3. Keep to the right side of the road, drive with the traffic in a straight line, and ride single file.
4. Never hitch a ride on other vehicles or carry other riders or packages that obstruct vision or interfere with proper control of the bicycle.
5. Always use proper hand signals to indicate turning or stopping.
6. Avoid cycling at night, but if you must do so, wear light or reflective clothing and use lights and reflectors on your bike.
7. Watch for doors opening from parked cars, for drain grates, wet leaves, potholes, stones, glass, or other obstacles on the road, and for pedestrians. Cross railroad tracks at a 90-degree angle to avoid catching the wheel in the tracks.
8. Be sure your brakes are operating efficiently, and keep your bicycle in perfect mechanical condition.
9. In rainy weather, caliper brakes lose up to 90 percent of their stopping power. Allow extra stopping distance and don't take corners too fast. Pump the brakes occasionally to wipe water off the wheel rims.
10. Keep alert. Look out for cars pulling out into traffic or turning. Listen for traffic approaching out of your line of vision. Anticipate traffic conditions rather than simply react to them.

Road Signs

The cyclist should be familiar with traffic signs and markings. These may be found in a driver's manual. Refer to it for rules specific to your state regarding cycling.

Dogs are potential hazards. If you see a dog at a distance, you can probably outrun it. Water from your bottle might scare it off, or you can stop, keeping the bike between you and the dog. Walk away slowly. Generally, it will leave you alone, but watch it carefully before you get under way again. *Do not try to run over or kick the dog because you may cause an accident and/or harm the dog.*

Group Riding

When riding as part of a group, the front rider should call and signal (point to) road hazards such as holes, loose gravel, bumps, and so forth (Figure 8-4). The rear rider should call, "Car back," to alert the group when an overtaking car is approaching. When "Car back" is called, all riders should quickly get in single file to allow the car to pass safely. While experienced riders may draft off each other to cut wind resistance, novice riders should avoid overlapping wheels, because a sudden unexpected swerve or bump could cause both to crash.

Ride single file unless traffic is light and you can see and hear approaching traffic well in advance.

Hand Signals. *Always* use hand signals when turning or stopping to alert other drivers to your intentions and to allow them time to react appropriately (Figures 8-5 and 8-6). Automobile drivers can anticipate moves and give a cyclist more respect and maneuvering room

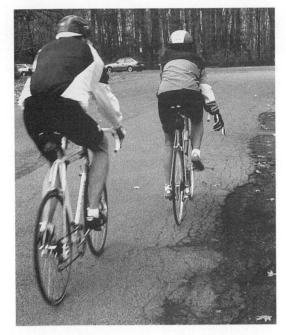

Figure 8-4 Front rider signals road hazard.

when she uses hand signals than when she simply stops without warning or suddenly cuts across traffic.

➤ **Practice/Organizational Suggestions**

1. a. Ride a mapped route. Practice braking and signaling before every intersection or stoplight.
   b. Stop or slow. Downshift into a lower gear, signal with the left hand, then squeeze the brakes.
   c. Turns. Downshift and slow down before turning. Keep the right hand on or near the

brake at all times, make sure traffic is clear both ways, signal the appropriate turn with the left hand, then proceed when safe. Do not brake while turning.

2. Ride route in groups of three to six. Have front rider call road hazards and rear rider call approaching traffic. Switch group positions at intervals so each person rides front and rear. Discuss different road hazards encountered.

3. Before riding route on which dogs may be encountered, discuss strategies for dealing with them.

Suggested Learning Sequence

A basic learning progression for the beginning cyclist is listed below.

1. Bike safety inspection (complete checklist)
2. Rules of the road (signaling, group riding)
3. General practice skills for bicycling
4. Physical fitness
5. Parts of the bicycle and terminology
6. Preventive maintenance and adjustment
7. Bicycle selection
8. Bicycle clothing and accessories
9. Clubs, organizations, racing, touring, bikeways, and so on.

Skills and Techniques
Mounting and Dismounting

When mounting, straddle the frame, place one foot on the pedal, raise the pedal to a high position, then push off and sit down on the saddle. You may dismount from a stationary or moving bike. For a stationary

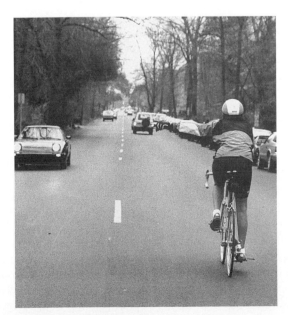

Figure 8-5 Hand signal—left turn.

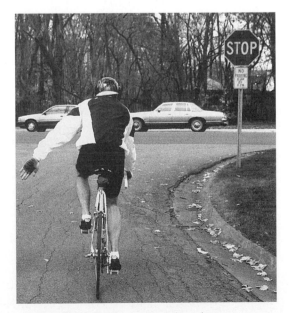

Figure 8-6 Hand signal—stop or slow down.

dismount, coast and brake with one pedal high and one low. Stop, then step down first with the higher foot. When both feet are on the ground, swing one leg over the top bar. For a moving dismount, coast with one pedal low, bring the other foot over the frame and downward as you leave the saddle, then apply the brakes and touch the ground.

Mounting and Dismounting with Toe Clips

After mastering mounting and dismounting, if you wish to ride with toe clips, you will want to practice getting your feet into and out of them. Toe clips keep the ball of the foot firmly centered over the pedal. They may seem more trouble than they're worth at first, but most people who make an effort to use them feel they are indispensable.

Mounting. Practice in an open area where you are not likely to run into anything. You may first wish to use just the clip without the strap. Straddle the frame, place one toe in the clip, push off, and get going a few strokes; then use your unclipped toe to flip the pedal so you can slip your toe into the clip. While you are doing this, you must steer the bike straight.

Dismounting. Use just the clips or keep straps loose. Stop and slide the foot on the higher pedal backwards, not sideways, out of the clip. Practice stopping quickly and taking the feet out of the clips without looking at the pedals.

Control and Balance

Cycling on the road requires straight-line riding, ability to maneuver quickly around obstacles, ability to stop quickly without skidding or being tossed over the handlebars, and ability to glance back at traffic without losing balance. To set up a practice course, locate an empty parking lot or other flat surface, and use chalk and sponges or empty milk cartons to mark lanes.

➤ Practice/Organizational Suggestions

1. *Balance.* Pedal 50 feet very slowly within a 2-foot-wide boundary, taking as much time as you can, with feet remaining on the pedals and moving only in a forward direction.
2. *Speed and Coordination.* Begin 30 feet before the starting line and pedal quickly through a course that is 8 feet wide but gradually narrows to 2 feet during the 50-foot run.
3. *Steering.* Place sponges 10 feet apart on each side of a 50-foot line. Weave in and out of the line of sponges with both front and rear wheels without knocking over the sponges. Experienced cyclists steer by leaning the body as well as turning the handlebars.

Figure 8-7 Twelve-sponge pattern for practicing evasion technique.

4. *Left and Right Spiral.* Follow a spiral to the center without touching any lines on the 2-foot-wide course. This tests left and right turning skill and balance.
5. *Emergency Braking.* Caliper brakes are so powerful that they can throw you over the front handlebars if applied forcefully. To brake safely, keep your weight far back in the saddle while applying both brakes simultaneously, just below the point where they skid. Pedal at average speed toward a goal and stop the bicycle 10 feet short of a marked line without skidding.
6. *Evasion.* Set up 12 sponges in the pattern shown in Figure 8-7. Place one sponge, then 4 feet later, two sponges 1 foot apart. Ride around the single sponge, then between the pairs of sponges. A skilled cyclist should be able to quickly skirt an obstacle, yet remain on course.
7. *Checking Traffic.* Signaling turns requires that the rider first glance back at traffic without steering off course or losing balance. Ride a straight line in a chalked-off lane, and on signal, look back over the left shoulder and tell your partner how many fingers she is holding up.
8. *Signaling and Turning.* Quickly glance back over the left shoulder to check traffic without wobbling; downshift; demonstrate proper signals for turns in both directions or stopping; then execute the maneuver.

Gearing and Cadence

When you can skillfully mount and dismount, start and stop, ride a straight line, and make turns, you are ready to use the gears. The purpose of gearing is to be able to maintain a steady pedaling cadence, regardless of terrain, wind, or weather conditions.

There are several gearing errors commonly made by beginners. Many people gear too high and pedal too slowly. They don't feel like they're doing any work unless they're pushing against resistance. This is inefficient and can produce sore knees. It is better to pedal quickly against less resistance in lower gears. While beginners may pedal at a cadence of 60–70 rpm, experienced tourists often maintain cadences of 90–100 rpm.

Second, in climbing a hill, beginners often wait to shift until they're halfway up the hill and pedaling cadence has slowed. To maintain your cadence, downshift in advance of need.

Finally, beginners seldom downshift when approaching stop signs or stop lights. They end up having to stand up on the pedals to get going again. While it takes practice to coordinate the downshift, signal, and braking, it is more efficient and kinder to the knees to pull away from an intersection in a low gear, upshifting as speed increases.

➤ **Practice/Organizational Suggestions**

1. *Gearing.* To practice shifting gears:
    a. On a straight road with little traffic, maintain normal pedaling cadence (about 65 rpm) but ease up on the pedal pressure.
    b. Without taking your eyes off the road, move a shift lever slightly forward or back. You will hear a brief rattle, then a click as the chain moves to another sprocket. If the rattling continues, the chain is between gears. Adjust the lever until there is no noise from the chain.
    c. Shift through several gears, using first the left, then the right shift levers, until you can shift into a higher or lower gear by feel.
    d. To achieve the lowest gear, the chain must be on the innermost chainwheels (small front and large rear). In the highest gear, the chain will be on the outermost chainwheels (large front and small rear). Avoid using the large front-large rear or small front-small rear chainwheel combinations. These force the chain to cross at the most extreme angle, producing excessive wear and tear on the chain.
2. *Cadence.* While cycling at a steady cadence, time and count your pedal strokes for 1 minute. How does your cadence compare with the suggested cadence?
3. *Hill Climbing.* Ride a course that includes one or more hills. As you approach each hill, keep well to the right. Try to downshift early enough so that you maintain an even cadence as you climb the hill and keep your hands on top of the brake hoods. You can lean forward and either pull on the handlebars with each push of the pedals or practice standing up on the pedals for maximum power. As you pick up speed on the downhill side, get down low and keep your weight well back in the saddle. Pump the brakes on-off to control speed.
4. *Ankling.* Ankling involves applying equal force, with the foot pushing and pulling throughout the pedaling cycle. Adding toe clips and straps enables you to pull on the upstroke as well as push on the downstroke, doubling pedaling efficiency.

➤ **Practice/Organizational Suggestion**
During part of a ride, concentrate on ankling technique.

Modifications for Special Populations

Orthopedically Impaired

1. Allow the student using a wheelchair to push the chair manually during the cycling session.
2. Commercial armcrank and rowcycles are available for persons with lower extremity injuries.
3. Use adult tricycles for students with balance deficiencies.
4. Depending on the student's disability, use of a scooter board may be appropriate; for example, the student can push from a prone position using the arms.
5. Use of stationary cycle is advised if safety or fitness issues predominate.

Cognitively Impaired

1. Safety issues are a concern. Make sure to provide a "biking buddy" for all trips off site.
2. Use adult tricycles for balance.
3. Tandem cycles may be appropriate.

Sensory Impaired

1. Use of tandem cycles is advised for students who are blind or have a visual impairment.
2. Use of stationary cycle is advised if safety or fitness issues predominate.

Cycling for Physical Fitness

Bicycling offers all the benefits of any cardiorespiratory activity, plus it is non-impact. However, the bicycle is so efficient that cycling short distances won't get you in shape. You'll have to put in some effort and sustain a training heart rate of 150–160 beats per minute (age 20 and under) if you want to improve your aerobic capacity. The sample workouts below are a good way to begin.

Sample Workout Program

Directions: Ride the recommended number of days and time at your training heart rate; rest one day between rides.

Beginning
Weeks
1. Ride 3 days × 15 minutes
2. Ride 3 days × 20 minutes
3. Ride 3 days × 25 minutes
4. Ride 3 days × 30 minutes
5. Ride 3 days × 35 minutes

Intermediate

6. Ride 4 days × 30 minutes
7. Ride 4 days × 35 minutes
8. Ride 4 days × 40 minutes
9. Ride 4 days × 45 minutes

Maintenance

10. Ride 3–5 days × 40–60 minutes

Physical Fitness Evaluation: Take a 5-mile time trial and record your time. After 8 to 12 weeks, repeat the ride and see how your time compares with the first trial.

The route, weather conditions, time of day, and type of clothing worn should be similar on both rides in order to make a valid comparison.

Terminology

Ankling Pedaling technique in which the foot applies equal force on both the upstroke and downstroke.

Bikeway Paths or roads designated as bicycle routes.

Cadence The number of rpm (revolutions per minute) a pedal makes.

Caliper brakes Hand brakes.

Clincher Common tire and tube combination rim.

Coaster brakes Foot-activated internal-hub rear brakes.

Derailleur Device that moves the chain from one gear to another.

Down tube Part of frame extending from the steering head to the bottom bracket.

Head tube Tube holding front fork assembly.

Saddle Seat.

Seat tube Part of frame extending from the bottom bracket to the seat.

Toe clips Metal cages or straps that hold the foot on the pedal.

Top tube Part of frame extending horizontally from the head tube to the seat tube.

Tubular tire (Sew up) Tire glued to rim of wheel.

Wheel Includes the hub, rim, spokes, and tire.

Further References

Baker, Arnie. *Smart Cycling: Successful Training and Racing for Riders of All Levels.* New York, NY: Fireside Press, 1997.

Ballantine, Richard and Grant, Richard. *Richard's Ultimate Bicycle Book.* New York, NY: Dorling Kindersley, 1992.

A Bicycle Built for You. *Women's Sports and Fitness,* 16(3): 51–60, 1994.

Bicycling Magazine Editors. *Bicycling Magazine's Bike Touring in the 90's.* Emmaus, PA: Rodale Press, Inc., 1993.

Bicycling Magazine Editors. *Bicycling Magazine's Training for Fitness & Endurance.* Emmaus, PA: Rodale Press, Inc., 1992.

Bicycling Magazine Editors. *Bicycling Magazine's Bicycle Commuting Made Easy.* Emmaus, PA: Rodale Press, Inc., 1992.

Burke, Edmund and Carmichael, Chris. *Fitness Cycling.* Champaign, IL: Human Kinetics Books, 1994.

Burke, Edmund. *Cycling Health & Physiology: Using Sports Science to Improve Your Riding & Racing.* Brattleboro, VT: Vitesse Press, 1992.

Burke, Ed, Pavelka, Ed and Burke, Edmund R. *The Complete Book of Long Distance Cycling: Build the Strength, Skills and Confidence to Ride as Far as You Want.* Emmaus, PA: Rodale Press, 2000.

Cuthberson, Tim and Morall, Rick (Illustrator). *Anybody's Bike Book.* Berkeley, CA: Ten Speed Press, 1998.

Edwards, Sally and Reed, Sally. *The Heart Rate Monitor Book for Outdoor and Indoor Cyclists: A Heart Zone Training Program.* Boulder, CO: Velo Press, 2000.

Fehlau, Gunnar. *The Recumbent Bicycle (Tour Cover Edition).* Williamston, MI: Out Your Backdoor Press, 2000.

Kennedy, Martha J., et al. *Fat Tire Rider: Everyone's Guide to Mountain Biking.* Brattleboro, VT: Vitesse Press, 1993.

Matheny, F. The 10 Simplest Things You Can Do to Improve Your Fitness. *Bicycling Magazine* 35(10): 84–85, 1994.

Mellion, Morris B., M.D. Bicycling. In *Sports Medicine Secrets.* Philadelphia, PA: Hanley & Belfus, Inc, 1995.

Oliver, Peter. *Bicycling: Touring and Mountain Bike Basics.* New York: W.W. Norton & Company, 1995.

Pavelka, Ed (Ed.). *Bicycling Magazine's Cycling for Health and Fitness.* Emmaus, PA:Rodale Press, 2000.

Pavelka, Ed (Ed.). *Bicylce Magazine's Mountain Biking Skills, Tips, Techniques, to Master Terrain.* Emmaus, PA: Rodale, Press, 2000.

Snowling, Steve and Evans, Ken. *Bicycle Mechanics.* 1990. Leisure Press, Div. of Human Kinetics Publishers, Inc., Box 5076, Champaign, IL 61820. Tel. 1-800-DIAL-HKP.

Strassman, Michael. *Basic Essentials Mountain Biking.* Guilford, CT: Globe Fequot Press, 2000.

Van der Plas, Rob. *Choosing, Riding, & Maintaining the Off-Road Bicycle.* 3rd ed. Mill Valley, CA: Bicycle Books, 1993.

Weaver, Susan. *A Women's Guide to Cycling.* Berkeley, CA: Ten Speed Press, 1998.

Periodicals

Bicycle Guide. 10/yr. Winning International, Inc. 744 Roble St., Ste. 190, Allentown, PA 18103.

Bicycle USA. 8/yr. League of American Wheelman, 6707 Whitestone Rd., Ste. 209, Baltimore, MD 21207. (General, beginning to advanced.)

Bicycling. 10/yr. Rodale Press, Inc., 33 E. Minor St., Emmaus, PA 18049. (General, beginning.)

Mountain Bike. Rodale Press, 33 Minor Street, Emmaus, PA 18098.

Recumbent Cyclist News. P.O. Box 58755, Renton, WA 98058-1755.

Audio-Visual Materials

AIMS Media. 6901 Woodley Ave., Van Nuys, CA 91406. Telephone 1-800-367-2467. *Bicycle Driving Tactics,* 14 min; *Bicycling for Physical Fitness, Health & Recreation,* 14 min; *Bikes Are Back,* 9 min; *Bicycle Basics,* 10 min; *Get to Know Your Ten Speed,* 19 min.

Beacon Films. An Hschul Group Company, 930 Pinter Ave., Evanston, IL 60202. Telephone 1-800-323-5448. *Bike Style.*

Centron Education Films, Supplementary Education Group, Simon & Schuster, 108 Wilmot Rd., Deerfield, IL 60015. Telephone 800-323-5343. *Safe Bicycling in Traffic,* 1981, 19 min.

Do-It-Yourself, Inc. 5250 77 Center Dr. , Suite 340, Charlotte, NC 28210. *Anybody's Bike Video—Bicycle Repair, Vol. 1,* 40 min; *Bike Tripping,* 40 min.

Elliot Bay Film Company (206-784-4666) or Back Country Bookstore (206-290-7652). *Fundamentals of Bicycle Maintenance, Fundamentals of Bicycling Touring.*

Iowa State University. 121 Pearson Hall, Media Resources Center, Ames, IA 50011. *Bicycling Safely on the Road,* 25 min.

L.L. Bean, Freeport, ME (800-221-4221). *L.L. Bean Guide to Bicycle Touring.*

National Safety Council. 425 N. Michigan Ave., Chicago, IL 60611. *Bike Safety: Making the Right Moves,* 15 min.

New & Unique Videos (619-282-6126). *Great Mountain Biking Video.*

Pyramid Film and Video. 2801 Colorado Ave., Santa Monica, CA 90404. Telephone 213-828-7577. *Everything About Bicycles,* 15 min.

Organizations and Clubs

American Bicycle Association. P.O. Box 718, Chandler, AZ 85244. (Off-road bicycle racing.)

American Cycling Union. C/o Estelle G. Black, P.O. Box 6099, Newark, NJ 07106. (Cycling for recreation and competition.)

Bicycle Federation of America. 1818 R St., N.W., Washington, DC 20009. (Promotes bicycle transportation, recreation, and programs.)

International Bicycle Touring Society. P.O. Box 6979, San Diego, CA 92106. (Bicycle tours.)

International Mountain Bicycling Association. P.O. Box 412043, Los Angeles, CA 90041-9043.

League of American Wheelmen. 67 Whitestone Rd., Suite 209, Baltimore, MD 21207. (Bicyclists and clubs.)

National Bicycle League. P.O. Box 729, Dublin, OH 43017. (BMX racing.)

National Off-Road Bicycling Association. 1750 Boulder, Colorado Springs, CO 80909.

Rails-to-Trails Conservancy. 1400 16th Street NW, Suite 300, Washington, DC 20036.

Women's Cycling Coalition. P.O. Box 7313, Loveland, CO 80537.

Web Sites

www.BikesRNotToys.com Offers tips on how to buy a bike, safety, and fitness, and other useful information.

www.bikeroute.com/WhyBent.html Offers history about recumbent bikes.

www.bentrideronline.com Offers Bent Rider, an online magazine with much helpful information, articles, message board, and terminology.

www.bikeroute.com/Recumbents Offers questions and answers about recumbents, terminology, medical benefits of recumbents, history, and much more.

www.helmets.org Site for Bicycle Helmet Safety Institute offers law, statistics, standards, services, buying a helmet.

www.webmountainbike.com Offers trail riding trips, product reviews, terminology, maintenance, mountain bike basics, tips, and much more.

www.bicyling.about.com/recreation/bicycling/mbody.htm Offers quizzes, tips on buying, clothing, workouts for cycling.

mountainbike.miningco.com/recreation/mountainbike Offers Mountain Bike 101, maintenance tips, organizations, magazines.

www.mtbinfo.com Offers product reviews, travel guides, message board, tips on maintenance, links to other sites.

www.usacycling.com Site for USA Cycling Association.

world.std.com/~jmf/biking/slang/htm Offers mountain bike slang from A to Z.

www.railtrails.org Site for Rails-to-Trails Conservancy, with many links to greenways appropriate for cycling, walking, jogging, and in-line skating.

www.ibike.org Site of the International Bike Fund, an advocacy organization promoting sustainable transportation; includes valuable information on youth bike programs, bike education, safety, bike mechanics, and much more.

www.yellowbike.org Site offers information about how to begin yellow bike programs in a community.

CHAPTER 9

Dance

- Folk Dance
- Country Western Dance
- Social Dance
- Square Dance

Nature and Purpose

Dance can be defined as any patterned, rhythmic movement of the human body in space and time as a means of expression.

Since prehistoric times, humans have always had the desire to dance. Today that desire is still with us: people dance (1) for self-expressive purposes; (2) for religious, ritualistic, or ceremonial purposes; and (3) to entertain or please others. Dance will never die because it is constantly being reborn through different dancers, different environments, and different cultures.

Unlike other art forms, the art of dance is the only art form whose sole necessary tool is the human body. As with other structured or creative physical activities, it is important not only to understand the objectives and basic patterns of dance, but also to practice the skills necessary to achieve a level of proficiency in this highly expressive art form.

This chapter will look at four forms of dance commonly taught in educational institutions: folk dance, counry western, social dance, and square dance. Other popular dance forms such as ballet, tap, and jazz dance are not included because of space limitations.

Movements Common to All Dances

All forms of dance involve movement. Although dance movement may at times be confined only to the body (nonlocomotor or axial movement), more commonly it requires the use of various forms of locomotion in which the body weight is transferred to the feet or from one foot to the other. All forms of locomotion can be reduced to five fundamental steps: walk, run, leap, jump, and hop. Any other type of locomotor activity is a combination of these basic steps. Closely related to the five fundamental steps are the skip, slide, and gallop, and often reference is made to the eight fundamental means of locomotion.

Walk. The weight is transferred from one foot to the other, alternately, one foot always being in contact with the ground. The usual foot action is a transfer of weight from the heel to the ball of one foot, during which time the other leg is pushing off, then swinging through to assume its position in the sequence of action.

Run. The speed of the walk is increased, and there is a brief period when neither foot is in contact with the ground. A run is usually a quicker progression than a walk.

Leap. A leap is a spring into the air by means of a strong pushoff from one foot, returning to the ground on the opposite foot. The leap differs from the run in that more energy is needed, and there is a longer period between transfer of weight due to a longer period of suspension in the air. The leap may be done either for height or for distance.

Jump. The body springs into the air by a two-foot takeoff, landing on two feet. Other types of jumps that you might see include: (1) a single-foot takeoff, landing on two feet; and (2) a two-foot take-off, landing on one foot. A jump may be made for either height or distance.

Hop. A hop is a spring into the air by means of a strong pushoff from one foot, returning to the ground on the same foot.

Graphic Representation. A walk, leap, jump, and hop are all done to an even beat, sometimes designated as long, and represented graphically as follows:

——————   —————   —————

A run can take just as much time, but is usually twice as fast and represented as

— — — —

In relation to the long beat, it is shown

— — — — — —

and so on. Should the pattern become uneven (long-short), each of the three remaining related forms of locomotion would fit into this rhythm: skip, slide, gallop. The graphic representation would be

——— — ——— —

the total time of which is equivalent to one beat, thus

——— — ——— —

Skip. A combination of a step and a hop, done to an uneven beat in which the step is given the long time value (———) and the hop the short value (—):

step   hop   step   hop   step   hop   step   hop
——— — ——— — ——— — ——— —

Note: Were each part given equal time value, a step-hop would result instead of a skip:

——— — ——— —   ——— — ——— —

    step   hop   step   hop

In performing the skip, there is a feeling of elevation resulting from the natural tendency to swing the free leg forward and upward.

Slide. The weight is transferred from one foot to the other by means of a step on one foot followed by a quick drawing up of the other foot, with an immediate transfer of weight to it, resulting in a sideward movement.

Gallop. A gallop is similar to a slide, except the gallop moves forward, and the foot executing the leap is brought up to but not beyond the foot that has completed the step. The leap, a forward movement, is done with slight height; distance is not a factor.

FOLK DANCE

A Brief History

They are of all ages, from all societal levels, and have vastly different backgrounds, yet individuals gather to participate in the shared activity of folk dance. Since the early 1940s in the United States, there has been increased interest and participation in international folk dance. This activity has become a common

element in education, recreation groups, dance clubs, and senior citizen programs.

Folk dances are sequences of movements, formations, and rhythmic patterns that have been created by people of different cultures. Although many of these international dances have the same steps and movement patterns, the stylization and the purposes for these particular dances are what adds to the rich cultural expression of each dance. Most dances are performed solely for recreational purposes; however, some international folk dances are performed for ritualistic ceremonies or for celebrating special occasions (Figure 9-1).

Suggested Learning Sequence

The following progression is recommended for beginners. Each step will be fully described below.

1. Two-Step
2. Schottische
3. Polka
4. Mazurka
5. Waltz Box

Basic Folk Dance Steps

The following abbreviations and terms (also used in social dance) will be used in describing the basic folk dance steps:

Fwd = Forward
Back = Backward
Q = Quick
S = Slow
L = Left
R = Right
FD = Forward Diagonal

The term *close* is commonly used in folk and spiral dance to mean that the free foot is moved toward the supporting foot. The free foot then becomes the supporting foot, and the supporting foot is now free to move.

➤ Learning Hints

Two-Step. Three steps are taken in the rhythm quick, quick, slow, using four counts. Thus, step left, closing step right to left, step left, and hold. The pattern may be repeated, starting with the right foot.

1	2	3	4
Step QL	Close QR	Step SL	Hold

Schottische. This four-count pattern is most frequently done by taking three small steps followed by a hop, each using one count. It is an easy, smooth pattern that is sometimes done with small runs instead of steps.

1	2	3	4
Step L	Step R	Step L	Hop L

Figure 9-1 International folk dancers enjoy the exhilaration of this rhythmic group activity.

Polka. Two long-short intervals based upon two counts make up the timing for one polka step. Depending on which part of this step one selects as a starting point, a polka becomes either (1) a hop-step-close-step or (2) a step-close-step-hop. The polka that is performed most is the (1) type.

(1)	&	1	&	2
	Hop L	Step R	Close L	Step R
(2)	3	&	4	&
	Step L	Close R	Step L	Hop L

Mazurka. This step is commonly executed diagonally forward and requires three even, long counts to be performed once. A gliding step is taken with the left foot to the front diagonal on count one; a closing step is taken with the right foot to the right; and a hop is taken with the right foot on count three. At the time of the hop, the left leg swings out, then the left knee immediately bends so that the foot comes close to the right shinbone. The left foot is then lowered to prepare for the next mazurka step. This is a strong, vigorous step, done continuously to the same diagonal unless a variation is introduced.

1	2	3
Step FDL	Close R	Hop R

Waltz Box. This step is a six-count pattern consisting of step, step, close, step, step, close. It must be remembered that the weight is evenly transferred from one foot to the other. Thus, step forward with the left foot, step side with the right foot, closing step left to right, step backward with the right foot, step side with the left foot, and closing step right to left.

1	2	3
Step Forward L	Step Side R	Close L
4	5	6
Step Backward R	Step Side L	Close R

Combinations of the above-noted basic folk dance steps are then used to perform specific international folk dances. Stylization, formations, and music allow these basic steps to become more exciting to perform and to watch.

➤ Practice/Organizational Suggestions

1. The primary concern of the teacher should be the selection of dances that are suited to the level of ability of the dancers. While there are many values of international folk dancing, it should also be a joyous activity. There is no better way to discourage students and to create dislike for the activity than to attempt to teach beginners a long, complicated dance.

2. Before teaching a new dance, the teacher should review the basic step or steps that are involved. Basic steps may be practiced in an open, a single, or a double circle, moving counterclockwise, which is the most common line of direction in international folk dances.

3. The teacher should be thoroughly familiar with the dance and the music before attempting to present the material. A short background introduction to the dance may be given, which should include the dance's native country, but students should get into the activity as soon as possible. The teacher should then demonstrate the complete dance to music.

4. In the starting formation, the teacher can break down the parts of the dance into small units while verbalizing with one descriptive word for each action. If necessary, this may be done somewhat slower, speeding up until the skill approximates the rhythm of the dance. In beginning any dance part, the teacher might give a two-word signal such as "Ready, and . . ." to alert dancers and allow for reaction time. When combining a part, the teacher may cue the dancers as to what will be next. Upon completion of the dance, corrections in skill, techniques, or stylization may be given to the entire group. When the dance is repeated, any errors may be corrected individually.

Suggested Folk Dances for Beginners

Dance	Basic Step
Alunelul	Walk
Black Forest Mazurka	Mazurka
Doudlebska Polka	Polka
Hora	Walk
Jugo	Schottische
Kalvelis	Polka
Korobushka	Schottische
Laz Bar	Two-Step
Little Man in a Fix	Waltz Box
Miserlou	Two-Step
Polka zu Dreien	Polka
Salty Dog Rag	Schottische

COUNTRY WESTERN DANCE

Brief History

Country Western dance has become an integral part of American social dance. Originally this type of dance was called American novelty individual or couple dance. Today it is referred to as Country Western dance. Country Western dancing has expanded its formerly limited repertoire to a very broad selection of dance forms and styles, from line dancing to stylized couple dances.

Each Country Western dance has a sequence of movements, a rhythmic structure, and its own form. Each dance also has subtle differences in the dynamics of performance. For example, the "Texan walk" and "Californian run" are not actual dance steps but rather characteristic ways of traveling across the dance floor. These characteristic ways are the "style" of a dance or a group of dances from one area or people. It is in these different styles that the important differences among Country Western dances are found.

Music plays an important role in the enjoyment of the dance. The new rock style of country music has increased the popularity of Country Western dancing. It has a more upbeat style and has allowed for a greater variety of dance forms. This contemporary music has also attracted people from all walks of life, many of whom are not necessarily fans of country music.

Executing the style and mannerisms inherent in the dance is as important as being able to dance the steps and pattern sequences. The dancer or student must develop style in order to achieve the fullest enjoyment of the dance. The following are guidelines dancers can follow to achieve the correct style in a dance or dances:

1. Study the background of the dance.
2. Develop an awareness of the characteristics of different styles.
3. Develop an understanding of the step patterns.
4. Be knowledgeable about the formations and positions.

On a dance floor, wherever in the world it may be, dancers must follow certain etiquette. Couples always move in Line of Dance (counterclockwise) around the floor. There are two imaginary outside lanes on a dance floor. The outside lane is used for couples doing progressive dances. The inside lane is used for couples who do not travel as far. In Country Western dances, the center of the floor is used for line dancing and stationary couple dances.

Suggested Learning Sequence

1. Vine (Grapevine)
2. Shuffle
3. Strut
4. Jazz Box
5. Stamp
6. Stamp Up
7. Scuff
8. Triple Step
9. Break Turn
10. Cha Cha
11. Butterfly
12. Hip Bump
13. Grapevine
14. Hook Step
15. Hook
16. Coaster
17. Paddle Turn
18. Rock
19. Kick Ball-Change
20. Waltz and Waltz variations

Basic Steps

Basic steps are any combination of one or more locomotor and/or nonlocomotor movements. They include the following: Break Turn, Butterfly, Cha Cha, Coaster, Diamond, Grapevine, Hook Step, Jazz Box, Kick Ball-Change, Paddle Turn, Rock, Shuffle, Strut, Triple Step, Vine, Waltz, and Waltz variations.

Break Turn. Step forward with one foot, turn a ½ turn on the supporting foot, and shift weight to the opposite foot. It is also called a *Pivot turn*.

Right Break Turn

1 Step right forward.
2 Pivot on right while turning a ½ turn to left (counterclockwise); shift weight to left.

Left Break Turn

1 Step left forward.
2 Pivot on left while turning a ½ turn to right (clockwise); shift weight to right.

Butterfly. Butterfly, also known as Heel Splits and Toe Splits, is a 2-count basic-step. Turn heels out and return heels to place.

Butterfly (heel splits)

1 Turn heels out.
2 Turn heels in.

Butterfly (toe splits)

1 Turn toes out.
2 Turn toes in.

Cha Cha. A Ballroom basic-step. In Ballroom, the Cha Cha has five steps. The last three steps in the Cha Cha sequence are described here. In a "quick, quick, slow" rhythm, step right to right, step left beside right, step right to right.

Right Cha Cha (in place)

1 Step right in place.
& Step left on ball of left foot beside right.
2 Step right in place.

Left Cha Cha (in place)

1 Step left in place.
& Step right on ball of right foot beside left.
2 Step left in place.

Right Forward Cha Cha

1 Step right forward.
& Step left beside right.
2 Step right forward.

Left Forward Cha Cha

1 Step left forward.
& Step right beside left.
2 Step left forward.

Right Backward Cha Cha

1 Step right back.
& Step left beside right.
2 Step right back.

Left Backward Cha Cha

1 Step left back.
& Step right beside left.
2 Step left back.

Right Side Cha Cha

1 Step right to right.
& Step left beside right.
2 Step right to right.

Left Side Cha Cha

1 Step left to left.
& Step right beside left.
2 Step left to left.

Coaster. A three-step sequence done in a "quick, quick, slow" rhythm. Step right back, step left beside right, step right forward. Can be done with either foot.

Right Coaster

1 Step right back.
& Step left back beside right.
2 Step right forward.

Left Coaster

1 Step left back.
& Step right back beside left.
2 Step left forward.

Diamond. A basic step that is typical to Country Western dancing. Point the toes forward, side and back.

Right Diamond

1 Touch right toes forward.
2 Touch right toes to right.
3 Touch right toes back.
4 Step right beside left.

Left Diamond

1 Touch left toes forward.
2 Touch left toes to left.
3 Touch left toes back.
4 Scuff left forward.

Grapevine. One foot steps to the side while the opposite foot steps in front or behind. Example: Step right to right, step left across right, step right to right, step left behind right. Can be done with either foot in any direction.

Right Grapevine (to right)

1 Step right to right.
2 Step left across right.
3 Step right to right.
4 Step left behind right.

Right Grapevine (to left)

1 Step right across left.
2 Step left to left.
3 Step right behind left.
4 Step left to left.

Left Grapevine (to left)

1 Step left to left.
2 Step right across left.
3 Step left to left.
4 Step right behind left.

Left Grapevine (to right)

1 Step left across left.
2 Step right to right.
3 Step left behind right.
4 Step right to right.

Hook Step. The Hook is both a single action movement and a basic step. As a basic step, it is a 4-count step. Touch right heel forward, swing right heel across left shin, touch right heel forward, step right beside left. Can be done with either foot.

Right Hook Step

1 Touch right heel forward.
2 Hook right in front of left shin.
3 Touch right heel forward.
4 Step right beside left.

Left Hook Step

1 Touch left heel forward.
2 Hook left in front of right shin.
3 Touch left heel forward.
4 Step left beside right.

Jazz Box. Jazz Boxes can be executed in many different ways, and they can take three, four, or five counts. It all depends on the type the dancer is asked to perform in each dance. The basic Jazz Box is as follows: Step right across left, step left backward, step right to right, step left beside right. Can be done with either foot in any direction.

Right Jazz Box

1 Step right across left.
2 Step left back.
3 Step right to right while turning a ¼ turn to right (clockwise).
4 Step left beside right.

Left Jazz Box

1 Step left across right.
2 Step right back.
3 Step left to left.
4 Step right beside left.

Right Jazz Box with a ¼ turn

1 Step right across left.
2 Step left back.
3 Step right to right while turning a ¼ turn to right (clockwise).
4 Step left beside right.

Left Jazz Box with a ¼ turn

1 Step left across right.
2 Step right back.
3 Step left to left while turning a ¼ turn to left (counterclockwise).
4 Step right beside left.

Kick Ball-Change. A 3-step sequence done in a "quick, quick, slow" rhythm. Kick right forward, step backward on ball of right beside left, step left forward. Can be done with either foot.

Right Kick Ball-Change

1 Kick right forward.
& Step on ball of right foot slightly back.
2 Step left forward.

Left Kick Ball-Change

1 Kick left forward.
& Step on ball of left foot slightly back.
2 Step right forward.

Paddle Turn. A basic step, consisting of two actions and two counts. Lead forward, with a given foot and shoulder. During the second action, turn a ¼ turn.

Right Paddle Turn

1 Step right forward.
2 Pivot on right while turning a ¼ turn to left (counterclockwise); shift weight to left.

Left Paddle Turn

1 Step left forward.
2 Pivot on left while turning a ¼ turn to right (clockwise); shift weight to right.

Rock. Rock is 2-count basic step. Step in a given direction and follow with a step in the opposite direction.

Right Forward Rock

1 Rock right forward.
2 Rock left back.

Left Forward Rock

1 Rock left forward.
2 Rock right back.

Right Backward Rock

1 Rock right back.
2 Rock left forward.

Left Backward Rock

1 Rock left back.
2 Rock right forward.

Right Cross Rock

1 Rock right diagonally forward across left.
2 Rock left back.

Left Cross Rock

1 Rock left diagonally forward across right.
2 Rock right back.

Right Diagonal Backward Rock

1 Rock right diagonally back behind left.
2 Rock left forward.

Left Diagonal Backward Rock

1 Rock left diagonally back behind right.
2 Rock right forward.

Shuffle. Shuffle is a 2-count basic step. It is counted as "1&2" and described as "step together step."

Right Forward Shuffle

1 Step right forward.
& Step left beside right.
2 Step right forward.

Left Forward Shuffle

1 Step left forward.
& Step right beside left.
2 Step left forward.

Right Backward Shuffle

1 Step right back.
& Step left beside right.
2 Step right back.

Left Backward Shuffle

1 Step left back.
& Step right beside left.
2 Step left back.

Right Side Shuffle

1 Step right to right.
& Step left beside right.
2 Step right to right.

Left Side Shuffle

1 Step left to left.
& Step right beside left.
2 Step left to left.

Strut. A stylized walk, leading with the heel or toes and transferring the weight to the whole foot. Usually takes 2 counts. Can be done with either foot, forward or backward.

Heel & Toe Strut

1 Touch right heel forward.
2 Shift weight to right.
3 Touch left heel forward.
4 Shift weight to left.

Toe & Heel Strut

1 Touch right toes forward.
2 Shift weight to right.
3 Touch left toes forward.
4 Shift weight to left.

Triple Step. The triple step is a basic step that has three actions done to 2 counts. It is counted as "1&2." It is also the basic step for the Triple Lindy or East Coast Swing.

Right Triple Step

1 Step right in place.
& Step left on ball of left foot beside right.
2 Step right in place.

Left Triple Step

1 Step left in place.
& Step right on ball of right foot beside left.
2 Step left in place.

Turn. Turn is a movement that progresses in a circular direction. You can turn a ¼ turn, a ½ turn, a ¾ turn, a full turn or more than a full turn. The type of turn to be executed will be specified in each dance.

Vine. Vine is short for grapevine. In Country Western dance, the Vine has become a standard for three steps and a fourth action that could be a brush, hitch, hook, kick, scuff, step, stomp, stomp up, or touch.

Right Vine

1 Step right to right.
2 Step left behind right.
3 Step right to right.
4 Do any of the following: brush, hitch, hook, kick, scuff, step, stomp, stomp up, or touch.

Left Vine

1 Step left to left.
2 Step right behind left.
3 Step left to left.
4 Do any of the following: brush, hitch, hook, kick, scuff, step, stomp, stomp up, or touch.

Right Forward Vine

1–3 Take 3 steps forward: right, left, right.
4 Do any of the following: brush, hitch, hook, kick, scuff, step, stomp, stomp up, or touch.

Left Forward Vine

1–3 Take 3 steps forward: left, right, left.

4 Do any of the following: brush, hitch, hook, kick, scuff, step, stomp, stomp up, or touch.

Right Backward Vine

1–3 Take 3 steps back: right, left, right.

4 Do any of the following: brush, hitch, hook, kick, scuff, step, stomp, stomp up, or touch.

Left Backward Vine

1–3 Take 3 steps back: left, right, left.

4 Do any of the following: brush, hitch, hook, kick, scuff, step, stomp, stomp up, or touch.

Waltz (Basic). Step right forward, step left beside right, step right beside left. Can be done with either foot in any direction.

Waltz Balance. Step right to right, step left beside right. Step right beside left. Can be done with opposite footwork in any direction.

Waltz Half Box. Step right forward, step left to left, step right beside left. Can be done forward or backward with either foot.

Waltz Box Quarter Turn. A basic turn in the English Waltz. When executing the right turn (clockwise): step right forward, step left to left while turning a ¼ turn to right (clockwise), step right beside left. When the left foot is the active foot, the turn will be done as follows: Step left backward, step right to right while turning a ¼ turn to right, step left beside right.

Waltz Half Turn. The same as in the Box Turn, except turn a ½ turn.

Waltz Full Turn. Turn a full turn with 3 steps.

Waltz Twinkle. A basic step used in the waltz. Step right across left, step left beside right, step right beside left. Can be done with either foot in any direction.

Single Action Movements

These are all the single action movements: brush, bump, clap, hitch, hold, hook, kick, pivot, scoot, scuff, stomp, stomp up, swivel, touch.

Brush. A movement where the toes or ball of the foot come in contact with the floor. Swing either leg in any direction while touching the floor with the toes or ball of foot. Can be done with either foot in any direction.

Bump. Move a hip in any given direction with an accent.

Clap. Strike hands together in any manner asked for.

Hitch. Lift the knee of the inactive leg, bending knee in a 45-degree angle. For example, step right forward while lifting the left leg with a bent knee. Can be done with either leg.

Hold. Hold a position for a given amount of time.

Hook. Swing the heel across the opposite shin. Can be done with either foot.

Kick. A sharp swinging action of the leg from the knee down. Usually in a forward direction. Can be done with either foot in any given direction.

Pivot. A turning motion on the ball of the foot that has the weight. Step right forward, turn on the ball of the right in any given direction and maintain the weight on the right. Can be done with either foot in any direction.

Scoot. A movement forward on the active foot, similar to a hop without leaving the ground.

Scuff. A movement where the heel comes in contact with the floor. Strike the floor with the heel in a forward motion without a shift of weight.

Stomp. An accented step with a shift of weight.

Stomp Up. An accented step without shifting weight to the active foot. Step right beside the left with an accent, without shifting weight to right. Can be done with either foot.

Swing. A forward or backward movement of any leg or arm.

Swivel. Turning of heel or toes from side to side on the ball or balls of the feet or heels.

Touch. Touch the floor with the heel or toe without shifting of weight. Can be done with either foot in any direction.

Suggested Country Western Line Dances for Beginners

Dance	Basic Steps
Arkansas Strut	Strut, Jazz Box
Barn Dance	Vine
Bartender Stomp	Vine
Boot Scootin' Boogie	Scoot, Vine
Canadian Stomp	Vine, Jazz Box
Celtic Cross	Shuffle, break Turn
Country Walkin'	Jazz Box, Swivels
Cowboy Boogie	Vine, Hip Bumps
Cowboy Cha Cha	Rock, Cha Cha, Break Turn
Cowgirl's Twist	Strut, Swivels
Cruisin'	Rock, Cha Cha, Break Turn, Vine
Electric Slide	Vine
Lazy Shuffle	Shuffle, Rock
Pure Country	Vine, Coaster
Rebel Strut	Break Turn, Shuffle

Dance	Basic Steps
Rocky Mountain Scramble	Vine, Diamond
Ski Bumpus	Shuffle, Break Turn, Kick Ball-Change
Tush Push	Hip Bumps, Shuffle, Rock
Waltz Across Texas	Waltz and variations

SOCIAL DANCE

Brief History

Social or ballroom dancing really began in the United States at the time of World War I with the introduction of many new forms of couple dances. The Charleston was followed by a series of "jitterbug" dances and the Latin-American rhythms that were performed to big swing bands. Rock-and-roll music influenced an individual type of dance that led to performances of disco. Novelty and fad dances seem to fill a need at a particular time and may reflect changing trends in music. They may stimulate interest and participation, but they seldom last long enough to merit a place in the repertory of traditional social dances. The following discussion focuses on basic elements used in social dance.

Dance Positions

Closed. (Used in waltz, fox-trot, and polka) Partners face each other, standing toe to toe, looking over each other's right shoulder, the man facing the line of direction. With his style arm (left), the man's left hand holds the woman's right hand at about shoulder height; arms are relaxed and slightly bent at elbows. With his lead arm (right), the man's fingers are closed and on the woman's back slightly above her waist. The woman's left hand is placed on the man's right shoulder (Figure 9-2).

In Latin dances (tango, samba, merengue), rumba, mambo, and cha cha cha, the man's lead arm (hand on partner's back) should be above the small of the back, and the elbow should be slightly higher than in the above-mentioned closed dance position. The man's style arm (left) is also placed higher when performed.

Semi-Open. From the closed position, partners turn slightly away from one another, looking in the line of direction—man's right and lady's left sides are near each other (Figure 9-3).

Open. From semi-open position, turn apart so that both are facing in line of direction.

Reverse Open. Partners turn so that both are facing in reverse line of direction—man's left and woman's right sides are near each other. Man's right arm and woman's left arm may hang down at side (Figure 9-4).

Line of Direction

In general, couples move about the floor in a counterclockwise circle known as the line of direction

Figure 9-2 Closed position.

Figure 9-3 Semi-open position.

Figure 9-4 Reverse-open position.

(LOD). Couples may, however, move forward, backward, or sideward within this pattern; and, there are many new dance steps in which the couples dance in much the same spot.

Style and Etiquette

Every type of dance is performed with a certain style. The particular dance form, its tempo, and rhythm determine the style with which a particular dance is executed.

A man asks a woman to dance in a simple and direct way: "May I have the next dance?" or "Will you dance with me?" are the two customary approaches. It is polite to escort the woman to and from the floor and to thank her for the dance. Usually a man may cut in on a couple at a private party, but at a public dance, cutting in is not condoned. Dancers should always be courteous and well mannered on the dance floor.

How to Lead and Follow

The man must indicate his steps and lead sufficiently in advance so that the woman can follow with confidence. He does this primarily with his upper torso, shoulders, and right arm and hand. The right hand becomes the steering rudder.

The woman's principal method of following is to remain relaxed so that her partner may guide her easily.

Suggested Learning Sequence

There is no set sequence for learning basic social dance patterns. The teacher might consider the interests and ages of the students, variety in rhythm, available music, and then select the order of dances that best fits the students. The following dances are described later in detail:

Fox-trot
Waltz
Tango
Rumba
Cha Cha Cha
Jitterbug

All steps indicated as slow (S) use two beats of the music, and all steps indicated as quick (Q) use one beat of the music. Unless otherwise indicated, the steps described are for the man's (or lead) part; the woman's is opposite. For example, the man's "forward left" would mean the woman's "backward right." (Note: Review the abbreviations listed in the Folk Dance section.)

Fox-trot (4/4 Time)

The fox-trot is an American ballroom dance first introduced by Harry Fox to ragtime music in a 1913 musical. A fox-trot may vary in tempo, but for beginning students, a slower version is more appropriate. Although it began as a trotting dance, the fox-trot developed into the smoother, gliding dance that is performed today.

Magic Step. Basic Rhythmic Pattern: S S Q Q
1. Closed Position
   Fwd left-S
   Fwd right-S
   Side left-Q
   Close right to left-Q
Lead Cue: Lift right arm, lean forward.
2. Semi-open Position
   Side left-S
   Cross right over left-S
   Side left-Q (return to closed position)
   Closed right to left-Q
Lead Cues:
   Pressure with heel of right hand.
   Pressure with finger tips of right hand.
3. Turn-Under
   Man's part same as semi-open position
   Lady's part:
   Side R: start to turn under R arm-S
   Complete turn under R arm onto L foot-S
   Side R-Q (return to closed position)
   Close L to R-Q
   Lady's right and man's left hands are released during turn.

Box Step. Basic Rhythmic Pattern: S Q Q
> Fwd L-S
> Side R-Q
> Close L to R-Q
> Back R-S
> Side L-Q
> Close R to L-Q

Waltz (3/4 Time)

The waltz is the oldest form of ballroom dance, and it is credited as being the first of its kind to be performed in the basic closed-couple dance position. It was not accepted when first introduced in America; however, composers such as Johann Strauss, Von Weber, and Franz Shubert gave the waltz a dignified grace through their smooth and flowing musical styles.

It is important to note that the heels stay off the ground when performing this dance pattern.

Basic Rhythmic Pattern: Q Q Q

1. Box step
   Same as Fox-trot except each step is Q.
2. Crossover
   Do one-half Box
   Cross R over L (semi-open position)
   Slide L (return to closed position)
   Close R

Lead Cues:
> Pressure with heel of right hand.
> Pressure with finger tips.

Tango (4/4 or 2/4 Time)

Some scholars believe the tango is derived from the "milongo," a dance that originated in Andalusia, Spain; others feel that the tango's roots lie in an Iberian gypsy dance resembling flamenco. Regardless of its beginnings, the tango is characterized by low, lingering steps followed by quick directional changes.

Basic Rhythmic Pattern: S S Q Q S

1. Basic step (closed position)
   Fwd L-S
   Fwd R-S
   Fwd L-Q
   Fwd R-Q
   Draw L to R, weight remaining on R-S
2. Semi-open Position
   Side L-S
   Cross R over L-S
   Fwd L-Q
   Side R-Q
   Draw L to R-S

Lead Cues:
> Pressure with heel of right hand.
> Pressure with finger tips.

Rumba (4/4 Time)

The rumba came to America in the late 1920s from Cuba. This Latin American dance was originally performed by African slaves living in South America. One of the main characteristics of the rumba is the smooth lateral swaying of the hips, a movement known as Cuban Motion.

Basic Rhythmic Pattern: Q Q S

1. Box (closed position)
   Side L-Q
   Close R-Q
   Fwd L-S
   Side R-Q
   Close L-Q
   Back R-S
2. Cuban Walk
   Walking forward or backward in the Q Q S rhythm.

Cha Cha Cha (4/4 Time)

The cha cha cha, which is a combination of the swing and mambo, became popular during the 1950s. The cha cha cha has Mexican, Afro-Cuban, and American influences, and was probably named after the three quick rhythmic sounds that the feet make when executing the steps. Like the rumba, the cha cha cha uses Cuban Motion.

Basic Rhythmic Pattern: S S Q Q S

1. Basic Step (closed position)
   Dancing toward each other with hands held:
   Fwd L-S, Back R-S
   Back L-Q, Back R-Q
   Back L-S, Back R-S
   Fwd L-S, Fwd R-Q
   Fwd L-Q, Fwd R-S
2. Cross-Step
   Cross L-S (reverse open position) Man's L and Lady's R hands joined
   In place R-S
   Side L-Q, Close R-Q, Side L-S
   Cross R-S (open position) Man's R and Lady's L hands joined
   In place L-S
   Side R-Q, Close L-Q, Side R-S

Jitterbug (4/4 Time)

The jitterbug evolved from the lindy hop, an American novelty dance that was named after the famous pilot, Charles Lindbergh, in 1927. As the movement of the lindy hop evolved into more exaggerated hopping sequences, viewers remarked that the dancers looked like "jittery bugs," thus giving the jitterbug its name.

Basic Rhythmic Pattern: S S Q Q

1. Basic Step (closed position)
   Touch L, then take weight on L-S
   Place R, then take weight on R-S
   Back L-Q (semi-open position)
   Fwd R-Q (return to closed position)
2. Basic Turn Man's Part same as Basic Step
   Lady's Part:
   Start to turn to R under R arm on R foot-S
   Complete turn under R arm on L foot-S
   Back R-facing partner-Q
   Fwd L-Q
   Start to turn to L under R arm on R foot-S
   Complete turn under R arm on L foot-S
   Back R-facing partner-Q
   Fwd L-Q

Lead Cues:

Pressure with heel of right hand.
Pressure with finger tips.

Once the basic step patterns are learned, the teacher may introduce variations or the students may be encouraged to create their own modifications.

➤ Practice/Organizational Suggestions

Because leading and following are basic elements for partner dances, the teacher should introduce them by using a simple dance walk. Today's young persons are not accustomed to dancing in contact with a partner, traveling on a dance floor, or following a definite basic step. The teacher, therefore, should try to begin in a fundamental manner.

Using a free formation, the student should learn the basic step of any social dance without a partner. The teacher, prior to presenting the foot pattern, might have students clap hands to the music that will be used for the dance, because being able to recognize the underlying rhythm is essential. The basic step pattern should be performed next with partners, all couples moving in line of direction. While the individuals keep dancing, the teacher may give verbal cues in relation to position, rhythm, or step pattern. If necessary, individual assistance may be continued through additional demonstration or dancing with the student. Students may receive extra ideas or be encouraged to create variations with partners learning together.

In the teaching of social dance, it is important to provide a relaxed learning atmosphere, to suggest and implement partner changes, to build confidence through words of encouragement, and to give opportunities for everyone to practice good social etiquette.

SQUARE DANCE

A Brief History

Although square dancing originated in 17th-century England with the English country dances (as well as the French contra dances), square dance has been labeled "America's Folk Dance." (Note: Some scholars believe that the dances of the Native Americans are the true American folk dances.)

The early New England colonists brought with them these pompous and precise line dances in which the couples faced each other. However, as American square dance evolved, the less rigid and the more recreational and social these dances became. In fact, square dancing was one of the most popular and satisfying forms of social recreation because it was something in which all generations could participate and enjoy.

The "caller" was introduced to American square dance in the early 19th century. The caller enabled dancing participants to execute the basic patterns without having to memorize the dances. Square dance calling requires a good deal of practice, understanding, voice control, and ability to handle large groups. Anyone who attempts calling must have a distinct and pleasant voice, a sense of timing so that the calls will immediately precede the figure and produce continuity in the dance, and a thorough knowledge of the dance figures. Excellent recordings of square dance music with calls are also available.

Although there have been radical changes in the calls, style, and music of contemporary square dance, the basic patterns and figures have been standardized, making it possible to enjoy this popular recreational art form all over the United States and abroad (Figure 9-5). Today, this popularity has created avenues in the competing commercial market for professionally trained callers, square dance retreats and vacations, and square dance clothing and accessories, for those who desire the latest square dance fashions.

Suggested Learning Sequence

Honor	Couple Promenade
Shuffle	Grand Right and Left
Forward and Back	Star Left (Right)
Do-sa-do	Pass Through
Seesaw	Ladies Chain
Allemande Left (Right)	Right and Left Through
Swing	Square Positions
Promenade Single File	Half Promenade

Figure 9-5 Square dancing has become a popular recreational art form in the United States and abroad.

These steps, terms, and figures are described below, along with a few other important square dance terms, in alphabetical order. The number of counts usually used to fully execute the figures and steps are also indicated where appropriate.

Square Dance Terms, Figures, and Steps

Allemande Left.   Man gives his left hand to the woman on his left. With left hands joined, they shuffle around one another (exchanging places) and then both return to place. This figure is sometimes followed by an allemande right, in which the man executes the same figure but with his partner. More frequently, the allemande left is followed by a grand right and left (8 counts).

Circle Left (or Right).   Three or more dancers circle to the left or right, as directed. Hands are joined with elbow comfortably bent so that the hands are above the elbow, man's palm up, woman's palm down (16 counts for a full circle, 8 counts for half).

Corner.   The person to the man's left or the woman's right is the corner person.

Courtesy Turn.   The man takes the woman's left hand in his left, then places his right hand in her right, which is at her back, waist high. Turning counterclockwise, the man backs up and the woman walks forward one half turn.

Do-sa-do.   Do-sa-do is a French term meaning back to back. Two dancers face each other and advance,

passing right shoulders. Each person slides behind the other person passing them, then moves backward into place (8 counts).

Forward and Back.   The persons or couples designated move four steps into the center of the circle, then move four steps backward out of the circle (8 counts).

Grand Right and Left.   In a square or circle formation, the partners face and take right hands. Men going counterclockwise and then women clockwise, each partner moves ahead, giving the left hand to the next person and pulling by, giving the right hand to the next person and pulling by, giving the left to the next, and stop. In square formation, the original partners will now be facing each other and ready for the next call (16 counts).

Honor.   The men bow while the women curtsey to their partners (or to the "corner" person, depending on the call). "Honor your partner" is an acknowledgement of your partner, usually at the beginning of a dance.

Ladies Chains
1. *Two Ladies Chain.* With couples facing each other, men stand still as the women shuffle forward, take right hands, pull by them, then give the left hand to the opposite man, who completes a courtesy turn (8 counts).
2. *Four Ladies Chain or Ladies Grand Chain.* In square formation, all four women star right and move

clockwise to their opposite man, who gives them a courtesy turn (8 counts). Partner: The woman on the man's right, the man on the woman's left. Sometimes partners are changed temporarily before returning to the original partners.

Pass Through. Two facing couples move forward, pass right shoulders, and remain facing in the same direction until the next call.

Promenade
1. *Couple Promenade.* The most commonly used promenade in square dancing is the couple promenade. Standing side by side, couples join left hands, then join right hands on top of their left hands. The couple then moves forward in a counterclockwise direction.
2. *Half Promenade.* Two couples, indicated by the call, use a couple promenade position to move counterclockwise and exchange positions in the square (8 counts).
3. *Promenade Single File.* Dancers face counterclockwise and move one behind the other.

Right and Left Through. With couples facing, each person gives a right hand to the person opposite them and pulls by. The left hand is immediately given to the partner, and each couple does a courtesy turn (8 counts).

Seesaw. Two dancers face and pass left shoulders. Each slides to the left while back to back, then backs up to original position (8 counts).

Separate. Each dancer turns his back on his partner, then they move in opposite directions. This movement is followed by a directional call.

Shuffle. A walking pattern in which the feet alternately slide in short, smooth steps along the floor in time with the music. A shuffle step is executed in an even rhythm, unlike the boisterous skip or hop of the early square dances, which is now regarded as an unacceptable style.

Square Positions. A square is an arrangement of four couples who stand facing the center in a square formation. The couples are numbered consecutively to the right, beginning with couple number 1, whose backs are closest to the music or caller. Couples 1 and 3 are the "head couples"; couples 2 and 4 are the "side couples."

Star Left (or Right). If couples or ladies star, those involved touch fingers of the designated hand, elbows bent, and shuffle forward. If men star, each turns the designated side toward the center of the star, and with an overhand grip, takes the wrist of the man in front of him. Dancers move around the circle to return to their original positions (8 counts).

Swing. This is a modified social dance position in partners. The man's left arm is extended to the side, his right arm around the woman's waist. The woman puts her right hand in the man's left, her left hand is on the man's shoulder. They stand to the side so that right hips and right feet are in line with one another and almost touching. Using the right foot somewhat as a pivot, they push with the left foot so that partners circle about in place, in a clockwise direction. As the swing is performed, partners look at each other and lean away, which results in a quick, vigorous turn (8 counts).

➤ Practice/Organizational Suggestions
1. The most common mistake made by the inexperienced square dance teacher is selecting a specific square dance and then directing the dancers to walk through the basic movements and figures of the dance. The movements from these dances require a great deal of practice and probably cannot be performed with music, resulting in uninteresting drills more than an enjoyable dance. Basic calls should be taught in a single circle. This method enables the teacher to see quickly all dancers, to use music immediately, and to eliminate the necessity for a specific number of students for squares. A simple dance to music can begin, for example, with

    Honor your partner
    Honor your corner
    Join hands, circle left, circle right
    Walk into the middle
    Come right back

2. When the movements can be done effectively, teach a Do-sa-do, Seesaw, Swing, Allemande Left, and a Couple Promenade. All calls may be combined then in varied sequence or in the following manner:

    Face your corner, do a Do-sa-do
    Seesaw your partner
    Join hands, circle right
    Circle left
    Face the center, go forward and back
    Allemande left your corner
    Allemande right your partner
    Swing your corner
    Swing your partner and promenade
    Go single file
    Face the center
    (Repeat)

3. A Grand Right and Left may be taught by designating a certain number of hands until a new partner is reached. For example, a right hand to the partner would be "one" and a left to the next would be "two." Any number may be chosen, but seven hands enables the dancers to learn the

principle involved and eliminates the confusion of counting a large number of hands. Once the Grand Right and Left is mastered, an Allemande Left with the corner may precede this figure. These movements are ready to be combined with those already learned.

4. The group of dancers may then move smoothly from the single circle formation to a double circle with partners facing. One may direct calls already acquired to make dancers comfortable in this new formation, for instance,

Honor your partner
Do-sa-do your opposite
Swing your partner
Circle left, circle right
Allemande right your partner
Allemande left your opposite
Do-sa-do your partner
Seesaw your opposite
Swing your partner

5. In the double-circle formation, Star Left and Right and Pass Through may be taught rapidly. This permits dancers to work with different couples while being at ease with the basic calls. Two Ladies Chain and Right and Left Through may be added to the figures. All basic calls except the Grand Right and Left and the promenades may be combined to music.

The teacher will be able to teach the square formation using previously taught calls and may add more advanced figures as the selected dances below require. Many of these are performed to music that has a familiar melody; therefore, the callers may choose to sing their calls. Happy dancing!

Selected Square Dances for Beginners

Big Daddy
Buffalo Girls
Gentle on My Mind
If You Knew Susie
Little Ole Winemaker
Little Red Wagon
Marina Just Because
Oh, Johnny
Ragtime Banjo Ball
Winchester Cathedral

Modifications for Special Populations

Orthopedically Impaired

1. Keep movement patterns slow, and avoid quick changes for students with movement difficulties, such as students with cerebral palsy, muscular dystrophy, or spina bifida.

2. Keep tempo of music moderate.
3. Emphasize concepts of high, low, soft, hard, rough, smooth, and so on, and have students interpret movements.
4. Minimal modifications are needed in square dance for students using a wheelchair, such as larger work area.

Cognitively Impaired

1. Follow suggestions for the orthopedically impaired.
2. Keep concepts and movement patterns simple.

Sensory Impaired

1. Use peer teachers and paraprofessionals for students who are blind or have a visual impairment.
2. Individual considerations need to be made to determine the appropriateness of dance for students who are deaf or have a hearing impairment.

Further References

Folk Dance

Cavalier, D. *Folk Dances from around the World*. Miami, FL: Warner Brothers Publications, 1997.

Gunzenhauser, M. *The Square Dance and Contra Dance Handbook: Calls, Dance Movements, Music Glossary, Bibliography, Discography and Directories*.

Jefferson, NC: McFarland and Company, Inc. Publishers, 1995.

Harris, J., Dark, C., Waller, M., and Pittman, A. *Dance a While: Handbook for Folk, Square, Contra and Social Dance*. Needham Heights, MA: Allyn & Bacon, 1999.

Weikart, P. *Teaching Movement and Dance: A Sequential Approach to Rhythmic Movement*. Ypsilanti, MI: High/Scope Foundation, 1998.

Country Western Dance

Woodruff, N. and Nielsen, P. *The Big Book of Country Western Line Dancing*. Curtis, WA: NAP Productions Publishers, 1996.

Social (Ballroom) Dance

Darnel, A. and Wals, P. *Beginners Only How To Dance Book: Learn Social, Ballroom, and Latin Dances*. Houston, TX: Beginners Only Publishing Company, 1999.

Harris, J. A., et al. *Dance a While: Handbook of Folk, Square, Contra, and Social Dance*. 6th ed. New York: Macmillan Publishing Co., 1988.

Moore, A. *Ballroom Dancing*. 9th ed. London: A & C Black, 1986.

Schild, M. *Social Dance*. Dubuque, IA: Wm. C. Brown Publishers, 1985.

Wals, P. and Wals, R. *Beginners Only How to Dance Book: Learn Social Level Dancing for Youth to Seniors.* Houston, TX: Beginners Only Publishing Company, 1997.

Wright, J. *Social Dance: Steps to Success.* Champaign, IL: Leisure Press, 1992.

Square Dance

Casey, B. *The Complete Book of Square Dancing and Round Dancing.* Denton, TX: University of North Texas Press, 2000.

Gunzenhauser, M. *The Square Dance and Contra Dance Handbook.* Virum, Denmark: Square Dance Partners, 1996.

Harris, J., Dark, C., Waller, M., and Pittman, A. *Dance a While: Handbook for Folk, Square, Contra and Social Dance.* Needham Heights, MA: Allyn & Bacon, 1999.

Schild, M. *Square Dancing Everyone.* Winston-Salem, NC: Hunter Textbooks, Inc., 1987.

Trimmer, G. *Singing Thru Mainstream.* Marlborough, NH: Supreme Audio, Inc., 1995.

Web Sites

Folk Dance

www.folkdancing.org Offers an extensive list of folk dance varieties with a description of each. Searchers can identify themselves as a newcomer, intermediate, or experienced dancer, thereby accessing relevant information more quickly. Additional information is available about Western Square Dance.

www.ifdo.pugmarks.com/dancepage.html The "International Folk Dance Resources Pages" in the index provides numerous links to a variety of dances, especially the "Folk Dance Notes" link.

Country Western Dance

www.sapphireswan.com/dance/links/western.htm A site with several Country Western dance links. The two "Let's Dance" selections provide an extensive listing of dances.

www.cwdi.org A resource guide for Country Western dance information. The dance resources selections on the site are beneficial to the learner.

Social (Ballroom) Dance

www.dancetv.com A site on ballroom dancing with tutorials on the waltz, fox-trot, and swing, plus a section on dance tips.

www.vidbook.com/titles.htm An alphabetized index for selecting a variety of dance steps.

www.socialdanceseries.com/more.html A contact for an integrated dance program for learning eight different dances: waltz, fox-trot, tango, rumba, cha cha, east coast swing, and city swing.

Square Dance

www.dosado.com A very comprehensive site index with over 40 various selections, including other dance forms.

www.heritagedance.com An extensive site featuring articles and links to the history of square dancing.

CHAPTER 10

Field Hockey

This chapter will enable you to

- Identify the field markings
- Describe the basic rules of the game
- Analyze and demonstrate the techniques of holding the stick, dribbling, the hit, fielding, various passes, the tackle, the dodge, the penalty corner, the free hit, defense hit, and push in
- Identify and describe the common goalkeeping techniques
- Describe basic offensive and defensive tactics
- Understand and use the basic terminology

Nature and Purpose

Field hockey, recognized as one of the most popular sports throughout the world, is an Olympic sport for both men and women. In the United States it has been played predominantly by women; however, men do play in various locations. The United States Field Hockey Association, through its sponsorship of youth hockey programs, encourages both girls and boys to become involved in the sport.

The game is played by two teams of 11 players usually designated as forwards, midfielders (links), defensive backs, sweeper, and goalie. The forwards are offensive players and therefore must be quick, possess good stickwork and ball control skills, and shoot well. The midfielders serve as links transforming the game from defense to offense. Midfielders must be in good physical condition to play both offense and defense; they must be good playmakers to set up the forwards and sure tacklers to stop the offensive thrust of the opponent. Defensive backs must be aggressive and possess good marking skills in addition to being strong tacklers. The sweeper, the last line before the goalie, directs play and shores up the defense. Sweepers must have patience, good fielding skills, and a "nose" for the ball. The last link in the defensive chain is the goalie, who must have catlike reflexes and be aggressive. Although some players are by nature offensive or defensive, an emphasis should be placed on total team offense and defense.

Field hockey has changed significantly in recent years. Although a traditional 5-3-2-1-G alignment is still used, most teams are moving to a style of play that is more characteristic of soccer. Spectators may

expect to see a variety of system alignments (3-3-3-1-G, 4-2-3-1-G) being employed by a team based on the talents of individual players (Figure 10-1).

Each player carries a hockey stick, which is the only means employed to move the ball in this game. The one exception to this rule is that the goalkeeper has kicking privileges.

Goals count one point and can be scored only if an attacker's stick touches the ball inside the striking circle.

Figure 10-1 Starting alignment of 4-3-2-1-G. Note team balance (depth), possible passing routes, and opportunities for 2-on-1 or 3-on-2 situations.

The official game is played in two halves with time out between halves, at which point the teams change ends. Note: The rules for high school, college, and international play vary in length of halves and half-time.

Because of the vigorous nature of the game and the skill, coordination, and conditioning needed, field hockey is an acceptable activity for both boys and girls and men and women in a school or college physical education program. Whether played by all boys, all girls, or on a coeducational basis, it is important to emphasize the rules of play, particularly those governing the hockey stick. Emphasis should also be placed on the wearing of shin guards and other protective gear.

For coeducational play, any or all of the following rule modifications may be made:

1. Use a larger, softer rubber ball rather than the official field hockey ball (especially in youth hockey).
2. Alternate positioning of girls and boys on the field to encourage participation and passing to one another.
3. Reduce the size of the field and the number of players (6 on 6) so the emphasis is on skill rather than on speed or strength.
4. Involve both boys and girls in specialty situations, such as penalty corner plays (i.e., boys push out and girls stop and hit) and penalty strokes.
5. Eliminate the hit and allow only a push.
6. Eliminate the flick when shooting at goal.

As in soccer, an indoor version of field hockey has become very popular. Indoor hockey is played on a gym floor (similar to street hockey) with six players on a team. With large classes, use the additional players for sideline play. There are rule modifications involved with indoor play, the most significant of which eliminates the hit and thereby encourages controlled passing with a push pass. Indoor hockey can be an excellent rainy day or cold weather activity as well as a complete unit.

Playing Field

The field is about the size of a football field, 100 yards long and 60 yards wide, with a goal at each end (Figure 10-2). Goal posts are 4 yards apart and 7 feet high, joined by a crossbar. The posts and cross-bars should have a square front and be painted white. The goal is usually enclosed with a net or screening.

The striking circle is placed on the field by starting with a straight line drawn 16 yards in front of the goal and 4 yards long. This line is continued to the end line by quarter-circle arcs of a 16-yard radius with the goal posts as centers.

Figure 10-2 The hockey field.

Basic Rules

The following basic rules may require modification for coeducational play and perhaps additional rules for safety.

Fouls

1. Taking part in the game without a stick
2. Using the rounded side of the stick
3. Advancing a ball off the body. Note: Only the goalkeeper is permitted to kick the ball or block the ball with the body. The goalie shall not be penalized if the ball is deflected off the body, provided it is not dangerous to another player and the goalie contacts the ball within the striking circle.
4. Hitting the ball in a dangerous manner (i.e., into a player at close range, a hard hit that rises, or a ball that is hit on the fly)
5. Using the stick in a dangerous manner (i.e., following through into another player, tripping, or slashing)
6. Obstruction: placing the body (feet, shoulder, or any part) between an opponent and the ball. A player may not obstruct an opponent from playing the ball by shielding the ball with their body

or stick. If a player keeps moving with the ball, obstruction can be prevented.

7. Stick obstruction: interfering with an opponent's stick (i.e., strike, hook, hold)
8. Pushing, charging, shoving, tripping, or in any way interfering with an opponent

Penalties for Fouls

A. Outside the circle. A free hit is awarded to the team fouled against on the spot of the foul.
B. Inside the circle
   1. Foul by the attack—a defense hit that is outside the circle and 16 yards out from the end line. This also applies when the foul occurs outside the circle but within 16 yards of the offensive goal. The 16-yard distance is designated by a hash mark on the sideline.
   2. Foul by the defense
      a. A penalty corner is awarded to the attacking team.
      b. A penalty stroke is awarded if the foul stopped a sure goal or was flagrant.

Out-of-Bounds Play

In all cases, the line is considered "in the field of play" whether it be the circle, sideline, end, or goal line. The umpire must decide which team touched the ball last, because there is no provision in the rules for co-responsibility (off two sticks).

A. Over the sideline. A hit-in (hit or push) by a member of the team opposite that of the player who last touched the ball before it crossed the sideline
B. Over the end line but not between the goal posts
   1. Off the attack—a defense hit
   2. Off the defense
      a. When the ball is unintentionally hit over the end line—a long hit
      b. When the ball is intentionally hit over the end line—penalty corner
      c. Over the end line between the goal posts
         (1) A legal goal when the ball was touched by the stick of an attack inside the striking circle. Play resumed by a center pass on the center line. The goal counts even if the ball was last touched by the stick or person of the defense.
         (2) When the ball was not touched by a stick of the attack inside the circle and
            (a) was touched by a stick of the defense—a long hit is awarded.
            (b) was last touched by a stick of the attack—a defense hit is awarded.

Equipment

The Ball

The official ball is hard and slightly larger than a baseball. For class purposes, a seamless polyurethane ball is most practical.

The Stick

The hockey stick ranges from 26 inches (youth sizes) to 38 inches in length and generally weighs from 16 to 23 ounces. The thin portion above the heel has a wrapping (usually fiberglass, although other materials are used) around the wood to give greater strength to this critical area. The blade is generally made of mulberry wood and is somewhat shorter today than it used to be. The left side of the blade is flat and is used for contact with the ball. The right side of the blade is rounded and may not be used for contact with the ball at any time (Figure 10-3).

When selecting the stick, it is important that the handle be comfortable, thin, and strong. The stick should be light enough to facilitate technique and ease of control. To determine the suitable stick length, the individual should stand, grasp the stick as for a hit, and swing it in front of the body. The stick should "feel" comfortable and should not hit the ground behind the ball at contact. For elementary age physical education classes there are junior hockey sticks available that are shorter and lighter than typical adult sticks.

Protective Equipment

Shin guards are wise protection for all field players. The padding should cover the ankle bone as well as the shins. Mouthguards are also recommended and are generally a requirement in competitive play.

Goalkeeper's pads should cover the leg from the thigh down. In addition to pads, kickers are worn to provide padding over the goalie's field shoe. Required protection for goalies also includes a helmet with a face guard and throat protector. Chest, shoulder, groin, arm, and elbow pads are also encouraged.

Figure 10-3 The hockey stick, right and left view.

Suggested Learning Sequence

There are numerous ways to arrange the sequence of skill development for field hockey. In the one proposed, dribbling and passing skills are introduced early along with teaching students to move into space and use support passing to beat a defender. Fielding should be taught with the push pass and hit so that students can stop a ball coming toward them. As a general guide, it is best to introduce a technique along with its definition, a rule that may apply, and some strategy involved.

A. Nature and purpose
B. Conditioning aspects—plan drills and exercises that might be related to movements found in field hockey. Emphasis of all areas of fitness, particularly upper body (forearm, wrist) strength, agility, speed, and flexibility.
   1. Circuit training with stickwork
   2. Footwork and acceleration moves
C. Basic game concepts
   1. Field of play
   2. Use of equipment
   3. Playing courtesies
D. Skills and strategy—introduce rules and terminology as well as combination skills and strategies at most appropriate times.
   1. Skills
      a. Gripping the stick
      b. Dribbling
      c. Push pass and fielding
      d. Hitting
      e. Reverse sweep
      f. Flicking
      g. Dodging
      h. Tackling
      i. Goalkeeping
   2. Tactics and strategy
      a. Offensive playing hints and passing combinations
      b. Defensive playing hints
      c. Game tactics: Center pass, free hit, defense hit, hit-in, penalty corner, penalty stroke, long hit.

Skills and Techniques

The proper relationship between ball and feet is most important and can only be gained by always practicing skills while one is moving. The essence of stickwork is footwork. Make the feet assume the proper relationship to the ball, not the ball to the feet. Be able to see the ball while also scanning the field for open space and passing options.

Gripping the Stick

There are three basic grips used in field hockey. The fundamental position is used for the basic dribble as well as hitting, pushing, and fielding. A grip change is required for reverse stick contact on the ball, as in the Indian dribble. A third grip is used in defensive play when utilizing the jab.

1. *Fundamental position.* With the heel of the stick resting on the ground in front of the body, allow the top of the handle to fall into the fingers of the left hand. This is basically a handshake position on the stick. Place the right hand 6 to 8 inches below the left. Grip the stick easily so the V formed by the thumb and index finger of both hands is in line with the top of the stick (Figure 10-4).

2. *Indian dribble grip.* A slight variation of the fundamental grip occurs when the player executes an Indian dribble or any reverse stick action of the ball. In this grip, the left hand slides right slightly. To assure correct positioning, place the stick flatside on the ground; reach down and place the V of the left hand on top of the stick (Figure 10-5). The right hand assumes its normal positioning. This grip allows the left hand to rotate the stick over the ball. The right simply acts as a sleeve allowing the stick to rotate in it.

Figure 10-4 Fundamental grip. Note the handshake positioning on the stick with V of left hand on side of stick when toe is up.

Figure 10-5 Assuming correct positioning for the Indian dribble grip. Note the V of left hand is on rounded side of stick.

Figure 10-6 Defensive grip. Note the V of left hand is on flat side of stick.

3. *Defensive grip.* Slide the left hand slightly left from the fundamental position. In this grip, the V of the left hand comes on the handle when the flat side of the stick is up (Figure 10-6).

➤ **Learning Hints**

1. Hold the stick firmly but comfortably.
2. Adjust grip appropriately according to the skill executed.

Dribbling

In the dribble, the fundamental grip position is used with the body in a crouched position for running. The stick is on the ball, which is in front of the body and slightly off to the right side (Figure 10-7). The arms are relaxed and away from the body, with the right arm extended beyond the left. The ball is moved forward by the stick as the player begins to run. The feet should stay behind the ball, and a change of direction is initiated by accelerating the feet in that direction. The ball should be kept close to the stick unless a player is in open field, in which case the ball can be pushed slightly ahead.

Indian Zigzag Dribble. This dribble is generally used in crowded areas and before attempting to move around an opponent. The ball is positioned in front of the body and is rolled over on alternate sides by the use of forehand and reverse stick taps (Figure 10-8). This movement uses the Indian dribble grip.

The zigzag motion with the stick around the ball allows the dribbler to disguise the dribble with faking moves, making it difficult for the opponent to tackle.

Figure 10-7 Dribble position. Ball is on the stick in front of the body. Player's eyes scan ahead.

A   B   C

Figure 10-8 Zigzag dribble. Forehand action on the ball. Stick rolls over ball with reverse stick action.

➤ Learning Hints

1. Keep the feet behind the ball.
2. Stay low and reach out for the ball.
3. Keep the stick close to the ball. Move the ball by accelerating with the feet.

➤ Practice/Organizational Suggestions

1. Begin by moving in a straight line—push the ball ahead with an emphasis on footwork and ball control. Concentrate on staying low by bending at the knees and keeping the head up. As they dribble, have the students call out the number of fingers held up by the teacher.
2. Move on diagonals and into open space with a change of direction. Emphasize that the feet initiate the action when changing direction.
3. Practice the technique of the Indian dribble stationary, then in a straight line, with direction change and around cones.
4. Use a designated grid area with 6 to 10 students and have them dribble around each other. Encourage dribbling into open space. Place cones on the grid and see how many cones the students can dribble to in one minute.

Fielding the Ball

The ball should be fielded or controlled when it comes to a player before it is passed or played. A "two-touch" sequence is used when thinking about fielding and passing. The first touch stops the ball, and the immediate second touch advances the ball. The right hand slides further down the stick (Figure 10-9).

➤ Learning Hints

1. Line the body up behind an approaching ball in a low position.
2. Let the ball come to the stick. Absorb the ball by having a "soft" right hand. Control deflections.
3. The left hand angles forward to trap the ball in the stick. Second touch the ball with pass or dribble.

➤ Practice/Organizational Suggestions

1. Have a partner roll a ball to a player with a stick. Emphasize lining up, absorbing, and trapping the ball.
2. Have a partner field a ball pushed or hit from another.
3. Introduce fielding on the move, i.e., shuttle passing, passing down the field with a partner.
4. Introduce a passive defender and play two-versus-one keep-away. Later, as proficiency in fielding is gained, add an active defender.
5. Add passing drills that encourage give-and-go passing, i.e., player A receives a pass from player B, A passes back to B, cutting to receive and hit on goal.

Figure 10-9 Fielding the ball. Left hand angles forward as right hand absorbs the ball.

Push Passing

The push pass is used for short, accurate passing or shooting when there is no time or necessity to hit the ball. The pass can be executed quickly off the dribble or after receiving a pass. There is no backswing on this skill because the stick stays on the ball as it is pushed forward. The approach on this skill involves starting with the left shoulder and foot forward in the direction of the pass, and the body in a low position (Figure 10-10). The ball should be contacted opposite the left foot.

➤ **Learning Hints**

1. With the body in the correct approach position, extend the arms out away from the body to push the ball forward. Let the wrists snap as the skill is completed.

2. The left side of the body initiates the action of this skill. Transfer the body weight from back to front foot, and finish with the head over a bent left knee.

3. Both hands need to push through and away from the body toward the intended direction of the pass.

➤ **Practice/Organizational Suggestions**

1. In a stationary position, push pass with a partner. Emphasize arm extension and follow-through.

2. Pass the ball off the dribble to a partner, as in a shuttle formation.

3. Move into give-and-go passing and keep-away as presented in #4, #5 for fielding.

Hitting

The hit is used for passing and shooting, and with proper execution will be quicker and harder than the push pass. The fundamental grip position is used, but the hands need to be brought together at the top of the stick. The stick swings in a perpendicular plane with a hip to hip pendulum-like motion in the direction the ball is to travel. The ball should be contacted opposite the left foot. On the backswing and follow-through, the toe of the stick is up (Figure 10-11). This is primarily a left-sided skill with a straight left arm pulling the stick through, with a weight transfer onto the front (left) foot. To be assured of an accurate hit, allow the hands to guide the stick in the direction of the pass.

➤ **Learning Hints**

1. Bring hands together (fundamental grip position).

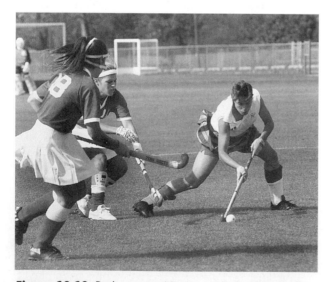

Figure 10-10 Push pass positioning. Left shoulder in direction of pass and low positioning.

Figure 10-11 The hit. Note the backswing and the beginning of weight transfer.

2. Transfer the weight to front foot. Initiate a left arm pull.
3. Let the arms swing freely.
4. Follow through with arms to intended direction of pass. Right hand helps guide the stick as the left arm pulls through.

➤ Practice/Organizational Suggestions

1. Let the arms swing the stick in a pendulum fashion. Recognize a relaxed and freely flowing arm position. Practice left arm swings.
2. Hit to a fence (or rebound board) and follow through with the stick to the fence.
3. In a stationary position practice the hit with a partner. Add hitting on the move (i.e., shuttle, passing down the field, dribbling, and hitting on the goal).

Reverse Sweep

The reverse sweep is used in the game as a technique to pass or shoot when the ball is on the left side of the body. The approach involves moving the right shoulder and foot forward in the direction of the pass. The grip has the hands sliding so the Vs are on the flat slide of the stick. On the backswing the stick and hands are close to the ground. Contact is made with the ball in front of the right foot with the shaft of the stick coming through the back of the ball (Figure 10-12). On the swing the toe of the stick comes through ahead of the hands, with a quick wrist action that brings the stick low and around in a sweeping motion on the follow-through.

➤ Learning Hints

1. Backswing is low with hands and stick close to the ground and knees bent.

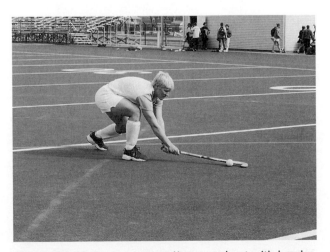

Figure 10-12 Reverse sweep. Knees are bent with hands and stick close to the ground.

2. Keep the body low, and let the arms, with an exaggerated wrist snap, swing through to ball contact off the right foot.
3. The follow-through carries the stick low and close to the ground as it wraps around the body.

➤ Practice/Organizational Suggestions

1. Practice the sweep in a stationary position with a partner. Emphasize allow hands and stick position. To help keep the body low, start with the left knee on the ground.
2. Pass the ball off the dribble by pulling the ball left and passing to a target.
3. Dribble toward goal, and pull and shoot with the reverse sweep.

Flicking

There is also no backswing on this skill, which is executed like the push pass. In the flick, however, the ball is slightly in front of the body so the stick can be placed under the ball. The left hand brings the top of the stick back and behind the right hand, which causes the stick face to open. Therefore, when the stroke is executed, the ball will rise with the height, depending on the angle of the stick. The flick is used as a technique for lifting the ball over a defender's stick, for penalty strokes, and for shooting. The flick is especially valuable for shooting at close range, since the ball comes off the ground. It is possible to execute the flick with a moving ball, but it is more difficult.

➤ Learning Hints

1. The stroke and follow-through are executed like the push pass.
2. Angle the stick by bringing the left hand back behind the right. This opens the stick face up and causes the ball to lift up.

➤ Practice/Organizational Suggestions

1. In a stationary position, practice the flick with a partner or into the goal.
2. Flick the ball to goal off a dribble.
3. Practice penalty strokes.

Dodging

The dodge is used when a player in possession of the ball wishes to evade an opponent who is approaching from the front. Because this technique is so useful, players should learn a variety of dodges. It is particularly important for beginners to learn how to dodge, thereby avoiding the natural tendency to move directly into an opponent—which is illegal. Teachers should introduce dodging at an early stage in the unit and provide for continued practice.

Figure 10-13 Diagrams of dodges: (A) non–stick-side dodge, (b) reverse stick dodge, (C) pull left dodge.

Non–Stick-Side Dodge. The player in possession of the ball sends the ball ahead and close to the non-stick side of the approaching opponent. The player runs to the stick side of the opponent. In other words, the ball goes right, and the player goes left (Figure 10-13A). This dodge (which is sometimes called Y dodge) is easily executed and very successful because it is played to the opponent's non-stick side. However, control of the ball is important because possession is temporarily lost.

Reverse Stick Dodge. Before the opponent can reach the ball, the player in possession pulls the ball with a reverse stick action laterally to the right. After this move, the player accelerates forward by the opponent (Figure 10-13B). The advantage of this dodge is it also goes to the non-stick side of the opponent, but with the player remaining in possession of the ball at all times. However, it is a more difficult dodge to execute.

Pull to the Left. On this dodge, both the ball and player go to the left of the approaching opponent. Shortly before the ball is within reach of the opponent, the player pulls the ball laterally to the left past the opponent's stick (Figure 10-13C). Upon completion of this move, the player should accelerate forward by the opponent. During this dodge, the ball remains in the player's possession; however, the timing must be accurate and the ball must be played laterally left, not diagonally, to avoid the opponent's stick.

► **Learning Hints**

1. Execute the dodge just before the opponent is within reach of the ball. Remember that both players are moving, thus this point will be considerably farther away than expected.

2. Keep the ball in control on the dodge to assure player possession.
3. Execute the dodge right off the dribble. Accelerate by the defender and cut in behind the defender to eliminate opponent recovery.
4. On lateral pulls, turn the feet and run with the ball. Avoid slide stepping.

► **Practice/Organizational Suggestions**

1. Practice dodge moves against a cone or a stationary defender. Be sure to emphasize lateral pulls as needed and footwork.
2. Dodge a passive defender who is standing but may use a stick to reach. Encourage early dodging by going against a defender who is using an ice hockey stick to extend the reach. The player must dodge before getting within a stick's reach of the opponent.
3. Carry this into one-versus-one play with an aggressive defender.

Tackling

The tackle is a technique used in attempting to take the ball away from an opponent. The key to becoming an accomplished tackler is preparation and patience.

In the preparation, a defender must establish a basic athletic stance: feet shoulder-width apart, knees flexed slightly, head up with eyes watching the ball, and feet moving. The stick is down low to the ground and extended toward the ball in a shadowing fashion (Figure 10-14). As the opponent approaches, the defender should establish an overplaying position (to

Figure 10-14 Defensive positioning. Note the stick is down, with player in a balanced position using the jab grip.

the left of the opponent), which forces the opponent to dribble into the defender's stick side. If the opponent dribbles to the right, the defender must quickly move the feet to constitute forcing the opponent right. If the opponent does get to the non-stick side (left) of the defender, the tackle must be made with a reverse stick, which is more difficult.

The defender's feet must be moving and giving with the opponent before a tackle can be made. This will allow the defender to be patient, and find the opportune time to steal the ball from the opponent. Caution must be made to avoid overcommitment and lunging, which makes the defender susceptible to being beaten with an opponent's dodge.

There are two basic approaches to tackling:

1. *Jab Tackle* (Figure 10-15) As the defender retreats with the opponent, extend the stick with the left hand to jab under the ball. If the attempt is unsuccessful, resume the position of two hands on the stick and attempt again. Fake jabs may be successful in confusing the opponent.

Figure 10-15 Jab tackle.

Figure 10-16 Block tackle.

2. *Block Tackle* (Figure 10-16) The defender gives with the opponent, stick down, and allows the opponent to bring the ball to the defender. For this tackle, the stick is held with the fundamental grip, and the defender extends the stick with two hands to block the ball. Avoid swinging and chopping with the stick.

► Learning Hints

1. Overplay to force opponent to the stick side.
2. Keep the feet moving with the opponent. Time the tackle so it is unexpected.
3. Continually jab and retreat, pressuring the ball.

► Practice/Organizational Suggestions

1. Without sticks and balls, have the defenders practice footwork against an opponent.
2. Have a defender move with an opponent who is dribbling straight ahead with the ball. The defender may not tackle, but should watch for the appropriate time to tackle. The defender can also make jab fakes.
3. Allow a defender to make a tackle against an opponent moving at half speed. Incorporate block and jab tackles.
4. Move into one-versus-one play with the defender tackling an aggressive dribbler. After the defender tackles and assumes possession, accelerate away from the opponent. Can also build in a passing option after possession is gained.

Goalkeeping

Goalkeeping requires skills different from those of other positions. The goalkeeper must be agile, quick, and have good concentration and anticipation. The goalie is well protected with a helmet, gloves, pads for the legs, and padded kickers that go over the regular field shoe. Pads to protect the chest, throat, groin, and elbows are recommended. The goalie has the privilege of using the feet for stopping and directing the ball and may also stop the ball with the hand and other parts of the body, as long as it is not batted or deflected in a dangerous manner.

Stance. A basic athletic stance with a few modifications would describe the goalie stance. The feet are shoulder-width apart, weight evenly distributed on the balls of the feet, legs slightly flexed, a slight lean forward, the arms hanging in front with the forearms parallel to the ground. Grasp the stick with palms facing out; the blade will be up and slightly pointing away from the right goal post. The head should be up watching the ball.

Goalkeeping Principles. The goalkeeper is the last line of defense. There are three important principles to follow and practice.[1]

1. In order to defend the goal line, the goalkeeper moves with small steps and drop steps in a triangular movement from the post to a point position 3 to 4 yards in front of the goal and back toward the opposite post. This allows the goalkeeper to narrow the angle to goal and thereby eliminate shooting space.

2. The goalkeeper should be set when a shot is made. This will allow the goalie to react to the shot. If moving on the shot, the goalie could be caught off balance and unable to change direction to react to the ball.

3. The goalkeeper should line up with the ball; i.e., the ball should be in line with the goalkeeper and the goal line.

Technique. The beginning goalkeeper should meet the ball with legs together and "give" on impact so the ball drops almost dead. It is then cleared with the inside of the foot or the toe, hard and accurately, to a space away from the opponent (usually along the sideline) or to a teammate ready to receive and relay the ball up the field. On the kick to clear the ball, the goalie must have the head over the ball and hold a balanced position. After contact, the knee follows through upward to bring the foot back into place alongside the other. With more experience, the goalie may learn to step out and redirect the ball with one foot, especially a well-directed shot that is impossible to get behind with two feet. The stick is used only for emergency clears.

With the development of foam kickers and leg guards, the technique of goalkeeping has changed. Due to the high rebound effect that the foam equipment offers, goalkeepers will go right into blocking the ball with the foot or leg to clear the ball out (Figure 10-17). Contact is made with the ball in front of the body, with the foot moving flat along the ground.

Figure 10-17 Goalkeeper blocks the ball off the foam kickers. The body is low with the head over the ball on contact.

Body weight will transfer into ball contact, and it is still most important for the head to be over the ball.

➤ Practice/Organizational Suggestions

Students should always wear protective equipment when practicing goalkeeping or in a scrimmage.

1. Reaction drills. Roll balls to the right, straight on, and to the left one at a time but quickly after each goalie clear. Emphasis is on getting behind the ball and maintaining balance and control.

2. Practice the application of basic goalkeeping principles. This can be accomplished by having a player push or hit on goal. Use caution to avoid players hitting when in very close to the goalie; instead, encourage players to use the more accurate push pass rather than the hit.

3. Place a goalie in the goal area with a 3-on-3 or 5-on-5 scrimmage situation. Emphasis should be placed on clearing the ball into space away from the rushing attack.

Modified Games

Sideline Hockey

Utilizing a grid area, divide the group into two teams and number off each side. Each team protects a line. Call out a number, and the player from each side with that number approaches a ball in the middle. The players compete one against one, trying to score by pushing the ball across the line of the opposing team. Repeat after a score. Develop the passing game by increasing the number of participants.

Keep Away

Divide into teams of three, four, or five and have teams work to keep the ball from the other through passing. Every three completed passes score a point. For beginners, it may be best to give the advantage to the team with the ball (i.e., 3 versus 1, 4 versus 2, 5 versus 3).

Six Aside

Half-field play utilizing six players against six attacking a goal. A smaller number of people participating will allow more touches on the ball for each player.

Playing Strategies

Offensive Strategy

Once the ball is in a team's possession, the players on that team must think about advancing the ball toward the goal. Advancement is executed by dribbling and through a series of passes. No matter which formation is being used, the following key principles must be employed if the attack is to be successful.

1. *Movement in Space*
   a. Players with the ball—a player in possession should move the ball into free space. This movement should result in the drawing of a defender, in which case the player should look for further options.
   b. Players off the ball—the responsibility here is for a player off the ball to move into a helping position for the player with the ball. These players are in a "support" role and need to position themselves in open space where the ball can be passed. A player standing behind a defender is considered in "dead space" where a teammate will have to pass through the defender in order to make the pass.
2. *Passing.* The ability to execute an accurate and well-paced pass to a teammate is the essence of field hockey. Passing includes the responsibilities discussed earlier of moving the ball to open space and support play. Teams that employ a hit-and-chase style of play will have minimal opportunities to establish a cohesive offensive plan. The team having the ability to make accurate, precise passes and maintain possession of the ball will have the most scoring opportunities and will control the tempo of the game.

   At any time during a game a player should have two to three avenues available to execute a pass if the team has established good field balance and depth (i.e., relationship of forwards, midfielders, and defense). Considerable practice time should be allowed for passing in combinations of 2, 3, or 4 players. Drills should be developed that include two-versus-one, three-versus-two, or four-versus-three situations where the passer and players without the ball must confront and get around a defender.
3. *Scoring Ability.* The team that wins is the team scoring the most goals. A constant offensive pressure employed by all members of the team will usually result in more scoring opportunities. Players must be able to get shots off quickly and accurately, and follow up on rebounds.
4. *Individual Ball Control.* Although creating space and passing are the most essential elements of the game, there are circumstances in which an offensive player must be able to get by a defender (one-versus-one) while carrying the ball. Successful dodging, acceleration, and stick and body fakes while maintaining tight ball control are necessities in developing success in the one-versus-one situation.

Defensive Strategies

Once the ball is in the possession of the opposing team, all players on the team without the ball must focus on defensive strategy. Defense involves total concentration on the game and an awareness of the offensive players in the vicinity. Various strategies are employed in the game involving player to player, zone play, and a combination of both. In general, though, a good defender must understand the following concepts.

1. *Pressure on the ball.* The first responsibility on defense is to provide constant pressure to the player in possession of the ball. When applying this pressure, it is important to channel the offensive player to a specific direction. In most instances, this should result in forcing the opposing player to the strong side or stick side. An exception would occur with left-side defensive players, who generally would channel the opponent to the sideline.
2. *Marking.* The second responsibility on defense is to apply pressure on the next opponent most likely to gain possession of the ball. Being able to mark an opponent without the ball in order to prevent that player from receiving a pass or to decoy that player is good defensive strategy. In such a situation it is important to know the position of the ball and the location of your own goal. The defensive player should stand ball side and goal side of the opponent when marking.
3. *Covering.* If an offensive player gets behind a defender assigned coverage, then another defender must be prepared to move in and accept the responsibility. The sweeper is most frequently found in a covering role. Once the opponent moves past a defender, it is important for that defender to switch into an unoccupied position (to cover) or to recover and catch the attacker (Figure 10-18).

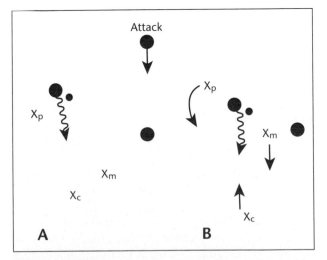

Figure 10-18 Defensive roles: (A) X_p pressure player with the ball; X_m marking ball side, X_c covering goal side; (B) when X_p is beaten and X_c moves to pick up the free offensive player while X_p recovers.

4. *Transition.* Being able to switch from offense to defense without a moment's delay is going to save valuable yards. It may also make the difference in regaining possession of a ball momentarily lost and turning it back to your advantage. The reverse is also true in changing from defense to offense. Upon changing possession, the defense needs to accelerate immediately into space, looking for passing options.

Situational Game Tactics

Center Pass. From the middle of the 50-yard line, the game is started with a center pass at the beginning, at halftime, and after a goal.

Formation. Both teams line up in any manner on their own respective halves. All opposing players must be 5 yards away.

Execution. The ball must be hit or pushed at least 1 yard in any direction. Emphasis should be placed on an accurate, well-paced pass.

Penalty Stroke. The penalty stroke is awarded to the attacking team when a foul (intentional or unintentional) is committed by the defending team inside the circle and a sure goal is prevented, or for a flagrant foul inside the circle.

Formation. The penalty shot is taken at a point 7 yards from the center of the goal line. Aside from the shooter and opposing goalie, the remaining players must remain outside the circle behind the 25-yard line until the ball is played.

The Play. The goalkeeper should be in a ready position on the goal line, not leaving the goal line or moving the feet until the ball is played. The player (on the 7-yard spot) taking the penalty shot must use a flick or a push (no backswing allowed). The referee asks the goalie, then the shooter if each player is ready and then whistles for the play to begin. The shooter has five seconds in which to execute the stroke and is allowed one stride to the ball before shooting. Faking or any other deceptive moves by either player are not allowed. After a successful goal, the play is restarted by a center pass. If the try is unsuccessful, the defense is awarded a free hit from the 16-yard area.

Penalty Corner. This formation is awarded as an advantage to the attacking team. It occurs when the defense fouls in the circle or when a defender intentionally sends a ball out-of-bounds over the end line.

Formation. The ball is placed on the end line 10 yards from the nearer goal post on either side of the goal, according to the choice of the attacking team. A member of the attacking team hits the ball out to a designated teammate on the circle. At different play levels, rules vary as to whether the ball must be stopped in or outside the circle. However, to score,

Figure 10-19 (A) Formation for penalty corner; (B) defensive zone alignment with rusher, trailer, cover, post, and goalie.

the ball must be hit from inside the circle. Other attacking players arrange themselves around the circle and, when the ball is hit, move in to rush the shot and play any rebounds. There needs to be additional players backing up the forwards to provide support in case the ball is missed or is hit out of the circle by the defense (Figure 10-19A).

The defending team has five players (including the goalie) who start with sticks and bodies behind the end line. No player may be nearer than 5 yards to the player hitting the ball out. These players may move as soon as the ball is hit. Usually a zone formation (Figure 10-19B) is used to defend against the initial shot. The other six members of the defending team are behind the 50-yard line, and may not cross it until the ball is hit out.

The zone formation usually involves a rusher who pressures the initial shot. This player must approach in a stick-to-stick position (defender on attack) to avoid being hit with the shot. A trailer also follows out stick-to-stick but behind the rusher in case that individual is beat. A cover moves by the goalie to assist with any rebounds and to get the ball out of scoring range. The goalie moves out from the goal line to narrow the angle and play the shot. Last, but certainly not least, is a post player who positions on the goal line (to the goalie's non-stick side) to stop any shots that may get past the goalie. Once support from other players is available, the defense moves into marking position on the opponents.

The Play. The designated offensive player pushes or hits the ball along the ground to a teammate, who must stop the ball. After the stop, the ball should be hit to goal or passed to another teammate to hit to goal. In circumstances in which field hockey is played on astroturf, a corner frequently involves a stick stop. In this case, after the ball is hit out, a teammate stops the ball for a second player to hit immediately. A variety of alignments and plays can be developed to assist in getting a shot off to goal. However, the success of a corner basically lies in a good initial pass, consequent stop, and hard, accurate hit to goal.

Free Hit. A free hit is awarded to the opposite team when a foul is committed anywhere on the field, except inside the circle (in which case a defensive hit or penalty corner is awarded according to the circumstances).

Formation. For a free hit outside the circle, the ball is placed on the spot where the breach occurred and is usually played by a midfielder or defensive player of the team fouled against. However, a forward can also play the ball, especially if it can resume play quickly and help gain an advantage. For any free hit, all opposing players must stand 5 yards away. Within a team's offensive 25 yards, teammates must be 5 yards away as well. The ball must be motionless before the hit can be taken.

The Play. The player taking the free hit may hit or push pass the ball, and the ball must move at least 1 yard. In high school play, the ball may also be lifted, but in college play, the ball must remain on the ground. After taking a free hit, a player may not play the ball again until it has been touched by another player. When possible, a free hit should be taken quickly, so as to take full advantage of the penalty, before the opposing team gets placed to block the play. A free hit should be passed to a teammate or into open space for a teammate to run immediately onto the ball.

Defense Hit. A defense hit is awarded to the defending team when an attacking player hits the ball over the end line or commits a foul within the attacking 16-yard area.

Formation. The ball is placed 16 yards from the end line exactly opposite the spot where it left the field of play (and should be outside the circle). It is usually taken by a defensive player in whose area the ball is placed. The ball must be motionless, and all opposing players shall be at least 5 yards away.

The Play. The ball is put in play as for a free hit.

Hit-In. When the ball has completely rolled over the sideline by one team, the opposing team is awarded a hit-in.

Formation. The ball is placed on the sideline and can be hit or pushed in by any member of a team. The hitter may have the feet in bounds or over the sideline as the hit-in is being executed. The defending team must remain 5 yards away from the ball.

The Play. Successful execution will result when the hit-in is made quickly since the defenders are 5 yards away. Once the whistle blows, indicating the out-of-bounds, the hit or push may be executed without another whistle to start play. The premium is on getting the ball to the point where it crossed the line and getting it in play. Once the ball is hit by the player, it cannot be played again by the same player until it is touched by another player.

Long Hit. A long hit is awarded to the attacking team when the ball is hit unintentionally over the end line by a defending player.

Formation. The ball is placed on the side line, 5 yards in from the sideline. Any team member may hit or push the ball into play, and opposing team members must position themselves 5 yards away.

The Play. The player taking the hit will try to direct the ball onto a teammate's stick or try to hit the ball across to the goal mouth if an opening is available. Note: A team cannot score directly off of a long hit. The defending team will attempt to block the hit with one or more players, while other players attempt to deny the ball to the opponent.

Modifications for Special Populations

Orthopedically Impaired

Individuals who use wheelchairs will have to play in a gymnasium. Floor hockey is the recommended modification for students with movement difficulties. Contact Special Olympics for the rules of floor hockey.

Cognitively Impaired

1. Follow suggestions for the orthopedically impaired.
2. Keep concepts and movement patterns simple.

Sensory Impaired

1. Use peer teachers and paraprofessionals for students who have visual impairments.
2. Individual evaluations should be made to determine the appropriateness of field hockey for students who are blind or have a visual impairment.
3. Minimal modifications are needed for students who are deaf or have a hearing impairment.

Terminology

Advancing Foul committed when the ball rebounds from a player's body (i.e., kicked).

Center pass Technique used to start a game at the beginning or at halftime and to restart play after a goal.

Covering A back-up defensive position used to support a teammate who is beaten or to pick up a free player moving into attack position.

Defense hit Term used to denote how play is resumed when the attacking team hits the ball over the end line or commits a foul within the attacking 16-yard area. The ball is placed 16 yards from the end line opposite the spot where it left the field or the foul was committed.

Dodge Play used to evade an opponent while maintaining control of the ball.

Dribble A skill used to move the ball on the field while maintaining constant control.

Fielding Controlling an approaching ball before it is passed or played.

Flick A skill that causes the ball to lift off the ground in a controlled fashion. Useful for shooting, lifting the ball over an opponent's stick, and in penalty strokes.

Foul Infringement of rules. Penalty may be a free hit, penalty corner, or penalty stroke.

Free hit A method used to restart play following certain infringements of rules. It is taken by a player on the team fouled against.

Hit A skill used to pass the ball that provides power and distance. This skill involves backswing into the ball.

Long hit A method used to restart play after the ball is hit unintentionally over the end line by the defending team.

Marking Guarding an opponent without the ball, which is performed with ball side–goal side defensive positioning.

Non-stick side A player's left side, which is not easily defended by the stick.

Obstruction A foul made by placing the body between the opponent and the ball so as to interfere with the opponent's effort to play or reach the ball.

Penalty corner The play awarded to the attacking team for a foul by the defense inside the circle or when the defense intentionally hits the ball over the end line.

Penalty stroke A shot awarded to the attacking team when a defensive player commits a foul to prevent a sure goal or flagrantly fouls the opponent in the circle.

Push back Technique used to start a game at the beginning or at half time and to restart play after a goal.

Reverse stick Turning the stick over to play a ball on the left.

Stick side A player's right side, where the stick can easily be extended to play the ball.

Tackle A skill used to dislodge the ball from an opponent.

Reference

1. Gros, V. *Inside Field Hockey.* Chicago: Contemporary Books, 1979, pp. 58–59.

Further References

*Anders, B. *Fitness Training for Field Hockey.* Parkerford, PA: Longstreth, 1995.

*Anders, B. *Lessons in Field Hockey.* Parkerford, PA: Longstreth, 1996.

*Anders, E. *Field Hockey Steps to Success.* Champaign IL: Human Kinetics, 1999.

USA Futures 2001 Coaching Manual. The Official Manual of the United States Field Hockey Association's Futures Program. Published by the USFHA National Office, One Olympic Plaza, Colorado Springs, CO 80909.

*van Asselt, B. *The Hockey Coaching Guide—Part 1.* Greenford, Middlesex. Harrow Press, 1993.

*van Asselt, B. *The Hockey Coaching Guide—Part 2.* Greenford, Middlesex. Harrow, 1996.

*van Asselt, B. *The Hockey Coaching Guide—Part 3.* Greenford, Middlesex. Harrow, 1999.

Periodicals

Field Hockey News. Published by USFHA National Office, One Olympic Plaza, Colorado Springs, CO.

National Field Hockey Coaches Association Newsletter. Published by NFHCA National Office. 11921 Meadow Ridge Terrace. Glen Allen, VA 23059.

Audio-Visual Materials

Play Hockey Slazenger Style. Produced by Slazenger, 1989.

Keeper 2000. Produced by Reedswain, Inc., 1996.

Skills 2000. Produced by Women's Hockey Australia, 1999.

---

* Sources marked by an asterisk are available from Longstreth Sporting Goods, P.O. Box 475, Old Schuylkill Rd., Parkerford, PA 19457.

*Wein, H. *The Key to Better Hockey.* A book on CD produced by International Educational Management System, 2000.

Web Sites

www.usfieldhockey.com Offers information about the history of field hockey, camps and grants for field hockey, and international events. Offers links to national and international organizations and clubs.

www.fh1fieldhockey.com Offers information on field hockey equipment and tips.

www.fieldhockeytraining.com Offers information on teaching ideas, a discussion forum and links to various related sites.

www.fieldhockey.com Offers field hockey news and updates on rules, etc. Has information on coaching/teaching, umpiring, and links to more sites.

CHAPTER 11

Football: Touch and Flag

This chapter will enable you to

- Discuss the key points of the games of touch and flag football
- Identify the differences in equipment, rules, and strategy between flag football and touch football
- Describe the rules governing play
- Analyze and demonstrate the various skills and techniques, including the stance, passing, catching, blocking, tackling, and kicking
- Describe the offensive and defensive strategies utilized
- Take proper safety precautions
- Use the basic terminology associated with the game

Nature and Purpose

Touch Football

The object of the game of touch football (and its variation, flag football) is to advance the ball over the opponent's goal line without being "tackled." Points are awarded for a touchdown (6 points), a point after touchdown (1 point by kicking, 2 points by running or passing), a field goal (3 points), a safety (2 points), a forfeit (1 point), and by penetration in the event of a tie (1 point).

Informal games of touch football are often played in areas any size large enough to give the players running and passing room. In schools and recreation leagues, in which the game is played on an organized basis, a regulation football field equipped with goal posts and yard lines is used. A regulation football is used, but players are not required to wear the heavy official football equipment because tackling is not permitted. Runners are stopped by a touch with one or both hands instead of a tackle. The fact that expensive equipment is not needed makes this game appropriate for use in recreational programs and in schools that do not have funds available for outfitting a regular football team.

The game retains most of the fundamentals of regular football, which gives it a popular appeal in the fall, when sport pages are filled with news about forward passes, touchdowns, and long runs. An official touch football team is usually composed of seven players, but variations (from five to eleven players) may be used with very little rules adaptation. The game provides an opportunity for the individual interested in football to duplicate in a relatively safe situation many of the skills utilized by widely publicized members of the gridiron game. Most present-day versions of the game resemble regulation football to the extent that names of positions of players, running and passing plays, punting, place-kicking, first downs, and scoring are used. The tackling element is eliminated in favor of the touch, and in most versions of touch football certain limitations are placed on blocking. In many cases, no limitations are placed on eligibility of pass receivers, making it possible for any player to receive a forward pass. This factor makes the game more interesting to players on the line of scrimmage, who seldom have an opportunity to score or handle the ball in regulation football.

Flag Football

Flag football is a variation of touch football in which cloth or plastic flags are worn on both hips by all players. In lieu of a touch, the flag is detached or stripped from a belt (worn by all players) by the defensive player. Flags are generally 12 to 15 inches long and 2 inches wide and are attached to the belt by an adhesive substance such as Velcro or by plastic snaps (Figure 11-1). A different colored flag is used by each team.

The basic rules governing flag football are similar to those used in touch football. Holding an opponent or holding onto the flag to prevent detachment are common infractions in flag football and must be closely regulated. Some contend that utilization of

Figure 11-1 Flag and belt worn in flag football. Flag is attached by Velcro.

the detachable flag in lieu of the one- or two-handed touch tends to minimize roughness in team play. Officiating is easier in flag than in touch football, since detachment of the flag is readily discernible, while there may be arguments regarding the touch.

From a strategic standpoint, flag football would appear to orient itself better to all-around offensive and defensive strategy because of the increased difficulty in detaching a flag. Teams will be more prone to include a more balanced running and passing attack; defenses will have to be designed to prevent both strategies.

In order to minimize hazardous play in flag football, the following precautionary measures are suggested:

1. Eliminate the blocking, tackling, or holding of the ball carrier by a defensive player attempting to secure the flag.
2. Defensive players must maintain contact with the ground when attempting to secure the flag—no jumping or diving.
3. The ball carrier may not employ a straight-arm or utilize body contact against a defensive player in order to prevent him from securing the flag.

Basic Rules

There are many sources of rules for flag and touch football. Although there may be some variations, generally they are very similar. When playing flag football, however, the rules for blocking, fumbling, and tackling must be strictly enforced. In flag football, any ball carrier without two flags is considered tackled.

Playing Field and Equipment

Playing Field. An official touch football and flag football field is 40 yards wide by 100 yards long (Figure 11-2). The field is divided into four 20-yard zones and two end zones, each 10 yards deep.

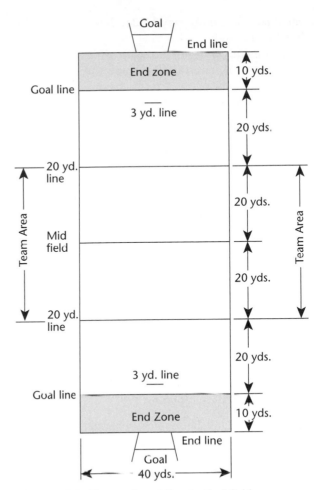

Figure 11-2 The touch and flag football field.

Goals. Goal posts are not a necessity; however, lack of goal posts eliminates points after touchdown by kicking and field goals. In these cases, points after touchdown are gained by running or passing.

Uniform. No special uniform is required. The use of football helmets and football pads is prohibited, although tennis shoes or soccer shoes with molded rubber cleats may be used.

Ball. A regulation leather or rubber-coated football can be used. It is recommended that a junior-sized football be used by younger children.

Flags. Flags should measure 12 to 15 inches in length and 2 inches in width. They can be made of cloth and tucked in the elastic top of the gym trunks if belts are not available.

Length of Game. Four ten- to twelve-minute periods constitute a game, with a one-minute rest between periods and a five-minute rest between halves. Games may also be divided into two 20-minute halves with a 5-minute rest period.

Overtime. Tie games may be decided by one of the following methods:

1. Award the game to the team with the greatest number of penetrations inside the opponent's 20-yard line.
2. Award the game to the team with the greatest number of first downs.
3. Give each team four downs from the 20-yard line and award the game to the team advancing the ball the farthest.

Forfeits. If a team is not ready to play within ten minutes after the scheduled starting time, the opponents are awarded the win on a forfeit. A team refusing to resume play after an order to do so by the referee forfeits to the opponent.

Timeout. Each team is allowed two timeouts per half. Timeouts are also taken under the following conditions:

1. When ball goes out of bounds
2. After a score is made
3. While a penalty is being enforced
4. At the discretion of the referee
5. At the end of each period

Scoring. Scoring is the same as in regulation football:

touchdown	6 points
field goal	3 points
safety	2 points
point after touchdown	1 point by kick; 2 points by run or pass

Players and Officials

Players. A team consists of seven players, although fewer or more players may be used by mutual consent. The offensive team must have at least three players on the line of scrimmage when the ball is put in play.

Substitutes. Any number of substitutions may be made at any time during the game. Substitutes must report to the referee.

Officials. Officials consist of a referee, an umpire, and linesmen.

Playing Regulations

Starting the Game. A toss of a coin by the referee determines which team has the choice of kicking off, receiving, or goals. The loser of the toss has the choice of remaining options. Privileges of choice are reversed at the beginning of the third period.

Putting the Ball in Play. The ball is put in play at the start of the game, after a score, and at the beginning of the third period by a place kick from the kicker's 20-yard line. Defensive team members must be 10 yards away when the ball is kicked, and members of the kicking team must be behind the ball. If the ball does not go 10 yards, it must be kicked again. If the ball goes out of bounds after 10 yards, the opponent has a choice of beginning play where the ball went out of bounds or on their own 20-yard line. If the ball is kicked into the end zone and the opponents elect not to run it out, play begins on their 20-yard line.

Fumbled Ball. A fumbled ball at any time is dead and belongs to the team that fumbled the ball at the point of the fumble, the down and point to be gained remaining the same. A fumbled forward pass is ruled as an incomplete pass.

Downed Ball. The ball is dead and the player downed when an opponent touches him with one hand somewhere between his shoulders and his knees. In flag football, the ball is downed or player tackled when one flag is detached from the belt or the ball carrier loses a flag.

First Downs. A team has four chances to move the ball from one 20-yard zone to the next. If a team does not advance the ball from one zone to the next in four downs, the ball goes to the opponents at that spot.

Passing. The following regulations govern passing:

1. All players on both teams are eligible to catch passes.
2. Forward passes may be thrown from any point back of the line of scrimmage, and lateral passes may be thrown from anywhere on playing field.
3. Any number of passes may be thrown in a series of downs.

Penalties

5-Yard Penalty Infractions. (from line of scrimmage)

Offside
Delay of game
Fewer than three players on line of scrimmage
Illegal motion or shift
Illegal forward pass

15-Yard Penalty Infractions. (from spot of foul)

Illegal use of hands
Illegal block
Unnecessary roughness (push, tackle, shove, trip, holding)
Unsportsmanlike conduct
Clipping
Pass interference

Flagrant violations of rules should be met with automatic disqualification of the players who commit them.

Rules for Coeducational Flag Football

Coeducational flag football is becoming an increasingly popular game. Many variations and modifications can be used. Modifications can be found in *Rules for Coeducational Activities and Sports,* published by the American Alliance of Health, Physical Education, Recreation, and Dance, 1977 and 1980.

Suggested Learning Sequence

A. Nature and Purpose of Touch Football/Flag Football

B. Conditioning Aspects—plan drills and exercises that might be related to movements of touch and flag football.

C. Basic Game Concepts
   1. Field of play
   2. Equipment
   3. Safety
   4. Playing courtesies

D. Rules/Coeducational Rules—rules should be introduced when appropriate and at a time that relates to a specific skill or strategy. This does not mean that all rules must be discussed at one time.

E. Skills and Techniques—skills should be taught in combinations whenever possible; the sequence that skills are taught is up to the individual preference of the instructor.
   1. Stances
      a. Three-point stance
      b. Upright stance
   2. Ball Carrying
   3. Passing and Receiving
      a. Pass Patterns
   4. Kicking
      a. Punting
      b. Place kick
      c. Kickoff
   5. Blocking
   6. Tackling
      a. Touch
      b. Flag detachment
   7. Centering
      a. Direct snap
      b. Long snap

F. Strategies—offensive game concepts as well as defensive game concepts should be introduced as early as possible so that skills can be practiced within the context of a game.
   1. Offense
      a. T-formation
      b. Shotgun formation
      c. Single wing
   2. Defense
      a. Pass defense—pass rush
      b. Running defense

G. Game Play

Skills and Techniques

The techniques and fundamental skills associated with touch football and flag football are identical to regular football in most instances. There are two areas, however, in which touch and flag football differ from the parent game; these are in tackling and blocking. The tackle in touch football refers to a touch between the shoulders and knees, while the tackle in flag football refers to the detachment or stripping of a flag by an opponent from a belt that circles the waist.

Figure 11-3 Stance. The people on the line are in a three-point stance; the backs are in an upright stance.

In both touch and flag football, players cannot leave their feet when blocking. There are other skills that all players must work on because the skills will be used regardless of the position played.

Stances

The stance will vary according to the position played and the function of either the offense or defense. Generally speaking, the three-point stance is used by the players on the line on offense and defense and sometimes by the offensive backs. The upright stance may be used by linebackers, defensive backs, and sometimes, the offensive backs (see Figure 11-3).

➤ Learning Hints—Three-Point Stance

1. Feet are shoulder-width apart, one foot slightly ahead of the other in a heel-toe relationship.
2. The supporting arm hangs vertically, the back is nearly horizontal, the head is up looking ahead, the weight is on the support hand.
3. The free arm rests on the knee of the forward leg.

➤ Learning Hints—Upright Stance

1. Foot position is much the same as in the three-point stance.
2. Hands are placed just above the knees, the back is slightly bent at the waist, the head is up, and the player is focused downfield.
3. Weight is on the balls of the feet.

Ball Carrying

Because of the rules governing play, most players have an opportunity at one time or another to carry the football. The effective ball carrier is one who can start quickly, change direction, dodge, side-step, and execute fakes that will throw the defensive player off stride. It is important that the ball carrier follow the blockers in order to elude the defensive players.

➤ Learning Hints (Figure 11-4)

1. Carry the ball in outside arm furthest from the defensive player.
2. One end of the football is placed in the armpit and the other end is held in the palm of the hand with fingers spread comfortably around the end to provide a firm grip.

➤ Practice/Organizational Suggestions

1. Align a ball carrier facing a defensive player standing 10 yards away. On the signal, have the ball carrier run toward the defensive player, changing the ball as the player changes direction.
2. For the same type of formation, have the ball carrier run toward the defensive player, using a series of fakes to try to avoid being tackled.

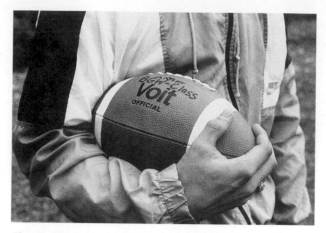

Figure 11-4 Proper way to carry a ball.

3. Using a blocker, have a ball carrier try to set up the block on the defensive player by following the interference and setting up a series of fakes.

Passing

The forward pass assumes an important role in touch football and flag football because rules permit everyone to be an eligible receiver. A good passing attack will loosen up the defense and allow the running game to become more effective. There are two types of passes commonly used: the forward pass and the lateral pass. The lateral pass may be thrown in an overhand motion or it may be "pitched" to a player in an underhand motion. The lateral, which cannot be thrown forward, adds much interest and excitement to the game because it can be used anywhere on the field.

➤ Learning Hints—Forward Pass

1. The ball is gripped by the hand on the top; the thumb is opposite the middle finger; the other fingers are spread on the laces (Figure 11-5).
2. As the ball is brought up behind the ear, plant the rear foot, step with the opposite foot in the direction of throw as the arm is brought forward.
3. The wrist is snapped downward and the palm of the throwing hand is rotated outward as the ball is released, thus giving the ball a spiral motion.

➤ Practice/Organizational Suggestions

1. Place players opposite each other and throw ball back and forth. Begin at a distance of 10 yards and move further away.
2. After you have reviewed certain pass receiver patterns, form two lines, have a player center the ball back to the quarterback, with receivers going out for a pass. First begin with short passes and then progress to longer passes.
3. Same formation as #2 but add two defensive linesmen; force quarterback to throw on the run.

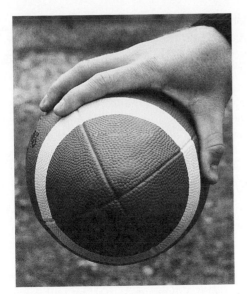

Figure 11-5 Proper grip for a forward pass. Note that the middle finger and thumb are opposite.

Figure 11-6 Catching the ball above the waist, with thumbs turned in.

Figure 11-7 Catching the ball below the waist, with thumbs turned out.

Another variation is to add two defensive backs and attempt to complete a pass.

Receiving

Pass receivers should become adept at eluding their opponents by dodging, faking, and using a change of pace that will enable them to move past the defensive player. It is important for the pass receiver to focus in on the ball as soon as it leaves the passer's hand, watching all the way to his own hands. Some basic fundamentals must be remembered.

➤ Learning Hints

1. Palms face out, thumbs toward the incoming pass. Catch with the hands and pull into the body.
2. On passes above the chest, thumbs are turned in; below the waist, thumbs are turned out (see Figures 11-6 and 11-7).
3. As the receiver moves away from the passer, fingers are extended, thumbs are turned out; give with ball on contact.
4. On passes caught over either shoulder, the thumbs are turned out; the arm on the ballside (nearest the body) is held below the shoulder; the forearm is held at eye level (Figure 11-8).

➤ Practice/Organizational Suggestions

1. Form two parallel lines and have passes thrown above chest and below chest to pass receivers.
2. Two lines, passer drops back and throws pass over the receiver's head for over-the-shoulder catch.
3. Two lines, receivers practice pass patterns and catches. Add defensive backs as a variation.

Figure 11-8 Catching the ball over the shoulder.

Kicking

The kicking game consists of kickoffs to begin play, punting, and place kicks.

➤ **Learning Hints—Punting**

1. The punter stands 13 yards behind the line of scrimmage, awaiting the center snap; the kicking foot is slightly ahead of the non-kicking foot, arms are relaxed, palms open and up, and the trunk is slightly flexed.
2. Follow the ball into the hands; the ball is held in the hand of the kicking foot toward the end and underneath. The other hand is placed on the ball with laces up to the front and side. The ball should be slightly tipped, nose downward just below the chest.
3. The kick and step is a step with the right foot, a hop with the left, and a follow-through with the right leg. The kicking foot may finish above the head.
4. The ball is released with the non-kicking hand after being guided to the correct position of the foot by the kicking hand prior to release.

Place Kicking and Extra Point. There are two types of place kicks, the traditional head-on approach and the soccer-style instep kick, which is described in the chapter on soccer. Some key points to remember for the traditional kick:

1. Assume a stance two steps behind the spot of the kick; the right foot takes a longer step and the left foot a short step.
2. The non-kicking foot is placed approximately two feet behind and a foot to the side of the ball.
3. With the head down and eyes on the contact point, the body leaning forward, the right leg follows through with a definite leg snap coming at the contact point.
4. The ball is contacted just below the center of the football; the leg should be extended at impact.

The Kickoff. The kickoff follows the same mechanics, except that the kicker is stationed 8 to 10 yards behind the ball prior to kickoff. Practice and timing are essential in executing the correct form for the place kick during a kickoff.

Blocking

Since the player is not permitted to leave the feet in executing a block, he/she must become adept at maintaining balance while retaining a position between the defensive person and the ball carrier. It is important to try to maintain contact with the defensive player and draw her away from the ball carrier. The blocker is not allowed to hold the defensive person, so the hands must be held in close to the body at all times.

➤ **Learning Hints**

1. Assume a three-point stance opposite your opponent; the initial steps are short, choppy steps to the opponent.
2. The body is in a semi-crouch position, the shoulder and forearms make contact with the opponent's midsection, and the head is placed between your opponent and the ball carrier.
3. Drive your opponent away from the ball carrier; use short, choppy steps.

➤ **Practice/Organizational Suggestions**

1. Form two parallel lines 2 yards apart. On the signal, block right or block left; the blocker attempts to maintain contact on a blocking position for 3 to 4 seconds.
2. With a center, a ball carrier, defensive player, and offensive player, on signal the ball carrier runs behind the blocker and cuts right or left, depending on the direction of the block.

Tackling

Tackling is the term used to denote the touching of a ball carrier to stop play or, in flag football, the detachment or stripping of the flag to stop play. An important point to remember is that, for the tackle to be valid, both feet of the tackler must be on the ground. A legal touch is between the shoulder and knee of the opponent. The game may be played using a one-hand touch or it may be increased in difficulty by making it a two-hand touch game (Figure 11-9). In flag football, one flag must be detached from the belt (Figure 11-10). Body balance and control of body movement and speed are important factors to practice.

Centering

The center plays an important part in touch and flag football. The center snap is executed at close range (direct snap) if a team uses a T-formation, but at longer range if a team uses a shotgun or single wing, and at still longer range on punts and extra point tries. Note that in touch or flag football, if the center snaps the ball on the ground before getting to the receiver, it is a dead ball.

➤ **Learning Hints—Direct Snap**
(Figures 11-11, 11-12)

1. Feet are shoulder-width apart. Bend at the waist, knees flexed, arms hanging comfortably in front, head up.
2. Quarterback places hands under the crotch of the center, fingers spread, heels of palms together.
3. The center places one hand on top of the ball (laces up) and the other hand alongside and toward the end of the ball. On the signal, the arms

Figure 11-9 Tackling: A two-handed touch above the waist.

Figure 11-10 Tackling, flag football style. The ball carrier's hand may not protect the flag.

Figure 11-11 The snap. Note quarter turn of the ball as it is given to the quarterback.

Figure 11-12 The direct snap.

Figure 11-13 The long snap.

are rolled toward the quarterback, and the ball is snapped back to the quarterback, with the right hand turning the ball a quarter right turn so the ball is placed in the quarterback's hands on its side.

➤ **Learning Hints—Long Snap** (Figure 11-13)
1. Same starting position, although weight may be forward and head lower than the buttocks.
2. Arms are swept toward the receiver, with wrist snap to impart spiral on the ball.

Strategy for Touch or Flag Football
Offensive Strategy

Touch football permits the use of a wide range of offensive plays because of the emphasis on passing and the fact that everyone is eligible to receive a pass. In arranging the offensive strategy, a team should plan a signal system that will denote the kind of play to be used (pass, run, punt), who is to carry the ball, and where the ball is to go. Plays should be kept as simple as possible. Numbers may be employed to represent the type of play, the player executing the play or carrying the ball, and the side of the line where the play is to go. The line may be numbered with odd numbers on the left side and even numbers on the right (Figure 11-14). The backs may be numbered: 1—quarterback, 2—right halfback, 3—fullback, and 4—left halfback. Thus, after the ball has been centered, the signal "Run 14" indicates a running play through the number 4 hole, with the number 1 back carrying the ball.

Offensive strategy should combine running and passing plays in order to create confusion for the defense. It is not good strategy to constantly employ all passing plays or all running plays. Try to keep the de-

fense guessing; attempt running plays on second down with a lot of yards to go for first down.

Offensive Formations. There are a number of formations that can be created by the offense as long as three people line up on the line of scrimmage before the ball is snapped. Three common formations used in touch football and flag football include (1) the T-formation, (2) the shotgun formation, and (3) the single wing formation (Figure 11-15).

Defensive Strategy

Teams should agree on a plan for the pass and the run defense. For a passing defense, certain players on the line of scrimmage should be assigned to rush the passer, while other players drop back to help the defensive backs cover possible receivers. Generally a person-to-person assignment is made for the deep pass receiver, while a zone defense is employed by the remaining defensive players to watch for the short pass receivers. Figure 11-16 illustrates four types of pass patterns.

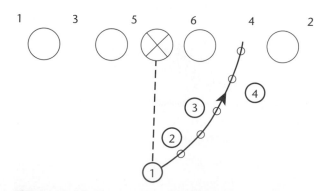

Figure 11-14 Numbers for offensive holes.

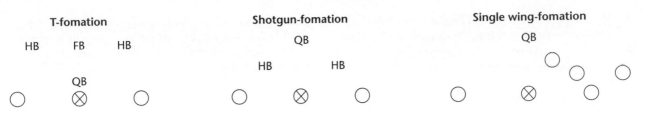

Figure 11-15 Types of offensive formations.

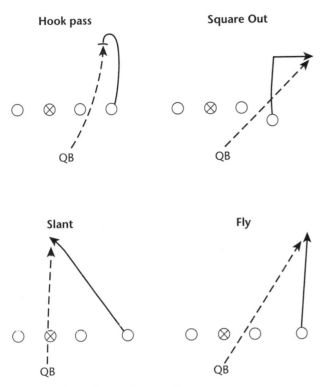

Figure 11-16 Types of pass patterns.

➤ **Defensive Hints**

1. Assign rushers to contain the passer or runner inside, not allowing the ball carrier the opportunity to break outside the defensive containment.
2. Learn to recognize the opponent's formations and most effective players; set up your defenses accordingly.
3. Listen to see if an opponent is continually using the same cadence; occasionally time your rush to the cadence.
4. Defensive backs should not turn their backs on the pass receiver; learn to run backwards or sidewards so that you can always see the ball and the pass receiver.
5. Use different pass rushers to confuse the offense; send in linebackers at times as an element of surprise.

➤ **Offensive Hints**

1. Keep the defense guessing by varying running and passing plays.

2. If the defensive secondary plays deep, use many of your players in short passing patterns. When the defensive draws in, use the deep pass.
3. If you receive a long penalty, do not try to make it up on one play; use a run and perhaps some short passes.
4. Change your cadence occasionally to pull the defensive team offside.
5. Utilize a quick kick on third down to get your team out of a defensive hole.
6. Let your field position help dictate the type of plays you will use—long passes are dangerous near your own goal line; plays involving deception are best in the vicinity of midfield; use quick hitting or pass plays near your opponent's goal line.

Modifications for Special Populations

Orthopedically Impaired

1. For students using wheelchairs, the games need to be played on the gymnasium floor, and a foam rubber football is recommended. Students without disabilities could play while positioned on a scooter. For students with functional upper body skills, no modifications would be needed for throwing and catching. Forward passes to students using motorized wheelchairs would be considered complete if the football struck any part of the wheelchair above the waist area, e.g., chair arms, seat back.
2. Students using crutches, canes, and/or walkers should be able to participate on an outdoor or indoor field. These students could be positioned as defensive linemen and coached to raise their assistive devices to block forward passes. Quarterbacks would not be allowed to move when throwing against this defense.

Cognitively Impaired

1. Concentrate on teaching the concepts of the game, e.g., offsides, line of scrimmage, offense, defense, first downs.
2. Make sure to use some means of designating team players in play demonstrations, e.g., green and red pennies.

3. Stationary lead-up games might be helpful, e.g., stationary passing relays the length of the field.

4. Reduce the size of the playing area and the number of players per team.

Sensory Impaired

1. Minimal modifications would be needed for the students who are deaf or hearing impaired. You will need to develop some visual system for stopping play, e.g., cue cards, waving a towel, or hand signals.

2. Individual considerations must be taken into account to determine the appropriateness of football for students who are visually impaired or blind. You might consider using a "double pass" system, in which the student who is blind or visually impaired is required to pass the ball to a sighted teammate before the defensive rush could occur. The sighted player would then be considered the second quarterback, who must continue the play.

Safety

Observance of the following safety precautions will minimize the incidence of injuries.

1. Do not wear any equipment possessing sharp or projecting surfaces that may injure teammates or opponents. This includes rings, belt buckles, and watches.

2. Use rules that prevent leaving the feet in executing the block.

3. Declare the ball dead on all fumbles.

4. See that the playing area is smooth and free from holes and projecting objects that may prove a hazard.

5. Use competent officials who enforce the rules and eliminate rough play.

6. Be sure adequate treatment is available for players in case of injury during play.

7. Players who wear glasses should wear a headband or eyeglass guard.

Terminology

Backs Players who ordinarily carry or pass the ball on offense. Stationed behind the linemen.

Backward pass Play in which the ball is thrown or passed in any direction except toward the opponent's goal. Any player may make a backward pass.

Balanced line An offensive formation that has an equal number of linemen on each side of the center. Line is unbalanced if more linemen are on one side of center than the other.

Block Action of offensive linemen and backs in which they use their bodies to ward off defensive players from the ball carrier.

Bootleg play An offensive play in which a back fakes handing the ball to a teammate, conceals it on his hip, and turns in the opposite direction.

Brush blocking Momentary blocking by an offensive player.

Button hook A forward pass play in which the receiver runs toward the defender, turns, and runs back toward passer to receive the pass.

Clipping A blocking action in which a player throws her body across the back of the leg(s) of a player not carrying the ball. This can cause injury, and is a personal foul.

Cross-buck An offensive play in which two backs cross paths in moving toward the line of scrimmage, one faking to receive the ball and the other actually taking the ball.

Cut-back An offensive maneuver in which the back starts wide and then cuts back toward center of the line.

End around An offensive maneuver in which one end wheels around, takes the ball from a teammate, and attempts to run for a gain.

Fair catch A player may make a fair catch on a kick-off, return kick, or kick from scrimmage by raising his hand clearly above his head before making the catch. He may not be tackled, and must not take more than two steps after receiving the ball. The ball is put in play from the spot of the catch by a free kick or scrimmage.

Flanker An offensive maneuver in which a player lines up nearer the sideline than a designated opponent.

Flat pass A forward pass that travels chiefly in a lateral direction and is usually thrown with a flat trajectory.

Forward pass An offensive play in which the ball is thrown toward the line of scrimmage.

Handoff An offensive play in which one back hands the ball off to another back who attempts to advance the ball.

Lateral pass An offensive play in which the ball is passed sideward or backward to the line of scrimmage.

Line of scrimmage An imaginary line, or vertical plane, passing through the end of the ball nearest a team's goal line and parallel to the goal lines. Thus there is a line of scrimmage for each team, and the area between the two lines is called the neutral zone. Any player of either team is offside if she encroaches upon the neutral zone before the ball is snapped.

Naked reverse An offensive play in which the ball carrier takes the ball from another back and attempts to advance without benefit of backfield blockers.

Neutral zone The imaginary line that passes between the lines of scrimmage for each team. Either team is offside if it moves across the neutral zone before the ball is snapped.

Offside When an offensive or defensive player is ahead of the ball before it is snapped. (The penalty is 5 yards.)

Safety A score made when a free ball, or one in possession of a player defending his own goal, becomes dead behind the goal, provided the impetus that caused it to cross the goal was supplied by the defending team.

Screen pass An offensive maneuver in which a wave of eligible receivers converge in area where a pass is to be thrown.

Shotgun offense A formation in which the quarterback lines up five to six yards behind the center. Usually one or both halfbacks may line up one to two yards on either side of the quarterback and one yard in front of the quarterback.

Shovel pass An offensive maneuver in which a pass is thrown, underhand, usually forward to a back behind the line of scrimmage.

Touchback When the ball becomes dead behind the opponent's goal line legally in possession of a player guarding his own goal, provided the impetus that caused it to cross the goal line was supplied by an opponent. No points are scored on the play, and the ball is put in play by a scrimmage at the 20-yard line.

Further References

American Association for Health, Physical Education, Recreation, and Dance. *Rules for Coeducational Activities and Sports and Dance.* Revised ed. Washington, DC: AAHPERD Publications, 1980.

American Association for Health, Physical Education, and Recreation, and Dance, Division for Girls' and Women's Sports. *Soccer-Speedball-Flag Football Guide.* Current ed. Washington, DC: AAHPERD.

Cihon, Michael. *USFTL Rule Book & Officials Manual.* Cleveland, OH: United States Touch and Flag Football League, 1988.

Dintiman, G. B. and Barrow, L. M. *A Comprehensive Manual of Physical Education Activities for Men.* Englewood Cliffs, NJ: Prentice Hall, 1970.

Frommer, H. *Sports Lingo: A Dictionary of the Language of Sports.* New York: Atheneum, 1979.

Little, M., Dowell, L. and Jeter, J. *Recreational Football: Flag and Touch for Class and Intramurals.* Minneapolis: Burgess, 1977.

Mood, D., Musker F. F. and Rink, J. E. *Sports and Recreational Activities.* 11th ed. St. Louis: Mosby, 1995.

National College Physical Education Association. *Touch Football—Official National Touch Football Rules.* Current ed. Chicago: The Athletic Institute.

Stanbury, D. and DeSantis, F. *Touch Football.* New York: Sterling Publishing Co., Inc., 1979.

The United States Flag and Touch Football League. *The United States Flag and Touch Football Rules.* Mentor, Ohio, 1992.

Skills Testing

Brace, D. K. *Skills Test Manual: Football.* Washington, DC: American Association for Health, Physical Education, and Recreation, 1965.

Hewate, C. and Reynolds, J. "Flag Football." *Soccer-Speedball-Flag Football Guide.* Washington, DC: American Association for Health, Physical Education, and Recreation, 1972.

Audio-Visual Materials

AIMS Media, Inc., 6901 Woodley Ave., Van Nuys, CA 91406. *Playing Touch Football* (¾ or ½ inch video, 12 minutes).

Clearvue Inc., 5711 Milwaukee Ave., Chicago, IL 60646. *Touch/Flag Football I: How to Play* (Filmstrip/Guide).

Clearvue Inc., 5711 Milwaukee Ave., Chicago, IL 60646. *Touch/Flag Football II: Rules of the Game* (Filmstrip/ Guide).

NIRSA: Flag and Touch Football Rules. NIRSA, 850 SW 15th St., Corvallis, OR 97333.

Web Sites

www.ehow.com/ehow/ehow.jsp?index=1077&id=3987 Brief overview of how to play touch football, along with some playing tips.

www.ehow.com/ehow/rhoe.jsp?index=1077&id=3988 Brief overview of how to play flag football, along with some playing tips.

www.afafootball.com American Football Association web site offers complete rules, a glossary, and other information.

www.agflag.com NFL flag football site, with rules and information about how to form leagues.

www.ruf.rice.edu/~ims/flag/html Rice University intramural department flag football rules. Also contains coeducational recreation rules for flag football

Note: Many universities with recreation departments have sites posted on the web with rules used to govern a variety of games.

CHAPTER 12

Golf

This chapter will enable you to

- Identify the parts and features of a golf course
- Identify the various clubs and other equipment, and know their function and proper care
- Describe and after practice execute the following skills: grip; stand; swing (irons and woods); pitch, chip, and sand shots; putting; and various golf exercises
- Identify and carry out the courtesies associated with the sport
- State and interpret the major official rules of golf

Nature and Purpose

One of the greatest advantages of golf lies in the age range of those who are able to participate. Both young boys and girls and mature men and women can be found participating at many golf courses. In recent years the United States Golf Association has sponsored Junior Golf Programs (ages 9 to 17); therefore, more and more children are becoming interested in playing at a very early age. Many private and public golf courses have extensive instructional programs for the junior golfer and sponsor golf tournaments all summer long. Most public and private clubs have also set aside specific playing times for the juniors in order to encourage their participation.

Golf may be played by strokes or by holes. The objective is to play a ball from a teeing area to a hole, a prescribed distance from the tee, in the fewest strokes possible. An official round is 18 holes. In stroke play, the winner is the person taking the fewest number of strokes over an entire 18 holes of play. Each hole receives a rating of par determined by the length of the hole (Figure 12-1). In match play, or play by holes, the winner is the golfer who wins the greater number of holes despite the final total in strokes. Stroke play is considered more exacting, because each shot is of equal value, whereas in match play, a loss of 2 or more strokes on a hole may be recouped by a 1-stroke victory on a later hole.

Golf is one of the few sports that allows a handicapping system among participants. Handicapping is a means of equalizing competition among golfers of differing abilities. The player with the lower average score is required to give strokes to the higher average

golfer. In stroke play, the higher average player subtracts these strokes from his total to get a *net* score. This is compared with the other player's *gross* or total score to determine the winner. In most handicap play, the strokes are usually computed in relation to the difference between par and the average score of the player. Thus, many can compete in a tournament on a handicap basis. In match play, the strokes are subtracted from the higher average player's score on holes designated as the most difficult. That is, a handicap of 5 would allow the player to subtract one stroke from his score on the five most difficult holes.

The Course

The course is the whole area within which play is permitted, and it is the duty of authorities in charge

For men	
Par 3	Up to 250 yards, inclusive
Par 4	251 to 470 yards, inclusive
Par 5	471 yards and over

For women	
Par 3	Up to 210 yards, inclusive
Par 4	211 to 400 yards, inclusive
Par 5	401 to 575 yards, inclusive
Par 6	576 yards and over

Figure 12-1 Directions for computing par on a golf course.

of the course to define its boundaries accurately. Most courses consist of 18 holes; however, there are many 9-hole courses. Golf scores are based on 18 holes of play, with the par usually varying between 70 and 72. Each hole consists of many common components and some not so common components (see Figure 12-2). A player tees a ball up on a wooden tee in the teeing area, in line with or no more than two club lengths behind the tee markers. Generally there are three sets of markers on a tee: the farthest from the hole are for championship play; the middle markers are generally for men; and the markers closest to the hole are where women may initiate play. From the tee, the golfer hits to a fairly well-groomed area called the fairway and from there, hits to a closely cut area of the hole called the green. Generally the area to the right and left of the fairway where the grass is long and other obstacles may be found is known as the rough. Most courses include obstacles such as sand traps, bunkers, water hazards, out-of-bounds, and trees placed in strategic positions to penalize a poor shot made by a golfer. There are

specific rules governing play that the golfer must understand when confronted by one of these obstacles. These are discussed later under "Rules of Golf."

Scoring

Figure 12-3 represents a typical score card. The golfer will note the yardage given for each hole, dependent on the set of markers from which play is initiated. Also included is information on the course rating, the par designation for a particular hole, as well as the hole's difficulty as expressed in men's or women's handicap. Thus the hole having the men's handicap designation of 7 (hole number 6) means that it is the seventh hardest hole on the course. If the golfer had a handicap of 7, he would be given a deduction of 1 stroke from his score in order to equalize the competition. In this example, the golfer would also receive a stroke deduction on holes 7, 11, 2, 13, 1, and 12.

The par designation is the number of strokes that an expert would take to play a hole. It is usually the number of shots from the tee to the green plus two strokes for putting. Thus an expert playing a par four hole would take two shots to reach the green and two putts to hit the ball into the hole. Sometimes a golfer will hit a ball from the tee into the hole in less than par. A score of 1 under par is a birdie, 2 under par is an eagle, 3 under par on a par 5 is a double eagle, and 2 under on a par 3 is a hole in one, the golfer's dream.

Equipment

Clubs

A set of golf clubs consists of woods, irons, and a putter (Figure 12-4). The beginner may not wish to invest in a complete set of expensive clubs and can initially get along with less expensive clubs. A minimum set should contain two woods, four irons, and a putter. The recommended choices would be a driver and a number 3 wood, the 3, 5, 7, and 9 irons, and a putter. While it is possible to obtain a full set by gradually adding the missing clubs, such as the number 4 and 5 woods and the 2, 4, 6, and 8 irons, as well as the sand wedge, a better plan is to play with the basic set until a fairly high level of skill is reached. At that time, a golf professional should be consulted to fit the player with a better and completely matched set of 14 clubs. The most popular 14 clubs are the driver, numbers 3 and 5 woods, numbers 2 through 9 irons, a pitching wedge, a sand wedge, and a putter. A set of clubs may cost anywhere from around $75 to over $1000. Generally the

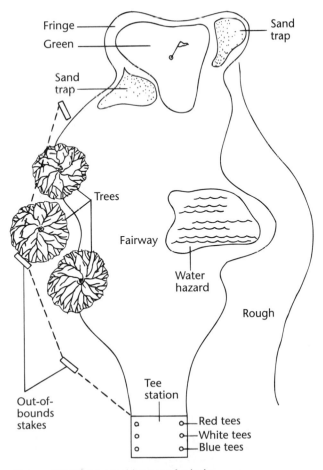

Figure 12-2 A typical layout of a hole.

SCORE CARD

HOLE	1	2	3	4	5	6	7	8	9	OUT	10	11	12	13	14	15	16	17	18	IN	Total
Championship BLUE	440	545	250	350	175	385	420	385	480	3430	520	440	525	420	205	350	385	185	405	3435	6865
Men's WHITE	365	515	245	325	160	380	415	350	455	3210	450	420	510	405	150	325	380	180	395	3215	6425
PAR	4	5	3	4	3	4	4	4	5	36	5	4	5	4	3	4	4	3	4	36	72
Men's handicap	5	3	13	15	17	7	1	11	9		12	2	6	4	18	14	10	16	8		
Won + Lost - Halved O																					
Women's YELLOW	360	490	245	320	160	365	410	350	440	3140	440	405	510	405	150	320	370	175	395	3170	6315
PAR	4	5	4	4	3	4	5	4	5	38	5	5	5	5	3	4	4	3	4	38	76
Women's Handicap	5	1	17	9	15	7	11	13	3		4	10	2	16	18	12	8	14	6		

COURSE RATING 70.5

DATE _____   PLAYER _____   ATTEST _____

Figure 12-3 Score card.

Figure 12-4 Parts of a wood club and an iron club.

beginning golfer can purchase a starter set for approximately $100 to $175.

The Putter. The putter is a golf club carried by all golfers; it is used primarily on the putting green to hit the ball into the cup. Today there are as many putter designs as there are golfers. The putter comes in various sizes, shapes, and colors. In choosing a putter, the key points to look for, according to the noted golf instructor Dick Aultman, are first, that the putter when soled flat on the ground allows you to look directly over the putting line; secondly, that it should be simple to aim, and thus, that it be easy to control.[1]

Choosing Clubs

Golf clubs are precision instruments and vary in design for men, women, and children. A golfer's shot-making ability is affected by many factors directly related to the construction of the golf club. Among these factors are swingweight, length of the club, shaft flexibility, clubhead design, and the grip.

Swingweight. Determined by a swingweight scale, swingweight is the relationship among the weights of a club's component parts—grip, shaft, and head. Scales to measure swingweight may be found in most pro shops. Swingweights are usually designated by the symbols C and D followed by a number ranging from 0 to 9. Women usually use a lightweight club that has a swingweight of C4 to C7; stronger women might use a C9 or even move to the D classification. Men's clubs start at D0; an average male golfer would use a swingweight of D0 to D4. Children's clubs are generally lighter.

Club Length. An important point to remember is that the higher the *number* of the club, the shorter

the club's *length*. The woods have the longest shafts while the 9 iron, pitching wedge, and sand wedge have the shortest shafts.

In addition, the shorter clubs have a more sharply angled club face (greater degree of loft). The combination of club length and club loft determine in part the distance a golf ball can be hit under normal conditions. If a golfer can execute a good shot each time, there is an approximate 10-yard difference between each club used. Figure 12-5 indicates the degrees of loft of specific clubs.

Women's golf clubs are 1 to 2 inches shorter than men's clubs, and children's clubs are shorter still. Some companies make fully matched sets of junior clubs, but they are quite expensive.

Shaft Flexibility. Matching the correct shaft flexibility to a golfer's swing is important. Most men golfers should use a golf club with a shaft flexibility rating of R, meaning regular. This shaft is also recommended for stronger women players. An S shaft means *stiff* and should be used by stronger male players. Most women golfers will use a golf club with an L (Lady)-rated shaft because these shafts have more flexibility.

Clubhead Design. In recent years significant advances have been made in clubhead design in both woods and irons. The topic is too extensive and technical for discussion here. Almost any golf clubs can be used to get you started. When your skill level increases, you can consult a local golf professional for the latest clubhead information.

Grip. Grips are generally made of synthetic rubber, although other materials such as leather or cord also are used. The standard size grip put on the club in the

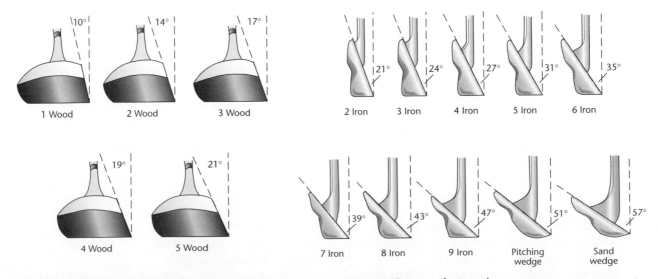

Figure 12-5 Club lofts. The loft of any one club will vary a few degrees. The manufacturers' recommendations are shown here.

factory can be changed to accommodate different hand sizes. A good general rule is, "If it feels right, it probably is."

Balls and Tees

Golf Balls. Golf balls come in a variety of types and in a wide price range. Beginners do not need to buy the most expensive ball.

Golf balls have two kinds of covers. Balata is a soft rubber cover that damages easily but is preferred by better golfers because they claim it has better feel. Surlyn is a sturdier cover made of plastic and some golfers claim surlyn-covered balls can be hit farther. Beginning golfers should use a surlyn-covered ball at first, but may have a different preference as skill develops.

The inside of a golf ball can be manufactured in two ways: (1) A small rubber core is covered by a thin rubber string wound tightly around the core; (2) The center of a golf ball can consist of synthetic material. Combinations of both styles of covers and insides are available.

Tees. The best tees are made of wood and come in various lengths; the standard is $2^{1}/_{8}$ inches. Tees made of other materials should be avoided.

Suggested Learning Sequence

Golf can be taught a number of different ways and from various starting points. Many of the skills can be learned and practiced indoors as well as outdoors. The availability of space and equipment (clubs, balls, screens, rugs, or mats) are important factors to consider. For beginning golfers, audio-visual aids can play a significant role in the learning process, for they reinforce many of the concepts explained during the initial stages of instruction. Another point to remember is that psychomotor and cognitive material is much better learned when presented together at the appropriate time. For example, etiquette and the rules governing play on the putting green are more meaningful during a lesson on putting than during a lesson devoted to the rules of golf. Finally, it is important to become proficient in the basic swing techniques before attempting to move on to the more advanced skills and techniques.

A. Introduction to Golf
　1. Nature and purpose of the game
　2. Choosing the right equipment
　3. Care of equipment
B. Etiquette and Rules of Golf. These should be introduced as deemed most appropriate for learning during different class intervals.
C. Skills and Techniques. Golf skills are best learned starting with the shorter clubs. Putting should be

introduced very early. As skill increases, the longer clubs can be introduced with the wood clubs coming last. Chipping can be introduced following putting and full swing fundamentals.
　1. Putting. Grip, stance, alignment, pendulum stroke, lag putting, short putts, reading greens, rules and etiquette.
　2. Pre-swing fundamentals. Grip, club face alignment, body alignment, stance, target selection and strategy.
　3. Full swing techniques. Take-away, backswing, downswing, follow-through, balance and tempo.
　4. Special shots. Chipping, pitch and run, sand trap shots.
　5. Strategy of golf. Best taught on the golf course during play, or as deemed most appropriate for learning.

Skills and Techniques

Pre-swing Fundamentals

It is very important to have a good understanding of the pre-swing fundamentals. These fundamentals—grip, club face alignment, body alignment, stance, and target selection—should be mastered before proceeding with the swing fundamentals. These fundamentals should be reviewed before every practice session and before playing a round of golf. Should a swing problem occur during a round of golf, a review of these fundamentals most often will solve the swing problem.

The Grip

The correct grip is the most important fundamental skill to be learned by golfers of any skill level. It can determine in great part the path of your swing, and consequently the directional flight of the ball. There are three types of grips used in golf: the overlapping (or Vardon) grip, the interlocking grip, and the ten-finger grip (Figure 12-6). The overlapping grip is the one most commonly used. In this grip, the little finger of the right hand overlaps the index finger of the left hand (for right-handed players). The interlocking grip is used by the golfer who has small hands and short fingers. In this grip, the little finger of the right hand *interlocks* with the index finger of the left hand. Both grips have the advantage of having the hands work as a unit, because the hands are joined together. The ten-finger grip is used by the golfer who has small hands; it is used frequently by beginning junior golfers. The ten-finger grip enables the golfer to take a strong hold, but there is a tendency for the hands to slip apart at times.

When assuming a grip, the golfer should not assume that because the grip is uncomfortable it is

Figure 12-6 Types of grips. (A) Overlapping, (B) interlocking, and (C) the ten-finger grip.

incorrect. However, the grip should not feel like a vise; rather it should feel firm yet somewhat relaxed. Tenseness in the grip will cause a restricted swing; the golf swing should flow.

➤ Learning Hints—Overlapping Grip (Right-handed Golfer)

1. A good golf grip starts by using the same hand position used when standing erect. As you stand erect with your arms hanging freely from your sides, notice how both hands turn slightly inward (Figure 12-7A). Extend your left hand and arm as though to shake hands. Close the thumb next to the first finger. The line formed by the thumb and first finger should be pointing toward the right eye. The back of the left hand should be pointing in the direction you want the ball to travel.

2. Extend your right hand in the same manner as above. Close the right thumb next to the first finger. This line formed by the thumb and first finger should also point toward the right eye. The palm

of the right hand should be pointing in the direction you want the ball to travel.

3. Extend both hands at the same time, as described above. Place the right hand slightly forward of the left hand. (The right hand will be below the left hand when gripping the club.) The palms of your hands should be facing each other (Figure 12-7B). The lines formed by the thumb and first finger of each hand should be pointing at the right eye. Later you may want to strengthen the grip by pointing the lines toward the right shoulder, as most women golfers do. You may want to weaken the grip by pointing the lines toward your nose if your hands are very strong.

4. Using a 7 iron or a 5 iron, attempt to grip the club. Be sure the sole of the club is flat on the ground and the club face is pointed toward the direction you want the ball to travel. Place the left hand on first, using the correct hand position. Grip firmly with the last three fingers of the left hand. The thumb and index finger grip with less pressure.

Figure 12-7 Assuming a grip.

Use both palm and fingers to hold the club firmly and securely, but do not squeeze too hard. (Figure 12-7C).

5. The left-hand grip, for a right-handed golfer, should have the end of the club cross the palm of the hand from the base of the index finger, diagonally to the heel of the hand (Figure 12-8A). Closing the fingers around the club will ensure a good firm grip. Left-handed golfers will use the same grip using their right hand.

6. The right-hand grip is mainly a finger tip grip. First place the two middle fingers on the club next to the index finger of the left hand (Figure 12-8B). Use only fingertips. Overlap the little finger between the index and middle finger of the left hand. The index finger of the right hand is formed like a trigger finger and placed gently on the club. Let the thumb find a natural place as you form the line mentioned above. The palm of the right hand covers the left thumb but does not touch the golf club.

7. Close the right hand; the life line of the right palm should be placed over the left thumb.

8. The palms should face each other; the line formed by the index finger and thumb of the right hand should also point toward the right eye; the club face should be square to the line of flight.

A

B

Figure 12-8 (A) Left-hand grip—fingers and palm. (B) Right-hand grip—two middle fingers.

➤ **Practice/Organizational Suggestions**

1. Place class in groups of two. One student works on acquiring a correct golf grip aided by the second student.

2. Grip with the left hand only. Hold the 7 iron at arm's length using only the left arm and hand. Remove all of the fingers from the club except the index finger. The club will be held with only this finger and the base of the hand.

3. Have the student helper attempt to pull the club from the golfer's grip. The club should not come out easily, if at all. If the grip is incorrect, the club will be very difficult to hold at arm's length and can be removed easily by the student helper.

4. Correct right-hand position must be observed by a qualified instructor.

5. Grip aids can be purchased and placed on a dowel rod. Grip aids come pre-molded for both right- and left-hand golfers. Normal, strong, or weak grips are also available. Home practice with a grip aid will speed learning (Figure 12-9).

The Stance and Address

The stance and address first involve assuming a good grip. Next, the feet, hips, and shoulders are properly aligned along with the club face. The stance is completed with two bends and a tilt. The first bend is in the waist, the second bend is at the knees, and the right shoulder is dropped to form a tilt.

Although there are three styles of stances, the square stance is used by most golfers for most all shots (Figure 12-10). The open stance is used for special shots, such as a sand trap shot. The closed stance is usually used to compensate for certain types of body builds. The open and closed stances can produce altered ball flight patterns, such as a slice or a hook.

➤ **Learning Hints**

1. Always choose a target before attempting the address and stance. Stand in line with the ball, select

Figure 12-9 A grip aid helps place hands in perfect grip.

A

B

C

Figure 12-10 Three types of stances: (A) closed, (B) open, (C) square.

a target, and draw an imaginary line from the ball to the target. A second imaginary line must be drawn parallel with the first line. These two lines must run parallel and not converge.

2. After securing a correct grip, place the club face on the target line, with the bottom of the club face at a right angle to the line.

Fiugre 12-11 Ball positions.

3. The second line is used to align your feet, hips, and shoulders at a right angle to the club face. The feet, hips, and shoulders should be pointing in the same direction.

4. In a good stance the arms will hang freely from the shoulders and straight down. Standing too far from the ball will cause a poor swing plane, and poor shots will result.

Ball position is determined somewhat by experimentation. As a general rule, the golf ball will be placed near the inside of the left heel for all full swing shots. You may need to move the ball nearer the center of your stance for the shorter clubs. Place the ball right of center for special shots or unusual circumstances (Figure 12-11).

Swing

The swing is a long, large elliptical circle. The radius of the circle is the firm left arm and the club. The left arm, wrist, and hand must be in control from the takeaway, through the backswing, especially at the beginning of the downswing, and on into the follow-through. Any undue influence by the right arm or hand will distort the swing circle and ruin the shot.

Swing the club back and up as far as you can, maintaining your balance. The right knee should remain inside the right foot during the backswing. The wrists will fall into a cocked position, with the thumbs under the shaft. This will occur near the top of the backswing. You will have turned your back to the target, but your head has remained steady. Your right elbow will be pointed downward.

The forward swing is started by replacing the left heel in the original address position. You should strive for the feeling of stepping into the shot. Your left heel may not come off the ground for all clubs, but the feeling of stepping into the shot is the same for all clubs. As you step into the shot, you must keep your head positioned behind the ball. Avoid anxiety and an urge of the right shoulder to take over the swing.

The wrists will remain cocked during the beginning of the downswing. They will uncock automatically without thinking about it.

During the forward swing, you should have a sensation of the right side working underneath the left side, causing a bowing action in the waist. With the irons, you should feel as though you are swinging down and through, and with the woods, you should feel a more level swing.

The entire swing lasts but a short time and does not require complicated thought processes. If you follow the above description of a golf swing and with good tempo, you will have the sensation of swinging the club through the ball and down the target line. The swing will finish as you face the target, with most of your weight on the left foot. The right foot will turn up on the toes. Your hands will finish high, and the weight will be equally distributed between the outside of the left foot and the right toes.

Although we frequently think of the adage "practice makes perfect," the truth is that "practice makes permanent." Therefore, haphazard practice is worse than no practice at all. Plan your practices well, concentrating on one phase of the swing at a time. Remember that you will probably get worse as your mind and body attempt to learn or relearn this new skill. Be patient and give yourself time to succeed.

➤ Learning Hints (Figure 12-12)

A. *Takeaway.* The takeaway is the act of moving the club away from the ball. The length of the takeaway is determined by how far the club moves away from the ball yet remains close to the ground. The longer the club, the longer the takeaway. The speed of the takeaway also determines the overall tempo of the entire golf swing.

　1. With the left hand, wrist, and arm in control, start moving the club straight back away from the ball. Do not pull the club inside the target line. The club will eventually begin an inside route as the club rises from the ground and is lifted into the backswing.

B. *Backswing.* This is not really a swing, but the act of turning and lifting the club into position.

　1. With the left arm still in control, begin coiling the body as you lift the club upward. The left shoulder will begin turning to a behind-the-ball position.

　2. As the club reaches waist level, you should see the left arm still firm and in control. The right elbow has begun to hinge. The left knee has begun to turn inward. The right leg is still braced, with the knee turned inward to prevent a lateral sway and loss of balance. The head has also begun to rotate slightly, but does not move laterally.

C. *At the Top*

　1. The club should be horizontal for the longer clubs, near horizontal for shorter clubs. The left side is still in control. The thumbs are under the shaft to support the club.

　2. Sometime during the backswing, usually near the finish, the wrists move to a cocked position. This action should happen naturally and is caused by the speed of the backswing.

　3. Your back should be turned to the target. The head will have continued to rotate but with no lateral movement. The right elbow is pointing toward the ground.

　4. The right leg has remained in the braced position. The left knee has turned inward, and the left heel may have been pulled off the ground.

D. *Downswing*

　1. The initial movement is made by replacing the left heel. A feeling of stepping into the swing should occur. As you step into the swing, the hips will begin to slide on a line parallel with the target line.

　2. With the left side still in control, you should pull the club on a downward angle. You will attempt to swing down and through the ball.

　3. The right side is active as it works under the left side. You will feel a bowing sensation in the waist.

　4. The wrists will uncock naturally; correct timing of the wrist cock will be obtained by practice.

　5. The head must remain behind the ball. Swing the club beyond your face before you allow head movement.

E. *Follow-through.* The follow-through is a reaction to all that has gone on before. If all has gone well, the hands will finish high, and you should be facing the target. You will be equally balanced between the outside of your left foot and the toes of the right foot.

➤ Practice/Organizational Suggestions

Many warm-up exercises can be used that approximate the rhythm and pattern of a full swing. In addition, golf is a target game and therefore a target should be selected and used as a reference in all drills.

A. *Without a Ball or Club*

　1. Assume a golf stance and grip, arms hanging straight down from your shoulders, knees and waist bent slightly. On command, pivot and swing to a position with arms horizontal to the ground. Stop and check for correct balance and body position. Continue on to the top of the backswing and stop. Execute a downswing, stopping at a point where the

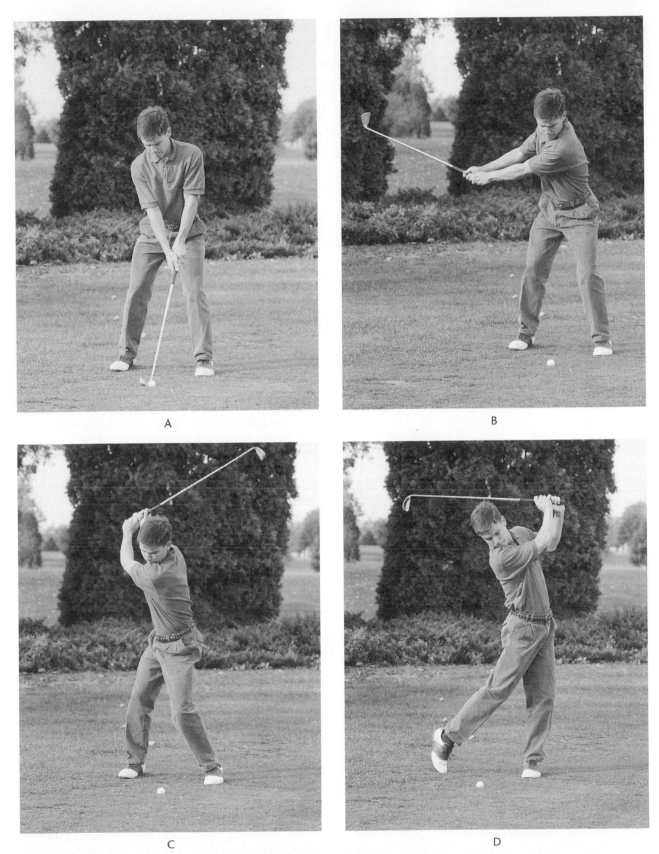

Figure 12-12 Swing sequence: (A) Takeaway, (B) backswing, (C) at the top, (D) flow-through.

ball would be struck. Finally, finish the swing. Each stop should be examined for correct body balance and position.

2. With a towel rolled and grasped at either end, assume a stance, then execute a golf swing. (A golf club can be used.) Make sure your weight is kept inside the rear foot on the backswing. Avoid excessive lateral movement.

B. *With a Club and Ball*

1. Assume a golf stance. Note the position of your left foot. Next, place your left foot next to your right foot. From this position, execute a backswing and come to a stop. The downswing is started by lifting your left foot from the ground and beginning to step this foot toward its original position. At the same time, begin to pull downward with your left arm. Complete the swing by replacing the left foot in its original position. Correct execution will teach the sensation of weight transfer in the golf swing. Practice this drill without a ball first, until you gain control. Add the ball to the drill only after you have good balance and control.

2. To learn control of the clubface, choke down on a 7 iron. Put your feet together and practice hitting balls. When a majority of the balls are flying toward your target, try a regular grip or move to a longer club. This drill can be used with any club, including the woods.

3. Stand on the left foot only, using only the right toes for balance. Hit balls toward a target from this position. This drill simulates body position at ball contact.

Suiting Clubs to Shots

Woods

The woods are used for the longest shots in golf. The driver, the longest club, is used for shots from the teeing ground on the longer holes. The first shot on every hole may be teed.

The 3 and 5 woods are also used for distance. They may be used for teeing off, but their primary use is from the fairway. They do not afford as much distance as the driver, but are more accurate. A near-perfect lie is necessary when using a wood from the fairway or rough. If in doubt as to the lie, it is best to use an iron.

Long Irons

The 2, 3, and 4 irons are considered the long irons. They produce less distance than the woods but are more accurate. Most long par 3 holes require a long iron for the first shot. These clubs are good for fairway and rough shots. They can also be substituted for a wood in a bad lie situation.

Some golfers find the long irons too difficult to use. A 7 wood can substitute for the 2 and 3 irons, leaving room for an extra club.

Medium Irons

This name applies to the 5, 6, and 7 irons. Remember, as the number becomes higher, so does the flight of the shot produced. Increased height gives less distance and less roll, but more accuracy.

Medium irons are versatile and can be used for several different kinds of shots. Par 3 golf holes of medium length require a medium iron for the first shot. On any hole, the medium irons should be considered as you near the 150-yard marker. A medium iron is a good choice from a fairway bunker with a large front lip. Near the green, if you desire a shot to land on the green and roll toward the hole, a medium iron works well. From deep rough, these clubs can get you back in play.

When first learning the golf swing, the medium irons are an excellent choice as the clubs with which to begin. Most golf drills require a medium iron.

Short Irons

This category includes the 8, 9, and pitching wedge (10 iron). These are the most accurate of all the irons and are used inside the 150-yard marker. Since the shots will fly much higher, you can expect less roll. You may now shoot more toward a specific target, such as the green or the hole, rather than a landing area.

During your practice sessions, learn how far the shortest club in your set will travel with a full swing under normal circumstances. On the golf course, once you are located at a distance that requires less than a full swing, adjustments will have to be made.

To curtail distance, first open your stance slightly. This will help shorten the backswing. Choking down on the club can also reduce distance. Narrow the stance in conjunction with the short irons for shorter shots. See "Chip Shots" and "Pitch Shots" for further ideas.

Special Shots

The short approach shots discussed in this section—the pitch, chip, sand shot, and putt—are frequently called the golfer's scoring strokes. A high percentage of shots taken during a round of golf consists of these four types; therefore, the more proficient you become, the lower your scores will be. One of the key elements in these shots involves "feel"; consequently, the shots must be practiced frequently in order to develop a comfortable feeling. Most of these shots, with the exception of a fairway sand shot, are executed near the green or on the green itself.

Pitch Shot

The pitch shot is characterized as a high-flying, minimum-roll type of shot. This shot is generally executed with a high-lofted iron such as the 8, 9, or pitching wedge. Less than a full swing is required.

The pitch shot is a good choice for a golfer faced with a hazard, sand or water, blocking the entry to the green. Many golfers use the pitch shot as a substitute for the chip shot, even though it is more difficult (Figure 12-13).

➤ Learning Hints

1. Assume a square or open stance. Use your normal grip.
2. The feet are moved closer together.
3. Play the ball slightly left of center.
4. Pick the club up early in the backswing by cocking the wrists (Figure 12-13A).
5. Swing down and through, making sure the hands do not stop at ball impact (Figure 12-13B).
6. Shift the weight slightly to the left foot, and avoid trying to scoop the ball in the hitting area. The arms, hands, and club generally reach waist high at the finish (Figure 12-13C).

Chip Shot

The chip shot is characterized as a low-flying, maximum-roll type of shot. Generally, the ball will be in the air one-third of the time, rolling two-thirds of the time. Any club—5 iron through pitching wedge—may be used. More lofted clubs produce less roll.

Most instructors suggest that the beginning golfer select one club, 7 or 9 iron, to develop the necessary experience. Since the chip shot is largely roll, the shot must be treated much like a putt. Select a landing spot, then read the green to the hole (Figure 12-14).

➤ Learning Hints

1. Narrow stance, square or slightly open.
2. Normal grip. Some golfers prefer a putting grip.
3. Play ball left of center. Hands, head, and weight center must be in front of ball. This delofts the club, allowing maximum roll.
4. The arms, hands, and club act as one unit and move back in a small arc in the backswing; in a right-handed golfer, the weight remains on the left foot (Figure 12-14A).
5. The arms, hands, and club are brought forward on the downswing, the butt of the club is kept ahead of the hands and arms through the hitting area. Make sure to accelerate the movement through the hitting area (Figure 12-14B).
6. The follow-through is generally the same length as the backswing (Figure 12-14C).

➤ Practice/Organizational Suggestions

1. Experiment with different clubs at 10-yard intervals, starting 10 yards from the green.

A   B   C

Figure 12-13 Pitch shot. (A) Note wrists cocked in backswing. (B) Note hands ahead of ball. (C) Follow-through.

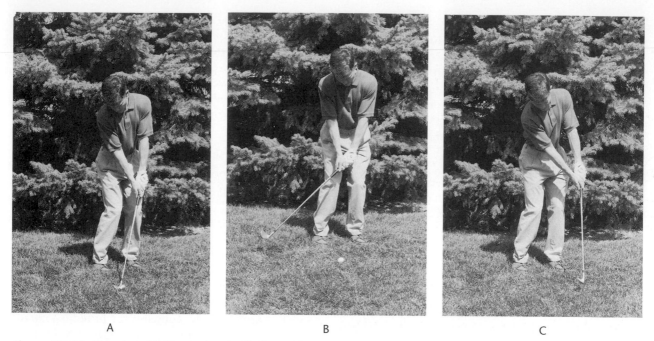

A   B   C

Figure 12-14 Chip shot. (A) Hands ahead of ball at address. (B) Club head low, wrists not cocked. (C) Club head low on follow-through.

2. Hit pitch shots over a barrier, such as your golf bag.
3. Hit chip shots onto a practice green. Notice how far the ball rolls when using different clubs.
4. Practice both chip shots and pitch shots with the same club. Note how changes are made to produce each shot.

Sand Shot

The sand shot is usually a difficult shot for the beginner to master because sand does not have the firmness of the fairway and the ball does not set up as it does on grass. A specially designed club called a sand wedge is used to execute the shot. Again, the element of "feel" can determine success. Getting out of a sand trap requires various strategies. With traps that are flat, near the green, and with no lip, the beginner might try putting the ball out of the trap, provided the ball is not buried. For shots with a low lip near the green, the golfer may try a chip shot. However, for shots in a deep trap and with the ball buried in the sand, the golfer must execute an explosion shot. Remember, a golfer may not ground a club in a trap without incurring a penalty.

➤ **Learning Hints**

1. Address the ball with an open stance. Wiggle the feet into the sand to secure a good foothold and prevent slipping.
2. The ball is played right of center. Preshift some weight forward prior to the swing, but maintain your head position behind the ball during the entire swing. Open the club face slightly.

3. Cock the wrists early in the backswing, much like the pitch shot. Focus on a spot an inch or so behind the ball.
4. Explode the clubhead onto the spot behind the ball. You must hit sand—not the ball.
5. Be sure to keep the clubhead traveling through the sand, under the ball, and into a good finish (Figure 12-15).

The Putt

Putting is probably the most important phase of the game, and too often one of the most neglected. Concentration and confidence are two of the primary requirements for good putting, and can be gained best through practice of fundamental techniques. Forms of putting differ widely, but basic fundamentals are much the same.

➤ **Learning Hints**

1. Grip the club with your fingers, palms facing each other and in line with the putter face. All five fingers of the bottom hand grip the club. Overlap the index finger of the top hand (Figure 12-16).
2. Any stance that is comfortable and allows you to place your eyes directly over the ball is acceptable.
3. Both elbows must be bent to allow you to stand close to the ball. You must also crouch down slightly for comfort.
4. The ball is played left of center. The putting stance may seem awkward at first, but give it a chance (Figure 12-17).

A   B   C

Figure 12-15 Sand shot.

Figure 12-16 Putting grip. Note overlap of index finger.

A   B

Figure 12-17 Putting stance. (A) Front view. (B) Side view.

5. The backswing should be kept low. It is initiated with the arms with little or no wrist break.
6. The forward stroke should return along the same line, keeping the putter face square to the intended putting line.

The Sweetspot. This name is given to an eighth-inch wide vertical area located on the face of the putter. The most successful putts occur when the sweetspot strikes the center of the ball. Missing the sweetspot towards the heel of the putter will cause the loss of distance and some control. Missing the sweetspot towards the toe of the putter will cause even more loss of distance and even more loss of control.

Of all putting fundamentals, striking the sweetspot to the center of the ball ranks as the most important. Regardless of which putting style you choose or change to later, striking the sweetspot to the center of the ball will always be your number one goal.

Finding the Sweetspot. To find the sweetspot, using your thumb and first finger, hold your putterhead in front of your face, putter face facing you. Using a golf ball, begin dinging the putter's face. Find the area that will allow you to drive the putter straight back and forth with no gyrations or shaft vibrations. Note the spot. Make a line on top of the putter to align with this sweetspot. Some putters already have a line marked for you; this line may or may not be correct.

The Putting Stroke. The putting stroke can be described as a sweeping motion. There should be no lower body movement. Your head should also be kept still until the putt is well on its way. The amount of wrist break depends on the individual. Generally, the closer to the hole, the less wrist break needed to putt. Be sure to keep your hands moving with the putt. Many beginners stop the hands at ball impact causing mis-hit putts.

Finally, learn to read the greens. A putt seldom rolls perfectly straight to the hole unless it is a very short putt. Since no green is perfectly flat, study which way the ball will turn and to what degree. The most important factor in reading a green is judging distance. Misjudging distance and missing the sweetspot are the main causes of missed putts.

Judging distance on a putt must include factors along with distance. How fast the ball will roll on a green can be affected by the grass length. Greens are mowed early each day and are much faster early in the morning after being mowed. Soft greens are usually slower than hard greens. A putt traveling downhill will roll much farther than one going uphill. In some areas, the grain of the grass is a factor to be considered. Since putting can account for nearly half or more of your total strokes, be sure to devote plenty of time to developing your putting skills.

Helpful Hints

1. Always select a target when planning any shot or putt. Stand at least ten feet behind the ball, plan your shot, then choose a club.
2. During the swing, concentrate on ball contact and direction rather than distance.
3. Know what club to use from 150 yards. Generally, men can add or subtract 10 yards and women 7 yards when choosing clubs for other distances.
4. For downhill shots, use a lofted club, wide stance, and play the ball back in the stance.
5. For uphill shots, use a less lofted club than normal, wide stance for balance, and play the ball forward in the stance. In both uphill and downhill shots, adjust your shoulder position and swing to match the contour of the hill.
6. For sidehill shots with the ball above your feet, take more club than normal, but choke down and swing easy. Expect the ball to travel in the direction of the contour of the hill.
7. For a sidehill shot with the ball below your feet, take more club than normal and plan to use a short, easy swing. This is one of the more difficult trouble shots in golf.
8. Consider weather conditions when planning shots. A golf ball will fly farther in warm, dry air. Consider the velocity and direction of the wind and how it will affect your ball flight.
9. Do not practice swing before you hit a normal shot. Use a practice swing after you have made a poor swing, and only if it will not delay play.
10. A practice swing may be used before playing an unusual or difficult shot to help determine how the normal swing must be altered.
11. Immediately after you play, analyze your game. Decide which part of your game needs the most practice or more instruction.
12. Most amateur golfers make three mistakes: They underclub themselves, then overswing, and finally overestimate their ability. Try to play within your own abilities and when in trouble, get back in play. Avoid attempting the miracle shot. It is better to accept a score of one or two strokes over par on a hole, rather than a very large score made by using poor judgment.

➤ **Practice/Organizational Suggestions—Indoor Work**

Sometimes the instructor is confronted with situations that will not allow outside practice and is forced to teach indoors. With a little ingenuity and the use of typical types of equipment found in most physical education departments (track hurdles, gymnastic mats, badminton nets, hoops, balance beam, rope circles, waste baskets, portable pitching net, tires, goal cage), it is possible to continue the unit without interruption. Many of the following suggestions can be organized into stations for practice. Plastic, hard rubber, foam rubber, or other softer synthetic practice balls should be used in most situations for safety reasons. Most equipment catalogues will have a listing of such equipment. Many carpet stores are willing to donate carpet samples for use as teeing areas and carpet remnants for use in putting, chipping, and pitching stations.

The most important phase of station work inside is to recognize the space required for stations, the type of golf ball (plastic or real) required for the station or skill being used, and the position of the student in relation to the station set-up and to other stations. Care must be taken to ensure a safe area where students are not in-line with clubs during a swing. Consideration should be given to using mats that are propped up or tied up to a wall for stations where golf balls are being chipped or pitched or where a full swing (without a golf ball) is being practiced.

1. There are several instructional videos (see further references section) that can be used when the class is forced to stay indoors because of weather.
2. Worksheets can be developed to help students understand terminology normally associated with golf.
3. Rainy-day weather is a perfect time to review the basic rules governing golf. Situations can be developed and presented to the class for answers and interpretation.
4. Divide the gymnasium into stations to practice putting, the full swing, the chip, and the pitch shot.
5. From a mat, the pitch shot can be practiced, using a mat draped over a track hurdle. Rolled-up mats can be used as obstacles for the golfer to pitch over.
6. From a mat, the chip shot can be practiced by extending a net between volleyball or badminton standards and having the students keep the chip under the net.
7. Putting can be practiced on large carpet remnants. Be sure to ask for pieces of carpet that have a close nap so the surface nearly approximates the feel of putting on a green.
8. A miniature putt-putt course can be developed in the gymnasium by using a variety of equipment as obstacles.
9. With a mat, the full-swing can be practiced, with a partner offering corrections as the instructor leads the students through a swing. Careful attention must be given to placing the partner behind and far enough away so as not to be in direct line with the swing. Swing toward a wall that has been padded or draped with netting.
10. The instructor can develop cue cards for the non-swinging partner to observe key points as the golfer is practicing the swing.
11. A variety of contests using targets (hoops, rope circles, cardboard circles, baskets, etc.) can be implemented to help students practice various beginning skills.
12. Stations can be set up with defining conditions typically involved in golf that would involve the student in making the correct rules or etiquette interpretation.

Modifications for Special Populations

Orthopedically Impaired

1. Allow students who use wheelchairs to play from their chairs, using a standard position for striking, e.g., perpendicular to the ball. Reposition striking position to accommodate the swing, e.g., facing the green and striking with one arm if necessary.
2. If outdoor facilities are not accessible, e.g., terrain is rough or the student's orthopedic condition is too severe, develop an indoor putting course. Use carpet remnants for greens and tees, and boards for side rails.
3. Modify the length of the club.

Cognitively Impaired

1. Keep the concept of the game simple. Do not stress various club selections for various conditions; e.g., suggest that a student select a driver for the tee, an iron for the fairway, and a putter for the green.
2. Refer to #2 under "Orthopedically Impaired."

Sensory Impaired

1. Allow students who are blind or have a visual impairment to "feel" someone complete a golf swing.
2. Allow students who are blind or have a visual impairment to pace off the distance on the putting surface to the hole.
3. Minimal modifications are needed for individuals who are deaf or have a hearing impairment.

Safety Considerations

Golf can be a dangerous game if attention is not given to your play and the play of others. Whether golf is being played in a class situation, on a practice range, or while playing a round, basic safety rules must be observed.

1. Never hit a shot until you are sure those in front of you are out of your range. If you hit another player, you may be liable for damages.
2. Never swing a club, especially on the tees, unless you are sure no one is standing close to you.
3. If the warning "Fore" is given, it is often dangerous to turn to see where the ball is coming from. It is best to cover the head for protection and turn away from the direction of the warning.
4. In the event of a thunderstorm, it is not wise to remain outdoors. Shelter should be sought in a closed building protected against lightning. Large or small unprotected buildings are alternatives in the order given. If remaining outdoors is unavoidable, keep away from open spaces and hilltops, isolated trees, wire fences, and small shelters in exposed locations. Shelter may also be sought in caves, depressions or deep valleys and canyons, the foot of a cliff, or a dense stand of trees. Umbrellas held overhead in exposed places are dangerous.
5. Never practice in an area where others are playing. Most golf courses have special practice areas.

6. Never hit practice shots while playing a round. It not only wastes time but also is dangerous.
7. Only one person should hit at a time. The person farthest from the hole should play first.
8. Knowing and applying the rules of golf and golfing etiquette will increase your safety on a golf course.
9. Carry a towel and wipe hands dry, particularly on hot, humid days and rainy days.
10. Know the distances of specific clubs and distances you can hit the ball.

In Class—Rules for the Instructor

1. Plan the lesson well in advance, checking such things as formation, target areas, methods of retrieval.
2. Allow no one to swing a club unless instructed to do so.
3. Provide plenty of space between golfers.
4. If stations are used, provide for adequate distance between groups.

In Class—Rules for the Student

1. Do not retrieve a golf ball until asked to do so; never step out of line to pick up a "muffed" shot.
2. Do not walk too close behind other golfers who are swinging their golf clubs.
3. If working with a partner, stand in front and to the side of your partner, not behind.
4. Listen to instruction and follow prescribed rules.

Etiquette and Playing Courtesies

Because golf is a polite game with a well-defined code of ethics, it is important for every golfer to observe common courtesies while on the course.

In General, While Playing the Course

1. Be polite at all times; know the rules of golf so decisions can be made quickly without causing undue delay.
2. Be aware of the local rules and regulations that govern play on a course.
3. Do not hit practice shots between regular shots—it is an infraction of the rules.
4. Abstain from obscene language, loud talk, and club throwing.
5. Plan ahead and be ready to play your next shot without undue delay. The player farthest from the flag stick shoots first.
6. Do not talk, move around, stand too close or directly in line of a shot when another player is preparing to shoot.
7. Never play a shot until the group ahead is completely out of range.

8. While looking for a lost ball, do not unduly delay the play of others. Allow a group playing behind you to go through by signaling them to do so, and do not resume play until they are out of range.
9. After each shot, pick up the divot or loose grass and replace it with your hand in the divot mark. Pat it down with your foot.
10. Fill holes made in bunkers and smooth the sand after playing from a trap. Be sure to rake all sand traps before leaving them.
11. Keep pull carts and motorized carts off the green area.
12. Yell "Fore" if a ball is in danger of striking another person.
13. The person having the honor (lowest score on the preceding hole) tees up first.
14. Notify your partners when you wish to change a golf ball.

On the Putting Green

1. As soon as a hole has been completed, the player should leave the green. Do not total the scores and record them on the green.
2. Allow the person farthest from the hole to putt first.
3. When lifting a ball on the green, mark it with a coin.
4. Never lay a bag of clubs down on the green.
5. Do not throw the flag stick off to the side. Always lay it down gently, away from all play, and replace it when the hole has been completed.
6. Do not damage the hole with the stick or by standing too close to the hole.
7. Repair ball marks on the green.
8. Upon completion of the hole, the group should move off the green to record scores.
9. Do not drag your feet or in any way scuff the green.

Rules of Golf

The rules of golf have been developed and are periodically upgraded by two coordinating bodies—the United States Golf Association (USGA) and the Royal and Ancient Golf Club of St. Andrews, Scotland. The rules undergo continual study and are revised by these two bodies every four years. The USGA publishes a rule book each year and offers it for sale at a minimal cost. It is strongly recommended that serious students obtain a copy. A booklet entitled *Easy Way to Learn Golf Rules* is available at a minimal cost from the National Golf Foundation.

Local Rules

In constructing the rules that uniformly govern all golf play in the United States, the United States Golf

Association recognizes that certain local conditions such as climate, variable physical conditions, and characteristics of golf courses may necessitate modifications of the rules. These modifications are termed Local Rules and are designed to protect the golf course and make the game more enjoyable. A player is responsible for becoming acquainted with the Local Rules before playing. Sources of information concerning Local Rules include the golf professional, the score card, golf course bulletin board, and players familiar with the golf course.

The United States Golf Association limits the extent to which Local Rules may modify the USGA rules. Players should refer to the United States Golf Association Rules of Golf Appendix to familiarize themselves with the limitations.

Summary of Important Golf Rules

1. A player may have a maximum of 14 clubs in the golf bag at any one time. The penalty for exceeding the maximum is (1) *match play:* one hole for each hole at which the breach occurred (maximum per round: two holes) or (2) *stroke play:* two strokes for each hole at which the breach occurred (maximum: four strokes per round).

2. A player must tee up her ball between the tee markers or anywhere in the rectangle two club lengths behind them. Violation of the rule is a two-stroke penalty.

3. An intentional swing at the ball must be counted as a stroke, even if the player "wiffs" it.

4. A ball is considered lost outside of a hazard if not retrieved in 5 minutes. The player must hit the ball from the previous spot and take a one-stroke penalty.

5. A ball must be played as it lies except as provided for in the rules.

6. Loose impediments such as leaves, sticks (anything of nature lying around) may be removed outside of a hazard, so long as the ball does not move.

7. For relief from artificial obstructions, drop the ball within one club length of the point of nearest relief without penalty, but no closer to the hole. See rule book for exceptions.

8. If a player hits a ball out-of-bounds, the player must take a one-stroke penalty and play the ball from the original spot.

9. When a ball is hit into a water hazard, the player may drop a ball behind the hazard, keeping the spot at which the ball crossed the hazard between herself and the hole. The penalty is one stroke.

10. A player, while in the act of putting on the green, whose ball hits another player's ball or the flag stick, is assessed a two-stroke penalty. Putting from off the green is not considered a putt.

Terminology

Ace A hole in one.

Address The position taken by a player when preparing to start a stroke.

Apron The area immediately surrounding the green.

Banana ball A slice

Best ball tournament Competition in which the better score of a partnership on each hole is used as the team score.

Birdie The score of one under par on a hole.

Bogey A score of one over par on a hole (United States rules). In countries playing the British rules, a bogey is the score an average golfer should make on a hole; on easier holes, par and bogey might be the same score.

Casual water Temporary accumulation of water that is not recognized as a hazard on the course.

Course rating The comparative difficulty of a specific course. Usually computed by a committee of a local association in order to have uniform handicapping for all courses within a district.

Divot Sod cut with the clubhead when executing or attempting to execute a shot.

Dogleg A hole that has a sharp bend in the fairway.

Driver Number 1 wood.

Eagle A score for a hole played in two strokes under par.

Fairway The course between the teeing ground and the putting green, exclusive of hazards.

Flag Banner on top of the flagstick identifying the cup.

Fore A warning cry to anyone of a stroke about to be played or one that has been played.

Go to school Learning the roll of a green by watching a previous putt over the same area.

Ground under repair Any portion of the course so marked that includes material piled for removal or a hole made by a greenskeeper.

Hazard Any bunker, water hazard, or lateral water hazard.

Hole Small cup sunk into the green, into which the golf ball is hit. The hole is 4¼ inches in diameter and at least 4 inches deep.

Honor The side entitled to play first from the teeing ground is said to have the honor. This is usually determined by a coin flip on the first tee. Once play begins, the player having the lowest score on the previous hole is said to have the honor thereafter.

Hook A ball in flight that curves from right to left (for a right-handed golfer).

Lie The position of the ball on the playing ground. Also refers to the angle of the clubhead.

Loft The slope given to the face of a golf club to aid in knocking the ball in a high curve.

Loose impediments Natural objects not fixed or growing and not adhering to the ball, and including stones not solidly embedded, leaves, twigs, branches, and the like, dung, worms, and insects, and casts or heaps made by them.

Match play Competition in which the winner is decided by the number of holes won.

Mulligan Permitting a second hit of a badly played ball—usually on a tee shot. (Not permitted under the rules but by mutual agreement in friendly matches.)

Obstruction An artificial object erected, placed, or left on a course and not an integral part of the course.

Par The standard score for a hole.

Pull-shot To hit a ball straight, but to the left of the target (for a right-handed golfer).

Push-shot To hit a ball straight, but to the right of the target (for a right-handed golfer).

Rough The unmowed terrain on either side of the fairway.

Scotch foursome A competitive round in which two partners play the same ball, taking alternate shots.

Slice A ball in flight that curves from left to right (for a right-handed person).

Stroke play (medal play) Competition in which the winner is decided by the total number of strokes taken from a specific number of rounds, not by individual holes won, as in match play.

Summer rules Playing the ball as it lies from tee through green.

Teeing ground The starting place for the hole to be played.

Trap A hazard, technically known as a bunker.

Waggle Body or club action prior to starting the swing.

Wedge A heavy iron club that is used to loft the ball high into the air. It is also used for special situations, such as getting out of heavy grass or sand.

Winter rules The privilege of improving the lie of the ball on the fairway of the hole being played.

Reference

1. Aultman, Dick. Golf Primer. *Golf Digest* (May): 113, 1979.

Further References

Aultman, D. *The Masters of Golf: Learning Their Methods.* New York: Atheneum, 1989.

Ballingall, P. *DK Pocket Guide to Golf: Practice Drills.* London: DK Publishing, 1995.

Casten, C. M. *Lesson Plans for Pangrazi & Darst: Dynamic Physical Education for Secondary School Students (Golf).* Boston: Allyn & Bacon, 1997.

Clarke, G. *Golf Rules Illustrated.* New York: Callaway Editions, 2000.

Curtis, B. *Beginning Golf.* New York: Sterling Publications, 2000.

Dobereiner, P. and Elliot, B. *Golf Rules Explained.* London: David & Charles, 2000.

Fisher, A. G. *Golf: Your Turn for Success.* Boston, MA: Jones and Bartlett, 1992.

Folio, M. R. and Nichols, R. W. *Skill Building for Beginning Golf.* Boston: Allyn & Bacon, 1997.

Gensemer, R. *Beginning Golf.* 2nd ed. Englewood, CO: Morton Publishing Company, 1995.

Hogan, B. *Free Lessons: The Modern Fundamentals of Golf.* Trumbull, CT: Golf Digest/Tennis, Inc., 1985.

Jacobs, J. and Newell, S. *50 Greatest Golf Lessons of the Century: Private Lessons With Golf Greats.* Harper Resources, 2000.

Lopez, N. *The Complete Golfer.* Chicago, IL: Contemporary Books, Inc., 1988.

McCord, G. *Golf for Dummies.* 2nd ed. New York: Hungry Minds Inc., 1999.

Nance, V. and Davis, E. *Golf.* 6th ed. Dubuque, IA: Wm. C. Brown, 1990.

National Golf Foundation. *The Easy Way to Learn Golf Rules.* Jupiter, FL: National Golf Foundation, 1986.

Nicklaus, J. *My 55 Ways to Lower Your Golf Score.* New York: Simon and Schuster, 1985.

Owens, De De. *The American Coaching Effectiveness Program.* Champaign, IL: Leisure Press, 1991.

Pelz, D. and Frank, J. A. (Contributor). *Dave Pelz's Putting Bible.* New York: Doubleday, 2000.

Pelz, D., Frank, J. A, and Janzen, L. *Dave Pelz's Short Game Bible.* New York: Broadway Books, 1999.

Snead, J. C. and Johnson, J. L. *Golf Today.* St. Paul: West Pub. Co., 1989.

United States Golf Association: *Rules of Golf.* Far Hills, NJ: United States Golf Association, 2000–2001.

Watson, T. and Hannigan, F. *The New Rules of Golf.* Latest ed. New York: Random House.

Wiren, G. with T. Dawson. *Golf's Common Errors and What to Do About Them.* Chicago: Contemporary Books, Inc., 1987.

Wiren, G. *Golf: Building a Solid Game.* 2nd ed. Englewood Cliffs, NJ: Prentice Hall, 1992.

Audio-Visual Materials

Other excellent material and films can be obtained by writing to the following:

Champions on Film & Video, 745 State Circle, Box 1941, Ann Arbor, MI 48106. *Golf for All Ages* (VHS only).

Also from Champions on Film & Video: *Beginning Golf for Women* (VHS, 40 minutes); *Ben Crenshaw and the Art of Putting* (VHS, 40 minutes); *Golf with Bruce Fossum* (VHS, 15 minutes); *The Rules of Golf* (VHS); *Stretching for Better Golf* (40 minutes); *Chipping and Putting* (30 minutes).

Karol Videos, 350 No. Pennsylvania Ave., Box 7600, Wilkes-Barre, PA 18773-7600. *Teaching Kids Golf* (VHS, 70 minutes).

Also from Karol Video: *Golf the Easy Way* (VHS, 50 minutes); *A Guide for the Woman Golfer* (40 minutes); *Golf for Kids* (30 minutes); *Rules of Golf* (30 minutes).

Heather Productions, 68 Mayfair Dr., Pittsburgh, PA 15228. *The Etiquette of Golf* (VHS, 35 minutes).

National Golf Foundation, 200 Castlewood Dr., North Palm Beach, FL 33408.

St. Johnsbury Academy, Seven Main St., Saint Johnsbury, VT 05819. *A Guide to Proper Etiquette* (VHS).

United States Golf Association, Golf House, Library Corner Rd., Far Hills, NJ 07931.

Web Sites

http://womensgolf.about.com/recreation/womens Site devoted to women's golf. Contains information about choosing clubs, history, handicaps, fitness and more.

http://golf.about.com/recreation/golf/mbody/htm General golf site contains information about fitness for golf, golf wear, governing bodies, history, instruction, life on the tour, and much more.

www.pga.com Up-to-date tour happenings, with excellent sections that cover instruction, fitness, golf equipment, rules, and a host of other topics.

www.learn-sports.com/golf/etiquette Site devoted to golf etiquette, in-depth explanations, and video clips with explanations.

www.randa.org/home.default Web site for the Royal and Ancient Golf Club. Contains rules of golf, etiquette, and definitions; discusses golf around the world.

www.mrgolf.com/ A primer about golf etiquette.

www.lpga.com/ Official site of the Ladies PGA Tour; contains biographies of players, tips for improving your game, history, and information about junior golf programs.

http://teetimefit.com An excellent site about fitness for golf; it also includes specific information on injuries and their treatment.

www.nmgf.com The National Minority Golf Foundation site; contains a number of topics, including information about junior programs, scholarships, and links to other golf organizations.

www.golfonline.com/ Site covers a broad spectrum of golf topics developed by the editors of *Golf* magazine. There is an excellent section on rules, instruction, junior golf, women's and men's golf, and more.

www.golfdigest.com/ Site developed by *Golf Digest* magazine includes good feature articles on the various aspects of golf, has an interactive swing sequences of players, provides equipment reviews, and more.

www.pga.com Professional Golfers of America site; good section on instruction and junior golf for kids as well as other up-to-date information.

www.golf101.com/ Site includes a large section on instruction, suggested videos, books, and more.

www.usga.com Site for the United States Golf Association; contains an information section about rules, including modified rules for golfers with disabilities. The USGA governs rules for the United States.

CHAPTER 13

Gymnastics and Tumbling

This chapter will enable you to

- Understand gymnastics as a competitive sport
- Identify the various events that comprise competition in gymnastics for men and women
- Appreciate the importance of acquiring safety attitudes and habits in gymnastics
- Understand how to introduce a tumbling and/or gymnastics unit in the classroom
- Identify basic body positions, grasps, and moves used in beginning tumbling and gymnastics

Nature and Purpose

Many people find it hard to think of gymnastics as a sport. It does not have the same tangible, competitive aspect that spectators see in other sporting events. We cannot yell "defense" or "get the ball," nor can we measure the performance of the gymnast with a stop watch or measuring tape. Gymnastics is the performance of a routine on a piece of apparatus. The routine is a combination of stunts and moves that have been practiced and improved over a period of time. The gymnast is actually competing against herself or himself, trying to improve upon the last performance. The sport of gymnastics involves individual effort; however, the gymnast's score is added to that of his or her teammates to obtain a team score.

One reason that makes it difficult for the uninformed spectator to grasp the concept of gymnastics is that there is no scoreboard or clock to watch during a gymnastic performance. In gymnastics it is not only *what* is performed, but also *how* it is performed that is important.

Gymnastics, like figure skating and diving, are judged by qualified individuals. Although judging may sometimes seem too subjective, there are specific guidelines that judges must use in scoring. A judge is considering the difficulty, the execution, and the composition of the routine. These three aspects are fundamental in scoring, but other areas also enter into a score—among them, amplitude, creativity, elegance, risk, and so forth.

All parts of the body benefit in the sport of gymnastics. It promotes strength, agility, flexibility, coordination, kinesthetic sense, and balance. Furthermore, mastery of a stunt or routine develops more than the physical aspects; it also improves the participant's self-image.

The Participant

As in other sports, size may determine the future and success of a gymnast. However, in gymnastics someone small in stature is more likely to succeed than the usual stereotyped 6'5", 220-lb. athlete. This does not mean that a tall gymnast will be unsuccessful, but generally a gymnast is shorter than 5'10".

Today's gymnast must be above average in strength for height and weight. Flexibility is another needed physical attribute. Also required are a good kinesthetic sense (awareness of where one's body and body parts are in space) and a sense of balance. In addition, a well-developed sense of timing along with good coordination are important.

Cardiorespiratory endurance does not play as vital a role in gymnastics as in other sports; however, a gymnast must have muscle endurance. Although a gymnastic routine may last only from one to two minutes, the abdominal or quadricep muscles may be contracted throughout that time. Also, a gymnast must have muscle power to be able to use the body and muscle groups with explosive force. Timing plays a part with the burst of energy, but unless the strength is there to call upon, the gymnast may end up on the floor.

Along with the physical attributes, there are also psychological aspects to be considered. The participant is individualistic, self-motivated, confident, and self-assured. The sport involves perseverance and a drive for perfection. The gymnast is subject to taking risks but not to the extent that safety is sacrificed.

Gymnastics is a team sport, but as a member of a team, a gymnast is also competing against his or her teammates. As previously mentioned, a gymnast is actually competing against himself or herself, always striving to perfect the routine. The individual's score will not only determine his or her place among the competitors, but also will be added to the team scores to determine its final standing.

The Competition

The gymnastic meet is an event in which more than one thing is happening at once. In large meets, all pieces of equipment may be worked at once. Judges will be at every station, and the gymnasts rotate to each station to perform.

On a smaller scale, for instance a women's college meet, the balance beam and floor exercise may be judged at the same time by different sets of judges. Later, the uneven bars and vaulting are judged. There are usually two judges per event at these meets. One set of judges may score the balance beam and unevens, while the other set will judge the floor exercise and vaulting.

At a gymnastic meet, the judges watch and score the performance. The average of scores is flashed (open scoring) or a runner will take the score to the scorer's table (closed scoring) where it will be tallied. Individual gymnasts' scores are added together to form a team score. A gymnast may score differently on each piece of equipment. For instance, he may be first on the pommel horse and third in vaulting, etc.

The "all-around" event comprises a total of the scores of a gymnast who competed in every event. The gymnast who wins the all-around is considered the top gymnast of the meet. A gymnast who does not compete all-around is called a specialist and may work only the floor exercise and vaulting. In most countries gymnasts are always all-around. Only in the United States do we continue to have gymnastic specialists, and many argue that this system enables more people to participate.

Each piece of equipment or event is unique, requiring a different strength from the gymnast. For example, a performer on the still rings would require more upper body strength than someone working floor exercise. However, the gymnast who specializes on rings may not be as flexible as the floor exercise specialist. The balance beam requires the athlete to have some dance background and a good sense of balance, while vaulting centers more on the gymnast's speed and explosive power. The all-around gymnast is able to compete in all areas at the meet.

The Rules and Judging

In 1968 the Fédération International Gymnastique (FIG), or International Gymnastic Federation, published a Code of Points, which has been the basis for the rules in gymnastics. Although it is not possible to state the universal rules, we will specify the rules that apply in each meet or competition described below.

Unless otherwise agreed upon by the teams involved, the men's gymnastic competition has six events and the women's four events:

Men	Women
1. Floor Exercise	1. Floor Exercise
2. Horizontal Bar	2. Balance Beam
3. Parallel Bars	3. Uneven Parallel Bars
4. Pommel Horse	4. Vault
5. Rings	
6. Vault	

For both men and women, there is also the all-around event, which is the total of either the men's six events or the women's four events.

To qualify as a judge, one must first be certified. To earn certification involves passing a written test, attending workshops, and paying a fee for certification. A judge must be aware of the rules of the meet and the sport of gymnastics. He or she must try to watch the performance with complete concentration and be as objective as possible. Judges consider three major areas when scoring a gymnastic routine:

Difficulty (what has been performed). Most stunts have been given a difficulty value that the judges have learned.

Composition (the way the routine is put together). Each event has certain requirements that must be incorporated in a routine.

Execution (how the routine is performed). These three areas make up the greatest part of a judge's score sheet.

Depending on the level of competition, the judge may have a point with which he or she may judge risk, elegance, amplitude, and so on. Usually deductions are made on the floor exercise area each time the gymnast goes out of bounds. Deductions are also made for falls, spotting, and not meeting time requirements on balance beam and floor exercise.

One other aspect of judging that is usually seen in private clubs is *compulsory routines*. This is a routine that is constructed for each piece of equipment at different skill levels. A gymnast learns the routine for her skill level and competes against other gymnasts at the same level, performing the same routine. As the gymnast becomes more skilled, she may move to harder "class levels" and learn more difficult compulsory routines. When judging this type of competition, the judge has also learned the routine and is aware of the specific deductions.

The types of routines used in the Olympics or in intercollegiate meets are those constructed by the gymnast, called *optional routines*. These routines contain certain difficulties, but each one is as different in composition as each gymnast.

Suggested Learning Sequence

A. Stretching, sit-ups and push-ups
B. Introduction—nature and purpose
C. Basic rules and safety conditions
D. Fundamental skills
  1. Tumbling
     a. Forward roll
     b. Backward roll
     c. Tripod balance
     d. Headstand
     e. Prone headstand
     f. Kip (neckspring)
     g. Cartwheel
     h. Round-off
     i. Back walkover
     j. Front walkover
     k. Headstand and forward roll
     l. Tinsica
     m. Valdez
     n. Back handspring
     o. Elementary combination
  2. Pommel horse
     a. Feint
     b. Front support and swing
     c. Single leg circle forward
     d. Simple travel
     e. Elementary combination
  3. Vaulting
     a. Squat vault
     b. Straddle vault
     c. Front vault
     d. Rear vault
     e. Stoop vault
     f. Thief vault
     g. Handspring vault
     h. Elementary combination
  4. Rings
     a. Inverted hang
     b. Nest hang
     c. Forward single leg cut
     d. Backward double leg cut dismount
     e. Elementary combination
  5. High bar
     a. Backward hip circle
     b. Knee circle
     c. Kip

     d. Squat dismount from support
     e. Elementary combination
  6. Parallel bars
     a. Forward hand walk
     b. Hip roll
     c. Corkscrew mount
     d. Flank dismount
     e. Elementary combination
  7. Uneven parallel bars
     a. Back hip pullover
     b. Mill circle
     c. Pop-up
     d. Straddle sole circle
     e. Elementary combination
  8. Balance beam
     a. Squat mount
     b. Chassé
     c. Back shoulder roll
     d. Arabesque
     e. Leap
     f. Forward roll
     g. Cartwheel dismount
     h. Elementary combinations

Skills and Techniques

Basic gymnastic teams refer to body positions utilized in many of the events. A simple understanding of the basic body positions helps performance. Following are the positions a gymnast uses when performing different stunts in a routine:

1. *Tuck*—The knees and hips are bent, and the head is in a chin-down position.
2. *Pike*—The legs are straight, but the torso is bent at the hips.
3. *Layout*—The entire body is straight.
4. *Puck*—This position is a combination of tuck and pike. There is only a slight bend in the knees.

There are also different grasps used when working the pieces of equipment. The grasps are generally changed a number of times in a routine.

1. *Over grasp*—The palms of the hand are on top of the bar (Figure 13-1).
2. *Under grasp*—The palms of the hand are under the bar (Figure 13-2).
3. *Mixed grasp*—One hand is an over grasp, and the other hand is in an under grasp.

The following are specific terms for the way the body moves in gymnastics:

1. *Somersault*—This is a rotation around a horizontal axis. The somersault could be in the tuck, pike, or layout position.
2. *Twist*—A rotation around a vertical axis. Again, it can be done in different body positions or in combination with a somersault.

Figure 13-1 Over grasp.

Figure 13-2 Under grasp.

3. *Kip*—The kipping action is a skill involving the flexing of the body and then finishing in the extended position. It is done quickly and is used in all events.
4. *Extension*—This is the opposite of the kip because you extend first and then achieve the move due to flexion. A good example of the use of extension would be a back handspring.

In order for the beginning gymnast to master some elementary combinations, a learning series (Practice/Organizational Suggestions) is given at the end of each apparatus and tumbling section.

Men's Gymnastics

Although both women and men vault and work floor exercises, the way they perform in these areas is completely different. We will describe first the six men's gymnastics events and then the four women's events.

Pommel Horse

The pommel horse is 64 inches long and 14 inches wide. It stands 45½ inches tall, with two handles extending up from the leather body. The height of the handles is 4¾ inches, which makes the overall height 50 inches. The pommel horse is divided into three sections: The left end, as you face it, is called the neck; the middle is called the saddle; and the right end is called the croup. All three areas must be worked in a routine, without hesitations or stops, or deductions are made by the judges. The pommel horse requires a great deal of upper body strength and balance and is considered by many to be the most difficult men's event. This is one event in gymnastics in which a spotter seems only to be in the way. Because of the scissor and leg circles, there is a greater chance of the spotter being injured than the performer.

Figure 13-3 Front support and swing.

➤ Learning Hints

Feint. A feint is used on the pommel horse primarily to initiate movement. A feint helps the gymnast gain momentum to perform a stunt. The gymnast would swing one or both legs in the direction opposite to which the stunt is performed. Many think of a feint as an extra swing or pumping action. In competition, a feint is considered unnecessary movement, and its use would result in points being deducted.

Front Support and Swing (Figure 13-3). Jump to a front support. Hands are in an over grasp on the pommels. The arms are straight, and the body is straight, with the legs spread wide apart. The swing is initiated from the hips, going side to side. The entire body moves side to side so the swing encompasses the shoulder joint as well as the hips. The gymnast tries to attain as much height as possible on the swing. There is a slight shift of weight as the body swings from pommel to pommel.

Single Leg Circle Forward (Figure 13-4). This can most easily be learned by placing the right hand on the pommel and the left hand on the neck of the horse. Jump to a straight arm support and immediately begin the move. Bring the right leg to the left between the horse and the left leg, twisting the hips slightly and leaning on the right arm. Bring the right leg over the neck of the horse and under the left hand, which regrasps the pommel (neck of the horse)

Figure 13-4 Single leg circle forward.

after the left leg passes under it. Continue the right leg circling by passing under the right hand and over the croup. This is considered one circle. It should be rhythmic and repeated, making continuous clockwise circles. There is a certain timing to this movement that helps with the momentum and support, making it much like a pendulum swinging.

Simple Travel-Through. Though this is called a simple travel, it is anything but simple and requires a lot of practice to master. Begin by placing the left hand on the neck and the right hand on the left pommel. Jump to a front support. Swing the left leg forward, cutting away the left hand and replacing it. Swing the right leg forward; now both legs are forward. The right hand is between the legs, with the left hand balancing on the neck. Swing the left leg back and shift the weight to the right hand and the pommel. The left hand regrasps the left pommel. Both hands are now on the pommel. Swing the right leg back and regrasp the right pommel again by shifting weight. This travel is repeated. Swing the left leg forward and under the left hand, which replaces itself on the pommel. Swing the right leg forward, and again the right hand is between the legs. Swing the left leg back and shift the body weight to regrasp the right pommel with the right hand. Swing the right leg back and shift the right hand off the pommel to the croup. At this point, the performer can dismount, having performed a simple travel. When the gymnast is moving from the neck to the pommels, it is considered an uphill travel, and when moving from the pommels to the croup, it is considered downhill.

➤ Practice/Organizational Suggestions

Jump to front support, single leg circle forward, simple travel, dismount.

Vaulting

The pommel horse may be used in this event. Remove the pommels and tape the holes to prevent any injury to the fingers. The horse is placed with the croup nearest the vaulter at a height of 53 inches. The male gymnast's hands must land only in the middle area of the horse to prevent a .5 deduction in competition.

When working with a beginning gymnast, it is advisable to lower and turn the horse sideways. Women gymnasts vault with the horse in this position, and it is much less intimidating to a beginner. The horse can be lowered to a height comparable with the gymnast's skill level.

The other piece of equipment used in vaulting is the spring board or reuther board. It is placed in front of the horse, and the gymnast hits the board with both feet to initiate the takeoff over the horse. The pre-flight is the time between hitting the board and the gymnast touching the horse. The vault is performed and then the after-flight begins until landing. All three phases of the vault are judged. The run to the board is not judged. Judging begins with the board takeoff. The vaults are presented and illustrated in Figures 13-5 and 13-6 with the horse turned sideways to decrease difficulty for beginners.

➤ Learning Hints

Flank Vault (Figure 13-5). The flank vault is so named because the side (flank) of the body passes over the horse. The flank vault is performed by swinging upward from the board and swinging the body and legs to the right over the horse. The right hand is cut away and the left hand leaves the horse just before landing. The gymnast lands facing forward. To spot this vault, the spotter is on the side opposite the passing legs. The spotter helps support and keep the arm of the vaulter stationary by grasping above the elbow. The spotter moves with the gymnast as he passes over the horse.

Front Vault. As with the flank vault, the front vault is so named because the front of the body passes over the horse. On takeoff, the body makes a quarter turn to the left. The legs swing up to the right so that the front of the body passes over the horse. The right arm

Figure 13-5 Flank vault.

Figure 13-6 Rear vault.

supports most of the weight, and the left arm pulls out to counteract the legs. The right arm leaves the horse just before landing. The gymnast lands with his left side to the horse. The spotter again stands away from the legs and helps support the shoulders.

Rear Vault (Figure 13-6).   The rear of the body passes over the horse. On takeoff from the board, the hands hit the horse, and the body quarter turns to the right as the legs are swinging sideward. The rear of the body is passing over the horse, and the legs are parallel to the floor. The right hand leaves the horse on the quarter turn, and the left hand releases as the body passes over. The right hand reaches for the horse on the landing for stability. The gymnast lands with the right side toward the horse. The spotter grasps the arm closest to him (away from the legs), moves with the gymnast, and releases the arm when the vault is being completed.

The Thief Vault.   The thief vault is different from most vaults because it doesn't use a two-foot takeoff. The takeoff is from one foot; as the other foot swings upward, the takeoff foot joins it. Both legs pass over the horse, followed by the rear. The hands touch the horse as the body passes over in a sitting position. The hands give a downward and backward push. Two spotters are used for the thief vault: One spotter stands on the vaulter's side to support the gymnast's shoulder and arm in case it is needed; the other spotter stands on the board side of the vault to help prevent a fall backward in case the vaulter does not clear the horse.

Rings

In competition the rings are called still rings. The performer not only controls his body movement but also that of the rings. It is important in a learning situation to have plenty of mats below the ring station. Women lack the upper body strength to compete on the rings; however, the stunts listed here can be taught to both men and women because they do not rely on a great deal of upper body strength.

Figure 13-7 Inverted hang.

➤ Learning Hints

Inverted Hang (Figure 13-7).   Jump to grasp the rings and at the same time flex the arms and tuck the knees to the chest. Lean back with the upper body and stay in a squat position until the head is down, arms are straight, and the inverted position is attained. Extend the legs, using the ropes to stabilize the body if needed, then bring the legs together. The inverted hang can be done in a squat position or a straight position. To return to a starting position, simply flex at the hips and slowly bring the upper body forward. The spotting is either one or two spotters on each side of the performer. Grasp the performer's wrist, and with the other hand assist by lifting up and back if help is needed. Once the inverted hang has been attained, remain near the performer to steady him by placing a hand in front and back.

Nest Hang (Figure 13-8).   Jump to hang and bring the feet up to the rings in a tuck position. Hook the feet through the rings and then push the body through the arms by arching the back. Raise the head. Return by reversing the process. Spotting is done by grasping the performer's wrist and supporting his midsection in case the feet slip out of the rings.

Forward Single Leg Cut and Catch.   Attain an inverted squat hang and straighten legs. The position is an inverted pike with the legs parallel with the floor. Both legs are going to move quickly forward, with the left leg straddling out to cut away the left hand from

Figure 13-8 Nest hang.

the ring. Regrasp the ring with the left hand as the legs move down to a hang. The performer keeps the arms slightly flexed and bears the weight on the right arm before releasing the left. Keep the ring as still as possible on the release and look for the ring on the re-grasp. The spotter supports the performer's upper back and hips after he has reached the pike position. The spotter can help by lifting, once the "cut" has been made, so the performer can regrasp the ring.

Backward Double Leg Cut Dismount. The rings must be high enough so that the performer cannot reach the floor in a hang. Momentum is the key to successfully completing this dismount. In a hanging position, arch and flex the body to gain some momentum and then raise the legs up and back over the head, bending at the hips. As the feet approach the arms, straddle the legs and look back with the head. Release the rings and raise the chest as the momentum carries the performer to a stand. For the beginner, two spotters are advisable. The spotter on the left side uses his right hand under the performer's shoulder and the left hand on his back. It is important to support the shoulder, especially if momentum is lost or the performer releases the rings too soon.

➤ Practice/Organizational Suggestions

Swing to an inverted hang, nest hang, forward single leg cut and catch, backward double leg cut dismount.

High Bar (Horizontal Bar)

The high bar is perhaps the most exciting piece of equipment to watch the male gymnast work. It has constant motion and moves quickly so that the spectator is often left wondering, upon completion of a routine, what the gymnast actually did! The steel bar is 7'10½" wide and is 8'4⅜" off the floor. A routine flows with no stops or pauses. The stunts performed on the high bar are much like the stunts performed on the women's uneven bars. If there is no high bar available, the top bar of the unevens can be used to learn beginning moves. Spotting of the performer on the high bar is virtually impossible without a spotting belt attached to the ceiling with pulleys. Spotting without a belt means that the spotter is in a position to catch the performer when difficulty arises.

Chalk (magnesium carbonate) is used when working the high bar to prevent the performer from slipping when hands are sweaty.

➤ Learning Hints

The following movements can be spotted by lowering the bar. These are beginning moves with which the student can attain success.

Backward Hip Circle (Figure 13-9). The performer jumps to a straight arm support. The hands are in an over grasp. Cast the legs back by flexing at the hips, lifting the heels backward (legs straight and toes pointed) toward the ceiling. As the body comes back to the bar, the head and upper body drop back, and the momentum helps the hips circle around the bar. Keep the hips next to the bar. The spotter or spotters are next to the performer. If standing on the performer's right side, the spotter helps secure the performer's arm with his left hand and uses his right hand to help guide and lift the performer's hips as he circles the bar.

Knee Circle. To prepare for a knee circle, the performer jumps to a front support and then lifts the right leg over the bar and between the hands. The performer sits on the right leg as he changes his hands or an under grasp. The performer circles the bar with the knee by moving in a forward motion. Before this can happen, he raises the hips so the bar is placed in the bend of the knee. Once in position, the performer lifts his head and chest to begin the forward motion. He circles and returns to the sitting position on the right thigh. The arms cannot collapse in the circling motion, and the head and chest remain up. The spotting for this act requires almost as much technique as the stunt itself. The spotter or spotters stand beside the performer. If the spotter is on the performer's right side, he uses his right hand

Figure 13-9 Backward hip circle.

to reach under and around the bar to grasp the performer's wrist. The grasp used is inverted, and the knuckles will be facing the spotter. The left hand helps support and lift the performer on the back as he circles the bar. The performer may want to chalk the back of the knee to prevent chafing.

Kip (Figure 13-10). There are many variations of a kip (glide kip, drop kip, reverse kip, etc.). The kip can be used as a mount, a stunt within a routine, or a connecting move between stunts. A kip requires strength, but the key is timing. It usually takes a lot of practice to master. Stand facing the bar with hands in an over grasp. Jump, flexing the hips, and bring the ankles forward. As the body swings slightly forward, prepare to whip the legs out and downward. The reaction to the whip with the legs is an upward

motion; bear down with the arms and end in a front support. The spotter is on the performer's side and has a sense of timing to assist with the kip. The spotter on the right side of the performer places his left hand on the performer's back and the right hand on his calves. Move with the performer. Help lift the legs, and after whip, lift lower back.

Squat Dismount from Support. From a straight arm support, cast the legs back and tuck the knees to the chest. At the same time, move the feet between the arms and over the bar. Land facing forward in a standing position. Once the momentum is established from the cast, the body continues forward with the head up. The spotters are on either side of the performer in front of the bar he is going to squat over. With the spotter's closest hand, grasp the performer's wrist, and

Figure 13-10 Kip.

with the other hand grasp his upper arm. Spotters need to move with the performer on the dismount.

➤ **Practice/Organizational Suggestions**

Jump to front support, backward hip circle, squat dismount from support.

Parallel Bars

Only men compete on the parallel bars, but there is no reason why women cannot successfully learn to work the parallel bars, too. The parallel bars are wooden bars measuring 11'6" in length, and they are adjustable in height from 5'7" to 5'9" and in width from 18" to 20". Many beginners lower the bars and adjust the width according to the length of their forearm and hand.

➤ **Learning Hints**

Forward Hand Walk. Jump to a straight arm support between the bars and move one hand at a time down the bars in a walking motion. Keep the head up and do not let the shoulders depress or sag. Take short hand steps and transfer the weight to the opposite arm on each movement. The spotter grasps the performer's thigh under the bar to support or lift if the performer becomes fatigued.

Hip Roll. Sit in a straddle seat in the middle of the bars and place both hands in an over grasp on the right bar. The right hand is the hand closest to the right leg. Lower the upper body and bring the head and shoulders under the right bar. At the same time lift the right leg, maintaining the straddle position, and roll across the hips on the left bar. Still in the straddle position, the performer rolls across the right thigh as the left leg crosses over to the right bar. The upper body lifts as the performer ends in a straddle seat, facing the opposite direction from which he started. The spotting for this is done from underneath the bars at the shoulders to support the performer, and another spotter may be helpful in guiding the leg placement.

Corkscrew Mount (Figure 13-11). This is a fun mount to teach beginners. The name matches the movement of the body, and the success rate is great. Stand facing the middle of one side of the bars. Grasp the near bar with the right hand in an under grasp and the left hand in an over grasp. Jump, lifting the legs toward the far bar, landing on the back of the left thigh. Begin turning over the bar with the right leg extended and moving downward toward the bar where the hands are grasped. As the legs are twisting, the chest and head stay near and under the grasped bar. When the legs are straddling the bars, the upper body rotates, and the left hand releases to grasp the far bar. Push up with both hands to finish in a strad-

Cross right over

Both legs straight

Elbow up

Land high on left thigh

Chest close to bar

Figure 13-11 Corkscrew mount.

dle seat. Spotting, like the hip roll, is done from under the bar, but this time, the spotter supports the performer's hips. Again, it may be helpful as a teaching aid to have another spotter helping to guide the performer's legs.

Flank Dismount. Jump to a straight arm support. The body is between the bars. Begin swinging. When the legs are forward, lean on the left arm and release the right hand. Pass the body over the bar, making a quarter turn, and pushing off with the left hand to land with the back toward the bar. The spotter stands to the outside and slightly behind the performer. Grasp the performer's left arm at the wrist with the spotter's left hand and above the elbow with the right. As the performer dismounts, the spotter would help guide him over the bar.

➤ **Practice/Organizational Suggestions**

Corkscrew mount, hip roll, flank dismount.

Floor Exercise

The floor exercise mat is 42' by 42' and at least 1 inch thick. The floor exercise event is the longest of the men's events, lasting 1 minute and 30 seconds. Along with tumbling, the performer displays strength, agility, and balance. The routine moves smoothly and covers all the corners and area of the mat. (Tumbling dominates the floor exercise routine and will be covered later in this chapter.)

Women's Gymnastics

Women's competitive gymnastics consists of four events. Two of the events are timed (balance beam and floor exercise) and must be completed in the allotted time to avoid score deduction. Both balance beam and floor exercise require dance and tumbling. The uneven bars are similar to the men's horizontal bar. The use of two bars reduces the need for upper body strength on the part of the woman gymnast. The uneven bars require circling moves, changes of direction, and changes in hand grips. Lastly, the vault

Figure 13-12 Back hip pullover.

is performed with the vault positioned sideways. The run and takeoff are like the men's vault. The women's performance in gymnastics centers around dance and the ability of the gymnast to perform difficult moves with ease. Unlike the men's gymnastic performance, a woman gymnast does not display strength throughout her routines.

Uneven Parallel Bars

This event is done with two parallel bars at different heights. The top bar is 7'6½" above the floor, and the lower bar is 4'11" high. The width between the bars can be adjusted out to 2'9⅞". Routines are constructed to flow smoothly without stops or pauses.

➤ Learning Hints

Back Hip Pullover (Figure 13-12). Stand between the bars with the hands shoulder-width apart in an over grasp. Keeping the shoulders and chest close to the bar, kick one leg forward, up and back over the bar. As the first leg travels up, the second leg joins it, and the head drops back. The performer pulls the hips back over the bar and ends in a straight arm support. The spotter stands on the side of the bar opposite to the performer. The spotter on the performer's right places her left hand on the performer's lower back and helps lift the legs with the right hand.

Mill Circle (Figure 13-13). The mill circle is very much like the knee circle explained on the horizontal bar. The difference is that the knee is not bent during the stunt. The performer is astride the bar with both legs straight. The bar is resting on the front of the back thigh. The hands are in an under grasp. Keeping

the bar in place on the back thigh, the performer lifts her hips up and thrusts the chest forward with the head up. Remaining in this position, circle the bar and finish in the starting position. The spotter stands on the same side of the bar as the back leg of the performer. If the spotter is on the performer's left, she uses her left hand to reach under the bar and grasp

Figure 13-13 Mill circle.

the performer's wrist in a reverse grip. As the performer circles the bar, the spotter helps lift the hips with the right hand.

Pop Up. This is an elementary transition from the low bar to the high bar. As the performer jumps to a long hang on the high bar, hands are in an over grasp. Place the left foot on the low bar, with the knee bent. The right leg is straight, toe pointed on top of the low bar. The move is very much like a back hip pullover. As the left foot pushes off the lower bar, the head drops back and the arms pull the hips to the high bar. The right leg joins the left as they circle the high bar ending in a straight arm support on that high bar. The performer keeps the hips close to the high bar and attempts to lift them up and over the bar. The spotter stands on either side of the performer. The spotter will help lift the hips up and back over the bar. On completion, grasp the calves of the performer to help steady the straight arm support.

Straddle Sole Circle Underswing Dismount (Figure 13-14). To learn this dismount the performer stands between the bars facing out. Grasp the bar in an over grip and jump up, placing the soles of the feet on the bar outside of the hands. The arms and legs remain straight as the body swings downward. The arms are pulling against the bar to keep the feet on as the performer circles under the bar. As the height of the swing is reached, the feet release from the bar and extend outward to land. The body follows in an arched position. The spotting for this move is done at the outside of the low bar. Because of the straddle position, the spotter reaches in for the upper body after the feet have passed. The spotter helps lift the upper body on the landing and follows the completed move.

➤ Practice/Organizational Suggestions

Back hip pullover, mill circle, straddle sole circle underswing dismount.

Balance Beam

The balance beam is 3⅞" wide, 16'4" long, and 3'11¼" above the ground. The gymnast is required to work from end to end on the beam, using tumbling, dance, and poses. The event is timed and the routine must be completed in 1 minute and 30 seconds to avoid penalty. A deduction is also made for each fall, and the gymnast is allowed only 10 seconds to remount the beam after a fall.

➤ Learning Hints

Lower the beam when teaching beginning students, or use lines on the floor.

Squat Mount. Place the spring board at a right angle to the beam. Stand on the board with the hands shoulder-width apart on the beam. Jump from the board, pressing down on the beam. At the same time, raise the hips and tuck the knees to the chest, placing the feet on the beam. The spotter stands on the opposite

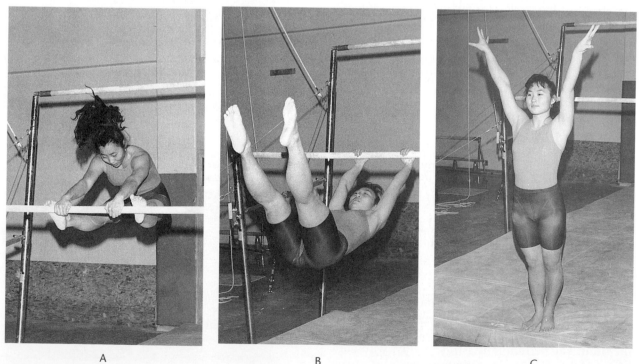

A   B   C

Figure 13-14 Straddle sole circle underswing dismount.

side of the beam and grasps the performer's upper arms to prevent her from falling forward.

Back Shoulder Roll (Figure 13-15). Lie back on the beam and drop the head to one side. Bring the legs back over the head to the beam, bending one knee to place on the beam. The hands move to the top of the beam and both hands push up. End in a knee scale.

A

B

C

Figure 13-15 Back shoulder roll.

The spotter is on the opposite side of the performer's head. Facing the direction of the roll, the spotter grasps the performer's hips and guides them until the knee scale is attained.

Forward Roll. Standing on the beam, bend at the waist and extend the arms to grasp the beam. Lower the upper body to the beam by bending the arms. Tuck the head by pressing the chin to the chest. Raise the hips, roll to the back of the neck, and continue forward. Allow one leg to bend, and place the foot on the beam as the other leg extends forward. Complete the roll by coming to a stand. The spotter stands to one side of the beam and guides the performer's hips. Follow the performer until she is balanced.

Leap. The leap is the transfer of weight from one foot to the other with neither foot touching the beam during the transfer. A leap is actually an isolated running step. The beginner may be hesitant to leave the beam for much height. Arms are out to the side at shoulder level for balance. Try to spot the end of the beam with the eyes and not look directly down. Spotters are on either side of the beam with the near arm extended toward the performer. The performer can then use the spotter's arms for balance when needed.

Chassé (Figure 13-16). The right leg is in front of the left and remains in front throughout. Step forward with the right leg and bring the left leg from behind to take its place. The weight shifts from the right to the left as the right leg is replaced with the left. Continue again, stepping forward with the right, and repeat. Spotter again walks along the side of the beam as the performer travels down the beam.

Arabesque (Figure 13-17). This is generally considered a momentary balance or pose. Step forward on one leg and lift the other leg to the rear as high as possible. Chest and head are raised by arching the back. Extend the arms to the side. The arms may be changed to different positions. Be creative. Use spotters on either side of the beam if needed.

Cartwheel Dismount. In order to do a cartwheel dismount, the performer should first be able to do a good cartwheel on the floor. Stand approximately one step back from the end of the beam. Execute a cartwheel, placing the hands at the end of the beam. Legs travel overhead and land together, much like a round-off (see "Tumbling"). The performer ends facing the beam for better balance. Keep arms straight, and push off to land. The spotter may want to stand on a bench or a stable chair to approximate the performer's height. Stand on the side of the beam at the performer's back when the cartwheel is performed. If the performer is placing her right hand down first, the spotter will cross her arms with the right arm on top

Figure 13-16 Chassé.

Figure 13-17 Arabasque.

and grasp the performer's waist. The spotter moves with the performer, and as the cartwheel is done, the spotter's arms uncross and end with the left over right. Reverse when spotting is on the other side.

➤ **Practice/Organizational Suggestions**

Squat mount, leap, forward roll, cartwheel dismount.

Vaulting

When teaching a beginner to vault, you should begin with the run and hurdle step. An instructor may want to first use the takeoff board without the horse. The student can run, use the two-foot takeoff, and land on a layer of mats. The hurdle step precedes the two-foot takeoff. The hurdle is a step onto one foot in front of the board and a two-foot jump onto the board. The takeoff from the board is explosive. With practice, the run and takeoff become second nature, and the gymnast concentrates on the actual vault.

In women's vaulting, the horse is sideways and 47 inches high. Women can perform two separate vaults, but only the better vault is scored.

➤ **Learning Hints**

Squat Vault (Figure 13-18). The lead up to a squat vault could be a squat mount onto the horse. After leaving the spring board, tuck the knees to the chest and place the hands on the horse. Land in a squat position on top of the horse. As soon as the student masters the squat mount, she can try the vault. The performer will again draw the knees to the chest, but as the hands land on the horse, she pushes downward and keeps the head and chest up. Pass over the horse in the squat position to land facing forward. The spotter is on the far side of the horse, ready to grasp the performer above the elbows if she should need assistance.

The Straddle Vault. The lead up to the vault can be the straddle mount. After hitting the spring board, the performer straddles (spreads the legs) and lands

Figure 13-18 Squat vault.

Figure 13-19 Stoop vault.

in a straddle position on top of the horse. The head is up, with the feet and hands in contact with the horse. The spotter is in front of the performer on the opposite side of the horse, grasping the upper arms, to prevent her from falling forward. The vault is done the same way as the mount, only the hands push downward and the performer clears the horse. The head remains up, and the hips travel in a forward motion over the horse. The spotter is in front of the performer, ready to grasp the upper arms if the performer should catch a toe while passing over the horse. If the performer clears the horse, the spotter moves quickly out of the way.

Stoop Vault (Figure 13-19). This vault is very much like the squat vault except the legs are kept straight. The hips are raised high enough to clear the feet between the hands. The head is up, and again the performer is pushing down against the horse with the hands. As the hips travel forward, the chest lifts upward to prepare for the landing. The spotter stays to the side to assist by grasping the performer's upper arm.

Handspring (Figure 13-20). The handspring is a more difficult vault to master than the previous vaults because the performer needs a great deal of momentum to accomplish it properly. The performer must have a good approach and takeoff. The hips bend slightly on the takeoff as the hips and legs pass overhead. The arms remain straight, and the head is aligned between the arms. There is a push on the horse that actually originates from the shoulders to

the hands. The contact with the horse is short and explosive. The after-flight is approximately the same distance as the pre-flight. The spotter stands on the far side of the horse. Beginners should have spotters on each side. Grasp the performer's shoulder and upper arm to prevent the arms from folding. Sometimes a spotter can also stand between the spring board and horse, lifting the vaulter's hips to attain the needed height.

Floor Exercise

Floor exercise for women is similar to the men's event in that the same equipment is used and the routine lasts no more than 1½ minutes. However, the requirements for the women's floor exercise are considerably different. The women's routine is choreographed to music, which must be instrumental only. Women must show dance skills, tumbling, and acrobatic skills, and they must work on the floor level sometime in the routine. The difficulties required in the composition of the routine may be derived from a gymnast's dance skills as well as from her tumbling. The beginning tumbling skills in floor exercise will be covered in the tumbling section.

Tumbling

Tumbling does not require the use of apparatus. Mats of different thicknesses are used as the tumbling stunts become more difficult or in the learning process of a certain skill. School programs from elementary

Figure 13-20 Handspring.

through high school would do well to include a tumbling unit in their curriculum. Most tumbling stunts require some courage and determination to accomplish; thus a student can gain self-confidence by mastering these new skills. The physical attributes attained through tumbling are increased balance, agility, coordination, and flexibility. Tumbling units can incorporate partner stunts, pyramids, and tumbling routines for variation.

The squad method of teaching a tumbling unit has been highly successful. Six to eight students on each mat is the preferred number. The mats are placed in a three-sided square or horseshoe formation, with the demonstration mat at the open side. The instructor can demonstrate or have a student demonstrate and then let the class practice the skill. Always explain and show spotting techniques.

There are many ways of evaluating a tumbling unit. The instructor can compose a short routine that all students must perform, or the students can compose their own routines, which must include certain tumbling stunts. The instructor can evaluate certain predetermined tumbling skills at the end of the unit and may find it beneficial to have a testing day every three or four days in the tumbling unit. On this day, the students may choose to be evaluated on skills they have mastered. The more skills they master by the end of the unit, the better the evaluation. The instructor can be creative in her methods of teaching stunts and tumbling and in evaluations. The important thing to remember is that each student should feel successful. The stunts introduced must be challenging and yet not be too difficult, so the majority of students can master them by the end of the unit. A

good instructor will keep the entire class involved and be generous with praise.

➤ Learning Hints

Forward Roll (Figure 13-21). The forward roll is one of the basic skills in tumbling. The student squats and places the hands, shoulder-width apart, on the mat. Next, tuck the chin to the chest, bend the arms and raise the hips. The back of the head touches the mat and continues to roll onto the feet to a stand. The hands *do not* touch the mat again. Some students find it helpful to grasp the shins and tuck more tightly on the roll. The spotter assists by placing one hand on the head (not the neck) and the other on the upper legs. The hand on the head keeps the chin tucked, and the hand on the upper legs assists with the roll.

Backward Roll. The backward roll is another basic skill and is sometimes more difficult to master than the forward roll. Again, the student begins in a squat position. The hands begin on the mat, but as the backward roll starts, they move upward to the shoulders, fingers pointing back and palms up. It is essential that the chin be tucked. The hands reach back and are placed on the mat beside the head, under the shoulders. As the hips come over the head, the hands push off the floor. Remain tucked, never allowing the knees to touch the mat, and land on the feet. The spotter may have a more difficult time helping the student complete the roll. If possible, try to lift the hips as the roll begins. Many students will roll backward crooked. This usually indicates they are not pushing evenly with both hands at the same time.

Figure 13-21 Forward roll.

Tripod Balance (Figure 13-22). Place the hands, shoulder-width apart, on the mat. The head is placed on the mat to make the third point of a triangle with equal sides. The balance is done on the roof of the forehead, not the crown of the head. Raise the hips and place the knees, one at a time, on the elbows. Balance. The spotter is behind the student to steady her at the hips.

Headstand. The headstand can be done out of the tripod balance. Straighten both legs slowly, with toes pointed. Once the balance is achieved, return to the tripod slowly. The spotter stands behind the student,

Figure 13-22 Tripod balance.

making sure that the balance is maintained by steadying the legs. This stunt is readily adaptable to a uniform count, so that everyone can try it at once; e.g.:

1. Hands down
2. Head down
3. Legs up (tripod forward)
4. Headstand
5. Legs down
6. Head up

Make sure that students are far enough apart that a loss of balance won't cause an injury.

Prone Headstand. Begin in a prone position, lying flat on the mat with the hands placed under the shoulders, fingers pointing forward. Pressing down with the hands, lift and bend at the hips. Keep the legs straight and raise the hips as if a string attached to the ceiling is pulling them up. Drag the feet along the mat. At the same time, place the forehead on the mat. Once the hips are overhead, raise the legs into a headstand. Once balance has been achieved, reverse the procedure, or roll out of the headstand by tucking the chin to the chest and rolling. The spotter stands behind the student and helps her maintain her balance. If the student has trouble lifting the legs off the floor, pull the hips slightly toward the spotter. Continue to spot at the hips when the student returns to the starting position.

Kip (Neck Spring) (Figure 13-23). Lying on the back, flex at the hips and bring the legs straight back so the knees are over the face. The hands are beside the head under the shoulders (same position as a backward roll). The hips begin to move slightly forward toward the floor and just at the off-balance moment, the legs snap upward and forward. Simultaneously, the hands push against the floor, and the feet come under the student to land on the mat. The hips must be kept high, and the legs remain straight on the whip. The spotter must have a feel for the timing of this stunt in order to help the student effectively. Kneel on the student's left side and place the left hand on the small of the back and the right hand on the upper arm. Help the student feel the slight movement forward before the whip. Lift at the small of the back on the whip, and continue lifting with the right hand as the student stands.

Cartwheel. The cartwheel (Figure 13-24A) is a basic move in tumbling. The student can visualize the spokes of a wheel when performing this move. The cartwheel is performed to either side (usually there is a preference). Stand with the right side to the mat. The legs are spread slightly more than shoulder-width apart and arms are overhead. Bend sideways, placing the right hand (straight arm) on the mat, and at the same time raise the left leg up, followed by the right, as the left hand goes down onto the mat. The left foot follows, and then the right foot arrives. As the feet are landing, the hands are coming off the mat. As with a wheel, the spokes (hands and feet) move in a straight line and hit the floor in an even count. The cartwheel can be modified by beginning facing the mat and bending forward instead of sidewards. The hand and foot placement are the same. The spotter (Figure 13-24B) always stands to the student's back to avoid being struck by her legs. If the student is going to her left, the spotter grasps the student's hips with the left arm crossed over the right. Move with the student, lifting at the hips as needed. Reverse hand placement if performing to the left.

Round-Off. The round-off should be attempted after the cartwheel has been mastered. The round-off is done from a short run. Perform as if doing a cart-

Figure 13-23 Kip (neck spring).

A

B

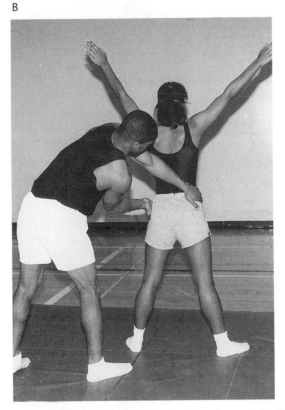

wheel, and as the legs are overhead, snap together and quarter-turn the trunk. The legs snap down together, and the hands push off the floor together (mule kick). The student will end facing the direction from which she started. The hands and feet are not in contact with the floor at the same time. It is difficult to spot a round-off because the student must learn to snap down and push off. If the cartwheel has been sufficiently mastered, there is little chance of injury. Verbal cues will be the greatest aid to the student in learning a round-off.

Back Walkover (Figure 13-25). This stunt requires back flexibility. Stand with hands stretched up overhead, abdomen pulled in, and the torso stretched. One foot is pointed in front of the body, and all the weight is on the back foot. Stretch up and look back, keeping the arms on either side of the head. As the head and shoulders move back and down toward the floor, the support leg may bend slightly, the pointed toe lifts off the floor and travels back. The legs remain split and move over the inverted torso to the floor. As the first foot lands, the hands push off the floor. The spotters may kneel or stand. If there is only one spotter, stand on the side of the forward leg. Place the closest hand on the student's back and the other hand on the back of the lead leg as it goes over.

Front Walkover. The front walkover requires even more flexibility than the back walkover and therefore is considered by many to be more difficult. Essentially, it is the reverse of the back walkover. Stand with the hands overhead and one foot pointed forward. Place the hands on the mat, shoulder-width apart. The weight transfers to the front foot as the back leg raises behind and upward. The leg continues to travel overhead, and the legs are in a split position. The back leg becomes the lead leg, or the leg that will contact the floor first. As the foot lands, the hands push off the floor. There is no period of flight. The leg that is still moving through the air drives downward and forward, with the upper body trailing behind. The spotter supports the student throughout the walkover. It may be easiest to kneel beside the stu-

Figure 13-24 (A) Cartwheel. (B) Spotting the cartwheel.

dent, supporting the shoulders with one hand and the small of the back with the other.

Handstand to Forward Roll. To achieve a handstand, the student places the hands shoulder-width apart on the mat and kicks one leg back and up overhead. The other leg quickly raises upward to join the first. The head remains aligned with the rest of the body, ears next to the arms. A tight, straight body makes maintaining a balance easier. After the balance is maintained, the student shifts the shoulders to the back to create a loss of balance. At the same time, tuck the chin to the chest and slowly bend the arms, lowering the upper body toward the floor. As the back of the head contacts the floor, begin the roll by tucking the legs to the chest. Finish the roll to a

A

B

Figure 13-25 Back walkover.

stand. The spotter stands to the side of the student, moving slightly to the back as she kicks to the handstand. Spotting at the legs helps the student attain balance. When the roll begins, the spotter makes sure the student is leaning off balance in the direction of the roll before the head begins to lower toward the ground. The spotter helps control the momentum of the roll by controlling the legs of the student.

Tinsica. The tinsica is a cross between a cartwheel and a front walkover. It is advisable that the student be able to do both before trying the tinsica. The student

begins with the hands overhead and the preferred foot forward. Place the same hand down on the mat in front of the foot that is forward. As the back leg rises, the other hand is placed ahead of the hand on the mat. The back leg continues overhead, followed by the forward foot, which has pushed off. The legs remain spread apart, and the student walks out of the stunt, one leg landing at a time. The student visualizes doing a front walkover on a balance beam with the hands and feet landing in a cartwheel-type rhythm. The hands and feet arrive at four different times, moving forward in a straight line. The spotter kneels and supports the student's back and upper body at the shoulder, moving and lifting with the student as the tinsica is being attempted.

Valdez (Figure 13-26). Sitting on the floor, extend the left leg and bend the right knee, placing the right foot close to the buttocks. The right hand is placed on the floor behind the buttocks, with the fingertips pointing away from the body. With a vigorous push off the right foot, swing the left arm back from the shoulder (backward and upward) and place the left hand on the floor. The legs remain split as they proceed overhead, finishing as if doing a back walkover. The right hand, which is on the floor, executes a half-turn during the inverted period. This usually happens naturally as the valdez is being performed. The spotter kneels beside the student on the side of the extended leg. Place the hand nearest the student's back on the lower back and the other hand on the extended leg's upper thigh. As the push-up and back is made by the student, the spotter lifts and guides the leg back and over.

Back Handspring (Figure 13-27). This tumbling stunt should be taught with two good spotters. The student stands with the feet shoulder-width apart and the arms extended in front, shoulder level. Lower backward as if to sit in a chair. When balance is lost, push against the floor with the legs and vigorously swing the arms up and back, stopping beside the head. The head looks back when the arms begin the move upward; however, it is best not to overemphasize this aspect in order to prevent the student from traveling straight back. The motion is explosive, and the body is extended as the hips thrust upward. The back arches slightly as the hands reach for the mat. When the hands hit the mat, they push off and the legs snap down after having passed through the overhead inverted position. The spotters stand on either side of the student. The spotter on the student's right places her left hand on the student's lower back and the right hand on the back of the upper thigh. The spotter on the student's left reverses the hand placement. The spotters are careful not to lift the student through the handspring but rather to provide support.

Figure 13-26 Valdez.

Figure 13-27 Back handspring.

In order to master the back handspring, the student must "feel" the sense of timing that is needed. The spotters can help by providing the security needed in attempting a backward tumbling move.

➤ **Routine Practice/Organizational Suggestions**

Prone headstand, tripod, forward roll, cartwheel, handstand, forward roll, round-off.

Safety Considerations

The nature of tumbling and gymnastics makes safety a major concern of those supervising the program. It is recommended that the participant warm up before beginning any work on the equipment. Warming up helps prevent muscle pulls and strains and makes an individual aware of his body's limitations. Stunts often require assistance (spotting), which aids in safety. The facility, equipment, and area organization can also assist in providing a safe environment.

Spotting

The purpose of spotting is to aid the gymnast to master a stunt safely. This aid can be either manual or via the use of a spotting belt.

A participant should not attempt a new stunt without having performed the progressions and lead-ups and without the confidence and ability required to succeed. The spotter should be used only as assistant or teaching aid, not as a guarantee of protection from injury.

Manual manipulation—the use of hands and/or body to assist the performer—is a valuable learning tool for students of gymnastics. A good spotter can apply just the right amount of support and protection needed. Of course it helps if the spotter has also tried the stunts, but that is not always necessary. A person can be an excellent spotter without ever having trained as a gymnast.

The Spotting Belt. The "hands-on" method of spotting seems preferable to the spotting belt, but for hazardous stunts, the belt is a necessary safeguard. The belt fastens around the performer and has ropes on either side that are attached with hooks that swivel. The spotters stand on either side of the performer and hold the ropes. Depending on the stunt, the spotters move and lift with the ropes to assist or secure the performer. With the belt, it is much harder to attain the feel of the stunt, and the timing may not be as precise, but safety is always assured.

There is also an overhead spotting belt, which is attached to the ceiling through pulleys. Only one individual assists the gymnast. The overhead belt can be helpful on the balance beam, high bar, and floor exercise (if it can travel). The spotter *must* have experience with this type of spotting method because it requires a good sense of timing for both the gymnast and the spotter.

Facility and Equipment

Having the proper facility and equipment is important in providing a safe environment. Most schools use the gymnasium, which has plenty of space and overhead clearance. Equipment cannot be too close to existing walls or other pieces of equipment. For example, there must be ample distance for the run and pre-flight in vaulting, but also for the after-flight of the vault. The high bar and uneven parallel bars need overhead clearance. A low ceiling limits the use of these pieces of equipment.

Gymnastic equipment is expensive and must be kept in good repair, not only for safety reasons, but to prolong its life. Individuals need to be instructed in how to adjust settings and properly move the equipment. It is a good idea to show those involved how each piece is set up and to have safety checks done on each piece of equipment before performing.

Those responsible must continually emphasize that the gymnasium and equipment may not be used without proper supervision. No one should be allowed on the equipment at any time without prior permission from the instructor, coach, or supervisor.

Organization

To provide a safe, controllable learning environment for a gymnastics unit, the instructor can organize the class into squads. By dividing a class into groups and then instructing by either rotation or at each station, the instructor can make sure a safe teaching progression of skills is used.

Teach the lead-ups and fundamentals of each skill before progressing. This not only makes it easier for the participant to learn and master the more difficult skills, but also is a safety factor. One of the main reasons participants are injured in the gymnastic or tumbling units is due to the individual's lack of understanding the skill he is executing. Mind and body cannot work together unless they both have a basic understanding of the skill. This can be accomplished only through lead-up and mastery of elementary progressions. The responsibility ultimately lies with the instructor's knowledge of these progressions. The "Further References" section provides resources for enhancing one's knowledge of proper progressions for any of the stunts and apparatus.

Modifications for Special Populations

Orthopedically Impaired

1. Create obstacle courses using gym mats draped over classroom chairs, balance beams, and similar apparatus, and allow wheelchair users to travel the course out of their wheelchairs. Emphasis should be placed on traveling over, under, around, and through the course. (Consult with the adapted physical educator and/or physical therapist before removing the student from the wheelchair.)

2. Students using canes and/or crutches should be able to participate with upper body activities, e.g., parallel bars.

Cognitively Impaired

1. Contact the Special Olympics for their gymnastics units.
2. Contact AIM, Adventures in Movement for the Handicapped, Inc., in Dayton, Ohio. (See Paciorek and Jones, 1989, listed in "Further References.")

Sensory Impaired

1. Use peer teachers for blind students.
2. Contact the United States Association of Blind Athletes in Muskogee, Oklahoma. (See Paciorek and Jones, 1989.)

Terminology

Amplitude The extent or degree to which a skill or routine is performed.

Balance The body weight is supported by the hands, upper arms, head, or forearms in an inverted position, with the shoulders above the point of support.

Dismount A stunt that moves the performer from the apparatus to a stand on the floor. Also the last moves of a floor exercise routine.

Grasp The placement of hands upon a piece of apparatus with the thumb and fingers wrapped around.

Hang A position on a piece of apparatus in which the weight is borne by the hands, knees, and so on, with the shoulders below the base of support.

Kinesthetic sense The self-awareness of one's body parts.

Layout The entire body is straight.

Mixed grasp A grasp in which one hand is in an over grasp position and one hand is in an under grasp position.

Mount A stunt that moves the performer from a stand on the floor to the apparatus. Also can be the first moves of a floor exercise routine.

Over grasp A grasp in which the palms of the hand are on top of the bar.

Pike The legs are straight, with the body bent at the hips.

Puck A combination of the tuck and pike, bent at the hips with a slight bend in the knees.

Roll A rotation of the body in contact with a surface.

Routine A combination of stunts in a series. A routine begins with a mount, followed by stunts, and ends with a dismount.

Seat A position on a piece of apparatus in which the weight is borne by the thighs or buttocks: *Straddle seat*—legs apart with the weight borne evenly. *Side seat*—legs are together with the weight borne by the buttocks or legs on one side of the apparatus.

Somersault The rotation of the body in the air around the horizontal axis.

Stand A fixed position, with the body weight supported by the feet.

Support A position on a piece of apparatus in which the weight is supported by the hands or arms, with the shoulders above the base of support.

Tuck The knees and hips are bent, with the head in a chin-down position.

Twist The rotation of the body around the vertical axis.

Under grasp A grasp in which the palms of the hand are under the bar.

Further References

Cooper, P. and Trinka, M. *Teaching Basic Gymnastics: A Coeducational Approach.* 3rd ed. Boston, MA: Allyn & Bacon, 1994.

Gula, D. *Dance Choreography for Competitive Gymnastics.* Champaign, IL: Human Kinetics.

Lihs, H. *Teaching Gymnastics.* Boston, MA: American Press, 1990.

Murray, M. *Women's Gymnastics: Coach, Participant, Spectator.* Boston, MA: Allyn & Bacon, Inc., 1979.

Paciorek, M.J. and Jones, J.A. *Sports and Recreation for the Disabled.* Indianapolis, IN: Benchmark, Inc., 1989.

Ryser, O. et al. *A Manual for Tumbling and Apparatus Stunts.* 8th ed. Dubuque, IA: Wm. C. Brown Co., 1990.

Taylor, B. et al. *Olympic Gymnastics for Men and Women.* Englewood Cliffs, NJ: Prentice Hall, 1972.

Turoff, F. *Artistic Gymnastics.* Dubuque, IA: Brown & Benchmark, 1991.

Audio-Visual Materials

Gymnastics Tumbling Video: How to do a Better Back Handspring. www.coachwayne.com.

Men's Gymnastics I, II and III. Champions on Film & Video, 745 State Circle, Box 1941, Ann Arbor, MI 48106. VHS.

The Foundations of Gymnastic Excellence Series (No. 1 Pad Drills; No. 2 Beginning Tumbling; No. 3 Intermediate Tumbling; and No. 4 Advanced Tumbling). Champions on Film & Video, 745 State Circle, Box 1941, Ann Arbor, MI 48106. VHS.

USSR Tour (Men's Tour and Women's Tour). Champions on Film & Video, 745 State Circle, Box 1941, Ann Arbor, MI 48106. VHS.

Women's Gymnastics I and II. Champions on Film & Video, 745 State Circle, Box 1941, Ann Arbor, MI 48106. VHS.

Web Sites

www.usa-gymnastics.org/ USA Gymnastics Online: the official Web site of USA Gymnastics offers live events, athlete biographies, member services, games, and more.

http://gymnastics.about.com/index.htm Offers a starting point for finding information on the Internet related to gymnastics. Gymnasts, coaches, and fans will find useful material to improve involvement in and understanding of the sport.

CHAPTER 14

Handball and Racquetball

This chapter will enable you to

- Select equipment necessary to play handball and racquetball
- Identify and put into practice the rules governing handball and racquetball
- Identify and develop the basic skills, namely the forehand stroke, the backhand stroke, the serve, and the back wall shot
- Employ the basic strategy necessary to play the game
- Identify and put into practice the safety considerations necessary for a successful game of handball or racquetball

Nature and Purpose

Handball and racquetball are related competitive sports in which the hand (or a racquet) is used to serve and return the ball. In their principal variations these games can be played by two opponents (as a singles game), by three opponents (as a cutthroat game), or by two opposing pairs of players (as a doubles game). In this chapter, all that is said about handball also applies to racquetball, unless otherwise stated.

Although the game can be played on one or three walls, the four-wall enclosed court provides perhaps the greatest challenge to skill and the most competition. Primarily the four-wall game will be discussed here, but most of its related description applies to the other variations of the game.

The first side scoring 21 points wins the game (in racquetball, first side to reach 15 points), and the first side winning two games wins the match. The third game, or tie-breaker, is usually played to only 11 points. There is no tie score nor requirement to win by two points, as in some games.

A player may use either the right or left hand for hitting the ball (or holding the racquet), but only one hand at a time may be used to play the ball, and the ball must be struck only once in each instance.

Playing Area and Equipment

Court. The standard four-wall handball court is 40 feet long × 20 feet wide × 20 feet high (Figure 14-1). An outdoor single-wall court is 34 feet long × 20 feet

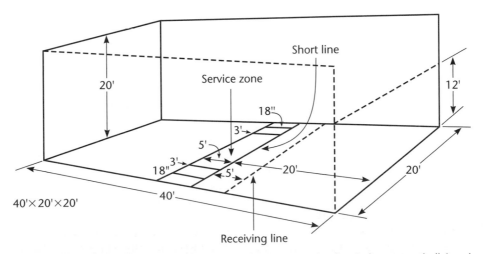

Figure 14-1 Four-wall handball court. The dotted line behind the short service line is for racquetball (receiving cue).

Figure 14-2 One-wall handball court.

wide × 16 feet high (Figure 14-2). The four-wall court is divided into a front court and a back court of equal dimensions by a line called the *short line,* running parallel to the front wall. Five feet in front of the short line is another parallel line called the *service line.* The area between the short line and the service line is called the service zone. Eighteen inches from and parallel with each side wall a line is drawn to form a box, termed the *service box,* where the partner of the serve (in doubles) must stand while the ball is being served. Three feet from and parallel with each side wall is the drive serve line. A player can drive serve to the same side of the court on which he is standing as long as his racquet does not break the plane of that drive serve line.

The racquetball court has a *receiving line,* which is marked as a broken line parallel with the short line. The back edge should be 5 feet from the back edge of the short line.

Ball. The handball is made of rubber, has a diameter of $1\frac{7}{8}$ inches, and weighs 2.3 ounces. In racquetball a seamless rubber ball is used that is $2\frac{1}{4}$ inches in diameter and weighs approximately 1.4 ounces. If one-wall handball is to be played in a physical education class, it would be advisable to use the racquetball ball.

Gloves. The rules of handball require that gloves be worn. This is not only for protection but to keep perspiration off the ball as much as possible. In racquetball, gloves are not required by the rules; however, many players prefer to wear them for a better grip and reduced slippage due to perspiration.

Racquet. The racquetball racquet length must not exceed 21 inches. There should be a thong attached to the bottom of the racquet handle that should slip over the player's wrist to secure the racquet to the wrist. The racquet frame may be of any material judged to be safe; popular types are made of aluminum, steel, fiber glass, graphite, or a combination of materials. The strings of the racquet must be gut, monofilament, nylon, graphite, plastic, or a combination of these.

Whatever the material, it should not leave a mark or deface the ball. The frame comes in three sizes—regular, mid-size, or full size. The price of the racquets ranges from \$20 to \$200. For physical education classes, a less expensive solution is to use wooden paddle racquets that cost much less.

Eyeguards. Eyeguards should be required of all racquetball players. Guards are available in various price ranges and styles.

Basic Rules

A strong point in favor of handball is the simplicity of the rules governing the game. Any person can become familiar with the basic rules in one or two class sessions. In 1958 the Amateur Athletic Union, the U.S. Handball Association, and the YMCA agreed upon a unified set of handball rules that would be applicable throughout the country, and in 1959 these rules were adopted by the Jewish Welfare Board. A summary of the latest rules is given below.

The Game

In the act of serving, the server drops the ball on the floor (between the short and service lines), and on the first rebound the ball is struck in such a manner that it will first hit the front wall and on the rebound land upon the floor back of the short line, either before or after striking one of the side walls, but in front of the back wall. After the ball is legally served, one of the receiving team players returns the ball by striking it either on the fly or on the first bounce so that it will strike the front wall before striking the floor, either directly or after having struck one or both of the side walls, back wall, ceiling, or any combination of these surfaces. The receiving side then returns the ball to the front wall, and play continues until one side is unable to return the ball legally, which will then constitute either a point or a handout or sideout. You must have served to score a point after winning a rally, and you continue to serve until you lose a rally.

Playing Regulations

The choice for the right to serve is decided by the toss of a coin, and the player or side winning the toss has the option to serve or receive at the start of the first game. The second game begins in the reverse order. The team or player with the highest total points in games one and two has the option to serve or receive in the tie-breaker game. The server may stand any place in the service zone. When the server or serving side loses the rally, she or they become the receiver and the receiver the server; they alternate in this fashion in all subsequent services of the game. The serve must be made within the service area; stepping on the line, but not beyond, is permitted. In racquetball, however, you may step over the service line, provided that some part of both feet remains either on or inside the service line. The server may not step over the short line until the ball passes the short line as it rebounds from the front wall.

In serving, the ball must be bounced on the floor and struck on its first rebound from the floor. If the server attempts to hit the ball on this rebound, and fails, the server is out. The server may not bounce the ball more than one time in the service zone in making a service. Violation of this rule retires the server. A server may not serve until the opponent has had a fair opportunity to get placed. The server's partner, in doubles, must stand within the service box with her back to the side wall, both feet on the floor, until the ball passes the short line on its return from the front wall.

If a player's partner is hit by a served fly ball while standing in the service box, it counts as a "dead ball" without penalty, but does not eliminate any short or long fault preceding this service. If one is hit by a served ball on the bounce, it is a short ball. If the served ball should pass behind the partner and strike the floor back of the short line, it is a dead ball.

In doubles, the side starting each game is allowed one handout only. After that, both partners are permitted to serve. Players in doubles must follow the same order of service throughout the game. It is not necessary for players to alternate serves to their opponents.

If a ball is swung at and missed, it may be played again, providing it is hit before bouncing twice on the floor. If a player swings at and completely misses the ball and if in her or her partner's attempt to again play the ball there is an unintentional interference by an opponent, it will be a hinder. If the completely missed ball should on the fly or first bounce strike an opponent, it is a penalty against the opponent—a point, or handout, as the case may be.

Receiving Service

The receiver or receivers must stand at least 5 feet back of the short line while the ball is being served. In racquetball, the receiver stands behind the receiving line while the ball is served. The receiver may play the ball on the first bounce or volley it, provided he does not cross the short line. In racquetball, the receiver may not play the ball until the ball either bounces or breaks the plane of the receiving line. The receiver may not play an illegally served ball.

Illegal Service

Any two of the following fault serves in succession retire the server:

1. Short serve: When the served ball hits the front wall and fails to strike the floor back of the short line on the fly.

2. Three-wall serve: When a served ball hits the front wall and two side walls before striking the floor.

3. Long serve: When a served ball hits the front wall, side wall, and back wall before striking the floor.

4. Ceiling serve: When a served ball hits the front wall, then the ceiling before striking the floor.

5. Foot fault: When the server steps beyond the short line or over the service line in the act of serving.

6. Screen serve: A served ball that first hits the front wall and on the rebound passes so closely to the server, or server's partner in doubles, that it prevents the receiver from having a clear view of the ball.

7. A served ball hitting the ceiling, floor, or side walls before striking a front wall.

8. Crotch ball: A served ball that hits the front and side wall, or front wall and floor, or front wall and ceiling at the same time.

9. A served ball that hits the front wall and rebounds back to hit the server.

Note: In racquetball, #7, #8, and #9 are out serves. The server gets only one attempt.

Suggested Learning Sequence

A. Introduction
   1. Origin and development
   2. Equipment
   3. Safety
B. Rules and Procedures of Play
   1. Playing area
   2. Scoring
   3. Serving
   4. Hinders
C. Skills and Techniques
   1. Forehand shot (sidearm stroke)
   2. Overhead stroke
   3. Overhead ceiling shot
   4. Back wall shot
   5. Backhand shot (Racquetball)
   6. Service
      a. Forehand serve
      b. Drive serve
      c. Lob serve
      d. Z serve
   7. Kill shot
D. Playing Strategy

Skills and Techniques

Forehand or Sidearm Stroke

The forehand stroke is the primary offensive stroke in handball and its mastery is essential in order to achieve a winning game. The most efficient stroke occurs at knee height and is similar to the motion of bending over to skip a flat stone across a body of water or throw a sidearm pitch in baseball.

➤ Learning Hints

1. Position your body as if you were a baseball batter, facing the side wall.
2. Raise the striking hand to the height of your ear in a "cocked" position (Figure 14-3).
3. As the ball is struck, step forward with the front foot, shifting weight from back to front foot (Figure 14-4).
4. Simultaneously with the step, drop your striking shoulder, rotate your body to enable your forearm and hand to move forward in a plane parallel with the floor.
5. Contact the ball at the vertical center of your body.
6. The wrist moves past the elbow in a snapping motion.
7. The ball is struck by the hand at the base of the fingers or in the "sweet" part of the racquet.
8. Follow-through ahead of the front knee.

➤ Practice/Organizational Suggestions

1. Stand facing the side wall in a ready position. Bounce the ball in front of you easily, striking the ball as it rebounds at about knee level. Start a series of practice shots near the short line, then move back 5 feet and hit a series, then back 5 feet more, and so on.

Figure 14-4 Contact point, forehand stroke.

2. Stand facing the side wall (5 feet away) in a ready position. Toss the ball easily against the side wall so that the ball will rebound up from the floor into a striking position for a forehand shot.

Overhead Stroke

The overhead stroke is used to strike the ball at eye level or higher and is very similar to a baseball catcher's throw or a quarterback's pass in football.

➤ Learning Hints

1. Position toes toward the side wall and open shoulders to the front wall.
2. Weight is on the rear foot.
3. Bring cupped hand to the ear, cocked (Figure 14-5).
4. Weight shifts to the front foot as the arm moves up and forward.
5. Ball is struck above and in front of the head.
6. Ball is struck by the fingers with a wrist snap.
7. Follow-through in the direction you wish the ball to take (Figure 14-6).

➤ Practice/Organizational Suggestions

1. Stand in a ready position deep in the court. Bounce the ball vigorously on the floor so that it rebounds up into a striking position for the overhead.
2. From a position deep in the court, throw the ball high against the front wall so that it bounces high to you, returning it with an overhead stroke. Move your body as soon as possible to the striking position.

Figure 14-3 "Cocked" position, forehand.

Figure 14-5 Overhead "cocked" position.

Figure 14-6 Overhead follow-through.

Overhead Ceiling Shot

The overhead ceiling shot, fundamental to racquetball, can be used effectively as either an offensive or defensive strategy. It can be hit with the side arm, forehand, backhand, or underhand strokes; the overhand ceiling shot is described here. The motion is very similar to a tennis serve, the objective being to hit the ceiling first, the front wall, and the floor, and then land deep in the court.

► Learning Hints

1. The body should be facing the side wall, with shoulders open to the front wall.
2. The weight is on the rear foot and will transfer forward as the contact and follow-through are executed.
3. The racquet arm is cocked, elbow up, and racquet dropped behind.
4. The non-hitting arm should be pointed upward, overhead, almost pointing to the ball.
5. As the racquet arm snaps upward, the ball should be contacted at the midline of the body. Too far behind will cause the ball to hit the ceiling directly overhead and too far forward will cause the ball to hit the front wall.
6. Follow through in the direction you wish the ball to take.

► Practice/Organizational Suggestions

1. Throw ball against the ceiling to get the feel of the ball rebounding off the ceiling, then against the front wall and the floor.
2. Toss ball overhead, using the same drill as #1; gradually increase the force at point of contact.
3. Repeat drill #2 and begin placing the ball in different parts of the court, trying to hit the ball consistently to the corner of the back court.

Back Wall Shot

The back wall shot, unique to handball and racquetball, rebounds from the front wall to the floor and then off the back wall before the opponent can get into position to play the ball. If you want to become an above average player, you have to learn to play this shot successfully. The stroke most applicable for the back wall shot is the forehand stroke in which the forearm is swung parallel with the floor. This offers a balanced and powerful method of hitting the ball.

► Learning Hints

1. Face the back wall or the area of the back wall that the ball is in.
2. Move the ball toward the front wall.
3. As the ball rebounds from the wall and begins to descend, pivot on your right foot (for a right hand shot) and turn your body, stepping toward the front wall.
4. Hand and arm locked above the ear.
5. Strike the ball at the vertical midpoint of your body.
6. Let the ball drop as low as possible.
7. Follow through in the direction you want the ball to follow.

➤ Practice/Organizational Suggestions

1. Facing the back wall, toss the ball against the back wall, letting it bounce toward the front wall from the floor. Move with the ball, positioning yourself for a back wall shot.
2. Facing the back wall, toss the ball against the floor to the back wall, but before it bounces on the floor, position yourself for a back wall shot.

Backhand Shot

While the handball player needs to develop both hands equally well in playing both sides of the court, the racquetball player must learn to use the backhand shot. The backhand shot is a mirror image of the forehand shot, but the stroke is much shorter and uses more wrist snap.

➤ Learning Hints

1. Position your body by facing the side wall (opposite side of the forehand stroke).
2. Rotate the racquet in your hand one-eighth of a turn toward the front wall.
3. Cock the racquet back near the ear, with pelvis turned (Figure 14-7).
4. As the ball is struck, step forward with the front foot, shifting the weight from the back leg to the front leg.
5. Simultaneously with the step, bring the racquet forward and contact the ball in line with the front foot, but away from the body using a level swing (Figure 14-8).

6. As the ball is struck, uncock the wrist, snapping the ball toward the front wall using a full follow-through.

➤ Practice/Organizational Suggestions

1. Standing at midcourt, facing the side wall, bounce the ball easily into the backhand hitting area. Hit a series of shots from this area, back up 5 feet, hit another series, back up another 5 feet, and repeat.
2. Stand at midcourt, facing the side wall. Toss the ball easily into the floor to the side wall so it will rebound into the striking area for a backhand shot. Repeat this series from deeper in the court.

Service

The service, the beginning stroke of each point, must be placed successfully in order to continue the point, but the service can also be an offensive weapon if developed to its potential. You may serve from anywhere in the service area, the most advantageous spot being in the center, so that you may direct your serve to either side. You must drop the ball into the serving zone and strike it on the first rebound, causing the ball to strike the front wall and rebound over the short line and land on the floor.

Drive Serve. The drive serve is a low, hard serve placed so that it returns close to the side wall and drops dead in the back corner; or a low, hard serve that strikes the floor and wall just behind the short

Figure 14-7 Backhand "cocked" position.

Figure 14-8 Backhand position on contact.

line. If possible, the drive serve should not rebound off the back wall, thereby giving your opponent a back wall shot. The drive serve should be struck with the same techniques described in the forehand stroke.

Lob Serve. The lob serve is a high ball placed on the front wall, which permits the ball to return in an arc, hugging the side wall, and striking the floor a few feet past the short line in such a manner that the ball rebounds again and drops gently into the corner. The lob serve may be struck with either an underhand or an overhead stroke, the underhand stroke being generally easier to develop in the beginning.

Z Serve. This serve is named from the Z pattern formed by the ball. Standing near the left wall of the service area, serve the ball so that it strikes the extreme right side of the front wall about a racquet's distance from the corner, approximately 4 feet above the floor. It should then strike the right wall, angle past in front of the server, strike the floor, and finally strike the left side wall from which it spins off nearly parallel with the back wall (Figure 14-9). The Z serve should be struck with a low forehand, almost an un-derhand stroke. The Z serve also could be executed from the right side of the service area.

Kill Shots

A "kill" shot is actually of such a low placement that there is little or no possibility of a return. Generally hit with a forehand stroke, a kill occurs not when the player hits "down" on the ball but lets the ball drop to knee height or lower before contacting it with a powerful stroke. Kills can either be front wall kills or corner kills. The front wall kill is stroked straight ahead, hitting so low on the front wall that the ball bounces twice before your opponent can hit it. The corner kill is hit low, but is aimed toward either corner formed by the front and side walls. The ball should strike either the front or side wall, and then it immediately will carom into the side or front wall, producing an angled return that is low and considerably slowed by the ball striking the two wall surfaces.

Playing Strategy

Handball and racquetball are games in which a premium is placed on analyzing the opponent's strengths and weaknesses. Some players are unable to use their left hand with much effectiveness in handball, or they have not developed a strong backhand shot in racquetball. When facing such an opponent, a player should direct a majority of the shots so the opponent is placed at a disadvantage. Players should vary their strategy by employing fast balls alternated with lobs (high, soft shots) in sufficient frequency to get the opponent off balance. The change of pace is particularly effective on the serve, and many good players use it to advantage. In playing doubles, partners should agree on the area that each is to cover and assign the areas so each player may take advantage of any particular strong points she may have.

Players should work for a desirable position on the court. It is usually good strategy to maintain a position in the well—near middle of the court and close enough to enable one to play low balls and corner shots. By skillfully placing shots, a player can keep an opponent in such a position that the opponent will be at a disadvantage in returning crosscourt angle shots. Think ahead and make the first play a forerunner to a second or third play that will result in an error by the opponent, or afford the opportunity to place a passing or kill shot. An opponent who persists in playing close to the front wall can be driven out of position by high lob shots that go overhead but do not strike the back wall with sufficient force to rebound any distance. In the final analysis, a careful scrutiny of your opponent's style of play is the first step in planning a campaign that will be most effective. Identify the opponent's weak points and take advantage of them.

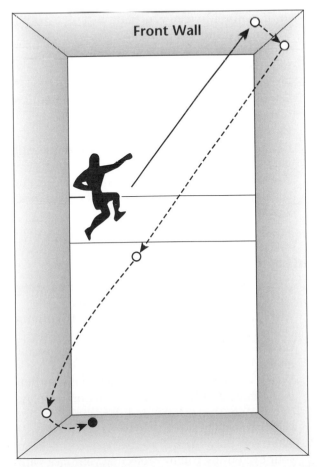

Figure 14-9 The Z serve.

Modifications for Special Populations

Orthopedically Impaired

1. Follow rules from the Wheelchair Racquetball Association, and allow students who use wheelchairs two bounces before a return shot is required.
2. For students with movement difficulties, tether a ball to an assistive device, such as a walker or crutch.
3. Use a larger size ball or one made of different material, e.g., Nerf ball.
4. Use Velcro strapping to secure a racquet to the player's hand during play.
5. Instead of a racquet, use a fat paddle-type board secured to the player's hand.
6. Commercial extension devices are available for students who have amputations and/or grip limitations.

Cognitively Impaired

1. Reduce the court size and responsibility for court coverage.
2. Use one-walled courts or stations in the gymnasium.
3. Refer to #3 in Orthopedically Impaired.

Sensory Impaired

1. Individual considerations need to be made to determine the appropriateness of handball or racquetball for students who are blind or have a visual impairment. Set up a lead-up game, in which the student rolls or throws an audio ball against a wall to practice movement and appropriate positioning. Make audio balls by placing small bells inside whiffleballs.
2. Minimal modifications would be needed for students who are deaf or have a hearing impairment. To enhance instruction, use sign language, videos, and pictures.

Other Considerations

Helpful Hints—Handball

1. Practice "kills" alone. Play the ball around an imaginary opponent and work on the various arm strokes.
2. If your hands swell from playing, soak them in hot water before entering the court. This helps to minimize the swelling.
3. Gloves are worn by a majority of handball players. Your enjoyment of the game will be increased if you wear a pair of gloves that fit your hands well. Always hang gloves up to dry after using them.

4. Do not rush the ball. Wait for it, and you will not only save energy but also play a better game.
5. Control is more desirable than speed.
6. Serve each ball so that it is difficult for the opponent to return it. Try to get several ace serves in each game.
7. A ball hit close to the floor has less bounce and is more difficult to return. The forehand stroke is best for this shot; practice regularly on this play.
8. Watch good players and pattern your play after those who have mastered the game.
9. As a playing courtesy, the opponent is entitled to a fair and unobstructed opportunity to play the ball.
10. If there is any doubt about a play, it is advisable to play the point over.

Helpful Hints—Racquetball

1. "Think" your serve before serving it; you have 10 seconds—use them.
2. Back out of the serving zone as soon as the ball crosses the short line, keeping your eye on the ball the entire rally.
3. Remain in a set position until you see if your shot will be a forehand or a backhand; then turn facing the correct side wall and move to properly align yourself to take your shot.
4. Return to center court. Try to place your shots to keep your opponent out of center court so you can remain there.
5. Place the ball away from your opponent.
6. Try to get the ball to take two bounces before reaching the back wall.
7. Hit with 80 percent power for control.
8. Running around the forehand and backhand will pin you against the side walls.
9. Your shoulder level should equal the ball height.
10. Let any ball at chest level in center court go past you and play it off the back wall.

Safety Considerations

1. Dress properly for the game. Always wear rubber-soled court shoes to ensure firm footing.
2. Always warm up thoroughly before beginning competition.
3. Do not play a dead ball, because your opponent may turn and get struck in the face.
4. Do not deliberately hit an opponent with the ball in the hope that he will call a hinder on the play. You may both get hurt, and ill feeling will develop.
5. After you play the ball to the back court, keep your eye on the ball by protecting your face with your shoulder or looking through your racquet.

6. Allow your opponents room to make the play. Don't crowd or you may be struck.

7. Wear eyeguards at all times.

Terminology

Ace A service that completely eludes the receiver.

Back wall shot A shot made from a rebound off the back wall.

Box See Service box.

Ceiling shot A shot striking the ceiling first, then the front wall.

Crotch shot A ball simultaneously striking two surfaces —two walls or a wall and the floor—is not good.

Cutthroat A three-person game in which the server plays against the other two players, with each player keeping an individual score. Not played in official competition.

Drive shot A power shot against the front wall that rebounds fast, low, and in a straight line.

Fault An illegally served ball, given a second attempt.

Handout The loss of service by the player on a doubles team who is the first server on that team.

Hinder Accidental interference or obstruction of the flight of the ball during play. Point will be played again.

Kill A ball directed to the front wall in such a way that it rebounds so close to the floor that it is impossible to return.

Passing shot A placement driven out of opponent's reach on either side.

Rally Continuous play of the ball by opponents from the serve until the ball is dead.

Receiving line A broken line parallel with the short line on a racquetball court. The back edge of the receiving line is 5 feet from the back edge of the short line.

Run-around shot Ball that strikes one side wall, the rear wall, and other side wall.

Safety zone A 5-foot area bounded by the back edge of the short line and receiving line. The zone is observed only during the serve in racquetball.

Screen A hinder due to an obstruction of vision by opponent.

Server Person (or persons, in doubles) in the "hand-in" position and eligible to serve.

Service box Area within the service zone bounded by the side wall and a parallel line 18 inches away; denotes where server's partner must stand in doubles when the serve is being made.

Service court The area in which the ball must land when returning from the front wall on the serve.

Service line The service line is parallel with and 5 feet in front of the short line. The front line of the service zone.

Service zone The area where the server must stand when serving the ball. Located between the service line and the short line, usually 5 feet wide and extending across the court.

Short line A line on the floor parallel with front wall and equidistant from front and back wall. Serve must carry over this line on its return from the front wall.

Shoot To attempt kill shots.

Side out The loss of serve by a player or team.

Thong Strap attached to the bottom handle of the racquetball racquet, worn around the player's wrist.

Volley To return the ball to the front wall before it bounces on the floor.

Z-ball A defensive shot that strikes three walls before touching the floor. The ball strikes the front wall, a sidewall, and then the opposite side wall.

Further References

Allsen, P. and Witbeck, A. R. *Racquetball.* 6th ed. Dubuque, IA: William C. Brown, 1988.

Amateur Athletic Union. *Official Handball Rules.* Current ed. 231 West 58th Street, New York, NY 10019.

American Amateur Racquetball Association. *Official Rulebook.* 815 N. Weber, Suite 203, Colorado Springs, CO 80903.

Edwards, L. *Racquetball.* 2nd ed., Scottsdale, AZ: Gorsuch Scarisbrick, 1992.

Goldblum, E. et al. *Racquetball Today* (West Activity Series). Toronto: Thompson Publishing, 1999.

Hiser, J. *Racquetball: Winning Edge.* New York: McGraw-Hill, 1998.

Isaacs, L., Lumpkin, A. and Schroer, D. *Racquetball Everyone.* 3rd ed. Winston-Salem, NC: Hunter Textbooks, 1992.

Kittleson, S. *Racquetball: Steps to Success.* Champaign, IL: Human Kinetics, 1992.

Lowy, C. *Handball.* 2nd ed. Boston, MA: American Press, 1991.

Mand, C. L. *Handball Fundamentals.* Columbus, OH: Charles E. Merrill Publishing Co., 1976.

Metzler, M. *Racquetball: Mastering the Basics with the Personalized Sports Instruction System: A Workbook Approach.* Boston: Allyn & Bacon, 2000.

Roberts, T. and Dewitt, J. L. *Racquetball: Learning the Fundamentals.* 5th ed. Dubuque, IA: Kendall/Hunt, 2000.

Sauser, J. and Shay, A. *Beginning Racquetball Drills.* Chicago: Contemporary Books, 1981.

Turner, E. and Clouse, W. *Winning Racquetball: Skills, Drills & Strategies.* Champaign, IL: Human Kinetics, 1995.

Verner, B. *Racquetball: Basic Skills and Drills.* Mountain View, CA: Mayfield Publishing, 1991.

Walker, D. P. et al. *Skills, Drills, and Strategies for Racquetball.* Buena Park, CA: Hathaway Publishing, 1999.

Audio-Visual Materials

Racquetball. Champions on Film & Video, 745 State Circle, Box 1941, Ann Arbor, MI 48106. VHS.

Racquetball with Dave Peck. Champions on Film & Video, 745 State Circle, Box 1941, Ann Arbor, MI 48106. VHS.

Racquetball for All Ages. Champions on Film & Video, 745 State Circle, Box 1941, Ann Arbor, MI 48106. VHS.

Web Sites

www.ushandball.org/ U.S. Handball Association web site; includes complete rules, court dimensions and layout, and tournament information.

www.racquetball.org/ Web site of U.S. Racquetball Association.

www.racqmag.com *Racquetball Magazine* web site; includes past issues with articles covering rules, instruction, techniques, and more.

www.racquettballcentral.com Includes useful information about history, rules, safety, fitness activities, drills, listing of books and videos, links to other sites, and much more.

www.racquetballkevin.com/ Offers links to other sites, long and short versions of the U.S. Racquetball Association rules, and links to various manufacturers.

CHAPTER 15

Orienteering

This chapter will enable you to

- Identify the parts of a liquid-filled compass and how it works
- Utilize fundamental topographic map reading techniques and skills
- Utilize basic compass techniques and skills
- Navigate an orienteering course using a topographic map and a liquid-filled compass
- Identify the basic terminology necessary to understand the activity and sport of orienteering

Nature and Purpose

Orienteering is a cross-country activity in which the participant utilizes topographic map reading skills and follows directions by compass or other means to navigate over unfamiliar terrain. The skills of orienteering can be used to enjoy many outdoor pursuits, such as camping, backpacking, hiking, cross-country skiing, fishing, and hunting, or for competing in the sport of orienteering. Called "the thinking sport," competitive orienteering requires great mental acuity, problem solving, and decision making, along with cardiorespiratory fitness, as the orienteer can cover distances from 2 up to 10 miles in navigating an orienteering course. With today's back-to-nature interests of people of all ages, orienteering skills can be valuable in improving environmental awareness and self-reliance in the out-of-doors.

Participants of all ages and levels of ability can take part in orienteering as a recreational activity or competitive sport. In competitive orienteering, courses with various degrees of difficulty are set up to allow for differences in skill levels; therefore, all participants can achieve success. For many, just completing the course can be a satisfying experience.

Orienteering is an excellent coeducational activity. The techniques and skills can be easily taught to boys and girls and men and women. The environmental setting makes for social acceptance. Since outstanding physical ability is not necessarily the limiting factor, girls often achieve the same success as boys.

Competitive Orienteering

Point-to-point or cross-country orienteering is the most common type of competition. This event requires the competitors to navigate through a pre-scribed series of control points shown on a topographic orienteering map (Figure 15-1), with all competitors visiting the controls in the same order. At the start of the event, competitors receive a clue card (Figure 15-2). The clue card identifies the control markers by letter code and describes a prominent feature in which the control marker has been set. The competitors leave the starting line at equal intervals of time, for example, 1-minute intervals, so that the event becomes for each a contest of route selection and physical skills, with the time to complete the course determining the order of finish. To ensure that each competitor has visited the control markers, a code or punch is located at each control and must be marked on a competitor's scorecard (Figure 15-3). In competitive orienteering, courses of different levels of difficulty are set up to allow for the differences in navigational and physical skill abilities of the contestants. These courses are designated by colors: white, yellow, orange, green, red, and blue, with white and yellow being for the novice, orange and green for the intermediate, and red and blue for the advanced orienteer. Course difficulty is determined by the number of controls, distance between the controls, and the difficulty of the placement of the controls in the field. For example, compare the distance between controls and the total distance of the red course shown in Figure 15-4 with the distances of the white course shown in Figure 15-1. The red course is obviously much more difficult.

Equipment

Maps. The most essential item of equipment for successful orienteering is the map. For children just beginning, a map of a schoolyard, local park, or forest pre-

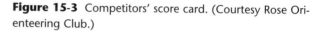

Figure 15-1 Topographic orienteering map showing a white course used by beginning orienteers. (Map courtesy of the St. Louis Orienteering Club and Dewayne Holloway.)

Day 1 White Course 2.7 km.

1	(WA)	The trail junction
2	(WB)	the re-entrant (head)
3	(WC)	The trail junction
4	(WD)	The re-entrant
5	(WP)	The junk
6	(WE)	the fence corner
7	(WF)	The depression
8	(HW)	The earth bank

Follow streamers to finish

Figure 15-2 Competitor's clue card for the white course. (Courtesy of the St. Louis Orienteering Club and Dewayne Holloway.)

ROSE ORIENTEERING CLUB CONTROL CARD

Name

Course   Class

Finish

Start   ○○

Elapsed

11	12	13	14	15	16	17	18	19	20
1	2	3	4	5	6	7	8	9	10

Figure 15-3 Competitors' score card. (Courtesy Rose Orienteering Club.)

serve, drawn to scale, is sufficient; however, for the advanced orienteer, large-scale topographic maps showing selected artificial and natural features are necessary. These topographic maps, usually drawn on a scale of 1:24,000, are produced by the United States Geological Survey (USGS) of the Department of the Interior. Recently, more accurate and highly developed

orienteering maps have been produced. These maps, usually drawn on a scale of 1:15,000 and developed from current aerial photographs, have been accurately field checked and printed in the standard international orienteering colors: blue (water features), black (artificial features), green (vegetation features), brown (contour features), and yellow (clear areas). Although colored maps are more meaningful and precise, black-and-white maps can be successfully used and are less expensive.

Figure 15-4 Topographic orienteering map showing a red course used by advanced orienteers. (Map courtesy of the St. Louis Orienteering Club and Dewayne Holloway.)

Orienteering maps provide the following important information to the orienteer:

1. *Map scale.* Each map contains a certain scale that is proportional between a distance on the map and the actual distances in the field. For example, a scale of 1:15,000 on a topographical map means that one unit of distance on the map equals 15,000 units of actual distance in the field. A bar scale representing map distance is located in the margin of the map.

2. *Directions.* The top of an orienteering map represents geographic north; therefore, the other cardinal directions are south (the bottom), east (the right), and west (the left). Most orienteering maps will have the magnetic-north lines already drawn on the map. These lines, called the declination lines, represent the degree difference between the magnetic north direction and true north direction. The angle of declination on USGS topographic maps can be found in the margin.

3. *Elevation features.* A topographic map is distinguished from a planemetric map (roadmap) in showing the shape and elevation changes of the terrain by brown contour lines. Each of these lines represents a constant elevation, in feet or meters, above sea level. The space between each line on a topographic map represents a vertical distance, called the contour interval. The contour interval is given below the bar scale at the bottom of the map sheet. In areas of the United States with little elevation, the contour interval will be 5 to 10 meters (or feet) to more accurately represent the land features, while contour intervals of 10 to 20 meters (or feet) are found in more mountainous areas.

4. *Other map features.* Other important artificial or natural features, such as power lines, roads, trails, bridges, buildings, fences, boulders, cliffs, streams, lakes, marshes, or ponds are also shown on the map. These features are either drawn to actual scale or displayed symbolically with the description of each symbol found in the map's legend (see Figure 15-1).

Compass.   The second most essential item of equipment for successful orienteering is the compass. The protractor-type compass with the liquid-filled housing (Figure 15-5) is the most widely used compass in

Figure 15-5 The protractor compass.

5. *Orienting lines.* Located inside the compass housing and running parallel with the orienting arrow are the orienting lines. These lines assist in determining declination by setting them parallel with the magnetic lines on the map, with north on the compass pointing to north on the map.

6. *Direction-of-travel arrow.* At the upper end of the base plate is located the direction-of-travel arrow, which is used for determining the direction of travel when the compass is oriented.

Suggested Learning Sequence

Whole Method

The direct, or whole, method is recommended for teaching younger children and novice orienteers. In this method, beginners walk or run an orienteering course in the field with suitable terrain as their first introduction to orienteering. The only preliminary learning prior to this field work is a knowledge of map symbols, an understanding of how to "orient the map," and the ability to map read by using the thumb—the first basic skills of orienteering.

It is important during these first learning sessions that orienteering courses be set that are good illustrations of those points that are to be learned. Therefore, the course-setter must understand that during the first few sessions, the courses should be set in such a way that the beginner needs only to follow roads, edges of fields, trails, and other similar objects.

The course-setter must never be enticed to set what we might normally call "good" controls, but instead, must always keep in mind that the purpose is to show what the map symbols and definitions mean. The control points should be typical for the symbol and definition. All controls should be so distinct that no one can be uncertain as to what is meant.

The following factors must be carefully attended to when course-setting:

1. *Terrain.* There must be lots of trails, open country, roads, and similarly distinct and easily read features. Then it is important to make proper use of these.

2. *Map.* The map should be drawn according to the norms, have the correct colors, be easily read, and preferably be 1:15,000 although it is possible to use 1:24,000. (It is a good idea to enlarge the normal maps for beginner courses).

3. *Control choice.* The aim of the control has been mentioned. Besides the above points, the control should be such that even without a compass, the novice can match the map with the terrain and find the control.

4. *Route choice.* Route choice, as we usually mean it, should not be introduced at the novice level. There are lots of things that must be learned

orienteering because it permits the orienteer to take a bearing and measure its distance quickly and accurately. The parts of the compass and their basic function are as follows.

1. *Base plate.* The transparent rectangular plate on which the compass housing is mounted is called the base plate. The front edge and one of the side edges are marked off in inches and millimeters for measuring map scale or distance.

2. *Compass housing.* The degree markings are found on the outer rim of the rotating compass housing. Each mark represents 1 degree, and they are numbered in intervals of 20. (It should be noted that 0° and 360° coincide and are both north.) Once the compass is set correctly, the degree bearing is taken at the index pointer on the rim of the housing.

3. *Orienting arrow.* Located inside the compass housing is the orienting, or north-seeking, arrow. Its function is to assist in orienting the compass. The compass is oriented by holding it in such a way that the orienting arrow is lined up with the magnetic needle, both of which will be pointed north.

4. *Magnetic needle.* The free-floating needle located inside the compass housing is called the magnetic needle. The north end is painted red and always points to magnetic north unless affected by a metal object.

before you start on route choice. "Route choice" that comes in a later part of the course means only that the novice, for example, chooses the correct path at a path junction.

5. *Orienting the map.* The controls and the legs between controls should be such that the novice can always match (orient) the map with the terrain without using the compass. It is important that the novice be taught always to have the map oriented. This is the most important point in the entire course, and it should be introduced right from the beginning.

After these basic techniques and skills are mastered and confidence gained, more advanced techniques and skills, such as a knowledge of contour lines, map scale, handling a compass, measuring distance, use of attack points, off-aiming, and pace counting, may be introduced.

Part-Whole Method

While the "whole" method of teaching is often used with children and novice orienteers, the most widely used and accepted method of teaching is the "part-whole method." In this method, the basic and advanced techniques and skills of using the map, the compass, and map and compass together are taught in a classroom/field setting before the orienteer attempts to navigate an orienteering course. In attempting to navigate an orienteering course, an orienteer using this method should start with a novice yellow or white course (such as shown in Figure 15-1), gradually progressing to an intermediate, orange or green, and then to a more advanced blue or red course (such as in Figure 15-4)—once the basic orienteering skills and techniques are mastered.

Skills and Techniques

Map Reading. Because the map is the primary tool for navigation in orienteering, it is essential to teach basic map-reading techniques and skills first.

1. *Orienting the map.* Orienting the map simply means keeping the map turned so that north on the map corresponds to north in the field, regardless of the direction the orienteer travels. Orienting the map can be done either by inspecting the surroundings and aligning the terrain features with those on the map or by using the compass. The steps in using the compass to orient the map are as follows:
   a. Set the compass dial at 360 degrees. Then place the compass on the map with the edge of the base plate parallel with one of the magnetic north lines, making sure the direction-of-travel arrow points north.
   b. Rotate the map and compass until the magnetic needle is over the orienting arrow. The map is now oriented with respect to magnetic north.

2. *Map reading by thumb.* In using this technique, fold so that it can be easily held and read, with only the immediate area in which you are orienteering showing. Then place the tip of the thumb on the map corresponding to the place in the field where you are standing and pointing in the direction you will travel. As you travel along, move the thumb to the place on the map corresponding to the location in the field where you have traveled. This technique helps keep you oriented, allowing you to easily analyze and check the terrain features that lie ahead.

Compass Reading. The compass can be used with a map or by itself. For the beginning orienteer, the steps in taking a bearing and traveling with the compass by itself should be taught first. These steps are as follows:

1. Stand facing the direction of the intended destination. With the direction-of-travel arrow pointed in this direction, turn the compass housing until the north end of the orienting arrow is lined up with the north end of the magnetic needle.

2. Once the compass is set, pick out a prominent feature, such as a tree or hilltop, in line with the direction-of-travel arrow. Travel to that feature, take another bearing, and continue toward the desired destination.

Additional Procedures. Taking a bearing and traveling with a compass and map involve additional procedures and should be done with precision. Three basic steps are used in this process:

1. Put the edge of the base plate from the present place of location to the intended destination, making sure the direction-of-travel arrow is pointing in the direction of travel (see Figure 15-6).

2. Turn the compass housing until the orienting lines are parallel with the magnetic lines and the orienting arrow is pointing north on the map (see Figure 15-7). When magnetic north lines are not present, the orienting lines can be set parallel with the meridian lines—the lines running true north to south. In this case, the declination (angle of difference in degrees between true north and magnetic north) must be added or subtracted to the final bearing. This degree difference is given in the margin on topographic maps. To decide whether to add or subtract, think of the rhyme "East is least and West is best." If the angle of declination is *east*, the degree of declination is *subtracted;* if the declination is *west*, it is *added.*

Figure 15-6 The first step in taking a bearing with compass.

Figure 15-7 The second step in taking a bearing with compass.

3. The final important step is to turn yourself until the north end of the magnetic needle points to the north end of the orienting arrows (Figure 15-8).

Safety Considerations

Although orienteering is a relatively safe activity, there are some precautions that must be followed:

1. Orienteers should be cautioned to avoid potentially dangerous obstructions and features shown on the map, such as cliffs, rock faces, barbed wire fences, or deep rivers and streams.

2. The orienteer should be instructed to wear protective clothing when heavy brambles, briar patches, or thick vegetation exist in the terrain.
3. Before embarking on a course, a safety bearing should be given that will lead the orienteer to a large catching feature such as a road or trail in the event he becomes lost or totally disoriented.

Competitive Strategies

In competitive orienteering, the orienteer must know special techniques and skills in order to select the fastest and least tiring route between control points (Figures 15-9 and 15-10).

Figure 15-8 The third step in taking a bearing with compass.

1. *Pace counting.* Pace counting involves a two-step approach:
   a. In step one, the orienteer measures the distance on the map by using the marked edge of the compass and the map bar scale.
   b. Step two involves measuring the distance in the field by pace counting. In pace counting, you count your double step, or each time the same foot hits the ground. This can be practiced by measuring an exact 100 yards or 100 meters over different terrain and counting the number of double steps taken in covering this distance.
2. *Attack points.* Sometimes called secondary controls, these are large, prominent features such as a cliff, building, bridge, trail junction, or other features near the control that can easily be found and identified on the map. Finding an attack point makes the final approach to the control much easier.
3. *Check points.* After finalizing the route, the orienteer should visualize certain prominent features (check points) she will see along the way that will indicate she is on the correct route.
4. *Handrails.* Linear features running parallel with the direction of a control point or an attack point are called handrails. These can take the form of natural features such as a stream, the edge of a

Figure 15-9 A young orienteer, using her map and compass, takes a bearing to the next control point.

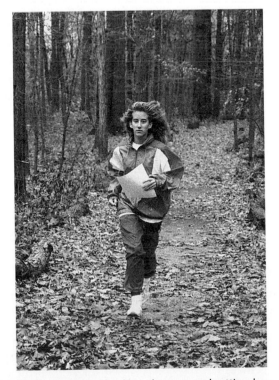

Figure 15-10 After checking the map and setting her compass, the orienteer has selected the woods trail to the next control.

field, or a ridge or artificial features such as a road, trail, fence, or power line. Handrails are used by the orienteer as a natural guide to follow toward the control point.

5. *Catching features.* Long features running crosswise to the orienteer's direction of travel are called catching, or collecting, features. These features can assist the orienteer in navigation, as upon reaching the catcher, the orienteer needs only to turn in the proper direction and follow it until the attack or control point is reached. These catchers include the same linear features described as handrails.

6. *Aiming off.* When control or attack points are located on linear features such as roads, streams, fences, and so forth, the orienteer aims off, that is, sets the compass toward a point 40 to 60 meters to the right or left of the control point rather than right at it, so that upon arriving at the linear feature, the orienteer knows exactly which way to turn, right or left, to find the control point.

Modifications for Special Populations

Orthopedically Impaired

Work on special "searches" within the gymnasium using maps and other coded documents. Designate each wall in the gym a color, and have the students follow the colored map; e.g., travel to the yellow wall, then the green wall, and find the hidden treasure.

Cognitively Impaired

Have the student work on making special compasses to learn north, south, east, and west; e.g., color code the directions.

Sensory Impaired

1. Use peer teachers and paraprofessionals for students who are blind or have a visual impairment.
2. Use visual cues, e.g., posters and notebooks, for students who are deaf or have a hearing impairment.

Terminology

Aiming off A technique in which the orienteer purposely aims to one side of a control point so that he or she will know which way to turn.

Attack point A large, prominent visible feature both on the map and in the field, from which the final approach of attack to the control can be made.

Bearing Sometimes called an azimuth, it is a direction measured in degrees from north with a compass.

Cardinal points The four basic directions on a compass: north, south, east, and west.

Catching feature A long natural or artificial feature running perpendicular to the orienteer's direction of travel.

Contour interval The vertical distance in height between contour lines on a topographic map.

Control Marker of two colors—usually red and white or orange and white—placed in the field before the orienteering meet starts; used for locating control points on the map.

Control description A word description for the location of a control point.

Declination The degree difference between the magnetic north direction and the true north direction.

Handrail Linear features running parallel with an orienteer's direction of travel that are used to navigate to a control or an attack point.

Magnetic north The direction to the magnetic north pole located north of Hudson Bay.

Map symbols Designs found in the legend on a map; used to indicate landscape features.

Meridians Real lines on the map or imaginary lines in the terrain running true north to true south.

Orienteering The skill or the process of finding your way in the field with map and compass combined.

Orienting the compass Turning the compass until north on the compass is the same as north in the field.

Orienting the map Turning the map until north on the map corresponds to north in the field.

Pace counting Method used to measure distance in the field by counting each time the same foot strikes the ground.

Scale A proportion between a distance on the map and the actual distance in the field.

Topographic map A map showing elevation changes by means of contour lines.

True north Geographic north (the North Pole).

Further References

Boga, S. *Orienteering: The Sport of Navigating with Map and Compass.* Mechanicsburg, PA: Stackpole Books, 1997.

Crouch, G. *Route Finding: Navigating with Map and Compass.* Helena, MT: Falcon Publishing, 1999.

Geary, D. *Using a Map and Compass.* Mechanicsburg, PA: Stackpole Books, 1995.

Kjellstrom, B., Heisley, N. and Assoc. Staff of the U.S. Geological Survey Orienteering Services. *Be Expert with Map and Compass.* New York: Hungry Minds, 1994.

McNeil, C., Renfrew, T. and Cory-Wright, J. *Teaching Orienteering.* Champaign, IL: Human Kinetics, 1998.

Palmer, P. *The Complete Orienteering Manual.* North Pomfret, VT: Trafalgar Square, 1998.

Audio-Visual Materials

Silva, 2466 State Road 39N, LaPorte, IN 46350.

Web Sites

www.us.orienteering.org/ Site of U.S. Orienteering Federation (USOF) offers information on books, meet competition, clubs, equipment, Web sites, and more.

www.orienteering.org/ International Orienteering Federation home page; offers information on books, news, events, clubs, Web sites, and more.

http://dir.lycos.com/sports/orienteering/ Offers a complete guide to orienteering from A to Z, including books, equipment, games, techniques, and more.

CHAPTER 16

Recreational Sports

- Angling
- Flying disc
- Horseshoes
- Pickle-ball
- Shuffleboard
- Table Tennis

ANGLING

Nature and Purpose

Angling is fishing for sport. More specifically, it is the use of the skill of casting to catch fish. Angling has increased steadily in popularity, and today countless people of all ages engage in the sport. Over 30 million fishing licenses are issued in the United States each year, and millions of people fish without a license. With so many participants, it is quite possible that more money is spent on angling than on any other sport. Wherever fish and water are to be found, anyone can enjoy this lifetime recreational activity.

The basic skill in learning to become an angler is casting. Despite the fact that this is a relatively simple skill, very few master it because they neither learn under proper guidance nor take the time to practice the skill once they have acquired it.

There are two types of casting: fly and bait or spin casting. There are some similarities between the two, but they employ different tackle and very different techniques. In *fly casting,* a longer, more flexible rod is used, the line is controlled from the hand, and the light fly is propelled entirely by the weight of the line. The technique of fly casting makes it possible to use small, light "lures" (i.e., artificial flies) and to cast with a great deal of precision and accuracy. *Bait/spin casting* requires a shorter, less flexible rod. Distance is gained by the weight of the bait or lure, and the line is controlled at the reel.

Equipment

Fly-Casting Tackle

The beginner should try to enlist the assistance of an experienced fly fisher to help with the selection of proper equipment. With the recent upsurge of interest in fly casting and fly fishing, this should not be a difficult task, because most fly fishers are willing to provide basic instruction as well as other information about getting started in this recreational activity.

Rod. The most important piece of equipment is the rod. Fly rods come in different lengths and have different actions. An 8½- or 9-foot graphite rod with a medium to fast action is probably the best choice for the beginner.

Reel. A single-action fly reel is recommended. This reel should have an adjustable drag (a mechanism that increases or decreases the resistance on a line once a fish is hooked), an interchangeable spool, and the capacity to hold enough backing line in order to play the fish. Figure 16-1 shows fly casting as well as bait and spin casting reels.

Line. The manufacturer's recommendations of line size for the rod should be followed closely. Fly lines are usually constructed of a core of braided dacron or nylon fibers covered by a plastic or other synthetic coating. They come in various tapers (thicknesses) and weight. To balance an 8½- or 9-foot rod properly, the beginner should select a weight forward floating line in a six or seven weight. These lines would be listed as a WF6F or WF7F on the manufacturer's box.

Figure 16-1 Types of reels.

Bait/Spin-Casting Tackle

Once again, the advice of an experienced bait/ spin caster is invaluable and would save the beginner a great deal of time in getting started.

Rod. The beginner should select a rod that is 5 to 6 feet long and has a medium action. Most rods are constructed of fiberglass, graphite, or some combination of the two.

Bait-Casting Reel. The beginner should select a "level-wind" reel, meaning that the line is wrapped evenly on the spool. The reel should fit the length and action of the rod.

Spinning Reel. Spinning reels are divided into two general classes. In the *open type*, the spool upon which the line coils has no cover, leaving the spool and line fully exposed. In the *cone type*, a cone covers the spool and line to protect the line from dirt and to prevent its being touched by lures, twigs, weeds, and other foreign objects. The line passes through a hole in the center of the cup, directly in front of the axis of the spool shaft.

The action of the reel spool is the basic difference between the spinning, spin-casting, and standard bait-casting outfit. The spool of a spinning reel does not rotate to release the line on the cast or to respool it during the retrieve. On most reels, it advances and recedes as the line is being coiled on, in order to

spool the line uniformly—but it never rotates. On the cast, the line slips off the exposed end of the spool. This action can best be visualized by thinking of a spool of thread. If one end of the spool of thread is held firmly in one hand and the thread end grasped by the other hand and stripped off straight over the opposite end of the spool, the action would be similar to that of the spinning line leaving the reel. The spool also remains stationary on the retrieve. A metal "finger" rotates around the spool, picking up the line and placing it back around the spool.

Line. Generally speaking, a light to medium monofilament line is recommended for the beginner. When putting the line on a spinning reel, it is very important to follow the manufacturer's instructions carefully in order to avoid twisting the line. Usually, a braided monofilament line is used for the bait-casting (level-wind) reel because many anglers feel it is less likely to backlash.

Skills and Techniques

The ability to cast the line onto the water is the most important skill the angler must learn. Indeed, the development of a good casting stroke is the key to success in any type of fishing. As the various techniques are described in this section, you will notice some similarities in the use of the fly rod, bait-casting rod, and spinning rod; however, there are important differences. Reference will be made to the positioning of the casting arm in relation to the hands on a clock. Most of the movements center on the ten o'clock and two o'clock positions. Therefore, if you think of the movement in terms of the hands of a clock face, you should have relatively little difficulty in understanding the action of the arm and rod in the learning sequence.

Fly Casting

There are two important things to remember when learning to fly cast: First, the right hand will grip the handle and become part of the execution of the cast, and second, the other hand must control the feed of the line as the cast is being made. After sufficient practice, the sequence and action of the two hands will become smooth and rhythmical. (Left-handed individuals should reverse the described procedure.) Another key point for the beginner to remember is that the cast is primarily a result of the action of the hand and the forearm and less of the wrist.

To practice the cast, begin by pulling 15 to 20 feet of line from the tip of the rod and placing it on the ground in front of you. Grip the rod on the handle, with the thumb placed on top in line with the rod. Wrap the fingers comfortably around the handle. The wrist is bent until it becomes a parallel extension of the forearm. The stroke itself is best executed between the ten o'clock and two o'clock positions. The greatest problem novice flycasters have is using their wrist too much, resulting in a casting action like a "buggy whip" (Figure 16-2).

➤ **Learning Hints**

1. Begin by lifting the tip up, rapidly accelerate from the ten o'clock to one o'clock position. The space between the wrist and handle opens slightly.
2. The rod stops at the one o'clock position, and the line drifts behind the shoulder. Wait until the line is almost completely unrolled, then begin the forward cast.
3. Accelerate the rod forward to the ten o'clock position, stop quickly, and allow the line to unroll forward. The line should land softly on the surface as the follow-through is completed.
4. Since the basic principle of fly casting is to cast ("roll" and "unroll") loops of line, the beginner should watch the back cast to be certain that these loops are rolling and unrolling properly. Indeed, fly casting is a recreational skill that requires the caster to apply equal power to *both* the back cast and the forward cast. Even more specifically, a proper forward cast is impossible to execute after an incorrect back cast.

➤ **Practice/Organizational Suggestions**

The left hand plays an important role in the cast because it feeds line to the rod on the forward cast or draws line from the reel during a false cast.

1. Slack is taken, and the line is grasped between the thumb and forefinger and stripped (drawn) from the reel. Repeat this action two or three times so additional coils are formed.
2. At the end of the forward cast, the line is released from the coil in the left hand, the loop nearest the ends of the finger being released first. It is important to keep the loops separated.
3. As soon as sufficient line is drawn for the length of the cast, complete the cast, releasing the loops of line referred to previously. The release of these loops of line into the cast is called "shooting the line" and is usually used to add distance to the cast.

Bait Casting

The grip for bait casting is different in that the thumb must be placed on the spool flange for the conventional type, and the reel turned sidewise so that the handle points straight up. The index finger should grip the finger trigger, while the other fingers grasp the handle firmly but not rigidly.

In fishing, a good caster learns to cast from any position and with either hand. In target casting, which is the only method of learning accuracy, the caster may stand directly facing the target or slightly sidewise, with the right side (if casting right-handed) toward the target and the right foot slightly advanced. The arms should be held in a relaxed "natural" position, with the elbow at or near the side. The target should be aligned by looking at it through the top of the tip.

The overhead casting action has two parts: the backward motion and the forward motion. Each is equally important.

➤ **Learning Hints**

1. Stand comfortably; the elbow should be clear of the body, while the forearm becomes an extension of the rod.
2. Bring the rod up quickly and stop at a two o'clock position; the weight on the lure will bend the rod further back.
3. With no hesitation, bring the rod swiftly to a ten o'clock position and ease the thumb off the line on the spool.
4. While the lure is in flight, gently apply pressure with the thumb, braking the spool, and allow the rod to follow through in the direction of the line of flight. The spool is braked to a complete stop as the lure reaches the surface of the water. The rod must be shifted to the left hand in order

A

B

C

D

Figure 16-2 Overhead fly cast (sequence). Note wrist is firm, not fixed.

to retrieve the plug. The right hand then grasps the handle of the reel and begins to reel in the line. The method of retrieving depends on the type of bait being used. Often the manufacturer supplies printed instructions on proper manipulation so the angler may secure the best results from each type.

Spin Casting

Remembering that there are two types of spinning reels, the open and the cone type, the cast for both is made in the same manner as with the bait-casting outfit. The only difference is in the control of the line during the cast. With the closed-type reel, the thumb button is pressed then released at the ten o'clock position, and the left hand helps to feather the line and eventually brake it. With the spinning outfit, the caster places pressure upon the line between the forefinger and the rod grip *after* the line has left the spool.

In starting the cast, hold the line (ahead of the reel) firmly against the rod grip with the forefinger of the hand with which the cast is made. While holding the line securely, release the pick-up bail or finger, and move aside so that it will not interfere with the line during the cast. This is done by turning the handle very slightly in reverse, by pressing a release button, or as required for the particular make of reel. The pressure upon the line is released at the same time and in the same manner as the thumb pressure upon the spool would be released with a bait-casting outfit. During the flight of the lure, exercise control by decreasing or increasing the index finger pressure on the line against the cork grip.

As with the conventional rod and reel, the direct overhead cast is recommended until proficiency with the new outfit is acquired.

➤ Practice/Organizational Suggestions

The beginning angler must not only learn accuracy and form but also develop a "feel" for the casting technique being learned. Distance is secondary in the beginning. Use a dummy lure (no barbs) when practicing. *Teaching Note:* In all instances, whether dealing with beginners or more advanced anglers, make sure there is adequate space between participants. Single line formations with two or three arms' length between participants are safest.

1. Pick up the rod and practice the forearm and wrist action without casting.
2. For a class, place a series of plastic hoops at a standard distance and have students hit the target. As proficiency is gained, move the hoops to varying distances, designate high scores for those hoops farthest away and lower scores for those that are nearest to the angler. Individual and team competition can be promoted.
3. Because many people fish from a boat, bring a bench or low-backed chairs to class so students can practice each method of casting from a sitting position.

Skill Testing—Skish

Skish is a dry-land game designed to improve one's skill in casting with regular bait/spin-casting and fly-casting tackle. It is an excellent way for all casters to master the skills of accuracy and the control of distance.

Bait Casting. Bait-casting rules call for the plug not to exceed five-eighths of an ounce, and the line must be no smaller than 9-pound test. Ten targets, rings not to exceed 30 inches, are randomly scattered with distances unknown to the caster. The closest target is not less than 40 nor more than 45 feet from the casting box (4 × 4 feet), while the farthest one should not be more than 80 nor less than 70 feet away. Each target has its own casting box, and the contestants move from box to box, taking two casts at each target (Figure 16-3).

Scoring: Six points are scored for a perfect cast on first trial; 4 points for a perfect cast on second trial. The cast must fall within the target to score. In the event of a tie score, the one having the greatest number of points on initial casts is declared the winner.

Fly Casting. Fly-casting rules for regular fly-casting tackle require a fly tied in approved dry fly style with the hook broken off back of the barb. Five targets are placed at distances unknown to the casters, between 20 and 40 feet from the casting boxes.

First round. The caster must start with fly in hand and no slack in the line, and is given 2½ minutes at each target to make three casts,

Scoring: Five points are scored for a perfect cast on first trial; 3 points for a perfect cast on second trial; 2 points for a perfect cast on third trial; and a maximum score is 50 points. (On water, the fly must rest on the water until the judge calls for the score.)

Second round. The time limit is one and one-half minutes (90 seconds) for each target. The caster roll casts until a "perfect" has been scored on all five targets or until the official calls time. Time begins when the fly drops on the surface. Each perfect score counts 5 points, with a possible score of 25.

Third round—with fly. The time limit is 1 to 1½ minutes. The caster starts with fly in the hand and no slack in the line. To begin, the caster extends the line to the nearest target by false casting, and time begins when the fly drops on the surface as a measured cast. Two casts are made, without false casts, at each of the five targets from left to right, stripping the necessary line and shooting it to reach each target.

Scoring: Three points are scored for a perfect cast on first trial; 2 points for a perfect cast on second trial. The maximum possible score is 25 points. In case of a tie, the caster having made the greatest number of initial perfects is declared the winner.

Safety Considerations

1. *All* anglers should carry or have access to a first-aid kit at all times. Hooks, whether on flies or lures, occasionally end up in one part or another of an angler's anatomy!
2. Anglers must be constantly aware of the dangers of being in the sun too long. Use a sunscreen or sunblocker and wear a hat (which is also good to ward off hooks on errant casts) and polaroid sunglasses—for safety and to see fish.
3. Anglers often, probably too often, fish in places where there are lots of insects, especially of the flying variety. Be certain to carry appropriate repellent.
4. Wading with boots in unknown waters or wearing them in a boat is hazardous, so the angler must avoid such risks.

Modifications for Special Populations
Orthopedically Impaired

Modifications must be considered for several aspects of fishing, baiting the hook, holding and casting, reeling, and removing the catch. Several adaptations can

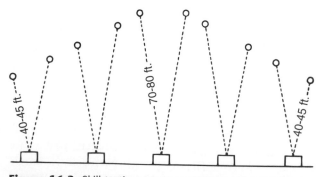

Figure 16-3 Skill testing set-up or skish game using ten targets and five stations.

be made for grasping the rod (see chapters on hand-ball/racquetball and tennis). Electronic devices exist to help casting and reeling; the simplest modification, however, would be to eliminate these sub-tasks and use a simple "cane pole" arrangement.

Cognitively Impaired

Minimal modifications are needed.

Sensory Impaired

Minimal modifications are needed.

Terminology

Back cast   Drawing the rod back; the initial movement in the cast.

Backing line   Thin braided line put on the reel before the fly line to fill up the spool and for insurance against a fish making a long run.

Backlash   A faulty casting technique that results in a tangling of the line.

Bait casting   The throwing and placing of a lure and line from the rod and reel.

Dry fly fishing   Casting a surface fly so that it resembles an insect on the water.

False cast   A fly-casting cast in which line is held in the air and not allowed to fall to the surface. Usually used to increase the length of a dry cast or to cause a fly to change direction.

Ferrules   The connections between the sections of the rod.

Fly   Natural and/or synthetic materials tied on hooks.

Fly casting   Throwing a line with an artificial lure by means of a fly rod.

Forward cast   The last movement forward with the rod that throws the lure or the fly to the desired spot.

Guides   Small loops on the rod through which the line is run.

Leader   The strong, transparent material that connects the line to the hook or lure.

Level-wind reel   A reel that has a carriage that distributes the line evenly on the spool.

Lure   Artificial or natural bait used to attract fish. A hook or hooks is/are attached to the lure.

Net   A device to take the fish safely out of the water.

Power stroke   The brief time in fly casting between the forward and backward cast when power is applied by the caster.

Reel   The mechanism that winds or unwinds the line.

Reel seat   The part of the rod handle to which the reel is attached.

Rod tip   The top end of the rod.

Roll cast   A fly cast in which line is rolled out over a surface without utilizing a backcast.

Shoot   Feeding out extra line during a fly-casting forward or backward cast. Also used to increase the distance of a cast.

Spinner   Artificial lure that spins when it is drawn through the water.

Spoon   Artificial lure shaped something like a spoon.

Strike   When a fish grasps the lure or fly as well as the angler's response to set the hook.

Tackle   Fishing gear; usually refers only to the rod and reel.

Thumbing   Controlling the speed of the cast by means of thumb pressure on the reel.

Further References

Borger, G. *Presentations.* Wausau, WI: Tomorrow River Press, 1995.

Bronquell, P. *Fly Fishing with Children: A Guide for Parents.* Woodstock, VT: The Countryman Press, 1994.

Budsworth, G. *The Complete Book of Fishing Knots.* New York: Lyons Press, 1999.

Circle, H. *Bass Wisdom.* New York: Lyons Press, 2000.

Cooper, G. and Haas, E. *Wade a Little Deeper, Dear. A Woman's Guide to Fly Fishing.* New York: Nick Lyons Books, 1989.

Gerlach, R. *The Complete Book of Casting.* New York: Winchester Press, 1975.

Kamininsky, P. *Fly Fishing for Dummies.* New York: Hungry Minds, Inc., 1998.

Kreh, L. and Walinchus, R. (Illustrator). *Presenting the Fly.* New York: Lyons Press, 1999.

Kreh, L. *Solving Fly Casting Problems.* New York: Lyons Press, 2000.

Lord, M. and Rowinski, J. *L.L. Bean Fly Fishing Handbook.* New York: Lyons Press, 2000.

Martin, D. and Leeson, T. *The Fly Fisher's Illustrated Dictionary.* New York: Lyons Press, 2000.

McClane, A. J. *Secrets of Successful Fishing.* New York: Henry Holt, 1979.

Meade, T. and White, J. R. *Essential Fly Fishing.* New York: Lyons Press, 1995.

National Skish Board. *National Skish Guide.* Current ed. Washington, D.C.: NSB (Bond Building).

Owen, P. *L.L. Bean Outdoor Knots Handbook.* New York: Lyons Press, 1999.

Pfeiffer, C. D. *The Field and Stream Bass Fishing Handbook.* New York: Lyons Press, 1999.

Pfeiffer, C. D. *The Field and Stream Tackle Care & Repair Handbook.* New York: Lyons Press, 1999.

Rosenbaur, T. *The Orvis Fly-Fishing Guide.* New York: Nick Lyons Books, 1984.

Rosenthal, M. *The Freshwater Fishing Book.* New York: Macmillan, 1989.

Rutter, M. and Card, D. *Fly Fishing Made Easy.* Old Saybrook, CT: The Globe Pequot Press, 1994.

Schaupmeyer, C. *The Essential Guide to Fly-Fishing,* Renton, WA: Lone Pine Publishing, 1998.

Schultz, Ken. *Ken Schultz's Fishing Encyclopedia.* New York: Hungry Minds, 1999.

Shook, M. and Kreiger, M. *The Complete Idiots Guide to Fly Fishing*. New York: MacMillan Distribution, 1999.

Sosin, M. *The Complete Book of Light-Tackle Fishing*. New York: Lyons Press, 2000.

Vliet, J. V. *The Art of Fly Tying*. Minnetonka, MN: Cowles Creative Publishing International, 1994.

Wright, L. *First Cast: The Beginner's Guide to Fly Fishing*. New York: Simon and Schuster, 1987.

Audio-Visual Materials

Dierks, R. *Introduction to Fishing*. Prior Lakes, MN: Mintex Entertainment.

Krieger, M. *The Essence of Fly Casting*. Sebastopol, CA: Sonoma Video Productions.

Penguin Productions. Vero Beach, Florida. *The Art of Fly Casting*.

Scientific Anglers. *Fly Fishing Made Easy*. Minneapolis, MN: 3M Sportsman Video Collection.

Note: The number of videos on all aspects of angling increases monthly. We urge you to check fishing publications for the latest releases.

Software

ESPN Interactive Fly Fishing School. Intellimedia Sports, Two Piedmont Center, Suite 300, Atlanta, Georgia. Windows or Macintosh format.

The Art of Fly Tying. Cy DeCosse Incorporated, Cowles Enthusiast Media, 5900 Green Oak Drive, Minnetonka, MN, 1996, Windows or Macintosh format.

Web Sites

www.tu.org Trout Unlimited site; includes up-to-date articles about environmental issues, conservation issues, and more.

www.fly-fisherman.com/main.cfm *Fly Fisherman* magazine site; includes good articles on a variety of topics.

www.flyfishingreview.com/ Offers resource for fly fishing equipment, a variety of articles, listing of fly shops worldwide, and much more.

www.myhost.com/flyfishing101 Site devoted to the beginning fly fisher; includes information on equipment, knots, casting, books, and more.

www.flyanglersonline.com/main.htm Online fly fishing magazine; includes many articles.

www.flyshop.com1 The fly fishing online network; offers a wealth of information.

www.fedflyfishers.org Federation of Fly Fishers site; offers comprehensive information.

www.flyfishing.about.com/recreation/flyfishing/mbody. htm Useful site that offers several topics about fly fishing, including a beginners' corner.

FLYING DISC

The flying disc traces its origins back to the Frisbie Pie Company and its predecessor, the Olds Baking Company in New Haven, Connecticut. The actual disc was either a pie or cookie tin, which was turned upside down and tossed. Students at Yale University played an early version of a flying disc game, in which the thrower would signal the receiver by calling "Frisbie."

Walter Frederick Morrison, the son of an inventor, is credited as the first to develop metal pie tins for commercial purposes following World War II. He eventually turned to plastic to manufacture a disc that would be used as a toy. The original was a flop, but in 1951 he developed an improved model, which eventually was purchased by a toy company and called "Wham-O's Pluto Platter." Because the activity was slow to catch on, the Wham-O company decided to distribute the disc to all parts of the United States. While visiting Harvard's campus, distributors first heard the term "Frisbie." The students said they had been tossing pie tins for years and called it "Frisbie-ing." The company borrowed the term and spelled it "Frisbee." Ed Headrick is credited with the development and patent of the modern Frisbee and with marketing the disc, millions of which have been sold.

Today, there are many varieties of activities that incorporate a flying disc. Ultimate frisbee, disc golf, freestyle, double disc court, guts, field events, and discathon are a few of games that have official rules for participation and/or national organizations. Many new flying disc activities are created regularly by individuals who enjoy throwing the flying disc.

Presented in this text is one team activity, ultimate frisbee, and one individual activity, disc golf. Each is presented separately following the chapter format for all activities. The Web sites listed at the end of this chapter provide more extensive details on these two disc sports and links to a wide variety of disc activities.

Nature and Purpose— Ultimate Frisbee

Ultimate Frisbee is a non-contact team game consisting of throwing and catching the disc continually without holding it too long and without running with it. The objective is to score a goal by catching a thrown disc while in the end zone of the field. The opponents gain possession of the disc on a turnover, which occurs when a pass is knocked down, incomplete, intercepted, or out-of-bounds. The disc is immediately put back in play with a throw from the spot where the infraction occurred. The strategies of the game are similar to those of football, soccer, and basketball. The participant needs good hand-eye coordination, speed, quickness, and agility. The spirit of the game embraces sportsmanship, fair play, player respect, self-officiating, and the joy of playing.

Rules

Ultimate Frisbee rules are easily modified to meet the needs of the participants.

Players. A team consists of seven people: "handlers, mids, and longs."

Field. The area is a rectangle with a playing surface of 70 yards by 40 yards and end zones at each end 20 yards deep.

Start of Play. A throw-off initiates play, and the members of the team throwing the disc must be in their own end zone. A throw-off is repeated after each score and after each period.

Scoring. A point is awarded for catching a throw in the opponent's end zone.

Disc Movement. The player in possession has 10 seconds to throw the disc while the defender loudly counts the seconds. The player with the disc may not run but attempts to complete a pass, after establishing a pivot foot, in any direction.

The receiver must take no more than two steps to establish a pivot foot for the next throw. If the receiver wishes to avoid stopping when catching the disc, he or she must throw it before taking a third step and may not change direction, increase speed, nor purposefully bobble it to himself or herself, which constitutes traveling.

Possession Change. Possession of the disc changes to the defending team if it is intercepted, blocked, dropped, or goes out-of-bounds. With the possession change, the defender (marker) must be no closer to the thrower than one disc diameter, and there may be only one defender. The new thrower establishes a pivot foot, may not pivot into the defender, and must throw before 10 seconds have elapsed. Stalling to restart play is not allowed; in such cases, the defender, who immediately starts the 10-second count, calls "delay of game."

Contact. No contact is allowed, and picks/screens are illegal.

Fouls. Any contact with another player results in a foul. If it is a foul of the player in possession, play immediately resumes.

Length of Game. There are two 24-minute halves with a 5-minute overtime period.

Equipment

The disc comes in a variety of sizes and weights. The team captains may choose the disc. Protective gear is allowed, provided it is not dangerous to others. No cleated shoes are allowed. A team is required to wear uniforms of the same color.

Skills and Techniques

All the disc activities revolve around throws, including grips and catches. It is important for beginners to focus first on the various ways to grip the disc and only then on throwing. Developing good grip technique is an often overlooked factor of playing the game well.

Grips

Backhand beginner. The thumb is on top of the disc, the index finger is along the rim, the middle finger extends toward the center, and the remaining two fingers are under the rim. Alternatively, the middle, ring, and little fingers can be under the rim, producing more power.

Backhand power. The thumb is on top of the disc, and all fingers grip the rim tightly. The position of the thumb can vary from along the edge of the rim to pointing toward the center of the disc.

Backhand hybrid. This is a combination of the two foregoing grips. The difference is that the middle finger flexes toward the disc, so that the top of the finger applies pressure to support the disc.

Backhand thumber. The thumb is under the disc, and all four fingers are on top.

Forehand beginner. The thumb is on top of the disc, the index finger is underneath pointing toward the middle, the middle finger is along the inside of the rim, and the remaining two fingers are clenched toward the palm, with no clutching on the disc.

Forehand power. The thumb is on top of the disc, the index and middle fingers together are pressed hard against the rim, and the remaining two fingers are clenched toward the palm with no clutching on the disc. One alternative is to curl the index and middle slightly rather than extend them fully. Another alternative is to place the side of the middle finger against the rim rather than pressing, the pads of the index and middle fingers against the rim. This promotes a palm up follow-through.

Forehand hybrid. The thumb is on top of the disc, the index finger is bent slightly and pressed firmly on the rim, while the middle finger is extended also on the rim. These two fingers are no longer parallel, because the index finger is bent. The remaining two fingers are clenched toward the palm with no clutching on the disc. *Forehand thumber.* The thumb is under the disc, and all four fingers are on top.

Throws

Throws may be made using a variety of grips. A basic throwing strategy is to step forward with the foot opposite the throwing hand/arm. The difference between the backhand and forehand throws is the point where the hand/arm start the throwing action. The backhand throws are across the body with the disc starting on the opposite side of the throwing hand/arm, which is coiled across the chest.

Backhand Throw Strategies (right-handed)

Air bounce. The air bounce is a slower throw that hangs in the air, allowing the receiver to run under it.

Inside out. The path starts to the opposite side of the body and curves back to the other side. To start the throw, the thrower tilts the outside of the disc down.

Reverse curve. The path starts to the non-throwing arm side and curves back toward the opposite side. To start the throw, the thrower tilts the inside of the disc down.

Blade. The outside of the disc is tilted down but is released so that it goes high into the air above defenders, curving to the left of the thrower.

Scooper. The grip on the disc is like holding a hammer. The arm is in an overhand vertical position moving slightly forward, releasing the disc with all wrist action.

Catches

Sandwich catch (pancake). Use two hands to catch the disc, with one hand on top and the other on the bottom. Alternating hands on the disc is an advantageous strategy.

C-catch. Form a C with the thumb and fingers, and close them to grasp the disc. The fingers are up for catching high throws, whereas the thumb is up when receiving low throws.

➤ Practice/Organizational Suggestions

Start 5 to 10 yards apart with a partner when initially practicing grips, throws, and catches. Gradually increase the distance as skill improves. Increasing the distance results in less accuracy and more movement of the disc, so safety in aligning the players becomes a greater concern. Additionally, as the disc moves greater distances, the receiver has more opportunity to run and catch, which compounds the difficulty of the game. By requiring the players to stop within three steps of the catch and to restructure the time before the next throw, the instructor can foster the players' application of skills to competition level. A final step might be to add defenders, more teammates, and restrictions for field size in a game of keep-away.

Playing Strategies/Tactics

In offensive play, the basic individual strategies for Ultimate Frisbee are very similar to many field games. The strategies include quick passes, becoming a receiver after passing, fast cutting, avoiding "bunching," maintaining balance among teammates, maintaining control of the disc, and moving the disc upfield toward the goal.

Offensive Formation and Strategies

The "stack" is an often used formation in which the players line up near the middle of the field in a line parallel with the sideline and in advance of the thrower. The player closest to the thrower positions himself or herself 15 to 20 yards ahead, with each succeeding player about 5 to 10 yards ahead of each other. The players closest to the thrower are called "handlers," those in the middle are called "mids," and the ones toward the end of the stack are "longs." This formation, due to its alignment, provides open areas to either side for passes to be thrown.

The tactics are for the players to systematically, starting with the one closest to the thrower, run back toward the thrower and make a cut to an outside open space. Timing of when to cut and when the next player starts is very important. A cutting player who does not receive the pass rejoins the stack after clearing the area.

Offensive and cut strategies include the following: gain the most yardage possible with each throw; move the disc to a better position on the field; maintain possession; start long cuts when close to thrower, not from the top of the stack; stay away from a deep cutter so one defender cannot cover two players; and clear the deep area.

Strategies to improve scoring opportunities include having the good handlers utilize the give-and-go, designating one person as the scorer near the end zone, and assigning the fastest players to long cuts. End zone scoring failures usually result from too many cuts or no cuts, not because of great defensive efforts.

Defensive Strategy

A person-to-person defense is most often used at the beginning levels of play. There are three positional tactics for the defender. First, face the receiver, attempting to stay at least 3 yards away, and focus solely on the player. Second, position to the open field side of the receiver and attempt to see the disc and receiver at all times. Third, face the thrower while glancing over the shoulder at the receiver. Another possible alternative for a defender covering a deep receiver is to play behind that player in an attempt to assist a teammate who has lost his or her player. It is not wise to attempt to block the disc, because if the player misses the block, the opponent will be open and the teammates will therefore have to switch. Switches leave receivers open and result in quick passes by the offense, making it difficult to reestablish defensive continuity.

Etiquette and Playing Courtesies

The spirit of the game embraces sportsmanship. A win-at-all-costs attitude is not acceptable in a player. One does not attempt to circumvent the rules and take unfair advantage. Players are expected to self-officiate. They call their own fouls. Players respect one another and play for the joy of the game.

Nature and Purpose—Disc Golf

Disc golf involves throwing the disc with power plus accuracy, utilizing the nuances of golf. The objective is to cover the course in the fewest number of throws. Play starts with a throw from the tee area, is followed by succeeding throws from where the disc comes to rest, and concludes when the disc is thrown into the above-ground target. The course, consisting of 9 or 18 holes, often includes trees, water, and other obstacles, which add difficulty to the activity. However, due to the adaptability of the game, a course can be set up in open areas. The activity appeals to all ages, sexes, and ability levels and also to the physically challenged.

Scoring and Rules

Scoring (same as golf). The score for each hole is determined by the total throws it takes to complete the hole, plus any penalties. The final score for the course is determined by comparing each player's score to par. Par for each hole depends on the difficulty and usually ranges from 3 to 6.

Penalties (one stroke assessment each). A disc that goes out-of-bounds is placed 1 yard from where it went out (penalty stroke). A disc that comes to rest above the ground (e.g., in a tree or bush) is placed directly below (penalty stroke). If the lie is unplayable or unsafe, the disc is placed at a spot 5 yards from the original location but not closer to the hole (penalty stroke). A "falling putt," where the player steps past the disc marker without the body momentarily stopping, is illegal (penalty stroke).

Order of Play. On the first hole, the order for throwing is determined by the names listed on the scorecard. All succeeding throws on that hole are by the player furthest from the hole. On succeeding holes, the first throw from the tee is determined by the best score on the last hole. If the score is tied, the order is the same as that for the previous hole.

Throws. The lie on each throw is marked at the spot where the disc comes to rest. On the "drive" and "approach" shots, the player must not step in front of the marker before the disc is released. Any throw within 30 feet of the target is considered a "putt." The player must not step in front of the marker on the "putt" until balance is demonstrated (penalty stroke).

Equipment

One of the advantages in disc golf is that there is very little equipment needed, and the equipment that is needed is inexpensive. A player needs only one disc. However, it is an advantage to have two available. One disc may be used to mark the lie and is available if the original disc is lost or damaged. Advanced players carry different types of discs, which are designed for the drive, approach, and putts. The disc for golf is different in that it is thinner with sharper edges. The target (hole) may be a post, tree, basket, or official target. The official target is an upright pole with a basket suspended by chairs. When the disc hits the suspension chains, it falls into the basket. There are several official targets on the market.

Skills and Techniques

The basic skill is throwing. The throws require power and accuracy. The layout of the course often demands various flight paths in order to navigate doglegs and hazards. A reference to the skills section on Ultimate Frisbee in this chapter describes various grips and throws. The beginner needs to master the backhand throw before attempting other more advanced varieties.

Backhand. The grip is the key to good throws. The thumb is on top of the disc near the edge. The index finger is under the rim edge of the disc. Most of the pressure is supplied by the thumb and index finger in a pinching action. The other three fingers are under the disc and are used to help make the grip stable or change the angle.

In the drive and approach throws, the body stands sideways to the target, with the throwing shoulder pointing toward the target. The feet and shoulders are in a straight line to the target.

The backswing starts with a slight flexion of the knees. The disc is at chest level as the straight throwing arm reaches backward across the body as far as possible. That arm is parallel to the ground. The wrist cocks, so that the disc touches the inside of the throwing arm like a coiled spring. The non-throwing arm is extended backward in a straight line pointing away from the target. The pulling action of the straight throwing arm leads with the elbow as the coiled wrist leads the disc. The arm continues forward rapidly as the wrist uncoils (snaps), releasing the disc. Simultaneously, the lower body unwinds and the upper body rotates as the arm extends. The torso twists outward vigorously as the feet stay stationary on the follow-through.

➤ Learning Hints

1. The harder the thumb and index finger pinch, the harder the throw.
2. Practice throwing using only the thumb and index finger as the grip.
3. Do not bend the throwing arm.
4. Make a complete throwing action without stopping short.
5. Do not release the disc too late.
6. Do not let the nose of the disc be in an up-leading position.
7. Arm speed and wrist snap are the most important factors for distance.
8. If the disc leads the wrist, the throw will be to the side of the dominant arm.
9. Snap the wrist like a whip.

Putt. The putt is the most important throw. The grip is the same as in the drive or approach throws. The only difference is the foot position, which provides an open stance. The stance is 45 degrees from the line to target as the front foot drops, allowing the upper body to more closely face the target.

➤ Learning Hints

1. Check body alignment.
2. Focus on a specific spot on the target.
3. Visualize the throwing action.
4. Develop a consistent pattern for the putt, and don't deviate.
5. Make the swing automatic; groove it.
6. Wind from the side is not important unless you are throwing a curve. A front wind causes the disc to rise, and a wind from the back causes it to drop.

Playing Strategies

1. Visualize the shot before throwing the disc. Look for any potential hazards or obstacles. Visualize the flight over or around these elements.
2. When a disc lands in a bad spot, throw it out into an advantageous area in preparation for the next throw. Attempting to take risks often leads to a

bad score. Another option is to take a stroke penalty and move the disc 5 yards from the trouble spot for an open throw.
3. Don't gamble by attempting a putt that is too long. Lay-up with the throw, placing it close to the target. The long putt often leads to worse problems.
4. Master the backhand first. Later, learn new throws that help you get out of tough spots.

Etiquette and Playing Courtesies

Disc golf is a polite game, just like regular golf. Refer to the chapter on golf for an extensive list.

Terminology

Ultimate Frisbee

Air bounce A throw aimed downward, which results in the disc's being buoyed by a cushion of air.

Backhand A throw across the body, where the disc is gripped with the thumb on top and fingers underneath.

Blade A forehand throw that goes high in the air and curves to the left of a right-handed thrower.

Check Restarting play following a stoppage where the marker touches the disc before the thrower is allowed to pass it.

End zone The area on the field where a score is made if the disc is caught by the team attacking that end.

Forehand A throw where the arm starts on the dominant side of the body and makes a sidearm action.

Hack A foul.

Handler A team's primary thrower.

Marker The defensive player who guards the thrower.

Mid A receiver who cuts for shorter passes rather than deep.

Receiver The offensive player who is in the act of catching the disc or not in possession of the disc.

Stack An offensive strategy where players position up and down the field in a vertical line.

Strip An illegal act by the marker attempting to touch or touching the disc while in thrower's possession.

Thrower The offensive player in possession of the disc or who has just released it.

Throw off The lining up of the offensive team in their own end zone and throwing the disc to the opponents, which initiates play.

Traveling Throwing the disc before establishing the pivot foot when changing from marker to thrower.

Turnover A pass that is incomplete, knocked down, intercepted, or out-of-bounds, which results in loss of possession.

Disc Golf

Refer to the golf chapter for additional terms.

Ace A hole in one.

Birdie A score that is 1 under par.

Casual A hazard that is not designed as part of the course, such as standing water.

Clear A term indicating that a hole is ready for play.

Lie The spot where the disc comes to rest and where the next throw is taken.

Mandatory A flight path that is designed as a path that must be followed on a hole.

Mini A small disc used to mark the lie.

Par A score that is required in order to complete the hole.

Putt A throw made from within 30 feet of the target.

Roller A disc that advances by rolling.

Safari golf When players make up different holes from an existing course.

Taco A term for a warped disc that has been damaged by hitting a hard object.

Tee pad The area on each hole that is designated as the place to begin.

Worm burner A disc that takes a down angle, resulting in a premature landing.

Further References

There are very few books, periodicals, or videos devoted to disc activities. The Web sites listed provide the best references and most up-to-date information.

Web Sites

www.frisbeehunter.com. A comprehensive site with a variety of links to sites about Ultimate Frisbee, disc golf, freestyle, and Frisbee dogs. Also describes equipment and costs for each activity.

www.discgolfassoc.com Provides history, products, course design, promotional assistance for educational groups at various levels, rules, other disc games, and additional links.

www.upa.org A great site with extensive information and links concerning Ultimate Frisbee.

www.wfdf.org An excellent site for official rules for all forms of flying disc activities (Ultimate Frisbee, disc golf, double disc court, freestyle, guts, field events, and discathon).

www.ultimatehandbook.com Addresses beginner, intermediate, and advanced skills/knowledge. Other highlights are history, drills, rules, media, glossary, and other links.

www.discgolfing.com A very inclusive site with good references for new players on rules, history, skills, terms, and tips on playing the game. Also includes a large number of links to other related sites.

HORSESHOES

Nature and Purpose

Horseshoe pitching has been popular for a long time, both as a recreational and a competitive sport. The formation of the National Horseshoe Pitchers Association in 1921 has given rise to chapters in nearly every state as well as Canada. The NHPA sanctions local and regional meets for men, women, boys, and girls. A World Tournament is held each year for Men and Women, while a Junior Boys and Junior Girls World Champion is also decided.

The game is played by pitching horseshoes toward a metal stake some 40 feet (30 for women and juniors) from the pitching point. Points are scored for shoes landing closest to the stake, provided the shoe is not farther than six inches from the stake. A ringer (shoe that encircles stake) counts 3 points. The winner is the player who first scores 21 points (informal play) or 50 points (official tournament competition). Players alternate in throwing shoes, with the player who scored one or more points on the previous pitch throwing first. In singles play, the players move from stake to stake after each throw, but in doubles, one partner is stationed at each stake and makes all throws from there.

Playing Area and Equipment

The Court. The official horseshoe court (Figure 16-4) is a minimum of 6 feet wide and 46 feet long, with 1-inch metal stakes placed 40 feet apart (30 feet for women and juniors). The stakes are centered in a 6 × 6–foot pitcher's box. An extended platform and additional 10 feet should extend beyond the pitcher's box to allow for pitching at shorter distances. For informal recreational games, the distance between stakes may be arranged to fit the available space. If courts are to be built on a school ground, it is advisable to build back stops behind each pitcher's box to prevent the horseshoes from rebounding into a student. In schools that lack the space or do not wish to build permanent courts, temporary ones can be built in a place of convenience.

Horseshoes. Horseshoes may be bought at local hardware stores or discount department stores, or may be specially ordered from a number of companies approved by the NHPA. For schools, several physical education and recreation equipment companies sell either official metal shoes or indoor and outdoor rubber horseshoes that are used with wooden stakes. An official shoe should not exceed $7\frac{1}{4}$ inches in width and $7\frac{5}{8}$ inches in length, and should weigh

Figure 16-4 Typical horseshoe court (NHPA dimensions).

no more than 2 pounds 10 ounces. The opening can be no more than 3½ inches from point to point.

Basic Rules

The National Horseshoe Pitchers Association establishes the official rules of horseshoe pitching. The simplified rules are listed below.

1. A game is divided into innings, and each contestant pitches two shoes in each inning. The length of the game is determined before play begins. There are two options: (1) the game can be played to a predetermined point limit (40 points is suggested); or (2) the game can be played by a predetermined number of shoes. An even number of shoes must be thrown. In event of a tie, an extra two innings may be played.

2. The choice of the first pitch to start the game is decided by the toss of a horseshoe or a coin.

3. A shoe that has left the pitcher's hand is ruled a pitched shoe.

4. A pitcher's opponent must stand behind the person in action and may not interfere with the pitch in any way.

5. A contestant may not walk to the opposite stake or be informed of the position of the shoes until the inning is completed.

6. Shoes thrown when a foul has been committed are considered shoes pitched; however, they may not receive any point value. Fouls may be assessed for the following:
   a. Illegal delivery of shoe
   b. Failure of opponent to stay behind the pitcher, or interfering in any way while the opponent is in the act of pitching
   c. Touching thrown shoes before a measurement has been made
   d. Thrown shoes that strike part of the pitcher's box or land outside the foul lines and that then rebound into the box
   e. Stepping on or over the foul line

7. Ties are broken by pitching an extra inning(s).

Scoring

1. The shoe nearest to the stake scores one point, provided it is within six inches of the stake.

2. Two shoes closer than opponent's shoe score 2 points.

3. One ringer scores 3 points and two ringers, 6 points.

4. A player having two ringers to one by his opponent scores 3 points.

5. All shoes equally distant from the stake count as ties and no points are scored.

6. A leaning shoe has the same value as that of a shoe lying on the ground and in contact with the stake.

Skills and Techniques

Players must stand behind the foul line on the pitching platform when pitching. Most players assume a starting stance with the pitching arm closest to the stake and in a position that permits a forward step in the act of delivery of the shoe. The number of turns that the shoe takes in flight usually determines the style of grip to be used. Regardless of the grip used, there are several factors common to all pitches:

1. The shoe should be held parallel with the ground, with calks down.

2. The rotation of the shoe should be clockwise.

3. The open end of the shoe should face the stake when landing.

There are four standard methods of delivery, so the beginner should do some experimenting to determine which method is best.

1. In the single-turn delivery (Figure 16-5), the open face of the shoe is directed toward the stake.

2. In the one and one-quarter–turn delivery (Figure 16-6), the open end of the shoe faces the pitcher's left and the thumb is across the top.

3. In the one and one-half–turn delivery (Figure 16-7), the open end of the shoe faces the pitcher.

4. In the one and three-quarters delivery (Figure 16-8), the open end of the shoe faces the

Figure 16-5 The single turn delivery.

Figure 16-6 The one and one-quarter–turn delivery.

Figure 16-7 The one and one-half–turn delivery.

Figure 16-8 The one and three-quarter–turn delivery. Two different grips are illustrated.

pitcher's right and either of two shoe-holding methods may be used.

➤ **Learning Hints**

1. Weight evenly distributed on both feet in the stance, step off on opposite foot, knees bent, eyes on the target, shoulders square to target.
2. While the player is slightly leaning forward, the arm remains straight and falls down and back and retraces the same arc on the forward swing. The pitch must be smooth and rhythmical.
3. At the release, the body and arm extend, giving proper lift, and the forearm rolls in order to turn the shoe.

➤ **Practice/Organizational Suggestions**

1. Experiment with deliveries; usually the one and one-quarter–turn delivery is best for a beginner.
2. Practice the step and throw without a shoe, and then add the shoe. Partner should check to see

that arc is straight, shoulders are square, and delivery is rhythmical.
3. Juniors and school-age children might start closer to the stake and work their way back to 30 feet.

Safety Considerations

1. Stand well away from the pitching court when not involved.
2. Be aware of people around you when swinging the horseshoe. Pitch only in the designated area.
3. If setting up courts for a class, make sure there is adequate distance between courts to compensate for erratic throws of beginners.

Playing Courtesies

1. Observe all the rules.
2. Do not disturb a person who is in the process of pitching.

3. Keep emotions under control.
4. Be aware of the game and the position in the game so you are ready to pitch when your turn comes.

Modifications for Special Populations

Orthopedically Impaired

1. Able-bodied students can be placed in a regular classroom chair if mainstreamed with students using a wheelchair.
2. Distances can be shortened.
3. The target for the horseshoe can be placed next to the student with grasp and release difficulties.
4. Small rings can be made from old jump ropes to replace the actual horseshoe, or hula hoops can be used for more severe mobility impairments.

Cognitively Impaired

Minimal modifications are needed.

Sensory Impaired

1. Some type of audio device can be placed as the target, e.g., buzzer or bell, and positioned inside of a hula hoop. Blind and/or visually impaired students could toss bean bags instead of horseshoes inside the hoop.
2. No modifications should be needed for the deaf and/or hearing-impaired.

Terminology

Calks Raised areas on the heels and toes of one side of the pitching shoe that tend to make the shoe less likely to skid when striking the surface of the pit area.

Double ringer Two successive shoes that encircle the stake by the same player in the same inning.

Flipped-up shoe Flipping shoe in air to determine which player takes the first pitch. Instead of calling heads or tails, a player calls smooth or rough.

Heel The ends of the prongs on each side of the open end of the shoe.

Inning The pitching of two shoes by each player.

Leaner (also **Hobber**) Shoe that leans against a stake.

Pit The area in that the shoe lands.

Pitcher box The area that includes the pitching platform and the pit.

Ringer A shoe that encircles the stake.

Further References

Boga, S. *Horseshoes (Backyard Games)*. Mechanicsburg, PA: Stackpole Books, 1996.

National Horseshoe Pitchers Association of America. *Official Rules for Horseshoe Pitching*. Current ed. Federation of 54 State Associations in the U.S. and Canada. (Contact local association for state address.)

The Horseshoe Pitchers' News Digest, published monthly, PO. Box 1606, Aurora, IL 60507.

Web Sites

www.gcforge.com/backyardcourt.htm Offers instruction on how to build your own backyard court; also includes backyard rules.

www.geocities.com/Colosseum/sideline/7 American Horseshoe Pitching Association (AHPA) site offers links, rules, information about AHPA, and more.

www.horseshoeonline.com/ National Horseshoe Pitching Association of America site offers sections on how to pitch horseshoes, court materials, backyard courts, court construction, game etiquette, and more.

PICKLE-BALL

Nature and Purpose

Pickle-ball is a fast-paced, fun-filled game for individuals of all ages. Developed first as a recreational backyard game, it has found popularity among racquet enthusiasts and in physical education programs. Combining the court markings and dimensions of badminton, skills associated with tennis, a net that is 3 feet high, solid wooden racquets, and a plastic whiffle ball, the game can be played in a singles format or doubles format. The premium is on ball placement rather than strength or size of the players. For this reason, it can be played as a coeducational activity and as a recreational activity by boys and girls and men and women. The winner of the game is that player or team to reach 11 points first; however, an individual or team must win by a margin of 2 points.

Pickle-ball can be played in a number of venues; the surface of the court must be hard enough so that the plastic ball will bounce. Therefore, it is not unusual to see pickle-ball courts set up inside on a gymnasium floor or on a concrete or blacktop playground surface. While official pickle-ball equipment can be purchased at a reasonable price from a number of physical education equipment suppliers or from Pickle-Ball, Inc., in Seattle, Washington, the square-headed paddles can be made from a good-quality plywood, a piece of nylon for a safety strap, and wooden handles. Whiffleballs the size of a baseball or softball may also be used, and generally the smaller the ball, the quicker the game. A badminton net strung across a series of wooden standards 36 inches high will meet the requirements of the net needed for the game. Because the equipment is relatively inexpensive, pickle-ball is an attractive game not only for class but also for recreation and intramural tournament play.

The game itself uses skills associated with tennis. Some physical education instructors use the game as a good skill developer for the forehand and backhand drives, lobs, and volleys. Because the player has to bend his knees to get low enough to stroke the ball properly, it is a good developer for this element of tennis. The game is played on a court with the same dimensions as a badminton doubles court. While the service areas retain their markings, the pickle-ball court has a non-volley zone seven feet on either side of the net. For the gymnasium that has a permanent badminton court painted on it, the short service area may serve as the non-volley zone.

Most important of all, it is a safe game not requiring size or strength to enjoy. The fact is, the person who has difficulty with tennis, racquetball, or handball because of the speed of the ball will find greater success with the moderately paced pickle-ball game.

Basic Rules

1. *Court.* The size of the court is 20 × 44 feet for both doubles and singles. The net is hung at 36 inches on ends, and hangs 34 inches in the middle. When laying out a court, allow adequate space—3 to 5 feet at each end and 1 to 2 feet at the sides—of the court boundary lines for player movement. However, it should be noted that many families play pickle-ball with little or no back and side court and enjoy the game (Figure 16-9).

2. *Serve.* The player must keep one foot behind the back line when serving. The serve is made underhand. The paddle must pass below the waist. The server must hit the ball in the air on the serve. Bouncing the ball before hitting it is not allowed. The service is made diagonally crosscourt and must clear the non-volley zone. Only one serve attempt is allowed, except if the ball touches the net on the serve and lands in the proper service court. Then the serve may be taken over. At the start of each new game, the first serving team is allowed only *one* fault before giving up the ball to the opponents. Thereafter, both members of each team will serve and fault before the ball is turned over to the opposing team. When the receiving team wins the serve, the player in the right hand court will always start play.

3. *Volley.* To volley a ball means to hit it in the air without first letting it bounce. All volleying must be done with player's feet *behind* the non-volley zone line (Figure 16-10). Note: It is a fault if the player steps over the line on his volley follow-through.

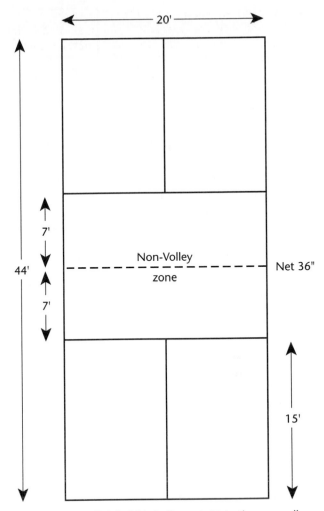

Figure 16-9 Official pickle-ball court. Note the non-volley zones. (Diagrams of Figures 16-9 through 16-13 courtesy of Pickle-Ball, Inc., Seattle, WA.)

Figure 16-10 Position of players at net when volleying.

4. *Double-bounce rule.* Each team must play its first shot off the bounce. That is, the receiving team must let the serve bounce, and the serving team must let the return of the serve bounce before playing it. After the two bounces have occurred, the ball can be either volleyed or played off the bounce (Figure 16-11).

Figure 16-11 Illustration of double-bounce rule.

5. *Fault*
   a. Hitting the ball out-of-bounds
   b. Not clearing net
   c. Stepping into the non-volley zone and volleying the ball
   d. Volleying the ball before it has bounced once on each side of the net, as outlined in Rule 4

6. *Scoring.* A team shall score a point only when serving. A player who is serving shall continue to do so until a fault is made by his team. The game is played to 11 points; however, a team must win by 2 points.

Position of Players for Doubles at Start of Game

Determining Serving Team. Players may toss a coin or rally the ball until a fault is made. Winner of the toss or rally has the option of serving first or not serving first.

Doubles Play. Two alternate positions for players are shown in Figures 16-12 and 16-13.

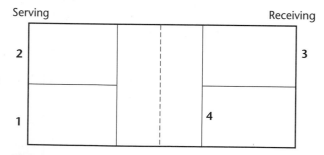

Figure 16-12 Position of players for doubles at start of game.

1. Player 1 in right-hand court (see Figure 16-13A) serves diagonally across court to receiver (3) in opposite right-hand court. The ball must clear the non-volley zone and land in the right-hand serving court. The receiver (3) must let the ball bounce before returning the serve. Serving team must *also* let the return bounce before playing it (Rule #4: Double Bounce Rule). After the two bounces have occurred, the ball may then be either volleyed or played off the bounce until a fault is made.

2. If the fault is made by the receiving team, a point is scored by the serving team. When the serving team wins a point, its players will switch courts and the *same* player will continue to serve. When the serving team makes its first fault, players will stay in the same court, and the second partner will then serve (see Figure 16-13B). When they make their second fault, they will stay in the same courts and turn the ball over to the other team. Players switch courts only after scoring. A ball landing on any line is considered good.

Singles Play. All rules apply, with the following exception: When serving in singles, each player serves from the right-hand court when his score is zero or an even number, and from the left-hand court when his score is odd numbered.

Equipment

Paddle

The official pickle-ball racquet is generally made of hardwood or a good quality plywood. The squared-off head should not exceed 8 inches in width nor

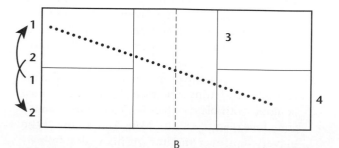

Figure 16-13 Doubles play: (A) Serve by Player 1; (B) serve by Player 2.

Figure 16-14 Note cord around wrist to prevent paddle from slipping from hand.

15½ inches in length. A racquetball paddle, any strung paddle, or paddle with holes is not legal. A cord should be attached to the butt end of the handle for safety purposes; the wrist should be inserted through the cord so the paddle does not come off during play (Figure 16-14).

Balls. The official perforated ball used in pickle-ball is 3 inches in diameter. Various sizes of whiffle balls may be used in a physical education class. Generally, the larger the ball, the slower the game. For smaller children, the larger ball is easier to strike and to "watch" into the hitting area.

Net. A badminton or a tennis net may be used in the game of pickle-ball. Wooden standards may be constructed and strung across a gymnasium floor to make up several pickle-ball courts for class play.

Suggested Learning Sequence

A. Nature and purpose of pickle-ball.
B. Acquainting players with equipment, court size.
C. Skills and techniques. Relate skills to tennis techniques; use drills to develop forehand and backhand drives, lobs, service, and volleys. Use practice drills using rebound volleying against a wall; play mini-games using only the forehand or backhand. Combine game-like drills as you begin introducing rules of the game.
   1. Grip, stance, and footwork
   2. Forehand and backhand drives
   3. Service—lob, drive
   4. Volley—forehand and backhand
   5. Lob
D. Rules of the game. Introduce the rules when appropriate; introduce the non-volley zone and rules governing net play as soon as possible.

E. Strategy. Strategy can be introduced with a skill as soon as appropriate levels of skill are attained. Game-like drills that combine elements of strategy and are introduced early help the player learn more quickly.
F. Game play.

Skills and Techniques

The techniques and skills required to play pickle-ball are identical for the most part with those used in tennis. Refer to Chapter 23 for the skill breakdowns for the eastern grip, the stance or ready position, forehand and backhand drives, the forehand and backhand volley, and the lob. Good footwork is also essential in pickle-ball. For movement to the ball requiring two steps or less, slide your feet into position. Use drills placing the player in a ready position and sliding the feet from side-to-side in that position. For balls hit further away, such as the lob over the head to the backcourt, turn and run to the ball while looking over the shoulder toward the net to note where opponents may be moving.

Service. There are two types of service. The first drives the ball over the net in a flat arc, while the second type of service results in an arc best describing a lob. When initiating the serve, there are three important rules to remember: (1) The paddle must pass below the waist in the serving motion; (2) the ball must be dropped and hit out of the air; and (3) one foot must remain behind the back line.

Lob Serve. The lob serve (Figure 16-15) is used as a defensive technique to keep the opponents in the backcourt area. This high arcing serve will tend to bounce higher and keep the opponent in a defensive mode.

▶ **Learning Hints**
   1. Standing with the paddle side foot behind the other and facing the net, the body is in a ready position.
   2. The weight is transferred from the back foot to front foot, the ball is dropped just forward of the front foot.
   3. The paddle arm swings forward and with the face of the paddle perpendicular to the direction of the serve, the paddle makes contact with the ball opposite the front foot.
   4. The arm continues forward and upward giving the ball the necessary lift for a high arcing serve.

Drive Serve. The drive serve (Figure 16-16) is an effective defensive serve when executed correctly. This low, flat arcing serve will land deep in the opponent's backcourt, forcing the player away from the volley zone.

Figure 16-15 The lob serve. Note that racquet contacts ball below waist.

Figure 16-16 The drive serve.

➤ Learning Hints

1. Standing with the paddle side foot behind the other and facing the net, the body assumes a ready position (knees flexed, bent at waist).
2. The weight is transferred from the back foot to the forward foot, and the ball is dropped opposite the forward foot.
3. The paddle arm swings forward; the wrist is cocked.
4. At contact opposite the front foot, the wrist is snapped through, and the forearm is pronated as the follow-through is executed.

➤ Practice/Organizational Suggestions

It is important to emphasize that the serve must be in play in order to score points; therefore, consistent serving is essential to the game. Practice serves for 5 to 7 minutes at the beginning of each class period.

Zones can be outlined on the floor and serves directed toward specific zones. Players will get a feel for how hard to hit the two serves.

The key to the lob serve is the height and depth of the serve. Standards with a badminton net placed across the back of the non-volley zone at a height of 10 to 15 feet will force the server to practice hitting the ball high enough to carry to the backcourt.

The key to the drive serve is also the height and depth. For helpful practice, use standards with a string across the court at a height of 4 to 5 feet above official net height; direct the server to hit the ball over the regulation net height but below the string.

Practice drills for the other strokes can be adapted from those described for tennis in Chapter 23.

Playing Strategy

1. Serves are most effective when hit into the far backcourt and into the corners. It is best to vary the serve, however, to keep your opponent off balance.
2. To receive the serve, place yourself in a ready position behind the back line; this enables you to return either a drive serve or a lob serve. Return the service in the backcourt and corners. Vary the placement of the shot so your opponent is forced to hit a backhand or a forehand.
3. Force your opponent to move from side to side and up and back.
4. In doubles, try to take control of the net by forcing your opponents to hit shots from the backline.
5. In doubles, hit the ball down the center of the court occasionally; this forces opponents to make choices that sometimes put them out of position to hit the return.
6. Use a lob shot occasionally when you have drawn your opponent to the net. If you and your opponent are near the net, however, use a lob as a defensive technique to allow you to get back into position.

Safety Considerations

1. Always wear the strap around your wrist so if the paddle slips from your hands, it stays with you.
2. Warm up properly before starting the game. Stretching exercises for the shoulder girdle, hamstrings, and abductors of the legs are recommended.
3. Get used to calling for the ball so as to minimize impact with your doubles partner.

Modifications for Special Populations

Orthopedically Impaired

See modifications discussed in Chapter 23 (tennis) and Chapter 14 (handball/racquetball).

Cognitively Impaired

Minimal modifications are needed.

Sensory Impaired

See modifications discussed in the Chapter 23 (tennis) and Chapter 14 (handball/racquetball).

Terminology

Approach shot A shot hit inside the baseline while approaching the net.

Backcourt The area near the non-volley zone and baseline.

Backhand Stroke hit on the opposite side of the hand holding the paddle.

Baseline The end line of the pickle-ball court.

Down-the-line A shot hit near a sideline that travels close to, and parallel with, the same line from where it was initially hit.

Drive A low shot that is hit near the opponent's backcourt.

Drop shot A ground stroke hit in such a way that the ball drops just over the net into the non-volley zone.

Error A mistake made by a player during competition.

Fault A serve that lands out-of-bounds or out of court area.

Foot fault Failure on the server's part to keep at least one foot behind the baseline during the serve.

Forehand The shot hit on the right side of a right-handed player.

Game A game is determined in pickle-ball when one side has reached 11 points; however, a team must win by 2 points.

Half-volley A ball hit only inches from the court surface after the initial bounce.

Let Any point that must be replayed.

Let serve A serve that touches the top of the net and falls in the proper service court; it must be replayed.

Lob A ball hit sufficiently high to pass over the reach of an opponent but falls within the court.

Non-volley zone The 7-foot area on either side of the net. A player may not step into the non-volley zone to play a ball before it bounces or on the follow-through of a stroke.

Pace The speed of the ball.

Passing shot The shot that passes beyond the reach of the net player and lands inbounds.

Placement A shot hit inbounds and untouched by an opponent.

Poach To cross over into your partner's territory to play a ball normally played by your partner.

Serve The lob or drive stroke used to put a ball into play at the beginning of the point. The serve must be using an underhand motion.

Smash A shot hit forcefully from above the player's head.

Volley To hit the ball in the air before it bounces on the court.

Further References

Clark, J. F. *Pickleball.* Dubuque, IA: Eddie Bowers Publishing Co., Inc., 1994.

Curtis, J. M. *Pickle-Ball for Player and Teacher.* 2nd ed. Englewood, CO: Morton Publishing, 1989.

Friedenberg, M. *The Official Pickle-ball Handbook.* Federal Way, WA: PB Masters, 1999.

Pickle-Ball Incorporated. Rules and other publications, 3131 Western Ave., Seattle, WA 98121.

Squires, D. *The Other Racquet Sports.* New York: McGraw-Hill, 1978.

Web Sites

www.pickleball.com/ Offers information about the court and history; also offers products and instructional materials.

www.uspa.org/pickleball.htm United States Pickle-Ball Association site; offers an explanation of pickle-ball, information about the USPA, message board, and a source of products.

SHUFFLEBOARD

Nature and Purpose

Shuffleboard may be played by two people *(singles)* or by four *(doubles)*. The game is played by propelling round wooden discs by means of a cue stick with a curved end over a hard, smooth surface on which the outlines of the court have been drawn.

The Court. The court is 52 feet long and 6 feet wide, with a triangular target and scoring diagram at each end (see Figure 16-17). One end of the court is designated as the head of court and the other as the foot of court.

Equipment. Each player is provided with a cue stick measuring 6 feet 3 inches maximum; it must have no metal parts touching the playing surface. There are two sets of discs, four in each set—one set painted red and the other black. The discs must be 6 inches in diameter, weigh not less than 11½ ounces nor more than 15 ounces, with thickness ranging from ¾ inch to 1 inch. Shuffleboard can be easily adapted to many types of surfaces; shuffleboard courts can be painted on the floors of classrooms, gymnasiums, hallways, sidewalks, or other concrete surfaces found at schools. Shuffleboard sets are available from most suppliers of physical education and recreation equipment at a very reasonable price. The discs are usually made of a durable composition material that can be used both indoors and outdoors.

Choice of disc color is made by playing one disc to the farthest deadline, with the player of the disc closest to it receiving his choice of colors. In starting a game, the owner of red discs shoots first, followed by black, then by red, alternating thus until all discs are shot. In singles play, after all discs are shot from head of court, the players walk to foot of court and, after tallying the score, continue play toward head of court with the owner of black discs shooting first.

In doubles, with two players at each end of the court, a game is started with the owners of red discs

Figure 16-17 Shuffleboard court.

shooting all discs first from the head of court, followed by owners of black discs. Owners of red discs again shoot first from the foot of court, followed by black. On the second round, owners of black discs shoot first at each end of the court, followed by owners of red discs. Playing of all discs from one end of the court and back constitutes a round, so in doubles play, the lead in starting to shoot changes after each round, while in singles play, the lead changes after each half round.

Basic Rules

Scoring. The scoring area contains one 10-point area, two 8-point areas, two 7-point areas, and one 10-off area. In order to count, a disc must lie entirely within one of the scoring areas, with no part of the disc touching any side line, except that the separation line in the 10-off area is not considered. A game may end at 50, 75, or 100 points. Play continues until all discs have been shot, even if game point has been reached during the early part of a half round. In doubles, if a tie score results at game point or over, two additional rounds are played. If the score is still tied, play continues as outlined. In singles, one additional round is played to determine the winner in a tie game. In match play, the winner is determined on the basis of the best two out of three games.

Penalties. From 5 to 10 points are deducted from the player's score for certain infractions of playing rules. Five points are deducted for the following infractions:

1. All discs not in respective half of 10-off area when ready to shoot
2. Discs not played from respective half of 10-off (red played from right side, black from left)
3. Players stepping on or over baseline in making their shot
4. Players not remaining seated when play is toward their end of the court
5. Interfering in any way with opponent while she is making a play
6. Players touching live discs at any time

Ten points are deducted for the following infractions:

1. Player making hesitation or hook shot
2. Player making remarks to disconcert opponent
3. Making any remarks that may be construed as coaching a partner while making a play
4. Player shooting before opponent's disc has come to rest

Playing Rules. A disc returning or remaining on the court after having struck any object other than a live disc is called a *dead disc* and will be removed from the court before the play is resumed. If a dead disc strikes a live disc, that half round will be replayed. A disc that stops in the area between the farthest deadline and starting point will be considered dead and be removed from the court. Any disc that stops just beyond the farthest baseline will be moved a distance of at least 8 inches from baseline. Any disc stopping more than halfway over sidelines, or that rests or leans on the edge, will be removed from the court.

Skills and Techniques

The skills involved in playing shuffleboard are very few; however, it is a game requiring the development of touch—to know just how hard to push the disc. It is extremely important for the shuffleboard player to "read" the surface on which the game is being played, since the disc will react with different speeds on different surfaces. In executing the push or forward thrust of the cue, it is important to place the cue against the disc before the pushing action begins. Do not jab at the disc, because this will result in a loss of power. A few important points must be remembered about the push.

> ### ➤ Learning Hints
> 1. The handle is held at the end, weight forward on the feet, body slightly leaning forward.
> 2. Push by straightening out the elbow; the opposite foot steps forward, and the arm straightens and follows through toward the target, with knees flexed.

> ### ➤ Practice/Organizational Suggestions
> 1. Have students line up in squads, one behind the other. Place one student at the end of the court to retrieve discs and push them back to students awaiting their turn. Rotate students from pushing position to retrieving position.
> 2. Place discs in different scoring areas and allow the students to practice pushing the disc out of the area with their own disc.
> 3. Practice shooting for position. Develop "feel" for the push by attempting to push the disc to various boxes. Begin with no competition and then add competition.

Modifications for Special Populations

Orthopedically Impaired

See modifications discussed for field hockey (Chapter 10).

Cognitively Impaired

Minimal modifications are needed.

Sensory Impaired

See modifications discussed in Chapter 10 (field hockey).

Terminology

Cue Stick used to propel discs toward the target.

Dead disc A disc that returns to or remains on the court after having struck an object other than another "live disc." Disc is also dead that stops between farthest deadline and starting line.

Foot of court That end of the court opposite the head.

Head of court That end of the court from which play starts to begin a match.

Hesitation shot This is illegal—the forward motion of the disc must be continuous (no stopping and restarting during the attempt).

Round The playing of all discs from one end of court and back constitutes a round.

Further References

American Association for Health, Physical Education, Recreation and Dance. *Official N.A.G.W.S. Recreational Games and Volleyball Guide.* Current ed. Washington, D.C.: AAHPERD.

McKenzie, P. L. *How to Win at Shuffleboard.* New Smyrna Beach, FL: Luthers, 1989.

National Shuffleboard Association. *Official Rules.* Kissimmee, FL: NSA, Inc., 1965.

Web Sites

www.shuffleboard.net/ Offers information on a variety of shuffleboard games, including rules and the history of shuffleboard.

www.orbonline.net~sandy/home Offers explanation of the game, equipment, history, rules, information about tournaments, and more.

TABLE TENNIS

Nature and Purpose

Table tennis (popularly called ping-pong) may be played by two or four people. Equipment consists of a table with a smooth playing surface, a net, balls, and rackets (also called paddles). The game may be played by both old and young and seems destined to remain one of our most popular recreational activities.

Equipment

The equipment necessary to play table tennis is of simple construction and relatively inexpensive. School physical education programs can have rackets and tables made by the industrial arts department at a very nominal fee. Many physical education and recreation supply companies sell table tennis sets and balls for a very reasonable price. Obviously, as the competitive level and skill increases, more expensive rackets may be wanted.

Table. The table is 9 feet long and 5 feet wide, with a height of 30 inches from floor to top surface (Figure 16-18). Most tables are made of ¾-inch pressed wood or good quality plywood, but other materials can be used. Tables that come in halves and have a collapsible undercarriage are easy to store. Some are constructed so that one half can be folded up into a backdrop and used for a rebound wall in practicing various strokes.

Net. The playing surface is divided by a net secured in the center and parallel with the end lines. The top edge of the net is 6 inches above the playing surface.

Balls. The balls are constructed of celluloid, hollow, 4½ to 4¾ inches in circumference, and weigh between 37 and 41 grains. A good ball should be perfectly

Figure 16-18 Table tennis table.

round and without wobble when spinning. The United States Table Tennis Association seal of approval on a ball is a good indication of quality.

Racket. A variety of rackets (paddles) can be purchased at most sporting goods stores. Some have grips that will fit your hand size. All have a rubber or sponge covering of some type that covers the playing surface. A covering of inverted sponge is most often used and is recommended for all levels of players.

Basic Rules
Singles Game
Scoring. The winner of a match is the player who first scores 21 points, unless both players have 20 points, in which case the winner must gain a 2-point lead in order to win. The choice of ends and service at the start of the game is decided by toss.

Change of Ends and Service. A game is started with the server making five consecutive services. The receiver follows with five services, each player alternating in this fashion for the duration of the game, unless the score becomes 20-all, in which case the receiver will make one serve, followed by the original server with one serve, then the receiver, and so on, until a winner is declared. If the match consists of only one game, or in the deciding game of a match, the players change ends at the score of 10. The player who started at one end of the table in one game starts at the other end in the immediately subsequent game.

The Service. The service is delivered by releasing the ball, without imparting any spin upon release, and striking it with the paddle outside the boundary of the court near the server's end. Finger spins and rubbing the ball against the racket face are illegal. Any spin imparted to the ball must come from action of the racket upon impact with the ball. The ball shall be struck so that it first drops into the server's court and then into the receiver's court by passing directly over or around the net.

A Good Return. A ball having been served or returned in play shall be struck by the player so that it passes directly over or around the net and lands in the opponent's court; if the ball, during play, returns of its own impetus over or around the net, it may be played the same as a returned ball.

Let Ball. The served ball shall be a let if it touches the net or its supports, and later lands in the receiver's court. A let shall also be declared when a serve is made before the receiver is ready, unless the receiver makes an effort to strike the ball. It is a let if either player, because of conditions not under his control, is prevented from making a serve or a return.

Either player loses the point

1. If he or she fails to make a good service, unless a let is declared
2. If a good service or a good return is made by an opponent and the player fails to make a good return
3. If racket, or any part of a player or clothing, touches the net or its supports while the ball is in play
4. If the player moves the table in any way while playing the ball
5. If a player's free hand touches the table while the ball is in play
6. If, at any time, a player volleys the ball. (A volley consists of hitting the ball before it has bounced.)

Doubles Game
The rules for singles games apply to doubles, except as indicated below.

Service Line. A one-eighth-inch white line drawn down the center of the table parallel with the sidelines is called the service line.

A Good Service. The ball must touch first the server's right halfcourt or the center line on the server's side of the net, and then, passing directly over or around the net, touch the receiver's right halfcourt or the center line on the receiver's side of the net.

Choice of Order of Play. The pair who has the right to serve the first five services in any game shall decide which partner shall do so, and the opposing pair shall then decide similarly which shall first be the receiver.

Order of Service. Each server serves for 5 points. At the end of each term of service, the one who was receiving becomes the server, and the partner of the previous server becomes the receiver. This sequence, in which the receiver becomes the server and the partner of the previous server becomes the receiver continues until the end of the game or the score of 20-all. At the score of 20-all, the sequence of serving and receiving continues uninterrupted, except that each player serves only 1 point in turn, and the serve alternates after each point until the end of the game.

Order of Play. After the server makes a good service, a good return is made by the receiver, then by the partner of the server, then by the partner of the receiver, and then by the server, and thereafter each player, in that sequence, shall make a good return.

Skills and Techniques
Table tennis requires much concentration and excellent reactions. Because of the close similarity to tennis, the basic fundamentals regarding stroking the ball

may be applied in some instances. The discussion in this section will deal with some of the beginning skills needed to get the player started.

Grip

The most common grip used by a majority of players is the "shake hands" grip used in tennis (Figure 16-19). The great Chinese players use a grip known as the penholder grip (Figure 16-20); however, this style of grip is usually best only for an attacking type of game.

➤ **Learning Hints**

1. With the racket perpendicular to the floor, grasp the racket as you would shake hands.
2. The last three fingers wrap around the handle and the forefinger lies close to the lower edge of the racket face.

Figure 16-19 Standard "shake hands" grip.

Figure 16-20 Penholder grip.

Strokes

The forehand and backhand push shot should be mastered by the beginner before playing the game. For the right-handed player, the forehand stroke should be used when the ball approaches from the right, and the backhand when the ball approaches from the left. Preparatory to any stroke, the player should assume a good athletic stance in a ready position. The knees are bent, weight is evenly distributed on the forward half of the foot, arms are in front of the body, elbows are bent, and the racket is held parallel with the ground.

When executing both shots, it is important to remember that the ball is directed over the net by a pushing action, not a hitting action. Variations in arm movement and wrist movement will allow spin to be imparted to the ball.

➤ **Learning Hints: Backhand Push**
(Figures 16-21, 16-22)

1. The ball is played in front of the body at the point of highest contact.
2. As the ball approaches, the right arm is drawn back by pivoting at the elbow, the right shoulder back by pivoting past the elbow; the right shoulder turns and is pointed toward the table.
3. Push the racket forward toward the ball, extend the arm in a horizontal plane.
4. Body weight transfers from back foot to forward foot throughout the stroke.

➤ **Learning Hints: Forehand Push**
(Figure 16-23)

1. As the ball approaches, the racket is drawn back; shoulders turn so the left shoulder is pointed toward the table.
2. Push the racket forward toward the ball, arm extended in a horizontal plane; shoulders return.

Figure 16-21 Position of the hand in backhand push.

Chapter 16   Recreational Sports   **257**

Figure 16-22 Position of body during backhand push shot.

Figure 16-23 Position during forehand push shot. Note that the left shoulder is pointing toward the table.

3. Body weight transfers from the back foot to the forward foot throughout the stroke.

Serves

It is important for the beginner to remember that the ball must be stationary, resting freely in the palm of the server's free hand. The ball is then projected upward at least an inch without imparting spin and then falls without hitting anything before being struck. As the ball is falling, it is struck with the paddle. The ball must make contact with the server's side of the table first.

➤ Learning Hints: Topspin Serve (Forehand Side)

1. The body assumes a stance three quarters sideways to the table, the ball rests on the fingers of the left hand, racket assumes position of a forehand push shot (Figure 16-24).
2. The ball is tossed upward; the racket face (slightly closed) comes forward and continues forward after the contact.

Figure 16-24 Ready to serve on the forehand side.

3. As the racket face follows through, it rolls over the top of the ball, thus imparting topspin to the ball.

The mechanics for a backhand topspin serve will be essentially the same, except the serve is initiated from the left side for the right-handed player.

➤ Practice/Organizational Suggestions

1. If a folding table is available, fold up one side perpendicularly so that it can be used as a rebound wall to practice strokes and serves.
2. Practice the toss (6 to 8 inches high) needed for the serve, concentrating on a smooth, rhythmic toss.
3. Practice against a wall, either letting the ball bounce once or volleying the ball as long as possible. As a variation, mark a target (circle or square) on the wall and try to hit the ball into the target.
4. To develop a feel for the racket and ball, continuously tap the ball upward off the face of the racket, then downward, while walking. Note the importance of concentration as this drill is executed.
5. When practicing the strokes and the serve, give equal time to developing skills on the backhand side as well as the forehand side.

Modifications for Special Populations
Orthopedically Impaired

1. See modifications discussed in Chapter 23 (tennis) and Chapter 14 (handball/racquetball).
2. Set up a modified table-top tetherball game. Tether a small whiffleball with a string to a 12- to 16-inch vertical dowel rod. Instead of a regulation paddle, use a large square piece of cardboard strapped to the student's hand.

Cognitively Impaired

Minimal modifications are needed.

Sensory Impaired

See modifications discussed in Chapter 23 (tennis) and Chapter 14 (handball/racquetball).

Terminology

Ace A service that completely eludes the receiver.

Advantage (ad) Next point made after a deuce score. It is "advantage out" if the receiver wins it and "advantage in" if the server wins. The player wins the match who first wins a point after gaining "advantage."

All Term used to denote an equal score; e.g., 20-all.

Backhand Stroke frequently used by right-handed player when returning a ball hit to his left. The paddle is held so that the back of the hand faces the ball; the ball is usually hit with side of paddle opposite the side used in the forehand.

Backspin A ball hit so that top of ball rotates toward the stroker, bottom moving away.

Block shot A half-volley.

Dead ball A ball is dead if a let is called, if the ball bounces twice on the table, and at the conclusion of a point or rally.

Deuce When the score is even at 20-all. To win, a player must score two consecutive points.

Drop shot A shot played so softly that it dies before the opponent can reach it, or places her at a disadvantage if she does play it.

Finger spin An illegal procedure whereby spin is imparted to the ball by the fingers in serving.

Forehand A stroke or volley made in such a fashion that the palm is the leading part of the movement. Usually hit with the opposite face of the paddle than that used in the backhand. In this stroke, the left foot of a right-handed player is toward the table.

Let Means "play the point over" and occurs when the ball strikes the top of net and falls into the correct service court; also if a ball breaks or if a player is interfered with by an official or spectator.

Mixed doubles Doubles game in which each team has one man and one woman player.

Push shot A ball struck with a pushing motion of the paddle near the top of the bounce so that no spin is placed on the ball.

Service court In singles, the entire table area on the receiver's side, 5 by 4½ feet. In doubles, the table is divided by a center line so each service court is 4½ by 2½ feet.

Slice A stroke in which the ball is stroked late so that it tends to spin in a direction away from the paddle.

Topspin A ball stroked so that the top spins forward in the direction of flight. Is the opposite of backspin or underspin.

Volley Illegal stroking of ball while it is in the air and before it has touched the table.

Further References

American Association for Health, Physical Education, Recreation, and Dance. *Official N.A.G.W.S. Individual Sports Guide.* Current ed. Washington, D.C.: AAHPERD.

DeWitt, R. T. and Dugan, K. *Teaching Individual and Team Sports.* 2nd ed. Englewood Cliffs, NJ: Prentice Hall, 1972.

Miles, D. *Sports Illustrated Table Tennis.* Philadelphia: J. B. Lippincott Co., 1974.

Sklorz, M. *Table Tennis.* Yorkshire, England: E.P. Publishing Limited, 1973.

Varner, M. and Harrison, J. R. *Table Tennis.* Dubuque, IA: Wm. C. Brown Company, Publishers, 1968.

United States Table Tennis Association. *Table Tennis For You.* Current ed. Philadelphia: USTTA.

Web Sites

www.tabletennis.about.com/recreation/tabletennis/mbody.htm Offers useful coaching tips, rules, articles of interest, equipment, and what's happening in table tennis around the world.

http://peacock.tnjc.edu.tw/ADD/sport/faq.htm Offers frequently asked questions about table tennis including rules and history.

www.tabletennis.gr/ Offers information about tactics, coaching tips, basics of table tennis, rules, and more.

www.library.thinkquest.org/20570/ Offers information about the sport of table tennis, how to play, types of equipment, skill techniques, terminology, and more.

CHAPTER 17

Skiing: Cross-Country

This chapter will enable you to

- Select equipment best suited to your needs
- Consider the advantages and disadvantages of waxless skis and waxable skis, and know how to wax them
- Understand and apply the concept of "layering" in clothing
- Perform the techniques of getting up from a fall, poling, turning, and striding while moving on flat, downhill, and uphill terrains
- Know what safety precautions to observe when cross-country skiing

Nature and Purpose

The great increase in popularity enjoyed by cross-country skiing can be attributed to many factors. *First* is the relative ease with which Nordic skiing can be learned. To move from one point to another, the skier only has to initiate a walking action, so it is a very natural activity. Unlike the person who engages in Alpine skiing, the touring skier has no lines to wait in, no crowds to endure, no long rides to the ski area, and no tow tickets to purchase. *Second,* the individual can engage in ski touring almost any place where there is no traffic: a country road, over fields, through woods, on hills, or on prepared tracks—these are all appropriate places to cross-country ski. *Third,* there are no age or sex limits; touring provides a good, clean form of recreation for all. It is not uncommon to find family groups—children, parents, and grandparents—gathering on a crisp, winter weekend day to ski tour in local and state parks, woods, or other scenic areas. In addition, many touring centers or local clubs in the United States now sponsor Citizens Races of varying distances, much like the marathons engaged in by many joggers. The purpose of the Citizens Races is not only competition but also the opportunity to participate with hundreds of other people and to test yourself.* *Fourth,* ski touring is an excellent physical conditioner, especially when performed in a smooth, rhythmic manner over a prolonged period of time. Research studies indicate that the cross-country skier expends a great deal of energy in this physically demanding sport. *Finally,* ski touring equipment is reasonably priced at the beginner level; many stores offer ski packages that include bindings, boots, poles, and skis for $100–130. For the person who wishes to try out the activity, several outdoor stores or state parks will rent the necessary equipment for less than $15 a day.

School Programs. Several high school and college physical education programs include cross-country skiing as part of the regular curriculum. Many stores and state parks will rent equipment to schools for a reasonable price and in some instances will provide basic instruction. Many of the beginning techniques can be learned in two or three sessions, so the student can soon participate on flat and slightly rolling terrain. Obviously, the more rugged terrain and steeper hills and valleys require more advanced techniques that take longer to develop. Although advanced techniques are beyond the scope of this chapter, information may be found among the Further References.

Programs for the Physically Challenged. Cross-country skiing is an activity that also appeals to the blind and the partially sighted, the deaf, and those with limb amputations. Instruction programs for the physically challenged enable special populations to enjoy this wonderful form of exercise and recreation. Several organizations that can supply additional information are listed in Further References.

*Further information about the Citizens Race can be obtained by writing to the Citizen and Club Cross-Country Racing Committee, United States Ski Association, 1726 Champa Street, Denver , CO 80202.

Equipment

Twenty years ago, the individual interested in ski touring would have found a limited selection of equipment from which to choose. Today, however, almost every Alpine ski manufacturer has added a line of ski-touring equipment. For the beginning skier, the selection process can indeed be mystifying and frustrating; therefore, it is best to consult an expert before buying any equipment. The most important consideration for the beginner is that the equipment function properly and serve the skier through and after the initial stages of learning and participation.

Skis

Cross-country skis are categorized according to their use. *Racing skis,* which are narrow (35 to 45 mm) and very light, are designed specifically for competitive skiing. *Mid-touring skis* are heavier and slightly wider (40 to 50 mm). Beginners, novices, and recreational skiers frequently use the mid-touring ski. The *touring ski* is still wider (45 to 60 mm) and heavier than the racing or mid-touring ski. Many beginners learn on this type of ski because it is heavier, provides greater stability, and can withstand greater abuse. Many learn-to-ski programs rent this type of ski to the beginner. The touring ski is also used by the expert for deep-powder skiing, because the extra width helps keep the ski above the surface rather than sinking into the snow.

Skis come in assorted lengths and should be selected according to your body build and sex. The following is a general guide to use in selecting proper ski length. While standing on the floor, raise your arm straight up. For a woman or girl, the tip of the ski should come to the wrist; for a man or boy, the tip should come to mid-palm of the hand (Figure 17-1). If you are a heavy person, consider a stiffer ski; if you are light, consider a more flexible ski.

One very important factor is whether to choose the waxable or waxless type of ski. Cross-country skis are designed to grip the snow's surface in order to obtain a good forward motion. The gripping action of the ski bottom to the snow results from the use of various waxes (the points of the snow flakes actually penetrate the wax to allow it to grip when pressure is applied to the kick zone) or, in the case of waxless skis, a specially designed indented surface that grips the snow (Figure 17-2). Although cross-country skis are generally made of a combination of wood and synthetic materials, most bottom surfaces are synthetic rather than wood, making them more impervious to moisture.

The waxless ski is easy to maintain and for that reason would perhaps better serve the occasional skier. There are, however, some disadvantages to this type of surface. The waxless bottom is not as adaptable to changing snow conditions as are waxable skis. Application of different waxes in the kick zone is generally not possible, thus prohibiting maximum gripping performance. Additionally, the waxless ski sacrifices high-level performance and speed. However, a majority of beginners and recreational skiers find the waxless ski to be very satisfactory for their purposes.

Waxable skis are used by the ski purist and by the skier who wants the fun of waxing skis. The obvious advantage is that different waxes can be applied for different snow conditions, thus ensuring a good kick and glide. Waxing skis takes time and requires some basic knowledge of snow conditions. It is also an additional expense and bother that some

Figure 17-1 Determining proper ski length. Tip comes to mid-palm for men and to the wrist for women.

Figure 17-2 Types of bottom surfaces found on "waxless" cross-country skis: (A) fish scale pattern, (B) step pattern.

Figure 17-3 A three-pin binding.

skiers would rather do without. Waxing is described in detail at the end of this chapter.

Bindings

Bindings enable the boot to be attached to the ski. There are several types: Some have cables that go around the bottom of the boot; others have cables that clamp the top of the boot to the ski. For the beginner and recreational skier, the traditional three-pin binding is most commonly used (Figure 17-3). It consists of three pins that are projected or inserted into the sole at the toe end of the boot; a metal bar or clamp called a bale is then pushed down and held by a projection on the binding. The bale can generally be released by applying pressure to the projection on the bar or clamp. Most toe bindings are made of metal, although some manufacturers have developed a plastic binding. All bindings are "norm fitted;" that is, they will fit any size boot. There are various norm sizes. The general size for the recreational skier is either a 75-mm Nordic norm (width of the toe boot) or a 50-mm Nordic norm. Newer, more sophisticated binding systems are available that may use a different design to secure the boot to the binding. Most, however, require some type of clamp to secure the boot to the ski (Figure 17-4). Bindings can be purchased separately, but it is best that they be mounted by an expert.

Boots

A proper-fitting boot is perhaps the key to successful cross-country skiing. Boots should be selected on the basis of comfort to the skier. The boot should be flexible enough across the crease so that it does not cut off circulation to the toes or cut across the toes. The skier should try on the boot, wearing the socks used

Figure 17-4 A clamp binding found on some newer systems.

for skiing. The heel of the boot should be snug, there should not be much side-to-side flexibility, and there should be plenty of room in the toes. Generally, a space about the width of a finger at the end of the big toe indicates proper length.

A light touring boot is best for the beginner and recreational skier (Figure 17-5). This boot is usually made of leather and comes in either a low cut or a high cut (gives more warmth) and should be set in a reinforced plastic or metal plate. Boots usually range in price from $20 and up. Before the first use, it is important to apply a waterproofing conditioner and let the boots dry well. If properly taken care of, boots will last for several years.

Figure 17-5 A light touring boot.

Poles

Poles are used to aid in propelling the skier forward or as a means of balance and support. The pole consists of a grip, a strap, a basket, and a metal point that is bent to facilitate extraction from the snow. The poles can be made of a carbon fiber material, fiberglass, aluminium, or bamboo (Tonkin poles). Because poles tend to take a lot of abuse, the bamboo pole is the least durable. Most skiers prefer the fiber-material pole, which can be found in most stores.

The three key factors to look for when selecting a pair of poles are the length, the type of strap, and the size of the basket. To check for proper length, as you stand on the floor, the pole should fit snugly under your armpit (Figure 17-6). A pole that is too long or too short will hinder the skier's movement. The strap should be adjustable in order to allow the skier to make adjustments to the size of the gloves or mittens worn on the hand. Baskets, which are generally made of plastic, should be of medium size. Large baskets are used for deep-powder snow, whereas smaller baskets are used by the competitive racer. Poles usually begin at $10.

Clothing

In addition to comfortable boots, what clothing to wear and how much are very important considerations. Remember that cross-country skiing involves total body movement and a great expenditure of energy. As a result, tremendous amounts of heat can be generated, and therefore overdressing will result in overheating. The best way to dress, as recommended by many experts, is based on the "layering" principle (i.e., by wearing layers of loose-fitting clothing). Layering enables the skier to add or subtract articles of clothing according to the prevailing weather conditions. The following are important points to remember when selecting suitable ski wear.

1. A non–moisture-absorbing layer (polypropylene material) should be worn next to the skin. This enables moisture and perspiration to pass out to your middle layer of clothing.
2. Avoid fabrics that do not breathe, because they tend to hold in heat and moisture. Fabrics that are water repellent are preferable to fabrics that are waterproof.
3. Outer garments should be of a nonabsorbent material. Occasionally a skier falls and then snow clings to the material and may wet the inside layers.
4. Because much heat is lost through the head, wear a warm woolen knit hat or head covering big enough to be pulled down over the ears.
5. Loose-fitting pants or knickers are recommended to allow freedom of movement. A wool sweater or turtleneck shirt plus a nylon shell will keep the skier warm and dry under most conditions.
6. Wear a light inner pair of polypropylene socks and a pair of woolen knee-length socks on top to keep the feet and legs warm and dry.

Figure 17-6 Judging the length of the ski pole. It should fit snugly beneath the armpit.

Figure 17-7 A pair of gaiters helps keep boots and ankles dry.

7. Wear mittens with a down fill or a light wool lining and a leather outer shell. Leather gloves with a warm lining are preferred by many because they give better control in handling the poles.

Other accessories include gaiters, an outer covering that keeps the lower legs dry (Figure 17-7); a fanny pack or knapsack to carry emergency materials, a repair kit, waxes, or extra clothes; and insulated vests. The cost of these items varies with the type and the quality. The important thing to remember, no matter what you spend, is that the layering of loose-fitting garments permits the cross-country skier to adapt to all types of weather conditions.

Suggested Learning Sequence

Cross-country skiing can take place during various weather conditions and on different types of terrain (uphill, downhill, the flat). The sequence suggested here begins on the flat, preferably with prepared tracks, and then proceeds to the uphill and downhill. The skills and techniques described are for the beginner to beginner-intermediate level of recreational cross-country skiing.

A. Nature and purpose
  1. Ski touring as a recreational sport
  2. Selecting equipment
  3. How to dress—what to wear
  4. Safety—introduced at appropriate times, when most meaningful
B. Conditioning—should begin prior to instruction on the slopes and should continue during the ski season
C. Waxing techniques
D. Skills and techniques
  1. On the Flat
    a. Getting up from a fall
    b. Diagonal stride
    c. Diagonal stride/Single poling
    d. Double poling
    e. Double poling/Stride
    f. Kick turn
  2. Uphill
    a. Diagonal stride
    b. Side step
    c. Traversing
    d. Herringbone
  3. Downhill
    a. Straight running
    b. Snow plow turn
    c. Step turn
    d. Traversing

Skills and Techniques

The skills and techniques discussed in this section are for the beginner and beginner-intermediate recreational cross-country skier. There are several pretechniques that can be practiced prior to beginning on the snow. These can be done on a carpeted area. If waxable skis are used, they should be free of wax.

➤ Practice/Organizational Suggestions: Carpeted Area

1. Familiarize yourself with how the binding on the ski works. Put on the boots and insert the toe in the binding so that the three pins are inserted into the three holes at the bottom of the toe.
2. With both skis on, side step; move the tails of the skis, keeping the tips fairly stationary; move around in a circle.
3. Slide the skis forward, approximating a walking action. Get the feel of the opposite arm and leg moving forward as the skis slide forward.
4. Learn to grasp the pole properly (Figure 17-8). Insert the hand through the strap, with thumb up; grasp the strap and pole grip. The skier should feel pressure at the bottom of the V of the thumb and index finger if gripping properly. As the arm pushes backward during the poling phase, the hand will release the pole; however, pressure of the strap should always be felt at the junction of thumb and index finger.
5. Lift one ski, then the other, to note the action of the ski to boot and to develop a sense of balance. Because the heel is free from the binding, often the tail will fall, causing the beginner to catch the snow and fall during side stepping or a kick turn.

Skiing on the Flat

It is best to start learning to cross-country ski on the flat. A facility that has pre-made tracks aids the beginner by placing the skis in the proper track while

A

B

C

Figure 17-8 Grasping the pole. The strap lies beneath the palm of the hand.

skiing. (When skiing alone in the wilderness you are not very likely to find any pre-laid tracks.) If no tracks are available, any flat ground with a shallow covering of powder snow will also serve the purpose.

Getting Up from a Fall. All skiers at one time or another find themselves on the ground, either as a result of a fall or as a deliberate means of slowing down. If on a hill or flat, the following method will enable you to resume a standing position (Figure 17-9).

➤ **Learning Hints**

1. Holding a pole in each hand, assume a position perpendicular to your skis. If you are on a hillside, the skis must also be perpendicular to the slope, with the skis on the downhill side. Now tuck the knees up under the body.
2. Roll to a kneeling position on the skis, with poles planted and held to either side for stability.
3. Slide one ski forward so one knee is at a 90-degree angle; then merely stand up.

Diagonal Stride—Single Poling

The diagonal stride is to cross-country skiing as walking is to moving forward. The diagonal stride is a smooth, vigorous, rhythmical walking action that must be mastered by all beginners (Figure 17-10). Opposite arm and leg action are used, just as when walking in a vigorous fashion, while the other arm and leg serve as a counterbalance to maintain proper body position. The stride involves a kick (pushoff) of the ski and forward slide, followed by the repeat action of the other ski as it is brought forward. A planting and downward and backward push of the ski pole aids the glide forward. This skill is used on flats and going up slight inclines. An accentuated motion can be used for moving up steeper inclines.

➤ **Learning Hints**

1. The head is up, and the skier is looking forward; the body leans forward slightly. The knees are comfortably flexed, and the weight is forward over the center of the skis on the balls of the feet.
2. The right arm reaches forward as the left leg slides forward. Place the left pole opposite the left foot, push downward and backward with the pole and push off with the right foot. As the glide slows, repeat the action on the opposite side.
3. From the pole plant, the arm will extend behind as the push is completed, knees remaining flexed through the action. The pole is released from the snow, and the arm is swung forward as the pole is regripped.

Double Poling/Kick

Double poling is a variation used as a change of pace from the single poling done with the diagonal stride. It is a powerful action that may be used when the skiing surface is crusty or a bit icy. Both arms are brought forward, the poles are planted opposite the toes, and a vigorous downward and backward push of the arms combined with a bending and compression of the upper body forward at the waist is initiated (Figure 17-11). The arms travel past the hips,

A

B

C

D

Figure 17-9 Getting up from a fall. Note the skier rolls to his knees, with knees straddling the uphill ski.

A   B

Figure 17-10 The diagonal stride. Note weight is forward, knees are flexed.

and the hands are released from the poles. A kick or stride may be added to this movement by simultaneously sliding the right or left ski forward as the arms swing forward. The opposite leg initiates the kick; near the end of the push, the poles are planted and the arms and upper body execute the double-poling technique (Figure 17-12).

➤ **Learning Hints**

1. Weight should be evenly distributed on both skis—knees flexed, weight on the balls of the feet.

2. As the arms are brought forward and the poles are planted, the arms will be slightly flexed at the elbow.

A

A

B

B

C

C

Figure 17-11 Double poling. Note compression of the back and extension of the arms upon completion.

Figure 17-12 The double pole and kick.

3. The upper back is compressed forward at the waist as the arms continue to push downward and backward through extension.

Kick Turn

The kick turn is a technique used to change the skier to an opposite direction while standing on the flat or hillside. Although it may appear difficult, it is quite easy for the beginning skier to master.

➤ **Learning Hints**

1. While standing with the skis together, plant the poles (used as balance) behind the body.
2. Turn the body to the right, pick up the right ski and turn so it faces the opposite direction of the left ski.
3. With weight on the right ski, pick up the left ski and swing it around so that it is parallel with the right ski.

► **Practice/Organizational Suggestions: On the Flat**

1. Without poles, begin by walking with the skis, to develop a sense of balance and rhythm. Focus on sliding the skis forward.
2. Without poles, kick (push off) on one ski and return to starting position; then push off with the opposite ski. Combine a kick (push) followed immediately by the same action of the opposite ski. Add a vigorous pumping action with arms to approximate the action used with single poling.
3. Combine poling with the diagonal stride. Emphasis should be on the forward plant opposite the foot with one pole, while the other arm is fully extended behind, and then the consequent downward push and extension of arm. The same drill may be used to practice double poling.
4. To practice double poling with a stride, begin by striding with only the left or right leg until you feel comfortable coordinating the kick, pole plant, and push; then add alternating strides.
5. Practice the kick turn on the flat without poles; then try using poles. Next, proceed to the hillside and practice there.

Moving Uphill

Obviously not all cross-country skiing is done on a flat surface. The skier must learn to negotiate slopes as well. The easiest method for going uphill is using the diagonal stride described above. Where the slope is fairly steep, the action resembles a running motion with little or no glide during the concluding phases of the stride; thus the kick and stride will be shorter. It is important to remember to keep the weight well forward and knees flexed as you are moving uphill.

Side Stepping.   When the beginning skier encounters a slope too steep to execute by means of the diagonal stride, the side stepping skill may be used.

► **Learning Hints**

1. Assume a position crosswise to the hill.
2. With the edges pressing into the side of the hill, step off with the downhill ski, and step up with the uphill ski.
3. Use the downhill pole to help push off with the downhill ski, keeping your weight into the hill.

Traverse.   Traversing is another means to travel uphill. Traversing is merely a diagonal stride combined with a slight uphill movement. The skier strides toward a point, then executing either a kick turn or a turn using a herringbone side-stepping action, changes direction going uphill across the face of the slope. The skier actually will move back and forth across the face of the hill while moving uphill toward the top.

► **Learning Hints**

1. Setting the skis crosswise to the hill, move forward using a diagonal stride. The movement is slightly uphill.
2. Weight should be forward, keeping the edges of the skis set into the hill. The steeper the hill, the greater amount of edge setting will be necessary.

The Herringbone.   Although the herringbone is the most tiring way to climb a hill, it must be used when climbing up a steeper slope. The technique can best be described as a series of Vs made by an alternating series of steps in which the ski tips are spread apart and the tails are kept fairly close together (Figure 17-13). In a V position, the poles are planted behind the skis; the edge of the skis are set with weight on the inside edge. As the right foot picks up the ski, the right pole is planted and used to maintain balance and pushoff; the process is then repeated on the other side.

► **Learning Hints**

1. With weight forward and knees flexed, spread tips of skis apart and keep heels together.
2. Set the weight on the inside edges by shifting weight to the inside of each foot.
3. Plant one pole behind the skis; step up, plant the other pole, and step up.

► **Practice/Organizational Suggestions**

For the beginning skier, these uphill techniques can be practiced first on the flat, then on a gradual incline before attempting a steeper hill.

1. On a moderate incline, practice setting an edge as might be used in side stepping. Emphasis should be on rolling the ankle so weight is on the inside of the downhill ski and on the outside of the uphill ski. Practice climbing 10 to 12 steps.

Figure 17-13 The herringbone climb, a method of climbing uphill.

2. The same exercise may be used for the herringbone as previously described. However, note that the weight is set on the inside of each ski as the step is made.

Moving Downhill

Once the skier reaches the top of a hill, it is usually necessary to go down. On slight inclines, the skier may go straight down, but on steeper hills it becomes necessary to slow down and even to turn in some manner to avoid running into an obstacle. At times, the best way to slow down is simply by sitting down. Before you used this method, however, make sure you know how to assume a standing position once again.

In moving downhill, the skier must remember a few key points. First, the weight must be centered or slightly forward over the skis; if not, the skier may lose balance and fall. Second, the hands must be held in front of the body so that the weight is placed properly over the skis. If the hands are allowed to fall behind and to the back of the body, they cause the weight to shift backward, resulting in a loss of balance and control. Finally, the skier should prevent the poles from dragging behind or becoming snagged in the snow, on a bush, or on any obstacle, because this would also result in a loss of balance and possible fall.

Straight Running. As the name implies, in straight running, the skier goes straight down a hill. For the beginning skier, this technique is used on hills with a gradual incline. In addition to the points previously discussed, the following hints are important.

➤ Learning Hints

1. Body weight is over the center of the skis; the skis are shoulder-width apart.
2. The knees must be flexed, the upper body is bent at the waist, with hands held in front, head up and looking ahead, poles tucked under the arms, parallel to the skis.

Snow Plow—Snow Plow Turn. An easy method to learn for slowing down is the snow plow. To slow down, push the skis apart at the tails, and transfer weight to the inside edges; the tips remain 6 to 8 inches apart, forming a V. To turn in this position, merely transfer the weight to the inside of one ski.

➤ Learning Hints

1. The knees are flexed more than normal as the body is lowered slightly. By exerting pressure through the inside of the heels, the skier pushes the ski tails outward, while the ski tips remain close together.
2. Body weight is slightly forward; pressure is placed on the inside edges of the ski by moving knees inward and slightly rolling the ankles.

3. To turn in this position, merely transfer more weight to the inside of one ski, and you will turn in the opposite direction. Pressure to the inside of the left ski will result in a right turn, and vice versa.

Step Turn. A step turn is frequently used to change direction, to go around a corner, or to avoid an object on the ground (Figure 17-14). The turn is executed from a glide while running straight downhill or while on the flat. The skis should be flat preparatory to initiating the turn. The steps themselves are a series of short steps, tips leading to the side, rather than wide steps. If going downhill, the stepping action is quicker than on a slight incline.

➤ Learning Hints

1. Turn the head and drop the shoulder slightly in the direction of the turn.
2. While lifting the tip of the inside ski, shift the weight from the outside ski, stepping onto the inside ski in the direction of the turn.
3. For tighter turns, quicken the steps.
4. Keep the hands in front of the body throughout the movement.

➤ Practice/Organizational Suggestions: Downhill Techniques

Begin developing the downhill techniques on a gradual slope before moving on to a steeper slope.

1. On a long gradual hill, begin by first straight running. Execute a snow plow with tails apart, then allow skis to return to a straight run position, then repeat the snow plow. Practice using this combination several times.
2. For snow plow turns, place stakes several feet apart on a long gradual hill and practice turning around one to one side and then another to the other side. Practice until you feel comfortable turning in both directions.
3. For the step turn, use stakes to design a course that forces you to step in different directions while moving on the flat and downhill.
4. Practice getting up from a fall while on the flat and while on a hillside. Emphasis should be on assuming a good base of support (crouch position) and use of poles.

Waxing

The art of waxing becomes more important as the skier's approach becomes more serious. Waxing is optional on the waxless ski, but it is essential on the waxable ski. For the waxless ski (fish scale pattern or step pattern; see Figure 17-2), you may apply a base wax to the whole surface and a glide wax on the tips and tails of the skis. The base wax is applied with a

Figure 17-14 The step turn. Note the head and shoulder drop in the direction of the turn.

hot iron and then ironed on evenly onto the surface. Care must be taken to move the iron quickly over the surface so as not to burn the base. The glide wax may be rubbed on by hand and then smoothed down with a cork. Most recreational skiers will never need to wax their waxless-bottomed skis.

For waxable skis, a two-wax system is recommended: one for snow conditions below freezing and the other for above-freezing temperatures. The wax is applied to the kicker zone of the ski so that the ski will grip when pressure is applied to that area but will release and glide smoothly when the pressure (kick) is completed. Manufacturers have color-coded the waxes to give the best results at varying snow temperatures. Usually, the green- to blue-colored waxes, which are harder waxes, are used for lower temperatures, whereas the red- and violet-colored waxes, which are softer, are used for higher temperatures.

For the beginning skier using waxable skis, it is recommended that the base wax be applied at the ski shop at the time of purchase. For subsequent care, a ski wax kit can be purchased that contains all the equipment needed. Such a kit should contain two to three kicker waxes, two to three glide waxes, a scraper to remove old wax, and a cork to smooth the surface.

Safety and Courtesy

1. Check equipment before you begin to ski, and make sure it is in proper working condition.
2. Use good judgment when skiing with people of lesser ability. Make sure all people are familiar with the trail and ski within their physical limits and on terrain appropriate to their level of skill.
3. Get yourself in good physical condition several weeks before engaging in a vigorous touring or racing program.
4. If skiing on a course that has pre-made tracks, let faster skiers have the right of way.
5. Be aware that the wind chill factor can make the air feel much colder then the actual temperature, therefore causing the danger of frostbite. Cover and protect extremities—ears, nose, fingers, and toes are especially vulnerable.
6. Dress appropriately for the prevailing conditions. Remember that as the temperature falls, wet clothes become very uncomfortable. Wear a hat. One-third of the body's heat loss is lost through the head.
7. Wear a good pair of sunglasses on bright, sunny days to cut the glare and prevent possible snow blindness.
8. If touring all day long, carry an emergency kit that contains ski wax, extra clothing, a wax candle,

matches or lighter to start a fire, high-energy food bars, and duct tape for temporary repair of broken ski tips.

9. If skiing alone, let someone know where you are going and the route you'll be skiing.
10. When skiing in rural areas, request permission of the property owner before crossing someone's land.
11. Ski under control at all times; if you find yourself going too fast, sit down.
12. Ski in areas free of traffic, including automobiles and snowmobiles.
13. When in a crowd, be careful with your ski poles; the pointed tips can cause injury.

Modifications for Special Populations

Orthopedically Impaired

1. Review commercial products for "sit skis" for individuals with disabilities. Recommend reviewing journal articles in *Sport 'n Spokes*, published by the Paralyzed Veterans Association (PVA).
2. Additional supports (similar to outriggers for downhill skiing) can be used for traversing the country side.

Cognitively Impaired

1. Peer students might be needed to assist with ski outings.
2. Make sure students have developed good cardiovascular fitness prior to engaging in cross-country skiing.
3. Try to ski on level surfaces as much as possible.

Sensory Impaired

1. Students who are visually impaired or blind can be tethered to their sighted peers. Make sure to provide training sessions for the sighted peers prior to tethering with a partner.
2. Students who are visually impaired or blind can follow groomed or tracked trials whenever possible. The tracks should be approximately 3 to 4 inches deep.
3. Students who are deaf or have a hearing impairment will need minimal modifications. Make sure to maintain eye contact with these students during any trips through wooded areas.

Terminology

Alpine skiing Downhill and slalom skiing as opposed to cross-country or Nordic skiing.

Bale A metal device that presses the sole of the boot over three pins, thus securing the boot to the ski.

Basket Circular portion, usually made of plastic, near the bottom end of the ski pole that prevents the pole from sinking too deeply into the snow.

Binding Metal or plastic device for fastening the boot to the ski.

Camber The curved portion built into all skis that touches the snow when force is applied and lifts off when weight is lifted. The ski appears bowed as it lies flat on the ground.

Diagonal stride A skier's gliding action that resembles walking as it is executed.

Fish scale A type of surface resembling fish scales, found on the bottom of waxless skis.

Gaiter A water repellent covering that fits over the boot, ankle, and lower leg. It is designed to keep snow out of the boot.

Groove Indentation that runs the length of the bottom of the ski, allowing the ski to run straight.

Herringbone A technique used to climb uphill that leaves a V pattern on the snow.

Kick The force (push) that is applied during the stride, allowing the skier to glide on the snow.

Kick turn A technique used to change direction 180 degrees while standing still on the flat or hillside.

Klister A type of sticky wax used on the bottom surface of a ski. *Klister* is the Norwegian term for "paste."

Layering Wearing loose layers of clothes over undergarments so that the skier may easily add on for extra warmth or remove excess if too warm.

Nordic skiing Cross-country skiing and ski jumping.

Pin binding A type of toe binding that has three pins that are projected into the sole of the boot, securing the boot to the ski.

Pole plant Action in which the poles are put into the snow at a particular place and during a particular time.

Setting an edge A technique used to prevent a skier from slipping by angling the edge of the ski into the hillside.

Side step A technique used to climb a hill on skis. The skis are parallel with each other as the skier steps up along the length of the ski.

Snow plow A technique used to slow the skier down while going downhill by spreading the tails and keeping the ski tips close together.

Step A type of ski-bottom design found on waxless skis, resembling a series of steps.

Tail The back or end portion of a ski.

Tip The front end or leading point of a ski.

Track The trail that is left by skis as the skier moves through the snow. These may be machine-made.

Traverse Movement back and forth across the face of a hill; the technique may be done uphill or downhill.

Wax A petroleum-based product applied to the bottom of a cross-country ski that enable the ski to grip and also to slide.

Further References

Baldwin, N. *Skiing Cross Country.* Toronto: McGraw-Hill Ryerson Limited, 1977.

Brady, M. *Cross-Country Ski Gear.* Seattle: The Mountaineers, 1987.

Caldwell, J. *The New Cross-Country Ski Book.* 8th ed. Lexington, MA: The Stephen Greene Press, 1987.

Cazeneuve, B. *Cross-Country Skiing: A Complete Guide* (A Trailside Series Guide). New York: W.W. Norton, 1995.

Endestad, A. and Traford, J. *Skating for Cross-Country Skiing.* Champaign, IL: Leisure Press, 1987.

Gillette, N. and Dustal, J. *Cross-Country Skiing.* 3rd ed. Seattle: The Mountaineers, 1987.

Gullion, L. *Nordic Skiing.* Champaign, IL: Human Kinetics, 1993.

Gullion, L. *Ski Games.* Champaign, IL: Human Kinetics, 1990.

Hall, W. *Cross-Country Skiing Right.* San Francisco: Harper and Row, 1985.

Masia, S. *Cross-Country Ski Maintenance and Repair.* Chicago: Contemporary Books, Inc., 1987.

Older, J. *Cross-Country Skiing for Everyone.* Mechanicsburg, PA: Stackpole Books, 1998.

Petersen, P., Lovett, R. A., and Morton, J. *The Essential Cross-Country Skier: A Step-By-Step Guide.* Camden, ME: Ragged Mountain Press/McGraw-Hill. 2000.

Sheahan, C. *Cross-Country Skiing: A Complete Guide.* New York: Sports Illustrated Winners Circle, 1988.

Audio-Visual Materials

Available from The Travelers Film Library, One Tower Square, Hartford, CT 06115. *I Hope I Get a Purple Ribbon* (1977). Featuring Bill Koch—silver medalist, 1976 Olympic Games. (16-mm sound film, 15 minutes)

Available from The Travelers Film Library, One Tower Square, Hartford, CT 06115. *It's as Easy as Walking* (1975). (16-mm sound film, 10 minutes)

Champions On Film & Video, 745 State Circle, Box 1941, Ann Arbor, MI 48106. *Cross-Country Skiing with Jeff Nowak* (VHS only, 60 minutes).

Karol Video, 350 No. Pennsylvania Ave., Box 7600, Wilkes-Barre, PA 18773-7600. *Skating and Striding: Cross Country Skiing* (30 minutes).

Also from Karol Video: *ESPN-Cross Country Skiing: Skating Techniques with Bill Koch* (44 minutes); *ESPN-Cross Country Skiing for Beginners with Bill Koch* (75 minutes).

Pyramid Films, P.O. Box 1048, Santa Monica, CA 90406. *If You Can Walk* (16-mm, 3/4 or 1/2 video, 14 minutes). Techniques of natural stride.

PBS Video, 475 L'Enfant Plaza, SW, Washington, D.C., 20024. *Introduction and Diagonal Skiing* (3/4- or 1/2-inch video, 29 minutes). An overview of cross-country skiing and diagonal stride. *Turning and Review* (3/4- or 1/2-inch video, 29 minutes). Three most successful turns and review of other techniques.

RMI Media Productions, 2807 W. 47th St., Shawnee Mission, KS 66205 (1/2-inch VHS or Beta video, 45 minutes). Overview of cross-country skiing, including equipment selection and other skills.

Web Sites

www.xskiworld.com/ Features training and conditioning information, instruction for beginners and more advanced skiers, waxing techniques, where to cross-country ski, and a variety of links.

www.xcski.org/ Site sponsored by the Canadian Cross-Country Ski Areas Association; features equipment directory, information on snowshoeing, daily ski reports, terminology, and hints for getting started.

www.trailsource.com/index.htm Identifies over 400 trails in the United States and around the world, provides up-to-date information about snow conditions, and is also a source for hiking and mountain biking trails.

www.crosscountryskier.com Site of *Cross-Country Skier* magazine; features articles concerning instruction, equipment, ski reports, and more.

CHAPTER 18

Soccer

This chapter will enable you to

- Identify and put into practice the rules governing the game
- Practice and then execute the basic skills, including kicking, passing, trapping, heading, tackling, the throw-in, and goalkeeping
- Discuss and employ basic offensive and defensive strategy and tactics
- Identify and discuss the nature of the game, including player responsibilities, field markings, and player positioning
- Identify and use basic terminology associated with the game

Nature and Purpose

Soccer is played by 11 players from each team. The game starts at midfield with a free kick called the kickoff as each team is in its own half of the field. The offensive objectives are to maintain possession of the ball, keep the ball wide until near the goal, and then get the ball in front of the opponent's goal where a player can propel it between the uprights, beneath the crossbar, and completely across the goal line for a score. The ball may be propelled with any part of the body except the hands and arms; however, the foot, body, and head are the main parts of the body used.

The defense's main objectives are to contain the opponents and the ball, forcing excessive passes; mark (guard) opponents in scoring position; tackle the opponent, taking the ball away whenever possible; funnel the ball to the middle of the field toward their own goal; and concentrate in front of their goal when the ball is in scoring position. The goalkeeper provides great assistance to the defense by being allowed to use the hands to contact the ball, and he also attempts to clear the ball away from the scoring area by throwing, punting, or drop-kicking it.

Systems of play are comprised of attackers (strikers/wings/forwards), midfielders (linemen/halfbacks), and defenders (stopper/sweeper/fullbacks). The attacker's primary contribution to the system is scoring. The midfielders support the offense and are the first line of defense. The defenders support the midfielders and are the last line of defense. The defender's primary objective is defending against the opponent's attack. Systems are numbered from the defenders forward (e.g., 4-2-4), depending upon the number of players comprising each of the three lines, excluding the goalkeeper.

The game is continuous, with no timeouts allowed, and time is stopped only for an injury, a temporary suspension of play by the official, the end of a period, or a score.

The players use basic skills of kicking, trapping, dribbling, heading, tackling, and throwing (where allowable) to propel or control the ball. The game is low scoring due to the difficulty of executing the skills, plus the nature of some rules.

The game requires constant adjustments by all the players and calls for short sprinting plus slower jogging. Good physical conditioning is necessary. The constant activity, use of the big muscle groups, large numbers competing, and low equipment expense make the game highly suitable for competitors of all ages and sexes.

Field of Play

A regulation field measures 100 to 120 yards in length and 65 to 75 yards in width (Figure 18-1). The dimensions and areas can easily be modified to suit the number, age, and sex of the participants. The field can be made longer or shorter and various grids can be applied (as discussed later) to provide practice areas for modified games.

In the list below, the numbers correspond to the numbers in the diagram of Figure 18-1.

1. *End line.* When the ball goes out of play over this line, it is put in play with either (a) goal kick

Figure 18-1 Regulation soccer field markings. (For further explanation of numbers, see text.)

(offense last touched the ball) or (b) corner kick (defense last touched the ball).

2. *Goal area*—the area where the ball is placed for the defending team to take a goal kick. It is placed on the front line of the area in that half field in which the ball went out of play.

3. *Penalty area.* Restriction area where (a) the goalie is allowed to play the ball with the hands; (b) the offensive team has to stay out of when the defending team is taking a goal kick; (c) on the goal kick, the ball must be kicked out of this area for the ball to be legally in play; (d) if a foul committed in this area by the defending team results in a *direct free kick*, then a *penalty kick* is awarded to

the team fouled; (e) players from both teams must stay outside on a penalty kick with the exception of the goalie and the person taking the penalty kick.

4. *Side or touch line.* A ball going out of bounds over this line is put in play with a throw-in by the opposite team of the one that last touched the ball.

5. *Penalty kick mark*—the spot where the ball is placed when a penalty kick results.

6. *Penalty kick arc.* This arc is a 10-yard radius from the ball, and players from both teams must stay behind it. On a penalty kick, both teams (except one offensive player and the goalie) must be out of the penalty area and at least 10 yards from the ball.

7. *Center, mid, or halfway line.* This line (a) ensures that both teams are in their own half of the field on the kickoff, and (b) is used to help regulate the offside rule.

8. *Center circle*—a 10-yard radius circle to restrict players of the defending team on the kickoff. They must stay out of the circle until the ball is contacted.

9. *Corner arc.* One yard from each corner there is a corner arc. The ball is placed on this arc when the offensive team is taking a corner kick.

10. *Goal line*—the line between the uprights of the goal. When the whole ball crosses it below the crossbar, either on the ground or in the air, a goal results.

11. *Corner flag.* The flag is at least 5 feet high and located in each of the four corners to assist in locating the boundary lines.

Basic Rules

Kickoff. At the beginning of the game, choice of ends and the kickoff are decided by the toss of a coin. The ball is placed in the center of the field on the half-way line, and the team kicking off plays the ball forward from the line. The player usually kicks the stationary ball legally (one circumference of the ball) forward to her teammate, attempting to maintain control of the ball. All players from both teams are in their own half of the field, with the defending team at least 10 yards from the ball. A goal cannot be scored from the kickoff.

Fouls. Fouls and misconduct committed during the course of play result in a free kick to the offended team. The severe infractions, which are most often injurious, result in a direct free kick, meaning a goal can be scored directly from that kick. A direct free kick foul occurring in the penalty area and against the defending team results in a penalty kick, the most severe infraction. Less severe infractions result in an indirect free kick, meaning someone else must contact the ball following the kick before a goal can be scored. When making a free kick, the opponents must be 10 yards from the ball, unless standing on their own goal line between the uprights, until the ball is kicked. The ball must be stationary on the free kick, must travel the circumference of the ball to be in play, and may not be re-contacted by the kicker until someone else touches it.

Direct Free Kick Offenses

Offenses for which a direct free kick is awarded are

1. Handling the ball; intentionally contacting the ball with the hands or arms. This includes the goalies when outside the penalty area.

2. Holding an opponent with the hands or arms.

3. Pushing an opponent; includes the hands or arms.

4. Striking or attempting to strike an opponent; the goalie is also not allowed to use the ball to strike a player.

5. Jumping at an opponent.

6. Kicking or attempting to kick an opponent.

7. Tripping or attempting to trip an opponent.

8. Using the knee on an opponent.

9. Charging an opponent violently or dangerously; includes the goalie in the penalty area or from the rear unless being obstructed.

All direct kicks awarded to the attacking team in the penalty area are penalty kicks.

Indirect Free Kick Offenses

Offenses for which an indirect free kick is awarded are

1. A player playing the ball a second time before it is played by another player at the kickoff, on a throw-in, on a free kick, on a corner kick, or on a goal kick (if the ball has passed outside the penalty area).

2. A goalkeeper carrying the ball more than four steps or the goalie delaying getting rid of the ball.

3. A substitution or re-substitution being made without reporting to the referee, or a substitute replacing the goalie not informing the referee and then handling the ball in the penalty area.

4. Persons other than the players entering the field of play without the referee's permission.

5. Dissenting by word or action with a referee's decision.

6. Discourteous behavior. For persistent infringement of the rules, a warning, or expulsion may follow.

7. Dangerous play by raising the foot too high or head too low while attempting to play the ball, thus endangering a player.

8. Resuming play after a player has been ordered off the field.

9. Offside.

10. Charging illegally (not violently or dangerously).

11. Interfering with or impeding the goalkeeper in any manner until the goalkeeper releases the ball, or kicking or attempting to kick the ball when it is in the goalkeeper's possession.

12. Obstruction other than holding.

13. Player leaving the field of play during the progress of the game without the consent of the referee.

Physical Contact. Body contact is allowed provided it is legal. A legal charge consists of a gentle nudge (not violently or dangerously), shoulder to shoulder, in an upright position, at least one foot contacting the ground, the arms close to the sides of the body, and playing the ball at the exact moment (Figure 18-2). The body may not be used as an obstacle to shield an opponent from getting to the ball unless actually playing the ball at that moment. This is obstruction (Figure 18-3) and allows for an opponent legally to charge the person obstructing, provided the contact is not violent or dangerous.

Penalty Kick. The penalty kick (Figure 18-4) is taken from any spot on the penalty mark, and all players except the kicker and the goalkeeper must be outside the penalty area. The goalkeeper must stand, without moving the feet, on the goal line between the goal posts until the ball is kicked. For any infringement by the defending team, the kick is retaken, if a goal does

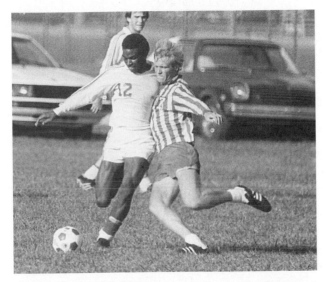

Figure 18-2 Legal charge.

Figure 18-4 Penalty kick.

not result. On an infringement by the attacking team, other than the player making the kick, the kick shall be retaken if a goal results. An infringement by the player making the kick results in an indirect free kick by the opposing team at the spot where the violation occurred.

Goal Kick. The ball is in play as long as it is not totally across the boundary lines (goal line or sideline), either on the ground or in the air. When it goes out of bounds over the goal line, the ball is put in play either with a goal kick (last touched by the attacking team) or a corner kick (last touched by the defending team). A ball put out-of-bounds over the sideline by a player is put in play with a throw-in by the opponents.

On the goal kick, the ball is placed on the front line of the goal area in that half of the field nearest to where it crossed the goal line (Figure 18-5). Any player on the team may take the kick. It is kicked from the ground. The opposing players remain outside the penalty area until the ball is kicked, and the ball must travel beyond the penalty area for it to be in play. The kick is retaken for any infringement.

Corner Kick. The corner kick is taken by the offense from the arc in that half of the field nearest to where the ball crossed the goal line. A goal may be scored directly from the corner kick (Figure 18-6).

Figure 18-3 Legal obstruction. Note use of body to protect the ball while playing it.

Figure 18-5 Goal kick.

Figure 18-6 Corner kick.

A   B

Figure 18-7 (A) Two opponents are nearer their own goal line at the moment the ball is played, *plus* the receiver is behind the ball at that moment—*not offside.* (B) Two opponents are *not* nearer their goal line—*offside.*

Throw-in. The throw-in is taken from where the ball went out of play. It is thrown equally with both hands on the sides of the ball from a point behind the head and delivered directly over the head. Both feet must remain on the ground during the throw and be either in contact with the sideline or outside the field of play.

Offside. The players must be concerned with their position in reference to the ball as play progresses. An offside infraction is called if a player is nearer the opponent's goal line than the ball at the moment the

ball is played, with limited exceptions. The offside rule is for assisting the defending team so that the offense will not be able to have players continually lurking in front of the goal. This would lead to an unskilled game with team strategy consisting of no more than long, uncontrolled kicks from one end of the field to the other, and back again.

A player nearer the opponent's goal line than the ball at the moment the ball is played is considered *offside* (Figure 18-7B) unless (1) he is in his own half of the field of play (Figure 18-8); or (2) there are two

Figure 18-8 Player is in own half of field—*not offside.*

opponents nearer their own goal line than he (Figure 18–7A); or (3) the ball was last touched by an opponent; (4) he received the ball directly from a dropped ball by the referee, a goal kick, a corner kick, or a throw-in; or (5) he is behind the ball. A player in an offside position does not have to be penalized except if he is gaining an advantage by his position, seeking to gain an advantage, or interfering with an opponent. Once offside, the only way for a player to put himself onside again is if (1) an opponent next contacts the ball; (2) he is behind the ball when it is next contacted by his teammates; or (3) there are two opponents near their goal when he is in an advanced position of the ball, and the ball is played to him by his teammates. The key factor for offside is always the position of the player in relation to the ball at the moment the ball is contacted.

Dropped Ball. Temporary stopping of play while the ball is still playable results in the game restarting with a dropped ball. Two opponents face each other and the referee standing between them drops the ball to the ground for either to contact. It is dropped where the ball was when play stopped unless in the penalty area. Then it is brought to the nearest point outside the penalty area and dropped. Common reasons for a dropped ball occurring are (1) simultaneous contact by opponents, causing the ball to go out of bounds; (2) temporary stopping for injury; (3) the ball becoming deflated; or (4) simultaneous fouls by both teams.

Goalkeeper. When the ball nears the scoring area, the goalkeeper enjoys certain privileges not granted to other players while in the penalty area. The goalkeeper may use the hand and arms to stop a ball from scoring; take four steps with the ball while in

possession; punt, throw, or drop-kick the ball; and is free from interference by opponents while in possession of the ball. The keeper loses these privileges when outside the penalty area.

Scoring. A goal is scored when the whole of the ball passes over the goal line, between the goalposts, and under the crossbar, provided it has not been thrown, propelled by hand or arm, or carried by a player of the attacking side (Figure 18-9). If a member of the defending team, other than the goalie, deliberately deflects the ball with his hand or arm attempting to stop a goal, it should be scored a goal if it crosses the goal line between the uprights. Goals also may be scored on direct free kicks, penalty kicks, and corner kicks. A goal counts one point for the team scoring the goal. After a goal is scored, a kickoff is made at the center of the field by the team scored against. Teams change ends after each regular and extra period.

Time and Players. The length of the game, number of substitutes, and when substitutes are allowed to enter the game vary depending upon the age and ability levels of the players. The organizations governing competition provide rule guides; however, there are only minor differences in them. Men and women are playing by basically the same rules regardless of the organization, and quite often at an early age (6 to 11), the game is played co-ed.

Equipment

The only equipment absolutely necessary for playing soccer are a ball and two goals. There are many makes and price ranges of soccer balls. The molded ball with a rubber bladder, nylon wound carcass, and compressed weatherproof leather or synthetic panels

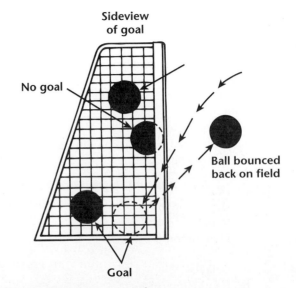

Figure 18-9 Scoring a goal.

is recommended. Goals can be purchased or may be constructed of 2 × 4s or pipe. Soccer shoes, shin guards, and nets for the goals may be added when progressing from physical education class to intramural to interscholastic competition levels. Gym shoes may be substituted for soccer shoes, thick magazines for shin guards, and chainlink fencing for nets. The fact that the game can be played by a large number of players at very little expense makes it particularly appealing. Competition apparel is not a major factor. Colored jersey vests and game jerseys are inexpensive. For pants, gym shorts, sweatsuits, or game trunks may be worn.

Suggested Learning Sequence
Beginning Level
A. Stretching and running
B. Basic rules
C. Fundamental skills
   1. Kicking
      a. Inside of foot push pass
      b. Instep
   2. Trapping (receiving)
      a. Sole of the foot
      b. Inside of the foot
      c. Chest
   3. Dribbling
      a. Inside of the foot
      b. Outside of the foot
   4. Heading; power standing
   5. Tackling: front
   6. Throw-in: standing
   7. Goalkeeping
      a. Catch—roll or bounce
      b. Catch—waist or chest
      c. Catch—head or above
      d. Punt
D. Strategies
   1. Tactics
      a. Possession
      b. Space—receiving ball
   2. Group
      a. Superiority around ball
   3. Team
      a. Communication
      b. Functional training combining two or more positional lines
E. Principles
   1. Attacking
      a. Depth/support
      b. Width
      c. Penetration
   2. Defending
      a. Delay
      b. Depth/support

      c. Width
      d. Balance
F. Systems
   1. W formation
   2. M-W formation
   3. Defensive style—zone
   4. Offensive style—static positioning, long pass, and short pass
G. Restarts
   1. Corner kick
   2. Goal kick
   3. Throw-in
   4. Kickoff

Intermediate Level
A. Partner stretching and interval training
B. Review beginning unit
C. Fundamental skills
   1. Kicking
      a. Outside of foot
      b. Lofting the ball
   2. Trapping (receiving)
      a. Outside of foot
   3. Dribbling
      a. Screening
      b. Sole of the foot
   4. Heading: power jumping
   5. Tackling: side
   6. Throw-in: running
   7. Goalkeeping
      a. Tip
      b. Throw—overhand
D. Strategies
   1. Review beginning unit
   2. Tactics
      a. Space-creating
   3. Group
      a. Space-restricting
      b. Tempo
   4. Team
      a. Rhythm
      b. Functional training involving tactical passing restrictions
E. Principles
   1. Attacking
      a. Mobility
      b. Improvisation
   2. Defending
      a. Concentration
      b. Control
F. Systems
   1. 4-2-4
   2. 3-3-4
   3. Defensive style—diagonal and player to player
   4. Offensive style—dribbling and fast/slow

G. Restarts
   1. Indirect free kicks
   2. Direct free kicks
   3. Defensive wall

Skills and Techniques

The fundamentals of soccer are dribbling, heading, trapping, kicking (shoot or pass), tackling, throwing, and goalkeeping. Because the game of soccer is primarily a kicking and trapping game, it is essential that players master the technique of controlling the ball without use of the hands or arms. In observing good soccer players, one sees that they control the ball and keep it reasonably close to their bodies when passing or advancing it down the field. The ball is kept close to the ground and not kicked into the air where it is difficult for the player to keep possession and control.

When learning or teaching each of the skills, keep in mind that the following factors are important for understanding common problems, both their causes and corrections:

1. Alignment to ball
   a. Position the body early in preparation to contact the ball.
   b. Position at the best spot in the line of flight for making initial contact.
   c. Prepare the contact surface at the proper angle required for optimum execution.
   d. Be as stable as possible.
2. Base
   a. Position the foot/feet for optimum stability.
   b. Position the foot/feet so that the contact surface can be at the proper angle for execution.
   c. Position the grounded foot/feet in the direction the ball is to be propelled or received.
3. Whole body position
   a. Position of specifically the feet, knees, hips, shoulders, arms, and head before, during, and after ball contact
4. Power/absorption
   Power
   a. Ball contact surface—speed of ball
   b. Joints providing force—range of motion and speed of motion
   c. Proper line of force (see #5)
   d. Total body parts alignment as they relate to the desired trajectory
   e. Follow-through (see #7)
   Absorption
   a. Ball contact surface—speed of ball
   b. Joints involved in receiving force
   c. Proper line of receiving force (see #5)
   d. Total body parts alignment as they relate to receiving the trajectory and force of the ball
   e. Direction (away from ball) of body parts used for absorbing the ball
5. Line of giving/receiving force
   a. Correct direction of all body parts related to the desired trajectory, rotation (spin), and final destination of the ball
6. Ball contact
   a. Surface and angle of body part used to make contact
   b. Exact spot on the ball to contact for accomplishing the desired end result
   c. Alignment to ball (see #1)
   d. Base (see #2)
   e. Whole body (see #3)
   f. Power/absorption (see #4)
   g. Line of giving/receiving force (see #5)
7. Follow-through
   a. The full range of motion (arc) of the primary power joints used and the exact point at which to stop in order to provide the desired power plus trajectory to the ball
   b. When receiving the impetus (trapping) of the ball, the primary joints used in recoiling, giving, or absorbing that lead to cushioning the impact—follow-through away from the line of flight of the ball.

Each of these factors will be considered as we discuss the learning hints for performing each specific skill or technique. Either a *B* (Beginning) or *I* (Intermediate) is indicated with each skill or technique to designate the appropriate ability level for presenting that skill. Where suitable, verbal learning hints are given in capital letters.

Kicking (Pass or Shot)

Kicking is primarily used for passing, shooting, and clearing. The rotation (spin) on the ball denotes proper or improper contact. Different parts of the foot can be used to contact the ball.

➤ Learning Hints: Inside of Foot Push Pass (B)

1. *Alignment to ball.* Quickly position as near the direct flight (180 degrees) of the ball as possible—alignment.
2. *Base.* Place grounded foot toward target and position it to the side of the ball approximately 6 to 12 inches and either even with or slightly behind the ball (Figure 18-10A), depending upon desired flight (on the ground or in the air)—GROUNDED FOOT. Knee slightly flexed.
3. *Whole body position.* Contact foot raised with toe pointed out—TOE OUT, knee pointed out—KNEE OUT, and ankle joint locked at 90-degree angle—

Figure 18-10 Inside of foot push pass.

Figure 18-11 Inside of foot push pass. Note leg, ankle, and knee of contact foot.

ANKLE LOCKED. Draw leg backward from the hip in a straight line. Raise the contact leg to the rear, bending the knee until the lower leg is close to parallel with the ground with the inside of the foot facing the ground—COCKED POSITION (Figure 18-10B). Position head directly above ball (to keep ball on ground) or slightly behind the ball (to loft off ground)—HEAD. Hips and shoulders near 90 degrees to approaching ball, with slight pivot out as the contact leg is drawn back. Arms comfortable, away from body for balance (Figure 18-10).

4. *Power.* Power results from the height that the contact foot is raised off the ground (Figure 18-10B), the speed that the contact leg is snapped forward to meet the ball, the speed of the approaching ball, correct ball/foot contact (hard surface), and the amount of follow-through.

5. *Line of giving force.* The foregoing power items applied in the correct line depend upon the approaching flight of the ball and the desired final destination. The correct line involves the body alignment to the ball (as near 180 degrees as possible), the direction the grounded foot is pointed (Figure 18-11A), straight linear (180 degrees) cocking of the contact leg, and the straight linear snap down plus follow-through of that leg—LINE OF FORCE.

6. *Ball contact.* The correct contact surface is the hard area near the heel of the foot and ankle

area (Figure 18-11B) with the inside of the foot facing the approaching ball. The ball is contacted near its midline and either high, middle, or low depending upon the desired speed and trajectory.

7. *Follow-through.* The height the contact foot and leg are allowed to lift after contact depends upon the desired trajectory and/or force.

➤ **Learning Hints: Instep Kick (B)**

1. *Alignment to ball.* Approach the path of the ball from a 45-degree angle—ALIGNMENT.

2. *Base.* Same as inside of foot push pass except the grounded foot is approximately 10 to 18 inches to the side of the ball—GROUNDED FOOT. Knee flexed.

3. *Whole body position.* Contact foot lifted with toe pointed down—TOE DOWN, knee rotated in—KNEE IN, and ankle joint locked as near 180 degrees with the lower leg as possible—ANKLE LOCKED (Figure 18-12). Lift heel upward toward the buttocks—COCKED POSITION. Hip extends and rotates slightly. Position head directly above the ball (to keep ball on ground) or slightly behind the ball (to loft off ground)—HEAD. Hips and shoulders should be near 90 degrees to approaching ball with slight pivot out as contact leg is drawn back. Arms should be comfortably away from the body for balance.

4. *Power.* Power results from the height that the contact foot is raised—HEEL RAISED, the speed that the contact leg is snapped forward to meet the ball—SPEED, the speed of the approaching ball, correct ball/foot contact, and the amount of follow-through.

5. *Line of giving force.* The foregoing power items applied in the correct line depend upon the approaching flight of the ball and the desired final

Figure 18-12 Instep kick. Note toe, ankle, and knee of contact foot.

Figure 18-13 Outside of the foot kick. Note toe, ankle, and knee of contact foot.

destination. The approach angle of the body to the flight of the ball approximates 45 degrees. The grounded foot is pointed toward the intended destination (Figure 18-12A) as the remainder of the power joints naturally correct to a direct alignment with the desired line of flight.

6. *Ball contact.* The correct contact surface is the hard area on the top of the arch (Figure 18-12B). The ball is contacted near the midline and either high, middle, or low depending on the desired speed and trajectory.

7. *Follow-through.* The height the foot and leg are allowed to lift is dependent upon desired trajectory and/or force.

> ▶ **Learning Hints: Lofting the Ball (I)**

1. *Alignment to ball.* Same as for instep kick.
2. *Base.* The grounded foot is approximately 10 to 18 inches to the side of the ball and slightly behind it. Knee flexed.
3. *Whole body position.* Same as for instep kick, except that the head is positioned slightly behind the vertical plane of the ball—HEAD BACK.
4–7.*Power, line of giving force, ball contact, follow-through:* All same as for instep kick.

> ▶ **Learning Hints: Outside of Foot Kick (I)**

1. *Alignment to ball.* Same as inside of foot push pass.
2. *Base.* Same as for inside of foot push pass.
3. *Whole body position.* Contact foot lifted with the toe extended down and rotated inward—TOE DOWN AND IN, knee rotated in—KNEE IN, and ankle joint locked—LOCKED ANKLE. Lift heel backward and upward toward the buttocks—COCKED POSITION (Figure 18-13).

Figure 18-14 Outside of the foot kick and dribble. Note toe, knee of contact leg, and contact surface.

4–5.*Power* and *line of giving force.* Same as for inside of foot push pass.
6. *Ball contact.* The correct contact area is the hard area on the top outside surface of the foot (Figure 18-14). The ball is contacted near the midline and either high, middle, or low depending upon the desired trajectory and speed.
7. *Follow-through.* Same as for instep kick.

Trapping

Many surfaces of the body can be used to trap (catch) the ball. Trapping means controlling a ball that is received by a player. There is "immediate" or "deflect" trapping. The first denotes control of the ball right where the player receives it, while the second means redirecting the ball close to the receiver (3 to 4 feet) to avoid an on-rushing opponent. When a body trap is used, a foot trap usually follows in order to "settle" the ball to the ground.

➤ **Learning Hints: Sole of Foot Trap (B)**

1. *Alignment to ball.* Quickly position as near to a direct line (180 degrees) with the path of the ball as possible—alignment.
2. *Base.* Body weight is totally supported by the grounded foot as the contact leg is raised with the sole facing the approaching ball.
3. *Whole body position.* Ankle of contact foot is flexed (90 degrees) with toe higher than heel, toe up, providing a wedge-like surface for ball contact. The contact leg and foot are extended in front of the body, and reach out, as the grounded leg provides support with a slight flexion of the knee. Hips and shoulders should be near 90 degrees to the approaching ball. Arms should be slightly away from body to provide balance and stability.
4. *Absorption.* The ball at contact is cushioned by slightly flexing the knee of the contact leg, and slightly flexing the knee of the support leg with a slight pike at the waist, which moves the head forward toward the ball—give.
5. *Line of receiving force.* The foregoing absorption factors are applied as near a direct line with the path of the ball as possible.
6. *Ball contact.* The ball is contacted on the top and slightly to the rear by the sole of the foot. The contact foot approximates a 45-degree angle with the ground, providing a wedge between the sole of the foot and the ground.
7. *Follow-through.* There is negative follow-through as the contact leg and foot at impact give in the same direction that the ball is traveling in order to stop the ball.

➤ **Learning Hints: Inside of Foot Trap (B)**

1–3.*Alignment to ball, base, and whole body position.* Same as for inside of foot push pass (Figure 18-15).
4. *Absorption.* The force of the ball is cushioned by the soft, relaxed contact surface, the wedging of the ball against the ground by the contact foot—WEDGE, and the movement of the contact leg away from the path of the ball at about the same speed of the approaching ball—GAME.
5. *Line of receiving force.* The foregoing absorption factors applied in the correct line depend upon the path of the ball and the desired final destination for the ball. The correct line involves the body alignment to the ball (as near 180 degrees as possible), direction the grounded foot is

Figure 18-15 Inside of the foot trap. Note alignment to ball, base, and whole body position.

pointed, angle of the contact foot, and direction the contact leg is moved upon impact.
6. *Ball contact.* The correct contact surface is the soft area on the inside of the foot near the arch. The ball is contacted on the top and back, wedging it to the ground to the rear of the grounded foot for "immediate" control. It is contacted nearer the bottom and back (imparting back spin) in advance of the grounded foot for "deflecting" the ball away from but close to the body.
7. *Follow-through.* The contact leg lowers the foot on the ball, wedging it (immediate control), or the leg and foot make a relaxed, sweeping action, "deflecting" the ball away from but close to the body.

➤ **Learning Hints: Chest Trap (B)**

1. *Alignment to ball.* Quickly position as near to a direct line (180 degrees) with the path of the ball as possible.
2. *Base.* The feet are in a staggered stance, with the body weight evenly distributed—STANCE.
3. *Whole body position.* The knees are flexed, hips thrust forward bending backwards, shoulders back further than the hips, placing the upper chest near parallel with the ground, the head away from the body for balance—BACKBEND (Figure 18-16).
4. *Absorption.* Upon ball contact, the knees flex deeper, allowing the chest to "give" quickly, absorbing the impact.
5. *Line of receiving force.* Same as #4 above. The ball rebounds off the chest in a low upward trajectory, falling to the ground near the feet. Turning the shoulders at impact causes the ball to rebound to the side of the body if desired.
6. *Ball contact.* The contact surface is the high flat part of the chest just below the throat.

Figure 18-16 Chest trap.

Figure 18-17 Outside of the foot trap.

7. *Follow-through.* Following contact and rebound, quickly stand straight and prepare to "settle" the ball to the ground by using one of the foot traps—SETTLE.

➤ **Learning Hints: Outside of Foot Trap (I)**

1. *Alignment to ball.* Same as for sole of the foot trap. The path of the ball is to the outside of the grounded foot—approximately 6 to 12 inches.
2. *Base.* Body weight is totally supported by the grounded leg while the contact leg is off the ground.
3. *Whole body position.* The contact leg reaches across and in front of the grounded leg—REACH ACROSS, with the ankle rotated inward and down, preparing the outside of the foot for contact. The upper body leans—LEAN, at an angle in the direction the ball is to be deflected. The arms are away from the body for balance.
4–5. *Absorption* and *line of receiving force.* The sweeping action of the contact leg from one side of the body to the other—SWEEP, absorbs force and controllably deflects the ball in the desired direction (approximately 90 degrees) away from the approaching flight of the ball. The ankle rotates out with a flicking action—ANKLE FLICK.
6. *Ball contact.* The contact surface is the outside of the foot, and the contact is high on the ball. The ankle that is rotated inward and downward before contact makes a forceful outward rotation at impact—ANKLE FLICK, flicking the ball to the side of the body as the whole contact leg sweeps across the body (Figure 18-17).
7. *Follow-through.* The contact leg sweeps across and in front of the body in the direction that the body is leaning, providing controlled redirection to the ball.

Dribbling

The skill of dribbling involves very controllably propelling the ball with the feet in an effort to move the ball to another area without relinquishing possession to another player. Different surfaces of the foot can be used to dribble.

➤ **Learning Hints: Inside of Foot Dribble (B)**

1. *Alignment to ball.* The body is directly behind the ball prior to contact.
2. *Base.* The grounded foot is behind and to the inside of the ball while the other foot is slightly off the ground for contact.
3. *Whole body position.* The body is in a continuous running action, with the ball making repetitive contacts with either foot (Figure 18-18).

Figure 18-18 Inside of the foot dribble.

4. *Power/absorption.* The contact surface (inside of the foot) can provide either force or absorption, depending upon how close to the body one wants to keep the ball.

5. *Line of giving/receiving force.* The speed of the running action provides force at contact. Contacting high on the ball takes away force and keeps the ball close, contacting near the middle applies force forward, and contacting low on the ball lifts the ball, which is desired.

6. *Ball contact.* The toe of the contact foot is pointed out; knee out, foot slightly off the ground, and sole parallel to the ground. The angle of the contact surface depends upon the path desired for the ball after impact.

7. *Follow-through.* There is a continuous running action, with repetitive contacts with the ball by either foot, TAP-TAP, propelling it along the ground in a controlled action.

➤ Learning Hints: Outside of Foot Dribble (B)

1–3.*Alignment to ball, base,* and *whole body position.* All same as for inside of the foot dribble.

4. *Power/absorption.* The contact surface (outside of the foot) can provide either force or absorption, depending upon how close to the body one wants to keep the ball.

5. *Line of giving/receiving force.* Same as for inside of the foot dribble.

6. *Ball contact.* The toe of the contact foot is pointed in and extended, down, with the knee inwardly turned. The contact surface is high on the outside of the foot near the ankle joint. The angle of the contact surface depends upon the path desired for the ball after contact (Figure 18-19).

7. *Follow-through.* Same as for inside of the foot dribble.

➤ Learning Hints: Screening (I)

1–2.*Alignment to ball* and *base.* Same as for inside of the foot dribble.

3. *Whole body position.* The body and ball are under definite control as the body is used to screen the opponent from the ball. Slight leaning contact against the opponent aids in protecting the ball plus determining the path the opponent desires to take to reach ball (Figure 18-20).

4. *Power/absorption.* None.

5. *Line of giving/receiving force.* Light leaning force against the opponent.

6–7.*Ball contact* and *follow-through*—depends upon which dribbling technique (inside, outside, or sole of the foot) the player decides to use to keep the ball away from the opponent. These techniques are often used in combination to feint the opponent prior to breaking away.

Figure 18-19 Outside of the foot dribble.

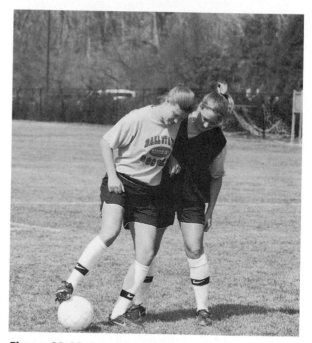
Figure 18-20 Screening. Note leaning body contact.

Heading

The head is used to play the ball when shooting, passing, or clearing the ball. Beginners use the *standing* approach; intermediates use the *jumping* play.

➤ Learning Hints: Power Heading, Standing (B)

1. *Alignment to ball.* Quickly position as near as possible to a direct line (180 degrees) with the path of the ball.

2–3. *Base* and *whole body position.* Same as for chest trap (see Figure 18-16).

4–5. *Power* and *line of force.* From the foregoing position the whole body snaps forward—SNAP (Figure 18-21). The upper body starts forward as the arms are vigorously thrust backward—ARMS; the weight transfers more to the front foot and the neck snaps—NECK SNAP, thrusting the head toward the ball. All are directed in a straight line toward the approaching ball.

6. *Ball contact.* The contact surface is near the hair line on the forehead. The contact on the ball is dependent upon the desired trajectory and target. Low ball contact propels the ball upward, middle contact propels the ball straight forward parallel with the ground, while high ball contact propels the ball downward to the ground.

7. *Follow-through.* All power components continue forward following contact, providing continued force and direction.

➤ **Learning Hints: Power Heading, Jumping (I)**

1. *Alignment to ball.* Same as for power heading, standing. Position in the arc of the trajectory where the ball can be contacted with a maximum height jump.

2. *Base.* A two-foot takeoff provides stability while suspended in air. A running one-foot takeoff provides height in jumping. Use both where desirable.

3. *Whole body position.* The arms are close to the side, the back arches, and the neck cocks in preparation for contact.

4. *Power.* The proper contact surface, back, neck, and proper jump timing assist with power as the upper body snaps forward to meet the ball while suspended in mid-air.

5–6. *Line of giving force* and *ball contact.* Same as for power heading, standing.

7. *Follow-through.* Same as for power heading, standing. A two-foot landing after execution of the skill is necessary for stability.

Tackling

The tackle is a skill used for taking the ball away from an opponent and maintaining control of the ball following that confrontation. Beginners use the frontal approach; for intermediates, tackling may be from the side.

➤ **Learning Hints: Front Tackle (B)**

1. *Alignment of ball.* Quickly position as near as possible to a direct line (180 degrees) with the path of the approaching player and ball (Figure 18-22).

2. *Base.* From a running approach, the grounded foot is positioned near and to the side of the ball as the full body weight is supported by that foot.

3. *Whole body position.* The head is above or slightly in front of the ball, grounded foot, and flexed knee. The arms are down and close to the body, and the hips are behind the ball. All are in a

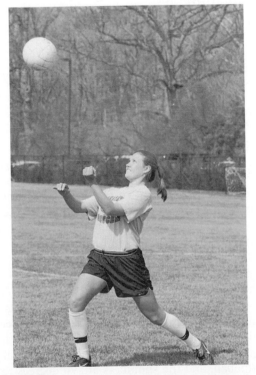

Figure 18-21 Power heading: Standing position.

Figure 18-22 Front tackling.

forward-leaning position. The contact foot is slightly raised backward, with the toe and knee out.

4. *Power.* The knee of the contact leg snaps forward as the contact foot blocks the ball—BLOCK, at the same instant that the opponent makes contact. Do not kick the ball but block it, attempting to simultaneously tie-up the ball.

5. *Line of giving force.* At that instant of contact, the near shoulder contacts the opponent with a gentle nudge. The straight contact leg is pushed/pulled forward from the groin—DRAG, as the whole body leans into the opponent, attempting to knock her off balance.

6. *Ball contact.* The ball is contacted exactly in the middle with the inside of the foot at the exact time the opponent makes contact, blocking the ball.

7. *Follow-through.* The whole body leans into the opponent as the contact foot lightly rolls over the top of the ball, causing it to roll over the opponent's foot and propelling it behind the opponent.

➤ **Learning Hints: Side Tackle (I)**

1. *Alignment to ball.* The approach angle is from the side at approximately 90 degrees to the path of the player.

2. *Base.* Same as for front tackle. The grounded foot is firmly planted in a direct line (180 degrees) with the path of the player and ball.

3. *Whole body position.* The firm plant of the grounded foot and transfer of total body weight to that foot allow the body to correct itself, facing the oncoming player as in the front tackle. (Refer to Front Tackle.)

4–7. *Power, line of giving force, ball contact, follow-through.* Same as for front tackle.

Throw-In

The throw-in is the only time that players, other than the goalkeeper, can use their hands to propel the ball. This is allowable only when the ball goes out of bounds over the touch line.

➤ **Learning Hints: Standing Throw-in (B)**

1. *Alignment to field.* Face in the direction that you intend to deliver the ball.

2. *Base.* Either a parallel or staggered stance can be used. The staggered stance (Figure 18-23) provides the best stability for a forceful throw.

3. *Whole body position.* From the stance, the back arches and arms raise the ball directly over and to a position behind the head.

4. *Power.* The snap forward of the arms, wrists, and upper body provides power.

5. *Line of giving force.* All power factors are delivered in a straight line as the body weight transfers to

Figure 18-23 Throw-in: Standing or running.

the front foot. The back foot must stay in contact with the ground throughout the throw.

6. *Ball contact.* The hands must be on the side of the ball and the ball delivered equally with both hands.

7. *Follow-through.* See #5.

➤ **Learning Hints: Running Throw-in (I)**

1. *Alignment to field.* Same as standing throw-in.

2. *Base.* A run prior to delivery, with a skip step followed by a stride (staggered), stance is used.

3–7. Same as for standing throw-in.

Goalkeeping

The goalkeeper uses skills for fielding and for clearing the ball. The hands may be used while in the penalty area. Catches are made in different positions, depending on how the ball arrives. Clearing involves either throwing or kicking skills.

➤ **Learning Hints: Kneeling Catch— Roll or Bounce (B)**

1. *Alignment to ball.* Quickly position in a direct line (180 degrees) with the path of the ball.

2. *Base.* Kneeling (Figure 18-24), the knee of one leg and foot of the other are placed on the ground on opposite sides of the path of the ball for stability and blocking purposes. Standing (Figure 18-25), the feet are placed together in a direct path with the flight of the ball.

3. *Whole body position.* Kneeling, the hands and arms are extended downward in front of the body to receive the ball. The lower leg of the kneeling limb is placed at an angle (45 degrees or greater) directly behind the path of the ball to block it if it gets past the hands. The head is directly above the ball, and the shoulders are 90 degrees to the path of the ball. Standing, the upper body bends

Figure 18-24 Kneeling catch: Roll or bounce ball.

Figure 18-25 Standing catch: Roll or bounce ball (front view).

over at the waist with both legs straight. The hands and arms are extended downward in front of the legs to receive the ball. The head is directly over the ball, and the shoulders are 90 degrees to the path of the ball.

4. *Absorption.* The soft contact surface (hands) makes initial contact as the ball is curled to the forearms, biceps, and chest.

5. *Line of receiving force.* The movement of the contact surface and absorption factors away from the

line of flight at about the same speed as the ball assist in receiving the force.

6. *Ball contact.* The little fingers of both hands are close together, all fingers are spread, and the palms are facing the approaching ball. This surface contacts the ball below its center, bringing it to the forearms, biceps, and chest in one smooth curling action.

7. *Follow-through.* Immediately stand up for balance and stability.

➤ **Learning Hints: Catch—Waist or Chest High Ball (B)**

1. *Alignment to ball.* Same as for catching a rolling or bouncing ball.

2. *Base.* The feet are even in a parallel stance.

3. *Whole body position.* The hips and shoulders are parallel with the goal line. The hands and arms are extended together in front of the body, reaching forward for the ball.

4. *Absorption.* A ball traveling at a slower speed is cushioned the same way as when catching a rolling or bouncing ball by first contacting the hands, forearms, biceps, and finally chest. A fast-approaching ball is cushioned by taking some of the impact immediately on the body while simultaneously curling the hands and arms around the ball as in catching a rolling ball. A slight jump in the air at contact also aids in absorption.

5–6. *Receiving force* and *ball contact.* Same as for catching a rolling or bouncing ball.

7. *Follow-through.* Bring the knee forward for protection against approaching players, if necessary.

➤ **Learning Hints: Catch—Ball Head High or Above (B)**

1. *Alignment to ball.* Same as for catching a rolling or bouncing ball (Figure 18-26).

2. *Base.* From a parallel stance, raise the knee of one leg forward, while the weight is supported on the other (exactly the same if a jump is required).

3. *Whole body position.* The hips and shoulders are parallel with the goal line, while the arms extend upward and forward to the desired height for fielding the ball.

4. *Absorption.* The soft contact surface (hands) makes initial contact as the ball is quickly brought to the chest area for protection.

5. *Line of receiving force.* Movement by the contact surface and arms is away from the line of flight at the same speed as the approaching ball.

6. *Ball contact.* The thumbs of both hands are close together, all fingers are spread apart, and the palms are facing the approaching ball. This surface contacts the ball near its center and brings the ball to the chest area in one smooth action.

Figure 18-26 Catch: Ball head high or above.

7. *Follow-through.* Land with two feet in a wide stride stance and lower the hips to a medium standing position for balance and stability.

➤ **Learning Hints: Tip (I)**

1. *Alignment to ball.* Same as for catching a rolling or bouncing ball.

2–3.*Base* and *whole body position.* Same as for catching a ball above the head.

4–5.*Power* and *line of giving force.* The contact surface (one or two hands) thrusts upward and backward, deflecting the ball over the crossbar.

6. *Ball contact.* The ball is contacted on its bottom area with the heel of the palm(s) as the wrist(s) is flexed for deflecting the ball upward and backward.

7. *Follow-through.* The knee is brought forward for protection, and the landing is on two feet for stability.

➤ **Learning Hints: Punt (B)**

1. *Alignment to ball.* The ball is held with both hands in front of the body.

2. *Base.* From a walking or running motion, the body weight is transferred to one foot while the other prepares to kick the ball.

3. *Whole body position.* The kicking leg is brought behind the body with a high heel raise as the arms are extended in front with the ball in the hands preparing to drop it.

4. *Power.* The proper contact surface, the height that the contact foot is raised behind the body, the speed that the contact leg is snapped forward to

meet the ball as it is dropped, and the amount of follow-through all provide power.

5. *Line of giving force.* The foregoing power factors applied as near as possible to a 180-degree angle with the intended flight provide the line and amount of force.

6. *Ball contact.* The ball is contacted in the back/bottom area. The closer to the ground that the ball falls prior to contact, the lower its trajectory. The contact surface is the top hard area of the foot (instep).

7. *Follow-through.* The contact leg continuing to lift following contact, provides both height and force as the body weight is supported by the grounded foot.

➤ **Learning Hints: Overhand Throw (I)**

1. *Alignment to ball.* The ball is held near the shoulder at the side of the thrower.

2. *Base.* A medium stride stance is used.

3. *Whole body position.* The ball is held in one hand and brought behind the body about head high with the arm flexed. The non-throwing arm is extended in front of the body for balance. The knees are slightly flexed. The hips and shoulders are slightly rotated toward the throwing arm.

4. *Power.* The distance that the ball is brought behind the body, the speed that the throwing arm is brought forward and the non-throwing arm is brought back, and the follow-through of the throwing arm plus the upper body all provide power.

5. *Line of giving force.* The foregoing power factors applied in a straight line provide maximum force and the desired direction.

6. *Ball contact.* The ball is held in the palm of the throwing hand and at the back/bottom of the ball.

7. *Follow-through.* As the ball is released overhand, the throwing arm continues forward and the body bends forward, providing force and direction.

Suggestions for Modified Practice Games and Areas

Figure 18-27 is a grid model showing various ways of modifying a regulation field to provide areas of different sizes. The larger the area, the more competitors possible. Examples are 2 on 1, 3 on 1, 2 on 2, 3 on 2, 3 on 3, 4 on 2, 4 on 3, 4 on 4, 5 on 3, 5 on 4, 5 on 5, and so on. A modified goal, objective, or soccer strategy and tactic are used in the games. Cones, flags, or other players are used as two-sided goals. These may be placed opposite each other on the end line of the area, slightly on the field with space behind them or in the middle of the area. One, two, or more goals may be used.

Figure 18-27 Grid for setting up practice areas.

Combining grids allows for actual games with modified field sizes. An example is using grids D, E, and F together, placing a goal on the sideline of the field and centered in the middle of the area. The size of the field is now 96 feet by 225 feet, where an actual game might consist of 6 on 6, 7 on 7, or 8 or 8. Two games may be played at once if grids G, H, and I are used similarly.

Combining areas A through F provides an even wider field, whereby more players can compete in an across-field game, as in the foregoing example. The same area (A through F) is used to practice offense (attackers and midfielders) versus defense (goalie, defenders, and midfielders) playing half field as on the regulation field. Scoring objectives are that the offense gets one point for scoring a goal, hitting the goalposts, or causing the goalkeeper to field the ball. Defense scores one point if they get the ball past the half-way line under their control.

Here are some other suggestions for playing games within a restricted area: A given number of consecutive passes without losing the ball receives a point; allow only one contact per player; allow no more than two contacts per player; after receiving the ball the player must out-dribble an opponent; the receiver of a pass must take the ball (pass or dribble) away from her

own goal before it next goes forward; every other pass must be in the air; no pass above knee height. The possible modifications are endless and dependent upon what skill or strategy one wants to stress.

Playing Strategy

Skilled execution of the techniques blended with knowledge of principles, tactics, and systems leads to a winning combination in soccer. *Principles* are factors that lead to skillful, organized, controlled play. *Tactics* denotes the execution of techniques and application of principles in a competitive situation. These fall into categories of individual, group, and team. *Systems* refers to the formational placement of players on the field where they apply techniques, principles, and tactics.

Principles

The basic principles are possession and space. Possession can be by one's own team (attack) or by the opponents (defend). The knowledgeable use of space when attacking or defending is the basis for successful play. The field size (space), understanding of the importance of each third of the field, attack principles and defense principles provide the initial foundation for team play.

Space. The position of players on the large (75 × 120 yd) field area presents a variety of available spaces. When in possession of the ball, the objectives are to attack the space behind, between, or in front of the opponents or to create new spaces by forcing them to move. The defensive objective is to deny the use of these spaces. The larger the space, the more time a player has to maintain possession, leading to more controlled play.

Strategic Field Areas. The field is divided into thirds (Figure 18-28). The following factors, when applied in each area, lead to systematic team coordination.

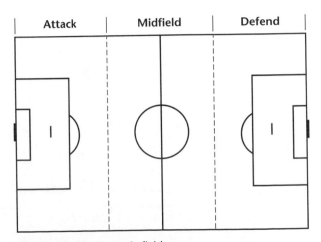

Figure 18-28 Strategic field areas.

Defend

1. The ball is distributed wide immediately upon possession.
2. Always provide support behind the teammate with ball.
3. Do not pass the ball across the goal mouth.
4. Do not give the ball away.
5. Control pass to midfield area as quickly as possible.
6. When in trouble, clear the ball (a) to midfield, (b) out-of-bounds over the sideline, (c) to goalie, or (d) over the end line (as a last resort).

Midfield

1. Slow down the tempo of the ball and the players.
2. Maintain control.
3. Diagonal cross-field flow of the ball.
4. Back pass to supporting players—reverse field to opposite side.
5. Penetrate to the attack zone.
6. Keep the ball wide.
7. Overlap extra players for numerical superiority.

Attack

1. Wide passes for control plus spread defense.
2. Penetrate with the ball when possible.
3. Center or cross the ball in front of the goal mouth, preferably in the air.

4. Short passes, one/two touch contact.
5. Back pass to maintain possession.
6. Shoot whenever possible.
7. Pressure the ball when it is lost.

Offensive Principles. As illustrated in the diagrams (Figure 18-29), the following principles aid the attacking team:

1. *Width*—distributing the ball wide spreads out the defense, opening larger areas for penetrating by either the ball or another player.
2. *Depth/support*—10- to 15-yard positioning ahead or behind the ball provides additional possible passing angles and enhances possession.
3. *Penetration*—the ball that penetrates past an opponent toward the end line is the most threatening pass to her. The deeper the controlled penetration, the better.
4. *Mobility*—the movement by players without the ball to different positions can provide superiority around the ball, create surprise, and create new situations to which the opponents must adjust.
5. *Improvisation*—the ability to adjust to ever-changing situations during the course of the play.

Defensive Principles. As illustrated in the diagrams (Figure 18-30), the following principles aid the defending team:

Figure 18-29 Offensive principles.

Figure 18-30 Defensive principles.

1. *Delay*—positioning in front of the player with the ball so that the ball cannot make immediate penetration, thus gaining the important defensive ingredient: time
2. *Depth/support*—positioning beside and behind teammates, restricting the space that the ball/opponent might move
3. *Balance*—the spread of players across the field, protecting all areas
4. *Concentration*—retreating by all defensive players funneling to the goal scoring area, causing congestion
5. *Pressure*—forcing mistakes through aggressive play
6. *Control/restraint*—applying all other principles of defense, awaiting the best opportunity for winning the ball; also not committing and being beaten by either the ball or the player

Tactics and Practice Suggestions

The execution of techniques and application of principles in a competitive situation is called tactics. These may be either individual, group, or team.

Individual. A player with the ball has the opportunity to dribble, pass, or shoot, and only has possession of the ball approximately two minutes of a 90-minute game. Developing technique and proficiency in the foregoing skills is important; however, it is more important to learn what to do for the other 88 minutes when one does not have the ball. One must learn how to use the available space for receiving the ball, how to create new space for either the ball or a teammate, and how to apply the principles of attacking or defending.

Group. The basic soccer objective of superiority around the ball initiates group tactics. When superiority is gained, the factors of using space, creating space, restricting space, and controlling tempo (time) are applied in small side games. Small side games (2 on 1, 2 on 2, 3 on 1, 3 on 2, 3 on 3, etc.) in restricted areas provide excellent opportunities for learning individual and group tactics.

Team. The grouping of a larger number of players leads to team tactics. Organizing restrictive games often with two lines of players (for example, 4 attackers and 3 midfielders versus 2 midfielders, 4 defenders, and the goalkeeper) requires additional continuity.

Playing within the boundaries of the suggested one-third field areas (see Figure 18-28), the players can concentrate upon the factors governing systematic team coordination. Communication becomes critical because more players are involved. Short one-word cues aid in communication. Using cue words such as *square, back, through, lead, leave, touch, carry, turn, settle,* and so on, lets teammates know what to do with the ball.

Special rules in such competitions help reinforce specific tactics. Examples of special rules are as follows: Allow only one or two touches per player; a back pass must be used before a penetrating pass; no passes over 15 yards; after receiving a pass, the player must dribble past an opponent; all passes must be longer than 15 yards; no passes above knee high; all passes above the head.

The next step in developing playing strategy is the application of principles and tactics within a specific system.

Systems

The formational placement of players on the field is called a system (Figure 18-31). The players are numbered, starting with the defenders (fullbacks), midfielders (halfbacks), and then attackers (forwards). The goalkeeper is not included in the numbering. The first attempt to develop new systems occurred when the five forwards of the 2-3-5 system changed their relative positions, thus forming either a W or M due to their alignment with each other on the field. Since that first change, many new systems have evolved, and all systems have strengths and weaknesses. Each evolved due to the specific abilities and knowledge of the players involved. The choice of which system to use should always depend upon those two factors—abilities and knowledge.

Figure 18-31 A systems alignment at kickoff. Number 2-3-5 (W) versus 3-3-4.

Style. Within a system, there are varying styles of play. Offensive styles are long pass, short pass, fast, slow, static positioning, improvisational movement, and dribbling. Defensive styles are zone, player to player, switching player to player, rotational, and diagonal.

Many current coaching books discuss principles, tactics, and systems in more detail. The "Further References" section lists several books for those requiring additional information.

Dead Ball Situations

When the ball goes out of play or there is an infraction of the rules, the game restarts from a dead ball situation. This allows a team the opportunity to initiate set plays. Goal kick, corner kick, kickoff, throw-in, or indirect and direct free kicks provide such an opportunity. The defending team also has time to prepare. There are many such plays and plans.

References in coaching books can provide a variety of set plays for dead ball restart situations.

Player Positional Responsibilities

Traditionally, the player positions have been called forwards, halfbacks, fullbacks, and goalkeeper. In recent years, the three basic lines are referred to more commonly as attackers, midfielders, and defenders. Each line has specific responsibilities related to that particular position. Listed below are the basic responsibilities for each line. Differing systems of play demand varying responsibilities, and the "Further References" section can provide more information.

Attackers

Attackers are the forward line players, who include wings, insides (strikers), center forward, or other teammates who overlap into the attacking area.

1. Scoring by shooting (head-foot)
2. Setting up scoring opportunities by dribbling to commit an opponent; center or crossing the ball in the air into the penalty area; running to create a new space for the ball or a teammate and to receive the ball; distributing the ball strategically and quickly wide, backward, or forward
3. Performing offensive restarts such as direct, indirect, and corner kicks in scoring area
4. Pressuring the opponents immediately upon their gaining control
5. Positioning for counterattacks upon regaining possession of the ball

Midfielders

1. Supporting the attackers on offense
2. Redistributing the ball wide, forward, or backward upon gaining possession for sustaining offense

3. Shooting outside the penalty area
4. Overlapping into the attack area for additional strength or surprise
5. Retreating, delaying the opponents upon their gaining definite control of the ball
6. Challenging for a loose ball when there is a 50/50 chance of gaining possession
7. Receiving goal kicks, both offensive and defensive
8. Taking a majority of the throw-ins
9. Defending against opponent's corner kicks
10. Positioning for counterattacks upon regaining control of the ball by one's own defenders or goalkeeper

Defenders

1. Supporting midfielders when attacking
2. Challenging for ball at midfield when there is a 60/40 chance of gaining possession
3. Retreating, delaying the opponents upon their gaining definite control of the ball in the midfield area
4. Funneling toward the goal and concentrating in the scoring area
5. Supporting each other when challenging for the ball
6. Clearing (kick or head) the ball out of the scoring area and when possible out of the defensive one-third
7. Keeping balance across the field; not allowing weakened areas
8. Positioning wide for counterattacking
9. Protecting the goal when the goalkeeper leaves the goal mouth
10. Forming walls for protecting against free kicks
11. Assisting or taking goal kicks
12. Overlapping occasionally for added superiority or surprise
13. Defending against corner kicks
14. Taking free kicks in the defensive one-third
15. Sprinting to the goal when beaten by both the ball and the player

Modifications for Special Populations

Orthopedically Impaired

1. Contact the United States Cerebral Palsy Athletic Association (USCPAA) at www.uscpaa.org for rules and information on indoor wheelchair soccer.
2. Allow students using crutches, canes, and/or walkers for ambulation to move the ball up and down the field or court with their assistive devices.
3. Use a commercial product called the Ominkin Ball, which is a large ball the size of a traditional cage ball. The Ominkin Ball is extremely light-weight and floats when tossed into the air. This is a great modification for students using wheelchairs. Contact the Omnikin Company at www.omnikin.com.

Cognitively Impaired

1. Contact your local Special Olympics for their soccer manuals and training programs.
2. Keep playing sessions short, allowing for frequent rest periods. Fitness levels are generally low in the student who is cognitively impaired.

Sensory Impaired

1. Individual considerations must be taken into account to determine the appropriateness of soccer for students who are visually impaired or blind. An appropriate alternative might be to tether a sighted student at the wrist to the student who is blind or has a visual impairment.
2. Minimal modifications are needed for students who are deaf or have a hearing impairment.
3. Review suggestions from the Orthopedically Impaired section for soccer.

Terminology

Center A pass from the outside of the field near the sideline into the center.

Charge The body contact between opponents that may be either illegal or legal.

Chip The lofting of the ball into the air using the instep kick technique; contacting the ball very low, causing it to loft quickly with back spin.

Clear Playing (kick or head) the ball a great distance, attempting to move it out of a danger area.

Corner kick A direct free kick awarded to the attacking player on the corner arc when the defending team last played the ball over their own end line.

Cross A pass from the outside of the field near the end line to a position in front of the goal.

Dead ball situation The organized restarting of the game following the stopping of play.

Direct free kick A free kick from which the kicker may immediately score from that initial contact.

Dribble The technique of the player self-propelling the ball with the foot so that he maintains control while moving from one spot to another.

Drop ball The method used for restarting the game after temporary suspension of play when the ball is still playable.

Goal area The rectangular area in front of the goal where the ball is placed for a goal kick.

Half-volley Contacting the ball just as it hits the ground after being airborne.

Head The technique of playing the ball with the head.

Indirect free kick A free kick from which a player other than the kicker must contact the ball before a score can result.

Kickoff The free kick that starts play at the beginning of the game, after each period, or after a score.

Obstruction The illegal use of the body to shield an opponent from reaching the ball.

One-touch Immediately passing a ball being received without stopping it.

Penalty area The large rectangular area in front of the goal where the goalkeeper is allowed to use the hands to play the ball.

Penalty kick A free kick awarded for a direct free kick foul in the penalty area against the defending team.

Settle The act of taking a ball that is off the ground and getting it settled on the ground so that it is rolling and no longer bouncing.

Square pass A pass that is directed toward the side of a player.

Tackle A technique for taking the ball away from the opponent.

Through pass A pass that penetrates between and past the defenders.

Throw-in The technique used for restarting the game when the ball goes out of play over the sideline.

Touchline The sideline of the field.

Trap The technique used for receiving the ball, bringing it under control.

Two-touch receiving Trapping a ball and immediately repassing it.

Further References

Buxton, T., Jago, G., Leith, A., and Drewitt, J. *Soccer Skills for Young Players*. Willowdate, ONT: Firefly Books, 2000.

Garland, J. *Youth Soccer Drills*. Champaign, IL: Human Kinetics, 1996.

Herbst, D. *Soccer, How to Play the Game: The Official Playing and Coaching Manual of the United States Soccer Federation*. North Hollywood, CA: Universe Publishing, 1999.

Luongo, A. *The Soccer Handbook for Players, Coaches and Parents*. Jefferson, NC: McFarland and Company, 1996.

McAvoy, N. *Teaching Soccer Fundamentals: A Progressive Guide to Maximize Player Development*. Champaign, IL: Human Kinetics, 1998.

Wein, H. *Developing Youth Soccer Players*. Champaign, IL: Human Kinetics, 2000.

Yakzan, R. *105 Practical Soccer Drills*, Orange, CA: Oceanprises Publications. 2000.

Yeagley, J. *Winning Soccer*. Indianapolis, IN: Masters Press, 1994.

Audio-Visual Materials

Head to Toe: Soccer for Junior Players. Champions on Film & Video, 745 State Circle, Box 1941, Ann Arbor, MI 48106. VHS.

Soccer for All Ages. Champions on Film & Video, 745 State Circle, Box 1941, Ann Arbor, MI 48106. VHS.

Soccer Fundamentals. Champions on Film & Video, 745 State Circle, Box 1941, Ann Arbor, MI 48106. VHS.

Soccer Defending: Individual and Team. Brown and Benchmark, 2460 Kerper Blvd., P.O. Box 539, Dubuque, IA 52001.

Soccer Goalkeeping. Brown and Benchmark, 2460 Kerper Blvd., P.O. Box 539, Dubuque, IA 52001.

Soccer Passing and Support. Brown and Benchmark, 2460 Kerper Blvd., P.O. Box 539, Dubuque, IA 52001.

Soccer Shooting: Attitude, Technique and Skill. Brown and Benchmark, 2460 Kerper Blvd., P.O. Box 539, Dubuque, IA 52001.

Soccer Tactics and Skills. (7 volumes: Passing and Support, Creating Space, Goalkeeping, The Attack, Set Plays, Shooting, and Defending.) Champions on Film & Video, 745 State Circle, Box 1941, Ann Arbor, MI 48106. VHS.

Teaching Kids Soccer. Karol Video, 350 N. Pennsylvania Ave., P.O. Box 7600, Wilkes-Barre, PA 18773-7600.

The Graduated Soccer Method (3 volumes). Champions on Film & Video, 745 State Circle, Box 1941, Ann Arbor, MI 48106. VHS.

Winning Soccer: The Basics of the Game. Champions on Film & Video, 745 State Circle, Box 1941, Ann Arbor, MI 48106. VHS.

Web Sites

www.socceramerica.com The search feature provides unlimited access to any topic.

www.usysa.org The site index lists numerous instructional tips under "Coaches Corner." The information ranges from skills, strategies, rules, and development to fitness training for youth.

www.finesoccer.com The Web site is designed specifically to help participants and coaches increase their knowledge of soccer; the search function allows for unlimited access to information.

www.nscaa.com The "Coaching Tips" feature addresses skill and strategy development in detail.

www.soccercoaching.net Presents skills and tactics each day of the week with a steady addition of new articles.

www.bysw.net The site is dedicated to youth soccer and lists many options for improving one's knowledge of the game.

CHAPTER 19

Softball

This chapter will enable you to

- Identify the basic equipment needed in softball and understand the rules pertaining to it
- Understand the rules of slow-pitch and fast-pitch games
- Demonstrate the skills of batting, baserunning, sliding, fielding, throwing, pitching, and catching; and of playing the infield and outfield positions
- Identify drills and lead-up games for the teaching of skills
- Identify the terminology necessary to understand the game
- Observe the procedures to make the game safe for participants

Nature and Purpose

In 1887 an indoor version of the game of baseball was developed by George Hancock of Chicago, Illinois. He used smaller playing dimensions and a larger and softer ball. The game became extremely popular and was moved outdoors. This game, softball, is now played by over 30 million adults and youths in the United States as well as in many nations throughout the world. Almost 5 million youths are estimated to participate in youth softball programs, making softball the most popular youth sport. Participation in softball games ranges from informal games at picnics, in parks, in backyards, and on the streets to formal leagues sponsored by schools, playgrounds, recreation departments, churches, and industrial organizations. The traditional forms of softball games included in league play are fast-pitch, 12-inch slow-pitch, and 16-inch slow-pitch games. With the variety of types and modifications of the basic game of softball, the game can be enjoyed by men and women of all ages. Softball is considered to be one of the safest sports for all ages.

Basic Rules

The rules of softball are patterned after those of baseball, making it very similar to the parent game. Pitching and several rules concerning field dimensions and equipment are different. A brief summary of the rules is given below, but players should study a copy of the Official Rules in order to become familiar with all regulations governing the game.

The games of slow-pitch softball and fast-pitch softball have many similarities: The ball must be pitched underhand, the game is 7 innings long, and the purpose is to get on base and score runs. The major difference, as the names imply, is in the speed of the pitched ball. In slow-pitch softball, the ball must be thrown underhand with a specific arc (6 to 12 feet), whereas in fast-pitch softball, the ball is thrown underhand with great velocity in a straight line—much like a baseball. Other differences are noted below.

Slow-Pitch	*Fast-Pitch*
No bunting	Bunting
No stealing bases	Stealing bases
Runners may leave the base after the ball crosses home plate	Runners leave base after the pitcher releases the ball
10 players per team	9 players per team
65-foot base paths (males) 60-foot base paths (females)	60-foot base paths
A mask and chest protector for the catcher recommended	A mask and chest protector for the catcher required

Game Regulations

The purpose of the game is to score more runs than the opponent. A regulation game consists of 7 innings, or $6\frac{1}{2}$ innings if the team second at bat has scored more runs than its opponent. The umpire may call (terminate) a game if five or more complete innings have been played or the team second at bat has scored more runs than the other team has scored in five or more innings. The score of a forfeited game shall be 7–0 in favor of the team not at fault.

Players and Substitutes

A team consists of 9 players in fast-pitch, 10 players in fast-pitch with a designated player (DP), and 10 players in slow-pitch. A team must have the required number of players to start or continue a game. A substitute may take the place of a player whose name is on the team's batting order. Any of the starting players, including a DP, may be withdrawn and re-enter once, provided such a player occupies the same batting position whenever he is in the line-up. A player, other than those in the starting line-up, removed from the game may not participate in the game again except as a coach. The DP may be used for any player, provided it is made known prior to the start of the game and his name is indicated on the line-up sheet. The DP must remain in the same position in the batting order, may enter the game on defense, and may be substituted for at any time by a player who has not yet been in the game.

Pitching Regulations

Fast-Pitch. In fast-pitch, the pitcher must take a position with both feet firmly on the ground and in contact with, but not off the side of, the pitcher's plate. Before pitching, the pitcher must come to a full and complete stop for a least one second and not more than 10 seconds, facing the batter, with both shoulders in line with first and third base and with the ball held in both hands in front of the body. The pitcher may not take the pitching position without the ball. The pitcher may wind-up in the delivery, provided there is no stop in the forward motion or reverse in the direction of the arm swing. The release of the ball and the follow-through of the hand and wrist must be forward past the straight line of the body, and, when the arm passes the body in the forward swing, the hand shall be below the hip and the wrist not farther from the body than the elbow. The pitcher shall not take more than one step, which must be forward toward the batter (within the length of the pitcher's plate), simultaneous with the delivery of the ball, and the pivot foot must remain in contact with the pitcher's plate until the stepping foot has touched the ground.

Slow-Pitch. In slow-pitch, the pitcher can take the pitching position with one or both feet touching the pitcher's plate, but both the pivot and non-pivot foot must be within the length of the pitcher's plate. A full stop must be made for 1 second and not more than 10 seconds, with one or both hands holding the ball in front of the body and the shoulders in line with first and third base, preliminary to pitching. The pivot foot must remain in contact with the pitcher's plate until the pitched ball leaves the

hands. It is not necessary to step, but if a step is taken, it must be forward toward the batter within the length of the pitcher's plate. The pitch shall be released at a moderate speed (umpire's decision—if warned about excessive speed and the act is repeated, the pitcher shall be removed from the pitcher's position for the remainder of the game), and at a perceptible arc of at least 6 feet and no higher than 12 feet from the ground.

Batting Regulations

The batter shall take a position within the lines of the batter's box and may be called out for stepping on home plate or having the entire foot touching the ground completely outside the lines of the batter's box when the ball is hit. A batter is removed from further participation in the game if an illegal bat is used. Players must bat in regular order, as indicated in the starting line-up. Batting out of order is an appeal play, and if the error is discovered while the incorrect batter is at the plate, the correct batter must replace the incorrect batter and assume the ball and strike count. If the error is discovered after the incorrect batter has completed the turn at bat and before there has been a pitch to another batter, the player who should have batted is out, and the next batter is the player whose name follows that of the player declared out. Any runs scored are cancelled, and baserunners must return to bases held when the incorrect batter came to the plate. If the error is not discovered until after a pitch is made to the next batter, no one is declared out and all play is legal.

A strike (fast-pitch) occurs when the ball passes over any part of home plate and is between the batter's armpits and the top of the knees when in a natural batting stance. In slow-pitch, the strike zone is over any part of home plate between the batter's higher shoulder and the knees when in a natural batting stance.

A foul tip is a foul ball that goes directly from the bat, not higher than the batter's head, to the catcher's hands and is legally caught. In fast-pitch, the ball is in play and baserunners may advance at their own risk. In slow-pitch, the ball is dead.

The batter is declared out when an infield fly is hit with baserunners on first and second or on first, second, and third with less than two out (infield fly rule). The batter is also called out in slow-pitch when the ball is bunted, is hit with a downward chopping motion, or is hit foul after the second strike.

Baserunning Rules

Baserunners must touch the bases in regular order and if forced to return while the ball is in play, the bases must be touched in reverse order. Two baserunners may not occupy the same base simultaneously. The runner who first legally occupied the base shall be entitled to it, and the other baserunner must return or be put out. A baserunner is out when she (1) runs more than 3 feet from a direct line between bases in regular or reverse order to avoid being touched by the ball in the hand of a fielder; (2) passes a preceding baserunner before that runner has been put out; (3) leaves a base to advance before a caught fly ball has been touched, provided the ball is returned to a fielder who touches that base while holding the ball, or a fielder with the ball touches the baserunner before returning to the base; (4) fails to keep contact with the base until a legally pitched ball has been released by the pitcher in fast-pitch (whether on a steal or batted ball); or (5) fails to keep contact with the base until a legally pitched ball has reached home plate in slow-pitch (batted ball only). A pitcher in slow-pitch who desires to walk a batter intentionally may do so by notifying the plate umpire, who shall then award the batter first base.

Dead Ball Rules

The ball is dead and not in play under the following circumstances: (1) on an illegally batted ball; (2) when the batter steps from one box to another as the pitcher is ready to pitch; (3) on an illegal pitch; (4) when a pitched ball touches any part of the batter's person or clothing; (5) when a foul ball is not caught; (6) when a baserunner is called out for leaving a base too soon; (7) when any part of the batter's person is hit with a batted ball while in the batter's box; (8) when a blocked ball is declared; (9) when a wild pitch or passed ball in fast-pitch goes under, over, or through the backstop; and (10) in slow-pitch after each strike or ball.

Scoring Regulations

A base hit results when a batted ball permits the hitter to reach first base safely when no fielding error is involved. A base hit shall not be recorded when a baserunner is forced out by a batted ball, or would have been forced outside, except for a fielding error.

Sacrifices are scored when with less than two out, the batter advances one or more baserunners with a bunt and is retired at first base, or when a run is scored by advancing runners after a fly ball is caught.

Assists are scored to each player who handles the ball in any play or series of plays that result in a put-out, but only one assist is credited to a player in any one put-out.

Put-outs are credited to players who catch a batted fly ball, catch a thrown ball that retires a baserunner, or touch a baserunner with the ball while the runner is off the base.

Errors are recorded for the player who commits a misplay that prolongs the turn at bat of the batter or the life of the baserunner.

A run batted in (RBI) is a run scored because of (1) a safe hit; (2) a sacrifice bunt or fly; (3) an infield put-out or fielder's choice; (4) a baserunner forced home because of interference, or in fast-pitch, the batter being hit with a pitched ball, or the batter being given a base on balls; and (5) a home run and all runs scored as a result.

Winning and Losing Pitcher

A pitcher is credited with a win if he or she starts and pitches at least 4 innings and the team is not only in the lead when the replacement occurs but remains in the lead the remainder of the game. When a game is ended after 5 innings of play and the starting pitcher has pitched at least 3 innings and the team scores more runs than the other team when the game is terminated, the pitcher will be declared the winner. A pitcher will be charged with a loss regardless of the number of innings pitched if replaced when the team is behind the score and the team thereafter fails to tie the score or gain the lead.

Playing Field

The regulation playing field is 60 x 60 feet square (Figure 19-1). The accompanying indications of the required distances for fast pitch and slow pitch are used in the majority of age groups. For official distances for specific age groups, consult a current Amateur Softball Association (ASA) rule book. Ground or special rules establishing the limits of the playing field may be agreed upon by leagues or opposing teams whenever backstops, fences, stands, vehicles, or other obstructions are within the prescribed area.

The home plate is made of rubber or other suitable material and is a five-sided figure, 17 inches wide across the side facing the pitcher, $8\frac{1}{2}$ inches long on the sides parallel with the inside lines of the batter's box, and 12 inches long on the sides of the point facing the catcher.

The pitcher's plate is made of wood or rubber and measures 24 inches long and 6 inches wide. The top of the plate must be level with the ground; the front line of the plate measures the following distances from the outside corner of home plate: male fast-pitch and slow-pitch and female slow-pitch—46 feet; female fast-pitch—40 feet.

The bases other than home plate must be 15 inches square and made of canvas or other suitable material and not be more than 5 inches thick. The bases should be securely fastened in position. A double base may be used at first base. This base is 15 by 30 inches. The half of the base in fair territory is white and the half of the base in foul territory is orange.

Figure 19-1 Softball field, official dimensions.

Laying Out a Diamond

The following directions are for laying out a diamond with 60-foot bases and a 40-foot pitching distance. Determine home plate position by running a line in the direction desired for the diamond. Place a stake at the corner of home plate nearest the catcher. Tie a cord to the stake with knots or other markings at the following distances: 40 feet, 60 feet, 84 feet-10¼ inches, and at 120 feet.

Place the cord along the direction line without stretching it. Place a stake at the 40-foot mark. This is the front edge of the pitching rubber. Also drive a stake at the 84 feet-10¼ inches mark. This is the center of second base.

Now place the 120-foot mark on the center of second base. Hold the cord at the 60-foot mark and walk to the right of the direction line. When the cord is taut, drive a stake at the 60-foot mark. This is the outside corner of first base. Walk across the field and do the same thing to mark the corner of third base.

Equipment and Clothing

Bats. The official softball bat is round and made of one piece of hardwood or bonded wood. Plastic, bamboo, or metal is also acceptable. The bat's maximum measurements are 34 inches in length, 2¼ inches in diameter at its barrel end, and 38 ounces in weight. Bats must be free of rivets, pins, rough or sharp edges, or any form of exterior fastener; metal bats must be free of burrs. The handle requires a safety grip of cork, tape (not smooth plastic tape), or composition material, and the bat must be marked "Official Softball" by the manufacturer.

Balls. A 12-inch ball is used for fast-pitch and men's and co-ed slow-pitch softball. An 11-inch ball is used for women's slow-pitch games. A larger 16-inch ball is also used for some slow-pitch games. The official 12-inch ball must be a smooth-seam concealed-stitch or flat-surfaced ball from 11⅞ to 12⅛ inches in circumference, and weigh from 6¼ to 7 ounces. (The official 11-inch and 16-inch balls have relative size and weight specifications.)

Gloves. Gloves (which have fingers) may be worn by any player, but mitts (which have no fingers) may be used only by the first baseman and catcher. The pitcher's glove must be a solid color other than white or gray. Multicolor gloves are acceptable for all other players, but gloves with white or gray circles on the outside resembling a ball are illegal.

Shoes. Shoes may have canvas or leather uppers or similar materials. The soles either may be smooth or have soft or hard rubber cleats. Ordinary metal sole and heel cleats may be used if the spikes on the plates do not extend more than ¾ inch from the sole or heel of the shoe. Shoes with rounded metal spikes are illegal. No metal spikes are allowed in any division of youth or co-ed play.

Protectors. Masks, throat protectors, and helmets must be worn by all catchers during a game and by anyone who is warming up a pitcher. Masks should be checked to be sure the wire eye opening is smaller than the bat barrel. Youth fast-pitch softball catchers must also wear shin guards and body protectors. Body protectors are recommended for slow-pitch games as well. Helmets are required to be worn by all adult fast-pitch players and youth fast- and slow-pitch offensive players. The helmets must be of similar color with double ear flaps. Helmets are not allowed for defensive players except the pitcher and the catcher and for medical purposes.

Uniforms. All players on a team must wear uniforms identical in color, trim, and style. Ball caps are considered part of the uniform and are required for all players under U.S. Slow-Pitch Softball Association (USSSA) rules and in Amateur Softball Association (ASA) rules for male players, including the catcher. Caps, visors, and headbands are optional for female players but may not be mixed on a team. No female player is required to wear headwear, but for those players who do so, the headwear must be alike. Plastic visors are not allowed as headwear.

Selected Learning Sequence

A. Nature and purpose of softball
B. Conditioning—exercises and drills for developing muscular strength, speed, agility, coordination, and balance.
C. Safety suggestions. Moving people and moving objects can create hazards; therefore, from the first day, safety precautions must be followed without fail.
D. Basic game concepts
   1. Field of play and player positions
   2. Equipment
   3. Safety
E. Skills and techniques
   1. Catching
   2. Throwing
      a. Grip on ball
      b. Arm motion
      c. Body movement
   3. Fielding the ball
      a. Ground balls
      b. Fly balls
   4. Batting
      a. Grip on bat
      b. Stance
      c. Stride
      d. Rotation of body and arms
      e. Follow-through
   5. Bunting
      a. Grip on bat
      b. Stance
      c. Direction of bunt
   6. Baserunning
   7. Sliding
   8. Pitching and catching
F. Rules—start with those essential to play the game and expand in depth and comprehensiveness as playing ability increases.
   1. Terminology
   2. Playing field
   3. Equipment
   4. Players and substitutes
   5. The game

6. Pitching regulations—fast- or slow-pitch, for whichever game is being taught
7. Batting
8. Baserunning
9. Dead ball—ball in play

G. Playing strategy. The fast-pitch game utilizes many strategies of baseball, whereas the slow-pitch game is the adaptation of field positions to batting strengths and/or weaknesses.

Skills and Techniques

While adaptable for general recreational use, softball is a game that demands a good performance of certain fundamental skills and techniques. Enjoyment from participation in the game intensifies as skills improve. Skill techniques are described below, followed by short hints to use in teaching each of the skills. Practice suggestions include drills and leadup games to enhance skill development.

Catching

Catching the ball is a fundamental skill that must be mastered before other skills are attempted.

➤ **Learning Hints**

1. Watch the ball into the hands or glove.
2. Position fingers up and thumbs together for balls chest high or higher. Position fingers down and little fingers together for balls waist high and lower.
3. Relax the fingers and arms.
4. On contact with the ball, absorb the force by bringing the ball close to the body—"Give with the ball."

➤ **Practice/Organizational Suggestions**

1. Provide each student with a ball. The students toss the ball up in the air and catch it, trying to toss the ball higher and higher and still be able to catch it.
2. A student tosses the ball up in the air and everyone claps and counts until the ball comes down and is caught. Take turns to see who can get the most claps.
3. Catch balls thrown by a partner from short range. Initially use foam balls or whiffle balls to eliminate fear of being hurt. Gradually increase the distance.
4. Catch balls a partner throws high, low, and to each side.

Throwing

Throws should be made quickly, accurately, and to the correct base or fielder. Players should be able to throw using an overhand, sidearm, or underhand motion. But spend more time on the overhand throw because with it one can attain the greatest accuracy.

The sidearm throw imparts a side spin on the ball that causes it to curve.

➤ **Learning Hints**

1. Grip the ball across a seam with index and second fingers (all four fingers if hand is small), thumb underneath, and third and fourth fingers to the side (Figures 19-2 and 19-3).
2. Point the elbow away from the body as the arm moves backward (Figure 19-4).
3. Move body weight to the foot on the same side (rear foot) and rotate the trunk in that direction.
4. Keep the wrist extended until just before release.
5. Push off with the rear foot and step with the other foot in the direction of the intended throw.
6. Rotate hips, trunk, and shoulders as the arm comes forward.
7. Lead with the elbow and snap the wrist as the ball is released opposite the peak of the cap.

Figure 19-2 Two-finger grip for adult.

Figure 19-3 Four-finger grip for children.

Figure 19-4 Overhead throw. As arm moves backward, point the elbow away from the body.

8. The throwing arm continues across the body for the follow-through.
9. Use a natural, rhythmical movement.

▶ Practice/Organizational Suggestions

1. Throw to a partner. Start with a short distance and then increase that distance. Throw to a specified target on the partner, such as the chest. Vary the target and the speed of the throw. Stay at a distance until accurate for four out of five throws (preferably all five).
2. Throw at a target from various distances.
3. Throw to different bases from different field positions.
4. Play "Beatball." A runner stands at home plate and a catcher has a ball, preferably a soft ball. On a signal, the runner begins running the bases. The catcher throws the ball to third base. The ball is relayed from third to second base and then to first base and home plate. The runner scores one point for each base touched before the ball returns to home plate. *Variation:* Allow the runner to continue around the bases until the ball reaches home plate prior to the runner on the same trip around the bases. Place a maximum of three trips around the bases.

Fielding Ground Balls

The ability to field ground balls is crucial to the success of any defense. With proper guidance, most players can learn to field routine ground balls successfully and improve their ability to field cleanly hard-hit balls and bad bounces.

▶ Learning Hints

1. Prior to the pitch, assume a ready position with the feet parallel and wider than shoulder-width apart. Flex the knees and hips and place the hands close to the ground (Figure 19-5).
2. When possible, move forward ("charge") toward the ball when it is hit.
3. Stay in front or get in front of ground balls. This enables you to handle them if they take bad bounces to the left or right.
4. Field ground balls with the feet in a stride position, knees slightly bent, and the body crouched (Figure 19-6): *wide stance.* On hard-hit balls, it may be advisable to close the feet or drop to one knee to block the ball.

Figure 19-5 Ready position.

Figure 19-6 Fielding ground ball position.

5. Catch a ground ball just as it leaves the ground on a bounce or after it has reached the peak of its bounce.

6. Keep the body and glove low on ground balls and move upward to make the catch. One can move more quickly upward, and because the body is already low, more bad bounces may be blocked by the body or glove.

7. Keep the glove open and watch the ball into the glove.

➤ Practice/Organizational Suggestions

1. Slowly roll ground balls between partners.

2. Increase the speed of the rolls and then increase the distance between partners.

3. Toss ground balls to the right and to the left of the partner.

4. Field ground balls with a partner tossing balls at varying speeds and in different directions.

5. Field ground balls hit by a partner at varying speeds and directions. Throws can be made to a catcher next to the hitter or to a base.

6. Play "Pegging First." One team is at bat and the other is in the field. Using a fungo bat, each batter hits the ball on the ground and runs to first base. If the batter reaches first before the ball, one point is scored. All members of the batting team bat before teams change positions.

Fielding Fly Balls

Catching fly balls can be a difficult skill for beginners to learn. Once the basic catching skill is mastered, judging the ball's speed and distance must be learned in order to field fly balls.

➤ Learning Hints

1. Get under the ball as quickly as possible. Use two hands.

2. To catch a ball hit over the head and to the right or left, pivot on the foot on the ball side, turn and run diagonally backward, and watch the ball over the shoulder opposite the ball side.

3. Relax the fingers slightly and have the hands and arms give with the ball as it is caught to reduce the force of impact.

4. Catch the ball, when possible, close to the throwing side so that the throwing arm can move into position for the throw as soon as possible.

5. Watch the ball into the glove.

6. Know where to throw the ball before you catch it, and then move quickly to accomplish the throw after the catch.

➤ Practice/Organizational Suggestions

1. Catch fly balls thrown by a partner. Gradually increase the distance.

2. Catch fly balls hit by a partner. Throw to a relay person, directly to a catcher next to the hitter, or to a player at a base.

3. Play "Five Hundred." Using a fungo bat, one player hits to a group of fielders. Fielders score successful catches. A fly ball is worth 100 points; a ground ball, 50 points; and a catch on a first bounce, 50 points. If a catch is tried and missed, the respective number of points is deducted. A player scoring 500 points exchanges with the batter.

Batting

The key to offensive softball lies in effective batting—a complex motor task—coupled with baserunning.

➤ Learning Hints

1. The basic position has the batter standing in the batter's box with feet slightly more than hip-width apart, knees relaxed and flexed slightly, and with the body bent slightly forward at the hips.

2. The bat is gripped by the handle in such a manner that the second joints of each finger on each hand are in alignment (Figure 19-7).

3. Before hitting, the bat is held in a position over the rear shoulder with the forearm (closer to pitcher) fairly straight and raised so that the elbow is chest-high. The back arm is bent slightly with the elbow away from the body (Figure 19-8).

4. The forward leg should step forward toward the pitcher, and during the swing the weight should shift over to the front leg, which should be straight.

Figure 19-7 Batting grip.

Figure 19-8 Batting stance.

Figure 19-9 Batting position at contact with ball.

5. In executing the swing, the body, arms, and bat first rotate slightly away from the pitcher. This gives the bat more distance over which to gain momentum and enables the body to exert more torque in hitting.

6. Rotate the hips as the bat comes forward. The arms should straighten, and the wrists should straighten forcefully just before the ball is hit and should continue to straighten very forcefully as the ball is hit.

7. The trunk and hips rotate until the batter almost faces the pitcher and the ball is struck about half an arm's length in front of the shoulder that is closer to the plate (Figure 19-9).

8. The rear foot initiates a push forward but should maintain contact with the ground as the ball is hit.

9. Watch the ball from the time the pitcher has it until just before hitting it.

10. Swing only at pitches in the strike zone.

▶ **Practice/Organizational Suggestions**

1. Strike the ball from a stationary tee or from a rope suspended overhead.

2. Using a fungo bat, hit fly balls, line drives, and ground balls.

3. Have a partner toss balls from a distance of 2 to 3 yards to the side (about a 45-degree angle). Students can hit the balls into the playing field or into a fence.

4. Get in groups of four or five with batter, pitcher, and two or three fielders. Hit 10 or 15 pitches and rotate. Position groups for safety.

Bunting

This is an effective offensive weapon in the fast-pitch game but is illegal in slow-pitch softball. Although the fielders are closer to the batter in softball than in baseball, it takes just as much time to field and throw a softball as a baseball. Therefore, the batter in softball should have a slight advantage over the baseball player in using the bunt as a means to reach first base safely.

▶ **Learning Hints**

1. The initial stance is the same as for hitting because it is most effective as a surprise maneuver, and its declaration must be withheld as long as possible.

2. Just before the pitcher releases the ball, the batter should pivot on the front foot and bring the back foot forward parallel with the front foot so that the batter is facing the pitcher and is near the front of the batter's box.

3. The knees should be bent and the body should crouch low, especially on low balls. Move the body up and down and maintain the bunting stance rather than moving the arms for high and low pitches.

4. The arms bring the bat downward to a position parallel with the ground in front of home plate and perpendicular to the ball's line of flight. As the bat comes down, slide the top hand up the bat to a position beyond the center of the bat, where the thumb and index finger grasp the bat on the rear side to avoid having the fingers hit. Arms should be half flexed (Figure 19-10).

Figure 19-10 Bunting position.

Figure 19-11 Path for running bases.

5. By flexing one arm a little more while extending the other arm, the ball may be guided down either the first or third base lines.
6. The ball should contact the bat slightly above the top hand.
7. The arms should give slightly as the ball hits the bat to keep the ball from rebounding too far into the playing field.
8. Keep the bat higher than the ball and hit the top half of the ball so that the ball is more likely to be hit downward.

➤ **Practice/Organizational Suggestions**

1. In front of a mirror, practice turning from batting stance to bunting stance.
2. Bunt balls that a partner tosses slowly.
3. Bunt to a glove placed on the ground at various positions.

Baserunning

In running the bases, follow the base lines and avoid making wide turns when rounding a base. The proper method is to pull out about 3 feet from the base line a couple of strides before reaching the base, and then by timing your steps, hit the inside corner of the base with the left foot. As the left foot hits the base, the body twists slightly to the left so that the right foot will land just beyond the next base line. The runner comes back to the base line and continues (see diagram, Figure 19-11).

When advancing from first to second, watch the third-base coach for directions. The coach is usually in a better position to see the entire field of play and tell the runner whether to stop at second or continue

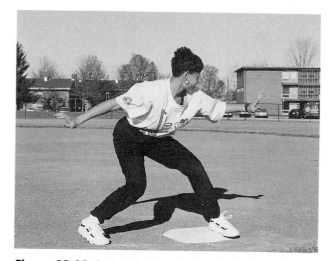

Figure 19-12 Sprinter's stance.

on to third base. Since the runner must remain on his base until the ball leaves the pitcher's hand (fast-pitch) or reaches home plate (slow-pitch), a sprinter's stance (Figure 19-12) should be taken with one foot on the base in readiness for a quick departure (whether on a steal or a batted ball).

➤ **Practice/Organizational Suggestions**

1. Run the bases after hitting in batting practice.
2. Practice hitting the ball and starting for first base.
3. Practice starting from a base with the sprinter's stance.

Sliding

To avoid injury, no one should attempt sliding without prior instruction and practice in the technique.

Knowing how to slide correctly will also prevent overrunning a base.

The *hook slide*, which is the most popular, is performed by sliding on a thigh and hip with the body leaning away from the base. When sliding on the right hip and thigh, the base is hooked with the left toe, and the right leg is either bent under the left leg with the right toe pointing backward (to keep from getting caught in the ground) or is extended forward in the air (to prevent the spikes from catching in the ground and injuring ankles and knees). The left leg is raised slightly off the ground and as the body, which is slightly to the right of the base line, approaches the base, the toe hooks onto the base (Figure 19-13). It is important to start the slide soon enough so that by the time the toe hooks the base, the body's momentum is slow enough to avoid pulling the toe off the base.

The *bent-leg slide* is used by players who wish to get to their feet quickly in order to advance to another base on an overthrow or misplay. In this slide, the player slides on the bent underneath leg, with the upper leg making contact with the base (Figure 19-14). The forward momentum of the slide is utilized to raise the body to an upright position after making contact with the base.

The *head-first slide* is often used when it becomes necessary to return to a base. The use of a head-first slide in any other situation should be strongly discouraged.

➤ Practice/Organizational Suggestions

1. Practice in a gym, on wet grass, or in a sliding pit. Wear long pants and socks, no shoes.
2. Judge one another on technique.
3. Slide for a square marked on the grass.
4. Slide into a base opposite a catch made by a partner who receives the toss from another player. Rotate.

Pitching

The success of a winning team depends largely on the consistency of its pitching. A good pitcher must have control and command a variety of pitches that can be used whether playing slow-pitch or fast-pitch softball. Special movement requirements are outlined under "Pitching Regulations" in the Basic Rules section.

Slow Pitching.   Place the foot on the throwing-arm side on the front of the pitching rubber. The opposite foot is behind the throwing-arm-side foot. The throwing arm is brought behind the body in an underhand, pendulum motion. The opposite foot steps toward home plate. The arm is swung forward, with the fingers under the ball. The ball should be released about shoulder high, which helps to attain the 12-foot arc and to drop the ball over the plate (Figure 19-15). Lower releases tend to flatten the pitch and give it more velocity. Varied spins as well as different speeds on the ball should be developed to keep the batter mixed up in the timing of the swing.

Figure 19-13 Hook slide.

Figure 19-14 Bent-leg slide.

Figure 19-15 Pitching delivery: Slow pitch.

Figure 19-16 Windmill pitch follow-through.

Fast Pitching. Several different types of deliveries are possible, including a sling shot or half windmill and a windmill. The beginning stance for each delivery is the same as for slow pitching except that the back foot must be in contact with the pitching rubber. The half windmill is the same motion as slow pitching but faster, and the release is by the hip with a snap of the wrist. A windmill involves moving the pitching arm through a full circle. The body is twisted away from the batter at the top of the swing. As the arm begins the downward swing, the hips are rotated to a position facing the batter. The leg on the throwing side pushes forcefully against the pitching rubber as the ball is released at the hip with a strong wrist snap (Figure 19-16).

➤ **Practice/Organizational Suggestions**

1. Throw to a partner who moves the target around the strike zone.
2. Throw to a target—such as an old mat tacked on a wall, fence, or backstop. In slow-pitch, place an empty bucket, milk crate, or circle on the ground as a target.
3. Play "Pitcher vs. Pitcher." Two players work together. One pitches and the other catches. The pitcher pitches to an imaginary batter. The catcher calls balls and strikes. The "batter" is either struck out or walks. "Runners" advance as additional "batters" become "runners." One player continues to pitch until three "batters" are out, then the players exchange positions. The

winner is the pitcher with the fewest "runners" scoring.

Playing Catcher

The catcher is frequently called the "defensive center of the infield" because the catcher handles all the pitched balls and is in a position to see all the infield proceedings. The catcher should call the player's name on infield flies, tell the fielder of a bunt where to throw, and keep all players informed of the number of outs. The catcher gives the pitcher the signal for the type of pitch to be thrown, gives a target to throw to, makes every effort to block wild pitches with runners on base, and makes plays at home plate. The catcher assumes a squat position as close to the batter as possible without interfering with the swing and with the weight forward on the balls of the feet so that quick movements in any direction can be made. In making a throw, the catcher brings the ball up to a position behind the ear, steps forward with the left foot, and throws by bringing the arm forward quickly and with a strong wrist snap just prior to release.

Playing First Base

The first-base player in fast-pitch softball must always be alert for fielding a bunt, because it is used frequently. The field position for this is in toward home plate 10 to 20 feet; a greater distance is used with no one on base, and a shorter distance is used with a runner on first and a double-play possibility. In slow-pitch, the playing position is approximately 10 feet behind the base but varies in depth and distance from the foul line according to the strength or weakness of the batter. To be in a position to receive a throw from another fielder, run quickly to the base when the ball is hit and assume a position facing the fielder, with the heels touching the inside edge of the bag. The first-base player should shift the body according to the direction of the throw. When the throw is to the left (toward home plate), bring the toe of the right foot to the edge of the bag by the left heel and then step toward the ball with the left foot. Reverse the procedure for a throw on the right (toward the outfield).

► **Practice/Organizational Suggestions**

1. Do the footwork without catching until it is an automatic response.
2. Have a partner toss balls to both sides of the base.
3. Have fielders throw balls to the base.
4. Have the coach hit ground balls to fielders and let them throw to first base.
5. Field bunts and ground balls hit to various spots in the first-base area.
6. Practice catching fly balls in the vicinity of first base.

Playing Second Base and Shortstop

The fielding position for the second-base player is approximately 15 feet from second base toward first base and about 12 feet behind the base line. The position varies with the strength and weakness of the batter. One should attempt to field all batted balls to the first-base side of second base. On a double-play situation from the third-base side, one should move quickly toward the base in a path that puts second base between the person fielding the ball and the second-base player. Time the move so that the ball is caught as the right foot hits the bag; step forward with the left foot toward the infield and first base to avoid the baserunner, and with a pivot, throw to first base.

The shortstop takes a field position similar to the second-base player's position but closer to third base; the position varies with the strength and weakness of the batter. One should attempt to field all batted balls to the third-base side of second base. In a double-play situation, move quickly to the base in a direct line with second base and the player fielding the ball. Time the move to catch the ball just before reaching the bag; step to the outfield side with the left foot; drag the right foot across the bag, and pivot and throw to first base. Both the shortstop and second-base player can stop just before they reach second base, catch the ball and touch second base with the left foot, push back with that foot, landing on the right foot, and then pivot and throw to first base.

► **Practice/Organizational Suggestions**

1. Field ground balls hit to various positions and with varying speeds.

2. Move across the bag and throw to first base.
3. Make the step-back-and-throw maneuver.
4. Complete the double-play situation after fielding ground balls.
5. Make the double play with a runner moving with the hit ball.
6. Tag runners stealing second base.
7. Catch infield fly balls.

Playing Third Base

The position of the third-base player in fast-pitch is similar to that of the first-base player—be in a position to field bunted balls by playing in toward home plate 10 to 20 feet, depending on the game situation. Attempt to field all batted balls hit down the third-base line and as many as can be reached that are hit to the second-base side, because the momentum developed by moving in that direction should aid the throw to first base.

► **Practice/Organizational Suggestions**

1. Field bunted balls and throw to first base and second base.
2. Field batted balls hit to various positions at varying speeds. Throw to first base and to second base.
3. Field batted balls and practice the double-play situation.
4. Catch pop-ups in the vicinity of third base.
5. Tag runners stealing third base.

Playing the Outfield

The position of the outfielders should enable them to cover their area from the infield to the fence, and it should vary according to the strength and weakness of the batter. The overhand throw is used when throwing to the infield because it is usually more accurate due to the fact that side spin is not put on the ball, which causes it to curve. Use the techniques for fielding ground balls and fly balls.

► **Practice/Organizational Suggestions**

1. Catch fly balls hit to various positions, including over one's head.
2. Field ground balls hit to various positions.
3. Make throws to second base, third base, home plate, and to a relay player. Do the same with players running the bases.
4. Throw to targets at the various bases.

Playing Strategy

Fast-pitch softball permits most of the team strategies used in baseball. It is varied according to any given game situation and the philosophical beliefs of the coach. One difference is that the second-base player covers first base on bunts rather than the pitcher. The winning team will be the one that not only masters individual fundamentals but also functions as a unit in the execution of team plays. In slow-pitch softball, there are no offensive plays, because a baserunner cannot leave the base until the pitched ball reaches home plate and cannot advance until the ball is hit or the batter is walked.

Safety Procedures

The following procedures should be observed to minimize the possibility of accidents and injuries.

1. Organize throwing and catching warm-up drills in parallel lines. Adjacent players should be a safe distance apart. When a ball is missed, it should be retrieved and the student should return to the line before making a throw to the partner.
2. The receiver should indicate the target before any ball is thrown.
3. Players should wear proper protection (helmets, masks, gloves, etc.) at all times.
4. Perfect sliding techniques before using them. Always avoid unnecessary slides.
5. Anchor bases firmly to the ground.
6. Students should swing bats only in designated areas, and no one should be allowed to enter batting areas.
7. Have batting practice organized so that one group does not hit toward another group.
8. Grip the bat tightly so it will not slip from the hands. Keep the hands dry and only use bats with the proper safety grip. After batting, *drop* the bat, do not throw it.
9. Players of teams waiting to bat should be in a specific safe area.
10. Keep equipment organized and in the dugout. Do not leave it scattered around or in the playing area.
11. Keep the playing area clear of rocks, depressions, obstructions, or any foreign objects.
12. To avoid collisions, learn the correct procedure for calling for fly balls and for covering bases.
13. Organize drills so that students are facing away from the sun.

Modifications for Special Populations

Orthopedically Impaired

1. Contact the National Wheelchair Softball Association.
2. Allow students using crutches, canes, or walkers to strike the ball from a stationary position, e.g., batting tee or traffic cone.
3. Use plastic bats and balls, e.g., whiffle ball.

Cognitively Impaired

1. Contact your local Special Olympics to obtain a copy of their softball manual.
2. Plan "one-base" softball, in which the batter runs only to first base and not the entire diamond. Add additional bases as skills and concepts of the game improve.
3. Do not play "three out"; allow all players from one team to hit before exchanging offensive and defensive positions.

Sensory Impaired

1. Contact the United States Association for Blind Athletes for the rules of "Beep Baseball."
2. For students who are blind or have a visual impairment, construct modified guidelines with jump ropes from home plate to first base.
3. Strike the ball from a stationary position, e.g., batting tee, and instruct the runners to move to an auditory cue, e.g., bell or buzzer at first base.
4. Minimal modifications are needed for students who are deaf or have a hearing impairment.

Terminology

Appeal play A play upon which an umpire cannot make a decision until requested by a player or a coach.

Assist Fielding credit for a player who throws or deflects a batted or thrown ball in which a put-out results, or would have resulted except for a subsequent error.

Battery The pitcher and the catcher.

Batting average The number of hits divided by the times at bat.

Blocked ball A batted or thrown ball that is touched or stopped by a person not engaged in the game, or that touches any object that is not part of the official equipment or official playing area.

Blooper A batted fly ball that goes just over the head of the infielders and just in front of the outfielders.

Cleanup hitter The number four batter in the batting order, a position usually occupied by the team's heaviest hitter.

Control The ability of a pitcher to throw the ball to a desired area when pitching.

Count The number of balls and strikes on the batter.

Cut-off A throw from the outfield that is intercepted by an infielder for the purpose of throwing out a runner other than the intended runner.

Double play Two consecutive put-outs occurring between the time the ball leaves the pitcher's hand and its return to the pitcher.

Error A misplay or mistake by the defensive team that results in prolonging the turn at bat of the batter or the time on base of the baserunner.

Fielder's choice   The batter is safe because the defensive player elected to retire a preceding baserunner.

Force out   An out as a result of a defensive player with the ball tagging a runner or the base to which the baserunner must go because the batter became a baserunner.

Fungo bat   A lightweight bat used in hitting balls to fielders during practice.

Grand slam   The batter hits a home run with the bases loaded.

Hit   A ball hit in such a way that the batter or preceding baserunners are not retired by good defensive play.

Hot corner   The third-base area.

Infield fly   A fair fly ball that can be caught by an infielder with runners on first and second, or first, second, and third, before two are out. The batter is declared out by the umpire.

Keystone sack   The second-base area.

On deck   The player in line to follow the batter at the plate. The place for waiting is the "on-deck circle."

Overthrow   A thrown ball that goes into foul territory beyond the boundary lines of the playing field on an attempt to retire a runner who has not reached or is off a base.

Passed ball   A legally delivered pitch that should have been held or controlled by the catcher, which allows a baserunner to advance. A dropped third strike that permits the batter to reach first base in fast-pitch is an error, not a passed ball.

Put-out   An out credited to the fielder who last handles the ball on a play that retires the batter or a baserunner.

Running squeeze   A play where the runner on third base starts for home with the pitch because she knows the batter is going to bunt the ball.

Sacrifice bunt   A play where the batter bunts for the ball to advance a baserunner and is thrown out at first base, or would have been if the ball were played properly.

Sacrifice fly   A fly ball that is caught and after which a baserunner crosses home plate to score a run.

Safety squeeze   A play in which the baserunner on third base starts for home after the batter bunts the ball.

Switch hitter   A batter who bats both right- and left-handed.

Texas leaguer   Same as a *Blooper*.

Wild pitch   A legally delivered pitch so wide or low or high that the catcher cannot stop or control the ball, which allows a baserunner to advance.

Further References

American Sport Education Program. *Coaching Youth Softball.* Champaign, IL: Human Kinetics, 2001. (Video also available.)

Blakemore, C., Hawkes, N., and Burton, E. *Drill to Skill: Teacher Tactics in Physical Education.* Dubuque, IA: Wm. C. Brown Publishers, 1991.

Garman, J. *Softball Skills and Drills.* Champaign, IL: Human Kinetics, 2001. (Three videos also available.)

Joseph, J. *Defensive Softball Drills.* Champaign, IL: Human Kinetics, 1998.

NAGWS Softball Guide. Reston, VA: AAHPERD, Current Ed.

Official Softball Rules. Oklahoma City, OK: The International Joint Rules Committee on Softball, Current Ed.

Potter, D. L., & Brockmeyer, G. A. *Softball: Steps to Success.* Champaign, IL: Human Kinetics, 1999.

Rikli, R. *Softball Skills Test Manual.* 1991.

Web Sites

www.usasoftball.com   The official site for USA Softball including information about the USA National Teams.

www.softball.org   The official site of the Amateur Softball Association (ASA), which is the national governing body of softball. Includes information about obtaining rule books, umpire programs, Hall of Fame, videos and books for players, and more.

www.angelfire.com/sd/slopitch/index.html   A slow pitch softball Web site that includes the history of slow-pitch softball as well as information about major tournaments and national champions.

www.softball.net/links/   A directory of other softball sites; includes a search option.

www.softball.net/Directory/Books/   Lists many outstanding softball books that can be ordered directly from the site.

www.serioussoftball.com/photos.htm   Includes lots of photos of softball players in action as well as team pictures. Is possible to post pictures to this site.

www.eteamz.com/NorthTexasBees/   Fast-pitch softball drills and tips as well as links to softball equipment vendors.

CHAPTER 20

Speedball

This chapter will enable you to

- Identify and put into practice the rules governing the game
- Practice and then execute the basic skills, including kicking, passing, catching, trapping, dribbling, and aerial ball conversions
- Identify differences and similarities of skills, rules, and strategies found in other sports
- Discuss and employ basic offensive and defensive strategies and tactics
- Identify and use basic terminology associated with the game

Nature and Purpose

The game of speedball is a combination of the skills, rules, and strategies of soccer, basketball, and football. It is a vigorous, continuous-motion activity involving running (sprinting and jogging) and changes of direction (dodging, cutting, stopping, restarting). It is played outdoors on a football- or soccer-size field by teams of 11 players, yet with limited modifications it can be played indoors in smaller areas and with fewer players.

Originally a men's activity, the game was modified for women's participation and has evolved into a sport that both can play by the same set of rules. Speedball is an adaptable game, and the leader can alter the rules to meet individual preferences.

The object of the game is to propel a ball to the opponent's end of the field and score points. The ball is propelled either as a ground ball (soccer skills) or an aerial ball (basketball and football). The skills involved are kicking, passing (hands or feet), catching, trapping, and dribbling.

In advancing the ball, the offense attempts to score either by a field goal, touchdown, drop kick, penalty kick, or end goal. The defenders attempt to impede the attack by guarding. Players on both teams are organized into forwards, halfbacks, fullbacks, and a goalkeeper, as in soccer.

Field of Play

A football, soccer, or field hockey field can be used. The regulation field is shown in Figure 20-1. The field consists of a middle/halfway line, restraining lines, end zone/penalty area, penalty kick mark, end lines, goal lines, and sidelines.

Middle/Halfway Line

The middle/halfway line is used on the kickoffs to ensure that the team taking the kick is in its own half of the field.

Restraining Line

The opponents of the team taking the kickoff must stay behind the restraining line until the ball is contacted. The ball must travel beyond (10 yards) the restraining line on kickoff, or be touched by an opponent, before those taking the kickoff can replay the ball.

End Zone/Penalty Area

The size of the end zone/penalty area may vary if using football field markings. The area has four purposes: (1) A ball thrown from the field of play, across the goal line, and caught in the end zone by the team attacking that end results in a score (touchdown as in football). (2) Any "contact foul" or "personal foul" committed in this area and against the team defending that end results in a penalty kick. (3) On a penalty kick, no player from the defending team except the goalie can be in this zone. (4) A legal attempt to score on a ground ball within this area by the offense results in an end goal if it crosses the end line but not in the goal.

Penalty Kick Mark

The penalty kick mark is the spot to place the ball for taking a penalty kick.

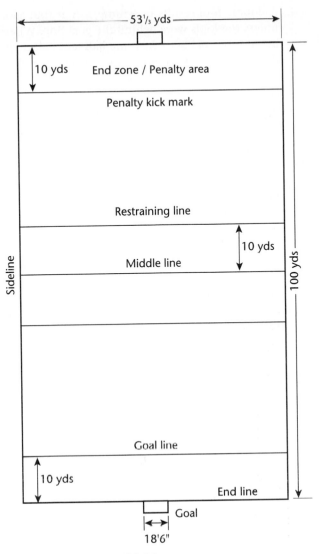

53⅓ yds

10 yds   End zone / Penalty area

Penalty kick mark

Restraining line

10 yds

Middle line

Sideline

100 yds

Goal line

10 yds

End line

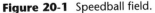

Goal

18'6"

Figure 20-1 Speedball field.

End Line

The end line serves as a boundary, and when the ball goes out-of-bounds without scoring, it is put back in play by the opposing team from that spot. The end line can also determine an end goal in men's rules (see End Zone/Penalty Area, purpose #4). On a penalty kick, the defensive players stand behind this line.

Goal Line

The goal line separates the field of play from the end zone/penalty area. On a penalty kick, players stand behind the goal line so that they are not in the penalty area.

Sideline

The sideline is a boundary line, and when the ball goes out of bounds it is put back in play with a throw by the opposing team from that spot.

Basic Rules

Although there are two sets of official rules for men's and women's competition, separate rules are no longer necessary. The following is a combined and simplified set of rules.

Scoring

The regulation methods for scoring are listed in Table 20-1 and described below. The points can be adjusted to meet the needs of varying age groups or for emphasizing specific skill usage. From experience, most individuals elect to overuse the "touchdown" method of scoring. Adding a higher point value than the one listed for a "field goal" leads to players using their kicking skills more often, thus de-emphasizing throwing and catching. Another suggestion is that the "end goal" method of scoring be eliminated.

> *Field goal:* propelling the ball with the feet or body (no hands or arms) into the goal—identical to a legal soccer score.
> *Touchdown:* throwing the ball across the goal line to a teammate who catches it in the end zone/penalty area—similar to a football touchdown.
> *Drop kick:* drop kicking the ball over the goal crossbar and between the uprights from outside the end zone/penalty area.
> *Penalty kick:* free kicking the ball as a result of a personal contact foul against the defending team when in their own penalty area. The ball is kicked from the penalty kick mark into the goal. It is suggested that the ball be placed on the ground (men's rules) similar to a soccer penalty kick rather than drop kicked (women's rules).
> *End goal:* the offense kicking the ball over the end line from within the end zone/penalty area without the ball going into the goal. It is suggested that this method of scoring *not* be used, but instead the opponents receive a pass/kick-in from the spot where the ball went over the end line.

Table 20-1 Speedball scoring: Official and recommended

	Official	Recommended
Field goal	3	3
Drop kick	2	2
Touchdown	1	1
Penalty kick	1	1
End goal	1	X

Violations, Fouls, and Penalties

The penalties for infractions vary according to the severity of the infraction. The following list combines the infractions and classifies them as either fouls (severe) or violations (less severe).

Violations

1. A ground ball touched with the hands or arms
2. Taking too many steps with the ball—two steps if received while running and one step while standing
3. More than one aerial dribble per possession
4. Holding the ball more than 3 seconds
5. Kicking or kneeing a fly ball before catching it
6. The offense drop-kicking the ball in the defense's penalty area
7. The offense throwing the ball to a teammate when both are in the defense's penalty area

Violation Penalties

1. A violation outside the penalty area results in an indirect free kick at the spot of the infraction. See Soccer, "Fouls—Indirect Free Kick."
2. A violation inside the opponents' end zone/penalty area gives the opponents a penalty kick.
3. A violation inside one's own end zone/penalty area results in an indirect free kick by the opponents at the spot of the infraction.

Fouls

1. Illegal contact with opponents
   a. Kicking
   b. Pushing
   c. Tripping
   d. Holding
   e. Blocking
   f. Charging—see Soccer, "Charge," for legality
   g. Hacking
   h. Obstruction—See Soccer, "Obstruction," for legality
   i. Unnecessary roughness
2. Illegal substitution
3. Unnecessary delay of game
4. Taking more than three time-outs
5. Having more than 11 players on the field
6. Unsportsmanlike conduct

Foul Penalties

1. A body contact foul (#1a–1i) by the defending team in their own penalty area/end zone results in a penalty kick by the opponents.
2. A body contact foul (#1a–1i) occurring other than in one's own penalty area/end zone results in an indirect free kick by the opponents.
3. A non-contact foul (#2–#6) results in a penalty kick to the offended team.

4. A double foul results in a jump ball at that spot unless the fouls were behind the goal line. When behind the goal line, the jump ball takes place on the goal line nearest where the fouls occurred.

Length of Game

Speedball is played in quarters, with intervals between each quarter and at the half. The time for each play period and for intervals can be modified to suit the physical abilities of the participants.

Kickoff

The ball is kicked from the ground forward from the middle line. All members of the kicking team remain behind the middle line until the ball is contacted. The receiving team remains behind the restraining line until contact.

The rules are identical to a soccer kickoff (see Soccer, "Kickoff"), but also allow the play to be turned into an aerial ball by lifting it with the feet to the hands of a teammate (not to self).

Playing the Ball

Ground Ball. The ball, when on the ground (rolling, bouncing, or stationary), is played as in soccer, with skills of dribbling, kicking, heading, or trapping. In order for the ball to be thrown, it must first be brought from the feet immediately into the hands.

Aerial Ball. The legal conversion of a ground ball using the feet to lift or kick it into the hands is called an aerial ball. When in the hands, it can be thrown, passed, and caught as in football and basketball. The ball can be air dribbled to oneself only one time each new possession. The air dribble consists of throwing the ball in the air and relocating to regain possession by catching it. On the air dribble, steps do not count while the ball is in the air. A player is legally allowed one step with the ball when holding it if obtained while standing, or two steps if running prior to receiving it. Additional steps are illegal and are called traveling. Holding the ball with the hands for more than three seconds without giving up possession is illegal. This speeds up the game and is a rule that can be modified.

Physical Contact. Rules allow for the same body contact as in soccer (see Soccer, "Physical Contact") when the ball is on the ground. With the ball in the hands, guarding as in basketball (see Basketball, "Fouls") is appropriate. Other personal contact fouls were identified in the foregoing listing of speedball fouls.

Jump Ball (Toss-up, Tie-ball). Two opponents simultaneously holding the ball results in a jump ball, Likewise, if it is not possible to decide which team put the ball out-of-bounds, a jump ball is held. The format is the same as in basketball, with two opponents facing each other and jumping to tip the ball, which is tossed between them. All other opponents must be at least 5 yards away on the toss-up. The ball remains as an aerial ball off the tip provided it does not contact the ground, in which case it is considered a ground ball.

Out-of-Bounds. A ball going off the field of play over the sideline is put back in play with a throw (overhand, underhand, two hands, one hand, etc.). A ball over the end line is either thrown or kicked into play.

Free Kick. Certain identified infractions result in a free kick as in soccer (see Soccer, "Fouls") except that the opponents only need to be 5 yards from the ball. The kick is taken at the spot of infraction. It can be turned into an aerial ball. Indirect free kick means that someone must touch the ball prior to a score.

Penalty Kick. Certain foul situations previously identified result in a penalty kick, which is a free kick. The ball is placed on the penalty kick mark (line), and one of the offended team members is allowed a free kick to score a field goal against the opposing team goalie. The offensive team members position outside the defenders' penalty area. The defensive players, aside from the goalie, position either behind the end line or outside the penalty area.

Goalkeeper. The goalie primarily defends the goal against the field goal attempts. The goalkeeper is bound by the same rules as all other players, with no special privileges or rules.

Equipment

The only necessary equipment is a ball and two goals. The regulation speedball is slightly larger than a soccer ball, but a soccer ball, which is more readily available, is most often used. Any type of goal (soccer, football, field hockey, team handball, etc.) can be used, but the soccer and football goals (uprights extending from the ground up) are most often available. The regulation goal is 18 feet wide for women and 18 feet 6 inches for men.

Suggested Learning Sequence

A. Stretching and running
B. Basic rules
C. Fundamental skills
   1. Passing
      a. Soccer—inside of foot, instep kick, lofting the ball, and punt
      b. Basketball—chest, overhead, and baseball
      c. Football—forward
      d. Speedball—drop kick
   2. Catching/Trapping
      a. Soccer—sole of foot, inside of foot, outside of foot and chest
      b. Basketball—two hands above and below the waist, pivoting
      c. Football—over the shoulder
   3. Heading
      a. Soccer—standing and jumping
   4. Dribbling
      a. Soccer—inside and outside of foot
      b. Speedball—aerial
   5. Individual defense
      a. Soccer—tackling from the front and side
      b. Basketball—guarding and denial of ball
      c. Football—pass defense
   6. Personal conversion to aerial
      a. Speedball—roll up, two-foot lift, and one-foot lift
   7. Goalie
      a. Soccer—catch at waist, chest, and above head; tip; throw and punt
D. Strategies
   1. Offense
      a. Soccer—possession, superiority around the ball, creating space, tempo, communication, depth/support, width, penetration, mobility, and improvisation
      b. Basketball—cutting, fakes/feints, attacking a player to player and zone defense, fast break
      c. Football—dodging, faking, and change of pace
   2. Defense
      a. Soccer—pressure, depth/support, width, balance, delay, concentration, and control
      b. Basketball—player to player, fast break, and zone
      c. Football—pass defense
E. Systems
   1. Style—long or short pass, static positioning, aerial or ground ball, player to player or zone
   2. Formations—(M or W as in soccer), V or inverted V
F. Restarts
   1. Kickoff
   2. Throw-in
   3. Free kick
   4. Penalty kick

Skills and Techniques

Only a few skills are specific to speedball. Most of the skills needed are described in the basketball, soccer, and football chapters. The skills from these sports are identified below, and a review of these sections will prepare the speedball player for skilled participation.

Basketball Skills: pivoting; chest pass; overhead pass—one hand overhead pass (baseball); two-hand catch and holding the ball; cutting; individual defense against a player with the ball, player without the ball and denial defense.

Soccer Skills: inside of foot pass; instep kick; lofting the ball; sole of foot trap, inside and outside of foot trap; chest trap; inside and outside of foot dribble, heading, standing, and jumping; tackling from front and side; goalkeeping—catching ball at waist, chest, and above head plus falling to side, tip, punt, and overhand throw.

Football Skills: forward pass and over-the-shoulder catch.

Aerial Conversions

Ball control and scoring opportunities are enhanced by having the ball in the hands. The ball must go from the feet directly into the hands for it to be a legal aerial ball. This may happen as a result of punts, soccer-style kicks, and drop kicks to other players. An individual can personally convert a ground ball to an aerial ball by using either a roll-up, two-foot lift, or one-foot lift.

➤ Learning Hints—Roll-Up

1. Stand erect with the ball wedged evenly between the feet (Figure 20-2).

2. Bend at the waist so the back is parallel with the ground.
3. Extend the arms downward and perpendicular to the ground.
4. Place pressure on the bottom half of the ball with the inside of one foot, rotate the knee outward, and roll the ball up the inside ankle and calf of the opposite leg (Figure 20-2B).
5. Grab the ball off the foot and leg with the hand, converting it to an aerial ball (Figure 20-2C).

➤ Practice/Organizational Suggestions

Wedge the ball with the inside of both feet and roll the ball up and down one lower leg by applying more pressure with the foot opposite that leg. Do not attempt to pick up the ball at this point, but repeatedly roll it up and down the leg to get the feeling so that control is not lost. Progress next to bending over to grab the ball off the foot and leg with the hands. Gradually attempt to speed up the whole process.

➤ Learning Hints—Two-Foot Lift

1. Stand erect with the ball wedged evenly between the feet as in Figure 20-2A.
2. Hop up, keeping the ball wedged evenly between the feet and lifting it higher toward the hands.
3. In the air, lean forward, extending the arms and hands downward to grab the ball from the feet (Figure 20-3A).
4. Catch the ball and land on two feet with the converted aerial ball, ready to pass it (Figure 20-3B).

A   B   C

Figure 20-2 Roll-up: (A) Wedge ball, (B) rolling ball up leg, (C) converting to an aerial ball by grabbing it with hands.

Figure 20-3 Two-foot lift: (A) Lifting the ball to convert to an aerial; (B) catching the ball from lift.

➤ Practice/Organizational Suggestions

Wedge the ball with the inside of both feet and hop in the air, attempting to lift the ball as high as possible. Keep the body erect and do not yet attempt to lean over to grab the ball. Continue this exercise, attempting to bring the ball higher each time. Progress next to leaning over to grab the ball with the hands before it drops to the ground.

➤ Learning Hints—One-Foot Lift

1. Stand erect with one foot extended in front of the body and the sole of that foot applying light pressure on the top of the ball (Figure 20-4A).

Figure 20-4 One-foot lift: (A) Rolling ball backward, (B) lifting backward rolling ball with toe, and (C) catching ball from the toe lift.

2. Apply more pressure on the top of the ball with the sole of the foot, and roll the ball quickly toward the body.

3. Place the toe of the foot rolling the ball under the rotating ball to lift it upward.

4. Bend forward at the waist, extend the arms and hands downward, and lift the ball with the toe toward the hand (Figure 20-4B).

5. Catch the ball with two hands as it is lifted waist-high into the air (Figure 20-4C), converting it to an aerial ball.

➤ Practice/Organizational Suggestions

In an erect position, reach forward with an extended leg and apply pressure on the ball with the sole of the foot. Roll the ball backward and forward, keeping foot pressure on it, to get the feeling of rolling. Gradually, on the backward roll, apply more pressure, causing rapid rotation on the ball as that foot releases from the ball. Next, attempt to place the toe of that foot quickly under the ball and lift the ball as high as possible into the air without catching it. Try to lift it at least waist-high. Finally, repeat all of the foregoing and lean forward to catch the ball. Once consistency is obtained, attempt to use the one-foot lift on an approaching ball that is already rolling toward you.

Drop Kick

The drop kick is used as one method of scoring. It also can be used to kick the ball a great distance, similar to punting, except that a drop kick tends to have a lower trajectory, which adds distance to the kick.

➤ Learning Hints

Refer to the soccer chapter learning hints on punting. Hints 1–5 apply to speedball. The following techniques differ for drop-kicking.

6. *Ball contact.* The ball is contacted with the instep (hard top surface) of the foot immediately upon the ball's touching the ground (bounce). The contact is in the back/bottom surface of the ball. The higher the contact surface on the ball, the lower the trajectory of the ball, and vice-versa.

7. *Follow-through.* A short follow-through by the contact leg results in a low trajectory, and a long one results in a higher trajectory.

➤ Practice/Organizational Suggestions

Face a wall 10 yards away and drop the ball, attempting to drop kick it with a low trajectory (no higher than the head). Allowing the ball to bounce too high from the ground results in a high trajectory, so attempt to contact the ball the instant it contacts the ground. Gradually attempt to kick the ball higher without sacrificing accuracy. Alternate between high

and low trajectories to reinforce the timing of ball/ground/foot contact.

Playing Strategies

The placement of players on the field assists continuity in offense and defense. Speedball players consist of forwards, halfbacks, fullbacks, and a goalkeeper, and their responsibilities are the same as in soccer. The basic strategies are for the players to position systematically on the field, maintain possession of the ball, propel the ball toward the opponent's goal line, and score points.

Offense

A quick reference to the Soccer chapter will prepare participants for offensive play. Note especially the information on space; strategic field areas; offensive principles; individual, group, and team tactics; and styles of play.

One difference in speedball offense is that there are several methods of scoring. One method (touchdown) can be accomplished any place along the entire width of the field, while others (field goal and drop kick) can only be accomplished at the goal on the endline in the center. Converting an aerial ball to a ground ball for a field goal attempt provides an opportunity to score more points. Due to this, the ball in the middle of the field near the goal is a good offensive strategy specific to speedball.

Because ball control and possession are easier in speedball than in soccer, and there is no offside rule, it is an advantage to have many players in front of the ball to increase penetration and scoring opportunities. Passers should immediately attempt to locate in advance of the ball upon relinquishing possession.

Varying the ways the team attempts to score makes it more difficult for the opponents to defend against the offense.

Defense

The soccer chapter identifies defensive principles that apply to speedball. The player-to-player defense is imperative in speedball because the offense can use the aerial ball, which leads to ball control. Defenders must be close to their assigned individual to disrupt the offensive advantage. Quick transition from offense to locating the assigned individual one is to guard is extremely important. The defenders need to know where their opponents are at all times and be close enough to protect against a pass.

The aerial ball rules in speedball make it important that the defender position far enough away from the player with the ball so that the player cannot air dribble quickly, getting behind the defender. The offensive player cannot move very far on one air dribble and has only three seconds to get rid of the ball. If the aerial ball is converted to a ground ball by the offense, the defender should immediately pressure the opponent and get closer so as to destroy control and reduce the chances of making a long kick or shot on goal.

Systems

The placement of players on the field and their responsibilities reflect systematic cohesion among teammates. The team systems indicated in the soccer chapter are appropriate for speedball. Field balance is important for either offensive or defensive success, and a system provides this. The system utilized is dependent upon what the opponents use and/or the strengths and weaknesses of one's own team.

Modifications for Special Populations

See modifications listed in the soccer and team handball chapters.

Terminology

Aerial ball A ball that has been thrown or propelled into the air by the feet and that can legally be played with the hands.

Air dribble A ball tossed to oneself in an attempt to relocate.

Double foul Two opponents simultaneously committing a foul, which results in a jump ball (toss-up).

Dribble Propelling the ball with the feet (soccer) so that the individual maintains control while moving.

Drop kick The skill of dropping the ball from the hands to the ground and kicking it upon ground contact; also a method of scoring.

End goal A score resulting from the offense kicking the ball across the opponent's end line while in the penalty area (men's rules).

Field goal A score resulting from the offense propelling the ball, as in soccer (no hands or arms), into the opponent's goal.

Foul An infraction of the rules that is penalized severely.

Free kick An unguarded kick from the ground, such as penalty kick, kickoff, or indirect free kick.

Goalkeeper The player responsible for protecting the goal against the field goal.

Ground ball A ball that cannot be touched by the hands but must be propelled as in soccer by dribble, kicking, heading, and so forth.

Guard The act of defending against an opponent.

Indirect free kick A free kick in which someone other than the individual making that kick must touch the ball before it can go into the goal.

Infraction A breach of the rules.

Jump ball (Toss-up) Tossing the ball upward between two players who jump to tip the ball, restarting play.

Kickoff A free kick at the middle line at the start of the game, following a score, and following suspension of play each period.

Kick-up The conversion of a ground ball to an aerial ball.

One-foot lift The skill of converting a ground ball to an aerial ball by rolling and lifting it with the foot.

Pass Propelling the ball, with either the hands or feet, to another player.

Penalty kick A free kick to attempt a field goal as a result of a foul.

Punt The skill of immediately kicking the ball after dropping it from the hands.

Roll-up The skill of converting a ground ball into an aerial ball by rolling it up the leg with the foot and grabbing it with the hands.

Throw-in Putting the ball back in play after it has gone out-of-bounds over the sideline.

Touchdown A score made when a teammate throws the ball to a partner who catches it in the opponent's end zone/penalty area.

Trapping The skill of receiving (catching) the ball with the foot or body to bring it under control.

Traveling Taking too many steps with the ball in the hands: one step if received while standing and two if while running.

Two-foot lift The skill of converting a ground ball to an aerial ball by hopping to lift the ball to oneself.

Violation An infraction of the rules that is not severely penalized.

Further Reference

Phillip, J. and Wilkerson, J. *Teaching Team Sports*. Champaign, IL: Human Kinetics, 1990.

CHAPTER 21

Swimming, Diving, and Water Exercise

This chapter will enable you to

- Understand and apply the principles of safety involved in aquatic-related activities
- Understand the fundamental skills, biomechanics of swimming, and progressions utilized in the beginning through intermediate levels of swimming and diving
- Identify and correct common errors of learning swimmers and divers
- Understand and participate in the benefits of water exercise
- Participate in and contribute to aquatic games and contests

SWIMMING

Nature and Purpose

Aquatic activities are among the leading forms of recreation in the United States. Over 75 million Americans enter the water in some form of recreational aquatic activity each year. An estimated 5,000 drownings occur annually in the United States. Many of these result from the inability to swim or from preventable accidents. These statistics indicate the importance of knowing how to swim; in fact, a knowledge of basic swimming skills may be life saving. The goal of physical educators who teach swimming and diving in our schools is to provide sound information to students who wish to utilize our nation's recreational aquatic facilities.

There are other advantages to be derived from swimming in addition to increased safety in the water. Participants may improve their cardiorespiratory fitness levels. Many aquatic activities may benefit those unable to jog or otherwise restricted from land activities due to physical handicaps, because the body's natural buoyancy in water reduces strain in the knee and hip region. Flexibility, agility, balance, and strength can be improved with regular participation in water activities.

Equipment

Most of the equipment needed for instruction, activities, and aquatic games is generally found in and around aquatic facilities. A well-equipped aquatic program would include but is not limited to the following:

kickboards, pull buoys, float belts, personal flotation devices (PFDs), instructional flotation devices (IFDs), masks, fins, snorkels, water volleyballs (rubber) and net, water polo equipment (balls, hats, flag, goals), inner tubes, rescue equipment (reaching pole, ring buoys, throw bag, backboard, head-immobilizing device, cervical collars, pocket masks, first aid kit, rescue tubes, rescue board, shepherd's crook, whistles), water basketball and goals, various types of floatable toys, hula hoops, rubber diving bricks and rings, resolite mats, and net bags for equipment storage.

A hose or water source other than the pool's should be available to rinse all equipment at the end of each session, and a preventive maintenance program should be developed to help keep all equipment in good working order. A planned equipment replacement and expansion budget should be instituted.

Suggested Learning Sequence
Beginning Swimming
A. Water orientation
B. Holding positions
  1. Entry
  2. Front
  3. Back
  4. Drafting
  5. Streamlining on front
  6. Streamlining on back
C. Skills
  1. Bubble bobs
  2. Safety bobbing
  3. Front float

4. Back float
5. Front glide
6. Back glide
7. Front glide with kick
8. Back glide with kick
9. Front beginner stroke
10. Back beginner stroke
11. Jump from wall (shallow water)

Intermediate Swimming

A. Strokes
   1. Front crawl
   2. Elementary backstroke
   3. Back crawl
   4. Breaststroke
   5. Sidestroke

Diving

A. Types of dives (in order of difficulty)
   1. Slide-in dive
   2. Sitting dive
   3. Kneeling dive
   4. Scale or tip-in dive
   5. Shallow push dive
   6. Deep push dive
   7. Forward standing dive (1 meter)
   8. Standing back dive (1 meter)

Beginning Swimming

Water Orientation

Beginning students may approach their first swimming session with great anxiety. It is important that the instructor create an atmosphere conducive to learning under these circumstances. The following gradual steps should be taken with the beginning swimmers. Instructors should demonstrate all skills immediately prior to students' attempt.

1. Sit on pool side with feet and lower legs in the water.
2. Use hands to splash water on themselves.
3. Slide into shallow water and remain holding the wall. Instructor may need to assist students into the pool.
4. Sink into the water and pull the warm blanket of water over the shoulders.
5. Instructor—demonstrate bubble blowing with chin and lips in the water. Student's turn!
6. Bubble blowing from mouth and nose
7. Face completely immersed—with bubbles
8. Head under

Note: The student should be asked to do these skills, never forced. Remember that fear levels may be high. The peer pressure of classmates doing the skill should be ample external motivation. Student readiness will determine the level of accomplishment.

Holding Positions

Entry. The beginning swimmer may need assistance entering the water. This is particularly true if she cannot touch the bottom. The instructor reaches under the armpits of the student and lowers her from a sitting position on the deck into the water. Students should be reminded to hold onto the wall.

Front. The front holding position, to be used when instructing the front float, front glide, and so on, is best accomplished by having the student cross one hand over the other and place both hands in one of the instructor's hands. The student's arms are then extended at the elbow and as the student stretches to the glide position, the instructor places his opposite hand on the student's hip (Figure 21-1).

Back. The back holding position provides the student with security when learning the back float, back glide, and so on. The student places both hands on the wall, pushes the abdomen toward the wall, and places the head back toward the instructor. The instructor cradles the head in one hand while reaching to the small of the back with the other. The student is instructed to straighten the elbows and to keep an arch in the back (Figure 21-2).

Drafting. Drafting helps students gain confidence in their ability to float. The student is held in either the front or back holding position directly perpendicular to the instructor. The instructor begins to move backward while pulling the student along. Once the student is moving, the instructor intermittently reduces support or, depending on the student's confidence level, lets go. The student's body will be pulled by inertia toward the instructor and follow in her wake (Figure 21-3).

Streamlining on the Front. Streamlining helps reduce water resistance. The most important part of this skill is the grab of the hands. While standing, students place both hands over their heads. Without grabbing their hands, they should try to squeeze their ears with their arms. Then, contrast this by having students place one hand over the other and lock the thumb of the top hand over the bottom hand. Now, squeeze the ears again. Students should note that they are much stronger with hands locked into position. Once accomplished, have students sink into the water and push off into a front or prone glide, keep-

Figure 21-1 Holding position for front/prone glide.

Figure 21-2 Holding position for back/supine glide.

A   B

Figure 21-3 The transition from back glide holding position to drafting.

ing arms straight, hands locked, finger tips pointed, and body in line.

Streamlining on the Back. Streamlining on the back can be accomplished in the same manner as the frontal streamlining, just turned over. However, when floating on the back, most beginning students find it easier to leave hands and arms straight down at the sides. This is acceptable at the beginning level.

Beginner Skills

Bubble Bobs. The student holds the wall with both hands approximately shoulder-width apart. Submerge and blow bubbles toward the wall. This should be done systematically at the beginning of each class, and students should build to about two sets of ten rhythmic bubble bobs. Emphasis is placed on blowing out under water, taking a breath above water, keeping eyes open during both phases, and not wiping face with hands.

Safety Bobbing. Once the student is comfortable with bobbing, safety bobbing can be taught. The instructor takes students one at a time into water slightly over their heads. Practice at 5 feet from the wall and have students bob to wall systematically and rhythmically, bouncing from the bottom and pushing toward the wall. The instructor should assist as much as needed.

Front Float. Students can achieve a front float once they are comfortable putting their faces in the water. With minimal support from the instructor, a student allows legs and arms to dangle in the water with the face in. Breath should be exhaled slowly from mouth and nose.

Back Float. With minimal support from the instructor, the student lays his head back in the water while pushing his hips and abdomen toward surface gently; arms are extended laterally and knees are bent.

Front Glide. From the front holding position, have student push gently away from the wall. Once moving, remove the support hand from the hip and then from the hands. If the student is comfortable in attempting, and can push from the wall in the streamline position and can maintain a glide for 5 to 10 seconds, move on to the front glide with kick.

Back Glide. Generally, students are less comfortable in the supine position. The instructor needs to assess student readiness before attempting any removal of support from the back holding position. To start, have the student ease off the wall in the back holding position; request that the student make eye contact with the instructor and keep the belly up. Drafting can be used to increase the student's confidence.

Front Glide with Kick. The flutter kick (freestyle) should be first practiced on the wall, using the wall holding technique shown in Figure 21-4. Simultaneous practice of the kick and head position for breathing can be done as shown. Once a satisfactory kick is established, the student may push off the wall in the streamline position, glide (5 feet), and begin kicking. The kick should generate from the hip area with knees flexing slightly and toes pointed on the downbeat; the kick is finished with a straight leg. The foot then moves upward until the heel breaks the water surface. Legs are alternated. The kick should not splash water. Proper head position is accomplished with the water line at the middle of the forehead.

Figure 21-4 Flutter kicking with head in breathing position.

Back Glide with Kick. The backstroke kick (flutter) is accomplished by allowing the foot to first sink in the water about 12 inches by bending the knees. The upbeat, which is the propulsive phase, is done by straightening the leg. The foot should not come out of the water but the leg and toes do come near the surface. This maintains proper body position. The student eases off the wall on the back, glides (5 feet), and begins a gentle backstroke kick. Arms should remain at side. Proper head alignment is indicated by the chin being slightly up and the water line just over the ears.

Front Beginner Stroke. This stroke is taught when the front glide with kick can be done for 10 seconds. The stroke consists of the front glide with kick and an armstroke. The armstroke is accomplished by alternating arms from the streamlined position to the thigh. The arms are moved in perfect alternation with an underwater recovery and pull, push, slice, reach action. The pull phase is initiated by pulling down and back on the water with the hand from the overhead position. Then, keep the elbow high and begin a bend at the elbow. The hand then passes down the centerline of the body. Once the hand passes mid-chest, a pushing action is made toward the feet. The hand should be angled so that the palm is facing and pushing toward the feet. Breathing can be accomplished by turning the chin to either shoulder. The breathing is timed so that when the hand of the desired breathing side is in the push phase, the chin should be turned to the shoulder of the breathing side. The breath pattern should be such that the student blows bubbles into the water with the face in, completes the exhaling phase when the mouth exits the water, and inhales with the mouth out of the water. Immediately after taking the breath, the student turns the head so that the face is in the water and begins to exhale. The breath is not held.

Back Beginner Stroke. The student streamlines from the wall in the back streamline position (arms down), glides (5 feet), and begins the backstroke kick. Simultaneous arm movement is started by running the thumbs up the sides of the body to the shoulders and then extending laterally. Palms should face the wall the body came from, and using straight arms, push the water toward the feet and hands to the hips, the start position. Arm cycle is repeated after a short glide. ARM CUE: Up, Out, Together, Glide.

Jump from the Wall (Shallow Water). This activity can be very exciting for the beginner. Although the skill is relatively easy, safety precautions must be given. Advise students not to turn around toward the wall when jumping into the pool. It's a good idea to assist the swimmer for the first few jumps. The in-

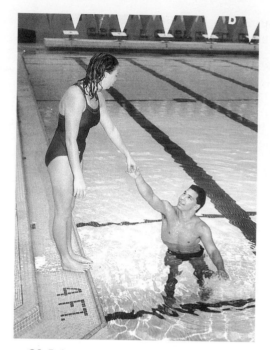

Figure 21-5 Instructor-assisted jump from wall.

structor stands facing the student, holds hands with the student, either right to left or left to right, then turns so that the student does not jump on top of the instructor (Figure 21-5). Students should look at the area where they are going to enter the water. The instructor can enhance this by placing the free hand in this area so that the student may spot it.

Intermediate Swimming

Before moving on to the intermediate level, students must thoroughly understand and be able to demonstrate the beginner skills in the previous section, and be able to swim approximately 2 widths of the pool. The intermediate skills described in this section will enable students to be more proficient in the water.

Stroke Skills

It would be helpful to review the section on the biomechanics of swimming and apply the principles to the teaching of the strokes. Similarities will be found among the strokes in propulsive force, pull patterns, rhythmic breathing patterns, and high elbow positions.

Front Crawl. The fastest of the strokes and also the one preferred for fitness swimming activities is the front crawl (freestyle). This stroke is characterized by the crawling motion of the arms.

1. The *arm cycle* is similar to that described in the beginner stroke, except that the arm recovery is above the water. The hand enters the water in front of the head, extending straight up from the

shoulder and entering with the thumb and forefinger side first (30- to 40-degree pitch). Upon entry, the arm should be extended fully forward and slightly downward. The catch of the stroke begins with the fingers pointing downward toward the bottom as the wrist and elbow begin to flex. Keeping the elbow above the hand, the swimmer begins to pull the body forward across the hand. The palm of the hand should face the wall the swimmer came from, the hand should move down the centerline of the body, and the elbow should bend to approximately 90 degrees to provide maximum leverage. The push phase is the final underwater stage and is accomplished by extending the elbow and pressing the hand to the thigh.

2. The *recovery* begins with the hand turning to the little finger side, by the thigh, and slipping out of the water. The elbow is lifted to a 90-degree angle at the elbow joint above the water, and the finger tips are carried close to the water surface to the entry point. ARMSTROKE CUES: Slice, Down the Hill, Up the Hill, Push to Thigh, High Elbow, Slice.

3. The *freestyle kick* is identical to the front kick in the beginner section, with a six-beat rhythmical pattern to stroke cycle.

4. Breathing is accomplished to either side with the head beginning the turn during the push phase of the armstroke to that side. The breath should not be held during any part of the stroke cycle.

Elementary Backstroke.

The elementary backstroke is a resting stroke that provides the swimmer with an opportunity to relax and breathe continuously.

1. The *arm cycle* is identical to that described for the beginner backstroke. The kick now becomes an inverted breaststroke kick instead of a flutter kick.

2. The inverted *breaststroke kick* is learned by sitting on the edge of the pool with legs together and extended over the water. Drop the heels to the pool wall by bending the knees. Keeping the knees close together (less than 6 inches) curl ankles away from each other and toes toward surface of the water. The propulsive phase is accomplished by straightening the legs and pushing water with the insoles of the feet. KICK CUES: Drop, Curl, Together.

3. Overall coordination begins with the thumbs up the side of the body to shoulder level, while the heels drop at the knee (Up); the arms reach laterally, while the ankles and toes curl up and out (Out); the pull begins slightly ahead of the extension of the legs; and hands touch thighs as toes come together (Together). CUE: Up, Out, Together, Glide.

Note: Hips, knees, and chest should remain in alignment throughout the entire stroke.

Back Crawl.

The back crawl is the second fastest competitive stroke and is characterized by the crawling motion in the supine position.

1. The *armstroke* of the back crawl begins with a straight arm entry of the little finger side of the hand, arms length, above the head (karate chop). The fingertips turn toward the bottom and sweep downward. The catch of the water takes place by an upward rotation of the hand and a bend of the elbow. The pull is an elliptical pattern and can be described as arm wrestling the water. The final underwater phase is a push downward and toward the feet. Arms alternate simultaneously.

2. The recovery begins by letting go of the water and bringing the hand out of the water with thumbs up. The arms remain straight during the above water phase, and the shoulder shrugs past the cheek. CUE: Karate Chop, Fingertips Down, Catch, Arm Wrestle, Push, Let Go, Thumb Up, Straight Arm, Shrug, Little Finger.

3. The kick is a six-beat flutter on the back similar to the beginner backstroke.

Breaststroke.

The breaststroke can be used as a resting stroke although it is one of the four competitive swimming strokes.

1. The armstroke of the breaststroke differs from the front and back crawl in that the arms do not alternate, and the recovery is underwater. The armstroke begins with the body in the streamlined position. The hands separate and press outward in a sculling motion. The hands rotate as the elbows bend slightly and move to an inward sweep. This phase ends as the hands come together beneath the chin. The hands then move upward and forward to the streamlined position with forearms close together. This movement can be described as drawing a heart on the pool bottom with the finger tips and then cutting the heart in half as the arms recover and extend forward.

2. Breathing takes place during the pull phase of the armstroke and is done simply by lifting the chin to water level. The breath should not be held during any phase of the stroke.

3. The kick is accomplished by taking the inverted breaststroke kick that was learned for the elementary backstroke and turning it over. A slight difference to be noted is that the heels should be pulled to the buttocks and the knees should not be pulled toward the abdomen.

4. The coordination of the stroke starts with the streamline, arm pull, breathe, extend arms and

recover heels to buttocks simultaneously, kick and glide into the streamlined position. *Hint:* Students may have trouble getting back to the streamlined position and holding it for the glide. Have students grab the thumb on the extension phase of the arms and hold the thumb until their toes touch from the kick, then glide, then separate and angle hands for pull. CUE: Hold Thumb, Pull, Breathe, Grab Thumb, Extend Arms, Kick, Toes Touch, Glide, Pull.

Sidestroke. The sidestroke is the stroke of choice used in lifeguard rescues. The sidestroke uniquely allows a rescuer to carry a victim comfortably and efficiently.

1. The arm cycle begins with the body on a preferred side with the top arm (trailing arm) extended over the hip and the bottom arm (leading arm) extended forward. The ear in the water (bottom ear) lies on the shoulder of the leading arm, and the water line runs down the cheek, with the mouth out of the water. Arms move simultaneously, with the leading arm sweeping downward and inward (Pull) in line with the body, while the trailing arm slices to position under the chin. With the hands near each other, the leading arm begins to slice forward as the trailing hand sweeps downward, backward, and upward (Push) in close proximity to the abdomen and finishing at the thigh.

2. The kick used in the sidestroke is the scissors kick, characterized by the scissor motion. The standard scissors kick begins with top leg resting on the lower, with knees straight and toes together and pointed. This is the start and end position. Legs are bent at the knees and drawn in line to the hips, with heels toward buttocks. The top leg and bottom leg separate simultaneously, with top leg forward, bottom leg backward, knees slightly flexed, and toes pointed, to the stride position. Legs can then be straightened to the glide position, producing propulsion with the back of the top leg and the front of the bottom leg.

3. The overall timing begins in the glide position on the side; as the pull takes place, the heels are drawn up, and as the hands meet, the legs separate to stride, then the push and kick occur together, and the stroke finishes with a glide. CUE: Pull and Draw, Push and Kick, Glide.

DIVING

Diving from the pool deck, dock, springboard, or platform can be exciting and exhilarating. Unfortunately, diving can also be dangerous if not taught and executed properly. It is estimated that 95 percent of all the diving injuries each year occur to the untrained diver and in less than 5 feet of water. This fact should make students and instructors follow proper progressions and make sure of the proper water depth when diving. The recommended depth for teaching diving from deck level is 9 feet or greater. The recommended depth for teaching from a 1-meter springboard is 12 feet or greater, with the board extending 6 feet over the water, and a landing area of the 12-foot depth extending forward 20 feet from the end of the board.

The following dives should be taught in sequence to ensure diving safety among participants. Dives must be taught in appropriate-depth water.

Slide-in Dive (9 feet deep). The slide-in dive is the most basic of all dives. The instructor has the student lie face down on a smooth resolite mat (preferred) or on the side of the deck, with arms extended overhead and body slightly arched (Figure 21-6). The instructor then holds the student's ankles, lifts the legs, and slides the student into the water. The student holds the body rigid and adjusts angle of entry by raising or lowering the arms and hands. If the student points the fingertips to the bottom, a deep dive will result; if the student raises fingertips and points to the other side of the pool, a shallow/distance dive will result.

Sitting Dive (9 feet deep). The sitting dive is the next in the sequence shown in Figure 21-6. Head position and arm position are essential. The early learning phase should consist of the chin being on the chest, arms over ears, and the student should remain in this position throughout the dive. This position will minimize the probability of smacking the chest and abdominal area. As the student becomes more accomplished, she will be able to adjust head and arm position to achieve desired depth or distance of dive. The instructor may assist from in the water by holding the student's fingertips and leading her down into the water.

Kneeling Dive (9 feet deep). The student positions on one knee, with toes of opposite foot over the pool edge (see Figure 21-6). Arms are extended overhead in the streamlined position, and the chin is placed on the chest. Initially, the student simply pivots over the knee and enters the water. As skill and readiness increase, the student can push with the foot of the non-kneeling leg. The instructor can assist in the same manner as for the sitting dive.

Scale Dive or Tip in (9 feet deep). The scale dive begins from the standing position, with arms placed overhead and in the streamline position. The diver then performs a gymnastic-type scale and balances with one leg vertically and one leg horizontally. The

Figure 21-6 Sequence illustrating (right to left) slide-in dive, sitting dive, kneeling dive, and shallow push dive.

instructor may assist the student by lifting the horizontal leg. The student pivots around the foot of the vertical leg and, while keeping knees straight, brings legs together with toes pointed as he enters the water fingertips first. Emphasis should be placed on keeping the chin on chest and keeping the vertical pivot leg straight.

Shallow Push Dive (9 feet deep). The shallow push dive starts with hands together in front of the body. The toes of both feet are over the pool edge and knees are bent (see Figure 21-6). The student begins the dive motion by extending the arms over the water surface, extending legs straight and pushing with the ankles. Emphasis should be placed on getting the heels higher than the head to achieve a fingertip head-first entry.

Deep Push Dive (9 feet deep). The deep push dive is used for reaching the bottom of the pool rapidly. As in all dives emphasis should be placed on keeping the arms overhead entering the water to prevent the head from striking the bottom or another object in the water. Additionally, the diver should always check the areas for swimmers or other obstacles before diving.

The diver begins in a more vertical position than in the previous dive. Arms are overhead in the streamline position, knees and hips are flexed, and toes are over the edge of the pool. The emphasis is on springing or jumping the hips up as the head and arms move downward toward the water. Once the diver is in the air, she must extend the body into a straight position to enter the water vertically and be projected to the pool bottom. It is helpful if the diver maintains a very slight pike at the hips upon entry so that the legs are not flopped over and the back arched.

Forward Standing Dive from the One-Meter Springboard (12 feet deep). This dive is performed in a similar manner as the deep push dive from the deck. The only notable difference is instead of jumping forcefully, the diver should utilize the spring of the board by extending the legs and riding the board to achieve maximum height. Body position upon entry should be stretched and rigid as shown in Figure 21-7.

Standing Back Dive from the One-Meter Springboard (12 feet deep). The back dive may cause some anxiety among students and instructors, but if proper safety precautions and instructional techniques are followed carefully, attempts will be more successful and less subject to trial and error or injury. The diving board must extend 6 feet over the water, and the depth from the end of the board back to the wall must be at least 12 feet, the distance of the diver's underwater path. Backward and inward dives should not be attempted from the pool side or from backyard pool diving boards because the diver may hit the pool wall.

The diver needs to understand that he or she will pivot around the tip of the board at the heels and that it is essential to keep straight legs. Also, the diver must realize that the body will follow the head and that the head must stay back, with eyes looking for the water. The diver then places the arms above the head, arches the lower back slightly, looks up at the hands, and falls head and shoulders first while keeping legs straight.

The instructor assists the diver by placing the student in proper body alignment. The instructor then places one knee against one of the student's knees, to keep him from bending the leg, and assists him in clearing the board. To maintain balance, the instructor must stand in the stride position. The instructor's

Figure 21-7 Standing dive from 1-meter board; water depth is 12 feet.

hands are placed on the student's sides level with the small of the back. The student is cued with Fall, and the instructor manages rate of fall by extending the arms. The instructor then moves hand positions to spot the diver by going to the back of the calf and adjusting the diver for a vertical entry (Figure 21-8).

Learning/Helpful Hints

The teaching of aquatic-related skills in schools since the advent of the YMCA and American Red Cross programs traditionally has been one of "assembly line"–like instruction. A recent contrast to this

approach comes in the contemporary prescriptive aquatic instruction or a developmental approach. This approach is based on the principles common to movement education. Both of these approaches should be given consideration and aligned with the goals of the particular instruction program offered at the institution.

This section outlines basic knowledge that many of the swimming/aquatic skills utilize. This section will include: methods of instruction, biomechanical/hydrodynamic principles related to swimming, effective pool use, water entry and exit, water orientation, bobbing and safety bobbing, buoyancy and

Figure 21-8 Standing back dive with instructor spotting from 1-meter board; Water depth is 12 feet.

floating, gliding, kicking, strokes, basic diving mechanics, and basic dives.

Teaching Methodology

Teaching swimming skills successfully depends upon the instructor's knowledge of mechanics, student readiness, the student's desire to practice, and the instructor's ability to communicate constructive observations. The method used to teach swimming is dependent on two factors: (1) the complexity of the skill to be learned and (2) the motor ability of the learner. For simple skills involving average to above-average ability, the whole method of teaching is used (verbal description, demonstration, and swimming of the whole stroke). For complex skills, the part method (breakdown of skill into body position, kick, armstroke, breathing, coordination) should be used.

For assessment of a swimmer's ability, a whole method is recommended because it allows the instructor to establish the overall ability of the class and ascertain levels of student fear. Where fear is not evident and swimmers are of average ability, swimming skills would be classified as simple and the whole method of instruction should be used.

Biomechanical Principles of Swimming

It is essential that the instructor understand how the biomechanics of the stroke affect swimming efficiency. A swimmer's forward progress through the water is affected by many factors—in particular, propulsion, resistance, and buoyancy.

Propulsion. The propulsive force is created by the different hand positions, pulls, and kicks utilized by the swimmer. Regardless of the stroke used, the hand should be held firm, slightly cupped, and the fingers relaxed but close together. The hands follow an elliptical pattern as opposed to a straight line. In the underwater phase of all strokes, the pull arm(s) come to a bent arm position, minimizing up and down movements in the water. Propulsion in all strokes must be optimized to overcome the laws of inertia. Other important laws of movement include the law of acceleration, whereby the swimmer must apply an equal force (even stroke) in the direction in which the force acts. A variation in application of force will be required in strokes other than the front and back crawl strokes. The law of action/reaction, which states that every action has an equal and opposite reaction, is also critical to the swimmer. For example, if a swimmer's armstroke in the front or back crawl is wide and sweeping, then the swimmer's legs and trunk will move in the opposite direction, thereby creating more resistance.

Resistance. Often referred to as drag, resistance is the combination of forces that slows a swimmer's forward progress. Frontal resistance is created by the water directly in front of the body: The more vertical the body is in the water, the greater the frontal resistance. Skin function resistance is created by the water that is flowing immediately next to the body. Tail suction, or "eddy" resistance, is caused by poorly streamlined body parts creating a momentary void in the water, making the body pull or suck water with it. All three of these resistance factors can be reduced by stream327us physical factors affect an individual's ability to float, among them bone size, fat tissue, muscular development, weight distribution, and lung capacity. A swimmer with dense bone structure and heavy muscle tissue will tend to sink lower in the water than a person with a higher body fat percentage. This explains why some swimmers float better than others.

The center of buoyancy is that point of the body around which it rotates in the water. The center of buoyancy is located higher in the body than the center of gravity. In general, on land a female's center of gravity is in the hip region and a male's is in the lower rib area. In the water, however, the center of buoyancy is generally located much higher in males than in females, likely due to the more dense leg structure of the male. This information is important when teaching floating and gliding skills, and explains why men find it more difficult to float and glide horizontally than do women. Another reason is that men float lower in the water, which requires them to overcome greater frontal resistance and skin friction due to the greater submerged body surface.

➤ Practice/Organizational Suggestions

Efficiency of pool use is necessary when classes are large. Beginner classes offer more restraints than advanced classes due to the use of only shallow water. The instructor will need to be in the water with the beginning-level swimming, while in teaching more advanced swimmers, the instructor may wish to be on the deck. In both situations, it is recommended that the instructor utilize the width of the pool for teaching and making corrections. Demonstrations should be done while swimmers are standing on the deck, with the demonstrator in the water. If the pool has windows, the students watching the demonstration should have their backs to the windows. These two recommendations allow students to get a better view of the demonstration by reducing glare.

Students need to be reminded that most accidents in the pool area occur on the pool deck and during water entry and exit. Reminders should be given at the beginning and throughout each pool session that students should enter by sitting on the pool side and slipping into the water or jumping in feet first and facing outward. Students should exit the pool by using the ladders.

In classes with swimming students of many different skill levels, the instructor should test students along the shallow end of the pool and divide them into groups according to their skill level: beginner, intermediate, or advanced. The advanced students can then assist the instructor. The advanced students will gain valuable insight into their own swimming by assisting in the instructional process. This also may entice these students into moving toward obtaining their water safety instructor certification in the future. The instructor should set aside time at the end of the class period to work with the advanced students on advanced skills, while beginners and intermediates practice basic skills unassisted, yet supervised. This strategy works well with the middle school ages and up. However, for the elementary students, the "divide-and-conquer" strategy, which groups swimmers by skill levels using the more advanced to work with the less skilled to assist the instructor, will difer.

First of all, the swimming instructors should request for prior grouping of students so that they teach beginners in one class period, intermediates in another class period, and so forth. Also, the instructor(s) should indicate what the appropriate student/instructor ratios are for the different skill levels. Recommendation:

Beginners: 10/1 maximum
Advanced beginners: 15/1 maximum
Intermediate: 20/1 maximum

If classes cannot be set up this way, the instructors must go to the divide-and-conquer method within the class period. Because many students of elementary age may not be able to stand even in the shallow end, it once again becomes imperative to have assistance in the pool classroom. A rule to which there can be no exception is to work with the student one on one. Stress that the students may not leave the wall, and maintain constant vigilance with the students on the wall. If the school is combined with older grade levels, utilize older volunteer students from study hall or activity periods to assist the teacher.

WATER EXERCISE

Nature and Purpose

Water exercise is one of the nation's fastest growing fitness activities. There are many advantages to this exercise venue. It is only in water that three-dimensional resistance to movement is possible. This provides improved muscle tone and joint stability. Water also provides smooth resistance that is accommodating over the full range of motion. The participant in water exercise is buoyed up by the water, which provides protection from injuries often associated with land exercise. This factor allows almost complete elimination of injurious ballistic stress on joints, connective tissues, and muscles. Water training allows the participant to simulate almost any sport movement, and if a proper program is adhered to for 20 to 30 minutes, three times a week, there can be an aerobic training effect for the heart and circulatory system. Clearly, therefore, water activity holds great value for rehabilitation, and in fact many individuals who cannot walk, run, or make ballistic movements on land can do so in the water.

Although it is recommended that participants know how to swim, it is not necessary that they have deep-water swimming ability, because water exercise can be taught completely in the shallow water. However, if water exercise classes wish to utilize deep water for conditioning, it is recommended that the instructor screen participants for deep-water swimming ability.

Equipment

Necessary equipment includes cassette player, audio cassette, battery-operated microphone, and amplification equipment.

Suggested Learning Sequence for Water Exercise

A. The instructor
   1. Instructor should teach from the pool deck. This allows students to see the techniques and allows the instructor to see students'
   performance. Additionally, this enables the instructor to access any audio-visual equipment that may be in use.
   2. The instructor's demonstration on deck must be slowed to allow the students who are in the water to keep pace with the instructor.
   3. Select music with lyrics appropriate for the students' age group.
   4. Music tempo should correspond to the students' ability to keep pace and to the desired physiological response, i.e., warm-up, aerobic, and so on.
B. The participant
   1. Appropriate swimwear should be worn (bathing suits). Cut-offs, gym shorts, and T-shirts should not be allowed.
   2. Participants may wish to wear aqua sock–type footwear to support the arches and protect the balls of the feet.
   3. Participants should take a soap shower and discard any chewing gum, candy, and so forth, before entering pool.
C. Teaching techniques
   1. Water should be approximately chest level for most exercises (3½ to 5 feet deep).
   2. Some participants may prefer to remain in the shallower water and squat down to chest level; this will increase their stability. Others may wish to reduce stability by standing in deeper water. Each participant should find a comfortable depth in which to achieve the maximum desired results.
   3. When exercising, the body weight should move in the same direction as the motion of desired area being exercised; i.e., if arms are moving forward, body weight should be moving forward.
   4. Leg position is the key to stability. Depending on the exercise goal, the feet should position either shoulder-width apart (straddle) or one foot in front, one foot in back (stride).
D. Exercises
   Table 21-1, on the next page, lists a number of common exercises that can be done in the water to work out muscle groups affected by each. Many other variations are, of course, possible. Water exercises are limited only by one's imagination and creativity. Instructors can readily select or design exercises to meet specific needs.

FITNESS SWIMMING

Nature and Purpose

Fitness swimming as an avenue for exercise has been popularized in recent years due to the concept of

Table 21-1 Water exercises for various muscles

Name	Muscle group	Body position	Foot position
Upper body			
Push/pull	Chest/back/arms	Standing/wall	Straddle
Push-down/pull-up	Shoulders/upper arm	Squat	Straddle
Lateral pull/press	Shoulders/upper chest and back	Squat	Straddle
Horizontal fly	Shoulders/upper chest and back	Standing	Stride
Front raise/press back	Shoulders/upper chest and back	Standing	Stride
Water punch	Upper arms	Squat	Stride
Arm circle	Shoulders/trunk	Squat	Straddle
Arm rowing	Upper back/trunk	Squat	Stride
Single-arm circle	Shoulders	Standing/wall	Straddle
Trunk			
Trunk rock	Abdomen/lower back	Standing	Straddle
Waist circle	Abdomen/lower back	Standing	Stride
Grapevine/cross-kick	Abdomen/lower back	Standing/wall	Straddle
Legs			
Walking/running	Buttocks	Standing/wall	Stride
Alternating leg kick—straight	Buttocks/thigh	Standing/wall	Stride
Alternating leg kick—bent	Buttocks/thigh	Standing/wall	Stride
Lateral leg kick—straight	Inner/outer thigh	Standing/wall	Straddle
Lateral leg kick—bent	Inner/outer thigh	Standing/wall	Straddle
Squat-tuck jump	Abdomen/thigh	Squat	Straddle
Knee lift	Abdomen/thigh	Squat/wall	Straddle
Roundhouse horizontal kick	Buttocks/abdomen/lower back	Standing/wall	Straddle
Leg circles front/back	Buttocks/thigh	Standing/wall	Straddle
Hamstring/quadricep curl	Thigh	Standing/wall	Straddle
Shuffle/run	Abdomen/thigh	Standing	Stride

cross-training and the increase in the number of triathalons. This section discusses the principles involved with fitness training and workout construction for swimming.

The three most common factors that must be adhered to in an effort to derive a benefit physiologically from any exercise program are frequency, intensity, and time (FIT). *Frequency* refers to the number of days per week that one should or can work out. Obviously, time constraints, schedules, and pool availability affect this factor. One should understand that swimming once per week is better than not swimming at all, but to obtain the greatest benefits, four to five times per week would be best.

Intensity is an indication of how difficult the training is physically. The principle of overload must be applied to improve physiological systems. The body, when trained at more intense rates than normal daily activity, will adapt accordingly with improved strength, endurance, and flexibility, as well as benefit the cardiovascular system. When overloading the systems, one must rely on proper progression and specificity, so as to avoid injury. Therefore, it is important to measure the intensity of workouts through one, or a combination, of four indicators: heart rate, time of swim, breathing rate, and perceived effort.

In terms of an aerobic training zone for adults, heart rate is best if between 120 and 170 beats per minute (bpm). To obtain the heart rate, one should take the pulse rate for 10 seconds at the carotid artery and multiply this number by 6. Note: Individuals who cross-train will generally find lower heart rates of 8 to 10 bpm in swimming as compared with land activities of equal perceived exertion. The physiological basis for this 8- to 10-bpm lowering stems from facial bradycardia, which is a result of the mammalian diving reflex. Simply, when a mammal places the face in the water, the heart rate is slowed.

The *time* of the overall training session should last 30 to 60 minutes to improve aerobic levels. Once again, proper progression should be utilized to avoid injury.

Breathing rate as an indicator of intensity is less exact than heart rate. Breathing rate can be assessed by counting the number of breaths taken in a 5-second interval. When training at an appropriate level, one should take three to four breaths in the 5-second interval.

Perceived effort can be determined through swimming speed. One can develop workouts by developing a baseline maximal-effort swim time, and then utilize percentages of this swim time to determine effort. For example, the swimmer swims and times an all-out maximal-effort 100-yard swim. The target, then, is to train at 75 to 90 percent of the maximal-effort time and identify the feeling of effort that accompanies the times. The aerobic range of perceived effort should fall in the 7 to 8 range on a 10 scale, with 10 being equal to the maximal-effort swim. This baseline may have to be adjusted as training levels and physiological conditioning improve.

Interval Training

There are several methods of training that can be applied to fitness swimming. Examples are straight long slow distance, fartlek, interval, speed-assisted, and speed-resisted. The most popular method is interval training because of the diversity of workouts that can be developed. The workouts are more interesting for the swimmer, therefore increasing motivation.

Interval training workout construction is best accomplished by utilizing four factors: distance, interval, repetition, and time (DIRT). *Distance* is the yardage of each repeat within a set of repeats. The distance per repeat for aerobic training generally ranges between 50 and 1,000 yards. *Interval* refers to the amount of rest between each repeat. The rest should be less than half the time required to swim the distance of the repeat, a 2:1 work-to-rest ratio. Short rest periods between repeats improve aerobic fitness due to the maintenance of the heart rate above 120 bpm. If longer rest periods were allowed, the heart rate would recover, thus limiting the aerobic benefit.

The number of *repetitions* per set should allow for aerobic overload. This overload can be accomplished by establishing a number of repetitions and rest intervals that take a minimum of 10 minutes to complete. Therefore, if the training period for a particular day is to last 30 minutes, three sets of 10 minutes will constitute the workout. The *time* for each repeat must be developed in accordance with the swimmer's ability, the goal of the workout (aerobic vs. anaerobic), and the desired intensity of the workout. Refer to the aforementioned information concerning intensity in the FIT principle.

The fitness swimmer may wish to utilize the following plan when constructing workouts:

1.	Warm-up	2–5 minutes
2.	Main sets	Aerobic 20–30 minutes
3.	Kick	5 minutes
4.	Pull	5 minutes
5.	Sprints	Optional
6.	Warm-down	2–5 minutes

The development of workouts in this manner will not only accomplish fitness goals, but also decrease boredom.

Safety Considerations

All swimming activities require a lifeguard on duty.

A. For progressive swimming levels
 1. Encouraged behavior:
  Soap shower
  Proper swimwear
  Care for others' safety
  Cooperation with lifeguards
 2. Discouraged behavior:
  Diving from starting blocks
  Diving from poolside into less than 9 feet of water
  Running, pushing, or other unsafe acts
  Swimming in springboard diving area
  Food, gum, or drinks in pool area

B. For springboard diving
 1. Divers must pass deep-water swim test.
 2. Check area in front of diving board.
 3. One person on diving board at a time
 4. No excessive bouncing
 5. Exit diving area promptly to nearest ladder.
 6. Difficult dives must be supervised.
 7. Reserve 3-meter diving boards for competitive use only.

C. For water exercise
 1. Permanently attach the pool safety lifeline, which separates the shallow and deep water sections.
 2. Before embarking on any physical fitness program, participants should consult a physician.
 3. Minimal instructor certification includes water safety instruction, first aid, and cardiopulmonary resuscitation.
 4. Instructor must understand physiological concepts of conditioning as they pertain to the aquatic environment, which differ considerably from those for land aerobic activity.

D. For fitness swimming
 1. A physical examination by a physician is recommended before starting any exercise program.

Failure to comply with the above-stated safety considerations may result in serious or fatal injury!

Aquatic Safety Standards and Accident Prevention

Instructor Certification

In most states, the Board of Education requires that the public school teacher teaching in the pool be currently certified as an American Red Cross Water Safety Instructor (WSI) or equivalent. An acceptable equivalent is the YMCA's progressive swimming instructor certification.

Lifeguards

A trained lifeguard certified through the American Red Cross or YMCA lifeguarding program must be on duty at water side for the duration of the activity, and may not be assigned any other duties than guarding the participants during the time they are in the water. If the school budget does not provide for a lifeguard, the teacher or coach may not also act as a lifeguard, which requires a specific certification.

Risk Assessment

The Aquatic Council to the National American Association of Health, Physical Education, Recreation and Dance established risk assessment procedures for aquatics in the AAHPERD publication *Principles of Safety in Physical Education and Sport.* Some of the topics to be considered in a risk assessment include design safety, hazard identification, maintenance, state regulations, pool checklists, remedial maintenance protocols, supervision/instruction, record keeping, insurance, and emergency accident management procedures.

Pool Safety Checklist

Pool safety is achieved only through a continuous program of quality supervision, maintenance, and inspection by trained and knowledgeable aquatic professionals. A pool safety checklist should be developed for the facility and should be used on a regular basis. The different areas of responsibilities may be assigned to different individuals according to their daily duties.

Emergency Accident Plan and Equipment

1. The pool must have a telephone accessible to the lifeguard and instructor with emergency numbers posted, a first-aid kit, towels, blankets, and an easily accessible emergency entrance/exit able to accommodate ambulance personnel and equipment.
2. A written emergency plan should be posted, and records of staff rehearsals kept on file. The local emergency medical services system should be consulted and utilized in the development of the emergency plan and subsequent rehearsals.

Attention

The instructor should have all equipment for the lesson moved to the pool edge prior to the participants' entry into the water. The lifeguard or instructor should not handle phone calls or other interruptions until the exit of all students from the water. It only takes 20 to 60 seconds for a swimmer to drown.

Modifications for Special Populations
Orthopedically Impaired

1. Use flotation devices, e.g., inner tubes, to play water games in shallow depths.
2. Use kickboards for stability in vertical positions.
3. Provide assistive stability, with peer teachers or paraprofessionals positioned behind student, stabilizing the trunk at the waist.
4. For striking games, use hand paddles attached with elastic.

Cognitively Impaired

1. Keep all activities in the shallow end until the student completely understands the rules of the game or task.
2. Keep your instructions very short and to the point, avoiding excessive directions.
3. Use peer teachers or paraprofessionals to provide manual assistance until the student completely understands the rules of the game or task.

Sensory Impaired

1. Use peer teachers or paraprofessionals until the student completely understands the rules of the game or test.
2. Allow students who are blind or have a visual impairment additional practice prior to initiating the game or task.
3. Use cue cards (symbols) to change direction for students who are deaf or have a hearing impairment.
4. Use cue cards (color codes) to represent a change in sequence and/or directions for the game or task.

Further References

American Alliance for Health, Physical Education, Recreation and Dance (1987). Principles of Safety in Physical Education and Sport. Reston, VA: Author, 1987.

American Red Cross. *Water Safety Instructors Manual: Swimming and Diving: Teaching Aquatics.* Boston, MA: Staywell, 2001.

American Red Cross. *Lifeguard Training.* Boston, MA: Staywell, 2001.

Clayton, R. and Thomas, D. *Professional Aquatic Management.* Champaign, IL: Human Kinetics, 1989.

Gabrielsen, M. A. *Swimming Pools, A Guide to Their Planning, Design, and Operation.* Champaign, IL: Human Kinetics, 1987.

Johnson, R. L. *YMCA Pool Operation on Location, YMCA of the USA.* Chicago, IL: YMCA, 1990.

Maglischo, E. W. *Swimming Faster: A Comprehensive Guide to the Science of Swimming.* Chico, CA: Mayfield Publishing, 1982.

Maglischo, E. W. *Swimming Even Faster.* Mountain View, CA: Mayfield Publishing, 1993.

Maglischo, E. W. and Brennan, C. F. *Swim for the Health of It.* Mountain View, CA: Mayfield Publishing, 1985.

United States Diving. *U.S. Diving Safety Manual.* Indianapolis, IN: United States Diving, Inc., 1990.

Web Sites

www.aquaweb.org Aquatic resources, including books, articles, and videotapes. Also includes excellent links, and clip art.

www.usdiving.org Official Web site for United States Diving. Includes information of diving safety, education, and resources.

www.usms.org Official Web site for United States Masters Swimming. Includes drills, resources, and a club finder.

www.aea.org Official Web site for the Aquatic Exercise Association. Includes resources, links, training ideas, and product information.

www.redcross.org Web site for the American Red Cross. Includes updates on the American Red Cross, first aid, CPR, water safety, and lifeguard training programs.

CHAPTER 22

Team Handball

This chapter will enable you to

- Identify and demonstrate the basic skills associated with team handball
- Develop at least one practice formation for each of the basic skills: pass, catch, throw, and dribble
- Understand and demonstrate simple rules and regulations
- Understand and demonstrate free throw, penalty throw, corner throw, throw-in, and throw-off
- Identify and name the positions of players

Nature and Purpose

Team handball may be played indoors or outdoors by children or adults of both sexes. Team handball employs fundamental motor skills such as running, throwing, catching, jumping, and defensive and offensive strategies similar to the motor skills used in basketball, soccer, and hockey.

The object of the game is to pass and/or dribble the ball toward the opponent's goal and then shoot the ball into the goal. The ball is played primarily with the hands; however, any portion of the body above the knee can be used to play the ball.

Court, Equipment, Players

The Playing Area

1. The playing area (indoors or outdoors) should be a rectangular surface with dimensions of 126 to 147 feet in length and 60 to 73 feet in width (Figure 22-1). For a physical education class, a basketball court can easily be adapted to an indoor playing court by taping the goal-area line and the free-throw line.
2. The goal area is a semicircular space marked off by the goal-area line, which is drawn in front of the goal at a distance of 20 feet, with a radius of 20 feet from the back inside edges of the goal posts.
3. The free-throw line is drawn as a broken line parallel with and 10 feet beyond the goal-area line.
4. The penalty-throw line is 3 feet 3 inches long and is drawn at a distance of 23 feet from the goal.
5. The goal is in the middle of each goal line and measures 6 feet 7 inches in height and 10 feet in width. If possible, a loose net, measuring 2 feet 8

inches at the top and 3 feet 3 inches at the bottom, should be attached behind the goal post. For a physical education class, two poles, such as volleyball or badminton poles, with a rope tied across them will serve as a goal.

The Ball

A round ball is used that will vary in weight and circumference according to the age and sex of the players. For males over age 15, the ball should weigh from 15 to 19 ounces and be 23 to 24 inches in circumference; for females and boys under age 15, the ball should weigh 11½ to 14 ounces and measure 21 to 22 inches around. For physical education classes, a playground ball or volleyball will serve the purpose of the game. However, basketballs and soccer balls should not be used.

Players

Each team consists of 7 players (6 court players and 1 goalkeeper) with 5 additional players for substitution. The positions of players are designated as goalkeeper, center half, right and left backs, center forward, and right and left wingers (see Figure 22-1).

Basic Rules

Duration of the Game

1. Playing times for a regulation game will vary depending upon the age and sex of the players: for men—two periods of 30 minutes, with an interval of 10 minutes; for women and junior males—two periods of 25 minutes, with an interval of 10

Figure 22-1   Team handball court and players' positions.

2. The ball cannot be held for more than 3 seconds if the player is not moving. (Otherwise, a free throw is awarded to the opposition.)

3. The ball can be bounced once or repeatedly with either hand while moving or standing—like a dribble in basketball.

4. Once the ball has been seized with one or both hands, it must be played off within three seconds or after three steps have been taken. (Otherwise, a free throw is awarded to the opposition.)

5. Any ball that touches a referee and/or goal post is still playable.

6. Players cannot dive for rolling balls that are on the ground.

7. The ball may be continuously rolled on the ground with one hand.

8. When the ball has passed the touch line, the ball can be put into play by the other team, as in basketball, and the throw-in should take place from the point where the ball crossed the touch line.

9. If the ball is touched by a defensive player, except the goalkeeper, and travels across the goal line outside the goal, a corner throw is awarded to the attacking team. The ball is put back in play by the goalkeeper with a throw-off if the goalkeeper last touched it.

Approach to Opponent

Players are not permitted to

1. Block an opponent with arms, hands, or legs (free throw awarded to opposition)

2. Hold, hit, push, run into, or jump at the opponent or throw oneself down in front of or endanger an opponent in any other way (free throw awarded to opposition)

3. Throw the ball intentionally at an opponent or execute a dangerous feint by moving the ball toward the opponent (free throw awarded to opposition)

The Goal Area

1. No player except the goalkeeper may enter the goal area.

2. A player of the defending team, provided the entry is intentional and for the clear purpose of defense, shall have a penalty throw (23 feet) awarded to the attacking team.

3. There shall be no penalty if a player enters the goal area after playing the ball.

4. Inside the goal-area line, the ball belongs to the goalkeeper. No other player shall touch a ball that is lying, rolling, or being held by the goalkeeper inside this area.

minutes; and for all other players—two periods of 20 minutes, with a 10-minute interval.

2. The winning team from referee's coin toss has the choice of either the end, defense, or offense.

3. By referee's whistle, the game must start at the center of the court only by passing the ball to another teammate. All players must be within their own half of the court at the beginning.

4. After each goal is scored, the other team will always start the game at the center of the court.

5. A goal cannot be scored directly from the throw-on.

Playing the Ball

1. The ball can be played in any manner with any part of the body except below the knee. (For violation of this rule, a free throw is awarded to the opposition.)

5. The ball shall neither be thrown into one's own goal area nor to the goalkeeper. (A penalty throw is awarded to the opposition team.)

6. A ball in the air is not considered to be in the goal area.

The Goalkeeper

1. As long as the goalkeeper remains inside the goal area, he/she is allowed to defend the goal in every possible way, including kicking the ball with the feet while the ball is moving toward the goal or is inside the goal area.

2. The goalkeeper is allowed to leave the goal area without the ball. When he/she does, the same rules apply to the goalie as to the rest of the team.

3. The goalie may not touch a ball that is lying or rolling outside the goal area.

Scoring

1. A goal is made when the ball has passed the goal line inside the goal with its *entire* circumference.

2. A goal made by the defending team is also scored as a goal.

3. After every goal is made, the other team should start the game from the center of the court.

Penalty Throw

1. When the offensive player has lost a clear chance of scoring by the defensive player's foul, the offensive player shall be awarded a penalty throw from the 23-foot line.

2. During a penalty throw, no other player except the goalkeeper shall be allowed between the goal-area line and the free-throw line.

3. The penalty throw shall be aimed directly at the goal.

Free Throw

1. All violations of the rules, except the penalty throw, shall have a free throw awarded to the opposing team.

2. All free throws are taken from the point where the violation occurred, except a violation between the free-throw line and the goal-area line, in which case the free throw shall be taken at the free-throw line.

3. During a free throw, players of the defending team shall stand 10 feet away from the player having the free throw.

4. A goal may be scored directly from a free throw.

Suggested Learning Sequence

Team handball is an activity that can be learned very quickly. It may be played at all levels by both sexes and on a coeducational basis. A basic game can be played at an early stage of the physical education class; offensive and defensive formations and styles of play may be added as the level of skill increases. It is important to discuss terminology, rules, skills, and strategies at a time when most appropriate and meaningful to the discussion of a particular concept.

A. Purpose of the game
B. Skills and techniques. The skills of passing, shooting, and dribbling are best taught in combination with each other.
    1. Passes for short distances
       a. Bounce
       b. Close hand-off
       c. Hook
       d. Chest
       e. Shovel
       f. Overhead
    2. Passes for medium distances
       a. Ground
       b. Jump
       c. Shoulder (baseball)
       d. Side arm
    3. Catching
    4. Dribble
    5. Shooting
       a. Jump shot
       b. Dive shot
       c. Underhand shot
       d. Reverse shot
       e. Side throw
       f. Lob shot
       g. Penalty throw
    6. Goalkeeping. Goalkeeping should be started early in the sequence. A few minutes' practice each day will add to the quality of the game.
C. Playing strategies
    1. Offensive
    2. Defensive
D. Rules. Discuss the rule when most applicable to a given situation or skill.
E. Terminology. Terms should be discussed as they arise in the normal progression.

It is recommended that scrimmage time be included in early lessons. The length of scrimmage time will increase as the unit progresses.

Skills and Techniques

The basic skills to be discussed in this section are passing, catching, dribbling, and shooting.

Passing

Passing is the most important element of team handball. It allows a player to move the ball quickly and accurately so as to advance the ball and set up scoring opportunities. Team handball passing fundamentals are quite similar to those utilized in basketball.

➤ Learning Hints

1. The speed of the receiver as well as the distance between the receiver and the passer will determine how hard the ball should be thrown and the type of pass to be used.
2. For practice purposes, point the non-throwing arm in the direction of the throw. (In actual game situations, more deception must be used to avoid "telegraphing" the pass.)
3. Use finger-tip control to ensure a more consistently accurate pass.
4. Maintain proper balance and distribution of body weight to ensure a more accurate pass. Shift your weight from the back to front foot, maintaining momentum behind the ball for a crisp pass. (Don't throw a pass when you are off balance except in improvised or emergency situations.)
5. Step forward with the leg opposite to the throwing arm.
6. Snap your wrist upon release.
7. Select a pass that is appropriate for a specific situation.
8. After you pass, always be ready to penetrate the defense and await a return pass.
9. A properly thrown pass will usually enable your teammates to catch the ball more easily.
10. A generalized rule to keep in mind when passing the ball is always to make a threatening motion (feint) to score before passing to a teammate.

Passes can be divided into three categories characterizing the distance, trajectory, and type (arm form) of the throw.

Short-Distance Passes. Passes that are normally used in short distances include the following:

1. *Bounce*—The ball should be thrown so that it bounces approximately 3 feet in front of the receiver. The receiver should move toward the ball and try to catch it on the short hop (as in baseball) in such a manner that he/she is immediately prepared to throw the ball.
2. *Close hand-off (front and back)*—In this pass (which usually occurs in close quarters around the goal area), the player merely hands the ball to a teammate in a manner similar to an "end-around" (reverse) play in football. Deception is of utmost importance in this pass. It should be used only after considerable practice and by players who are very familiar with each other, because the chance for error is much greater than with most other passes.
3. *Hook*—This pass is very useful when a player is closely guarded by two or more players. It can

also be used when a player is in the air for a jump shot. The player simply releases the ball at the top of his/her jump to a teammate who might be penetrating toward the goal. This pass is the same as the "hook shot" in basketball.

4. *Chest (push)*—This pass should be one of the most frequently used in short distances. It is one of the most accurate passes and relatively simple to learn. The same fundamentals can be applied as for the two-hand chest pass.
5. *Shovel (scoop)*—This pass is less frequently used than those passes described thus far. The player picks a low ball upon the short hop and remains in a crouched position while quickly tossing the ball (underhand) to a teammate.
6. *Overhead (two hands)*—One of the methods of putting the ball back into play after it has crossed one of the sidelines. The throw is taken by a player of the team that did not cause the ball to go out. The player making the throw must have both feet touching the surface outside the sideline and throw in to the playing area with one or two hands in any manner.

Medium Distance Passes. Passes that are normally used in medium distances include the following:

1. *Ground ("roller")*—When all other passing lanes are blocked it may, on occasion, be appropriate to roll the ball between a defender's legs. Also, when there is a "scramble" for a loose ball on the court and a player can't control the ball completely, he/she can roll it to a nearby teammate.
2. *Jump*—When normal passing lanes are impeded, a player can use this pass by jumping into the air and releasing the ball in a manner similar to the shoulder throw.
3. *Shoulder (baseball)*—When throwing, the player should not attempt to grip the ball as if it were a baseball. Rather, allow the ball to rest in the hand with a flexed wrist and fingers spread wide enough to cover as much of the ball surface as is comfortably possible.
4. *Side arm*—This pass is the same as the shoulder pass, except the positioning and action of the throwing arm may be likened to a three-quarters and/or "submarine" pitching motion, as in baseball. The length of stride for the lead leg should correspond (approximately) to the length of the pass. For a right-handed throw, the right foot can remain in place (with weight back), and the left foot can stride forward simultaneously with the arm-throwing motion.

Catching

An accurate throw will result in an accurate catch.

➤ **Learning Hints**

1. Whenever possible, players are to catch the ball with two hands to ensure best control.
2. The player should always attempt to catch the ball with the fingertips spread. Whenever possible, the ball should not be allowed to make contact with the palms.
3. The elbows should be flexed and the body relaxed to absorb the impact of a hand-thrown ball.
4. Whenever possible, the player should move forward to meet the ball, maintaining eye contact with the ball as it comes into the hands.
5. Upon receiving a pass, a player should be immediately prepared to shoot, dribble, or pass the ball again.

Dribble

In team handball, the dribble is used to advance the ball up the court when a player is not closely guarded and to gain "rhythm" when attempting to move the ball for purposes of attacking the goal or setting up a possible scoring play. Because of their strong basketball orientation, most Americans have a tendency to dribble too much in team handball.

The dribble is similar to that used in basketball except that the player may take three steps when the ball is seized by either one or both hands. When the ball is seized, it must be played off within three steps or three seconds.

Shooting

The primary objective of attacking the goal in team handball is to score. Shooting will not occur in team handball as frequently as in basketball. Players must learn to be patient and work for a good opportunity to score a goal. This does not mean that players should be overcautious, as team handball is an aggressive game in which the offense must continuously attack the goal and generate its own scoring opportunities.

➤ **Learning Hints: Basic Shooting Principles**

1. The shooter must have a definite throwing direction in mind prior to releasing the ball. Shots blocked and easily caught by the goalie often result in fast-break 2-on-1 situations for the opposing team. The most vulnerable shooting lanes are the high and low corners of the goal mouth. It is generally agreed that shots directed to the lower corners of the goal have greater scoring percentages.
2. The momentum of the shooter should always be toward or perpendicular to the goal.
3. The use of deception is of utmost importance. The shooter should attempt to draw the goalkeeper toward one corner of the goal and, depending upon

the commitment of the goalkeeper, the player should aim his shot for the opposite corner.

4. The shoulder pass is the most frequently used in team handball shooting.
   a. The ball is held behind the head, with the arm cocked to hide the ball from the goalie and make it more difficult for defensive players to take the ball away.
   b. The non-shooting arm remains forward to ward off defenders and assist in maintaining balance.
   c. The shot should be released with a snap of the wrist and follow-through (as in throwing a football or baseball).
5. Many foot-movement patterns can be utilized in team handball shots, including hop steps, crossover steps, and running steps. New players are encouraged to experiment with different step and dribble combinations that fit their individual abilities.

Specific Shots and Their Uses

Jump Shot. This shot simply involves the use of the shoulder throw (pass) in which the ball is released at the height of the jump, with the momentum of the body directed toward the goal rather than falling away. By jumping high in the air, the player is able to see the goal more clearly and determine the direction of his/her shots (Figure 22-2).

Dive Shot. This shot also utilizes the shoulder throw. The shooter stretches his body out and directs his momentum toward the goal. The ball is released at the last possible moment and as close to the goal mouth as possible.

➤ **Learning Hints**

1. The weight is evenly distributed on both feet as the shot is initiated.
2. The body is leaning, moving in a position parallel with the floor.
3. The upper body is thrust upward in a diving action toward the goal.
4. Snap the wrist and release the ball quickly.
5. Break the fall with your chest and both hands positioned at your side about chest level.

Underhand Shot. The side-arm or three-quarter pitching motion is used in this shot. The right-handed thrower turns (twists) the left side toward the goal. To generate increased power, a crossover step is used with the push-off coming from the rear foot. This shot is used when upper scoring lanes are cut off by the defense. The shot is on a low trajectory with a continuous follow-through.

Reverse Shot (circle). This shot is used around the goal area when the defender is playing behind and/or

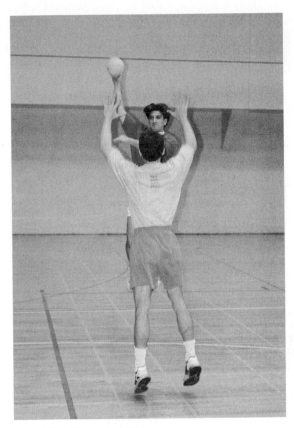

Figure 22-2 The jump shot.

overplaying to the shooting side (Figure 22-3). When you are unable to execute a normal shoot, lower your center of gravity (bend knees), fake to the strong (normal shooting) side, turn, and quickly pivot away from the strong side on your right foot (if you are right-handed), releasing the ball in a side-arm motion

(Figure 22-4). (This is similar to the initial backward motion in the discus throw.) As the ball is released, body momentum should be directed toward the goal.

Side Throw (twister). This is a relatively weak shot, but with the proper element of surprise, it can be successful. Most frequently, it is used in close to the goal area when an attempted shot with a regular shoulder throw is stopped by a defender. If you are right-handed, drop your left shoulder, step across your body with your right foot, then execute the same arm motion described for the reverse shot with body momentum directed toward the goal.

Lob Shot. This shot is often used in a 1-on-1 fast-break situation and also in certain 2-on-1 situations. When the goalie comes out to challenge, the offensive player lobs the ball over his/her head into the goal, or to his/her teammate if this is a 2-on-1 situation. Timing is of utmost importance in the execution of this shot.

Penalty Throw. This throw is taken at the 23-foot penalty-throw line. It is a 1-on-1 situation with the goalie as the only defender. The goalie may move about and come within 10 feet of the penalty line. The player who is awarded the penalty throw cannot move his/her foot or touch the penalty line until the ball is released. The offensive player has three seconds in which to shoot from the time the referee blows the whistle to begin the throw. The type of shot normally utilized in this situation is the shoulder or side throw. The other players must remain outside the free-throw line area until the shot is taken. They should strategically position themselves around the

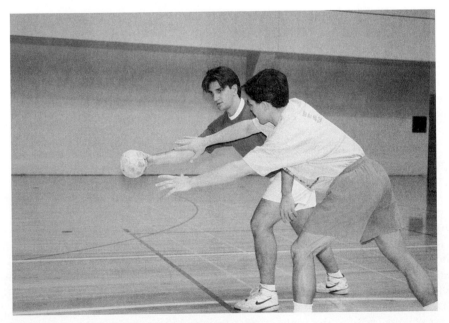

Figure 22-3 Setting up for the reverse shot: Fake to one side.

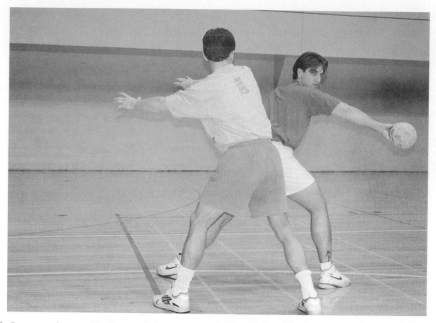

Figure 22-4 Reverse shot, release with side-arm motion.

goal to be ready for a blocked shot, which might possibly rebound out into the area of play.

➤ Practice/Organizational Suggestions—Basic Skills

Drills for team handball basic skills—passing, catching, and dribbling the ball—are similar to those used in basketball. Therefore, basketball drills should be utilized to practice the basic skills, particularly passing, catching, and dribbling the ball, with the following points in mind:

1. The ball is much smaller than the ball used in basketball. Therefore, the ball can be easily handled by either one or both hands.
2. It is permissible to take a maximum of three steps or 3 seconds with the ball in either one or both hands. For example, after catching the ball from another player, you may take three steps and start dribbling. When you stop dribbling, you must either pass or shoot after taking no more than three steps or three seconds.

Goalkeeping

The goalkeeper is the most important defensive player in team handball. The goalie should have quick hands and feet, be fearless of the ball, and be able to throw the ball well in initiating fast-break plays. The main task of goalkeeping is to stop the ball by any manner possible. The goalie can use any part of the body to deflect shots. Within the goal area there is no restriction on how many steps the goalie may take or the time the ball may be held. Without the ball, the goalie may become a court player at any time; in that case, all rules applying to court players apply to the goalie.

➤ Learning Hints: Goalkeeping Fundamentals

1. The goalie should know the position of the ball on the court at all times.
2. The goalie should maintain a low center of gravity, with weight evenly distributed on the balls of the feet.
3. In blocking shots, the goalkeeper's palms should always face out toward the field of play. The hands should be relaxed enough to "give" with a shot to keep it under control in the area and not allow the ball to rebound back out onto the field of play.
4. Low shots in close to the goalie's legs should be fielded (blocked) in a manner similar to an infielder fielding a ground ball.
5. On shots that are low and to the side, the goalie should stride to the side with hands and outside foot stretching simultaneously to block the ball.
6. Similar to the goalkeeping used in hockey or soccer, the goalie should move out away from the goal mouth in an attempt to cut down the best shooting angles.
7. On high hard shots, the goalie should not try to catch the ball, rather, he/she should deflect the ball over the top of the goal.
8. In defending against the penalty shot, the goalie should move out toward the 23-foot penalty line to cut down the shooter's angle.
9. The goalie should always play one foot out from the goal line to avoid a self-scored goal.
10. When the goalie recovers a blocked or missed shot, he/she returns the ball to play by means of a "throw-out." In this instance, the ball is free, and the defense can try and intercept the throwout and score directly.

11. It is recommended that the goalie wear a protective supporter, long pants, and a long-sleeved shirt to cut down on the "sting" of blocked shots.

Playing Strategies

Various defensive and offensive strategies are described below. These can be understood better and developed further with reference to similar team sports such as soccer, basketball, field hockey, and football.

Defensive Formations

When the ball is lost, all players of the team become defensive players with certain defensive responsibilities according to the defensive strategies employed. Generally, defensive strategies are divided into (1) player-to-player defense, (2) zone defense, and (3) a combination of the two. In defensive play, a player should always attempt to keep the opponent in front of him/her, or else the opponent should be slightly overplayed to the shooting-arm side. ("Stay between your opponent and the goal" is a general rule to follow.)

Player-to-Player Defense. Each defensive player must cover one designated player of the attacking team regardless of whether he/she has the ball. The offensive player is continually blocked off and hindered in attacking actions.

Zone Defense. Each defensive player is responsible for protecting a particular area against the attacker. Zone defense may require less running, but it requires more teamwork to be effective.

Combinations

6-0 Defense (Figure 22-5). Six court players stand alongside and in front of the goal-area line, each having the specific responsibility to protect a certain area.

The players must coordinate with each other to cover any space that may be left uncovered when a defensive player attempts to attack an opponent with the ball. Taller players should be placed in the center of the defensive zone and shorter players on the outside.

5-1 Defense (Figure 22-6). The 5-1 concept is similar to that of a box and 1 defense used in basketball. Five players stand in front of the goal-area line. One player, pulled out to the free-throw line, has the two assignments of covering the opponent with the ball and/or covering a good shooter. This player, who frequently originates the fast break, must be an all-round athlete.

4-2 Defense (Figure 22-7). Four defensive players are positioned on the goal-area line and shift as a unit. Two defensive players move out to the free-throw line in order to concentrate on intercepting passes and harassing the ball handlers to prevent their taking the most advantageous routes toward the goal area. These two players not only have to protect the central axis, but also are responsible for filling in gaps between defensive players behind them.

Man-to-man defense on outstanding shooter or playmaker

Figure 22-6 The 5-1 defensive formation.

○ Defensive player
→ Player's movement

Figure 22-5 The 6-0 defensive formation.

Figure 22-7 The 4-2 defensive formation.

Figure 22-8 The 3-3 defensive formation.

3-3 Defense (Figure 22-8). Three defensive players stand on the middle of the goal-area line, and the other three players stand in front of the free-throw line. These three players as a unit have to shift toward the attacking point of the offensive team to protect against long-distance shootings. This formation is vulnerable against the team having shots from angles and requires a capable goalkeeper.

Offensive Formations

In the deployment of any offensive alignment, every effort should be made to utilize the entire offensive floor area. Fast, continuous movement must be maintained at all times. Upon receiving a pass, every player should make a motion of threatening to score whenever in scoring range. In order to spread out the defense as much as possible, it is important that players maintain good spacing and that most plays be initiated from approximately 40 feet. Dribbling should be avoided if possible, and the ball should be passed quickly between players. Effective screening (similar to that used in basketball) is a key to the success of most offensive patterns. Screens and double screens can be improvised from any of the offensive formations presented. The following represent some common offensive formations.

2-4 Offense. This is the most frequently utilized offensive formation in team handball. In this formation, the two backcourt players are situated at around 40 feet. The wing players are spread out wide for the best possible shooting angles. The circle runners are strategically positioned between the two wing players at 20 feet. A variety of offensive maneuvers can be initiated from this basic offensive pattern. This offense will spread out most zone defenses and allow opportunities for scoring between the defensive players.

3-3 Offense. This offense is also effective in spreading out the coverage of a zone defense. If a team possesses three strong shooters, this is an excellent of-

fensive formation to employ. Constant movement of the ball is essential, and each player must threaten to score each time he/she receives a pass.

1-5 Offense. This offensive formation can best be employed by a team that has some strong inside players who are very physical. Effective inside screening is the key to a successful 1-5 offense. It is of utmost importance that one player always stay back to guard against a possible fast break.

1-3-2 Offense. One backcourt player is situated around 40 feet as a playmaker; three players are placed around the middle of the free-throw line; and two players become outside and circle runners between the free-throw line and the goal-area line.

The backcourt player passes the ball to make a play. The three middle players attempt to block defensive players by whatever means to create an opportunity for the two circle runners to make effective shooting chances. The two circle runners must constantly move and feint to confuse defensive players and at the same time make a good shot into the goal.

Modifications for Special Populations

Orthopedically Impaired

1. Contact the United States Cerebral Palsy Athletic Association (USCPAA) at www.uscpaa.org for rules and information on indoor wheelchair soccer. The game of indoor wheelchair soccer is actually a hybrid of soccer and team handball.
2. Set up stationary positions using desk chairs placed on the goal perimeter arch, and have students with and with disabilities try to score from there.
3. Allow students with limited grip to use smaller objects, e.g., bean bags, instead of regulation team handballs.
4. For students using wheelchairs, consider playing the game on a flat, hard-top surface.

Cognitively Impaired

1. Create smaller groups and lead-up games.
2. Allow students to move the ball up the field in any manner possible, e.g., with one or two bounces.
3. Spend considerable time teaching concepts of the game, e.g., offense, defense, goal area, penalties. Use visual prompts to help with your instructions, e.g, colored pinnies, colored signs to mark zones of the field.

Sensory Impaired

1. Individual considerations must be taken into account to determine the appropriateness of team

handball for students who are visually impaired or blind. One appropriate option may be to tether a sighted student to the wrist of a student who is blind or has a visual impairment.

2. When using tethered peers, do not allow defensive players within 10 feet of the offensive partners.

3. Designate students who are blind or have a visual impairment to be attackers, and position them in stationary positions. They must attempt a shot on goal once every two trips down the field by their team.

4. Minimal modifications are needed for students who are deaf or hearing impaired.

Terminology

Corner throw When a defending player (except the goalkeeper) plays the ball over his or her own goal line on either side of the goal, the game is restarted by means of a throw from the corner of the court by one of the attacking players. The player must place one foot on the corner and throw the ball in, using either hand.

Court player Member of the handball team actually playing on the court, except for the goalie.

Dive shot A means of trying to score a goal by launching the entire body into the air toward the goal in an attempt to gain more distance.

Free throw A throw awarded to the opposing team when the other team is in violation of certain rules of the game.

Free-throw line The broken line parallel with the goal-area line at an extra distance of 10 feet; from this line, free throws awarded near the goal area are taken.

Goal A goal is considered scored when the ball has passed wholly over the goal line between the uprights and underneath the crossbar of the goal.

Goal area The area of the playing court inside and including the goal-area line.

Goal-area line The semicircular line drawn in front of and on either side of the goal.

Goalkeeper (goalie) The player who is allowed to play freely inside the goal area to defend the goal.

Goal line The line forming the end of the court that runs between the uprights of the goal and meets the sidelines at the corners of the court.

Penalty throw A shot attempted by any offensive player when an offensive player is prevented from making a clear goal-scoring chance by foul means. The player attempting the penalty throw is required to make a direct attempt to score a goal from the penalty-throw line.

Referee's throw A ball bounced by the referee to restart the game after an interruption of play caused by players of both teams committing simultaneous infractions of the rules, or if the game has been interrupted for some other reason.

Throw-in The method of putting the ball back into play after it has crossed one of the sidelines. The throw is taken by a player of the team that did not cause the ball to go out. The player making the throw must have both feet touching the surface outside the sideline and throw the ball into the playing area with one or two hands in any manner.

Throw-off The means the goalkeeper takes of throwing the ball onto the court after obtaining possession of the ball in his goal area.

Throw-on The method of putting the ball in play at the start of the game and after a goal is scored. The throw is made from the center of the court.

Throw-out Same as a throw-off except that defensive players may place themselves at the goal-area line.

Further References

Clanton, R. and Dwight, M. *Team Handball; Steps to Success.* Champaign, IL: Human Kinetics, 1997.

Hamil, B. and LaPoint, J. *Team Handball Skills, Strategies and Training.* Dubuque, IA: Eddie Bowers Publishing, 1994.

Neil, G. I. *Modern Team Handball: Beginner to Expert.* Montreal, Canada: McGill University, 1976.

Official U.S. Team Handball Rules. Jayfro Corp., P.O. Box 400, Waterford, CT 06385.

United States Team Handball Federation (USTHF), 10 Nottingham Road, Short Hills, NJ 07078.

United States Team Handball Federation Business Office, 1750 E. Boulder, Colorado Springs, CO 80909.

Web Sites

www.hickoksports.com Provides an explanation of how the sport is played and its history.

www.usateamhandball.org/aboutb.html Presents the history and simplified rules of the game.

CHAPTER 23

Tennis

This chapter will enable you to

- Select tennis equipment that will be appropriate for you
- Demonstrate the proper grips and techniques for the following strokes: serve, return of serve, approach shot, forehand, backhand, volley, lob, overhead
- Understand the scoring procedures and the basic rules of play
- Identify the playing courtesies, safety considerations, and basic terminology associated with tennis

Nature and Purpose

Tennis has always appealed to both sexes, young and old. Many consider it to be one of the best forms of co-recreational sports. The pace can be adjusted to the players' abilities, ranging from a mild form of exercise to a strenuous test of strength and endurance. Speed, agility, coordination, and endurance can be developed, and indeed are needed, to play even a recreational game of tennis.

The game of tennis can be played as either singles or doubles. The singles game has two participants, one individual opposing the other. The doubles game has four participants, two individuals teaming up to compete against another team of two. The doubles court is 9 feet wider than the singles court, having a 4½ foot alley on each side of the singles court (Figure 23-1).

The basic rules are the same for men's and women's tennis. To start the game, the server stands just behind the baseline to the *right* of his or her center service line, and puts the ball into play by striking it in the air in such a manner that it lands in the opponent's right service court. The server has two chances to put the ball into play. The ball that does not land in the proper service court is called a "fault" and is not played. A served ball that touches the net during flight and lands in the proper service court is called a "let"; a let is not counted as a fault, nor is it played, but is served again.

The receiver must return the serve to the server's court on its first bounce. The rally continues until one of the players fails to return the ball, either on the fly or after the first bounce within the boundaries of his or her court.

When the point has been completed, the server stands just behind his or her baseline and to the *left* of the center service line and serves to the opponent's left service court, continuing to alternate left and right after each point until the game is completed. Upon completion of the game, the server becomes the receiver. Players change sides at the completion of each odd-numbered game.

In doubles, each player serves a game in turn—first a member of one team, then a member of the other team, and so on. The same order of serving is kept throughout the set.

Scoring

Points in tennis are called Love, 15, 30, 40, Deuce, Advantage, and Game.

0, or nothing, is called Love.

First point won by a player is called 15.

Second point won by a player is called 30.

Third point won by a player is called 40.

Fourth point won by a player gives him Game, provided his opponent does not have more than 30 (2 points).

If each player has won three points (40-all), the score is Deuce. The next point won by a player gives him/her Advantage. However, if the next point is lost, the score is again deuce. When either player wins two *consecutive* points following the score of deuce, the game is won by that player. The server's score is always given first. The score should be called loudly and clearly after every point.

In scoring, the player who first wins six games wins a *set*, unless both players have won five games;

Figure 23-1 Lawn tennis court, singles and doubles.

then it takes an advantage of two games to win, so the score could be 7–5, or 8–6, or 9–7, and so on.

In scoring the *match*, the player first winning two sets is generally declared the winner. In professional tennis matches, the winner of three sets is declared the winner of the men's match, while in the women's game, the winner of two sets is declared the winner of the match. For example, match scores could be 6–0, 6–3, 6–2; 9–7, 4–6, 10–8; 2–6, 6–4, 6–4; 6–1, 6–1, 6–3; 4–6, 6–4, 6–4, 6–4; 6–0, 5–7, 7–5, 2– 6, 8–6.

Tie-Breaker Procedures

A tie-breaker game has been put into effect in an attempt to reduce the length of a tennis match when the score is tied at six games all. The 12-point tie-breaker is what is most commonly used today. To win the tie-breaker, a player must win at least 7 points and establish a margin of 2 points. Score is kept numerically. When the score of the set reaches six games all, if it is your turn to serve, you begin serving in the tie-breaker. The first server serves only 1 point

from the right service court. The second server begins from the left court and serves 2 points. From this point on, the server will always serve 2 points in a row. The players change ends of the court after a total of 6 points have been played, with a continuation of the rotation. The first player to win 7 points with a 2-point margin is declared the winner of the set. The score of the set is then recorded 7–6, with the score of the tie-breaker in parentheses: 7–6 (7–5).

Selection of Equipment

The selection of proper equipment is of utmost importance to the beginning tennis player as well as to the professional player. With good equipment, the beginning player can eliminate many handicaps, and thereby get more enjoyment from mastering the fundamental skills.

Tennis Rackets

In selecting the racket, consider the weight, balance, grip size, stringing, and quality of the frame (Figure

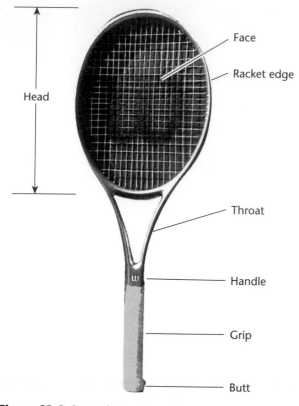

Figure 23-2 Parts of a tennis racket.

23-2). Rackets are manufactured in three different weights: light, medium, and heavy; they range from about 11 to 15 ounces. Women tend to prefer light rackets whereas men usually select medium or heavy racket frames. The "feel" of the racket as you swing it should be the most important consideration in choosing a new one. When shopping, you should make this comparison test and also take into account differences in materials and manufacture.

Most rackets are 27 inches long and measure 9 inches across the racket face. Currently, tennis rackets are being manufactured in different lengths, with oversized racket heads, and use various combinations of wood, aluminum alloy, steel, magnesium, fiberglass, and graphite. Choose a racket of good quality, with a frame sturdy enough to withstand at least four or five restringings. Cheap rackets soon lose their shape and are usually not a good long-term investment.

Basically, there are two types of strings: gut and nylon. Gut strings are more expensive but also more resilient and pliable. This type is preferred by most tournament players. Gut requires more care than nylon and is vulnerable to humidity and wetness. Nylon strings do not have the elasticity of gut but are still very comparable in play. Also, nylon strings are more durable, impervious to dampness, and less expensive. Nylon is adequate for the beginning player.

When you are purchasing a racket, the retailer will usually want to know your preference for string tension. The greater the tension (or tightness), the less control the player tends to have. Also, the racket frame cannot withstand as many restringings when it is strung tightly. The recommended string tension for beginning and intermediate players is between 55 and 57 pounds. Most rackets come with recommended tensions.

Rackets are manufactured to be evenly balanced, head-heavy, or handle-heavy. Head-heavy rackets are preferred by players inclined to be ground strokers or baseline players. Handle-heavy rackets are used by individuals who are predominantly net players. It is suggested that beginners select an evenly balanced racket to start with.

Another important factor in choosing an appropriate racket is the size of the grip. Grips usually range in circumference from 4 to 5 inches. The proper grip size depends upon the user's hand size, and selection may require professional assistance. If the individual grips the racket in an Eastern forehand grip (described below), the thumb should come just past the first knuckle of the middle finger. Correctly fitting a grip is of the utmost importance.

Tennis Balls

Most tennis balls are pressure-packed with compressed air and marked with numbers for identification. Manufactured according to United States Tennis Association (USTA) specifications, a ball must weigh two ounces, measure $2\frac{1}{2}$ inches in diameter, and have a wool-felt covering.

Tennis balls are also produced to be court specific. Some are made especially for hard courts (asphalt or cement) by having more felt on the ball's cover. Others are made for soft-court play on such surfaces as clay or grass.

Official Rules

Server and Receiver

The players stand on opposite sides of the net; the player who first delivers the ball is called the server, and the other the receiver.

Delivery of Service

The service is delivered in the following manner. Immediately before commencing to serve, the server stands with both feet at rest behind the baseline and within the imaginary continuations of the centermark and sideline. The server then tosses the ball by hand into the air and before it hits the ground, strikes it with her racket. The server is not permitted to touch the court inside the baseline until after the racket has made contact with the ball.

From Alternate Courts

In delivering the service, the server stands alternately behind the right and left courts, beginning from the right in every game. The ball served passes over the net and hits the ground within the service court, which is diagonally opposite.

Faults

The service is a fault if the server commits any breach of the rules of delivery of service or delivery of service from alternative courts; if he or she misses the ball in attempting to strike it; or if the ball served touches a permanent fixture (other than the net) before it hits the ground. However, if the server tosses the ball without making an effort to hit it, there is no fault.

Ball in Play Until Point Decided

A ball is in play from the moment at which it is delivered in service. Unless a fault or a let is called, it remains in play until the point is decided.

Player Hinders Opponent

If a player commits any act, either deliberately or involuntarily, that, in the opinion of the umpire, hinders the opponent in making a stroke, the umpire in the first case awards the point to the opponent, and in the second case orders the point to be replayed.

Ball Falling on Line

A ball falling on a line is regarded as falling in the court bounded by that line and is therefore a good ball.

Good Return

The return is good if

1. The ball touches the net, posts, cord or metal cable, strap, or band, provided that it passes over any of them and hits the ground within the court.
2. A player's racket passes over the net after the player has returned the ball, provided the ball passes the net before being played and is properly returned.
3. A player succeeds in returning a ball, served or in play, that strikes another ball lying in the court.

When Players Change Sides

The players change sides at the end of the first, third, and every subsequent alternate game of each set, and at the end of each set unless the total number of games in such set be even, in which case the change is not made until the end of the first game of the next set.

Doubles, Order of Service

Decided at the beginning of each set. The pair who have to serve in the first game of each set decide which partner shall do so, and the opposing pair decide similarly for the second game. The partner of the player who served in the first game serves in the third; the partner of the player who served in the second game serves in the fourth. The order of serving may be changed following the completion of any set.

A complete staff of officials for a tennis match includes a referee, an umpire, a net-court judge, and at least seven linespersons. However, most dual matches are played with only a referee or, at most, a referee and an umpire.

Doubles, Order of Receiving

The order of receiving is decided at the beginning of each set. The pair who have to receive the first game decide which partner shall continue to receive the first service in every odd game throughout that set. The opposing pair likewise decide which partner shall receive the first service in the second game, and that partner continues to receive the first service in every even game throughout that set. The order of receiving may be changed following the completion of any set.

Suggested Learning Sequence

In the beginning stages, it is important to stress that the learner acquire the ability to hit the ball consistently across the net. Early drills and skill development should focus on gaining familiarity with the basic stroke mechanics and racket skills. Students should be introduced to all strokes as quickly as possible; much time will be spent developing consistency in both the stroke and return of the tennis ball.

The following outline includes everything one would need to cover; the sequence might vary from teacher to teacher.

A. Basic racket skills
   1. Stance and basic foot movement—side-to-side, forward and backward
   2. Grips—eastern and continental
B. Strokes
   1. Forehand and grip
   2. Backhand and grip
   3. Service
   4. Return of service
C. Rules and etiquette (best to introduce when directly related to skill or strategy being taught)
D. Volley
E. Lob
F. Singles game—focus on consistently returning the ball into the court
G. Doubles game—regular and mixed

Skills and Techniques

The Grip

The importance of a proper grip cannot be stressed enough. There may be adjustments made in a player's swing, but a proper grip will last a player for a lifetime.

Special names have been given to the forehand grips, based upon the position of the palm against the racket handle:

When the palm sits upon the top right side, the grip is called the *Continental* (Figure 23-3). This grip requires a strong wrist and is used by some professionals for both forehand and backhand strokes.

When the palm sits on the back side of the handle, it is called an *Eastern* grip (Figure 23-4). The palm and the racket face are on the same plane, which gives the sensation of hitting the ball with the palm of your hand. This is the most common grip and the one strongly recommended in this chapter.

When the palm rests on the bottom of the handle, so that the palm points at the sky, it is called a *Western* grip (Figure 23-5). This is the least common grip, although some players use it to great advantage.

Eastern Grip. The Eastern grip is recommended for the forehand and is the only grip described in detail. A teacher without an extensive tennis background can't go wrong by suggesting this grip.

If you are right-handed, start by holding the throat of your racket with your left hand so that the racket face is vertical to the ground. Then hold the racket at waist level with the right palm vertical and your fingers pointing slightly downward at approximately a 45-0degree angle. The thumb should overlap and lie next to the middle finger, with the index finger spread. Now hold the racket out away from you and look at the top edge of your racket and the top edge of your right palm to see if they are both absolutely vertical. If you play this game correctly, you'll rarely hit a shot that requires the racket to vary more than 10 degrees from the vertical position.

Eastern Backhand Grip. The backhand grip advocated in this chapter is the Eastern backhand grip. This is attained by putting the palm on the top of the racket; the knuckle of the index finger rides the top right ridge, and the thumb can be placed either behind the racket or underneath. This grip position provides the most stability and requires the least amount of wrist adjustment in order to provide a vertical racket head at impact.

Two-Handed Backhand Grip. This grip uses a regular backhand grip with the dominant hand, which is at the base of the racket. The non-dominant hand should be placed comfortably above the other hand, similar to gripping a baseball/softball bat (Figure 23-6).

A   B

Figure 23-3 Continental grip (front and back views).

A   B

Figure 23-4 Eastern grip (front and back views).

A   B

Figure 23-5 Western grip (front and back views).

Figure 23-6 Two-handed backhand grip: (A) Front view, (B) top view.

Strokes

All the strokes are described in terms of a right-handed player's actions. There are some general principles that the player must be aware of:

1. Spin of the ball. The direction in which the ball spins is determined by the trajectory taken by the racket before and after contact with the ball. If the racket comes from below the ball, is vertical at impact, and finishes above the ball, topspin (low to high) will be attained. If the racket starts above the ball and sweeps down to the ball, underspin (high to low) will be attained.

2. Nearly every successful hit is accomplished with a vertical racket head. A player *does not* come over the ball for topspin or under the ball for underspin!

3. With the exception of the serve and overhead, all strokes in this chapter are to be hit with a locked wrist. The swing will come from the shoulder and not the wrist.

The Serve

The serve is the first ball hit in every point. The motion is very similar to that of a baseball pitcher's throwing motion. A good way to start teaching the serve is just to watch the student throw the ball over the net. Have the student pretend the ball is the racket, and don't be satisfied until the perfect motion is attained.

Many beginners prefer to use the regular forehand grip to hit a basic "flat" serve, but intermediate and advanced players should use the Continental grip, halfway between the Eastern forehand and Eastern backhand, in order to facilitate greater ball rotation with less stress on the wrist.

To attain a good service motion, it is necessary to coordinate two movements simultaneously—the ball

toss and the action of the racket. The toss is made by holding the ball near the finger tips, with the palm up, and then releasing the ball upward with all fingers letting go at the same time.

Achieving spin on the ball is an important aspect of serving. There are three kinds of serves recommended:

1. *Flat.* A totally flat serve is a myth because every ball has some amount of spin. This serve has the least amount of spin and is attained by snapping the wrist up and forward through the middle of the ball.

2. *Slice.* Very much like a curveball in baseball. The racket face must move across the backside of the ball on an almost horizontal plane, thus producing sidespin. Using the face of a clock as a reference, the right-hander would hit from nine o'clock to three o'clock.

3. *Topspin.* The principle of applying topspin on a serve is basically the same as on a forehand or backhand. Swing from low to high and brush the back side of the ball at about a 45-degree angle. On the imaginary clock, hit from eight o'clock to two o'clock.

The Serve Motion. Figure 23-7 shows the sequence of motions involved in the service (refer to views A–D):

A. *Ready position.* It is important to be totally relaxed before attempting to serve. The feet are shoulder-width apart, and the front shoulder is pointing in the direction the ball will be served.

B. To start the motion, the player's arms go down together and then start up together. Also begin to lean forward slightly.

C. Position C is crucial. At this point the ball is released and shoulder rotation must begin. The racket is slightly above the shoulder, and the tossing arm is pointing toward the right net post, so the toss will be 10 to 12 inches to the player's right. The height of the toss is 18 inches out of the out-stretched tossing arm. The object of the shoulder rotation is to let the right shoulder replace the position of the left shoulder. The weight at this point is mainly over the front foot, with both feet still in contact with the ground.

The racket is forming a loop behind the player's back. The racket *does not* scratch the back but forms a loop. This loop is accomplished by maintaining a loose arm and rotating the shoulders at the proper time. If the racket is hitting or touching the student's back at any time, the motion is out of sync.

D. *Point of contact.* At impact, the arm should be extended but not necessarily at the peak of one's reach (depending on spin desired). The chin is

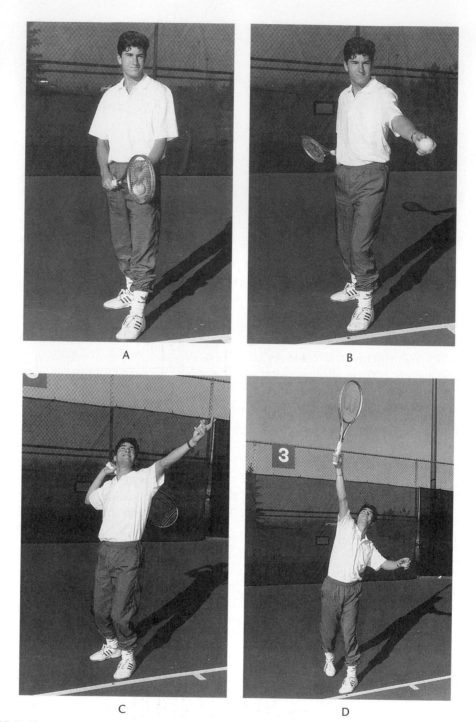

Figure 23-7 The service sequence.

held upward, and for optimal power both feet should be in contact with the ground, though the weight should have transferred forward. Notice that contact is made to the right of the player's head and in line with the hitting shoulder.

E. *Follow-through.* The right shoulder has replaced the position of the left shoulder, and the player's momentum following impact has brought the back foot a step into the court. If the player wishes

to serve and volley, this will naturally become the first step toward the net. If not, the participant may step back and rally off of the baseline.

Serve and Volley. The footwork recommended for serve and volley is to step with the right foot, left foot, right foot, and then bring both feet into alignment (Figure 23-8). This is called a "split step." The closer you can get to the service line, the better.

Figure 23-8 Footwork for serve and volley.

➤ Learning Hints

1. No fancy movements. Just relax and take your time.
2. To toss the ball, hold the ball with the finger tips and not the palm.
3. The toss must fit into the motion.
4. Chin up and hit up and out. This is true for all serves.
5. Think positive. Picture in your mind a successful serve before starting the motion.
6. Shoulder rotation, *not* the strength of the arm, is the main source of power.
7. Hit the second serve with the same motion as the first—just with more topspin.

➤ Practice/Organizational Suggestions

1. Hit buckets of balls at specific targets to each service court.
2. Before serving, determine the spin to be desired (flat, slice, topspin) and then evaluate your success accordingly.

One-Handed Backhand

Figure 23-9 illustrates the sequence of motions involved in executing the one-handed backhand (refer to views A–F):

A. *Ready position.* In a good ready position, the player's feet are shoulder-width apart and knees are slightly bent. Elbows are winged out, and the racket position is at a 45-degree angle to the ground. Note that the player is holding the racket with an Eastern forehand grip.

B. *Backswing.* The first move, once determining the ball is coming to the backhand side, is to turn the shoulder and change the grip simultaneously. The grip recommended is the Eastern backhand. The body should be turned enough so that the back of the shoulder is pointing at the oncoming ball.

C. Position viewed from behind. Notice how low the racket is and also that the racket face is slightly tilted downward. The arm is a radius, and if the racket is to be horizontal at impact and the wrist locked throughout the swing, the racket face must be tilted downward at this point. The left hand may be used to help push the racket downward, but this is optional.

D. Three movements happen simultaneously in this photo. The right foot steps into the ball, the racket drops to the bottom of the loop, and the knees bend to a crouch position. The racket must be below the level of the oncoming ball if topspin is to be achieved.

E. *Impact with the ball.* The racket face is vertical and the arm is extended well in front of the body (8 to 10 inches in front of the right foot). Eyes are focused right on the point of contact. The knees have lifted upward so as to help lift the ball up (topspin), and the hips have rotated toward the net. Body weight has transferred forward slightly before impact.

F. *Follow-through.* Following impact, let the racket face and knuckles follow the flight of the ball until the arm is fully extended. Freeze at this point and check to make sure that your weight is forward and over your front foot, and also the

Figure 23-9 One-handed backhand sequence.

racket should form an archway. If one were to drop the shoulder straight down, the racket should still form a perfect hitting position.

Two-Handed Backhand

If you lack strength, the two-handed backhand may be the stroke for you. It has its advantages in that you can hit a heavy ball that penetrates the court and you can disguise it easier than the one-handed backhand. Figure 23-10 illustrates the sequence of motions

involved in executing the two-handed backhand (refer to views A–E):

A. The grip. Use a regular backhand grip with the dominant hand, which is at the base of the racket. The non-dominant hand should be placed comfortably above the other hand, similar to gripping a baseball/softball bat.

Ready position. It is the same as the one-handed backhand, except for holding the racket with two hands on the grip out in front of the body.

Figure 23-10 Two-handed backhand.

B., C. *Backswing.* Turn your shoulders away from the ball, with the racket arms extended off the hip. Be sure the racket is pointed directly behind you toward the fence. The body should be perpendicular to the ball, with the majority of the weight on the back foot.

D. *Contact.* Weight is transferred from the back foot to the front foot. At the same time, the racket is brought around the body from slightly below the ball to make contact with the ball in front of the hip.

E. *Follow-through.* The racket should continue to move through the ball and diagonally across your body and wrap around your shoulders. The hips have rotated through the ball, but the feet remain in contact with the ground.

➤ **Learning Hints**
1. Change the grip and pivot the body as early as possible.
2. Concentrate on bending the knees and getting low. The legs are a tremendous source of power.

3. Work hard to swing easy.
4. Reach forward and out away from the body for contact.
5. Let the knuckles of the hitting hand be the guide for direction. As the knuckles go, so goes the racket head.
6. Reach out and upward for the follow-through.
7. Always check the follow-through at the completion of a swing.
8. While the body is lifting, the head must remain stationary. Leave head and eyes glued on the point of impact.

➤ **Practice/Organizational Suggestions**

1. Hit backhands toward a specific target area either from a ball machine or from someone feeding from across the net.
2. Hit off of a backboard.

Forehand

Figure 23-11 shows the forehand sequence (A–D):

A. *Ready position.* The feet are shoulder-width apart and knees are slightly bent. Elbows are winged out, and the racket is at a 45-degree angle to the

Figure 23-11 Forehand sequence.

ground. The player is holding the racket with an Eastern forehand grip.

B. *Backswing.* Turn the shoulders so that the back of the left shoulder is pointing toward the oncoming ball. It is important that this movement happens well before the ball crosses the net. The left hand is held in front of the body for balance and may also be an aid on the follow-through.

C. *Bottom of the loop.* Three movements happen simultaneously in this photo. The left foot steps forward, and the racket and knees drop down together. Notice that the racket face is turned slightly downward. The arm is a radius, and if the wrist is to remain locked and the racket face be vertical at impact, then the racket face must be tilted slightly downward at this point.

Impact with the Ball. The racket face is vertical, and the player's eyes are focused on the point of contact. Legs are lifting upward and hips are turning forward. Body weight has been transferred forward to the left foot.

D. *Follow-through.* There are two important points on the follow-through. One, the palm of the hitting hand should be pointing toward the intended target. Two, the hitting arm should be extended until the shoulder and chin touch, as shown in Figure 23-11D. Also, the legs are totally extended, and the majority of weight is on the left foot.

➤ Learning Hints

1. Rotate both shoulders together when turning the body.
2. Keep the wrist firm and let the palm be the guide for direction.
3. Synchronize the movement of the racket and body.
4. Keep the swing short. Don't let the racket get lost behind the body.
5. Power is generated from the leg lift and hip rotation—not just the arm.
6. On completion of the follow-through, the palm should face the intended target and the player's chin and hitting shoulder should touch.
7. Always check the follow-through at the completion of the swing.
8. While the body is lifting, the head must remain stationary. Leave head and eyes glued on the point of impact.

➤ Practice/Organizational Suggestions

1. Hit forehands toward a specific target area either from a ball machine or from someone feeding from across the net.
2. Hit off of a backboard.

Lobs

With some practice, the lob stroke should resemble the forehand and backhand ground strokes as much as possible. To conceal the lob, remember to turn the front shoulder and have a loop swing identical with the forehand and backhand ground strokes. This also means running to the ball with the racket head up and already back. But instead of turning the racket face down as the racket drops, work on a bevel (slight backward tilt of the racket face) and lifting the ball high into the air, using the opponent's baseline as a target.

Overhead Smash

Figure 23-12 shows the ready position for the overhead smash. The motion from this point is exactly like that of a flat serve. When teaching, stress keeping the chin up through contact and also reaching up for the ball.

Backhand Volley

The sequence of motions recommended for the backhand volley is illustrated in Figure 23-13.

A. *Ready position.* The player is waiting to determine the direction of the ball; he is holding the racket with an Eastern forehand grip.
B. *Backswing.* The player pivots the body and changes his grip (continental grip). Actually, there is little or no backswing. The racket should always remain out in front of the body. Notice

Figure 23-12 Ready position for overhead smash.

Figure 23-13 Motions recommended for backhand volley.

Figure 23-14 Motion recommended for forehand volley.

how the left elbow is held high to keep the racket face on line with the ball.

C. *Contact and follow-through.* The key points here:

1. The racket head must remain above the wrist.
2. The ball is contacted well in front of the body—8 to 10 inches.
3. The arm and racket form a V.
4. The player's head, racket head, and ball should all be on the same plane. During the follow-through, the racket head should remain above the wrist, and ideally the

racket face should follow the flight of the ball to gain depth on the volley. The follow-through is very short. From an instructional standpoint, it is good technique to try to have the student freeze the racket right at the point of impact to assure that the wrist isn't breaking.

Forehand Volley

The sequence of motions recommended for the forehand volley is shown in Figure 23-14 (A–C).

A. *Ready position.* The player assumes a ready position, holding the racket with a Continental grip.

B. *Backswing.* The player pivots the body, striving to get the shoulders sideways to the net. The racket should go back as far as the body turn takes it, yet never be out of the player's peripheral vision. The less backswing, the better.

C. *Contact and follow-through.* As the player reaches forward to the ball, impact should take place slightly in front of the left shoulder. The nature of the swing will give the ball natural underspin. Do not break the wrist or chop at the ball. The arm and the racket form a V, and the player's head, racket head, and the tennis ball should be at the same height at contact. During the follow-through, keep the wrist firm, and try to keep the racket face in line with the ball. Do not let the racket head drop if at all possible.

➤ **Learning Hints for Volleys**

1. Always step forward and attack the volley. Also, change the grip when necessary.
2. Use little or no backswing.
3. Contact well out in front of the body, especially on backhands.
4. Keep the wrist locked.
5. Finish with the racket head above the wrist.
6. Use the knuckles for direction guidance on the backhand and the palm on the forehand.

➤ **Practice/Organizational Suggestions**

1. Hit off a ball machine or a feeder with a specific target in mind.

2. Alternate hitting a forehand and then a backhand to get used to the shoulder rotation.
3. Hit off of a backboard.

Backhand Return of Serve

The suggested technique for backhand return of serve is analyzed in Figure 23-15.

A. *Ready position.* The player should be up on his toes, slightly leaning forward and holding an Eastern forehand grip.

B. The player pivots the body sideways while changing the grip to an Eastern backhand. The backswing is very short, the emphasis being on a blocking motion similar to the volley.

C. *Contact and follow-through.* At this point, it is crucial that the returner has stepped forward and is reaching out to contact the ball 8 to 10 inches in front of the body. This shot is hit with underspin. Concentration should be on putting the ball back in play rather than on hitting a winner. The follow-through is the same archway as described for the backhand ground stroke.

Forehand Return of Serve

The suggested technique for forehand return of serve is illustrated in Figure 23-16.

A. *Ready position.* Remember to keep the elbows raised, and be ready to move forward.

B. Rotate both shoulders sideways while limiting the length of the backswing. Hold the racket face

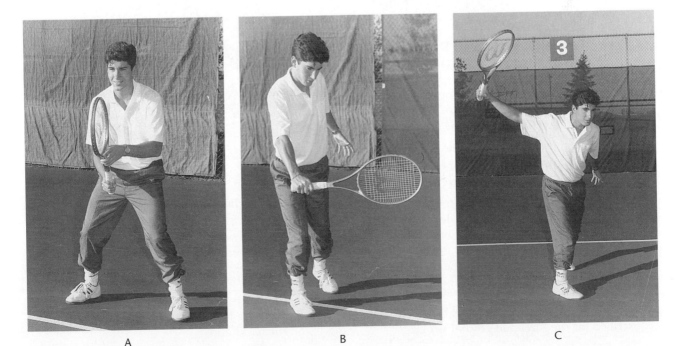

A   B   C

Figure 23-15 Suggested technique for backhand return of serve.

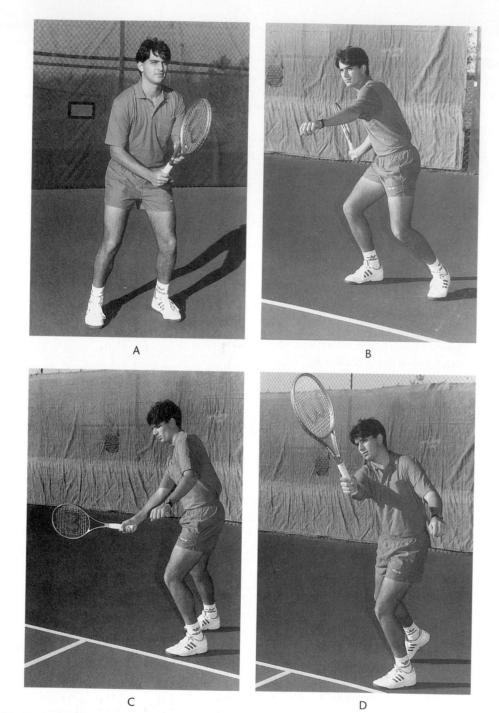

Figure 23-16 Suggested technique for forehand return of serve.

on the level of the ball and remember that a blocking motion similar to a volley is desired.

C. *Contact.* The ball is met just in front of the player's left shoulder. A step forward as well as body weight transfer is important. The shot is hit with slight underspin with emphasis on putting the ball back in play.

D. *Follow-through.* This position is the same as described for the forehand ground stroke.

➤ **Learning Hints**

1. Start with a forehand grip rather than in between the two grips.
2. Use a short backswing and a long follow-through.
3. Keep the wrist locked.
4. Always try to have the weight forward on the feet, never back on the heels.
5. Contact the ball in front of the body, especially on the backhand.

6. Follow-throughs are the same as for ground strokes.

➤ Practice/Organizational Suggestions

Have a fellow participant practice serves while you hit returns to a specific target area. Alternate between both service courts.

Playing Strategy

Singles Strategy

The game of tennis is usually won by forcing your opponent into making errors. Your second option is to place the ball where the opponent cannot reach it. Both of these strategies are good, whether you are a beginner or an advanced player.

Another option you have is to play a patient groundstroke game from the baseline. The object here is to move your opponent around the court and to keep the ball in play. This strategy requires a great deal of patience because the rallies are usually very long. A serve and volley style of game produces shorter points, but the individual is also taking a greater risk of making an error. Finally, your fourth option is an all-court game, which uses the baseline and the net play for an assortment of shots.

As an individual, you should choose which type of play best suits your personality and your skill level. Whichever style you choose, have fun with it!

Doubles Strategy

The game of doubles is entirely different from the game of singles, with the exception of which strokes are used. Besides the obvious difference of having two players on each side, doubles is an attacking game. Most doubles play is located at the net, and you will find that points are generally much shorter (usually 3–5 hits).

The beginner does not always experience the full challenge of the game because of its attacking nature, but usually enjoys working with someone for a common cause. For most, doubles will be the individual's first experience on the court, especially if being taught in a large group setting.

One-up and one-back strategy occurs when one partner plays the net position and the other plays the baseline position. If you are not confident with your transition game (moving from the baseline to the net), this is a good style of play for you. In the two players-back strategy, both players stay at the baseline for the majority of their points. This style of doubles is definitely for those who want to play a more defensive game. Two-up is the most assertive style of doubles. Both players, whether returning or serving, are always trying to get to the net. This is a very exciting style of play.

Most players will find themselves in the situation of playing more doubles than singles. Find the style of play that works the best for you and your partner.

Modifications for Special Populations

Orthopedically Impaired

1. Contact the United States Tennis Association at www.usta.org for the rules on wheelchair tennis.
2. Allow students using wheelchairs two bounces before returning a shot.
3. Students using assistive devices, e.g., canes, walkers, crutches, might play from a seated position with another student in a seated position. For the non-impaired student, you might be able to borrow a wheelchair from a local hospital's rehabilitation unit.
4. For students with limited grip, use Velcro straps to secure the racket to the student's hand.
5. Allow students with limited grip to use flat paddle boards instead of rackets. Secure the boards with strapping.
6. See modifications for handball/racquetball.
7. Use larger balls or ones made from different material, e.g., Nerf or beach ball.

Cognitively Impaired

1. Have students throw the ball back and forth across the net to help them understand the concepts of the game.
2. Have students practice in a smaller area, e.g., a smaller court, or rebound off of a wall.
3. Reduce the tension in the stringing of the racket to allow a slower moving ball.

Sensory Impaired

1. Individual considerations must be taken into account to determine the appropriateness of tennis for students who are visually impaired or blind.
2. You might consider playing lead-up games, such as goalball, for the visually impaired. You can obtain rules from the United States Association of Blind Athletes at www.usaba.org.
3. Place small bells inside whiffleballs and use as an audio ball for rebounding against a gym wall.
4. Minimal modifications are needed for students who are deaf or hearing impaired. Consider using visual stop-and-start signals for these students.

Etiquette and Playing Courtesies

To make the game more enjoyable for yourself and for others, you should follow certain court courtesies or rules of etiquette. If one of your tennis balls rolls into another court, wait until the players on the court have finished their rally before asking for your ball. When you return someone's ball that has rolled into your court, roll the ball back to the player asking for it instead of trying to gain some stroking practice. If they are engaged in playing a point, roll the ball back against the screen out of their field of play. If your opponent is interfered with in any way during the play for a point, stop the play, call a "let," and then play the point over. You call lines on your side of the net and let your opponent call lines on her side. When leaving or entering the courts, do not walk behind a player playing a point. Wait until the rally is over, then quickly cross the rear of the court close to the back screen.

Helpful Reminders

1. Keep your eye on the ball at all times.
2. Strive for accurate placement rather than speed.
3. Always play the game to win, but if you go down in defeat, give your opponent due credit.
4. Play to your opponent's weaknesses.
5. When calling the score, always call the server's score first.
6. Keep your weight on the balls of both feet so you can move in any direction with ease and speed.
7. Acquire an understanding of the fundamentals of stroking, and practice faithfully to master them.
8. Notice how your opponent strokes the ball so when he uses the chop or slice stroke, you can play the bounce accordingly.
9. Turn your body sideways to the net on all ground strokes.
10. When stroking the ball, avoid stiff leg action by keeping the knees loose and relaxed.
11. On ground strokes, return the ball deep into the opponent's backcourt near the baseline.
12. On ground strokes, attempt to hit the ball at waist level and on the rise.
13. Hit the ball squarely on the strings of the racket face by hitting "through" the ball instead of chopping under it.
14. The follow-through of the racket is in the direction of the intended flight of the ball.
15. After completing each stroke, return to a ready position, facing the net and loosely grasping the throat of the racket with the left hand to facilitate change of grip if necessary.

16. Well-placed lobs out of reach of the net rusher will help keep her away from the net.
17. When serving, attempt to get the first serve in the proper court as often as possible. Stress control and accuracy if a second serve is necessary and concentrate on getting the ball into the proper service area.
18. The server should always have two balls in his or her possession before starting the service.
19. The receiver should not retrieve or return the ball if the opponent's first serve is a fault, rather, the receiver should remain in receiving position so the server can immediately follow with a second attempt.
20. Devote periodic practice sessions to correcting specific weaknesses.

Safety Considerations

1. Warm up sufficiently before starting strenuous play.
2. If injured, stop and report the injury to the instructor.
3. Remove rings, bracelets, watches, and other objects that may cause bruises and cuts.
4. Check the playing surface for glass, nails, stones, slippery spots, and so forth.
5. Stay in line, on mark, or in your own area when swinging or hitting.
6. Control your emotions; do not throw the racket or hit a ball in anger.
7. Shout a warning when there is danger of a ball hitting someone.
8. Avoid showing off and "horseplay."
9. Be aware of the distances between the baselines and walls, fences, screens, and so on.
10. When playing in excessive heat, make sure to drink plenty of fluids.

Terminology

Ace A ball served and untouched by the opponent's racket.

Advantage (Ad) Scoring term: The next point won after the score is "deuce."

Alley The $4\frac{1}{2}$ foot strip on either side of the singles court, used to enlarge the court for doubles.

Approach shot A shot hit inside the baseline while approaching the net.

Backcourt The area between the service line and the baseline.

Backhand Strokes hit on the left side of a right-handed player.

Backspin Spin acquired on a ball dropping from a vertical position, which forces the ball to bounce back toward the hitter.

Backswing The beginning of all ground strokes and service motion requiring a backswing to gather energy for the forward swing.

Baseline The end line of a tennis court, located 39 feet from the net.

Break Relates to the act of winning a game in which the opponent serves.

Center mark Short mark that bisects the baseline.

Center service line The line perpendicular to the net, which divides the two service courts.

Center strap A strap placed at the center of the net and anchored to the court to facilitate a constant 3-foot height for the net at the center.

Center stripe Same as the center service line, which divides the two service courts into halves.

Chip Refers to the short chopping motion of the racket against the back and bottom side of the ball.

Chop Used in the same manner as "chip" by many. Refers to the placement of backspin on the ball with a short high to low forward swing.

Cross-court A shot hit diagonally from one corner of the court over the net into the opposite corner of the court.

Cut off the angle To move forward quickly against an opponent's cross-court shot, allowing the player to hit the ball near the center of the court rather than near the sidelines.

Deep (depth) A shot that bounces near the baseline on ground strokes and near the service line on serves.

Default A player who forfeits her position in a tournament through failure to play a scheduled match.

Deuce Scoring term used when the game score is 40–40.

Dink A ball normally hit very softly and relatively high to ensure its safe landing.

Double fault When the server has served two serves out-of-bounds on the same point.

Doubles line The outside sideline on a court—used in doubles only.

Down-the-line A shot hit near a sideline, which travels close to, and parallel with, the same line from which the shot was initially hit.

Drive An offensive shot hit with extra force.

Drop shot A ground stroke hit in such a manner as to drop just over the net with little or no forward bounce.

Drop volley A volley hit in such a manner as to drop just over the net with little or no forward bounce.

Error A mistake made by a player during competition.

Face The hitting surface of the racket.

Fault A serve that lands out-of-bounds or is not hit properly.

Flat shot A ball hit in such a manner as not to rotate when traveling through the air.

Foot fault Illegal foot movement before service, penalized by the loss of that particular serve.

Common foot faults are stepping on or ahead of the baseline before the ball has been contacted, and running along the baseline before serving.

Forecourt The area between the net and the service line.

Forehand The stroke hit on the right side of a right-handed player.

Frame The rim of the racket head plus the handle of the racket.

Game Scoring term when a player wins 4 points before his opponent and holds a minimum 2-point lead.

Grip That portion of the racket that is grasped in the player's hand.

Ground stroke Any ball hit after it has bounced.

Half-volley A ball hit only inches away from the court's surface after the ball has bounced.

Hold serve To win your own serve. If you lose your own serve, your serve has been "broken."

Let (ball) A point that is played over because of some kind of interference.

Let serve A serve that touches the net tape and falls into the proper square and is played over.

Linesperson A match official who calls balls "in" or "out."

Lob A ball hit sufficiently high to pass over the outstretched arm position of the net player.

Lob volley A shot hit high into the air from a volleying position.

Love Scoring term: zero points or games.

Match A contest between two or four opponents.

Match point The point immediately preceding the final point of a match. The player who holds this point is said to be serving for match point.

Midcourt The area in front or in back of the service line of the playing court.

Net ball A ball that hits the net and falls back on the same side as the hitter.

Net player The player who has gained position at the net and is prepared to volley.

No player's land A general area within the baseline and proper net position area; when caught in that area, the player must volley or hit ground strokes near his or her feet.

Offensive lob A ball hit just above the racket reach of an opposing net player.

Open face racket A racket whose face is moving under the ball. A wide open racket face is parallel with the court surface.

Overhead A shot hit from a position higher than the player's head.

Overhead smash A shot hit extremely hard from a position higher than the player's head.

Overhitting Putting too much force into each shot.

Pace The speed of the ball.

Passing shot A shot that passes beyond the reach of the net player and lands inbounds.

Placement A shot hit inbounds and untouched by the opponent.

Poach To cross over into your partner's territory.

Racket face The hitting surface of the racket.

Racket head Top portion of the racket frame that houses the strings.

Rally The act of hitting balls back and forth across the net. A rally includes all shots other than the serve.

Receiver The player about to return the opponent's serve.

Retrieve Normally refers to a fine defensive shot in response to an opponent's well-placed offensive shot.

Server The player initiating play.

Service line The end line of the service courts, running parallel with the net.

Set Scoring term: The first player to win six games with a minimum two-game lead has won a set.

Set point The point that, if won, will give the player the set.

Sidespin A ball hit and rotating on a horizontal plane.

Signals in doubles Signaling your partner that you are going to poach at the net.

Singles line The first sideline closer to the center mark and running the entire length of the court.

Slice Motion of the racket head going around the side of the ball, producing a horizontal spin on the ball.

Tape The band of cloth or plastic running across the top of the net.

Telegraphing the play To indicate the direction of one's intended target before actually hitting the ball.

Topspin The clockwise rotation of the ball at a 90-degree angle.

Touch The ability to make delicate soft shots from several positions on the court.

Twist A special rotation imparted to the ball during the serve, causing the ball to jump to the left (of right-handed server).

Umpire The official used in tournament play to call lines.

Underspin A counterclockwise spin placed on the ball by catching the backside and bottomside of the ball with the racket head.

Volley To hit the ball in the air before it has bounced on the court.

Further References

Barton, J. and Grice, W. *Tennis.* Boston, MA: American Press, 1994.

Bryant, J. *Game-Set-Match.* Englewood, CO: Morton Publishing, 1994.

Douglas, P. and Brown, D. *101 Essential Tips on Tennis.* New York: DK Publishing, 1996.

Early, F. *Tennis Strokes That Win: Breakthrough Techniques for Mastering the Game.* Chicago: NTC/Contemporary Publishing, 1995.

Faulkner, T. et al. *The Complete Idiot's Guide to Tennis.* New York: MacMillan, 1999.

Groppel, J. et al. *Science of Coaching Tennis.* Champaign, IL: Human Kinetics, 1989.

Johnson, M. and Hill, D. *College Tennis.* Winston-Salem, NC: Hunter Textbooks, 1990.

McEnroe, P. et al. *Tennis for Dummies.* New York: Hungry Minds, 1998.

Moore, C. and Chafin, M. *Tennis Everyone.* 5th ed. Winston-Salem, NC: Hunter Textbooks, 1992.

Murray J. and Frey. R. *Smart Tennis: How to Win the Mental Game.* San Francisco: Jossey-Bass, 1999.

Parks, B. A. *Tennis in a Wheelchair.* National Foundation of Wheelchair Tennis, 1988.

Stolle, F. and Knight, B. *Tennis: Let's Analyze Your Game.* Englewood, CO: Morton Publishing, 1992.

USTA Schools Program. Princeton, NJ: United States Tennis Association. Latest ed.

USTA Recreational Tennis Curriculum. Princeton, NJ: United States Tennis Association, 1989.

Van Collie, S. *Tennis, The Lifetime Sport.* San Leandro, CA: Briston Publishing, 1992.

Vasquez, R. *Kids Book of Tennis: Over 150 Tennis Games to Teach Children the Sport of a Lifetime.* Secaucus, NJ: Carol Publishing Group, 1997.

Zebas, C. and Johnson, H. *Tennis, Back to the Basics.* Dubuque, IA: Eddie Bower Publishing, 1991.

Audio-Visual Materials

ESPN-Maximizing Your Tennis Potential with Vic Braden. Karol Video, 350 N. Pennsylvania Ave., P.O. Box 7600, Wilkes-Barre, PA 18773-7600.

Hot Tips Presents the 30-Minute Tennis Lesson. Champions on Film & Video, 745 State Circle, Box 1941, Ann Arbor, MI 48106. VHS.

Playing Doubles. Champions on Film & Video, 745 State Circle, Box 1941, Ann Arbor, MI 48106. VHS.

Teaching Kids Tennis. Karol Video, 350 N. Pennsylvania Ave., P.O. Box 7600, Wilkes-Barre, PA 18773-7600.

Tennis. Champions on Film & Video, 745 State Circle, Box 1941, Ann Arbor, MI 48106. VHS.

Tennis for All Ages. Champions on Film & Video, 745 State Circle, Box 1941, Ann Arbor, MI 48106. VHS.

Tennis from the Pros. Karol Video, 350 N. Pennsylvania Ave., P.O. Box 7600, Wilkes-Barre, PA 18773-7600.

Tennis Our Way. Champions on Film & Video, 745 State Circle, Box 1941, Ann Arbor, MI 48106. VHS.

Visual Tennis. Champions on Film & Video, 745 State Circle, Box 1941, Ann Arbor, MI 48106. VHS.

Web Sites

www.tennis.com Offers instruction elements, including 101 tips, with drills, rules, history, tip of the week, grip guide, and frequently asked questions.

www.tennisserver.com An extensive site with multi-index references, including rules, code of ethics, book and video listings, and much more.

www.tennisone.com A top resource for instructional tennis hints, with an index that includes a lesson library, professional strokes, grips, rules, and much more.

www.tennisclinic.com Provides a multitude of services for improving one's game.

www.littletennis.com A site devoted to youth instruction, analogous to Little League instruction.

CHAPTER 24

Track and Field

This chapter will enable you to

- Understand the learning sequence for the hurdling, jumping, and throwing events
- Demonstrate and perform basic skills and techniques of various running, hurdling, jumping, and throwing events
- Set up a training program for a participant in various running and hurdling events
- Identify the basic terminology used in the sport of track and field
- Identify the basic rules of the sport

Nature and Purpose

The more than 30 different track and field events in the Olympic Games involve walking, running, jumping, and throwing. Each requires different combinations of sports fitness (endurance, strength, speed, flexibility) and motor skills to be successful. Yet this great variety of events requiring these different combinations of natural and acquired abilities gives practically every individual, no matter the body size, shape, or form, the opportunity to participate successfully. Often young boys and girls do not realize they have the natural ability to become successful in track and field until they give it a try. Many track and field stars "discovered themselves" in a physical education class or intramural sport. In fact, participants can easily assess their natural abilities of strength, speed, endurance, and power by performing specific tests. These talent tests could include a 30-meter timed sprint, standing long jump for distance, vertical jump for height, five alternate leg bounds for distance, 5-kg shot tossed backward overhead for distance, or an 800-meter timed run.

Basic Rules

Sprinting

1. For most elementary, middle school, high school, and college events, one false start disqualifies a runner.
2. For many youth, club, and international events, disqualification results on the second individual false start.
3. A false start is the result of the athlete moving or leaving his mark before the gun is fired.

4. A starter may not touch on or over the line before the firing of the gun.
5. Some part of each foot must be in contact with the track in the blocks.
6. The athlete is timed and places are determined when the torso crosses the finish line, which does not include the hand, arms, or legs.

Relay Races

1. The baton must be passed inside the 20-meter passing zone.
2. The baton must be carried in the hand throughout the race.
3. After passing the baton, the runner may not interfere with an opponent.
4. A baton dropped outside the zone must be retrieved by the runner who dropped it.
5. A baton dropped inside the zone may be retrieved by either runner.
6. For relay legs that are 200 meters or less, the outgoing runner may line up 10 meters in front of the exchange zone, but the pass must occur within the 20-meter zone.

Hurdling

1. The entire body must pass over the hurdle.
2. A hurdler may not interfere with a hurdler in another lane.
3. A hurdler may not intentionally knock over the hurdles with the hand or foot.

High Jump

1. The jumper must make a jump from one foot.
2. Three trials are allowed at each height.

3. Displacing a bar, passing under it, crossing the line of the bar extended, or leaving the ground shall count as a foul and trial.
4. The jumper goes out of the competition when he or she has three consecutive misses at any height. The participant is credited with the best mark that was successfully cleared.
5. Leaving the ground is not considered an attempt unless the plane of the crossbar is broken.

Long Jump

1. Touching the ground at any point past the foul line (the front edge of the takeoff board) as the participant jumps is considered a foul and not measured.
2. The jump shall be measured at right angles to the board and at the point of landing closest to the takeoff.
3. If the jumper leaves the pit to the side and moves backward to a point that is closer to the takeoff board than the mark made in the pit, it is considered a foul.

Triple Jump

1. The legal measurement of a jump is the same as described in the long jump.
2. A foul jump is the same as described in the long jump.

Shot Put

1. Touching on the top or outside of the circle or toe-board with any part of the body constitutes a foul.
2. The thrower must leave by the back half of the circle.
3. The shot must be thrown within a 60-degree sector (in high school competition and below) and within a 40-degree sector in college and international competition.

Discus Throw

1. The discus must be thrown within a 60-degree sector (40-degree in college). As in the shot put, after entering the ring, the thrower must pause before starting.
2. The thrower may not touch any part of a painted line, or the top of a band used to outline part of the ground outside the circle.

Equipment

The equipment required in track and field varies with the events. Proper equipment is important and can affect the learning of skills and technique as well as help to reduce injuries. Lighter-weight throwing implements for shot or discus should be used for smaller and younger athletes. For the beginning hurdler, modified hurdles using light-weight wooden rods placed upon small cones or bricks and easily displaced should be used instead of heavy solid hurdles. In the high jump, a soft foam pit made from gymnastic mats or high jump mats is essential. The crossbar should be of soft plastic rather than solid metal.

Spiked shoes must be worn not only for safety but also for optimal performance, particularly in the jumping events. For the elite performer, shoes designed specifically for the various events may be purchased.

Track and field shorts, shirts, and warm-up suits vary in price depending upon the quality of the material. These can be purchased from catalogue suppliers or sporting goods or department stores.

Suggested Learning Sequence

The running and field events described in this chapter may be taught in any order, taking into account particular student needs, the time available, and the type of facilities available. It is, however, important to follow a simple-to-complex progression leading up to the completion of a skill. Other important keys to successful learning include positive reinforcement through feedback and using good learning hints.

In all instances, rules, hints, cues, and terminology should be introduced only when significant to the learning progression and when dealing with the particular event. Safety considerations are of prime importance during the initial stages of learning.

A. Orientation
   1. Safety considerations
   2. Discussion of equipment
   3. Importance of warm-up and cool-down
B. Rules, skill development, terminology, and specific safety instructions are given in connection with the particular event.
C. Running events
   1. Sprinting
   2. Middle and long distance running
   3. Relays
   4. Hurdling
D. Field events
   1. High jump (flop style)
   2. Long jump
   3. Triple jump
   4. Shot put
   5. Discus throw

Specific Safety Instructions

Sprinting

1. Warm up thoroughly before starting.
2. Don't jump or lunge at the finish tape.
3. Don't take starts after a hard training session.

Relay Races

1. After passing the baton, remain in your lane until all others have passed.
2. Pass the baton to opposite hands, right to left or left to right, to avoid a collision.

Hurdling

1. Warm up and stretch well before hurdling.
2. Never attempt to go over a hurdle from the wrong direction.

High Jump

1. Make certain the pit is positioned correctly.
2. If using gymnastics mats, they should have a depth of 24".

Long Jump

1. Keep the landing pit area soft and smooth.
2. Wear jumping shoes with heel cups or rubber pads in the takeoff heel.

Triple Jump

1. Wear heel cups or rubber pads in both jumping shoes.
2. Keep the landing pit area soft and smooth.

Shot Put/Discus

1. Roll or carry implements back to the circle rather than throw them.
2. Practice in a protected area.
3. When retrieving implements, never turn your back to the throwing circle.

Skills and Techniques

Sprinting

While speed or sprinting ability is largely determined by inherited traits—the white muscle fiber composition of the body—a sprinter's innate speed can be greatly improved through technique work and training. Technique work involves improving a sprinter's start, ability to lift ("change gears"), and ability to relax, thereby sustaining speed.

The Start. The placement of the starting blocks is essential to a good start. Most sprinters favor the medium start. In this start, the front block is set in approximately 2-foot lengths from the starting line,

and the back block 3- to 4-foot lengths. These distances may vary according to the sprinter's body structure, height, and length of limbs.

The starting commands are "on your marks" and "set" and the firing of the gun.

In the on-the-mark position, the hands are parallel with the starting line, the arms are shoulder-width apart, the dominant leg is forward in the blocks with the opposite knee resting on the track, and the head is relaxed. After assuming this position, the sprinter will then slide or roll forward until the shoulders are over or in front of the starting line, with the pressure being on the knee and fingertips.

On "set," the sprinter raises the hips until slightly higher than the shoulders. In this position, the knees are parallel or at a slight angle to the track. The sprinter feels good power in both legs in this position if the blocks are spaced properly. The head is relaxed with no tension on the neck (Figure 24-1).

At the gun, the sprinter concentrates on good sprint form: opposite arm/opposite leg action while keeping the driving angle low and forward (Figure 24-2). It is important that the sprinter's movement be forward, not upward, which is the result of the proper "set" position.

Lifting. After coming out of the blocks, the sprinter concentrates on lifting, or "shifting gears," by driving the knees high, which will continue acceleration. This action continues until the sprinter has reached maximum speed, somewhere between 30 to 40 meters, at which time an upright running position and full running stride length will have been achieved.

Free-Wheeling. In this phase, which is also referred to as floating, the sprinter works to sustain speed through total body relaxation. Total relaxation is achieved by running tall while keeping the hands, arms, and jaw loose and the shoulders down to

Figure 24-1 An excellent "set" position is demonstrated by the two sprinters.

Figure 24-2 At the gun, these two sprinters demonstrate good sprint form and drive forward out of the blocks.

reduce tension in the antagonistic muscle groups of the neck (Figure 24-3).

The Finish. The sprinter drives or runs through the tape at the finish in regular sprint form and does not attempt to jump or lunge.

➤ **Practice/Organizational Suggestions— Training Workout**

In training for the sprinting events, quality work is important over quantity work. Basic sprint training should include *long sprints* consisting of 200 to 250 meters for the 100 meters, 250 to 300 meters for the 200 meters, and 500 to 600 meters for the 400 meters; *medium sprints* consisting of 50 to 75 meters for the 100 meters, 100 to 150 meters (around turn) for the 200 meters, and 300 to 350 meters for the 400 meters; and *short sprints* using a starting gun, consisting of 20 to 30 meters for the 100 meters, 50 to 75 meters for the 200 meters, and 100 to 150 meters for the 400 meters. A weekly competitive season training

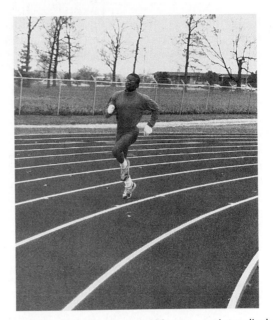

Figure 24-3 Free-wheeling. A 400-meter sprinter displays total relaxation, which is important in sustaining speed.

program is given in Table 24-1. Each of the workouts should be preceded by a good warm-up, which includes stretching and flexibility exercises, easy running, and sprint drills, and should be followed by a good cool-down of easy running and stretching.

➤ **Practice/Organizational Suggestions— Sprinting Skills**

1. *High knee drill.* Running 20 to 30 meters with knees lifted so that the thighs are at least parallel with the ground. Emphasize quality lifting; the drill should not be hurried. The vertical action is fast, but the horizontal movement forward is slow.
2. *Block drill.* Sprinter A gets into the blocks in the on-the-mark position. Sprinter B stands facing

Table 24-1 A weekly training program for sprinting events

	100 Meters	200 Meters	400 Meters
Monday	4 × 250 m at 95% effort/ walk 8 min.	3 × 300 m at 95% effort/ walk 10 min	2 × 600 m at 90% effort/ walk 15 min
Tuesday	Baton work; 8–10 × 30–40 m gun starts	Baton work; 8–10 × 75 m gun starts (around turn)	8–10 × 150 m gun starts (around turn)
Wednesday	5–6 × 75 m at all-out/walk back for recovery	6 × 150 m at all-out/walk back for recovery	2–3 × 300 m at race pace
Thursday	Baton work; 5–6 × 20–30 m gun starts	Baton work; 6–8 × 50 m gun starts	5–6 × 100 m at 95% effort
Friday	Meet	Meet	Meet
Saturday	1–2 miles easy distance golf course	1–2 miles easy distance golf course	2–4 miles easy distance golf course
Sunday	Rest	Rest	Rest

him with hands on the shoulders of sprinter A. Upon continued hand pressure, sprinter A comes to "set" position. On the command "go" from sprinter B, sprinter A drives out of the blocks, concentrating on driving the arms and lifting the knees while sprinter B continues to offer resistance.

3. *Figure 4 drill.* Running 20 to 30 meters, the sprinter concentrates on the heel coming up under the buttocks as the foot comes off the track; this will elevate the knee parallel with the track.

4. *Sprint-float-sprint drill.* The sprinter runs 150 meters, running the first 50 working hard, the next 50 meters floated (relaxed running), and the last 50 meters working hard. The sprinter runs the floated 50 meters within one second of the hard 50 meters by concentrating on good sprint form and relaxation, so as not to decelerate.

Middle and Long0 Distance Running

Middle distance races include the 800-meter, 1,500-meter, and mile races. Long distance races include the 3,000-meter steeplechase, 5,000-meter, 10,000-meter, and marathon races. Running form in these events is not significantly different from the sprinting events except that as the speed of a runner is reduced, the stride length becomes shorter, the body is more erect, and the foot strikes more on the heel in landing.

In training for these events, it is important to train both energy systems of the body—the aerobic and anaerobic.

Aerobic Training. This type of training, which improves a runner's endurance or stamina by increasing the ability to take in and utilize oxygen, is accomplished through runs of 3 to 10 miles or longer at different tempos (speeds). An easy tempo involves relaxed recovery running; a brisk tempo involves running at steady state or oxygen balance; and a hard tempo involves running beyond steady state but not all-out. Using all three tempos in a run produces a type of training called *Fartlek* (Swedish for "speed play") or playing with speed. Early training should include only easy and brisk tempo runs for several weeks; later, hard-tempo and hard Fartlek runs with hills may be alternated with easier runs. An example of this pattern of training is given in Table 24-2.

Anaerobic Training. This type of training, which improves the body's ability to run while under oxygen debt, is best developed through intermittent or interval-type training. Interval training consists of running a number of short distances at a given pace, interspersed by 1 to 5 minutes of rest or jogging fixed distances. For example: 8 × 200 meters at 30 sec/jog

Table 24-2 An aerobic training program

Sunday	3–5 times race distance or longer if mature enough (easy tempo)
Monday	2–5 times race distance (hard tempo)
Tuesday	3–4 times race distance (brisk tempo)
Wednesday	4–7 miles of Fartlek
Thursday	3–4 times race distance (brisk tempo)
Friday	2–5 times race distance (hard tempo)
Saturday	2–4 times race distance (brisk to easy tempo)

200 meters. Interval training is used basically to develop race rhythm and for sharpening speed.

➤ Training Workout Suggestions

A weekly competitive-season aerobic/anaerobic training program for high school and college is outlined in Table 24-3. These distances would be reduced for elementary/middle school runners.

Relays

There are two types of relays: *sprint relays* (400, 800, 1,600 meters) and sprint medley (200, 400, 800 meters) and *distance relays* (3,200, 6,000) and distance medley (400, 800, 1,200, 1,600 meters). Four runners compete for a team, each running an equal distance (except in medley relays), and pass a baton to the next runner. The baton must be exchanged within a 20-meter exchange zone. There are two general methods of exchanging the baton, the *blind pass* and the *visual pass.*

Blind Pass. The blind pass is used in sprint relays. In this exchange, the outgoing runner stands in a good sprint position at the back of the 10-meter fly zone located beyond the 20-meter zone (Figure 24-4). The runner stands on the left side of the lane if the baton is to be received in the right hand, and the right side of the lane when the baton is to be received in the left hand. When the incoming runner hits a predetermined mark on the track, called the "go mark," the outgoing runner leaves, concentrating on good sprinting action. This go mark may vary by 5 to 8 meters and is established by a trial and error method. The baton is exchanged at a given point in the zone, preferably in the last 10 meters of the 20-meter passing zone, without the receiver looking back. The exchange is made by the incoming runner extending the baton forward as far as possible and placing the baton downward into the receiver's opposite hand, which has been extended backward, palm up (Figure 24-5). In the 400-meter relay, it is best to handoff: first exchange (right to left), second exchange (left to right), and third exchange (right to left), to make it possible for curve runners to be on the inside of the running lane.

Table 24-3 A weekly competitive-season aerobic/anaerobic training program

	800 Meters	1500 Meters	5000 Meters
Sunday	6 miles (easy tempo)	8 miles (easy tempo)	10 miles (easy tempo)
Monday	1 mile (easy tempo) 2 × 600 m at race pace/walk 5 min; 15 min (easy tempo)	2 miles (easy tempo) 5 × 800 m at slower than race pace/jog 400 m; 20 min (easy tempo)	3 miles (easy tempo) 4 × 1200 m at race pace/jog 600 m; 25 min (easy tempo)
Tuesday	40 min (brisk tempo)	50 min (brisk tempo)	60 min (brisk tempo)
Wednesday	2 miles (brisk tempo) 4 × 400 m at faster than race pace/walk 4 min; 15 min (easy tempo)	3 miles (brisk tempo) 8 × 400 m at race pace/jog 200 m; 25 min (easy tempo)	4 miles (brisk tempo) 12 × 400 m at faster than race pace/jog 200 m; 35 min (easy tempo)
Thursday	20 min (brisk tempo) 4 × 200 m at 90% effort/ jog 200 m	30 min (brisk tempo) 6 × 200 m at 90% effort/ jog 200 m	50 min (brisk tempo) 8 × 200 m at 90% effort
Friday	20 min (easy tempo)	30 min (easy tempo)	40 min (easy tempo)
Saturday	Meet	Meet	Meet

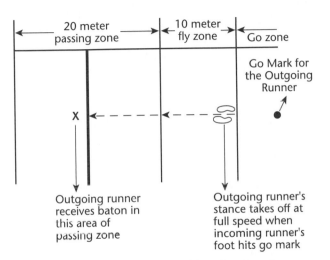

Figure 24-4 The blind pass, used for all sprint relays.

Figure 24-5 These two relay runners demonstrate excellent hand-off technique in the 400-meter sprint relay.

Visual Pass. The visual pass is used in all distance relays. It enables the outgoing runner to judge the speed and fatigue of the incoming runner. In this exchange, the outgoing runner, who is turned toward the inside of the track facing the pole lane, stands on the right side of the lane and receives the baton in the left hand, palm up, from the incoming runner's right hand. Upon receiving the baton, the outgoing runner should always immediately transfer the baton to the right hand.

➤ **Practice/Organizational Suggestions—Sprint Relay Drills**

1. *Standing hand-touch.* Two relay runners standing in their hand-off positions and moving their arms in a running motion touch hands on the command "reach" or "hand."
2. *Running hand-touch.* This drill is the same as for the standing hand-touch, but with the two relay runners now running at a slow pace.
3. *One-on-one drill.* Two relay runners first start at 2 to 5 meters apart and, running at 75 percent speed, pass the baton. The runner in front takes off when the back runner yells, "go." This drill progresses, with the incoming runner moving back 20 to 25 meters and hitting a mark set up 7 to 10 meters from the outgoing runner.
4. *Four-runner baton drills.* After mastering the first two drills, progress to using all four relay runners and a baton. First standing still and then running, the runners gradually increase the pace. The relay runners should be staggered to the right or left, according to the receiving hand. Care must be taken to keep the proper spacing between runners to allow good extension of the passing and receiving arms.

Hurdling

Hurdling is rhythmical sprinting and should be done with as little deviation from sprinting as possible.

Figure 24-6 Recommended form in the high hurdles. (From J. Kenneth Doherty, *Modern Track and Field.* Englewood Cliffs, NJ: Prentice-Hall, Inc, 1953.)

Clearing a hurdle is a *run over* action, not a jumping movement, and all hurdling is taught with this concept in mind (Figure 24-6).

The physical attributes of height or good leg split, speed, flexibility, and coordination along with the mental qualities of courage, patience, and concentration are important for success in hurdling.

➤ **Learning Sequence**

One of the best ways to teach hurdling is to use dowel rods and different-height cones or "sticks and bricks" so the hurdles may gradually be raised. The hurdler progresses through the following steps:

1. Set the first hurdle at 15 meters and three other hurdles at 7 or 9 meters apart, depending on the ability of the hurdler and her stride length.
2. Have the hurdlers sprint over the hurdles at full speed, with the sticks or dowel rods flat on the track, experimenting with the proper lead leg and steps to the first hurdle while taking three steps between the hurdles.
3. Have the hurdler run over the hurdles, gradually increasing the height while working on the correct stride pattern to the first hurdle and the three-stride pattern between the hurdles.
4. When the stick reaches 24 inches above the ground, introduce specific hurdling techniques—proper lead leg, trail leg, and arm action—by means of a wall drill.
5. *Wall drill—first part.* Work on the proper lead leg and arm action. The hurdler, standing a few feet

from a wall, starts by lifting the lead knee and leg toward the wall, letting the weight fall forward. The leg is planted on the wall at hurdle height, the chest drops down toward the knee, and the opposite arm is driven toward the opposite leg.

6. *Wall drill—second part.* Work on the trail leg. Standing facing the wall, the hurdler leans forward with both hands against the wall. The trail leg is brought up under the armpit and reaches out for a long step forward.
7. The next step is to walk over a 30-inch hurdle and then gradually increase the speed running over this hurdle height. As the speed of the hurdler increases, the distance between the barriers can be increased until the actual hurdle spacing is reached. However, never increase the distance between the hurdles if it causes the hurdler to stretch their stride, because it will lead to poor hurdle form. Also, do not raise the hurdle height if doing so causes the hurdler to jump rather than sprint over the hurdle.
8. The last step is to gradually increase the height of the hurdles as technique improves; however, the participant will learn correct form more readily if the hurdles are fitted to the participant rather than trying to fit the participant to the hurdles.

Hurdle Start. The hurdle start differs from the regular sprint start in that the hurdler must come up to the running position sooner. A high hurdler will take 7 or 8 steps to the first hurdle; an intermediate hurdler 21,

22, 23, or 24 steps. The hurdler who takes an odd number of steps to the first hurdle will have the same leg forward in the blocks as leads over the hurdle. With an even number of steps, the lead leg over the hurdle is the back leg in the blocks. The hurdler determines the lead leg by attempting to hurdle with each leg. The one most comfortable should be the lead leg.

Running Between the Hurdles. In the highs, a hurdler must take 3 steps and in the intermediates 13, 15, or 17 steps. The intermediate hurdler can use a 14-stride pattern if the lead leg is alternated. The hurdler must concentrate on good sprint action between the hurdles, running up on the balls of the feet, with knees high and arms driving hard with relaxation. Good sprint rhythm between the hurdles is important. The hurdler should never gallop or overstride, which often is caused by not getting a good step off the hurdle with the trail leg.

➤ Learning Hints

1. In the lead leg action, lead with the knee, not the foot.
2. Keep the trail leg flat, toe out and up, and bring it up high under the armpit and out.
3. The opposite arm/opposite leg action is used over the hurdle.
4. Sprint through the hurdle, rather than jumping over the hurdle.

➤ Practice/Organizational Suggestions— Hurdling Drills

1. *Wall drill.* (See Learning Sequence 7 and 8, above.)
2. *Lead leg over hurdles.* Performed with the lead leg over the side of four to six hurdles spaced 7 to 9 meters apart for the 3-stride rhythm, or 9 to 13 meters apart for a 5-stride rhythm. The hurdle height varies between 12 to 36 inches.
3. *Trail leg over hurdles.* Same as the preceding lead leg drill, except only the trail leg passes over the hurdle.

Table 24-4 presents a weekly competitive-season training program for hurdling. Each of these workouts is preceded by a good warm-up consisting of specific hurdling flexibility and stretching exercises, easy running, and sprint work, and is followed by a good cool-down of easy running and stretching.

High Jump (Flop Style)

The flop or back layout style of jumping, originated by the 1968 Olympic champion Dick Fosbury, is currently used by the majority of high jumpers. The technique can be broken down into three phases: approach, plant/takeoff, and bar clearance.

1. *Approach.* The "J" approach is used by most jumpers. This is a run of 3, 4, or 5 strides straight ahead, then 3, 4, or 5 strides on a curve (see Figure 24-7). Speed is important in the approach, so the jumper must lean to the inside of the arc in order to maintain velocity into the bar.
2. *Plant/takeoff.* The next-to-last stride is longer to enable the jumper to lower the center of gravity for the jump. The last stride (takeoff) is from the outside foot farthest from the bar and is shorter so that the body is in a lean-back position. The free-knee leg is kicked upward and coordinated with an upward swing of the arms (arm/knee drive). The kick combined with the curved approach and the takeoff foot planted toward the left standard causes the jumper's back to rotate toward the bar at takeoff. As the takeoff is being executed, the jumper should look over the inside shoulder.
3. *Bar clearance* (layout position). During bar clearance, the lead knee remains up with the plant by catching up to it. The legs are spread, with the knees out in a "frog" position and the feet together. The hands are placed alongside the body. There is a laying back of the head and an arching of the back until the bar passes along the back and hips. At this point, the chin is tucked down to the chest so that the body folds up in an L-position.

Table 24-4 Hurdling—A weekly competitive-season training program

	110m Hurdles	400m Hurdles
Sunday	2 miles (easy tempo)	3–4 miles (easy tempo)
Monday	Go over flights of 7, 6, 5, 4, and 3 hurdles 3 times at full effort, walk back for recovery 1 × 400 m at full effort	Go over flights of 8, 6, 4, and 2 hurdles, from blocks, working on stride pattern at race pace
Tuesday	"Five-step" 5 hurdles, 2–3 times 3–4 × 150 m at 90% effort/ walk back for recovery	2 × 300 m at full effort
Wednesday	Go over 5 flights of hurdles (70 meters) 5 times at full effort 1 × 300 m at full effort	Go over flights of 5, 4, 3, 2, and 1 hurdles at race pace
Thursday	5–6 gun starts over 2 hurdles 3–4 × 100 m at 90% effort/ walk back for recovery	4 × 200 m at 90% effort
Friday	Easy stretching and jogging "Five-step" 3 hurdles, 2–3 times	3–4 gun starts over 1st hurdle working on stride pattern
Saturday	Meet	Meet

Figure 24-7 The "J" approach used in the back layout (flop style) high jump.

➤ **Learning Sequence**

1. Arm/knee drive while standing still.
2. Running 2 to 4 strides with the arm/knee drive
3. *Arch drill.* Lie flat on your back, heels against buttocks, with heels shoulder-width apart and shoulders on the floor. Grab your ankles with your hands and arch your back.
4. *Back jump drill.* The crossbar is below hip height, with your back to the bar, and feet shoulder-width apart. Execute a 2-foot takeoff in front of bar, drive the body up, and arch over the bar to land on the mat.
5. Running 3 strides over bar with back jump
6. Running 3- to 5-stride approach jumps away from pit on "curve"
7. Running 5-stride approach jump
8. Running 7 to 9 strides with "J" or "curved" approach jumps

➤ **Learning Hints**

1. Approach the bar fast but relaxed with good sprint technique.
2. Use the same speed for all heights.
3. Quicken the last two strides and lower the hips.

4. Plant the foot farthest from the crossbar, heel first, and at an approximate 15-degree angle to the bar.
5. Drive the lead knee upward at takeoff.
6. At clearance, keep the legs apart—"frog" position—and squeeze the buttocks muscles together.
7. Drop the chin to the chest after the hips pass over the bar.

➤ **Practice/Organizational Suggestions—Drills**

1. *Plant/takeoff drill* (described in "Learning Sequence")
2. *Approach drill* (described in "Learning Sequence")
3. *Clearance drill.* Stand on a small box at the edge of the pit with your back to the pit. Jump up and backward, working on the clearance technique.

Long Jump

The long jumper must possess good sprinting speed, a rhythmic, consistent stride pattern, and powerful jumping ability. The basic technique of the long jump can be broken down into four phases: the run-up, plant/takeoff, flight, and landing.

1. *The run-up or approach.* During the approach, the jumper must get to the takeoff board with maximum controlled speed and be in a position to lift. Therefore, relaxation and consistency of stride length are important during the approach. To ensure that the jumper hits the takeoff board with consistency, checkmarks are established in the following manner:
   a. The jumper, one stride from the takeoff board, runs 12 to 16 strides in the opposite direction of the jumping pit until the same foot that is to hit the takeoff board lands on the track.
   b. The jumper continues with 4 to 5 runthroughs in this direction until the takeoff foot hits consistently at the same point.
   c. The jumper then places a checkmark at that point and, standing one stride away, hits the mark with the takeoff foot.
   d. Now running toward the jumping pit, the jumper makes 4 to 5 run-throughs until hitting the board consistently.
   e. The checkmark may be moved forward or backward depending on whether the jumper is over or under the takeoff board.
2. *Plant/takeoff.* Like in the high jump, the next-to-last stride is a longer, settling stride preparing for the lift. The last stride is shorter, and the takeoff hits in a heel-toe action. The free leg comes through as in a normal running stride.
3. *The flight.* After leaving the board, the jumper can use one of three types of techniques in the air:

Figure 24-8 Recommended form in long jump, using a modified hitch kick.

the hitch kick, hang, or sail. The *hitch kick* is done with a run-in-the-air action (see Figure 24-8). The *hang* is performed by letting the legs hang down, with the hips forward and the upper body back. In the *sail,* the legs are tucked up under the body. The purpose of these flight positions is to prevent forward rotation and to get good leg extension in landing.

4. *The landing.* Important in landing is getting good leg extension. This can only be achieved when the flight positions are done correctly. Upon landing impact, the jumper must work through the jump in order not to sit back. This is accomplished by dropping the chin to the chest and driving the arms back forcefully behind the body.

▶ Learning Sequence

1. *Arm/knee drive.* While standing, drive arm and knee upward. Takeoff as in plant/takeoff (see Figure 24-8).
2. Arm/knee drive, landing on two feet (emphasize vertical lift)
3. Running 3- to 5-stride approach with split landing on opposite foot from takeoff
4. Running 5-stride approach jump with switching legs (hitch kick)
5. Running 7-stride approach jumps off of an 8- to 10-inch box placed at the front of high jump mats
6. Running 9-stride approach jumps into the long jump pit

▶ Learning Hints

1. Work for a consistent stride pattern in the approach, using a gradual, uniform acceleration.
2. Run-up off the takeoff foot with 1—2-3 rhythm last 3 strides.
3. At takeoff, drive the free-leg knee up and push the hips forward.
4. After takeoff, the hips remain forward, and the arms are used for good balance (Figure 24-9).

5. Work through the jump and land with good leg extensions, sweeping the arms backward to prevent falling back.

▶ Practice/Organizational Suggestions

1. *Pop-ups.* Repeat 3- to 5-stride jumps, working on the 1—2-3 rhythm.
2. *Flight pop-ups.* Repeat 3- to 5-stride jumps from a box, working on the flight in the air technique, the sail, hang, and hitchkick.
3. *Landing and extension pop-ups.* Repeat 3- to 5-stride jumps from a box, concentrating on correct landing procedures as to leg extension, collapsing of the knees, and driving the arms back forcefully.

Figure 24-9 This NCAA all-American long jumper uses excellent in-flight technique after leaving the takeoff board.

Triple Jump

Formerly called the "hop, step, and jump," the triple jump is an event requiring good speed, great leg strength, and excellent coordination. Proper knee action, with thighs parallel with the ground, and equal rhythm are the keys to good performance.

The technique in the triple jump can be broken down into the approach, plant/takeoff, flight, and landing.

1. *Approach.* To ensure hitting the takeoff board with consistency, check marks are established using the same method as in the long jump. However, the approach is slower and more controlled than in the long jump.
2. *Plant/takeoff.* Since the movement at takeoff is more forward than upward as compared with the long jump, the jumper does not need to settle or gather at takeoff. The takeoff foot is planted flat, with the center of gravity directly over the foot.
3. *Flight.* The first phase of the flight is the hop. The *hop,* or first jump, is performed by bringing the takeoff leg forward after it has fully extended from the takeoff board. The thigh of the hopping leg is held parallel with the ground; the hopping foot lands flat in preparation for the next phase. The *step,* or second jump, is performed by bringing the free leg forward and parallel with the ground, riding it forward until there is a good thigh split (Figure 24-10). The third phase, or *jump,* utilizes the same technique as described in the long jump. However, the hang or sail should be used rather than the hitch kick because there is less time to perform the action.
4. *Landing.* The landing techniques are the same as those used in the long jump, except that some jumpers sit out in landing rather than falling forward, as in the long jump.

➤ Learning Sequence

1. Standing on one foot, the jumper performs a standing triple jump, saying out loud "same, other, both," which refers to the landing leg or legs.
2. The jumper progresses to 3-stride and then 5-stride short approach-run jumps. Cones are placed at equal distances for each phase of the jumps so that the jumper keeps a rhythmical pattern and equal distances.
3. Once proper technique is mastered, these short run jumps are transferred to the runway and jumping pit.

➤ Learning Hints

1. Run-off the board, emphasizing jumping out, not up, and keeping the legs low.

Figure 24-10 Excellent technique in the second phase of the triple jump. The "step" is demonstrated by this triple jumper.

2. The body remains upright throughout the jump.
3. Work through each phase of the jumps with active heel first or mid-foot landings.
4. Coordinate the arms with the leg action to maintain speed throughout the jumps.
5. Keep the rhythm even during all three phases of the jump.

➤ Practice/Organizational Suggestions

1. *Rhythm drills.* Use short 5- to 7-stride approach runs, working on the equal length of each phase and overall rhythm.
2. *Power-bounding drills.* Short 25- to 50-run intervals, on soft surfaces, hopping on either one leg or the other.
3. *Box drills.* Box drills are done jumping on or over various sizes of boxes. As technique improves, the boxes can be moved farther apart.

Shot Put

The world record for shot put distance has been increased through improved techniques and greater emphasis on speed, strength, and explosive power training. Today, putters use one of two styles of throwing: the glide (O'Brien) and the spin (discus-turn).

Glide Style. With the putter facing opposite the direction of the throw, he glides (shifts) across the circle, lifts the shot with the back, hips, and legs, and then explodes with the arm. In learning this technique, it is important to keep the legs and hips ahead of the upper body and throwing arm, thus utilizing the stronger, larger muscle groups of the lower body.

In learning this shot technique, it is helpful to think of the circle as the face of a clock with the twelve o'clock position at the back, and two lines dividing the circle in four equal parts: one a line of direction, the other, a cross-line.

1. *Grip.* The weight of the shot is placed where the fingers meet the palm of the hand. The thumb and little finger support and guide the shot. The three middle fingers are used for power.

2. *Shot placement.* The shot is held against the neck under the jaw bone underneath the ear.

3. *Starting position.* The putter stands at the back of the circle with the right foot in the eleven o'clock position on the line of direction. The putter keeps the eyes focused on a focal point in the back of the circle, with the non-throwing arm and shoulder kept square and held back.

4. *Glide.* From the starting position, the body weight drops down over the right leg, raising the left leg. The left leg makes an easy swinging motion toward the throwing direction. At the same time, the right leg begins its pushing action across the circle. This is a ball-to-heel motion that causes a stretching action, not a hopping or jumping movement. As the body weight moves toward the front of the circle, the right leg snaps underneath the thrower to the middle of the circle in the nine o'clock position. The left leg lands at the same instant in the five o'clock position just to the left of the line of direction.

5. *Throwing (power) position.* This position at the front of the circle is called the power position; it is the key to a successful throw. Hitting this position correctly for a right-handed thrower means the feet and hips are turned to the left side of the circle, the head faces the back of the circle, body weight is over the right leg, and the right and left legs are bent.

> ### ► Learning Sequence
1. Because 80 percent of the distance in the throw comes from the leg and the trunk, begin with standing power position throws, emphasizing the rotation of the right foot-knee-hip.

2. Next, the glide across the ring is developed, with concentration on getting the bent right leg up under the body and keeping the shoulders square to the back of the circle, which ensures a leg/trunk throw.

3. The finish of the throw emphasizes an explosive right-leg drive over a braced left leg.

> ### ► Learning Hints
1. Keep the shot against the neck during the movement across the circle.

2. Leg and hips lead and shoulders remain square to the back of the circle during the glide across the circle.

3. The right leg is snatched up under the body quickly during the glide across the circle and must remain bent.

4. Use concentration and explosive action from the power position—with the force coming from the ground up, through legs, hips to shoulders, and then the arm.

> ### ► Practice/Organizational Suggestions
1. *Standing throw drill.* Execute standing throws from the power position, concentrating on perfect technique and leg/trunk force.

2. *T-drill.* From a standing position, the thrower drops down in a T-position as if starting the throw.

3. *A-drill.* From the standing T-position, the thrower drops down and kicks the left leg until his body is in the A-position.

4. *Crossbar drill (right leg).* With arms draped over a crossbar, the putter snaps the right leg under; the crossbar prevents the shoulders from turning.

5. *Crossbar drill (left leg).* With arms draped over a crossbar, the putter concentrates on driving the left leg low and to the toe-board without turning the upper body.

Spin Style. In the spin (discus-turn) style, the thrower makes a 1¾ spin as in the discus throw. The thrower must accelerate across the circle gradually in order to hit the power position. As in the glide style, the legs and hips lead the throw, and the shot is held against the neck at the jaw.

Discus Throw

As in the shot put, world distance records for the discus have increased with improvement in techniques and greater emphasis on speed, strength, and explosive power training.

1. *Grip.* The thrower holds the discus on the last crease of the fingers with the fingers spread or the first two fingers placed together.

2. *Preliminary swings.* The thrower begins by standing at the back of the circle with the back opposite to the direction of the throw. With the legs bent slightly and the weight on the balls of the feet, the thrower initiates several preliminary swings, shifting the weight from the right foot to the left as the discus is swung back and forth in a horizontal plane.

3. *Turn.* At the end of the final swing to the right, with the discus as far back as the thrower can reach, the thrower prepares to enter the turn, pivoting over the left leg. The right leg is picked up and moves in an arc toward the front of the circle as the left leg drives forward. The legs and hips are kept ahead of the shoulders as the turn is performed.

4. *Power position.* After the right foot lands in the middle of the circle, the thrower keeps pivoting until the left leg lands slightly bent. The thrower is now in a power position with the legs bent and the shoulders and the throwing arm back in a torqued position.

5. *Follow-through.* The right hip drives through as the bent legs drive upward and the weight shifts to the left leg. The throwing arm is whipped through by this powerful leg/trunk action.

➤ **Learning Sequence**

1. The grip and release are taught first. The thrower, with legs bent, flips the discus in the air or bowls it on the ground, making sure the discus comes off the index finger in a clockwise rotation (for a right-handed thrower).

2. The standing throw is taught next. In the power position, with the bent right leg at the nine o'clock position and the left leg at the six o'clock position, the thrower, shoulders torqued and throwing arm back, performs a series of standing throws. Concentration is on a right foot/right hip action beginning the initial movement of the throws.

3. The step back throw is now introduced. The thrower, standing in the center of the circle with the feet together, steps back with the left leg while sinking on the right, which achieves a power position. From this power position, the thrower performs a series of throws.

4. The thrower is now ready for the 1¼-turn throw. Standing at the rear of the circle sideways to the direction of the throw, the thrower transfers weight to the left foot, pivots, and using a running sprint across the circle, lands in a good power position. From this position, the thrower performs the throw.

5. After mastering this progression, the thrower can learn the 1¾-turn discus throw.

➤ **Learning Hints**

1. Keep the throwing arm up at shoulder level throughout the turns.
2. Before starting the turns, the shoulders and throwing arm are torqued back as far as possible.
3. The shoulders remain level during the turns and the legs are bent.

4. Legs and hips always lead, which creates a "leg throw."

➤ **Practice/Organizational Suggestions**

1. *Flip and bowling drills.* Used to teach the release, these drills are best learned with partners.
2. *Swing drill.* With discus taped to the hand, practice the weight shift for the preliminary swings and getting the discus all the way back.
3. *Line-turn drill.* Facing the direction of the throw, the thrower pivots or turns on the right foot, ending up for a power position throw. To simulate the discus throw, cones may be used in this drill.
4. *Standing throw drills.* With a traffic cone or any other soft, weighted object, the thrower, with feet together and back facing opposite to the throw, steps with the right foot into the power position, practicing leg/hip pop throws.

Modifications for Special Populations
Orthopedically Impaired

1. Contact the National Wheelchair Athletic Association (NWAA), the United States Cerebral Palsy Athletic Association (USCPAA), or the United States Les Autres Sports Association (USLASA) for their information on track and field.
2. Hold mock track and field meets in the gymnasium using modified equipment, e.g., toss bean bags instead of shot puts; suspend a rope between two standards and throw Nerf balls over the rope to simulate the high jump; and vary the height of the rope.

Cognitively Impaired

Contact the local Special Olympics for their track and field manuals.

Sensory Impaired

Contact the American Athletic Association of the Deaf (AAAD) and/or the United States Association of Blind Athletes (USABA) for their track and field manuals.

Terminology

Aerobic running Running done at low-intensity speeds so that oxygen intake and oxygen output are the same; therefore, this type of running can be sustained for a long period.

Anaerobic running Running done at great-intensity speeds so that oxygen intake is less than oxygen output; therefore, this type of running can be sustained only for a short period.

Anchor leg The last leg for a runner on a relay team.

Baton The stick that is passed from one relay runner to another.

Blind pass A nonvisual baton exchange used in sprint relays.

Crossbar The bar that a high jumper or pole vaulter must clear.

Discus One of the field events in track and field in which a cylinder-like object is thrown. The weight and size of the discus may vary according to the age of the participants.

False start Moving or jumping before the gun is fired.

Fartlek Swedish term for "speed play," a type of training in which a runner varies running speeds over a long distance, usually in a forest, on golf course, or other non-track area.

Flight The in-the-air techniques for the long jump and triple jump.

Flop style The style of high jumping in which the jumper's back passes over the bar.

Fly zone The 10-meter zone outside the passing zone used by the outgoing runner to get a flying start.

Gather In jumping events, the settling or lowering of the hips during the last few strides prior to takeoff.

Heat Preliminary race whose winners qualify for the semi-finals or finals.

Hitch kick A running-in-the-air action during flight in the long jump, used to prevent forward rotation.

Interval training A type of running training containing four variables: the number of repetitions, distance, tempo of run, and rest interval.

Passing zone The 20-meter zone in which the baton in a relay must be exchanged (passed).

Relay leg The distance each runner travels in a relay.

Takeoff board The board from which the long jumper takes off.

Throwing sector The specified arc in which a thrown implement must land.

Toe-board A board, in the form of an arc, on which or over which the shot putter must not step.

Trial An attempt in a field event.

Visual pass The pass used in the distance relays in which the outgoing runner visually watches the incoming runner during baton exchange.

Further References

Bowerman, W. and Freeman W. *High-Performance Training for Track and Field.* Champaign, IL: Human Kinetics, 1991.

Powell, J. *Track and Field Fundamentals for Teacher and Coach.* 4th ed. Champaign, IL: Stipes Publishing, 1987.

Rogers, J. *USA Track and Field Coaching Manual.* Champaign, IL: Human Kinetics, 1999.

Santos, J., Shannon K., and Kuetmeirer, K. *Sports Illustrated Track and Field Event.* New York: Sports Illustrated Books, 1989.

Wallace, E. *Track and Field Coaches Guide: Practice Techniques and Materials for Building an Effective Program for Success in Every Event.* Englewood Cliffs, NJ: Prentice-Hall, 1999.

Audio-Visual Materials

The following sources have multiple listings:

Cambridge Physical Education and Health, P.O. Box 2153, Dept. PE15, Charleston, WV 25328-2153. *Fundamentals of Track and Field; Coaching Men's Track and Field (Shot Put, Long Jump, High Jump, Hurdles, Discus, Triple Jump, Javelin, Pole Vault and Training); Sprinting with Carl Lewis and Coach Tom Tellez; Coaching Women's Track and Field (Shot Put, Long Jump, High Jump, Hurdles, Discus, Triple Jump, Javelin, Plyometrics, and Strength Training).*

Karol Video, 350 N. Pennsylvania Ave., Box 7600, Wilkes-Barre, PA 18773-7600. *Conditioning, Discus, Hammer Throw, High Jump, Hurdles, Sprinting, Javelin, Long Jump, Middle Distance Running, Pole Vault, Relay Running, Road Running, and Shot Put.*

Champions on Film & Video, 745 State Circle, Box 1941, Ann Arbor, MI 48106. *Beginning Track and Field Video (Conditioning, Middle Distance Running, High Jump, Relay Running, Shot Put, Javelin, Discus, Sprinting, Hurdles, Pole Vault, Long Jump, Road Running, Hammer Throw); Women's Track and Field; Track and Field Training Techniques (Sprints, Hurdles, Long Jump, High Jump); Conditioning for the 400 Meter Runner and Intermediate Hurdler; Weight Events Conditioning.*

Web Sites

http://trackandfield.about.com/sports/trackandfield/ The ultimate site for track and field, cross-country, and major road races, including feature articles, links, and a race calendar.

www.american-trackandfield.com/ *American Track & Field* is a professional publication dedicated to the improvement of both the image and the performance of American athletes in the sport of track and field.

CHAPTER 25

Volleyball

This chapter will enable you to

- Describe the nature and adaptability of volleyball
- Apply basic skills in modified practice games
- Describe and execute in game play the skills of overhand pass, forearm pass, serve, spike, and blocking
- Describe, discuss, and put into practice the rules of power volleyball during a game or match
- Describe play in power volleyball using the correct terminology associated with the sport

Nature and Adaptability

Volleyball is an adaptable team sport that may be played by various numbers of players (from 2-on-2 to 6-on-6); by all-male, all-female, or mixed teams; with net height adjustments for men, women, co-ed, or age-group differences; and using a variety of playing surfaces (wood, rubberized material, sand, or grass).

Volleyball is a net game and a rebound sport in which, following the initiation of play (serve), the ball may not visibly come to rest. Each team is allowed a maximum of three contacts before the ball is returned across the net. A player may not play the ball twice in succession.

The basic objective of the game is to keep the ball, which is served over the net, from contacting the floor on your side and to return it so that it contacts the floor on the opponents' side before they can return it. Skillful, organized play involves using the three allowable contacts to pass, set, and attack the ball (offense). The opponents attempt to block the ball at the net before it crosses, dig it if the ball evades the block, or pass a nonforcefully returned ball, skillfully making the transition back onto offense. The continuous cycle repeats until the rally is terminated; hence, either a point is scored (serving team only) or a side-out is awarded, with the opponents earning the right then to serve. The sequence is repeated until one team reaches 15 points with at least a 2-point advantage. To shorten the length of time it takes to play a game/match, new scoring rules are used by various levels of play (club, high school, college, international), whereby a point is scored on every serve. A team wins on reaching 15, 25, or 30 points, with a 2-point advantage.

Because all players on the team must rotate one position clockwise each time they earn a side-out, this assures that one-half of the time, individual players have restrictions concerning net play. This controls domination of the net by taller players and requires that each individual become a more complete player, possessing a variety of skills and techniques.

There are five basic skills, each having a variety of techniques. The air skills of attack and block are normally performed in the attack area near the net, while the ground skills of forearm pass, overhand pass, and serve are utilized while in contact with the playing surface.

Teams involving six players use organized systems for serve reception, attack coverage, defense, and offense. The organized game involves specialization, using the individual talents and skills of players such as setters, attackers, passers, and so on.

The flexibility in number of players, sexes, equipment adjustments, variety of rules, and playing surfaces allows for individual preference and for selecting a variety of competition levels. Due to its adaptability, volleyball may be played on any level—from recreational to national, international, and professional.

Basic Rules

Players and Rotation. When the ball is not in play, the players must remain in the proper rotation order, which establishes the sequential service order. Proper rotation order (6-on-6) establishes three front row and three back row players (Figure 25-2). The back row players may not legally enter the front court attack area to block or attack the ball over the net. When the ball is dead, players may not overlap with a player who is in an adjacent position. "Adjacent" refers to the player in the corresponding position on the opposite row (example: center back with center front), plus the teammate(s) next to that player on the same row (example: center back with *both* left back and right back). The players all rotate one position clockwise following a rally in which they win the right to serve.

Serve. The player who rotates to the right back position serves, or if at the start of the game, is the first server. The serve is initiated from within the serving area (see Figure 25-1) behind the boundary line. The objective is to serve the ball across the net into the opponent's court. However, some levels of play now allow a "net serve" to be playable without ruling it a fault. It is a fault (illegal) if the ball contacts the net, or the antenna, or does not land in the court.

Playing the Ball. Each team is entitled to a maximum of three contacts each time the ball crosses into their court. A ball contacting the block does not count as one of the three allowable contacts. No player may play the ball twice in succession, except if they contacted the ball as a blocker.

The ball may not visibly come to rest; if it does, it is considered a held ball (fault). A held ball frequently results when a player uses the hands in exe-

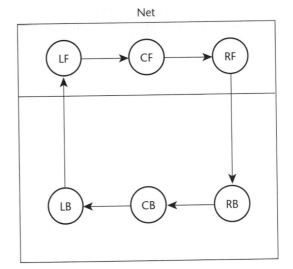

Figure 25-2 Team position and rotation.

cuting an overhand pass. The ball may not be guided, lifted, or pushed in an effort to redirect it.

Net Play. A player may not contact any part of the net, or it is a fault. A ball contacting the net is considered playable. A player may reach across the net to contact the ball on the opponent's side, provided it was attacked by the opponent. Likewise, a player may cross the net when attacking the ball, provided part of it was on the attacker's side when it was contacted. Opponents simultaneously blocking the ball may result in a held ball, which is then replayed with no point scored (play-over).

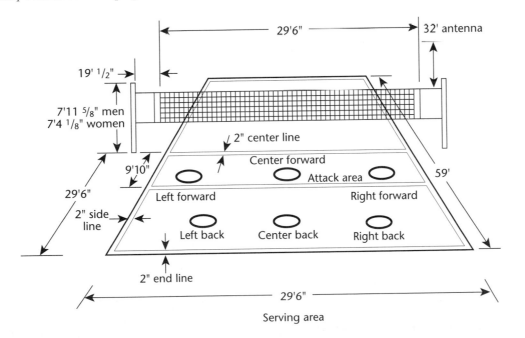

Figure 25-1 The official volleyball court markings and dimensions.

A player may contact the ball on the opponent's side *underneath* the net while attempting to save the ball. The boundary line below the net separating the court restricts players from stepping into the opponent's area. Standing on the line is legal as long as part of the foot is in contact with the line. Any other part of the body on the floor and across the line is illegal.

Scoring. The serve starts play, and the objective is to keep the ball from contacting one's own floor and, without violating the rules, rally until the opponents fail. When the team serving wins the rally, a point is scored. If not serving and the rally is won by the non-serving team, they earn a side out, rotate, and serve next. In rally scoring, a point is awarded to whoever wins each rally. The first team to score 15 points and be ahead by at least 2 points wins the game. Some levels of play go to 25 or 30 points. A match consists of either winning 2 out of 3 or 3 out of 5 games.

Equipment

Volleyball is an inexpensive activity. The player's equipment is minimal, requiring only rubber-soled shoes and possibly knee pads (individual preference) for hard playing surfaces or for safety. A ball, net, and net supports are the only other equipment necessary. Volleyballs are available in different sizes, weights, and coverings. The recommended covering is either synthetic leather or leather with a molded carcass. Care should be taken in selecting a ball that is not too hard and that meets the abilities of the players.

The Court

The court (Figure 25-1) is divided into equal halves separated by a center line and net. Each half has a front court attack area, which restricts back row players from attacking or blocking in that area. The boundary lines are considered a part of the court; thus, a ball landing on these lines is considered in-bounds.

Nets should extend at least one foot on each side of the court (32 feet), have 4-inch-square mesh openings, and a flexible cord or cable running through a 2-inch-wide white band at the top. The net supports should be located at least 19½ inches outside the sideline and anchored securely enough to allow the net to be safely stretched tight without any sag below the required height. Supports with easily adjustable settings assist in quickly varying net height.

The net height is adaptable for differences in player size, sex, and team composition. Men's regulation height is 7 feet 11⅝ inches and women's is 7 feet 4⅛ inches. A ball contacting the net within the boundaries of the court is considered playable. In regulation play, antennas extend upward from the net directly above the sideline to assist in determining whether the ball crossed the net within the court. A ball contacting the antenna is out of play.

Suggested Learning Sequence

Beginning Level
A. Running, stretching and explosive sprinting/jumping
B. Introduction—nature and purpose
C. Basic rules
D. Fundamental skills
   1. Movement skills
      a. Low Position
         1. Shuffle step
         2. Forward/backward
      b. Medium position
         1. Shuffle step
         2. Run lateral/forward
         3. Backpedal
   2. Serve
      a. Underhand
      b. Overhand floater
   3. Forearm pass
      a. Serve reception
      b. Free-ball pass
      c. Side to target
      d. Back to target
   4. Overhand pass
      a. Set forward
      b. Free-ball pass
   5. Attack
      a. Spike roll
      b. Spike
E. Strategies
   1. Use 3 contacts
      a. Pass to center front—8′ × 8′
      b. Set to left front
      c. Spike roll/spike
   2. Make opponents play the ball
   3. Serve in court 80–90 percent
F. Systems
   1. Five-person, "W" serve reception pattern
   2. Free-ball defense
   3. 6–6 or 4–2 offense
G. Play modified games (instant winner)
   1. 1 on 1, 2 on 2, 3 on 3
   2. Small court—½ wide front court
   3. Toss on serve
   4. Vary type of contact required

Intermediate Level
A. Running, partner stretching, and explosive sprinting/jumping
B. Review beginning unit

C. Fundamental skills
  1. Serve
    a. Overhead floater
      1. Deep
      2. Short
  2. Forearm
    a. Dig
      1. Stride and slide
  3. Overhand pass
    a. Set backward
  4. Attack
    a. Spike
      1. Power angle
    b. Lob
      1. Dink
      2. Roll
  5. Block
    a. One blocker
    b. Two blockers
D. Strategies
  1. Serve—weak opponent/deep corners
  2. Dig to middle of court 15 × 15 ft
  3. Set forward and backward—12 to 15 ft high to 3 × 3-ft target
  4. Spike crosscourt and lob over block-short
  5. Block
    a. Take away crosscourt
    b. No hole between blockers
E. Systems
  1. Repeat beginning unit
  2. Spiker coverage
  3. 2–1–3 defense
  4. 4–2 or 5–1 offense
F. Play modified games and 6-on-6
  1. Modifications (point on each serve—5 points winner stays)
    a. Court ½ wide, full length 3-on-3—must use 3 contacts
    b. Full court 4-on-4 (3 back, 1 at net)—no block
  2. Full game—6-on-6 with no modifications

Skills and Techniques

Volleyball comprises five basic skills: forearm pass, overhand pass, serve, attack, and block. Each skill uses a variety of techniques that players need as they progress from beginning to advanced levels of competition.

The ball handling skills—*forearm pass* and *overhand pass*—and their associated techniques constitute at least two-thirds of the ball contacts during play. The *serve* often dominates play both positively and negatively at the beginning to intermediate levels and is a crucial skill. The *attack* adds offense and power to the game but can only be utilized when the ball handling

skills become accurate and consistent. The *block* is used only when the opposing team consistently attacks the ball from a point near or above the net, forcefully driving it downward into one's court.

Forearm Pass

The forearm pass (also called "pass," "bump," or "dig") with its associated techniques is the most frequently used ball-handling skill. It is utilized to pass the serve, play balls below the waist, play hard-driven balls, and contact balls located far from the player. Employing this skill avoids official ball-handling violations.

➤ Learning Hints

1. Feet are shoulder-width apart, in a stagger stance (heel-toe relationship), and the body weight is forward on the inside front half of each foot with the heels slightly off the ground (Figure 25-3).
2. Knees are flexed approximately 90 degrees, inside the feet and in front of the toes.
3. The upper body is in a front-leaning position with waist flexed approximately 90 degrees and the shoulders in front of the knees.
4. Hands are connected by pressing the pads of both thumbs together with the base of the thumbs, even and level. The grip is relaxed, with the hands extended downward. Several methods for clasping the hands together (back of one hand across palm of other, interlocking fingers, fist of one hand cupped by fingers of other) are acceptable as long as they follow the foregoing (Figure 25-4).
5. Arms reach out in front of the body, and elbows rotate inward together and are locked exposing the fleshy part of the forearm. The arms are parallel with the thigh of the leading leg. Attempt to align with the approaching ball as near as possible to the midline of the body.

Figure 25-3 Body position for the forearm pass.

Figure 25-4 Hand position and forearm surface.

6. Ball contact is on the fleshy part of the forearm approximately 2 to 6 inches above the wrist. The trajectory angle of the rebound is dependent upon the angle of the forearms. The eyes focus on the ball until contact and following rebound.

7. Force is provided to the ball when needed by a slight bunting action of the arms, extension of the legs, and body lean toward the intended target. A hard-driven ball from the opponents might require absorption of the force at contact by dropping of the forearms upon contact as a cushioning effect.

➤ Practice/Organizational Suggestions

Use the part method for learning to isolate and reinforce correct contact. Start on one knee, leaning forward, and bunt a controlled tossed ball back to a partner standing 10 feet away. Establish accuracy standards to check progress and to motivate. Repeat, except from the correct whole-body position. Next, add lateral shuffle steps prior to the toss. Finally, attempt to pass the ball repeatedly back and forth between partners who are 15 feet apart. When control is achieved, move to a small court to play modified, small side competitive games (see "Modified Games").

Overhand Pass

The overhand pass is the most controllable of the ball-handling skills. It is used for accurately passing any ball above the head to a teammate and for the setting technique of passing the ball to an attacker with specific height, trajectory, and placement. Ball/hand contact and precise alignment with the ball make the skill more susceptible to official ball-handling violations.

➤ Learning Hints

1. Feet, knees, and upper body (same as "Forearm Pass," #1, 2, and 3)

2. Align ball with the forehead hairline (Figure 25-5).

3. Arms are raised, elbows are flexed (90 degrees) at approximately chin height, and the hands are equally positioned 6 inches above the forehead, with the wrist flexed back (Figure 25-6).

4. Fingers and hands are spread into the shape of the approaching ball, thumbs pointing toward the nose and wrist flexed back. The thumbs are approximately 3 inches apart and the index fingers about twice as far apart.

5. Ball contact is on the inside edge of the first digital areas of the thumbs, index, middle, and ring fingers, and the ball is allowed to almost slide through, with the hands on the side.

6. Force is initiated by the thighs, ball/hand contact is made, and finally the arms are extended fully. The synchronized action is THRUST (thighs)—CONTACT (hands)—EXTEND (arms) for the correct, smooth, and sequential action. Weight finishes forward on the front (right) foot, with all body action directed toward target.

➤ Practice/Organizational Suggestions

The part method aids in the development of the many aspects for skillful execution of the overhand pass. Start on the left knee with the right foot forward in a kneeling position. Place the arms and hands in the correct position for receiving the ball (see Learning Hints #3 and #4). The ball is tossed accurately and gently into the hands by a partner

Figure 25-5 Body position and alignment to ball on overhead.

who is just 3 feet away. Play the ball 6 feet straight up so it drops on the tosser's head. Use the "force" sequence of CONTACT-EXTEND to play the ball (see Learning Hints #5 and #6). Next, assume a full squat position and duplicate the foregoing, playing it 10 feet high. The "force" sequence now entails THRUST-CONTACT-EXTEND to play the ball.

When accuracy and synchronization are established, stand in a medium ready position (Figure 25-7) to receive a ball tossed from a partner 10 feet away. Adjust to the tossed ball and play it 10 feet high, returning it to the tosser. Finally, attempt to volley the ball repeatedly with a partner and move to modified, small side competitive games (see "Modified Games") when control and accuracy is achieved.

Serve

A consistent serve is important because only the serving team can score. The serve has an expected success rate that is 80 to 90 percent higher than the other skills because the server tosses the ball to himself rather than receiving the ball from another player. Equally important is the fact that the serve is the first opportunity a team has to put the opponent at a disadvantage. The overhand floater serve provides both power and consistency (Figure 25-8).

Figure 25-6 Arms, hand shaping, wrist flex, and finger/thumb position prior to overhand contact.

Figure 25-7 Whole-body ready position prior to overhead contact.

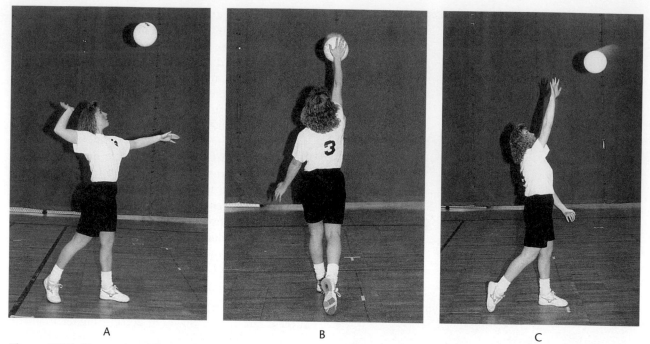

A　　　　　　　　　　B　　　　　　　　　　C

Figure 25-8 The overhand floater serve.

➤ Learning Hints

1. Stand or step and stride with the foot opposite the striking arm (left foot for right-handed person). That lead foot is positioned 2 feet in front of the back foot and is pointed directly toward the intended target. The stride starts as the ball is tossed into the air.

2. The toss is made in front of the striking shoulder and at contact is in front of the striding body parallel with the front foot. The ball is tossed low (1 to 2 feet above head height) for controlled accuracy. A two-handed spin free toss aids accuracy.

3. The striking arm action on the toss resembles an overhand throwing motion (Figure 25-9). As the ball is released (approximately shoulder level) on the toss, the arm flexes, the elbow draws back at shoulder height, and the upper body rotates so that the non-striking shoulder is in a leading position and the alignment of both shoulders is approximately 45 degrees with the back line of the court. The elbow snaps forward ahead of the wrist, and the forearm accelerates in preparation for ball/hand contact.

4. The wrist of the striking arm is tense and locked, the hand is open wide, presenting a flat contact surface, and the ball is aggressively contacted with the bottom half (heel) of the hand at a point slightly higher than head level.

5. Velocity is generated by the elbow snap throwing the forearm forward, and the ball accelerates rapidly as it is contacted with the hard surface (heel) of the hand.

6. Body weight transfers to the front foot, and the forearm of the striking arm is immediately stopped at contact, producing a recoil action.

7. Body balance is maintained as both feet remain in contact with the floor and all movement is directly at the target on the follow-through.

➤ Practice/Organizational Suggestions

Practice the toss and stride (Learning Hints #1 and #2), letting the ball drop to the floor. The ball should land to the side of the body, in front of the striking shoulder, and parallel with the front foot.

Progress to the whole skill with a partner. Students stand 10 feet from the net on opposite sides. The ball is tossed and served at the net (1 to 3 feet above) on a straight line, using the up-stretched arms and hands of the partner to check accuracy. Observe the served ball to make sure it is not rotating in flight but floating spin-free.

Gradually move back from the net, maintaining (1) a straight line trajectory, (2) spin-free (floater) flight, and (3) accuracy. The greater the distance, the more emphasis on providing force to ball contact (Learning Hints 3–6). Continue moving back until the serve can be initiated legally from behind the back line.

Attack

The attack is used in aggressive play against the opponents to keep them from returning the ball or making a transition to return it aggressively. The types of attack are the spike, lob, and drive, with the

Figure 25-9 The striking arm action for the overhand serve and the attack (ball/hand contact and wrist action are different).

emphasis on performing these techniques from as high a position off the floor as possible.

The *spike* is contacted above the midline and at the back of the ball, attempting to impart top spin and drive the ball downward into the opponent's court. The *lob* is contacted below the midline and at the back of the ball, attempting to play it up over the block. The *drive* is contacted in the middle back of the ball, attempting to propel it off the blocker's hands.

In beginning to intermediate levels of play, one does not consistently receive a ball from teammates in a manner that allows time to jump and attack the ball. The technique of the *spike roll* provides an intermediate step between returning the ball easily (free ball) to the opponents and jumping to spike the ball downward into the opponent's court. It also gives a short player an opportunity to attack the opponents, even though that player may be unable to contact the ball above the net.

➤ Learning Hints

Spike Roll

1. Align with the ball so that it is dropping directly above the striking arm's shoulder.
2. The feet are in a stagger stance (see the first sentence in "Serve," Learning Hints #1).
3. Both arms lift above the head. The shoulders rotate approximately 45 degrees with the non-striking arm in a leading position (Figure 25-10A). The non striking arm fully extends and points at the descending ball. The striking arm, in a motion resembling an overhand throw, flexes at the elbow as it draws back at shoulder height.
4. The non-striking arm starts the hitting action by pulling toward the hip on that side as the striking arm's elbow snaps forward, simultaneously lifting higher. The hand and forearm of the striking arm move from a lead position of the elbow to a position trailing it. The hand is open, fingers spread, and wrist flexed back fully (Figure 25-10B).
5. The firm, open hand is thrown at the ball, with initial contact made on the bottom back quarter of the ball, with the palm simultaneously snapping the wrist forward (SLAP and SNAP). The hand goes from a below-ball initial contact to one at follow-through, which is over the top. This imparts the essential topspin on the ball (Figure 25-10C).
6. Body weight transfers to the front foot, and the striking arm finishes in an extended high position, with the wrist fully snapped forward, fingers pointing toward the ground upon completion (Figure 25-10D).
7. Body balance (see "Serve," Learning Hint #7).

A   B   C   D

Figure 25-10 Spike roll: (A) Both arms positioned to strike; (B) non-striking arm pulls down and striking arm elbow snaps forward; (C) open hand contacts the bottom back quarter of the ball; (D) SLAP ball, SNAP wrist, and finish in high position.

Spike

1. The approach to jump is started from a point approximately 12 feet from the net, depending on the length of the attacker's stride. It is an angular approach directly to where the ball is descending, the angle dependent upon the approach position (left, center or right front) and the handedness of the attacker. A right-handed person's approach is 45 degrees toward the net from the left front (LF) position and increases moving to the remaining positions (CF & RF). A left-handed player also makes a 45-degree angle in approaching from the opposite side (RF), the angle increasing when in CF and LF positions. Figure 25-11 shows the approach to jump sequence.

2. The footwork consists of four final steps: a short step with the same side foot as the striking arm (Figure 25-11A), followed by an elongated running stride with the opposite foot (Figure 25-11B), followed by an almost simultaneous step, step/close gathering for a maximum vertical jump (Figure 25-11C, D). The length of the second step depends on the desired distance and speed. The next step, step/close is a breaking heel plant, rocking to the balls of the feet for a two-footed

A   B   C   D

Figure 25-11 Spike. Approach footwork and arm positions prior to jump in attack (right-handed).

takeoff in the jump. The feet are 8 to 10 inches apart on the step/close, with the foot opposite the striking hand ahead of the other foot (Figure 25-11D). The legs flex approximately 90 degrees for maximum jumping thrust.

3. The arms assist in providing force for jumping. They function identically during the approach and are extended straight, behind, and nearly parallel with the floor at the two-footed takeoff (Figure 25-11D). The arms thrust vigorously forward and upward for lifting force as the legs thrust for the vertical jump (Figure 25-12A).

4. The takeoff point aligns the body with the ball so that it can be contacted 6 to 18 inches in front of the body and in front of the striking shoulder.

5. The arm action for striking starts as the body leaves the floor (see "Spike Roll," Learning Hints #3 and #4 and Figure 25-12B).

6. The firm open hand is thrown at the ball, with initial contact made on the top back quarter of the ball (Figure 25-12D), with the palm simultaneously snapping the wrist forward (SLAP and SNAP) (see Figure 25-9). This imparts topspin on the ball and drives it downward toward the opponent's court.

7. The simultaneous coordination of the arm and leg action while suspended in air provides force and body control. The arm action is performed as the legs are flexed and then vigorously snapped down, providing a piking action by the upper and lower body (Figure 25-12C).

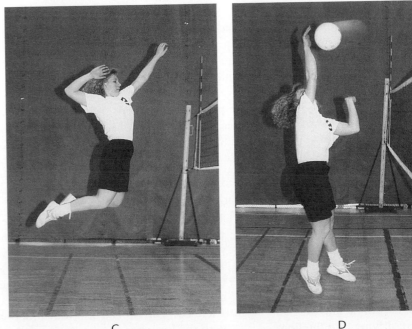

Figure 25-12 Attack: (A and B) actions of whole body in takeoff, (C) striking motion, (D) ball/hand contact.

8. The legs are flexed upon contacting the floor to prevent injury and to regain stability.

Lob

1. The approach, footwork, arm action, alignment to ball, upper and lower body coordination, and landing are identical to the spike (see "Spike," Learning Hints 1–5 and 7). The only difference is the ball/hand contact.

2. Ball/hand contact is made in the lower back quarter of the ball, causing it to take an upward trajectory over the block. As the hand comes forward on the striking action, the fingers and thumb are formed to make contact with the surface of the ball with the first digital area of each. The contact is referred to as a "dink," which is the most common type of lob used at the beginning to intermediate level of play.

Drive

1. As with the lob, the only difference between the drive and the spike is the ball/hand contact.

2. The ball is contacted in the middle back, causing it to take a trajectory parallel with the floor and deflecting off the blocker's fingers. The hand contact, as in the spike, is with the firm open surface of the palm but driving the ball straight ahead instead of downward.

➤ Practice/Organizational Suggestions

The ball/hand contact (SLAP) is developed by holding the bottom of the ball firmly with the nonstriking hand. Position the ball at arm's length in front of the striking shoulder and at head height. With the striking arm hanging straight down at the side, initiate the correct arm action by lifting it straight forward and upward until it is beside the ball. Use the throwing action (see "Spike Roll," Learning Hints #3 and #4) and ball/hand contact (see "Spike," Learning Hint #6) to aggressively "slap" the back/top quarter area of the ball, developing the feeling of the palm contact.

Repeat the foregoing, but hit the ball downward out of the holding hand to the floor. Stand 6 feet from a wall so that the ball hits the floor and then rebounds off the wall. Emphasize the ball/hand contact and power component (wrist snap) for force—SLAP and SNAP. Finish with the striking arm high and fully extended, with the palm facing the floor and fingers pointing down.

Next, toss the ball in front of the striking shoulder, using both hands to toss it precisely 4 feet high. Both arms extend up as if jumping (see "Spike Roll," Learning Hint #3) and duplicate the complete arm action (Learning Hints #3 and #4) contacting the ball (see "Spike," Learning Hint #6), driving it to the floor as in the foregoing.

Next toss and jump off 2 feet, repeating the foregoing arm lift, striking action (both arms), and ball/hand contact.

Practice the approach footwork (see "Spike," Learning Hints #1, 2, and 3) toward the net and mimic the correct striking arm actions previously described without using a ball. Next, place a tennis ball in the striking hand and repeat the approach, footwork, jump, and arm action, throwing the tennis ball over the net with an aggressive wrist snap. Emphasize the SNAP and a high straight arm finish of the throwing arm.

Proceed to hitting a volleyball over the net. A partner, with side to net and 3 feet from the net, tosses the ball 12 feet straight up so the attacker can approach, jump, and attack the ball. The tosser stands on the attacker's hitting-arm side and is careful to use a two-handed underhand toss such that the ball goes straight up and down directly in alignment with the attacker's striking arm. The tosser gradually moves laterally away from the attacker, tossing higher (15 to 18 feet) with a trajectory that drops in alignment with the approach path of the attacker.

Block

The block is used to counter a forceful attack defensively. This is accomplished by jumping and positioning the hands above and over the net, decreasing the area available for the attacker to drive the ball downward forcefully into the blocker's court. The use of two blockers on one attacker increases the area of the block, conversely decreasing the court area available for a downward attack. Defensive systems are developed around the block.

Not every attack calls for blocking, because the attacker controls the path of the attack. The objective of the block, aside from reducing the area an opponent can attack, is to render the ball unreturnable while it is in the opponents' court. The success rate for effective blocking is low and negative outcomes are possible. Therefore, the decision on whether to block is governed by the attacker's ability to drive the ball downward into the court from a position near or above the net.

➤ Learning Hints
Ready Position (Figure 25-13A)

1. The feet are in a parallel stance, shoulders parallel with the net. Stand 6 to 12 inches from the net, with knees slightly flexed for quick movement.

2. The hands are positioned between the net and the body at shoulder height, with fingers spread and palms facing the net.

3. The elbows are flexed and touching the rib cage, with the forearms perpendicular to the floor.

4. The back is straight.

Figure 25-13 Block: (A) ready position, (B) knee flex, (C) net penetration and piking action.

Jump

1. The knees flex to a near 100-degree angle for a quick and maximum jump (Figure 25-13B).
2. Thrust off from the floor equally with both legs, and thrust the arms straight upward parallel with the net.
3. As the hands clear net height, gently push them across as far as possible, being careful not to touch the net (Figure 25-13C). Position the outside hand slightly toward the court to deflect the ball inward.
4. Pike slightly at the waist for balance and power (Figure 25-13C).
5. Upon descending, gently withdraw the hands, returning them in front of the shoulders.
6. Upon floor contact, bend the knees to absorb shock and for balance. Pivot away from the net, following the direction of the ball.

Movement Footwork

1. To adjust 3 to 6 feet laterally, use one to two shuffle steps, keeping hands up, feet parallel, and shoulders parallel with the net prior to jumping.
2. A longer adjustment requires a step, run, and plant footwork:
    a. *Step.* Take a step with the foot nearest the ball, pointing the foot toward the sideline.
    b. *Run.* The shoulders rotate from a parallel position to perpendicular as the trail leg takes a running stride for distance and speed toward the sideline.
    c. *Plant.* Both feet hop into a plant, with both returning to a perpendicular position of toes toward the net. The hop is a breaking of momentum as the knees flex for a vertical jump.
3. The hands remain in the "ready" position throughout all footwork prior to jumping.

➤ Practice/Organizational Suggestions

A blocker stands facing a partner who is 3 feet away and holding a volleyball firmly with arms fully extended upward. In a standing "ready" position, the blocker thrusts the arms upward, surrounding the held ball to assume ball/hand contact. Next, duplicate the foregoing with both players squatting to jump prior to arm action and ball/hand contact. Movement footwork can be added, plus a net between partners.

Using a net between partners, the blocker assumes the "ready" position directly in alignment with the partner who is standing 3 feet away from net. The partner self-tosses the ball and jumps to spike (see Spike, Practice/Organizational Suggestions) the ball into the hands of the blocker, who has jumped to intercept it on the spiker's side of the net. Add two blockers to the foregoing drill.

Modified Games

It is not necessary that a skill be mastered or that all skills be taught before playing on the court. When players can adjust to a moving ball and perform the whole skill, it is time to play modified games on the court.

Modifications can be made in a variety of criteria: court size, height of net, number and alignment of players, number of contacts allowed, type and combinations of skills, special rules for desired outcomes, and so on. The games should have an immediate winner/loser so that everyone is participating quickly without waiting.

Games provide motivation, enjoyment, teamwork, communication skills, strategy, and most of all, immediate feedback on performance. Following is an example:

Court: ½ court wide and 10 ft front (10 × 15).
Players: 2-on-2
Rules:

1. Immediate winner of the rally; winner moves to winner's side of the net; losers move to end of waiting line; two new players challenge winners.
2. Play starts with an easy toss (serve) from the challengers to the winners.
3. Each side must make *two* contacts only.
4. First contact *must* be a forearm and second contact *must* be an overhand.
5. On each contact, that player *must* call "mine" (communication) prior to contact.
6. The rally continues until play terminates—rules are broken or ball is not returned.
7. A point is scored if the players on the "winner's side of net" win. If challengers win the rally, they change to the "winner's side of net" to have an opportunity to score a point, and their opponents rotate out to the end of the waiting line (Note: Have no more than 8 persons per ½ court—two volleyball courts equal 32 players).

8. Losers chase the ball. Each waiting couple has a ball.
9. The first to accumulate 5 points wins the game.
10. Option: Change partners each time the losers go to the end of the line. Each player would then carry the individual score forward instead of a team score.

Playing Strategies
Offensive Play

Offenses in power volleyball have developed widely in the past several years. Although the techniques of passing and spiking have changed relatively little, the methods by which the spike is obtained vary greatly.

In most beginning programs or physical education classes, the 6–6 offense would be the simplest to administer. In this offense, all six players spike when rotating to the spiking positions and any of them will also be setters when rotating into a setting position. The 4–2 offense is very similar, except that four members of the team are basically spikers and two members are used essentially as setters. For the alignment of the 4–2 offense, see Figure 25-14A.

The 4–2 offense can be used in physical education classes. It allows smaller players to develop skills as setters and become an integral part of the volleyball team. Although relatively simple, the 4–2 offense includes some of the concepts used in the more complex 5–1 and 6–0 offenses.

In preparing to receive a serve (Figure 25-14B), players face the server in a semi-crouched position,

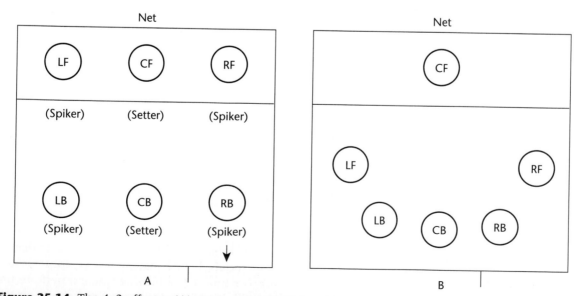

Figure 25-14 The 4–2 offense: (A) serving, (B) receiving.

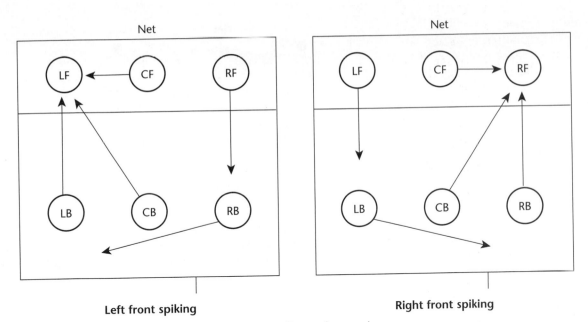

Left front spiking   **Right front spiking**

Figure 25-15 Coverage for the spiker in the 4–2 offense when serving.

prepared to return the ball with a forearm pass. Every attempt is made to direct the first pass to the center front position (setter, either with or without switching) with an arc of 12 to 16 feet. This high pass gives the setter ample time to get to the ball. The setter positions under the ball and faces the direction he plans to set the ball for the spiker.

The setter attempts to pass or "set" the ball 6 to 10 feet above the net, 2 to 3 feet from the net, and near the sideline. This sideline set gives the spiker three advantages: (1) the center blocker has a greater distance to travel; (2) the spiked ball may rebound back out-of-

bounds; and (3) a ball spiked diagonally across court has a greater area in which to land for a point.

Team coverages on the spike for the 4–2 offense are shown in Figure 25-15.

It is necessary for the spiking team to form a "cup" around the spiker to protect against a blocked spike that returns immediately back into their court. The players not in the cup follow the ball, looking for a ball that is blocked high and deep.

When the offensive team is serving, the front line players are close to the net in preparation for the blocking of a spike (Figure 25-16).

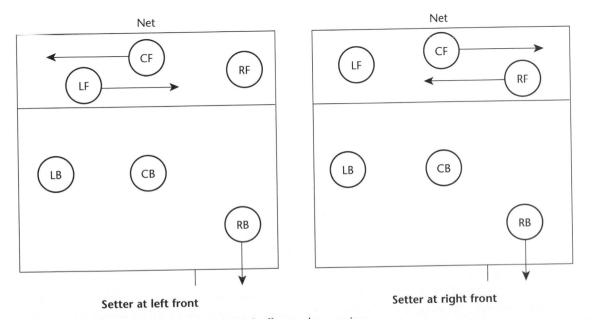

Setter at left front   **Setter at right front**

Figure 25-16 Switching the setter in the 4–2 offense when serving.

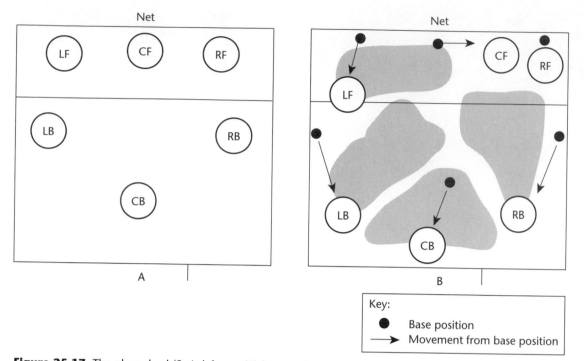

Figure 25-17 The player-back/2–4 defense: (A) base positions, (B) area responsibilities.

Defensive Play

Defenses in power volleyball may vary as widely as the offenses, but the primary job of the defense is to offset the spiking action of the opponents. This can be done by blocking and rejecting the ball or controlling it on your own side of the court, which results in a passing-setting-spiking combination.

Players move to base defensive positions when the ball goes into the opponent's court (Figure 25-17A). Switching positions between players is usually done to capitalize upon any specialization skills. For example, at the beginning level the setter might switch to the center front position to set.

Player-Back Defense

The player-back or 2–4 defense provides good deep coverage, with four players stationed near the court's perimeter and two blocking. The starting positions and areas covered by each player are shown in Figure 25-17B. The blockers attempt to protect more against the sideline spike by the positioning of the block. This defense is used by a team whose players are not particularly tall but very quick and agile.

Player-Up Defense

The player-up or 2–1–3 defense is shown in Figure 25-18. The player that is "up" is the center back, who moves to a position behind the block and covers all dinks, or deflections, that fall short. The blockers attempt to protect against a crosscourt spike by establishing their block to the inside ef the spiker. It is hoped that the spiker will attempt to hit down the line where

the right back defensive player is waiting. This defense would be used by a team that is tall and blocks well.

Serve Reception

The five-person "W" formation is used at the beginning level. It provides complete coverage of the court (Figure 25-19). The front row setter positions near the net in each of the three rotation positions in order to set the second contact. The setter is careful not to be out of position by overlapping with a teammate who is in an adjacent position until contact is

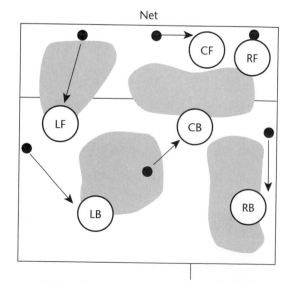

Figure 25-18 The player-up/2–1–3 defense and area responsibilities.

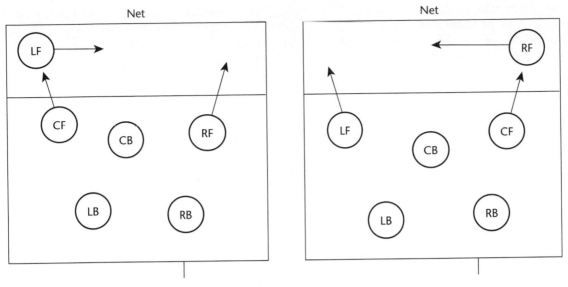

Net   Net

Setter at left front   **Setter at right front**

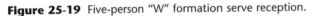

Figure 25-19 Five-person "W" formation serve reception.

made on the serve. Upon contact, the setter quickly positions with the right side to the net approximately 12 feet from the right sideline, keeping the middle of the court in front where the passed ball descends.

Modifications for Special Populations

Orthopedically Impaired

1. Contact the World Organization of Volleyball for the Disabled at www.WOVD.com.
2. Consider playing a modified game as a "table top" game using balloons or beach balls.
3. Allow students to sit on a padded floor and use a long jump rope for a net. Balloons or beach balls can also be used from the floor.
4. Tether the ball from an overhead height and allow students to push back and forth.

Cognitively Impaired

1. Contact the local Special Olympics for their volleyball manuals.
2. Play a lead-up game of Newcomb to develop a concept of the game. Newcomb is played like volleyball, except that the players are allowed to throw and catch the ball.
3. See suggested modifications for Tennis.

Sensory Impaired

1. Individual considerations must be taken into account as to the appropriateness of volleyball for the blind and visually impaired.
2. Minimal modifications are needed for deaf and/or hearing-impaired students.

Terminology

Attack Any method used to return the ball across the net in an attempt to put the opponents at a disadvantage.

Ball handling Execution of any passing fundamental.

Block The process of intercepting the ball just before or as it crosses the net. A block may be executed by any front-row player.

Bump (See Forearm pass)

Court coverage The court assignment of each player on defense.

Dig An emergency pass, usually used to defend a hard-driven attack.

Dink A soft shot off the fingertips, used to lob the ball over the block.

Double foul Infraction of rules by both teams during the same play.

Drive An attack contacted in the center that attempts to hit the ball off the blocker's hands.

Fault An infraction of the rules.

Forearm pass A pass made off the forearms. Used to play served balls, hard-driven spikes, or any low ball.

Free ball A return of a ball by the opponent that may easily be handled.

Front court The playing area in which it is legal to block or attack.

Held ball A ball that is simultaneously contacted above the net by opponents and momentarily held upon contact.

Kill An attack that cannot be returned directly as a result of that attack.

Lob A soft attack that is contacted in the back bottom quarter of the ball, causing it to take an upward trajectory.

Overhand pass A pass made by contacting the ball above the head with the finger pads.

Overlap An illegal foot position, when the ball is dead, with an adjacent player putting one out of position.

Play-over The replay of a rally due to a held ball or the official prematurely suspending play. The server reserves with no point awarded.

Point A point is scored when the receiving team fails to return the ball legally to the opponents' court.

Rally scoring In rally scoring, a point is awarded to whoever wins each rally.

Rotation Shifting of the players clockwise upon gaining the ball from the opponents.

Serve The method of putting the ball in play over the net by striking it with the hand.

Set The placement of the ball near the net to facilitate attacking.

Setter Player assigned to set the ball.

Side-out Side is out when the serving team fails to win a point or plays the ball illegally.

Spike A ball hit with topspin and a strong downward force into the opponents' court.

Spiker Player assigned to attack the ball.

Spike-roll An attack that first takes an upward trajectory using the spiking actions (with or without jumping).

Topspin (Overspin) Imparting of a forward spin to the ball during the serve, spike, or spike roll.

Further References

Asher, K. *Coaching Volleyball*. Indianapolis, IN: Masters Press, 1997.

Bertucci, B. and Peterson, J. *Volleyball Drill Book: Game Action Drills*. Indianapolis, IN: Masters Press, 1993.

Bertucci, B. and Peterson, J. *Volleyball Drill Book: Individual Skills*. Indianapolis, IN: Masters Press, 1993.

Davis, K. *Advanced Volleyball Everyone*. Winston-Salem, NC: Hunter Textbooks, 1992.

Frazer, S. D. *Strategies for Competitive Volleyball*. Champaign, IL: Leisure Press, 1988.

Goebel, K. and Kluka, L. and D. *Competitive Volleyball Drills*. Logan, UT: Kelcon, Inc., 1989.

Hebert, M. *Insights and Strategies for Winning Volleyball*. Champaign, IL: Human Kinetics, 1991.

Howard, R. E. *An Understanding of the Fundamental Techniques of Volleyball*. Needham, MA: Allyn & Bacon, 1995.

Iams, J. *New, Competitive Volleyball Games*. Evanston, IL: Sports Support Syndicate, 1990.

Kiraly, K. *Championship Volleyball*. New York: Simon & Schuster, 1990.

Neville, W. *Coaching Volleyball Successfully*. Champaign, IL: Human Kinetics, 1990.

Neville, W. *Serve It Up: Volleyball for Life*. Mountain View, CA: Mayfield Publishing, 1992.

Nichols, K. *Volleyball: The Skills of the Game*. North Pomfert, VT: Trafalgar Square Publisher, 1995.

Scates, A. *Winning Volleyball*. Dubuque, IA: Brown and Benchmark Publishers, 1993.

Scates, A. *Winning Volleyball Drills*. Dubuque, IA: Brown and Benchmark Publishers, 1989.

Selinger, A. and Ackerman-Blount, J. *Arie Selinger's Power Volleyball*. New York: St. Martin's Press, 1986.

Stokes, R. and Haley, M. *Volleyball Everyone*. Winston-Salem, NC: Hunter Textbooks, 1992.

Viera, B. and Ferguson, B. J. *Volleyball Steps to Success*. Champaign, IL: Human Kinetics, 1989.

Wise, M. *Volleyball Drills for Champions*. Champaign, IL: Human Kinetics, 1998.

Periodicals

American Volleyball. American Volleyball Coaches Association, 122 Second Ave., Suite 201, San Mateo, CA 94401.

Coaching Volleyball. Human Kinetics Publishers Inc., 1607 N. Market, Champaign, IL 61820-2200.

Volleyball. Western Empire Publications, Inc., 950 Calle Amanecer, Suite C, Box 3010, San Clemente, CA 92672.

Audio-Visual Materials

Beginning Girls' Volleyball—Individuals' Skills. Truckee River Studios, P.O. Box 1040, Alamo, CA 94507. VHS or BETA.

Beginning Girls' Volleyball—Team Tactics. Truckee River Studios, P.O. Box 1040, Alamo, CA 94507. VHS or BETA.

Men's Volleyball. Truckee River Studios, P.O. Box 1040, Alamo, CA 94507. VHS or BETA.

USA Volleyball. Athletic Institute, 200 Castlewood Dr., N. Palm Beach, FL 33408. $\frac{1}{2}$" VHS.

Volleyball. Champions on Film & Video, 745 State Circle, Box 1941, Ann Arbor, MI 48106. VHS.

Volleyball Drills. Champions on Film & Video, 745 State Circle, Box 1941, Ann Arbor, MI 48106. VHS.

Women's Power Volleyball Series. Champions on Film & Video, 745 State Circle, Box 1941, Ann Arbor, MI 48106. VHS.

Women's Volleyball—Series I. Truckee River Studios, P.O. Box 1040, Alamo, CA 94507. VHS or BETA.

Web Sites

www.usavolleyball.org Provides information on volleyball education, officiating, modifications for the disabled, tips on high performance, national teams, merchandise, and over 30 links to other volleyball sites.

www.emporia.edu/vball/drills An extensive site that lists 74 drills in 15 different categories.

www.coachingvolleyball.net The playbook, videos, books, and software selections provide extensive resources for skill development.

www.volleyball.org A special beginner's section on volleyball's characteristics, history, rules, basic skills, glossary, and books highlight the site.

www.vball.net A comprehensive site that addresses all aspects of volleyball.

www.about.com/sports/volleyball Lists a large variety of subjects. The section "Beginners Info and Drills" alone is worth visiting the site because it gives very descriptive explanations of how to perform basic skills and drills, with accompanying pictures and diagrams.

www.WOVD.com Site of the World Organization of Volleyball for the Disabled; provides rules for sitting volleyball.

CHAPTER 26

Weight Training

This chapter will enable you to

- Identify and compare the key points associated with Olympic lifting, powerlifting, athletic weight training, and bodybuilding
- Identify the differences and similarities among weight-lifting equipment
- After practice, demonstrate the various skills and techniques necessary to execute the various weight-training lifts
- Identify and discuss facts and myths related to female weight lifting
- Identify the necessary safety concerns of weight training
- Become familiar with basic terminology required to carry out a successful weight-training program

Nature and Purpose

During the past two decades, the effectiveness of carefully planned weight training as a method of improving body development and sports performance has been accepted on the basis of well-controlled studies. Although being musclebound, having reduced localized muscle endurance, and loss of speed and agility were once thought to result from weight training, such claims have no physiological basis.

Much may be gained from the systematic and intelligent application of modern weight-training principles. Using the principle of overload (taxing the muscles beyond their normal daily activities), coupled with progressive resistance through a full range of motion, appears to be the most effective means of acquiring dynamic strength. The closer the weight lifting movement simulates the actions in sports, the greater the transfer of strength to motor performance. Weight lifting is also an excellent way to develop flexibility, provided the exercise is executed through the entire range of motion. Muscle enlargement does not reduce muscle endurance, because an increase in capillarization usually accompanies the cross-sectional increase of muscle fibers, which helps to delay the onset of fatigue. Weight training does not necessarily affect cardiorespiratory endurance unless movements are executed for this specific purpose. Increasing cardiorespiratory endurance requires specific training. To achieve this, heart and respiratory rates must be intensely increased and maintained at higher than normal resting values for a duration of time. Systematic

weight training that applies the principles of resistance, overload, and specificity will have positive effects on motor performance parameters and contribute to successful participation in sports.

Many individuals become involved in weight training as a means of gaining or losing weight. The use of weight training is of greater benefit to gaining body weight than to losing it. This is due to the activities' physiological effect upon the body. The overload principle causes proteins to be readily incorporated into the muscle, thus increasing muscular mass (hypertrophy), while on the other hand, the energy expenditure of weight lifting is too low to be of much benefit in body weight reduction. However, the overweight person may want to include weight training as part of a weight reduction program to increase body tone while reducing weight with diet and an aerobic program.

Many centers of rehabilitation find the use of weights valuable in developing weak or injured muscles, strengthening underdeveloped muscles, or rebuilding muscles affected by atrophy following casting or hospitalization.

Equipment

Variable Resistance Machines

Variable resistance weight-training machines are manufactured by many companies under a variety of trade names. The most widely used are Cybex (Eagle) (Figure 26-1) and Paramount (Figure 26-2). These units consist of weight stacks connected by pulleys or

Figure 26-1 The Cybex chest press.

Figure 26-2 The Paramount machine.

cams to levers of lifting bars. The levers and pulleys allow a variable resistance through a fixed and often-times limited range of motion. This type of equipment is available in separate units and may also be found in a jungle gym arrangement on which several athletes can work out at one time. Weight-training machines offer a number of conveniences and time-saving features that appeal to the coach as well as the lifter. These machines may be placed within restricted space and offer the safety of confined weight stacks, which are not features of traditional "free weights." Because the amount of resistance can be changed rapidly by a pull of a pin in the stack, the amount of time required to complete a training session is also greatly reduced over free weights. One great disadvantage to all machines is in the transfer of strength gains to performance. While the machines can offer great safety, they also remove the interaction between the weights and the lifters needed to balance or coordinate movements while lifting. This interaction is of greatest importance for maximum benefit to performance. However, when time is a restricting factor, training on machines has been found by many coaches to be an excellent way to maintain strength in-season.

Isokinetic Equipment

Probably the most talked about and misunderstood equipment available today is isokinetic devices. The term *isokinetic* means "moving at a constant speed." These machines require no weights because the resistance felt from this equipment is self-generated. The machines can set at a variety of training velocities. If the athlete is capable of moving through a range of motion that approaches this velocity, then resistance is felt through that range. If the velocity is not reached, resistance is not felt. For this reason, to train on these devices requires a highly motivated athlete with constant supervision. The significance of training at a variety of velocities is found in the physiology of the muscle fibers. Because muscle fibers are of a fast and slow nature, it is felt that training at fast and slow speeds will increase recruitment of these fibers.

The value of isokinetic devices in rehabilitation is well founded. The Orthotron and Cybex 340 (Lumex Inc.) (Figure 26-3) are most commonly used for rehabilitation, whereas the Mini Gym is used for sports training. One problem with isokinetic devices is that they do not relate well with other forms of strength training. There is also doubt as to their effectiveness in building muscular bulk.

Free Weights

The oldest forms of weight training have been done with free weights. There are two types: the Olympic

Figure 26-3 The Cybex 340 isokinetic testing unit.

form and the standard 1-inch barbell. A well-equipped training room will have both types of bars. The Olympic bar offers more balance, is more durable, and is a must for power and Olympic lifts. If properly used with supervision from an experienced lifter, free weights offer the most substantial strength program available. The cost of equipment is low, but the risk may be high with improper accessory equipment or lack of supervision.

Other Equipment

The following items may become necessary to the lifter of free weights as the training becomes more intense.

Lifting Belt. The lifting belt is made of thick leather and is used to give physical support to the lower back and moral support to the mind. There are two types of belts: training and competition. The training belt is 5 inches wide and gives a wide support to the lower back. The competition belt is 4 inches wide and may not exceed this in Olympic and power lifting. The belt is generally worn with free-weight squats and cleans.

Lifting Straps. Lifting straps are loops of leather or canvas belting about 1 inch wide. The straps are placed around the hands and then under and around the bar. With an overhand grip, the lifter secures the strap, and the bar is held tightly to the hand. Straps are used with dead lifts and cleans for training only. Lifting straps may not be used in competition.

Knee Wraps (Super Wraps). Wraps are long, 3-inch-wide strips of tough elastic material. They are worn extremely tight around the knee to add spring to the rebound phase of the squat and clean. They

are needed only with heavy weights and may be worn in competition.

Super Suits. Super suits are made of tough elastic material and look like wrestling gear. The suit gives support and spring to the body during heavy squats and cleans. They are generally not worn in training but are normally always worn in competition.

The Female Weightlifter

The fundamentals, techniques, and training programs described in this chapter are directed at both sexes. Female athletes need strength training every bit as much as their male counterparts, if not more. Competitive power lifting and bodybuilding are also becoming very popular among women across the country. Coeducational weight-training classes offer no problems in terms of training programs; in fact, they are very effective ways of destroying weight-lifting myths concerning females.

Myth: Women are not as strong as men.

Fact: Through elementary school, middle school, and well into high school, females are as strong if not stronger than their male counterparts, although with age and training, men will surpass women pound for pound.

Myth: Women should execute lifts differently because they are built differently.

Fact: Anatomical differences in bone and muscle are so slight that they have no bearing on lifting technique.

Myth: Women will become extremely muscular if they lift heavy weights.

Fact: Women can increase strength up to 70 percent with little change in physical appearance. It is the male hormone (testosterone) that causes the noticeable hypertrophy in men. Most women have such small amounts of this hormone that bulk muscularity is next to impossible. Women bodybuilders who do show extreme hypertrophy have (1) very low body fat, (2) unusually high levels of testosterone, or (3) may take anabolic steroids (a testosterone-like drug).

Myth: Women (as well as men) are concerned that their muscles will turn into fat if they stop working out.

Fact: Just as lead cannot turn into gold, muscle cannot turn into fat. Muscle generally atrophies (becomes smaller) when training ceases. People who appear to have become fat after they stopped training may not have changed their eating habits and consequently may be gaining weight.

Myth: Women should not train during various stages of the menstrual cycle.

Fact: The overwhelming majority of female athletes report no adverse effects on performance due to this physiological process.

Most women who have begun training with weights find they have gained the following benefits:

1. Increased physical strength improves their performance in sporting events.
2. There is a decrease in overall body fat while muscular tone increases.
3. There is an improvement in self-image and a feeling of well-being.

Suggested Learning Sequence

Weight training as part of a physical education program should be approached as a skill-oriented class and not merely as an activity. Weight training requires an overall philosophy, the development of techniques, and the ability to execute the skills of each lift.

A 4-day-a-week lifting program is recommended that splits the various lifts into two groups. Monday and Thursday lifts emphasize legs and back while Tuesday and Friday lifts emphasize upper body. If time restricts the number of lifts that can be accomplished, then some leg and back lifts may be done on Monday and some may be done on Thursday. The same arrangement can be used with the upper body lifts. A practical approach for utilization of equipment would be to split the class into two groups containing subgroups of three students (matched for strength, if possible). By doing this, one group can do Monday/Thursday lifts on Tuesday and Friday, thus allowing the proper amount of time needed to execute a proper program. The subgroups of three students lift as a team and are responsible for spotting each other when this is required. Each member of the subgroup should complete a set before any member repeats a set.

The following instructional approach is recommended:

1. Students should be informed of the various forms of strength training and how they differ.
2. Each lift should be demonstrated to the student, with emphasis placed on key points as well as safety factors. Students should also understand the purpose of each lift. (Olympic lifts may be omitted from the demonstration as they are not part of the training program.)
3. If the course meets five times a week, the non-lifting day should be devoted to instruction about related areas (stretching techniques, aerobic exercises, guest speakers or lifters).

4. Begin the lifting schedule as soon as techniques have been demonstrated and safety tips have been emphasized.

Outlined below is a basic plan that may be adopted as is or with modifications. If this plan does not meet the needs of your program, many different lifting schedules may be found in the books listed in the reference section. This program may be done almost entirely on variable resistance machines (Universal Gym or Cubex and Paramount), totally with free weights, or in combination. Students should begin with an amount of weight that can be handled through the recommended number of repetitions (reps). The first set should be lighter than the second or third set. The student may increase the weight in a set when there is no longer difficulty in completing the last few reps of the second or third set.

FW = free weights; VRM = variable resistance machines.

Monday and Thursday Lifts:

Exercise	Sets	Reps
Back		
Dead lifts (FW)	2	5
Bent-over rows (FW)	2	10
Lat pullovers (FW)	2	10
Lat pulldowns (VRM)	2	10
Biceps and Forearms		
Barbell curl (FW or VRM)	2	8
Reverse curl (FW or VRM)	2	8
Legs		
Squats (FW)	1	10
	1	5
Leg lunge (FW)	2	10
Leg press (VRM)	2	10
Leg extensions (VRM)	2	10
Leg curls (VRM)	2	10
Calf		
Donkey calf raise	2	15
Dorsal flexion	2	15
Abdominals		
Sit-ups	2	15 (may vary)

Tuesday and Friday Lifts:

Exercise	Sets	Reps
Power cleans (FW)	3	5
Shoulders		
Military press front (FW or VRM)	2	10
Military press back (FW or VRM)	2	10
Dumbbell shrugs (FW)	2	10
Chest		
Bench press (FW or VRM)	3	5
Incline bench press (FW)	3	5
Triceps		
Lying triceps extensions (FW)	2	10
Calf		
Same as Mon/Thur		
Abdominals		
Same as Mon/Thur		

Skills and Techniques

The correct lifting form is essential not only for obtaining quick results but also for safety.

The Grip

The overhand, palms-down grip is used in practically all exercises. The thumbs may be hooked underneath the bar or in some instances, as in the bench press, may remain on the same side of the bar as the other fingers. This requires more balance and is not recommended to the novice lifter (Figure 26-4).

The underhand grip is the exact opposite of the overhand grip, with palms placed upward under the bar. This grip is used in executing the curl maneuver (Figure 26-5).

The alternating grip, with one hand palm down and the other hand palm up, is favored for dead lifts. Regardless of style, the hands must be spaced evenly on the bar in order to execute the lift properly as well as provide safety (Figure 26-6).

When involved in Olympic or power lifting, the use of chalk on the hands is recommended. The chalk will increase the bar/hand friction, thus facilitating a better grip.

The Feet

When the bar is being lifted from the floor, as in cleans or dead lifts, place the toes approximately under the bar, with the feet spread about 1 foot apart. The feet should always be in the same line, although the distance between them may vary. Many beginners make the mistake of not starting close enough to the bar; consequently, when they start the lift, the bar swings toward the feet instead of going straight up. Many experienced lifters find that a slight angling outward of the feet, not more than 15 degrees, is a more comfortable and efficient lifting style. This is a technique that should be developed as the lifter improves.

Breathing

Breathing should come naturally during the course of the exercise, letting the body regulate the demand. Forced gasping and hyperventilating (rapid puffs of breath) only interfere with proper breathing and may even lead to lightheadedness. The best pattern of breathing is to inhale during the lifting phase and to exhale with the return movement. As the weight increases, many lifters find it more effective to take one deep breath and hold it through the repetition of the lift. The lifter should never hold a breath for more than one repetition. This puts undue pressure on the body cavities as well as the blood vessels of the head. Getting a purple face in the weight room will not improve your lifting ability.

Figure 26-4 The overhand grip.

Figure 26-5 The underhand grip.

Figure 26-6 The alternating grip.

The Bar and Body Placement

A technique that is of utmost importance in a weight room is lifting a bar from a power rack or squat stands. Injuries that occur during this phase of lifting with free weights can most always be traced back to carelessness on the part of the lifter. To properly place your body under the bar to execute a lift, check the following items:

1. The bar should be no higher than the shoulder nor more than 3 to 4 inches below the shoulder.
2. Grip the bar evenly and space your hands wider than your shoulders.
3. Move under the bar in such a way that the midpoint of the bar is on line with your backbone.
4. The bar should rest on the base of the neck and the shoulders.
5. If the muscles of the neck and shoulders lack mass to cushion the bar, foam pads or towels should be wrapped around the bar so as to protect the bony parts of the back. This is extremely important for young lifters and, as a rule, is a good policy for women to follow.
6. By bending at the knees, align your body as vertically as possible under the bar.
7. With the head up, lift straight up with hip and leg power to a vertical position.
8. Step backwards out of the rack no more than 2½ feet.
9. With spotters on both ends of the bar, execute the lift.
10. Rerack the weights by stepping back into the rack, with alignment by spotters, and set the weight down.

Training Programs

As weight training has come of age and specificity has become a recognized factor in a successful program, it has become difficult to recommend training programs without knowing what equipment is available and what purpose the program will serve. There are publications that speak to many specific programs in weight training. For this reason, specific programs will not be proposed, but rather comments concerning programs will be presented. For training manuals, refer to the references at the end of the chapter.

Light-Conditioning Programs

Light-conditioning programs cover the broadest range of weight trainers from in-season athletic programs to the programs typically offered to the general public at health clubs. The programs generally consist of a three-day-a-week lifting routine. All of the basic lifts would be done at this time with a brief stretching and warm-up followed by one set of 10 to 15 reps of the various lifts. This is the "circuit" or "circus" training approach, also known as the "get them in—get them out" routine. This approach is a life-long battle that yields nondramatic results.

Heavy-Conditioning Programs

Heavy-conditioning programs in this area are practiced by a smaller group of lifters containing pre-season athletes, power lifters, Olympic lifters, and bodybuilders. The programs run from 4 to 7 days per week. On a given day, muscle groups, rather than the entire body, are worked. The average workout lasts around 2 hours; however, bodybuilders, prior to a contest, may actually train on a split-day routine, thus doubling the workout time. This is a very effective program for those who can afford the time. The general rule followed in heavy training is to thoroughly overload and exhaust the muscle each time it is trained, with at least one day between training of that muscle group again. Overtraining in heavy programs is a real problem, and it affects different people at different times. Constant muscular pain with a loss in strength are the warning signs. The large muscle groups are the first to be affected, especially the lower back.

A heavy training program, although there is much variation, may consist of a 5 × 5 approach of 5 sets with 5 reps, not including a warm-up or stretch. A current variation of the 5 × 5 approach is to include one day of extremely high rep work at around 50 to 60 percent of maximum.

An important point concerning heavy training for sport is that the movements of the sport should also be done before or after the lifting. This will allow new motor skills to develop with the new strength gains.

Description of Training Groups

Olympic Lifting

Olympic lifting requires strength, power, and quickness. In competition, there are two lifts: the two-hand snatch and the two-hand clean and jerk. Training for competition requires explosive lifts such as power cleans as well as bench press, military press, and parallel squats for strength development. Olympic lifters are also concerned with muscular endurance and often include running in a training regimen. Although Olympic lifting is an Olympic sport, its popularity in this country has dropped off dramatically in past years. This drop-off is due to several reasons:

1. The reluctancy of lifters to adopt modern training techniques
2. The lack of experienced strength coaches
3. A new emphasis on power lifting
4. The acceptance of bodybuilders in society

In competition, the competitor attempts to lift the heaviest weight he can in each lift, and the individual with the highest total is declared the winner in his body weight class as established by the Amateur Athletic Union.

Two-Hand Snatch

1. Place the bar on the floor horizontally in front of the lifter.

2. Grip the bar with both hands, palms down, at least shoulder-width apart.

3. With the legs bent, drive with the legs and pull with the arms until the bar is supported vertically above the head with straight arms.

4. The lifter may split the legs or squat with the weight in order to achieve the vertical arm position. The lifter must stand erect upon completion of the lift.

5. The lifter must stand motionless with feet in the same line to be judged a good lift.

Two-Hand Clean and Jerk

1. Place the bar horizontally on the floor in front of the lifter.

2. Grip the bar with both hands, palms down, at least shoulder-width apart.

3. The bar is brought to the shoulder from the floor in one continuous motion with bent or split legs.

4. The bar may rest on the chest while the feet must return to the same line with straight legs before continuing with the jerk.

5. By bending the legs and then extending them and the arms vertically, bring the bar to a vertical extension above the head.

6. The lift is complete when the lifter is motionless with the weight vertical above the head and with feet on the same line.

Power Lifting

Whereas flexibility and explosive power are of utmost importance in Olympic lifting, power lifting relies mainly on sheer strength. Although technique is important, the power lifts are easier to master than the Olympic lifts. The power lifts are the bench press, the parallel squat, and the dead lift. As in Olympic lifting, the competitor attempts to lift the greatest amount of weight in each lift. The largest total lifted

wins the individual weight class. The competition begins with the parallel squat, and the lifter must have one of three attempts judged good to continue into the other lifts. Although power lifting is not an Olympic sport, it is very popular in the United States with women as well as men.

Bench Press (Figures 26-7 and 26-8)

1. The lifter lies horizontally with head, trunk, and buttocks on the bench.

2. The palms are placed up against the bar, with the thumb placed on the same side as the other fingers or hooked on the opposite side. The hands may not be placed with more than 32 inches between forefingers.

3. The bar is pressed vertically to straight arm length and held for 2 seconds.

4. The bar is lowered to the region of the chest but may not sink into the chest.

5. The bar is then raised evenly to a vertical position without moving the trunk, buttocks, or feet. Movement is grounds for disqualification.

Parallel Squat (Figures 26-9 and 26-10)

1. Begin in an upright position with the bar resting across the shoulders.

2. Keep the head up.

3. Keep the back flat, arching the small of the back.

4. Keep the feet 12 to 16 inches apart and in the same line.

5. Keeping the back straight, squat slowly with the weight until the tops of the thighs are parallel with the floor.

6. From the squat position, drive with the legs and hips to an upright position. The small of the back should remain arched slightly so as to prevent leaning, which may lead to injury.

Figure 26-7 Starting position for proper execution of the bench press.

Figure 26-8 The bar is lowered to the chest region with the back flat on the bench.

Figure 26-9 Starting position for the parallel squat.

Figure 26-10 With the back flat, the weight is lowered to a position where the thighs are parallel with the floor.

Dead Lift (Figures 26-11 and 26-12)

1. Place the bar on the floor horizontally in front of the lifter.
2. Begin in the squat position, thighs parallel with the floor, head up, feet 12 to 14 inches apart, and back flat.
3. Place the palms on the bar approximately shoulder-width apart, using a palms-down grip or an alternating palms-up, palms-down grip.
4. The lift also may be done with the increasingly popular "sumo" style. The only difference is that the feet are spread widely apart, 36 to 40 inches, with the hands placed about 14 inches apart.
5. With the arms straight and the back flat, drive upward with leg and hip strength.
6. Pull with the back once the bar is past the knees.
7. The lift is complete when an upright body position is attained.

Training includes a few other lifts besides those that strengthen secondary muscle groups involved in the power lifts. These lifts will be discussed in the next section. For information concerning training schedules for Olympic and power lifting, consult the references listed at the end of the chapter.

Bodybuilding

Bodybuilding for men and women is an activity that is growing rapidly in this country. There are many reasons although media coverage and the popularity of self-improvement are the main contributors to its popularity. Bodybuilding is as much an art form as it

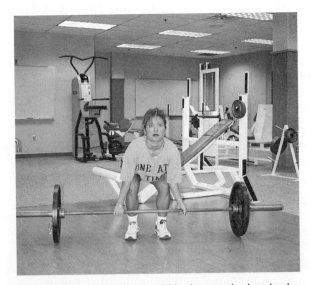

Figure 26-11 Begin the dead lift close to the bar, back flat and head up.

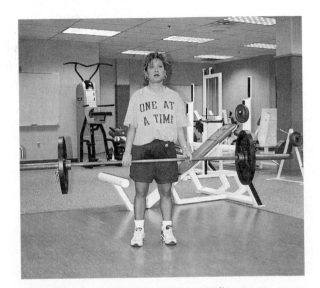

Figure 26-12 End the dead lift by standing erect.

is a sport and may well be called a form of kinetic sculpture. Bodybuilders are not concerned with muscular strength, although all maintain a strength that matches their muscular size. They do not train with the specificity needed for a particular sport activity, yet all are athletic. Bodybuilders train with weights to achieve muscularity with symmetry. This requires a multitude of lifts that are variations of the lifts described in the weight-conditioning section. Rather than attempt to describe each of these lifts in detail, the reader is referred to the literature suggested at the end of the chapter.

Weight-Training Conditioning

Weight training in the pre-season and during the season is important for every athletic team or conditioning class. The key to a successful weight-training program is specificity and supervision. Specificity means that the program should be designed to fit the needs and movements of the athlete. Supervision by a strength coach or a member of the teaching/coaching staff is important from a safety standpoint as well as a means of building morale. This section will describe a number of the lifts commonly used in building a strength program. It will not, however, attempt to put together any programs for different sports. For this type of information, the references section will be helpful.

Behind-the-Neck Press. The behind-the-neck is an excellent exercise for the development of the shoulders, especially the deltoid group. The exercise may be done with a barbell or with a machine (Figure 26-13).

1. With the barbell resting behind the head on the shoulders, inhale and press the weight to a vertical position above the head (Figure 26-14).
2. Lower the weight until it nearly touches the shoulders behind the head and exhale.

3. The exercise may be done standing or seated.

The Military Press. The military press is another excellent lift for shoulder development and may be done with free weights or on a machine (Figure 26-15).

1. With the barbell resting on the chest, inhale and press the bar to a vertical position above the head (Figure 26-16).
2. Lower the weight until it nearly touches the chest and exhale.
3. The exercise may be done standing or seated.

Bent-Over Rowing. Rowing has long been used as an overall back developer. It will add thickness and width to the "lats" while developing strength very quickly. This exercise must be done with a barbell.

1. Place the barbell horizontally on the floor in front of the lifter (Figure 26-17).
2. Bend at the hips and grip the bar palms down, shoulder-width apart. Bend the knees slightly to remove hamstring tension.
3. With the back stationary and flat, pull the bar to the chest (Figure 26-18).
4. Slowly lower the bar to near the starting position (bar need not touch the floor).

The Bench Press. Much controversy continues as to which muscle gains the principal benefit from the bench press. Most biomechanic experts would agree it primarily exercises the anterior deltoid and triceps, with the pectoralis major a secondary mover. To put more emphasis on the "pecs," the incline bench press may be incorporated in advanced training programs.

The correct procedure for the bench press has been outlined earlier under power lifting. It should be emphasized at this point that athletes, trainers, and coaches who recommend benching by bouncing the weight off of the chest or arching the back and pushing

Figure 26-13 Begin the behind-the-neck press with the barbell resting in this position.

Figure 26-14 Raise the bar to a vertical position above the head.

Figure 26-15 Starting position for the military press.

Figure 26-16 Raise the bar to a vertical position above the head.

Figure 26-17 Starting position for bent-over rowing.

Figure 26-18 Raise the bar to this height to complete the lift.

with the legs to achieve the lift are toying with injury. Many coaches boost their athletes' bench press achievements by actually teaching the bounce and arch as part of the lift. The athlete will gain more physiologically and mentally if taught the proper technique in this exercise. The lift should be done with free weights and spotters, but also may be done on a machine.

Upright Rowing. Upright rowing is often done to supplement training for Olympic lifting. The front deltoids and the trapezius musculature are thoroughly exercised. The lift must be executed with a barbell and may be done explosively or at a slower speed.

1. Grip the bar palms down, about shoulder-width apart.
2. Begin by standing with the bar held at the level of the thighs.

3. Pull the bar straight up the front of the body to the area of the chin (speed may vary).
4. Slowly return the bar to the front of the thighs.

Dumbbell Lat Pullover. The dumbbell lat pullover is a lift for all sports from tennis to the shotput. The exercise is designed to work the musculature of the back and rib cage. For this reason, it should be included in all training regimes for track events. The pullover should be done with a dumbbell but may be done with a light barbell. Traditional lat work is done on some form of lat pulldown machine and will not be described in this text.

1. Lie crossways on a flat bench, with only the upper shoulder region supported by the bench (Figure 26-19).
2. The knees should be bent, with the feet flat on the floor.

Figure 26-19 Start the dumbbell lat pullover with the thighs low and the shoulders flat on the bench.

Figure 26-20 Keeping the hips low, raise the arms to a vertical position above the head.

3. The buttocks should dip slightly to keep an arch in the small of the back.

4. Grip the weight by cupping the hands in such manner that the palms are against the weight plates. This will cause the weighted ends to be in an up-and-down position.

5. Extend the arms vertically so that the weight is over the face (Figure 26-20).

6. Lower the weight slowly in an arch so as to miss the head, until the weight is nearly touching the floor behind the bench.

7. Return the weight to the vertical position slowly by contraction of the lats, keeping the arms nearly locked out.

The Barbell Curl. The curl is well known to anyone who has ever touched a weight. The exercise builds the biceps and is tremendously overused, especially by teenage boys. It is most often used to increase the size of the arms for visual rather than functional reasons, and therefore should be considered a bodybuilding exercise. Coaches will generally have little trouble getting males to do an arm workout. The lift may be done with a straight barbell, a bent (E-Z curl) barbell, dumbbells, or machines. All provide slightly different results in terms of appearance.

1. Grip the bar palms up, about shoulder-width apart (Figure 26-21).

2. Begin with the bar in front of the thighs and the elbows kept at the sides.

3. Contract the biceps so that the bar moves in an arch toward the shoulders (Figure 26-22).

4. Slowly lower the bar against gravity to ensure a good stretch to the starting position and repeat.

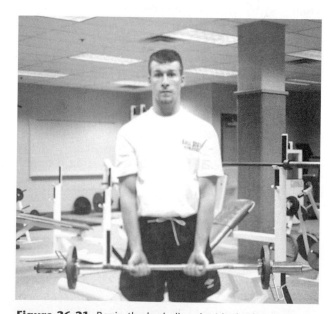

Figure 26-21 Begin the barbell curl with the bar in front of the thighs and the elbows at the sides.

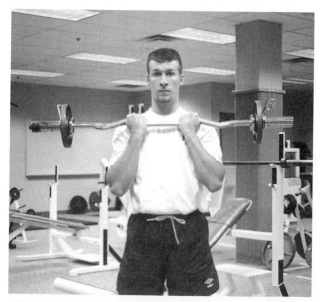

Figure 26-22 Contract the biceps and raise the bar in an arch toward the shoulders.

Figure 26-23 Begin the reverse curls with palms down.

Figure 26-24 Contract the biceps and raise the bar in an arch toward the shoulders.

The Reverse Curl. The reverse curl is done to strengthen the forearm and biceps. The lift is most effective when done with a barbell.

1. Grip the bar with palms down, about shoulder-width apart (Figure 26-23).
2. Start with the elbows at the sides and the bar in front of the thighs.
3. Move the bar in an arch toward the shoulders (Figure 26-24).
4. Lower the bar to starting position and repeat.

Donkey Calf Raise. When traditional calf machines are not available, the donkey calf raise will give the best all-around calf development. This exercise is done

with a partner and does not involve weights. The partners should be approximately the same weight.

1. Place the feet on a calf board (2 × 4 on 2 × 4 blocks), with the balls of the feet on the board and the heels off the board (Figure 26-25).
2. Bend at the waist until the back is flat while supporting the body weight on a chair or bench.
3. The partner should sit on the exerciser's back, on the hips if possible.
4. The lifter should then lift up as far as possible onto the toes (Figure 26-26).
5. Once the toes are locked out, lower the heels until they pass beyond the calf board, and then repeat.

Figure 26-25 Begin the donkey calf raise with the heels lower than the toes.

Figure 26-26 Complete the lift by raising up on the toes.

The Parallel Squat. The parallel squat, described in the power lifting section, is the ultimate exercise for leg development. It has long been used to develop strength and size in the leg. Done properly, the parallel squat will give very quick results. The current belief held by many coaches that the parallel squat will damage the knees is both biomechanically and medically unfounded. The use of a bench for the athletes to squat on is very popular but not necessary. In fact, bouncing up and down on the bench may lead to more serious injuries due to aggravation of the spine. If safety is the reason for bench use, the problem can be eliminated by using spotters at both ends of the bar or by the use of safety squat racks.

Leg Lunge. The lunge is done to strengthen the thighs and is an exercise that might be used as a means of stretching prior to doing squats. The motion of the lunge should be mastered without weights before actual weighted lifts.

1. Begin the lift with the bar resting across the back (Figure 26-27).
2. Take a lunging step forward, about 3 to 4 feet, so that the rear knee dips and touches the floor (Figure 26-28).
3. Return then to an upright, starting position.
4. Balance is of utmost importance with this lift, and any amount of weight should be worked up to gradually.

Dumbbell Shrugs. The shrug is probably the best exercise for development of the trapezius and neck muscles. It is a must for additional training in the power lifts. The lift may be done with a straight bar, but the best results are obtained with the dumbbell.

1. Begin the exercise with dumbbells in both hands, with arms at the sides (Figure 26-29).
2. Raise the shoulders as far as they will go toward the ears (Figure 26-30).
3. Hold that position for a 3-count and relax.
4. The lifter may also roll the shoulders while executing the lift.

Lying Triceps Extensions. The triceps extensions work to strengthen the posterior portion of the arm. This exercise should be done as a secondary lift with the bench press. The exercise may be done with a bar or a machine.

1. Lie on your back on a flat bench.
2. Grip the dumbbell, which should be behind your head on the floor, with a palms-up position about 12 inches apart.
3. Raise the dumbbell such that it is positioned vertically over the face, with the arms locked out (Figure 26-31).
4. Lower the dumbbell from the elbows while keeping the upper arm in a near-vertical position. The bar should be lowered to the forehead (Figure 26-32).
5. Extend the forearm back to the vertical position.

Leg Extensions. The leg extension works directly on the quadriceps muscle group. The exercise can be done with a weight boot, but most workout areas are now equipped with extension machines. The leg extension is generally part of a rehabilitation program

Figure 26-27 Begin the leg lunge in this position.

Figure 26-28 Lunge forward with a straight back until opposite knee touches the floor.

Figure 26-29 Begin the shrugs with dumbbells at the sides.

Figure 26-30 Keeping the arms straight, shrug the shoulders upward.

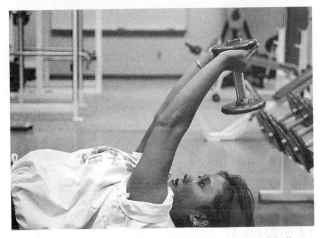

Figure 26-31 Triceps extensions begin with dumbbell held vertically over the face, arms locked out.

Figure 26-32 Dumbbell is lowered to forehead and then raised to a vertical position.

for people who have weak knees or who have recently undergone surgery.

1. Sit on the bench of the extension machine and put your feet behind the lower pad so that your toes point out. You should sit so that you are leaning slightly back (Figure 26-33). This will put the quadriceps at the optimal angle for maximum extension.
2. Hold on to the sides of the bench and raise the lower weighted bar so that your legs are parallel with the floor (Figure 26-34).
3. If the lifter cannot achieve full extension, there is too much weight on the machine.
4. Slowly lower the weight to the starting position.

The Leg Curl.   The leg curl is a most effective way of strengthening the hamstring muscles of the upper leg. Unless the athlete is on a good parallel squat program, there is a tendency for the "quads" to become too strong in relationship to total quad/hamstring

strength. While the exercise may be done with weighted boots, most workout areas are equipped with leg curl machines.

1. Begin by lying stomach down on the machine and position the heels behind the heel pad (Figure 26-35).
2. Prop yourself up slightly with your elbow so as to keep the hamstrings as prime movers of the lift.
3. Contract the hamstrings and attempt to touch the heels on the buttocks (Figure 26-36).
4. Slowly return to the starting position and repeat.

Dorsal Flexion of the Foot.   A group of muscles on the front of the lower leg are generally forgotten about in training, except by bodybuilders. It is this musculature, however, that causes many athletes a great deal of trouble in the form of shin splints. While the exact cause of all shin splints is not known, it generally results from an overdeveloped calf muscle

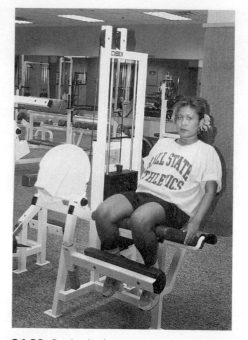

Figure 26-33 Begin the leg extension in this position.

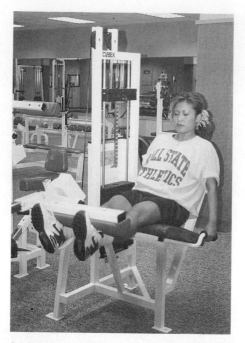

Figure 26-34 Extend legs so they are parallel with the floor.

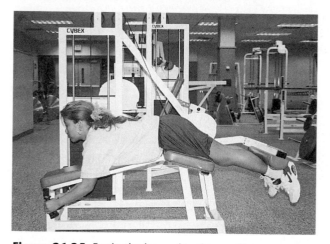

Figure 26-35 Begin the leg curl in this position.

Figure 26-36 Flex the legs so they are vertical to the floor.

and an underdeveloped anterior tibial muscle (front of the lower leg). This condition is found in many runners and also may result from prolonged wearing of high heels. The exercise is simple and really requires no equipment other than what may already be found around the home.

1. Begin in a seated position with the feet hanging freely above the floor.
2. A weighted device is hung from the toes so that resistance is felt. The weight may be as simple as a bucket filled with water or sand, which allows the amount of resistance to be altered easily.
3. Contract the foot so as to bring the toes up (Figure 26-37) and point to the knee (active dorsal flexion).

4. Relax the foot and repeat (Figure 26-38). Repetition is the key to this exercise.

The Power Clean. The power clean is probably the most total body lift that can be successfully executed short of the clean and jerk. More than any other single lift, the power clean will significantly improve the vertical jump with greater total body strength. All training programs should include the clean to some intensity. The lift must be done with free weights, preferably Olympic weights. The sequence is shown in Figures 26-39 through 26-43.

1. Begin with the bar horizontally at the feet of the lifter.

Figure 26-37 Contract the foot, and point the toes upward.

Figure 26-38 Relax the foot, and let the toes point downward.

2. Grip the bar, palms down, about shoulder-width apart.
3. The feet should be placed inside the hands so as to provide a firm base of support.
4. Squat low, as in the beginning dead lift position.
5. The head should be up, with gaze fixed toward the ceiling.
6. Drive with the hips and legs to lift the bar from the floor.
7. Continue to drive with the legs as the bar gains acceleration, and as the bar passes the knees, pull with the back and shoulders.
8. As the bar reaches the chest region, it will begin to lose momentum.
9. At this point, the body needs to move slightly under the bar as the elbows drive forward under the bar to catch the weights on the chest. This

Figure 26-39 The power clean starting position.

Figure 26-40 Initial pull phase should not be rapid.

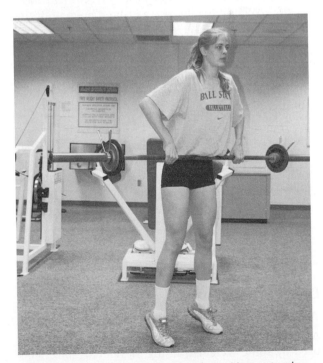

Figure 26-41 Rapid acceleration phase. Note extension onto the toes.

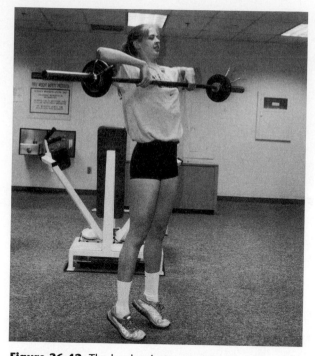

Figure 26-42 The bar has lost momentum—time to move under it.

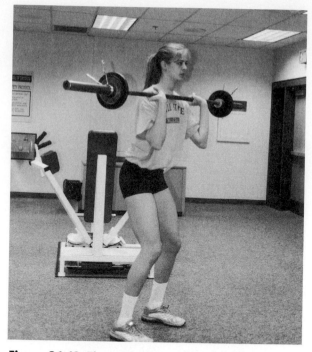

Figure 26-43 The catch phase—knees are bent.

arm movement should be somewhat passive, because this is not a reverse curl. If the lifter must reverse curl the weight, the weight is too heavy or there was insufficient momentum in the drive phase.

10. The lifter will find it necessary to bend at the knees in order to achieve the correct catch position. When bending occurs, stand erect with the weights before lowering them to repeat.

➤ Learning Hints

To ensure a successful training lift in the clean, be sure to follow these instructions:

1. The bar should move almost vertically up the front of the body.
2. This is an explosive lift; therefore, rapid acceleration of the bar is important.
3. Do not jerk the weight from the floor with the arms, rather drive it up with the legs.
4. Extend up on the toes when possible to increase leg-drive force.
5. Do not actively reverse curl the bar back to the chest.

Drug Education

Anabolic Steroids and Weight Training

Anabolic steroids are protein-building drugs that are used by some weight-training individuals for effects that are believed to enhance performance. These drugs may be legally prescribed only by physicians and veterinarians. Anabolic steroids are used in conjunction with weight training because they increase weight and because there is evidence that they help induce muscle hypertrophy (enlargement of individual muscle fibers, which results in increased muscle mass). They also are credited with enhancing endurance, improving recovery time, and increasing aggressiveness, but none of these claims has been objectively proven. Many of the drugs used come from black market sources. Since there is no regulation of these sources, counterfeit and deliberately misidentified anabolic steroids have become a widespread problem. The health risks of anabolic steroid use are not well known. There is little medical information on the effects of anabolic steroids at the doses used by weight-training individuals. However, their link with the development of liver tumors and a consistent decrease in HDL cholesterol with increased LDL cholesterol is well documented. The change in cholesterol fractions has been identified as a significant risk factor for heart disease. The health risks associated with anabolic steroid use are likely to increase with larger doses and longer use.

Modifications for Special Populations

Orthopedically Impaired

1. Follow the same guidelines used for students without movement difficulties, with the following adaptations:

a. Do not allow students with cerebral palsy to move the resistance too ballistically. Ballistic movements will increase flexor tone for students dominated by spasticity; therefore, concentrate on less resistance and more range of motion.

b. Before a student in a wheelchair begins to lift weights, make sure the brakes on all wheelchairs are locked.

c. For students with spinal cord injuries, be sure to identify the level of injury and consult with a physical educator and/or physical therapist prior to initiating a program.

2. Consult your local fitness clubs for commercial equipment modified for individuals with orthopedic impairments.

3. Wrist weights, weighted sandbags, and other homemade equipment make great modified equipment for fitness training.

Cognitively Impaired

1. Fitness levels for individuals who have cognitive impairments are generally very low; therefore, it is important to start a weight-training program very slowly. Take time to build in a solid base, and increase resistance very slowly in the early stages of the program.

2. Minimal modifications are needed; however, use of peer teachers and paraprofessionals, improvement charts, T-shirt clubs, and the like are excellent incentives for the student.

Sensory Impaired

1. During a lifting program, maintain close supervision of students who are blind or have a visual impairment.

2. Use weight machines to increase safety precautions.

3. Students who are deaf or have a hearing impairment require minimal adaptations. Visual cues need to be established for starting and stopping a lifting session when the hearing-impaired student works out with a large number of students in a small area.

Safety In The Weight Room

1. Stretching exercises and a warm-up should precede the training program.

2. Until you are familiar with the movements involved with the lift, do not attempt a great amount of weight on the bar.

3. Collars should always be used on the bars, and they should be secure.

4. Keep adequate distance between the lifters and the equipment in the training room.

5. Always use spotters on the squats and the bench press.

6. Avoid dropping weights any place other than on a lifting platform. Also, avoid banging the weight stacks up and down on machines.

7. It is always best to unload both sides of a weight bar partially before removing the final batch of weights.

8. When weight plate racks are available, replace all weights after use.

Terminology

Barbell A steel bar 5 to 7 feet long on which circular iron plates of known weight may be placed.

Cheating A lift that is executed with the addition of muscle groups other than the prime movers involved in the lift.

Clean The power clean or beginning phase of the clean and jerk.

Dumbbell A short barbell, 12 to 16 inches, with fixed or removable weight plates.

"Lats" The latissimus dorsi muscles of the back.

Overload principle Progressively increasing the intensity of the workouts over the course of the training program.

"Quads" The four quadriceps muscles of the thigh front.

"Pecs" The pectoralis major muscles of the chest.

Rep Repetition or the continuation of identical motions.

Set The completion of a predetermined number of repetitions.

Specificity The development of a training program aimed at increasing one's ability to succeed in a particular skill.

Spotter An individual responsible for the safety of the lifter. Generally, two spotters are used, one at each end of the bar, in lifts such as the squat and the bench press. They are not used in Olympic lifts.

Further References

Baechle, T. R. and Earle, R. W. *Essentials of Strength and Conditioning.* Champaign, IL: Human Kinetics, 2000.

Baechle, T. R. and Groves, B. R. *Weight Training, Steps to Success.* Champaign, IL: Leisure Press, 1992.

Faigenbaum, A. and Wescott, W. *Strength and Power for Young Athletes.* Champaign, IL: Human Kinetics, 2000.

Fleck, S. J. and Kraemer, W. J. *Designing Resistance Training Programs.* Champaign, IL: Human Kinetics, 1997.

Kraemer, W. J. and Fleck, S. J. *Strength Training for Young Athletes.* Champaign, IL: Human Kinetics, 1993.

Lombardi, V. P. *Beginning Weight Training*. Dubuque, IA: Wm. C. Brown Publishers, 1989.

Martens, R., Christina, R. W., Harvey, J. S. and Sharkey, B. J. *Coaching Young Athletes*. Champaign, IL: Human Kinetics, 1981.

Williams, M. H. *Beyond Training: How Athletes Enhance Performance Legally and Illegally*. Champaign, IL: Leisure Press, 1989.

Organizations

The National Strength Training and Conditioning Association, P.O. Box 9908, Colorado Springs, CO 80932.

Web Sites

www.nsca-lift.org National Strength and Conditioning Association site offers information about the organization, publications, and memberships.

www.ncsa-cc.org National Strength and Conditioning Association site offers information about certification for strength specialists and personal trainers.

www.acsm.org American College of Sports Medicine site offers information about health and fitness, publications, and membership programs.

www.yorkbarbell.com York Barbell Company site offers a free online journal, information about equipment, and more.

www.MH-18.com Men's Health site is the first of its kind for health and fitness information for teenage males.

www.WedMD.com User-friendly site for health, fitness, and medical issues.

CHAPTER 27

Yoga

This chapter will enable you to

- Provide an introduction to yoga and the ways in which it differs from other physical activities
- Present some of the benefits that follow the practice of hatha yoga
- Explore some of the principles of movement that underlie many forms of yoga
- Discuss practice and safety considerations
- Provide in-class activities for the physical education teacher
- Provide a map that will lead the interested teacher to yoga classes, practice manuals, yoga videos, and music that embodies the spirit of yoga

Yoga is the hottest fitness practice of the decade. As talk show hosts, rock stars, and athletes have praised its ability to strengthen, stretch, and tone the body, as well as to nourish the spirit and calm the mind, more and more not-so-famous people have felt encouraged to investigate the power of yoga to help them shape up and release stress, all in one practice session. Yoga has grown in popularity because it delivers on its promises. This chapter presents some of the critical hatha yoga concepts in a way that will make them useful to public or private school professionals in incorporating "health and fitness yoga" into their curriculum. These practices are, as Feuerstein notes, "technological" rather that philosophical in nature and can comfortably be used to the benefit of anyone who chooses to explore them.[1]

Nature and Purpose

In its broadest sense, yoga is a holistic discipline that is approximately 5,000 years old. In its original forms, yoga has something to say not only about movement, but also about personal behavior, diet, breathing, relaxation, and the meditative practices that open our spirits to joy as they discover their true identity. The word *yoga* can mean "union" or "integration" or "discipline" and is frequently literally defined as meaning "to yoke" or "to join" the small personal self to some much larger self. Much of yoga's enduring attraction lies in its nondenominational spiritual power.

As yoga has surged in popularity in the United States, hatha yoga practices also have been adopted by those who have little interest in yoga philosophy but who have much interest in yoga's stress-relieving and health-promoting aspects. Yoga expert Maria Carrico has called this approach "health and fitness yoga."[2] Hatha (pronounced "hah–tah") yoga—the yoga of health and the body—is the most popular form of yoga practiced in the United States today. Usually, a hatha yoga class designed for the fitness setting will consist of selected yoga postures (*asana*s) and a period of deep relaxation. It may or may not include some observation of or manipulation of the breath (*pranayama*). In the health and fitness setting, the yoga practice usually does not include chanting and other reminders of non-Western approaches to spirituality. It may or may not retain a spiritual flavor.

Postures

The postures are the most accessible part of yoga. In the classic *Light on Yoga*, B. K. S. Iyengar includes instructions for 216 postures, but only about 50 to 60 of these postures are commonly practiced.[3] Postures can be classified as standing, sitting, forward/lateral bending, balancing, backward bending/twisting, inversions, and the relaxation pose. Most types of yoga include poses of each type in every class. Poses are sequenced in a way that balances the whole body. The physical practice of hatha yoga is extraordinarily adaptable. Postures can be modified to provide nourishing movement for those with limitations in mobility, balance, or strength; they can be linked together to provide challenging workouts for even conditioned athletes; and they can be practiced by the young, the old, and all of us in between, as our own strength, flexibility, and desire dictate.

The usual yoga practice will move the spine in all six of its directions and will also take the joints through their full range of motion. Yoga postures lengthen, strengthen, and balance the musculature of the body, creating greater flexibility, strength, and stamina, and both the movements and the breath massage the internal organs. Gentle approaches emphasize relaxation and range of motion, whereas more athletic styles, such as power yoga–based and Iyengar-based practices, both demand and create strength, flexibility, and endurance. Yogis have long claimed that either type of practice can profoundly impact physiological and psychological states.

Breathing

The attention to the breath may simply teach students how to relax and breathe more fully, or it may involve breathing exercises, called *pranayama*. Some forms of yoga ask students to move with the breath—performing opening and stretching movements on inhalation, and forward bending and work on exhalation. Power yoga students learn a specific yogic breathing technique called *ujjayi* (pronounced ooo-jai), which creates heat and strength, as well as an audible rhythm with which to move. (Think of *Star Wars'* Darth Vader, but turn down the volume.) Breathing practices improve vital capacity and bring peace and clarity to the mind.[4] The ancient yogis claimed that pranayama practices can extend life and youthful vitality.

Relaxation

Relaxation at the end of the practice period brings much-needed balance to our typically overactive lives. Although there are different ways of approaching the relaxation period, generally students lie on their backs in a formal relaxation pose. The body is consciously relaxed in a systematic way for anywhere from 5 to 15 minutes (and in some practices, even more). Attention or awareness is brought to a part of the body, and it is encouraged to soften and to let go of all tension. Sometimes the scan moves down the body from the head to the toes and then back up again; sometimes it moves from the toes up. Sometimes, the technique is more complex and may include imagery or visualization.

Students are usually and accurately told that relaxation pose (Savasana—pronounced "Sha-vas-an-ah") is the hardest pose to do correctly. For most of us, it is the one we are most eager to practice over and over again because it is so revitalizing. The usual goal of the relaxation period is to release all mental and physical tension. The student is encouraged to broaden his or her awareness, to let thoughts pass like clouds, and to keep a light, clear awareness of the coming and going of the breath, relaxing the body a little more with each exhalation. Sleepiness is almost inevitable, and the challenge is to learn to remain in the pose in a tranquil yet alert state.

Benefits That Can Emerge from the Practice Of Hatha Yoga

- Less reactivity to stressors
- More energy
- Better sleep
- Better digestion
- Improved aliveness, vitality, and inner peace
- Great appreciation for the complexity of the union of body, mind, and spirit
- More ability to identify with others
- More interest in the health of the environment
- Interest in healthier diet and lessening or cessation in the use of mood-altering drugs, including tobacco and alcohol
- Ability to breathe diaphragmatically, thus improving vital capacity and heart health
- Ability to turn attention into (rather than away from) sensations within the body, thus becoming more able to respond appropriately to stress, ill health, etc.
- Ability to "watch the mind" at work and to simply choose to turn away from distraction to one's chosen object of attention
- Strength and length in the musculature of the body, which results in greater agility and fewer injuries among athletes
- Improved posture
- Appreciation for our similarities as human beings
- Appreciation for noncompetitive physical practices, as well as for the competitive spirit
- Improved coordination
- More centered energy
- Greater awareness of the need to rest and a willingness to balance rest and activity through more careful lifestyle choices

It is important to remember that these benefits come as the result of consistent, systematic practice. Some benefits may come quickly, some quite slowly. As George Leonard notes, it is the willingness to practice for the pleasure of practicing, rather than for the results, that characterizes the path of mastery.[5]

Equipment

The basic equipment required for yoga practice is a human body and a few square feet of space. However, having a warm, clean practice space with natural light and fresh air enhances yoga practice. Outdoor practice, when the sun is not hot and high, is delightful. Indoors, a yoga mat placed on a clean wood floor or firm carpet is the ideal underfoot surface. It can be helpful to have a mirror available so that students can check their alignment, but constantly facing a mirrored surface detracts from the inner sensing that is vitally important. Some teachers never use music; others use it all the time. Music is particularly useful in a classroom setting where noises from corridors or other rooms invade the yoga class, or when the teacher wants to create an atmosphere that says, "This isn't your usual gym class." In addition, yoga props can be very valuable in adding comfort and stability to otherwise difficult poses. Yoga props include the following:

1. Yoga mats
2. Yoga straps
3. Chairs
4. Foam or wood blocks
5. Eye pillows
6. Blankets and yoga bolsters
7. Balls
8. Headstanders, back benches

Mats. Mats are probably the most necessary piece of yoga equipment. Many yoga studios and programs ask their students to supply their own mats, a more sanitary practice than sharing mats. It is helpful to specify the type of mat the student will need because mats come in a variety of types and tend not to be interchangeable among types of yoga practices. For extremely gentle yoga, thick, padded mats are desirable. For more athletic yoga, in which standing poses are a central feature of the practice, the "tapas" mat or "sticky" mat is the mat of choice. Within this general category are mats of several different types.

Yoga straps. Yoga straps are used to extend the reach, to provide guidance and support for either a limb or a whole body, and to improve comfort in postures. The best straps for yoga are made of woven cotton, with either D-ring or quick-release buckles. Although it is possible to improvise straps from bathrobe belts and old neckties—and these can be great for personal use—it is safer to use an "official" yoga strap that is designed not to break under force and weight. This is especially important if you are going to support a whole body posture, as in downward-facing dog pose. Adjustable rings or buckles on the straps also provide more utility.

Chairs. Chairs are excellent yoga props. Many yoga studios use a special yoga chair, which looks much like a basic metal folding chair with the back support cut away, but the basic metal folding chair on which they are based also works quite well. Chairs can be used to facilitate standing stretches, as a training ground for "office yoga" postures, and as supports for those who need assistance with balance, who have muscular weakness, or inflexibility.

Foam and Wood Blocks. Foam and wood blocks can be used to raise the level of the floor for standing postures—an invaluable help for those who have limited flexibility in their hip flexors, legs, and backs—and as supports for a variety of other asanas. Foam blocks have the advantage (and disadvantage) of having some "give" to them, and they are more comfortable than wood to drop on your foot. Wood blocks have the beauty of wood and absolute sturdiness to recommend them. Blocks come in a variety of sizes. Having at least one per student is highly desirable.

Eye Pillows. Eye pillows are frequently the first yoga prop that the new yoga student acquires. They create total darkness for the relaxation period, and their weight gently reduces eye movement and encourages relaxation of the eye muscles. Covers are generally silk. Contents range from scented flaxseed to unscented plastic beads.

Blankets and Yoga Bolsters. Blankets and yoga bolsters are helpful in many postures. Both can be positioned under the knees to flatten the lower back during relaxation—a definite help to most people with lower back problems. Yoga blankets tend to be either cotton or wool. Cotton blankets can be used as covers in cool rooms, rolled to create breathing bolsters, and can be used to create special support for the neck and head that will allow the spine to lengthen comfortably. Official yoga bolsters come in several sizes and shapes and reduce the time required to provide support for many poses. These props tend to be used by people trained in the system of yoga developed by B. K. S Iyengar.

Balls. Physio balls (also called "fit balls" and "proprio balls") make great yoga props. They are inexpensive and facilitate a variety of movements, from back bends and side stretches to strength poses. They promote balance and even opening of muscles on both sides of the body.

Other Props. As yoga grows in popularity, so do the number of props available to aid in its practice. Two are worth mentioning. The headstander is designed to take weight off the neck while allowing the student to become inverted, as in a headstand. The back bench allows the student to gradually increase the extent of a backward bending posture. It prevents overarching of the lower back and provides support to those who are not strong enough to push up into a back-bending posture from the floor. Neither is an essential piece of equipment. Before acquiring any special props, try to use them in a yoga studio to assess their value in meeting your needs.

Suggested Learning Sequence

1. Appreciating the difference between yoga and other forms of exercise
2. Learning how to recognize the "edge" of a pose
3. Underlying movement principles
4. Relaxation pose (Savasana)
5. Breath observation
6. Diaphragmatic breathing
7. Pelvic rock (cat and dog tilts and pelvis-neutral position)
8. Fundamental standing pose
9. Shoulders back and down
10. Safe forward bending
11. Making waves
12. Extension through extended child's pose
13. Moving on into the dog
14. Floor sequence
15. Surya Namaskara—the sun salutation
16. A yoga game
17. Lee's chair suite

Skills and Techniques

Appreciating the Difference Between Yoga and Other Forms of Exercise

One of the key differences between yoga and other forms of movement is a responsive, nonjudgmental attention to internal sensations. The student is always engaged in a dance of balancing movements and opening lines of energy with awareness of the breath and with regard to joining comfort and muscular effort. Because most of us are unfamiliar with this type of observation, just learning how to start paying attention IN is also part of the yoga effort. Some styles of yoga seek to open access to a sensation of internal energy streams by insistence on a precise external form. Other styles emphasize allowing the physical body to open gradually as internal sensations direct the movement. Consciously feeling the internal sensations is important in both styles. This "tuning" IN, as well as out, is one of the qualities that distinguishes yoga. A second hallmark that makes yoga distinct is the attention paid to the breath and breathing.

Recognizing the "Edge" of a Pose

The "edges" of the pose have been described by Kramer[6] and by Schiffmann.[7] By "playing the edge," one can keep the body in a state where both it and the mind are in a state of pleasure. The edge of greatest importance is the boundary beyond which pain is felt. The delight of hatha yoga occurs in the exploration of the territory at the edge of a pose, where there is intensity and opening, but no pain—and this demands awareness of sensation and an ability to concentrate the attention inside the body. The edge is a flexible boundary that relaxes and moves with gentle attention, conscious movement of the breath into the area being opened, and relaxation. When the body knows that its limits will be honored, it will enter poses with much less background tension.

Movement Principles

Donna Farhi, international expert on yoga, discusses seven movement principles that underlie the practice of yoga.[8] She believes that these principles work with all the various styles of hatha yoga now practiced. When followed, these principles give rise to an expressive and satisfying external form as well as a stable and comfortable pose. Yoga asks that the student (1) develop a sense of being moved by the breath; (2) find the central balance (which Farhi calls "yielding") between collapsing toward the earth and hardening and lifting the body away from it; (3) have an awareness of the power center of the body and an ability to radiate energy from that core; (4) develop an awareness of the central axis of the body (the spine), its natural curves, and how to both extend and revolve around this central axis; (5) embody the importance of the foundation of the pose; (6) create alignment by following the lines of energy suggested by the bones; and (7) engage the whole body in the practice—muscles, organs, bones, and more.

Through focus on these principles of grounding, extending, and balancing, the student begins to improve his or her posture and vitality of movement, which can also be thought of as a fundamental expression of how one is in the world. All movement is affected by basic postural habits, and it is through changing this fundamental orientation of the body and its stereotypic response patterns that athletic performances improve, personal confidence changes, and a different sense of the self emerges. Because our habits blind us to what we are actually doing with our bodies, to move beyond the habitual usually requires observation by and feedback from an experienced teacher. However, yoga has a vast tradition of self-study, self-observation, and self-reliance. So it is very possible to begin this exploration on your own or with friends, using some of the excellent yoga manuals and videotapes that now exist.

Relaxation Pose (Savasana)
➤ **Learning/Helpful Hints**

1. Sit on your yoga mat with your knees bent.
2. Thread your spine onto the mat, maintaining both length and normal curves. When you are on your back, the line formed by the top of the head, nose, and chin should extend through the center of the body. The position should be comfortable

Figure 27-1 Relaxation pose.

for the lower back. If it is not, and the pose is going to be held, use a chair or a bolster to lengthen the lumbar curve (Figure 27-1).

3. Both feet and both hands should be equidistant from this midline and a comfortable distance apart. Usually the feet are about 18 to 24 inches apart. The hands are 8 to 12 inches away from the hips. Rotate the arms at the shoulders so that the palms of the hands face the ceiling.

4. To check your positioning, use your awareness to compare the places in contact with the floor on the right and left sides of the body. They should feel more or less the same in terms of size and shape. Make tiny adjustments until you feel you are well aligned in the pose.

5. Try to limit your consciously created movement in this pose to the first minute or so. You may well need to readjust as your body relaxes and lengthens, but the essence of the pose is mental and physical stillness while the mind remains tranquil and alert.

Breath Observation

Most of us have never spent any time noticing our breath, yet our breath is more important to our survival than our diet, which is often a focus of obsessive attention. While lying in relaxation pose, ask yourself some or all of the questions below. You may want to ask only one or two questions per relaxation, and you may want to observe your breath frequently over time.

➤ Learning/Helpful Hints

1. What does my breath feel like as it enters and leaves my nostrils?
2. Is one stream of breath freer and bigger than the other?
3. Where does the breath go? Where in my body can I feel evidence of my breathing?

4. Do I feel more movement on the right or the left side of my torso? On the top or bottom of my body?
5. What moves when I breathe?
6. Do I feel sparkles, waves, or a sense of current anywhere in the body?
7. Does my breath "hit a wall" or feel like it wants to have more room than it has?
8. If I place my left hand on my breastbone and my right hand on my abdomen, which hand seems to move up and down the most? (As diaphragmatic breathing is learned, the left hand will barely move.)

Diaphragmatic Breathing

Most of us have learned to tighten our abdominal muscles, and often the side ribs and chest, drawing them in and up. This chronic, often unnoticed tension inhibits our breathing. It may take a while to fully relax the musculature of the abdomen, chest, and side ribs, which is necessary for the downward movement of the diaphragm that comes with a full inhalation.

➤ Learning/Helpful Hints

1. Lie on your back with your knees bent. Place both hands on the lower abdomen, little fingers near the legs and thumbs above the navel. Feel the warmth of your hands melting any tightness in your abdominal muscles. Sense this warmth penetrating to the inner core of the body.
2. Begin to ask the breath if it is willing to come deep enough into the body to meet the warmth radiating from your hands.
3. Release any tension that you feel with each exhalation.
4. Continue to practice as long as it is both an interesting and gentle inquiry. If you become frustrated or think that you "should" be achieving more than you are, it's time to stop. Come back at another time and begin again.

Pelvic Rock

Most styles of yoga ask the student to become aware of the normal curves of the vertebral column and to maintain an awareness of the position of the spine in each of the postures performed. Both Jean Couch[9] and master teacher Erich Schiffmann[10] describe the basic orientations of the pelvis that impact the entire length of the spine (and hence the posture) as (a) cat tilt, where the back is rounded and the tailbone moved forward; (b) dog tilt, where the back is swayed, the buttock bones (or sit bones) and tailbone are lifted; and (c) pelvis neutral, where the tip of the tailbone is at its furthest extent from the crown of the head. These three positions are easily explored through pelvic rocking, performed on the back with the knees bent (Figure 27-2), or from the table posture described

Figure 27-2 Pelvic rock.

Figure 27-3 Mountain pose.

below in "Making Waves." It is useful to perform these explorations before attempting mountain pose (basic standing pose) because mountain pose requires a sensitivity to bringing the pelvis into the neutral position.

➤ Learning/Helpful Hints

1. Lie on your back with your knees bent. Synchronize your movements and your breathing.
2. As you exhale fully, press the lower back into the mat. Use the muscles of the torso, rather than pushing into the feet to accomplish this movement. Note that the tip of the tailbone rocks up toward the ceiling.
3. As you inhale fully, arch your back, moving the tip of the tailbone toward the floor.
4. Repeat, noting the place in the middle where the back is neither arched nor flattened.
5. Come to rest in the pelvis neutral position. Take a mental snapshot of the sensation you feel in this position.

Fundamental Standing Posture (Mountain Pose)

In yoga, the aligned body is the body characterized by the sense of lightness that comes when right and left and front and back are in harmony and balance. In this fundamental standing posture, the normal S-curvature of the spine is reinforced. Body weight is balanced front to back and side to side in both feet, and the musculature of the body balanced so that a plumb line would fall through the following points on the side body: ear lobe, shoulder, hip, knee, and the front edge of the ankle bone. The head is balanced and light over the shoulders. The toes point straight ahead. Arches are lifted into the feet, and the kneecaps are lifted and the knees pointed straight toward the center of the feet. There is both a sense of pressing down in the feet and lifting up through the crown of the head. The eyes are level and the chin parallel to the floor. This position is maintained with-

out hardness; it permits springy, fluid movement when the body comes into motion. All the standing poses begin and end with Mountain Pose (Figure 27-3). When we think of mountains, we think of majestic, enduring bodies that are undisturbed by all the things that happen on their surface. When they move, the movement comes from deep inside.

Shoulders Back and Down

Keeping the shoulders back and down is performed successfully when the pelvis is also maintained or moved into neutral position. It is a counter to all our head-forward, body-slumped activities, working at the computer and the TV slouch chief among them. There are different ways to achieve this posture. Here's a suggested sequence performed from standing.

➤ Learning/Helpful Hints

1. Begin by squeezing the shoulders up and in toward the ears.
2. Roll the shoulders back and down, broadening across the collarbones, feeling the shoulder blades slide, like hands, down the body toward the waist.
3. When accompanied by a slight firming of the abdominal muscles to maintain the neutral pelvic position and a resolution to avoid military hardness, this movement does much to bring the upper body into alignment.

Safe Forward Bending

Many students come to yoga looking for greater flexibility. Athletes tend to be most aware of the benefits they gain from increasing their flexibility. Many are also convinced that they are "just not very flexible" people. This often is a misconception based on long-term prior conditioning in poor "stretching" practices that only maintain their tight hamstrings and tight shoulders. Persuading athletes to give the following stretch a sincere effort can be a challenge in itself.

However, when performed exactly as described, the stretch is safe for the lower back, and it actually does isolate a controllable stretch in the belly of the hamstring muscle. According to Jean Couch, athletes need to consciously learn and use effective stretches for the legs and for the back. This movement accomplishes both a lengthening of the spine and a healthy stretch to the muscles in the backs of the legs.[11]

➤ **Learning/Helpful Hints**

1. Keeping the back extended so that it retains its normal curves, begin to sit down, as though you were going to sit in a chair.
2. Roll the abdomen and the ribs into contact with the thighs.
3. Relax the shoulders, neck, and jaw.
4. Begin straightening the legs; *do not* lose the contact between the thighs and the ribs.
5. Straighten the legs slowly, find the first "edge" of the pose, stop and breathe, allowing the backs of the legs to soften (Figure 27-4). Stay in the territory between the first and second edge of the pose, allowing the lengthening to occur.

Making Waves

Most of us have learned to alternate from a back rounded (cat tilt) position to a scooped-back (dog tilt) position by hinging in the lower back. It is also possible to move between these positions by making waves that travel up from the pelvis one segment of the back at a time. This is an amazingly satisfying and (for most people) healthy back movement that lengthens all the muscles of the back and also provides some toning of the abdominal musculature. It also often opens the window of internal awareness a little wider. As its name suggests, this movement also helps maintain a sense of the fluidity of the body, as well as teaching coordination of the breath and movement. This pose also goes by many other names, including the cat, cat-cow, and cat-dog tilt.

➤ **Learning/Helpful Hints**

1. Begin in the table posture, hands directly underneath the shoulders, fingers spread and pointing straight ahead. The knees are directly underneath the hips, with all the bones of the leg and foot in the same plane as the hip socket. When you peek down between your knees, you see only the inner soles of the feet.
2. As you exhale, curl the tailbone down, hollow the belly below the navel, then move this arch up through the rib cage and neck. Move one vertebra at a time. The head will move down as a natural result of the arching of the full extent of the back (Figure 27-5).
3. As you inhale, pull the tailbone back and up, focusing this time on lengthening the entire front of the body. As the wave travels from the seat toward the head, the breastbone also moves forward and up, and the neck and chin rise as a natural extension of this forward movement from the core of the body (Figure 27-6).
4. Each movement phase lasts only as long as the phase of the breath with which it is paired.

Figure 27-5 Making waves, back arched.

Figure 27-4 Safe forward bending.

Figure 27-6 Making waves, tailbone up.

5. The following tip will help you get the most from this movement: Stay wide across your collar bones, keeping the shoulders well away from the ears. It is fairly common for students to make a "tunnel" around the neck with their shoulders pulled close to the ears. Many times when this occurs, the student tries to compensate for the lack of movement in the core of the body by an extreme lift of the chin. Remember that you want to extend the entire length of the spine in an organic way—each segment of movement grows out of the last opening out, much like a tree grows in the spring.

Extension Through Extended Child's Pose

The extended child's pose broadens both the chest and the shoulders, evenly lengthens the muscles of the upper arms, helps correctly position the shoulders, and lengthens the lower back muscles. It is a wonderful resting pose that naturally follows the making waves movement (Figure 27-7).

➤ Learning/Helpful Hints

1. From the table position, let the seat come as close to the heels as possible. Keep the shoulders back, down, and wide.
2. The arms will lengthen and, by pushing, help bring the seat closer to the heels. The back lengthens, and, as the shoulders rotate into an arms-extended position, the head will naturally come between the upper arms. Instead of moving the forehead toward the floor, keep the neck extended and the ears directly between the upper arms. The neck should retain its normal curve and the throat feel open—just as though you were standing up.

Moving on into "The Dog"

An excellent posture for lengthening the entire back of the body is the downward-facing dog pose. All the principles explored in basic standing posture and the two postures above come into play in an open and extended dog pose.

➤ Learning/Helpful Hints

1. From the extended child's pose, curl the toes under; bring the weight onto the hands and the knees.
2. Rotate the pelvis into dog tilt, and push the body back and up—tailbone aiming toward the intersection of the wall and ceiling behind you. In dog pose, as in fundamental standing posture, the normal curves of the spine are maintained. As in fundamental standing posture and shoulders back and down, the collarbones are wide and the shoulder blades moved toward the waist. The body forms an inverted V; the space between the toes and the hands is about the same distance as the length of the legs. Generally this is the distance between the hands and the feet that occurs in extended child's pose. If the backs of the legs are tight, discomfort can usually be alleviated by bending the knees and by letting the heels come away from the floor. If the back of the body is very tight, raising the level of the floor through the use of yoga props under either the hands or the feet, can make an immense difference in the comfort and ease of this pose (Figure 27-8). Typically, if the legs are tight, props under the feet help, whereas if the shoulders are tight, props under the hands help.
3. From dog pose, return the knees to the floor and then move the body back into extended child's pose.

Figure 27-7 Extended child's pose.

Figure 27-8 Using props to increase comfort and ease in executing downward-facing dog pose.

Floor Sequence for the Whole Body

Doing a sequence on the floor eliminates the problem of maintaining balance, which for beginners can be an occasion of tightening and concern about alignment, rather than a pleasurable exploration of movement principles. Altough standing poses are critical to a beginning yoga practice, and in some systems are the heart of the practice for beginning students, it can be helpful to work with the principles of extension, grounding, and breathing before bringing the exploration to standing. This sequence moves the entire body, encourages the spine to move in all six of its directions, and is usually acclaimed by students for the wonderful feeling it leaves.

➤ Learning/Helpful Hints

Have a strap handy.

1. Stretch out on the front of the body. Place your right hand on top of your left, rest your right cheek on your right hand, and breathe deeply for about 1 minute, changing the hand on top and the resting cheek about halfway through. Focus on coming into the body, feeling the breath moving the ribs and feeling the lower back flex and the head move on inhalation and exhalation.

2. Bring your hands under your shoulders, fingers pointed straight ahead, and push back into extended child's pose on an exhalation. Keep your shoulders wide and away from the ears.

3. As you inhale, come up onto the hands and knees into cat tilt. Keep the head down (Figure 27-9).

4. Still inhaling, move into dog tilt, swaying the back, lengthening by moving both the breastbone forward and up and the tailbone back and up (Figure 27-10).

5. Push back into extended child.

6. Repeat steps 3, 4, and 5 a total of four times.

7. From extended child's pose, come onto the hands and knees. Hands are directly under the shoulders, knees under the hips.

8. Lengthen through the body and, on an inhalation, raise the right hand directly up toward the ceiling, looking at the fingers (Figure 27-11). Stay for one full breath.

9. As you exhale, rotate the extended arm down, then bend the elbow and slide the right hand straight out from the shoulder, back of the hand toward the floor. At the end of the extension, bring the right cheek and shoulder to the floor (Figure 27-12).

10. Repeat steps 7, 8 and 9 on the right three more times, then repeat steps 7, 8, and 9 on the left four times.

11. Level off in the table pose, looking straight down, lifted to the top of the range of motion in the shoulders.

12. Push back to extended child's pose. Lengthen the spine and breathe deeply. Balance your inhalations and exhalations.

Figure 27-10 Dog tilt, tailbone back and up.

Figure 27-9 Cat tilt, tailbone down.

Figure 27-11 Part of whole body sequence; note position of head, arms, and extended hand.

Figure 27-12 Part of whole body sequence, right cheek and shoulder to floor.

Figure 27-13 Part of whole body sequence, "wagging;" note position of head and shortened left side.

13. Come forward into the table posture. Make sure the fingers are spread and the middle fingers point straight ahead. Leave the arms fully extended. Curl the toes under, move the pelvis into dog tilt, and lift the sit bones toward the intersection of the wall and ceiling, coming into downward-facing dog pose. Lengthen the arms. Press firmly down into the index finger and thumb as you continue to lengthen through the sides and the back. The ears are between the upper arms. The arms form a straight line that extends through the hips.
14. Lift the buttock bones as much as the back and backs of the legs will allow. If the stretch is too intense, bend the knees.

Figure 27-14 Thunderbolt pose.

15. Remember to breathe and to be pliable in the pose. Stay for two or three deep, smooth breaths, then come down to the hands and knees and exhale into extended child's pose.
16. Come again into the table. Turn the head from eyes down to eyes to the right, and shorten the right side of the body, as though wagging to the right. This is called "wag the tail of the dog."
17. Turn eyes down and then to the left. Shorten the left side of the body, as though wagging to the left (Figure 27-13).
18. Repeat steps 16 and 17, wagging either two or four times to each side.
19. Level off in the middle, eyes down.
20. Push back into extended child's pose.
21. Roll up into thunderbolt pose, head coming up last, and sit with seat to heels, spine with all its normal curves, and the weight of the body over the heels (Figure 27-14). Do this only if you are able to sit back on the heels without pain in the knees or ankles. If this pose is painful, sit in simple cross-legged position. Sit for several breaths. Then roll onto your back for relaxation pose.

Surya Namaskara, The Sun Salutation

There are many versions of the sun salutation. This one is usually relatively easy for beginners to do. It warms and awakens the entire body.

➤ Learning/Helpful Hints

1. Come into mountain pose (Figure 27-15). Sense the balance and stillness of the body and the movement of the breath before going on to the next pose.
2. As you inhale turn the palms forward. As you exhale, bring the hands together at the center of the chest in "Namaste" position.
3. As you inhale, circle the arms out and up overhead, palms facing the midline of the body (Figure 27-16). Have the palms face the ceiling when the arms are at shoulder heighth and fully extended.
4. As you exhale, come into safe forward bend.
5. As you inhale, keep the fingers on the floor (or low on the legs) and lift the body parallel to the floor, lengthening the spine.
6. As you exhale, come into safe forward bend.

Figure 27-15 Sun salutation begins in mountain pose.

Figure 27-16 Sun salutation, arms overhead.

are either touching or no more than hip-width apart, the tailbone presses down to engage the abdominal muscles (which prevents overarching the lower back), and the hands are under the shoulders with the fingers spread and pointing forward. The lift is both forward and slightly up. The back of the neck remains lengthened (Figure 27-19).

Figure 27-17 Sun salutation, lunge position.

Figure 27-18 Sun salutation, plank position.

7. As you inhale, spread the arms wide, and come all the way up to arms overhead.
8. As you exhale, return to the Namaste position.
9. Repeat steps 3 through 7 to make this movement sequence a total of four times.
10. Inhale and circle the arms overhead
11. Exhale into safe forward bend, and step back with the right foot. In this version, the right knee comes to the floor (Figure 27-17).
12. Inhale and look up, lengthening the back, keeping the hips even and the shoulders away from the ears.
13. Move into plank position with the breath held. In plank, the hands and toes support the weight, and the body forms a straight line from the back of the head to the heels. The hands are underneath the shoulders, fingers spread and pointing forward (Figure 27-18).
14. Exhale both knees to the ground, and stretch into extended child's pose.
15. Inhale and flow forward into low cobra pose. In this version of the cobra, the toes point, the legs

Figure 27-19 Sun salutation, low cobra pose.

Figure 27-20 Sun salutation, lunge position.

16. On an exhalation, push back into downward-facing dog pose

17. On an inhalation, step the right foot forward into the lunge position, taking care to get the right knee directly over the right ankle and foot (Figure 27-20). Many people will find this the most difficult move in the sun salutation and want to leave the foot well behind the knee. It is much healthier for the knees to insist that the foot come directly under the knee. It can be picked up and placed if necessary.

18. On an exhalation, step the left foot forward, coming into safe forward bend.

19. On an inhalation, circle the arms overhead, remembering to turn the palms toward each other and to look up at the thumbs.

20. On an exhalation, return the hands to the Namaste position.

21. Repeat from steps 10 to 20, using the left foot to step into and out of the lunge positions. After the lunge in step 17, step the right foot forward into the forward bend.

A Yoga Game

The following game is a great deal of fun and can be used to encourage students to reflect on the values of cooperation, not taking mistakes too seriously, helping those less skilled, and more. This game, which is, essentially, group juggling, was taught at a mindfulness meditation retreat for health care professionals led by Jon Kabat-Zinn and Saki Santorelli.

Equipment

Bean bags with a variety of colors or patterns—having five to six different covers is helpful.

➤ Learning/Helpful Hints

Every student will need a beanbag. Students count off to form groups of five to seven players. This number can vary, but when groups are too small, the game is boring. When they are too large, the fun of getting all the bags in play at one time is lost.

Each group forms a circle. All but one person places the beanbags by their feet. The person with the beanbag starts by tossing the bag to another person in the circle; this one beanbag makes the rounds of every person in the group, without repetition, before returning to the starter. Players are asked to remember to whom they tossed the bag. The same pattern is repeated four or five more times, and then another bag is added. Players are reminded to follow the original pattern. If the group is too cautious and decides just to pass the bag around the circle, the teacher may want to invoke the "you can't just pass it around the circle" rule, unless the teacher wants to make the point that being too safe is pretty boring. Players *always* throw to the same person. Bags are added until all are in play (or until the teacher decides to end the game.) It is possible to debrief the game by asking a question such as, "If this were the game of life, and you were going to play life just like you played this game, what would the rules be?" It is also possible just to let students have the fun of it without the analysis.

Lee's Chair Suite

Lee's chair suite is pleasant, safe for most people, and can easily be performed by those who have desk jobs. Many people in wheelchairs can perform the first 12 steps. It is refreshing, relaxes shoulder and neck tension, and lengthens the lower back and the deep muscles along the length of the spine.

Equipment

A folding chair with a straight seat or other armless chair with a firm bottom cushion.

➤ Learning/Helpful Hints

1. Sit away from the back of the chair. Sit tall in a way that is both relaxed and erect. Have the normal curves in the spine. Place your feet at least as wide apart as the chair legs. Inhale and stretch your arms overhead. As you stretch your arms up, also keep your shoulders wide and away from your ears, so that your neck remains nice and long. You may want to arch back slightly as you stretch up. At a minimum, have your arms in line with the sides of your body, and tilt the head back enough to see your thumbs (Figure 27-21).

2. As you exhale, bend forward with the back extended. When your ribs meet your thighs, round your back so that your head and arms relax and extend between your legs (Figure 27-22).

3. Place your hands on your thighs, just above your knees, and slowly roll your body back to a sitting position. The movement is like the unfurling of a

Figure 27-21 Tilt head back enough to see thumbs.

Figure 27-22 Arms should be relaxed.

Figure 27-23 Lee's chair suite, using hands to bring knee into chest.

Figure 27-24 Lee's chair suite, twisting to right.

fern, with the head the last part of the body to roll into place.

4. Repeat steps 1 through 3 four times.

5. Move the feet closer together; thigh bones can come straight out from the hips, so that some space remains between the legs, but not as much as in step 1. Bring the right knee into the chest, assisting with the hands either interlaced over the shin or behind the thigh. Give a good squeeze on exhalation, and then replace the right foot on the floor. Follow the same sequence on the left (Figure 27-23).

6. Turn sideways to the left, then place the right hand on the right edge of the chair back and the left hand on the left edge. Inhale, sit straight, and

as you exhale, twist to the right (Figure 27-24). Start the twist deep in the belly behind the navel, and spiral up. Turn to the right side of the chair, and perform this same twist to the left.

7. Slide to the back of the seat, reach over the chair back and interlace the fingers, roll the shoulders back and down, straighten the arms as much as you can, and lift the center of the chest up toward the ceiling. (Do *not* leave the core of the body stationary and just lift from the chin.) Feel the elongation of the entire front of the body as well as the pleasant stretch in the neck and shoulders.

8. Slide forward again. Raise the arms to shoulder height (remember, normal curves in the spine, shoulders away from the ears!), then bend gently

Figure 27-25 Lee's chair suite, arms at shoulder height and body bent gently to left.

to the right on an exhalation; come up. Keep the arms up; bend gently to the left (Figure 27-25).

9. Lower the arms. Squeeze the shoulders toward the ears, then drop them three or four times.

10. Place the feet chair leg's width apart. Raise the arms to shoulder height (remember to elongate the back and drop the shoulders), then bend forward as you exhale, touching your left foot (or ankle, or shin) with your right hand. Come up on an inhalation. Repeat, this time touching your right foot with your left hand.

11. Repeat steps 1 through 3 again.

You can end here, or you can stand up and do a hip-opening forward bend, followed by the "chair dog," and chair relaxation.

12. Place the chair against a wall or piece of heavy furniture so that it cannot slide away from you as you push on the chair seat.

13. Stand to the left edge of the chair, and place your right foot on the chair seat toward the side edge closest to your right side. On inhalation, bring the arms up, and then fold forward on an exhalation, letting the arms come toward the floor in front of your body. You can assist yourself up by placing your right hand on the chair seat, or you can roll up as in step 3. Do this movement two or four times. Then move to the right side of the chair, and repeat the sequence with the left foot up.

14. To lengthen and balance the back, move on to the "chair dog." Facing the chair, place your hand on the outer edges of the seat. Walk back,

until your feet are three or four feet away from the chair; then, taking weight onto your hands, lengthen your back until your hips are squarely over your feet. Keep your shoulders away from your ears, your ears between your upper arms. Stay wide across your collarbones. Lengthen your back until it has all its normal curves again. Try to avoid (1) overarching the lower back, (2) hunching the shoulders, and (3) tucking the tailbone. If the stretch is too intense in the backs of your legs, bend your knees slightly.

15. If you can, end with the following relaxing posture. Lie down on the floor, put your lower legs on the chair seat, let your arms relax by the sides of your body, palms up, and let go! As you lie on the floor, let your lower back relax and lengthen, relax your lower belly, and watch the gentle rise and fall of your belly as you breathe diaphragmatically. Stay as long as you are comfortable.

Safety Considerations

The phrase "not every pose is for every body," is true. Most of us have been schooled into the "no pain, no gain" and "just do it," mentality, and this is about as far from yogic thinking as you can get. In yoga, you

- Listen to your body.
- Look for the edge (or edges) of the pose.
- Stay within your comfortable capacity.
- Avoid strain (but not work).
- Stay with your breath.
- Wait at least 2 and preferably 4 hours after eating to practice.

Most poses can be adapted to avoid causing or aggravating injury, and there is an evolutionary path to even the most difficult poses. However, actually practicing these principles is as great a mental challenge as practicing some of the more difficult poses is a physical challenge. We are so used to our habitual ways that we employ them even when they are not helpful.

Listening to your body means that you *evaluate* uncomfortable sensations. These can be out-and-out pain in the muscles, joints, or mind, or just a sense that something is not quite right. For muscular pain, you ask if it hurts "so good" or if it hurts "so bad." If the answer is the former, and the stretch seems to alleviate an existing discomfort, the feeling is fundamentally a positive one, which means that it really isn't pain. If the answer is the latter, it is probably advisable to back off until the pain returns to the "hurts good" category.

Joint pain is usually a sign of misalignment and a signal to stop whatever you are doing immediately. After you stop, the next step is to see how you can rearrange the pose to eliminate the discomfort. Rearranging may involve rotating a limb, shifting the body weight, lengthening the spine or lessening the arch of the back, shifting the weight from foot to foot, or something else. What is important is to be aware of discomfort and act creatively to alleviate it. It is suggested that this rearranging begin with an evaluation of the position of the feet (if the pose is a standing pose) or with the buttock bones and the pelvis, if the pose is a seated pose. Poses, like buildings, are best built from the ground up. Breathing more deeply and relaxing can also be powerful steps in the right direction. If discomfort persists, it is best to not do the pose and to seek some advice from an experienced teacher.

Schiffmann[12] notes that it is difficult for novices to distinguish between intensity and pain. Any time there is a fear about the experience of intensity or worry about getting hurt, a state of resistance is created, and resisted intensity is experienced as pain. Progress comes from the recognizing that one is either at a mental or physical edge, accepting it, and being willing to play at the edge, much as a child dances along the edges of the waves rolling into a beach.

As a culture, we have been taught to ignore information from the body. "It's nothing" is one of our favorite phrases about sensations arising from the physical body. Another example of our mental overriding of physical information is expressed in the phrase "no pain, no gain." Yet cultivating an awareness of internal feeling states actually helps prevent physical injury and also promotes empathy and compassion, two qualities not usually stressed in physical education, yet important to yoga and to living in a culture characterized by diversity and complexity.

Avoiding strain is *not* avoiding work. Yoga teachers frequently say, "Keep breathing." Breathing is especially important if the pose is difficult. It doesn't matter why the pose is hard; any difficulty tends to cause us to hold the breath. Holding the breath causes the body to become tighter. If you have to hold your breath to do whatever it is you are doing, or if your body shakes and the breath is ragged and uneven, you have exceeded your comfortable capacity and it's time to back off.

Staying with the breath means maintaining an awareness of the breath, whatever pose you are in. This is relatively easy when there are few demands for muscular strength or unaccustomed flexibility. The only way out of this dilemma is repetition. Only through repeated practice of any given pose, with the attention fully turned inward, will the posture begin to "flow" and "open up."

Learning Strategies

Practice. Find a good yoga class or a good manual or videotape, and make a commitment to regular practice. Look at your schedule, and pick a realistic time to practice. Start with short sessions, and increase your time as your pleasure grows. Practice at least 2 hours after eating a light meal and 4 after a larger meal. Make sure you have empty bladder and bowels before you start.

Setting. Practice in a warm room (or outdoors) on an even surface. Use a yoga mat suited for your type of practice (see below). Avoid direct sun. Try to have fresh, but not cold, air. Be sure that your cell phone, pager, and small children are not going to distract you. Yoga has its roots in observation of natural movement and conditions (both internal and external) and is, according to internationally acclaimed teacher Angela Farmer, deeply organic. So, try to have a view of the natural world.

Bare Feet and Comfortable Clothes. Yoga is traditionally practiced in bare feet. The feet appreciate the opportunity to strengthen, breathe, and be liberated from the prison of their shoes. Bare feet also allow you to have a sense of the ground on which you stand (literally and figuratively). Your clothing should not restrict your movement *or* distract you with the need to make adjustments every few seconds, such as having to tuck your T-shirt in.

Movement. Your movements need to be slow enough to allow you to maintain awareness. Be sensitive. If you use a video or manual, carefully look at the alignment of the pose BEFORE you attempt it. You want to be comfortable, able to breathe, aware of the edge, and consciously relaxing as much tension as you can while still maintaining the pose. Yoga asks you to eliminate all extra effort. So check in with your eyes, jaw, neck, throat, shoulders, lower back, belly, and seat to see whether you have tightened any body part you don't need to use to hold the pose.

Pain. If you feel pain or discomfort, you may begin to tighten both around the pain and in other areas of the body, such as the eyes and the jaw. When you observe this happening, instead of quitting, try softening as much as you can and begin to find out about the pain and tightness by observation and dialogue. If the tightness or pain is persistent, you might want to explore Phoenix Rising Yoga Therapy as a technique to bring greater understanding. Phoenix Rising Yoga promotes the integration of mind/body states. For more information, contact Phoenix Rising Yoga at www.pryt.com.

Turn Your Awareness In. As you hold the pose, stay present! Be aware of the constant stream of communication that comes from your body. Does the pose cause fatigue? Is the pose alive (can you feel the movement of your breath?) or cast in concrete? What do the emotions have to say? It is so important to be willing to hear what the body has to say in practicing yoga, and it can be a difficult process as well as a liberating and joyful one.

Injuries. Jean Couch[13] recommends that following an injury to muscles, tendons, or ligaments that you *not* do poses that stretch the area for at least 3 weeks. As you resume, start with the easiest pose for that area, and add only one pose at a time. Observe for a week before adding a second pose. Impatience and a "macho" attitude (and this can exist in women as well as in men) are enemies of full recovery, so be patient and observant as you resume.

Modifications for Special Populations

Orthopedically Impaired

1. Students who use wheelchairs and/or have mobility problems can perform poses while sitting in a chair or their wheelchair, or from a mat.
2. Use bolsters and wedge mats to assist in positioning student into poses.
3. Utilize peer tutors or paraprofessionals to manually guide students through the yoga poses.

Special Note: Consult with physical educator and/or physical therapist for procedures to use in removing students from wheelchairs, ways to use bolsters and to wedge mats for positioning and range of motion limitations.

Cognitively Impaired

1. Use peer teachers and paraprofessionals to guide students through the yoga poses.
2. Keep instructions very short and to the point, avoiding excessive directions.

Sensory Impaired

1. Use peer tutors or paraprofessionals to manually guide students who are blind or have visual impairments through the yoga poses. Their assistance can be gradually withdrawn as students learn the "feel" of the poses.
2. Minimal modifications are needed for students who are deaf and/or have hearing impairments. Instructional considerations include the use of sign language, videos, and pictures.

Terminology

Adho Mukha Svanasana Downward-facing dog pose.
Asana Pose or posture.
Hatha Sun and moon; active and receptive life forces.
Hatha yoga The yoga of health and physical discipline.

Namaste Term meaning "The center of spirit and love in me recognizes and salutes the center of spirit and love in you."
Prana Life force, energy.
Pranayama The studied practice of controlled breathing to increase vital life-force energy.
Raja yoga The royal path. It includes eight rungs, or limbs, of practices that lead the practitioner to a state of complete absorption in universal consciousness or bliss. The path of kings. This path that holds union with the supreme universal spirit; the eight-fold path of Patanjali, first codifier of yoga practice between 800 and 200 B.C.
Savasana The relaxation pose.
Surya Namaskara The sun salutation.
Ujjayi breathing "Victorious breathing;" a controlled form of nose-only breathing used to help focus the mind and pace the movements during yoga practice.
Yoga Union or to yoke.

References

1. Feuerstein, G. *Yoga: The Technology of Ecstasy.* Los Angeles: Jeremy P. Tarcher, 1989.
2. Birkel, D. and Edgren, L. "Hatha Yoga: Improved Vital Capacity of College Students." *Alternative Therapies*, 6, no. 6, pp. 55–63, 2000.
3. Carrico, M. "Contraindications of Yoga." *Idea Health & Fitness Source*, November–December 1998, pp. 34–41.
4. Iyengar, B. K. S. *Light on Yoga* (revised edition). New York: Schocken Books, 1977.
5. Leonard, G. *Mastery: The Keys to Success and Long-Term Fulfillment.* New York: Plume, 1991.
6. Kramer, J. "Yoga as Self-Transformation." *Yoga Journal*, May 1980.
7. Schiffmann, E. *Yoga: The Spirit and Practice of Moving into Stillness.* New York: Pocket Books, 1996.
8. Farhi, D. *Yoga Mind, Body & Spirit.* New York: Henry Holt and Company, 2000.
9. Couch, J. *The Runner's Yoga Book.* Berkeley, CA: Rodmell Press, 1999.
10. Schiffman, *op. cit.*
11. Couch, *op. cit.*
12. Schiffman, *op. cit*
13. Couch, *op. cit.*

Further References

1. Birch, B. *Power Yoga—The Total Strength and Flexibility Workout.* New York: Simon & Schuster, 1995.
2. Feuerstein, G. and Payne, L. *Yoga for Dummies.* Foster City, CA: I.D.G. Books, 1999.
3. Kraftsow, G. *Yoga for Wellness.* New York: Penguin/Arkana, 1999.
4. Lasater, J. *Relax & Renew: Restful Yoga for Stressful Times.* Berkeley, CA: Rodmell Press, 1995.

5. Schatz, M. P., *Back Care Basics, A Doctor's Gentle Yoga Program for Back and Neck Pain Relief*. Berkeley, CA: Rodmell Press, 1992.
6. Swenson, D. *Ashtanga Yoga: The Practice Manual*. Sugarland, TX: Ashtanga Yoga Productions, 1999.
7. Van Kooten, V. *From Inside Out—A Yoga Notebook from the Teachings of Angela & Victor, I & II*. Berkeley, CA: Ganesha Press, 2000.

CDs

Adagio—Music for Relaxation. Peter Davidson, Livingarts.

The Mask and Mirror. Loreena McKennitt, Warner Brothers.

Nada Yoga: The Ancient Science of Sound. Russill Paul, Healingmusic.

Music for Zen Meditation. Tony Scott, Verve.

Videos

Farmer, A. *The Feminine Unfolding*. Hohokus, NJ, 1999.

MacGraw, A. *Yogamind&body*. Warner Home Video, 1994.

Ray, K. *Tri Yoga*. Planet L Publishing, 1990.

Rich, T., and White, G. *Total Yoga*. White Lotus Foundation, 1994.

Wenig, Marsha. *YogaKids*. Livingarts, 1996.

Yee, R. *Yoga for Energy*, Livingarts, 1995; and *Yoga for Athletes*, Livingarts, 2000.

Web Sites

www.riverlightyoga.org The author's Web site, featuring occasional articles, information, and classes.

www.yogadirectory.com Has links to hundreds of teachers, centers, and retreats.

www.yogafinder.com Has a search engine that can locate sites by state or instructor's name.

www.yogajournal.com The Web site of *Yoga Journal* magazine. Features contents of the current issue, a book and tape source, articles on yoga and health, teacher directory, and more.

www.yimag.org The Web site of *Yoga International* magazine. Features contents of the current issue, access to yoga sutras chanted in Sanskrit, teacher directory, and more.

www.yrec.org Web site of the Yoga Research and Education Center, founded by Georg Feuerstein and others to promote education and research in traditional yoga. Features many links, including a link to Yoga Alliance, a teacher registry, as well as research articles and information on therapeutic yoga.

www.yogasite.com Offers a state-by-state listing of teachers, links to vendors, and more.

Overview of and Resources for Contemporary Activities

- Canoeing and kayaking
- Hiking and backpacking
- Inline skating
- Scuba diving
- Skin diving
- Skateboarding
- Snowboarding

INTRODUCTION

Several activities that are popular today are not typically included in most school physical education curricula. The activities have become popular as recreational pursuits and are enjoyed by thousands of participants throughout the world. Space does not permit a full discussion or skill breakdown of each activity. However, in this Appendix the authors present an overview of each activity, including basic equipment requirements and a list of the important skills and concepts the learner would be expected to master.

In addition, each activity is accompanied by a number of references that provide a description of the skills and a more thorough discussion of the specific activity. Many of the books can be purchased through Internet sources (e.g., www.amazon.com) or at national bookstores such as Borders, Barnes and Noble, Books-A-Million, Walden, and Dalton. National organizations through which instructional materials can be acquired and an extensive list of Web sites with many links will provide further invaluable information.

Some of the activities would be deemed high risk, and it is recommended that if they are included in a curriculum, the teacher be proficient in teaching the skill or identify someone who is an expert to provide instruction.

CANOEING AND KAYAKING

Nature and Purpose

Canoeing and kayaking are outdoor recreational activities that offer broad appeal to people of all ages. Both can be done individually or with groups or families. Canoeing and kayaking can be done in still or moving water, on lakes, rivers, or the ocean, and can be incorporated with camping and extend over a period of several days and weeks. On the one hand, these small craft may be used in a very leisurely fashion, allowing a person without a high degree of fitness to enjoy the freedom of the outdoors. On the other hand, when they are performed in fast-moving water that includes rapids and other obstacles, canoeing and kayaking can also satisfy the most ardent extreme sport enthusiast.

Canoeing and kayaking can provide a satisfying experience for people of all levels of ability. Both are skill-based activities, which require some instruction before beginning. First and foremost, any novice paddler should be able to swim a distance of 200 yards unassisted. Beginning instruction should be completed in a relatively sheltered open water area in calm, still water. Preferably instruction will take place in a small craft in a swimming pool before the student advances to open water. Prior to entering water in any small craft, boaters should first have a pool orientation. Skills to cover should include a swim test, basic paddling skills, self-rescue skills, and buddy rescue skills.

For the beginner, slow-moving rivers and relatively calm seas and lakes are essential for enjoying a positive first experience.

Equipment

Canoeing and kayaking require relatively little equipment—a craft, paddle, and personal flotation device. As the student becomes more skilled, equipment requirements may change. Beginners, however, should rent a canoe or kayak from a knowledgeable outfit that can place them into a craft that meets their needs. The remainder of this section will provide a brief overview needed for canoeing and then kayaking.

Canoeing

Canoes are commonly constructed of aluminum, fiberglass, kevlar, or wood and come in different lengths, widths, and hull shapes. Generally, the average canoe is 16 feet long; however, canoes can be longer. A shorter canoe is more maneuverable but is generally not a type that would be taken on a long trip or tour. A longer canoe can hold supplies for long trips and track better in the water. The width of a canoe at the waterline determines the canoe's stability. Wider canoes are more stable but are slower. Canoes have a variety of hull shapes—straight, flat bottom, round bottom, and a shallow V-hull. Each shape has an impact on performance. For the recreational canoeist, the shallow V-hull is the preferred shape because it is more stable and easier for the beginner to handle.

Other equipment needed by the canoeist includes a personal flotation device (PFD). This life-protecting device is required by many states. U.S. Coast Guard–approved PFDs are rated by the wearer's weight and are designed to keep the wearer in a vertical to slightly backward position in the water. Size and weight information is contained on a label affixed to the jacket. Preferably, the PFD should be orange, yellow, or red so that it can be easily spotted by rescuers. Other safety equipment includes an extra paddle and a throwable seat cushion or throw-bag to assist with a rescue.

Paddles enable the canoeist to maneuver the craft. Paddles used for canoeing are made of wood, fiberglass, or aluminum and come in different lengths, shaft shapes (straight or bent), and blade sizes (narrow to wide). The type of paddle is determined by the performance the canoeist wants, the type of conditions, and the canoeist's ability and strength. Generally, the paddle should be long enough for the grip to reach eye level while the tip rests on the ground.

Kayaking

Kayaks are made of plastic, fiberglass, kevlar, carbon fiber, or wood. They are either rigid, folding, or inflatable. Most beginners use kayaks made of plastic. They are rigid, durable, and can take more abuse. Folding or collapsible kayaks consist of a wood or aluminum frame with a fabric skin stretched over it. Inflatable kayaks are easily portable and can be folded up and easily stored in a basement.

There are two major types of kayaks: river and sea. River kayaks are smaller, have rounded hulls, and are generally fast and nimble. Sea kayaks are larger, with V-shaped hulls. Sea kayaks may also include hand-operated bilge pumps for bailing water, and sealed compartments for storing camping equipment. Sea kayaks are more stable than river kayaks but tend to be slower and have a much larger turning radius because of their size.

River kayaks are by the nature of their rounded hulls very unstable. They are highly susceptible to rolling. The kayaker should be able to re-right from a roll, but this requires a great deal of practice. It is essential that that those who wish to pursue this type of kayaking learn how to exit their craft while underwater.

The type of craft selected depends on where the boater will be kayaking (river, open lake, sea), experience in the craft (beginner to expert), the portability and weight of the craft (how much the kayak will be used, whether it will be stored), and the capacity needed (single-person or two-person kayak, storage for camping and long tours). An additional factor is the fit of the kayak. For high performance, a snug cockpit is necessary, whereas for long tours, a looser fit enables the kayaker to move around and stretch his or her legs.

In addition to the kayak itself, a two-bladed paddle is required. The blades are "feathered," or set at opposite angles, to provide a better angle of effectiveness for the paddler. Although there are some kayaks, called sit-on-top kayaks, that have no enclosed cockpit (the boater sits in a depression), most kayaks require the boater to sit "in" a cockpit that encloses the legs and lower torso.

Other equipment found in a kayak include a sprayskirt, which is a neoprene device that the kayaker wears around the waist and fastens to the edge of the cockpit. The sprayskirt helps keep water out of the enclosed kayak hull, which preserves the boat's integrity and helps keep the kayaker warm. Other personal equipment worn by the kayaker may include a neoprene wet suit, with gloves and boots for warmth.

The PFD used by the kayaker is slightly different from the canoeist's. It is designed to provide more freedom of movement. In cases of river kayaking in swift water, the boater may also wear a lightweight helmet to prevent head injuries and other injuries sustained from making contact with the bottom.

Basic Skills

Canoeing

Although one experienced boater may perform canoeing alone, two boaters can enjoy an activity called "soloing." The bowman is stationed at the front of the boat and normally paddles and performs lookout functions for obstacles and hazards. The sternman sits in the rear of the boat and paddles as well as steers the canoe. The more experienced boater should normally act as the sternman.

The direction of a canoe is controlled by a series of strokes, many initiated by the sternman, but sometimes in conjunction with the bowman. When paddling, the canoeist should submerge at least three-quarters of the blade in water. A person should expect to learn the following basic skills:

- Safety skills—swimming, self-rescue, buddy rescue techniques
- Selecting a canoe
- Selecting a paddle
- Choosing a right PFD
- Carrying a canoe
- Boarding a canoe
- Re-entering a capsized and upright canoe
- Rocking a canoe dry
- Strokes—forward stroke, C-stroke, J-stroke, sweep stroke, draw stroke, pry stroke

Kayaking

Unlike canoeing, kayaking is generally a solo sport performance performed by a boater using a double-bladed paddle. The paddle is gripped with both hands, approximately shoulder-width apart, and is alternately dipped on both sides of the kayak to move the kayak forward.

The beginner should be cautioned not to try to kayak without proper instruction. The beginner should learn the following basic skills:

- Safety skills—swimming, self-rescue, buddy rescue techniques

- Selecting a kayak
- Selecting a double bladed paddle
- Entering the kayak
- Falling out of a kayak
- Eskimo roll (righting the kayak)
- Forward stroke
- Reverse stroke
- Sweep stroke
- Draw stroke
- Reverse sweep
- Bracing
- Tracking

Further References

Gordon, H. *Canoeing Made Easy: A Manual for Beginners with Tips for the Experienced*. Old Saybrook, CT: Globe Pequoit, 1992.

Hanson, J. *Complete Sea Kayak Touring*. Camden, ME: Ragged Mountain Press, 1998.

Hanson, J. *Essential Sea Kayaking*. New York: Lyons Press, 2000.

Johnson, S. *Sea Kayaking*. New York: McGraw-Hill, 1998.

Stuhaug, D. *Kayaking Made Easy: A Manual for Beginners with Tips for the Experienced*. Old Saybrook, CT: Globe Pequoit, 1992.

Swenson, A. *L.L. Bean Canoeing Handbook*. New York: Lyons Press, 2000.

Organizations

American Canoe Association, Springfield, VA 22150.

Trade Association of Sea Kayaking, Mequon, WS 53097.

North American Paddlesports Association, Mequon, WS 53097.

Web Sites

www.canoekayak.com Site of *Canoe and Kayak* magazine offers tips, product information, articles, and trip advice.

www.canoeamerican.org Offers trip database, list of paddling organizations, and an online outfitter.

www.clubkayak.com Offers links to paddling sites, online classified section for buying and selling equipment, and news for the world of kayaking.

www.epaddler.com Offers news, events, a paddler directory, and more.

www.kayakonline.com Includes kayak buying tips, information on manufacturers of kayaks and kayaking gear, and links to sea and whitewater clubs and events.

www.paddlesource.com A comprehensive source for paddlers, with gauge readings, river descriptions, maps, classified ads, links, and more.

www.webcre8.com/canoe/index.html Offers an extensive list of Web sites.

www.infinitec.org/water_kayak.htm Offers information and listing of organizations related to kayaking and canoeing for disabled participants.

HIKING/BACKPACKING

Nature and Purpose

Hiking/backpacking is a fun-filled activity enjoyed by thousands of people throughout the world. A wide variety of trail systems has provided people with an opportunity to examine many wonders of the world. Hiking and backpacking can take place in many different environments—the heat of the desert, the coolness of the mountains, and the snow of the winter. Hiking can be done on mountain trails, through urban settings, on the network of rail-to-trails systems in the United States, through the forest and woods, through neighborhoods—in other words, it can be done anywhere.

Generally, hiking refers to walks that are taken for exercise or for pleasure, whereas backpacking refers to an activity that requires the hiker to take along everything needed (carry on one's back) to stay overnight (Seaborg and Dudley, 1994). The benefits far outnumber the dangers. If the hiker follows some simple rules, is properly attired, can read a map and a compass, and learns a few other "rules of the road," he or she can minimize potential dangers and look forward to a lifetime of adventure and pleasure.

The activity is relatively inexpensive. However, as the hiker gains more experience and extends the length of the trips, he or she will need more equipment and other skills.

Equipment

The types of equipment needed to enjoy hiking and backpacking will vary according to many factors, including but not limited to the length of the trip (day hike or overnight hike, weekend to week-long trek or longer), the temperature, the type of environment, the type of terrain, and the time of the year. The beginning to intermediate hiker and backpacker should consider the following types of equipment.

Footwear

Without doubt, the most important piece of equipment the hiker needs to consider is well-fitted footwear. Although tennis or running shoes may be comfortable to wear, they are not appropriate for hiking. Hikers should wear boots made of leather, leather and fabric, or fabric. The type of boot selected depends on the terrain, the distance the hiker wishes to walk, and the weight carried in the backpack.

Boots are designed to provide a hard sole to protect the hiker from sharp rocks and uneven surfaces. They are also designed to support the ankle, i.e., to prevent twisting. The weight of the boot is also an important consideration. Although a heavier boot may appear to be stiffer and therefore offer more protection, over a long, strenuous hike, added weight can quickly tire the backpacker. Some boots made for longer, more rugged hiking are made entirely of leather and serve to give support and maximum protection. Boots that are insulated and extend over the ankles are used for backpacking in snowy terrain. For day hikers moving over moderate terrain, a boot made of a combination of leather and fabric is lighter and more comfortable. All-fabric boots are most often used for moderate hikes on fairly smooth, consistent surfaces where protection isn't as necessary.

As with all equipment, it is best to try on the boots or to consult with an expert who can help fit you to ensure a proper fit. Remember that the most important piece of equipment is footwear. Boots can range from $50 to $300 or more.

Clothing

The type of clothing depends on many factors: the temperature, the type of terrain, the type of environment (the woods, the desert, mountains, heavy underbrush, etc.), and the intensity of the hike. Hiking is a physical activity, and as the hiker becomes more active he or she will generate more heat, even on cooler days. A simple rule is to dress in layers, that is, to wear layers of clothing that can be taken off as the hiker becomes warmer and added when the hiker becomes colder. Fabrics that are worn next to the body should be able to "breathe," that is, allow heat and air to escape and allow moisture to evaporate. Cotton does not "breathe well"; in fact, it retains moisture. Some experts recommend a three-layer system. The first layer should be a synthetic material (polypropylene) worn next to the body. The second layer should be a pile or fleece covering that serves to keep the hiker warm if necessary or helps to wick moisture away from the body. The final layer should be a breathable shell, such as Gore-Tex, or a fabric that is windproof and waterproof and helps to protect from the elements (Seaborg and Dudley, 1994). Layers can be taken off or added, depending on the weather conditions and the condition of the hiker.

The hiker must also be aware of the conditions of the hike. For example, even in warm weather, long pants might be necessary to protect one from the underbrush, from insect bites, and from thorns. On day hikes on a fairly flat terrain with a consistent surface, it might be necessary to wear only shorts, a light T-shirt, and a light pair of hiking boots. In other words, the hiker must know something about the route and the prevailing conditions in determining the type of clothing to wear.

Backpack

Selecting the proper backpack can be a bewildering experience. Backpacks come in many different sizes and shapes; some come with an external frame to which the backpack attaches, whereas others come with a frame that is built into the backpack. Generally, the external frame is used by the hiker who will be doing trail hiking. The frame keeps the backpack away from the body and allows air to circulate. However, the backpack itself may not move with the movement of the body, causing a loss of balance if the hiker decides to move off-trail. Backpacks with built-in frames are used in off-trail hiking and move more easily with the body. However, this type of pack is more difficult to fit and needs more adjustment (Seaborg and Dudley, 1994).

Beginners should consult an expert for help selecting a backpack. Before buying the backpack, the beginner should try it on, place the weight that might normally be carried in it, and walk around with it on his or her back. Other features to look for include adjustable straps to allow weight to be carried high on the shoulders, some type of padded hip belt that allows weight to rest on the pelvis, enough space to carry necessary items, and a padded back for a more comfortable fit.

Other important pieces of equipment to carry depend on the distance traveled. A person who is backpacking should carry a first-aid kit, some type of tent or portable shelter, a sleeping bag, cooking equipment including a stove, well-marked maps, and routes developed for the area. Other miscellaneous equipment to consider is a flashlight, a compass, a mirror, waterproof matches, sunglasses, sunscreen, a pocket knife (Swiss Army knife), water equipment (canteen and purifying tablets), rope, a candle, spare batteries, and insect repellant. Most camping books provide recommended checklists of the equipment that should be taken by the beginner as well as the advanced backpacker (McManners, 1998).

Basic Skills

Before considering hiking and/or backpacking, the hiker should possess a moderate level of physical fitness, including cardiovascular fitness, muscle strength and endurance, and flexibility. In other words, some physical preparation is necessary weeks before embarking on day-long and longer treks. If you are a teacher and considering this as a unit of instruction, then look for opportunities to engage in a multidisciplinary experience with other teachers in

the school. The physical educator can help prepare students to become fit to hike and teach them about how to set up a tent and campsite; the health teacher can teach basic first aid; the consumer science teacher can teach students about types of fabric to wear, food, nutrition needs, and cooking on the trail; the geography teacher can teach students how to read maps and provide information about the terrain they will encounter; and the life science teachers can contribute information about the environment, the vegetation, and the animals. Some of the skills needed by the beginning and intermediate hiker and backpacker include the following:

- Activities requiring a moderate level of fitness
- Proper hiking (walking) techniques on various terrains
- Selecting equipment—boots, backpacks, tents, sleeping bags, etc.
- Selecting clothing
- Reading a map
- Reading a compass
- Preparing a checklist
- Basic first aid
- Safety skills—the "rules of the road," survival skills
- Packing a backpack
- Planning for a trip
- Setting up a campsite
- Crossing streams
- Reacting to animals
- Dealing with the weather
- Basic cooking
- Building a fire

References

McManners, H. *101 Essential Tips: Hiking.* New York: DK Publishing, 1998.

Seaborg, E. and Dudley, E. *Hiking and Backpacking.* Champaign, IL: Human Kinetics, 1994.

Further References

Berger, K. *Advanced Backpacking (A Trailside Series).* New York: W.W. Norton, 1998.

Berger, K. *Hiking and Backpacking: A Complete Guide (A Trailside Series).* New York: W.W. Norton, 1995.

Berger, K. *Everyday Wisdom: 101 Expert Tips for Hikers.* Mountaineer Books, 1997.

Cary, A. *Parent's Guide to Hiking and Camping (A Trailside Series).* New York: W.W. Norton, 1997.

Curtis, R. *The Backpacker's Field Manual: A Comprehensive Guide to Mastering Backcountry Skills.* Maynard, MA: Three Rivers Press, 1998.

Fletcher, C. *The Complete Walker III: The Joys and Techniques of Hiking and Backpacking.* New York: Random House, 1984.

Hall, A. *Backpacking: A Woman's Guide.* New York: Mc-Graw-Hill, 1998.

Logue, F. (Contributor) et al. *Kids Outdoors: Skills and Knowledge for Outdoor Adventures.* New York: McGraw-Hill, 1996.

Randall, G. *The Outward Bound Backpacking Handbook.* New York: Lyons Press, 2000.

Townsend, C. *The Advanced Backpacker: A Handbook of Year Round, Long-Range Hiking.* New York: McGraw-Hill, 2000.

Townsend, C. *The Backpackers Handbook.* 2nd ed. New York: McGraw-Hill, 1996.

Organizations

American Hiking Society, Silver Spring, MD 20190.

Sierra Club, San Francisco, CA 94109.

American Volkssport Association, Universal City, TX 78148.

American Canoe Association, Springfield, VA 22150.

Appalachian Mountain Club, Boston, MA 02108.

National Audubon Society, New York, NY 10022.

National Parks & Conservation Association, Washington, DC 20036.

The Nature Conservancy, Arlington, VA 22209.

Rails-to-Trails Conservancy, Washington, DC 20036.

Web Sites

www.thebackpacker.com/ Offers a beginner's corner, backpacker directory, articles, a question-and-answer section, trail database, and more.

www.backpacking.about.com/recreation/backpacking/mbody.htm Offers information about getting started; topics include backpacking basics, family backpacking, lone backpacking, and discussion about gear, trails around the world, online magazines, and more.

www.trailsource.com/hiking Offers information about a variety of trails around the world; it allows the user to pick a specific state to locate trails and obtain a map and provides current weather information at that location. The site also offers guidebooks, articles, maps, and much more.

www.teleport.com/~walking/hiking.html Offers articles about walking and hiking, directories for hiking clubs, and information about gear, videos and book reviews; it also includes a how-to section on developing a walking program.

www.americanhiking.org American Hiking Society site offers information about trail conservation and policy, events around the country, information about the National Trail Endowment and more.

www.trailwalk.com/ Offers information about walking, hiking, trekking, backpacking, camping and outdoor gear. Also features a discussion forum.

www.bpbasecamp.com *Backpacker Magazine* site offers articles, technique suggestions, gear, and much more.

www.gorp.com/gorp/activity/hiking.htm The Great Outdoors Recreation Pages site offers information on where to hike, trail finders, how to hike, information about gear, Web links, discussion boards, and more.

http://outdoorphoto.com/hiking/ Offers essentials on getting started, hiking ethics, discussion about the layering concept, photography, and more.

INLINE SKATING

Nature and Purpose

Although skating has been around for hundreds of years, the type of skating that boys and girls and men and women participate in today is a far cry from what John Joseph Merlin envisioned in 1735. Gone are the metal skates with metal wheels that attached to a shoe or boot. It was not until the 1980s that the modern inline skate was developed in response to hockey players who wished to train off-season when no ice was available. Inline skates were developed in Minneapolis, Minnesota, by a company called Rollerblade Incorporated. Today you may still hear people refer to inline skates as rollerblades; however, the correct term to use is inline skates (Powell and Svensson,1998).

Since the introduction of inline skates in the 1980s, the activity has become significantly more popular. Now, millions of people participate in some form of skating throughout the world. Inline skating appeals to children; to athletes who use inline skating to cross-train for Alpine skiing, cross-country skiing, cycling, and running; to adults who wish to incorporate inline skating as part of their physical fitness routine; to others who like the social pleasure of recreational skating; and to some who participate in inline skating as a sport. Many skaters also use paved trails that are part of America's Greenway Systems, found in many states, as a venue for their recreation and fitness pursuits.

Inline skating can be practiced in many forms, including (1) aggressive skating, where stunts are performed on street courses or on specially designed ramps; (2) artistic skating, which features many of the movements and skills performed by ice skaters; (3) recreational skating, with a focus on the social aspects of skating with other people; (4) fitness skating, which focuses on a participant's physical fitness regimen; (5) inline hockey, which features all of the elements of ice hockey but without the ice; and (6) speed skating, which focuses on attaining high speed around an oval, much like speed skating on ice.

Inline skaters have exhibited many health benefits, including improved cardiovascular health, increased muscular strength and endurance, improved flexibility, reduced stress, and weight control. Inline skating is also a low-impact activity; it is easy on a person's joints. It is an activity that almost anyone can enjoy, one of its greatest attractions.

Equipment

As is the case with other activities described in this chapter, inline skating requires some specialized equipment. And as with skateboarding and snowboarding (discussed later in this Appendix), it is best to consult an expert before buying your first set of inline skates. Many experts would suggest that a beginner rent their first set of skates. Particularly if you do not go to an expert, be sure to try on the skates first because the fit of the pair you rented may differ from the brand that you want to buy.

Inline Skates

An inline skate has several components, including the boot, the frame, the wheels, the brake, and the bearings. The selection of an inline skate is directly related to the use of the skates (recreational, speed, aggressive, etc.), the size of the skater (large, small, heavy, light, etc.), the ability of the skater, the skating surface (indoor, outdoor, smooth, rougher), and the type of skating planned.

The boot can be a hard plastic shell or a soft durable material. Most boots used for recreation have a hard plastic outer boot with a high back that extends over the ankles and up the lower calf. There is an inner liner that keeps the foot secure and enables the skater to control movement and perform stunts if that is his or her desire. The boots either buckle or have laces. The lace enables the participant to sometimes better "fine tune" the boot to their foot. There are different boots and boot configurations for each type of inline skating (i.e., recreational, aggressive, fitness, racing, etc.).

Attached to the bottom of each boot is a plastic, metal, or composition frame that holds either four or five wheels. Frames vary in length depending on the type of skating you wish to do. The frame should be large enough to hold the largest wheel possible. Some frames will have an additional metal piece attached across the bottom of the frame to enable the aggressive inline skater to perform grinding stunts on curbs or railings (Powell and Svensson, 1998).

Each skate has either four or five hard rubberlike urethane wheels that fit into the frame. Some wheels are softer than other wheels; the wheel hardness needed depends on how the skate is being used, the type of surface, and the ability of the skater. Generally, a beginner is likely to prefer a softer wheel to absorb the bumps and provide a slower ride. Wheels vary in size from 55 to 82 mm. Smaller wheels are used by artistic skaters. Recreational and fitness skaters use wheels that are 70 to 76 mm, and speed skaters use wheels that may be 78 to 82 mm. Each wheel has a set of bearings that allow the wheel to spin smoothly as the skater is moving (Powell and Svensson, 1998).

Recreational skates have a brake on one of the skates attached to the back of the frame. Aggressive, artistic, fitness, hockey and racer skates generally do not have brakes.

Safety Equipment

There is an element of risk in all forms of activity; inline skating is no exception. In order to minimize the risk of injury, it is best to have the following pieces of equipment: (1) an ANSI-approved helmet (most bicycle helmets are approved helmets); (2) wrist guards with a plastic brace that is worn on the inside of the guard (these are essential; hand and wrist injuries are the most common form of injury); and (3) knee and elbow pads covered with hard-impact plastic that help dissipate the force of a fall and help prevent scrapes, bruises, cuts, and broken bones (Nottingham and Fedel, 1997).

Basic Skills

Before venturing out and engaging in any form of inline skating, each skater has to master some basic skills. Beginners should start on a level area that is relatively smooth and free of downhill slopes. Once they have mastered the ability to glide, skaters can then attempt terrain with a gradual downhill slope. But for beginners, it's best to master the basic skills listed below. If you are interested in a specific form of inline skating, consult the references or Web sites of interest listed at the conclusion of this discussion for further information (Powell and Svensson, 1998; Nottingham and Fedel, 1997).

- Warm-up (stretching the lower back, quadriceps, hip flexors, hamstrings, buttock, legs, and neck)
- Skating posture and weight distribution
- Striding (stroking)
- Stopping (brake or T-stop)
- Stopping on an incline
- Climbing a hill
- Turns
- Connecting turns
- Cross-over turns
- Traversing
- Stepping up and down curbs
- Skating backward

Once these basic skills are learned, beginner skaters are ready to move on and participate at a level that improves their fitness or provides an opportunity to make new friends.

References

Nottingham, S. and Fedel, F. J. *Fitness In-line Skating.* Champaign, IL: Human Kinetics, 1997.

Powell, M. and Svensson, J. *In-line Skating.* 2nd ed. Champaign, IL: Human Kinetics, 1998.

Further References

Joyner, S. *In-line Roller Hockey: The Official Guide and Resource Book.* Lincolnwood, IL: NTC/Contemporary Publishing Company, 1995.

Millar, C. *In-line Skating Basics.* New York: Sterling Publishing Company, 1996.

Miller, L. *Get Rolling: A Beginner's Guide to In-line Skating.* 2nd ed. New York: McGraw-Hill, 1998.

Nealy, W. *Inline: A Manual for Beginner to Intermediate Inline Skating.* Birmingham, AL: Menosha Ridge Publishing, 1998.

Official Rules of Inline Hockey. 3rd ed. Triumph Book Publishing Staff, 1999.

Siller, G. *Roller Hockey: Skills and Strategies for Winning on Wheels.* Federal Way, WA: Masters Press, 1997.

Organizations

Aggressive Skaters Association, Marina Del Rey, CA.

USA Roller Sports, Lincoln, NE.

Rails-to-Trails Conservancy, Washington, D.C.

American Trails, Prescott, AZ.

International Inline Skating Association, Wilmington, NC.

Web Sites

www.usara.com United States Roller Sports site features information about speed skating, roller hockey, roller figure skating, fitness skating, and recreational skating; also provides sources for videos on artistic skating, speed skating, and hockey.

www.crhl.net Collegiate Roller Hockey site features information about roller hockey in colleges.

www.iisa.org International Inline Skating Association site features information about the National Skate Patrol Program, how to buy inline skates, fast facts about inline skating, rules of the road, and start-up guide for building a skate park and more.

www.active.com Online newsletter that features information about inline skating events in the United States.

www.activevideo.com Lists many inline skating videos.

www.skatecity.com Contains information covering most forms of inline skating and more.

www.skatefaq.com Offers useful information on a variety of inline skating topics.

www.rollerblade.com/ Offers information about skating gear, skate maintenance, getting started, skating for fitness, an inline directory, and more.

SCUBA DIVING

Nature and Purpose

From early times, many divers yearned for the ability to stay underwater longer than the period of time they could hold their breath. Early attempts at providing a continuous air supply included diving from diving bells. A diving bell was essentially a large container, weighted upside down and open at the bottom. Air was trapped inside, and the diver would travel to and from the bell, getting a breath of air when necessary. The Industrial Revolution brought machines that could actually pump air through a hose down to a diver underwater. Extended dives were possible, but they were still limited to the length of the hose or distance the diver could swim from the bell. Divers longed to carry their air supply with them and swim freely for an extended period of time.

SCUBA, or "self-contained underwater breathing apparatus," was first invented by Jacques Cousteau in the late 1940s. This invention finally allowed divers the freedom to remain underwater for longer periods of time. Many had experimented with self-contained units, but Cousteau was the first to succeed in designing a demand regulator that would give a breath of air when the diver desired. Earlier regulators produced a constant flow, therefore wasting a lot of air and limiting underwater time. From Cousteau's early design, equipment has evolved to today's easy-breathing, comfortable items that are worn by thousands enjoying the sport all over the world.

Anyone 12 years old and older may participate. Basic swim skills and comfort in the water are essential. Because of the extended time spent underwater and the breathing of compressed air in a higher-pressure environment, formal training is required to dive safely. SCUBA dive stores will require a certification card as proof of training before selling SCUBA gear or taking individuals on dive excursions. Courses in beginning SCUBA generally require a minimum of 32 hours of instruction. The best courses will include instruction that begins with skin diving, then progresses to SCUBA. The course includes lecture instruction, work in the pool, and supervised SCUBA dives in the open water prior to certification.

Once certified, divers have a wide variety of choices of dive sites. From the warm, clear waters of the tropics, to the many inland freshwater lakes, rivers, and quarries, to the cold waters under the polar icecaps—divers have explored them all. These explorations are safely limited to depths of 100 feet. Beyond those limits, different equipment and a higher level of training are required.

Equipment

Basic equipment needed by the SCUBA diver includes a mask, snorkel, wet suit, fins, and SCUBA apparatus. Well-fitted equipment is essential for the diver's safety and enjoyment. It is best to consult an expert at a dive shop or an experienced diver before obtaining new equipment. The SCUBA unit and wet suit are described below. A description of fins and mask will follow under "Skin Diving."

The SCUBA Unit

The SCUBA unit itself consists of multiple pieces of equipment assembled and worn by the diver. Tanks, or air cylinders made of steel or aluminum, hold the supply of compressed air. A single hose, two-stage regulator attached to the tank transports air from the tank to the diver's mouthpiece. On a separate hose attached to the regulator is a gauge indicating the amount of air in the tank at all times. Additional gauges may be added to indicate depth and direction. The tank is strapped into the buoyancy compensator (flotation vest). The SCUBA unit is worn with the skin-diving equipment of mask, snorkel, fins, and any necessary thermal clothing.

Extensive instruction occurs in the classroom and pool concerning operation, selection, assembly, and use of this equipment underwater. The regulator and tank are the specific equipment items that can be purchased only with proof of certification. Use of this equipment without proper instruction and understanding can result in injury.

Wet Suit

A wet suit, made of neoprene, is thermal clothing worn in the water to slow heat loss from the body. Wet suits are available in a variety of thicknesses and designs. A full body suit keeps the SCUBA diver comfortably warm.

Basic Skills

Since Cousteau's invention of SCUBA, the sport has grown from one of relative obscurity to one that is enjoyed by many worldwide. Instruction is affordable, even in inland areas of the country far from the ocean. Proper instruction and regular practice reduces risk and eliminates most problems. SCUBA allows one to enjoy another dimension of the world that most people will never see. When taking a SCUBA class, the prospective diver should learn the following skills:

- Identification, selection, and operation of SCUBA equipment
- Diving physics, physiology, and medical aspects of diving
- Environmental factors (diving procedures, safety considerations, ecological concerns, interaction with marine life)
- Diver first-aid and rescue
- Entry-level swim test and fitness swims
- Use of mask, fins, snorkel, and flotation vest
- Assembly and use of SCUBA equipment underwater
- Safety techniques (buddy system, sharing air, rescue techniques)
- Required proficiency tests (in pool to demonstrate comfort and proficiency in use of skills and equipment)
- Open water dives (to test proficiency and skills)

SKIN DIVING

Nature and Purpose

Skin diving is an aquatic sport that can be enjoyed by all ages. Skin diving by definition is primarily a combination of floating and swimming on the surface of the water while wearing a mask, snorkel, and fins. However, the "skin diver" also will surface dive and swim under the water for a period of time that he or she can comfortably hold the breath. By strict definition, the "snorkeler" wears the same equipment but stays on the surface of the water enjoying the sights below. Often times, the two terms are used interchangeably to mean the same sport.

The risk of injury is very small in this sport. Because it is an activity involving water, the obvious precautions normally taken with any aquatic sport should be followed. Good swimming skills and comfort in the water are obvious prerequisites to participating in this sport. For optimum safety, skin divers should participate in small groups or, at a minimum, always with a buddy. Participants can take formal classes to learn techniques and procedures. However, the "water-oriented" person can easily learn to use the equipment and enjoy the sport with a little help from a friend or by reading one of the skin diving manuals on the market. Many of the swim strokes, kicks, and surface dives used in skin diving would have already been learned in the process of learning to swim. A little extra time is needed to learn to use the equipment that allows one to see, breathe, and swim early while skin diving.

Skin diving has existed as long as people have been living around water. Skin divers collected food and other items to be used from the sea. Written records have been discovered describing military and commercial salvage of sunken shipwrecks by skin divers as far back as 5,000 years ago. These activities usually occurred in coastal waters, in depths less than 100 feet. Divers with long breath-hold capability were prized by commercial salvage operations. Today, technology has provided better ways to explore, salvage, and conduct undersea operations. After World War II, Jacques Cousteau and his friends began to pursue skin diving for exploration and the hunting of fish with spear guns. It was Cousteau's love of his pursuit that led to his eventual development of SCUBA, or "self-contained underwater breathing apparatus." Today, skin diving is primarily pursued for fun and recreation.

Vacationers to warmer climates and island resorts include skin diving on their list of leisure activities. Entire families can participate, enjoying the fish, colors, shapes, and other visual thrills of the coral reefs that surround many islands in tropical seas. In temperate climates, when the water becomes warm during the summer months, skin divers can learn about, explore, and enjoy the creatures and plants found in many inland fresh-water lakes and quarries.

For those who wish to go on to the sport of SCUBA, skin diving is also an important first step. SCUBA courses should always begin with lessons in skin diving.

Equipment

Skin diving is a relatively inexpensive activity. Initial outlay for a good mask, fins, and snorkel is necessary. A wet suit, which is optional for most people, is not really needed unless the diver is planning to dive in colder waters. Equipment can be purchased from a retail dive shop. For those who wish to try the sport, rentals are also available through dive shops. As with all activities, well-fitted equipment is a key to maximizing the enjoyment of the activity. It is best to consult an expert before buying equipment.

The Mask

The mask used for skin diving is the same piece of equipment used in the sport of SCUBA. The first masks, or eye coverings, were goggles made of polished tortoise shell. These early goggles, like today's masks, restored the pocket of air in front of the eyes, thus enabling the skin diver to see clearly underwater. Early divers discovered, however, that although the tortoise shell goggles enabled them to see underwater, everything was out of focus. Today's masks are made of long-lasting silicone. The faceplate should always be of tempered glass for optimum safety. The nose remains inside the mask. Exhaling air into the

mask through the nose is important to prevent a malady called "mask squeeze." Squeezes are injuries that result from the increased pressure exerted by the water on the diver's body as he or she swims to depth. Avoiding these problems is easy and covered in any text or course on skin diving.

Masks come in a variety of sizes, colors, and price ranges. The most important consideration in selecting a mask is the fit on the face. To check for proper fit, place the mask on the face, and then inhale through the nose. No air should leak in around the seal during the inhalation. A proper seal will ensure a minimum of water leakage when the mask is worn in the water.

The Snorkel

The snorkel is simply a breathing tube. It allows one to comfortably rest the face in the water while skin diving and eliminate the need to continually lift the head out of the water to take a breath. The J-shaped tube comes in a variety of designs, colors, and price ranges; however, the length is critical. Twelve to 15 inches is the maximum length for ease of breathing. Snorkels may be continuous tubes or have one-way drains called "purge valves" that allow for easier clearing of water. The snorkel is attached to the left side of the mask strap by a device called the "snorkel keeper."

Fins

The fins increase the surface area of the foot for easier swimming. Fins come in two basic designs: full-foot, or bare-foot, fins; and open-heel fins. The full-foot fin is popular with skin divers. They are lightweight, cheaper in price, and easier to transport. Open heel-fins are designed to be worn with boots. The boots keep the foot warm and protect it when walking over rough or rocky shorelines. Open-heel fins are generally more costly and heavier, but more durable. They are popular among SCUBA divers but are certainly usable for both sports.

A properly fitting mask, snorkel, and fins are the minimum pieces of equipment needed to comfortably and safely enjoy skin diving. Additional equipment is sometimes used, depending on the circumstances. Flotation vests, also called "buoyancy compensators," may be used by skin divers. Commercial boat charters taking skin divers on an excursion to open water usually require vests. The very skilled and comfortable skin diver may elect not to wear a flotation vest, but should put one on a friend who is skin diving for the first time. Consider the skill level and water comfort of others in determining the use of this item.

Basic Skills

Many YMCAs include skin-diving technique as part of the progressive swim lessons they teach. Any dive shop or organization that teaches SCUBA will also be able to train people to enjoy skin diving. The YMCA of the USA SCUBA Program offers courses in skin diving for all ages. With minimal instruction and a reasonable level of water comfort, the entire family can enjoy skin diving. A prospective skin diver would expect to learn to demonstrate proficiency in the following skills:

- Selection of properly fitting mask, snorkel, and fins
- Use of equipment in pool or in shallow, open water—adjusting and sealing the mask
- Clearing water from the mask
- Clearing the snorkel—blast technique and displacement clearing
- Use of fins—the flutter kick, frog kick, and dolphin kick
- Water entries—standing and sitting
- Exit from water—on boat, on shore
- Surface dives (foot-first, head-first)
- Entry to surface—arm above head
- Safety considerations—buddy system, skin protection, temperature
- Equalizing pressure in ears
- Basic water physics
- Reacting to aquatic life—fish, jellyfish

References

Barsky, S.M. *A Simple Guide to Snorkeling Fun.* Flagstaff, AZ: Best Publishing Co., 1999,

Berger, K. *SCUBA Diving, A Trailside Guide.* New York: W.W. Norton, 2000.

Graver, D. K. *SCUBA Diving.* 2nd ed. Champaign, IL: Human Kinetics, 1999.

Joiner, J. (Editor). *NOAA Diving Manual: Diving for Science and Technology.* 4th ed. Flagstaff, AZ: Best Publishing Co., 2001.

Maas, T. and Sipperly, D. *Freedive.* Ventura, CA: Blue-Water Free Divers, 1998.

Organizations

YMCA SCUBA Program, 101 North Wacker Drive, Chicago, IL 60606.

Web Sites

www.leaird-scuba.com Offers courses in skin and SCUBA diving, information on equipment sales, and skin and SCUBA diving sites in central Indiana.

www.ymcascuba.org Details programs and instructors available throughout the nation for the YMCA SCUBA Program.

www.padi.com Professional Association of Diving Instructors site offers information about courses to take, articles, environmental news, products, places to travel, and more.

www.naui.org/index_side.html National Association of Underwater Instructors site offers information about SCUBA and snorkeling, programs offered, articles and essays on all aspects of diving, and more.

www.scubacentral.com/ Offers links to information about diving, shopping, photography, humor, and more.

SKATEBOARDING

Nature and Purpose

Skateboarding, enjoyed by over 9 million participants, is a high-risk activity that is similar to surfing and snowboarding. For the participant using safe equipment and possessing good balance and body control, it provides a thrilling and exhilarating ongoing challenge.

Much has been said in recent years about the risk involved in skateboarding. However, a review of such other activities as inline skating, gymnastics, football, basketball, cycling, and roller skating shows that skateboarding is as safe if not safer than these other activities. The key to minimizing the risk is proper instruction, body control, smooth surfaces or approved areas on which to ride, safety equipment, practice, and good judgment.

Skateboarding first appeared in the early 1900s, when children attached roller skate wheels to a board and played on the streets and sidewalks. The sport reached serious levels in the 1950s, when surfers looked for a way to tie their love for surfing to the streets. As the years progressed, the sport went through many highs and lows due to the public's perception of the reckless nature of the participants, the liability involved, insurance issues, and the development of materials for wheels and the board that would be durable and safe. Skateboarding began on the streets and sidewalks but made its way to pool skating, half pipes, and ramps. Skate parks were once popular, then lost popularity, but now appear to be making a comeback (Brooke, 1999).

California has long been a leading state in the development of skate parks. The International Association of Skateboard Companies has encouraged other states to follow California's example in constructing safe facilities (Brooke, 1999).

Equipment

The Skateboard

The skateboard consists of four primary parts: (1) the deck, on which the rider stands; (2) the trucks, which are the front and rear axle assemblies that are attached to the deck and hold the wheels; (3) the wheels, which are made of polyurethane; and (4) the bearings, which make the wheels go around.

The board is generally 28 to 34 inches long. The deck is concave, curved up at either end in order to perform specific tricks. Boards are made of thin layers of maple glued together to make a strong, durable surface. The deck is generally covered with a grip tape (with a sandpaper-like texture) that helps the rider grip the board with the feet.

The trucks should be made of metal. Anything less should be avoided. Good trucks are adjustable to allow the rider to steer and make quicker turns. The trucks are also the landing gear; the surface of the axle allows the rider to execute a skill called grinding.

The wheels, made of polyurethane, can be soft for a comfortable, smoother ride or hard for a fast ride. The softer wheel tends to wear out faster but grips the surface better. The diameter of the wheels ranges from 39 to 66 millimeters.

Bearings make the board go faster or slower depending on the bearing rating. A lower rating (slower ride) is best for a beginning rider.

Safety Equipment

While the board is important for performance, there are other types of equipment that must be worn to minimize the risk of serious injury. The pieces of equipment that are essential for the beginning skateboarder include (1) a well-fitted helmet with a chinstrap to help prevent head injuries; (2) wrist guards, which help prevent broken bones; (3) knee pads with a plastic cover, which slide over the surface and help disperse the impact when the skater falls; (4) elbow pads, which prevent broken bones, bruises, and scrapes; and (5) gloves, which also help prevent cuts and bruises.

Basic Skills

Experts concur that the first step to successfully negotiating the skateboard is to learn basic movements with the rider on the ground. Among the skills the beginner can expect to learn are the following (Werner, 2000):

- Standing on the board—right foot or left foot forward
- Moving the board forward—pushing with one foot
- Stopping
- Turning
- Gliding—down a gradual hill
- Kickturn—frontside and backside
- Carving
- Ollies

- Dropping in
- Fakies

There are many other tricks that can be learned when the rider becomes more comfortable and in better control on the skateboard. Many of these are completed in the air and in combinations as seen in some of the skateboard events on television. But even for beginners, a good board, well-fitting safety equipment, practice, and a safe place to skate with smooth surfaces can lead to a challenging and exciting activity.

References

Brooke, M. *The Concrete Wave: The History of Skateboarding*. Toronto, Ontario: Warwick Publishing, 1999.

Werner, D. with Badillo, S. *Skateboarder's Start-Up: A Beginner's Guide to Skateboarding*. San Diego, CA: Tracks Publishing, 2000.

Further References

Davis, J. and Phillips, S. *Skateboard Roadmap*. London, England: Carlton Books, 1999.

Freimuth, J. *Extreme Skateboarding Moves* (Behind the Moves series). Mankato, MN: Capstone Press, 2000.

Gutman, B. *Skateboarding: To the Extreme*. New York: St Martin's Press, 1997.

Gutman, B. *The Wild and Exciting World of Skateboarding*. New York: Tor Books, 2001.

Shoemaker, J. *Skateboarding Street Style* (Action Sports series). Mankato, MN: Capstone Press, 1995.

Organizations

Extreme Downhill International, San Diego, CA 92109.

International Association of Skateboard Companies, Santa Barbara, CA 93116.

Web Sites

www.skateboard.about.com/recreation/skateboard/mbody.htm Offers a great deal of useful information for the beginner and beyond; also includes health and safety information, references, hints for maintenance, and much more.

www.interlog.com/~mbrooke/history.htm Offers a concise history of skateboarding.

www.exploritorium.edu/skateboarding/ Offers clips of tricks, a glossary of terms, and information about equipment.

www.skatepark.org Serves as a resource for promoting skateboarding and for people actively working to get skate parks built, and much more.

www.skateboarddirectory.com/ Offers links to other skateboard sites, directs the reader to references, and contains information on snowboarding, BMX (Bicycle Motocross), and more.

www.skateboarding.com Site for the skateboader; offers information on live events, news, trick tips, skate parks, a chat room, and more.

www.boardpark.com Offers a comprehensive list of Web sites, companies, magazines, skate parks, online shops, and more.

SNOWBOARDING

Nature and Purpose

Snowboarding can be enjoyed not only by boys and girls but also by men and women well into their middle age. It requires a moderate degree of physical fitness, average coordination, and the ability to maintain balance while moving. Generally, skateboarders and skiers pick up snowboarding quite easily. The movements and some of the skills in these two activities are also used in snowboarding. Snowboarding is easy to learn, provides good physical activity, and is relatively safe; moreover, the equipment is easy to use and less expensive than skiing equipment (Carlson and Gross, 1998).

The sport became popular in the late 1980s and since then has grown throughout the world. For many people, snowboarding either complements or provides a viable alternative to skiing. As late as the mid-1980s, most areas did not allow snowboarding; however, today virtually every ski area accommodates it. A good deal of its popularity has resulted from television exposure and its inclusion as an Olympic sport (Bennett et al., 2000).

Equipment

Snowboarding requires some basic equipment, including a snowboard, bindings, boots, waterproof and windproof apparel, goggles or sunglasses, padded gloves, kneepads, a leash to keep the board with you if you fall, and a hat or, preferably, a helmet. Wrist guards, similar to those used in skateboarding, are additional equipment that can help to prevent sprains or broken bones.

Before trying this sport, beginners should rent equipment first and then purchase from a shop that specializes in snowboard equipment. There are variations in the equipment. Selection depends on the person's sex, ability (beginner or advanced), and the intended use or type of skiing the person wishes to do. There are four styles of snowboarding: (1) freestyle, (2) free riding, (3) Alpine, and (4) racing. Each style generally requires a different board, boot, and binding. So it's important that beginners consult an expert and be fitted for the snowboard, boots, and binding best suited to their ability.

The Snowboard

Snowboards come in different lengths, widths, flexes, and shapes. A snowboard consists of layers of laminated materials; the inner core is usually laminated wood or foam, and the outer layers are made of a variety of durable plastics. The anatomy of a snowboard can best be described as having the following parts: (1) a tip and a tail; the curvature and height of each depends on the type of skiing the person wishes to do (freestyle, free riding, Alpine, racing); (2) a base surface made out of a durable, polyethylene layer to withstand the ever-changing slope surface conditions; (3) the deck (top surface), where the bindings are mounted; (4) a plastic or rubber stomp pad, mounted between the two bindings, where the back foot is placed when it is not in the binding; and (5) steel edges built into the board, which run along the bottom edges of the board and enable the skier to turn and carve. The cost of a snowboard ranges from $100 to $500. The size ranges from 130 to 175 centimeters (Bennett et al., 2001).

When selecting a board, the snowboarder can choose from among a variety of lengths and widths; some boards will be more flexible, some will have greater camber, some will be stiffer, and some will be designed specifically for women. Beginners should look for a board that is wider and has a softer flex.

Bindings

Bindings are mounted on the deck of the snowboard, generally at an angle. The angle depends on the type of snowboarding the person wishes to do. There are three kinds of bindings: (1) strap bindings (soft) have two straps that secure the boot, along with a high plastic back that extends up over the ankles and lower calves, which enables the snowboarder to control the board for turning and other maneuvers; (2) step-in bindings allow the snowboarder to step into the binding without worrying about straps; and (3) the plate binding, which secures the boot to the board through the use of bails and a snap-down lever. The plate binding is generally used for a hard boot, which is used by racers or Alpine boarders (Bennett et al., 2001).

Boots

As with skiing, one of the most important pieces of equipment is a boot that keeps the feet warm, dry, secure, and comfortable throughout the day. There are three types of boots: (1) Soft boots have an inner bladder that keeps the feet warm, dry, and comfortable. The soft outer boot allows flexibility and movement of the ankle. Soft boots are generally used by freestyle snowboarders and for those who want comfort while snowboarding. (2) Hard boots have a sturdy inner boot but a stiff outer boot that increases edge control and allows the board to respond to the body as it leans into the heelside or toeside edges of the snowboard. Alpine racers use this type of boot. (3) Hybrid step-in boots generally have a hard sole and a flexible outer boot. A skier wanting both flexibility and stiffness uses hybrid boots. Boots range in cost from $50 to $300 (Bennett et al., 2001).

Other Equipment

Aside from water-repellant and windproof clothing, the snowboarder should have (1) a leash that attaches around the forward leg and to the binding and prevents a board from flying down the hill if it should come off; (2) sturdy, well-padded waterproof gloves, as the snowbaorder tends to continually touch the ground; (3) a hat, preferably a helmet, to keep the head warm and protect against head injuries; (4) goggles or UV-protected sunglasses to protect the eyes; (5) kneepads to protect the knees (some pants have kneepads sown in); and (6) wrist guards, much like those used by skateboarders to help prevent wrist injuries. Clothing should be comfortable. Avoid cotton clothing, such as jeans, because it retains moisture and can make for a long, cold day. Layering is a concept that should be understood by the snowboarder. For a discussion of layering, refer to Chapter 17, "Skiing: Cross-Country."

Basic Skills

Many of the tricks used in freestyle snowboarding are similar in name and execution to those in skateboarding. This listing includes the basic skills needed to begin this exciting activity. Discussions of other, more advanced, skills can be found in the references and on the Web sites of interest (Bennett et al., 2001; Carlson and Gross, 1998).

- Etiquette
- Parts of the snowboard
- How to buckle up
- Balance
- Stance—regular or goofy
- Falling down and standing up
- Getting on and off ski lifts
- Walking
- Skating
- Edging
- Steering and pivoting
- Straight glide
- Toeside and heelside turns
- Skidded turns
- Traversing
- Linked skidded turns
- Carving

Snowboarding can provide fun-filled challenges for almost anyone. The skills that can be performed and the tricks executed are directly related to the amount of time spent practicing. Whether one wants the rush of speeding down a mountain, the peace and rhythm that comes with linking a series of turns together in deep powder snow, or the daring of executing 360s or Ollies, snowboarding can be a viable alternative.

References

Bennett, J., Downey, S., and Arnell, C. *The Complete Snowboarder.* 2nd ed. New York: McGraw-Hill, 2000.

Carlson, J., and Gross, M. M. (Series Editors). *Snowboarding: A Women's Guide.* Camden, ME: Ragged Mountain Press, 1998.

Further References

Gutman, B. *Snowboarding.* New York: Tor Books, 2000.

Howe, S. *Sick: A Cultural History of Snowboarding.* New York: St. Martins Press, 1998.

Lurie, J. and Clarke, J. (Photographer). *Fundamental Snowboarding.* Minneapolis, MN: Lerner Publications Company, 1995.

Older, E. *Snowboarding.* Mechanicsburg, PA: Stackpole Books, 1999.

Ryan, K. *The Illustrated Guide to Snowboarding.* Dallas, TX: Master's Press, 1998.

Organizations

Canadian Snowboard Federation, Calgary, Alberta, Canada.

International Snowboard Federation of North America, Fergus Fall, MN 56537.

United States of America Snowboard Association, Truckee, CA 96160.

United States Ski and Snowboard Association, Park City, UT 84060.

Web Sites

www.snowboarding.about.com/recreation/snowboarding/mbody.htm Offers useful information for the beginner; also includes articles of interest, tips, tricks, information about protective gear, and more.

www.snowboardreview.com Offers what's happening in snowboarding, good section on snowboard 101, product reviews, other links, and more.

www.snowboard.com Offers the largest online snowboarding community on the Web, free membership, articles, tricks, film clips, places to ski, and much more.

www.usasa.org United States of America Snowboard Association Web site offers many links, information for the snowboarder, events, history of the USASA, and more.

www.ussnowboard.com United States Snowboard Association Web site offers information for beginners, competition, a glossary, books, code of conduct, and much more.

www.burton.com Site sponsored by Burton Snowboard Company offers information about a program called CHILL for underprivileged and at-risk children.

www.snowboardingtips.com Offers articles; information about safety; subscription to a free newsletter; and links to travel, schools, camps, instruction, magazines, and more.

www.theboarderline.com An online magazine for snowboarding; also offers games, technical (skill) help, product reviews, the beginner's corner, and much more.

www.heckler.com *Heckler Magazine* site for snowboarders and skateboarders; offers articles, news, product reviews, ramp plans, and more.

How to Conduct Tournaments

Types of Tournament Drawings

Various kinds of bracket arrangements may be used in conducting tournament competition. The type of elimination is usually determined by several factors: (1) type of activity, (2) number of entries, (3) amount of playing time, (4) playing space and equipment, (5) age of participants, (6) officials available.

With a large number of entries, it is sometimes desirable to run a combination tournament, for example, a double elimination–single elimination tournament. The winners of the double elimination brackets compete in a single elimination tournament to determine the ultimate champion.

Number of Byes. The first step before making a drawing for the bracket arrangement is to determine the number of entries.

When the number of competitors is 4, 8, 16, 32, 64, 128, or any higher power of 2, they meet in pairs. When the number of competitors is not a power of 2, there are byes in the first round. For example, if there are 13 entries, a bracket of 16 with three byes is required. The purpose of having byes is to bring into the second round a number of competitors that is a power of 2. To determine the number of byes, subtract the number of competitors from the next higher power of 2; to determine the number of competitors in the first round, subtract the number of byes from the total number of competitors. If the byes are an even number, half of them are placed at the top of the draw and half at the bottom of the draw; if they are an uneven number, there should be one more bye at the bottom than the top. The byes at the top half are the names drawn first. The next names drawn are placed in the first round. The byes in the bottom half are drawn last.

Seeding the Draw. It is a common practice to select the best teams or individuals and place them in the bracket so that they will not meet in the early rounds of the play. Two or more entries may be seeded— usually the 4 best are selected in a 16-name bracket and 8 in a 32-name bracket. The seeded entrants are usually placed in the 1st, 5th, 9th, 13th, etc., bracket positions. The No. 1 and 4 seeded teams are generally placed in the 1st and 5th positions of the top bracket and the No. 2 and 3 seeded teams in the 9th and 13th positions of the lower bracket, or the No. 1 and 3 in the upper with the No. 2 and 4 seeded teams in the lower half.

Single Elimination Tournament

If the contestants are of equal strength or their strength is not known, have a drawing for positions in the bracket. If the strength is known, seed the best teams so they will not meet in the early rounds. Place the seeded entries in the 1st, 5th, 9th, 13th, etc., positions.

All byes must occur in the first round of play. The total number of games played is always one less than the number of entries. To determine the number of games that the winner would have to play, count the powers of 2 in the number of entries; e.g., with 32 entries the winner plays 5 games.

Double Elimination Tournament

Two defeats eliminate an entry in the double elimination tournament. The losers in the first rounds move into the losers' bracket. The teams that advance farthest in either bracket meet each other in the final game. Should the winner of the losers' bracket defeat the winner of the first-round bracket, the teams are rematched for the championship when one team will have lost two games.

Byes are distributed in the first round of the original elimination brackets as in a single elimination tournament, but in the first round of the losers' brackets byes must be arranged to avoid giving a second bye to an entry that has already had a bye. Also, at all stages of the losers' bracket, avoid pairing entries that have met in earlier rounds, if possible.

This type tournament is seldom used unless the entries are 8 or less in number. If more than 8 entries, double the process. The 2 winners meet for the title.

Consolation Tournament

There are two types of general use: The consolation type tournament is generally used only when the number of entries is 8 or 16. In the No. 1 bracket

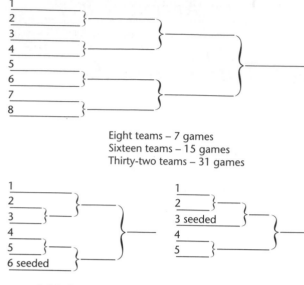

Eight teams – 7 games
Sixteen teams – 15 games
Thirty-two teams – 31 games

6, 12, 24 teams   5, 10, 20, 40 teams

Double elimination tournament

FIRST ROUND

8 Teams
Minimum games 14
Maximum games 15

Champion – A
Runner-up – B

Formula for total number of games, with N representing Number of entries 2(N-1) = Minimum Games to Play; 2(N-1)+1= Maximum Games to Play.

Double elimination tournament—byes

arrangement, only the losers in the first round of play compete for the consolation title. In the No. II, the losers in all the rounds except the final of the upper bracket compete for 3rd and 4th place.

In both tournaments, every team plays at least two games before being eliminated.

Round Robin Tournament

In the round robin, a simple but efficient method, each team plays every other team once, with the final standing determined on a percentage basis.

FIRST ROUND BRACKET – 16 ENTRIES

Champion

TYPE II – CONSOLATION BRACKET

B
3rd place

E
4th place

TYPE I – CONSOLATION BRACKET

Consolation winner

Consolation tournament

The following formula will apply to any number of teams, whether the total is odd or even. With an odd number of teams, there is the same number of rounds; with an even number of teams, there is one less number of games than teams.

For Odd Number of Teams. Assign a number to each team and then use only the figures in drawing the schedule. For example, in a league with 7 teams start with 1, putting down figures in the following order:

7	6	5	4	3	2	1
6–1	5–7	4–6	3–5	2–4	1–3	7–2
5–2	4–1	3–7	2–6	1–5	7–4	6–3
4–3	3–2	2–1	1–7	7–6	6–5	5–4

Note that the figures go down on the right side and up on the left. No. 7 draws a bye in the first round and the others play as indicated. With an odd number of teams, all numbers revolve, and the last number each time draws a bye.

For Even Number of Teams. With an even number of teams, the plan is the same, except the position of No. 1 remains stationary, and the other numbers revolve about it until the original combination is reached. For example, with 8 teams:

1–2	1–8	1–7	1–6	1–5	1–4	1–3
8–3	7–2	6–8	5–7	4–6	3–5	2–4
7–4	6–3	5–2	4–8	3–7	2–6	8–5
6–5	5–4	4–3	3–2	2–8	8–7	7–6

In essence, there are two things to remember: (1) With an even number of teams, No. 1 remains stationary and the other numbers revolve; (2) with an odd number of teams, all numbers revolve, and the last number each time draws a bye.

Ladder Tournament

In a ladder tournament, the competition is arranged by challenge, and the tournament requires a minimum of supervision. A player may challenge either of the two players above him or her in the ladder. If the challenger wins, he exchanges places with the loser in the ladder. All challenges must be accepted and played at an agreed time. Players draw for positions in the ladder; a starting and closing date for the tournament must be announced. Each player carries his or her handicap against all players, in case handicaps are used.

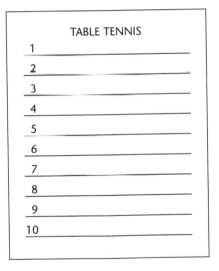

Table B-1   Tournament schedule calculator

Teams entered	Byes		Single elim.	Double elim.	Round robin
	Top	Bottom	No. of games	No. of games	No. of games
4	0	0	3	6 or 7	6
5	1	2	4	8 or 9	10
6	1	1	5	10 or 11	15
7	0	1	6	12 or 13	21
8	0	0	7	14 or 15	28
9	3	4	8	16 or 17	36
10	3	3	9	18 or 19	45
11	2	3	10	20 or 21	55
12	2	2	11	22 or 23	66
13	1	2	12	24 or 25	73
14	1	1	13	26 or 27	91
15	0	1	14	28 or 29	105
16	0	0	15	30 or 31	
17	7	8	16	32 or 33	
18	7	7	17	34 or 35	
19	6	7	18	36 or 37	
20	6	6	19	38 or 39	
21	5	6	20	40 or 41	
22	5	5	21	42 or 43	
23	4	5	22	44 or 45	
24	4	4	23	46 or 47	
25	3	4	24	48 or 49	
26	3	3	25	50 or 51	
27	2	3	26	52 or 53	
28	2	2	27	54 or 55	
29	1	2	28	56 or 57	
30	1	1	29	58 or 59	
31	0	1	30	60 or 61	
32	0	0	31	62 or 63	

Diagrams reproduced courtesy of Wilson Sporting Goods Co.

Pyramid Tournament

The pyramid tournament is similar to the ladder tournament, except the design allows for more participating and challenging. After the original drawings are made, any player may challenge any other player in the same horizontal row. The player who wins may then challenge anyone in the row above—the two change places in the pyramid.